Holy Madness

Also by Adam Zamoyski

Chopin: a Biography
The Battle for the Marchlands
Paderewski
The Polish Way
The Last King of Poland
The Forgotten Few

HOLY MADNESS

Romantics, Patriots and Revolutionaries
1776–1871

ADAM ZAMOYSKI

Weidenfeld & Nicolson
LONDON

First published in Great Britain in 1999
by Weidenfeld & Nicolson

A CIP catalogue record for this book
is available from the British Library.

ISBN 0297 81571 7

Typeset by Selwood Systems, Midsomer Norton

Printed in Great Britain by Butler & Tanner Ltd, Frome & London

Weidenfeld & Nicolson

The Orion Publishing Group Ltd
Orion House
5 Upper Saint Martin's Lane
London, WC2H 9EA

Contents

Illustrations

Preface

I have always been fondly amused by the romantic and often ridiculous national heroes gracing sleepy squares in minor European cities, who seem to want to leap from their plinths into some titanic struggle and by those who stare with missionary zeal from aged engravings or lithographs. The obvious intensity of their desire to liberate or resist is in heroic though doomed contrast to the pigeons placidly perched on the sabre they brandish or the foxing that spots their fading image. They are like the essence of the longings of another age, frozen in time.

Coming from a culture that took for granted not only the virtue of fighting for the national cause, but also the inherent desirability of staging hopeless risings, I found myself wondering where such assumptions came from, and why they held such enormous appeal. And having been brought up in the Catholic tradition, I could not help noticing the bits of ritual and imagery stolen from that faith, along with large tranches of dogma, which reinforced and bedecked those assumptions.

It seemed to me that this was no coincidence: as the state took more and more functions over from the Church, it assumed the trappings and the underlying belief-system. At the same time, the changing role or outright overthrow of monarchy gave rise to a new sense of the nation as a sovereign entity. The monarchy had always been invested with a degree of divinity, the king being the secular representative of God on earth. The nation necessarily inherited some of that divinity along with the function of sovereign. Intrigued by these connections, I set out to explore them. I had no particular agenda, and after years of research I can posit no theory and venture no argument. This is an essay, not an analysis. But it is by no means an idle exercise.

A great deal has been written on the subject of 'nationalism', a term used with diminishing degrees of discrimination to cover anything from mere attachment to tradition to crypto-Maoist terrorism. Since the Second World War, it has been regarded by the educated classes of Western societies as a kind of disease affecting those peoples who have not had the benefits of liberal-democratic inoculation. This is not an intelligent view. It misses the point and hinders any sensible reaction to the threat posed by nationalism today, and it is worth challenging. Rather than attempting a history of nationalism or an examination of its causes and effects, I have sought to do so with a thoughtful look at some of the spiritual and emotional conditions that gave rise to the cult of the nation.

This book will no doubt enrage specialists in every field I meander into, but such rage is both the prerogative and the bane of any specialist, and I make no apologies. There was nothing remotely methodical about my explorations, and as I re-read the manuscript I am constantly aware that more could have been said on every point and person I mention. I have probably placed too much emphasis on some phenomena and failed to cover others adequately; subjects not central to the general themes are treated with a mixture of brevity and impressionism bordering on the facetious. I sometimes quote people out of strict context, not to prove a point, but as an indicator of states of mind and lines of thought. There must be many sources I have missed, but this is only to be expected: there are no bibliographies of non-subjects such as mine, and whenever I attempted to quiz specialists, I encountered unhelpful degrees of incomprehension. For similar reasons, I have not gone in for the same rigorous verification of sources as I would when researching a closely defined subject. All of this is unavoidable in a work that ranges over such a vast area in both time and place. The choice of time and place itself is difficult to justify otherwise than by instinct, and I hope that a reading of the book will vindicate mine. If it does not, I hope that the reader will at least have enjoyed as much as I did the company of these blessed originals.

Holy Madness

1

Our Lord Mankind

On 21 January 1793 King Louis XVI was taken from the Temple prison and conducted in a tumbril to the place which had once borne his predecessor's name, and now bears that of Concorde. The sky was overcast, and there was a deathly silence as he mounted the scaffold. He began to address the crowd, but his voice was drowned out by a drum-roll. Denied even this chance of appealing to his people, he submitted to the guillotine. When the executioner held up his severed head for all to see, a few people in the crowd cut their own throats, others threw themselves into the Seine. A number went mad.

This was not because they bore any particular affection for the king. It was because he was the anointed of God, and it was he who gave validity to the ideological and cultural compound that was France. Writing one hundred and fifty years later, a man as modern as Albert Camus called this moment 'the turning-point of our contemporary history'. As far as he was concerned, the execution of the king had secularized the French world and banished God from the subsequent history of the French people.[1]

Traditionally, the death of a king of France was announced with the phrase: '*Le Roi est mort, vive le Roi!*', in order to stress the continuity of the institution of monarchy. When the king's head was held aloft on that sunless day, the crowd assembled around the scaffold shouted: '*Vive la Nation!*' The message was unequivocal. The nation had replaced the king as the sovereign and therefore as the validating element in the state. The dead king's God had been superseded by 'Our Lord Mankind', to use the words of one prominent revolutionary.[2]

This was the culmination of a long process, which began at the Reformation. The Christian religion, on which every throne in Europe rested, had been gradually undermined by the appliance of human logic to divine tenets and by scientific discoveries that brought into question aspects of the revelation and gave the impression that man could understand and control the world around him without recourse to God. Towards the end of the seventeenth century the French philosopher Pierre Bayle suggested that goodness and morality had nothing to do with religion, an idea supported by the accounts of travellers to distant places. The Siamese had never benefited from Divine Revelation, yet they had created a sophisticated society based on the practice of virtue. And virtue, according to Voltaire and most of the French *philosophes*, was glaringly absent from the Catholic Church and the ranks of its clergy. He identified it as the root of most of the evil in society and led his colleagues in an all-out war on it.

The element of Christian teaching that aroused the particular ire of the eighteenth-century clerisy was the doctrine of original sin – that all men are born with the taint of Adam and need to redeem themselves. They saw in this dogma not only an offensive notion that seemed to condemn the charming Siamese to eternal damnation, but also the ultimate instrument of control over the masses. What man needed, in their view, was not salvation but education, which would liberate him from all the superstitions born of ignorance. They heaped ridicule on the Christian belief in an afterlife and attacked the concept of abnegation and sacrifice leading to sanctity. They lampooned ritual, dismissed the veneration of saints and their relics as idolatry, and stridently condemned 'fanaticism', by which they meant faith.

But while they enjoyed nothing better than laying into what they saw as the superstition and flummery of the Church, only a handful were brave enough to deny the existence of God altogether. In the 1670s the Dutch philosopher Benedict de Spinoza had mooted the idea of a rational God, a sort of spirit of the universe, and the majority of his colleagues in the next century subscribed to some variant of this, usually labelled 'the Supreme Being'. As they were mostly convinced that there existed a *natura rerum*, a formula according to which the universe functioned, they tended to accommodate the Supreme Being within their quest for it. This was the first step in a gradual confusion of nature itself with God. The Baron d'Holbach's *Système de la Nature* opens with the assertion that 'Man is only unhappy because he does not understand nature', and several other philosophers made out that morality was no more than a natural attribute.[3] In 1750, Rousseau wrote his essay on the arts and sciences, arguing that man was born virtuous and civilization had corrupted him. The French explorer Louis Antoine de Bougainville's description of the mores of the Tahitian islanders seemed to bear this out, and in his *Supplément au Voyage de Bougainville*, Diderot posited a modern version of the Fall: man had been happy in an original 'state of nature', but then became tainted with 'artifice' and as a result has been in conflict with himself ever since. This notion was sentimentally appealing, and it stuck. At the beginning of the nineteenth century Mary Wollstonecraft was still laying down that 'a barbarian, considered as a moral being, is an angel, compared with the refined villain of artificial life'.[4]

While rejecting the notion of original sin and striving to eradicate it from the moral conciousness of their contemporaries, such writers were actually reinventing it in the guise of the imagined taint of civilization. And if it was man-made civilization that had brought about this secular Fall, then it was up to man to put it right. The terrifying inference was that redemption could, indeed must, be achieved through political means.

Rousseau was not only the most celebrated thinker of his day, but also a best-selling novelist. And fictional literature had to some extent hijacked the moral argument, developing a sensibility that transcended rules and suggested new assessments of right and wrong, based on emotional intention. An early example is the Abbé Prévost's *Manon Lescaut*, whose eponymous heroine is a prostitute whose sin is cauterized by the sincerity of her love for her reprobate beau. Thereafter the innocent sinner was no stranger to European literature, and misfortune itself became a morally ennobling condition. This was, in effect, a perversion of the Christian virtue of charity.

The writers of the eighteenth century, whether they were *philosophes* or hacks, believed that they preached a morality based on reason, nature and primal human instinct. But their minds and their hearts had been moulded by centuries of Christianity, and they could no more emancipate themselves from its influence than explain the existence of the universe without recourse to some benevolent deity. Their moral and emotional language was not, as they believed, universal. It was not that of the

Tahitians they idealized. What they were peddling was a mongrel Christianity.

In attacking the Catholic Church, the *philosophes* were not just demolishing some superannuated institution. They were undermining the central organizing principle underlying all the societies of Europe and its colonies. In all these societies, the Christian religion had furnished the basis of the educational canon, it had created the art, the music and the very language that made up the common culture, and it had provided the legal and institutional framework of all states, in which it still played a key role. By undermining it, the *philosophes* dislodged all the old certainties. By destroying the credibility of traditional ways of practising the faith, through feasts, rituals and displays, they created a vacuum. Man seeks ecstasy and transcendence, and if he cannot find them in church, he will look for them elsewhere.

Denied expression in its traditional area, the religious instinct naturally spilled over into alternatives such as the occult. It also flooded the arts. These had, until now, fulfilled the practical function of enhancing man's environment. They also served as vehicles for religious expression and elevation. In the course of the eighteenth century, as Christian devotions ebbed out of people's lives, the arts also drew away from formal religion. The Judaeo-Christian themes which had dominated seventeenth-century painting gave way to Classical, social and even political ones. The same is true of literature and to a lesser extent of music. But whether it was within a defined religious framework or outside it, the arts remained the chief means of expression of the longings and fears of mankind. As such, they became a substitute religion, providing consolation and solace, and offering the possibility of attaining the sublime. Over the next century, poets and other artists would assume the role and authority of high priests. The arts became subject to the kind of passionate fits of self-doubt and denunciation that usually characterized religious discourse. The arguments over questions of style were no longer about taste but about morality, and the arts were taken over by the same spasmodic rhythms of renewal and heresy as religion.

The rejection of Christian teaching and, with it, of the concept of an afterlife also gave birth to a new politics. Until now, political life had been circumscribed by the struggle for power and resistance to oppression. Curing the evils in society was left to God. From the end of the seventeenth century onwards, a number of philosophers addressed ways of making the world a more equitable place politically. The perceived ideal was a polity in which a maximum of personal freedom could be guaranteed within a strong and stable state structure. But by the middle of the eighteenth century the notion of personal freedom began to undergo significant change. For Diderot and Rousseau, 'freedom' began to mean much more than not being captive or physically oppressed. It embraced notions of self-fulfilment and empowerment. It necessarily meant freedom from the oppressive Christian dogma of the afterlife. And since this dogma rested on the premiss that the search for happiness on earth is pointless, as true happiness can only be found in paradise, freedom must ultimately mean achieving happiness in this life. As they associated true happiness with a sentimentalized vision of prelapsarian innocence, the *philosophes* were naturally drawn into the exercise of constructing heaven on earth.

Thus political life was transformed into a struggle for self-expression and the quest for happiness – conceived in highly religious terms. Discussion of how the blessed state was to be achieved generated mountains of print over the next two centuries. Attempts to put the more 'scientific' of the theories into practice would result in human misery on an unprecedented scale and leave behind them mountains of corpses. But in the latter part of the eighteenth century and the first half of the nineteenth, the quest for salvation drove many to immolate themselves rather than others. Fired by the urge to redeem mankind and themselves, many young men struggled and died in a kind of crusade whose Jerusalem was an idealized projection of 'Our Lord Mankind', the nation, death in the service of which brought martyrdom and life everlasting.

2
The American Parable

On 25 March 1777 an otherwise undistinguished French brig, recently rechristened with the resounding name of *La Victoire*, set sail for North America from the French port of Bordeaux. Dozens of taller ships left the port each week for the same destination, but this one was different. While it hardly measures up to those of the *Santa Maria* or of the *Mayflower*, her crossing was to prove just as rich in consequences. Yet its motives were as confused, and its execution verged as closely on the farcical, as the feelings and deeds of the young nobleman who had chartered the craft.

Marie Joseph Paul Yves Roch Gilbert du Motier, Marquis de Lafayette, was born on 6 September 1757. He never saw his father, a colonel of grenadiers who was cut in two by an English cannon-ball at the Battle of Minden two years later. He was brought up by a gaggle of doting female relatives in an old castle in the Auvergne, and then in Paris, where he went to school. His mother died in 1770, leaving him a considerable fortune, and four years later, when he was only sixteen, he married. His bride was the fourteen-year-old daughter of the Duc d'Ayen, a member of the Noailles family, whose influence was second to none in France at the time.

The young man was made a captain in the Noailles dragoons, and had to live with his in-laws, at Versailles and Paris. Daily contact with social superiors and with the court of the young Queen Marie Antoinette only served to accentuate certain personal problems. Lafayette was neither handsome nor imposing. He was physically awkward and lacking in social graces. He was not naturally gregarious or sociable, and to many he seemed taciturn and reserved. Aside from that implied by his birth and means, he was a young man of little consequence, and nobody took much notice of him.

Like every French nobleman of his generation, his national pride smarted under the humiliation of his country's defeat in the Seven Years War, which had ended in 1763. France had lost Canada and her possessions in India, as well as a string of other colonies, to her arch-enemy England. A desire for revenge combined with a burning need to distinguish himself animated the seventeen-year-old when he joined his regiment at Metz for manoeuvres in the summer of 1775. The commander of the forces stationed around Metz was the Maréchal de Broglie, an old soldier who had seen long service against the English. Like most Frenchmen, he was delighted by the news that on the morning of 19 April that year the dispute between the English colonists of North America and their government in London had turned violent, leading to an exchange of shots on Lexington Green.

Apart from feeling the natural restlessness of a soldier in time of peace, Broglie also nurtured a hurt pride, having been given less than his due for years of distinguished service. And in the American situation he saw opportunities. He began hatching plans for the unofficial despatch of a number of French officers to the American colonies to foment rebellion. He himself would stand at their head, and, as all the officers would have been chosen by him, he would be in an unassailable position. Behind this purely military plan to repay England for France's loss of Canada, lurked a personal dream. Lafayette was drawn into these plans, and they assumed immediacy for him when the Minister of War, the Comte de Saint-Germain, began slimming down the French forces in the interests of economy. On 11 June 1776, Lafayette was transferred to the reserve list. This meant that he would never make a career in the army, and a lifetime of inactivity at court and personal nonentity threatened.

By then, the American rebels had an agent in Paris, Silas Deane, who was procuring arms through Pierre Augustin Caron de Beaumarchais, businessman, spy, publicist, wheeler-dealer and later author of *The Marriage of Figaro*. Deane had no authority to do so, but under the influence of Broglie and others he also began to enrol officers for the rebel cause. By mid-December 1776 there were several ships in the roads of Le Havre with a quantity of arms and some sixty French officers aboard, mostly men proposed by Broglie. Lafayette badgered Broglie and Silas Deane to be included. The nineteen-year-old captain who owed his rank solely to his connections, and had never fired a shot in anger, insisted on being given the rank of major-general. When Deane balked at this, Lafayette countered by waiving the right to general's pay and by pointing out that his position in French society would bring with it valuable publicity for the cause of the colonists. On 7 December 1776 Deane signed his contract.

However much he might have wanted to exploit the difficulties of the English, Louis XVI was not inclined to support rebels against their rightful king. His chief minister, Turgot, was against getting involved in something that might lead to a war France could not afford. The men enlisted by Deane could only be sent to America clandestinely, albeit with unofficial clearance from the French Ministry. Lafayette knew that his family would block any attempt on his part to obtain such clearance. His brother-in-law, the Vicomte de Noailles, had tried and been firmly called to order. The same had happened to their friend the Comte de Ségur. But Lafayette was his own master insofar as he had money of his own.

He secretly bought a boat and offered to give passage to some of the volunteers. These made their way to Bordeaux individually, and on 25 March 1777 the *Victoire* weighed anchor, with Lafayette and twelve other officers on board. Instead of making straight for America, however, it sailed across the Bay of Biscay to the Spanish port of San Sebastián. Before going any further on his adventure, Lafayette wanted to ascertain the reactions to his escapade, and he rode back into France incognito.

News of his departure had caused consternation in Paris, where people could not believe that a young man with a fortune, a pretty wife and a title could possibly wish to forfeit everything in order to fight for a band of common rebels. His family were outraged, and Lafayette decided to submit to his father-in-law's instructions that he abandon the venture. Broglie, who had been following developments closely, did not want the young man's hesitation to jeopardize the despatch of the other officers to America, so he sent the Vicomte du Mauroy to intercept Lafayette. Mauroy caught up with the reluctant rebel outside Bordeaux. He convinced the young man to go ahead with his original plan, and the two made a dash for Spain.

The *Victoire* weighed anchor once again, and made directly for the new world this time. The crossing was dull, the only interesting figures among the other officers being du Mauroy and Captain de Valfort – who, as commander of the École Militaire, would one day teach strategy to Cadet

Bonaparte. Lafayette must have used the time to collect his thoughts and clarify his motives. In mid-Atlantic he penned a letter to his wife Adrienne, clearly meant to be some kind of testament, in which he declared his intention to fight selflessly in the cause of liberty. 'In working for my glory I work for their welfare,' he wrote. 'I hope for my sake you will become a good American. It is a sentiment meant for virtuous hearts. The welfare of America is intimately linked with the welfare of all humanity.'[1]

This sudden concern for humanity was a new departure for someone who had never shown the slightest interest in the condition of the peasants who toiled on his extensive estates. It was not a sentiment that ran very deep, any more than his new-found love for the colonists' cause. Six months later, he was writing to a brother officer that he longed for France to declare war on Britain so that he might fight under French colours. Elsewhere in his letter, he assured Adrienne that 'the rank of general has always been regarded as a title to immortality', which suggests that what was at stake was not so much the welfare of humanity, but the reputation of Gilbert du Motier, Marquis de Lafayette, backed up by a desire to escape the aristocratic mediocrity mapped out for him and prove himself to his peers. The fact that it was to North America that he had sailed was nevertheless highly significant.

European perceptions of America had a mythical quality from the moment Columbus discovered land beyond the ocean. What fascinated those who had never been there were an exoticism and an otherness that derived from it being the 'new world'. In 1704 the Baron de Lahontan published a book of 'dialogues' between himself and a Huron Indian, who lives 'according to the laws of instinct and of the innocent and wise conduct that nature impressed upon him in the cradle'.[2] With this book, the myth of the noble savage was born. Travellers were quick to point to the cruelty and often less than noble characteristics of many North American tribes. But the myth became deeply embedded in the European psyche as a kind of subconsciously felt poetic truth. And it was given substance by the circumnavigation of the globe by Louis Antoine de Bougainville, and the publication in 1771 of his account of the paradisical existence of the Tahitian islanders.

The English colonies of North America had little in common with Tahiti. But the mirage of a better form of life in the new world extended over them in the perspective of European dreamers. The *philosophes*' search for alternative systems of government and communal living had led them to look at some of the colonial congeries such as the Quakers. Voltaire was seduced by their pacifism and their rejection of superfluity. Without bothering to acquaint himself with their doctrines, he pictured them as rational deists, and went on to represent them as an ideal society on his own terms, a kind of Enlightenment Arcadia in Pennsylvania. This was the myth of the noble savage reinvented, or, what was even more dubious, a vision of civilized man undergoing regeneration in the beneficent climate of the new world.

In 1770, Guillaume-Thomas Raynal published his ten-volume *Histoire Philosophique et Politique des Établissements et du Commerce des Européens dans les deux Indes*; hardly a promising size or title for what was to become one of the best-selling and most influential books of the age, translated into five languages and reissued more than fifty times before the end of the century. It is a denunciation of European colonialism, short on sound facts but strong on sentimental outrage at the evils inflicted on the world by Europeans. Raynal was particularly interested in the English colonies of North America, about which he knew very little. In a lengthy passage on the mores of the New Englanders he painted a vision of paradise on earth, where 'people enjoy probably all the happiness compatible with the frailty of the human condition'. In these colonies, according to him, beauty and virtue reign, and there is no room for lust or base instincts. Even women 'are still what they should be, gentle, modest, compassionnate and vulnerable'.[3] The hallucinatory nature of some of these writings is remarkable. A French author who clearly liked the sentimental classicism of Watteau's figures posturing in Elysian landscapes explained that 'In Virginia the members chosen to establish the new government assembled in a peaceful wood, removed from the sight of the people, in an enclosure prepared by nature with banks of grass'.[4]

Hector St John Crevecoeur's *Letters from an American Farmer* represents the rural life of a settler in the colonies as a kind of Garden of Eden. In one passage, he describes how the new arrival from the old world undergoes a total metamorphosis. 'He begins to feel the effects of a sort of resurrection; hitherto he had not lived, but simply vegetated,' Crevecoeur argues.[5] As the two young American poets Freneau and Brackenridge put it in their poem 'The Rising Glory of America', written in 1772, it was 'a new Jerusalem, sent down from heaven'. Here 'myriads of saints' would 'live and reign on earth a thousand years, henceforth called millennium'.

The revolt of the English colonies appeared to some as a dramatic condemnation of the evils of Europe. Here was Europe's better nature, its reborn transatlantic self, raising its head and showing the world how to redeem itself. 'The epoch has come of the total fall of Europe and of the transmigration to America,' the Abbé Galliani wrote from Naples to Madame d'Épinay in Paris on 18 May 1776. 'Everything here turns into rottenness – religion, laws, arts, sciences – and everything hastens to renew itself in America.'[6] In 1776, while Lafayette was at Metz, his friend Ségur was taking the waters at Spa. 'Spa was then the café of Europe,' he explains, to which people flocked as much for reasons of pleasure as of health. It was while he was there, surrounded by the established society of a preponderantly monarchical Europe, that news arrived of the American colonists' Declaration of Independence. 'I was singularly struck to see the unanimous eruption of such keen and all-embracing sympathy for the revolt of a people against a king,' writes Ségur. 'The American insurrection took hold of the imagination like some fashion,' he adds, and indeed fashions changed overnight: the game of whist was replaced at the card-tables of Spa by 'le boston'.[7]

Nobody knew how to exploit this mood better than the 'apostle of liberty' Benjamin Franklin, who arrived in Paris as the agent of the American rebels in December 1776, just as Lafayette was preparing to leave. Franklin was famous for his discovery of the lightning conductor. In an age when thousands of houses were burned and people killed by lightning every year, this invention was as self-evidently salutary as any vaccine. In a climate where the useful was equated with the good and the moral, he appeared as a sort of saint. A native of Boston, brought up in poverty and the Presbyterian faith, he had educated himself, become a printer, graduated to journalism and risen to the office of Postmaster-General for the Colonies. He had visited England, moving in high circles and joining the Hell Fire Club. Even now he hedged his bets by serving British intelligence.

As he had no official accreditation, Franklin's only way of promoting the rebels' cause was by seducing French society. He rented a little house in Passy, just outside Paris, and settled into a modest way of life. His plain clothes hinted at fashionable Quakerism; his refusal to wear a wig or powder his hair, his sensible and thrifty lifestyle, his studiedly unceremonious deportment epitomized the Voltairian ideal of '*simplicité*'. He wore a trapper's fur hat, redolent of the virgin glades of the new world, and bifocal spectacles of his own construction that proclaimed his scientific credentials. He acted out for the French the ideal new man they fantasized about, and as a result soon became the object of a cult. His cane was copied, snuff-boxes, rings, bracelets and even shirts bearing his likeness were manufactured and sold. In Arras, an ambitious young lawyer by the name of Maximilien de Robespierre dedicated his first important court case to him.

It was on Friday 13 June 1777 that the *Victoire* came in sight of the promised land. Lafayette and two others climbed into a launch and made for the shore, but soon got stuck on a mudbank. Some black slaves in a dugout took them on board and, after splashing around in a great deal of mud, Lafayette and his companions reached a habitation. It was midnight, and Major Benjamin Huger of the South Carolina Militia, whose house it was, was unwilling to open the door at that late hour, but relented and gave them beds for the night.

They had made landfall about 25 leagues from Charleston, and the three men decided to go there on foot, letting the ship make the trip without them. Their reception at Charleston was disappointingly cool when they trudged into town weary and bedraggled, but improved when they were reunited with their ship and Lafayette's money. 'They are as friendly as my enthusiasm made me picture them,' he wrote to his wife after a few days at Charleston, retailing all the familiar prelapsarian virtues. 'What enchants me the most here is that all citizens are brothers. In America there are no poor, not even what one might call peasants.'[8] He kept up this blind optimism in Philadelphia, where he and his companions went next, and where attitudes were undeniably hostile.

Many of the colonists had fought against the French in the colonial militia during the Seven Years War. Most subscribed to the British view of the French as being untrustworthy, corrupt and degenerate; that they preferred garlic and frogs' legs to honest roast beef, and that they were all tailors, barbers or dancing-masters. Lafayette and his companions were told that there were no places for them in the army. Some of his group, already disillusioned by the realities of America, set off for home. But Lafayette was determined. While most Frenchmen were eloquent on the subject of their qualifications and social position, Lafayette quickly convinced the locals that his case was special. He wanted to serve without pay, he bought whatever he needed, and he even bailed out his less fortunate compatriots. Where other Frenchmen who had come to offer their services were haughty and insolent, he was unassuming and deferential. His boyish enthusiasm melted prejudice. Finally, it was widely noted that he did not look like a Frenchman, with his pale complexion and his sandy hair turning to red.

After persistent lobbying, Lafayette obtained the coveted general's sash, and on 31 July 1777 he met George Washington, whose staff he joined. The young man's initial admiration for the tall, elegant commander rapidly developed into adulation. One evening, Washington told Lafayette to treat him 'as a father and a friend', a natural enough show of avuncular concern in the circumstances.[9] To the French boy who had never known his own father, the offer meant far more, and he took it literally. He considered himself to have been adopted, and associated himself more firmly with the cause, whatever he might have thought this to be.

The thirteen English colonies of North America were politically and culturally very diverse. They had been founded individually, by groups of people who laid down their own sets of standards. There were hermetic religious settlements of Germans and Dutch that spoke their own language. The Quakers were a world unto themselves. Aside from the native Indians, the largest non-English group were the black slaves, numbering some 400,000 and making up about 17 per cent of the entire population. The next largest were the mainly poor Presbyterian Scotch-Irish Ulstermen, who were ardently disliked by the older English immigrants. There were plenty of Scots, many of them refugee Jacobites, and there were representatives of every nationality in Europe. 'Each settlement was a little world by itself,' wrote Andrew Burnaby, travelling through the colonies in the early 1760s, noting that they 'remained as much divided in their interests and affections as Christian and Turk'.[10] This state of affairs was frequently lamented by those like Franklin who believed that the colonies would benefit from a union of some sort. The economist Josiah Tucker was convinced that 'the mutual antipathies and clashing interests of the Americans' ensured they would remain 'a disunited people till the end of time, suspicious and distrustful of each other'.[11]

The only thing the colonies had in common was their Englishness. They were firmly anchored to the twin bases of British statehood – a militant Protestantism forged in perennial struggle against Papist France, and a dedication to the constitutional arrangements arrived at as a result of the 'Glorious Revolution' of 1688. The same shibboleths about 'the rights of Englishmen' were uttered on both shores of the Atlantic, and the same holidays celebrated. Most sacred was 5 November, the anniversary of the uncovering of Guy Fawkes' Popish Plot and that of the landing of the saviour William of Orange in 1688.

Politicians as well as churchmen frequently represented the English as the children of Israel, with the French or other enemies as the Moabites. The concept of the chosen people was strong across the Atlantic too. The staple popular text of the time, Bunyan's *Pilgrim's Progress*, was widely read as representing the English people picking their virtuous way through adversity and around temptation towards the ultimate goal, continuously threatened by the forces of evil. In America this vision was extended into a millenarian dream of breaking away from the old world altogether and founding a new social order based on religious principles, in effect a divine, theocratic polity. This lay behind the Great Awakening that had created a sort of ecumenical and multi-ethnic consensus in the early decades of the century. But if it united the colonists in an optimistic and assertive sense of destiny, this vision had little to do with the issues stirring Europeans at the time. While European intellectuals saw a new Athens in North America, its inhabitants were building a new Zion.

In political terms, the colonists were even more attached to the 'rights of Englishmen' than their metropolitan brothers. This was hardly surprising, since an element of personal freedom was inherent in the origins of the colonies, where rights and exemptions had been written down in charters and compacts. They also exceeded their metropolitan cousins in religious zeal. The decisive failure of the 1745 Jacobite rising suggested that the Hanoverian monarchy was now strong enough to withstand any threat of a reimposition of Catholicism in Britain through a Stuart comeback. With the victory of British arms in the Seven Years War (1756–63) the French threat receded as well. The result was a relaxation of anti-Catholic paranoia in Britain, which was noted with disapproval in the transatlantic colonies. Colonial visitors to London observed increasing corruption in private and public life, which reinforced traditional perceptions of the 'sinfulness' of the metropolis. When Parliament passed the 1774 Quebec Act, allowing the mainly French Catholic inhabitants of Canada to practise their religion freely, there was outrage in the colonies, accompanied by mutterings about imperial Popish Plots.

The metropolitan government, which was feeling the pinch after a victorious but expensive war, wanted the colonies to share the cost of maintaining troops for their defence. But the Stamp Act of 1765, which was intended to raise this contribution, caused uproar. The Westminster parliament was told that while it had every right to legislate in the colonies, it could not tax them as it did not represent them, and it was forced to back down. In 1767 it imposed indirect taxes, in the form of duties on imported goods. The ensuing legal argument sounded at times like a theological debate. The position of the colonists was represented as righteous and virtuous, that of the government was equated with corruption, 'sin', and 'debauchery'. The rejection of the English government's pretensions became confused with rejection of metropolitan evils. The government's case was labelled as 'popery in politics', and those voicing pro-British views were branded as 'apostate'; a Philadelphia Stamp Commissioner complained to his superiors in London in 1766 that the stamps were being described as 'the sign of the Beast'.[12] The colonists' point of view became 'the sacred cause'. Dissent was heresy, and from the late 1760s government agents and colonial Tories were castigated for being 'enemies of liberty', 'enemies of America' and even 'enemies of the people', a curious new phrase that was to have a long and bloody history.

The stridency of the language was curiously inappropriate. Westminster's right to govern and legislate for the colonies was not in dispute. The less than charismatic George III was widely held to be 'the best king any nation was ever blessed with', and the general consensus remained that the British constitution was the finest in the world.[13] To most people in the colonies there was nothing intrinsically wrong with the arrangements; governments naturally overreached themselves on occasion, and it was the duty of responsible citizens to check them. After the repeal of the Stamp Act, the Reverend William Smith, Provost of Philadelphia College, praised his fellow citizens for 'asserting our pedigree and showing that we were worthy of having descended from the illustrious stock of Britain'.[14] It is true that there was a sense of coming of age in the colonies, and a concomitant feeling that they ought to enjoy greater autonomy, but this in no way undermined their fundamental loyalty. According to John Dickinson, it would have been 'impossible to determine whether an *American's* character is most distinguishable for his loyalty to his Sovereign, his duty to his mother country [i.e. Britain], his love of freedom, or his affection for his native soil'.[15]

It was only gradually that the last two gained ascendancy. The British government's blundering and insensitive actions angered the colonists, and a degree of paranoia made them attribute sinister motives to trivial measures. The port city of Boston was particularly prone to this. Its wealth, its interests in trade and smuggling, and its vitality made it take a keen interest in, and a strong position on, every public matter. Its propensity for mob violence did the rest. Provocative demonstrations and riots against customs commissioners, representatives of the forces of law and order, or against local Tories, eventually led to confrontations with the troops stationed there. Rumour made mobs volatile and dangerous, and each clash engendered fresh grudges. In 1770 the new government of Lord North rescinded all the duties except that on tea, and the troubles died down. Three years later, in May 1773, the Tea Act awarded the monopoly of the tea trade to the East India Company. This did not increase the duty, but nevertheless provoked an eruption of public feeling. This groundless fury culminated in the famous 'tea-party' of December 1773, when a group of Bostonians stole aboard one of the company's ships in the harbour and dumped its cargo of tea overboard. Such actions incensed the metropolitan authorities, which saw the issue in terms of law and order. It did not occur to them to take a closer look or revise their policy. As late as 1775 the British Whig politician Edmund Burke observed that 'any remarkable robbery on Hounslow Heath would make more conversation than all the disturbances in America'.[16] This was to change only with the first skirmish, at Lexington Green on the morning of 19 April 1775.

The British commander in Boston, General Thomas Gage, decided to limit the potential of the local militias by confiscating their gunpowder stores and sent out a small force to secure those at Concord. But Paul Revere, a silversmith of Huguenot descent, had got wind of the plan and rode through the night to raise the alarm. When the column of Redcoats commanded by Major John Pitcairn reached Lexington, they found a force of militiamen formed up and waiting for them on the green. Instead of moving on towards Concord, Pitcairn ordered them to disperse, and, when they refused, opened fire. The skirmish resulted in the deaths of one soldier and nine colonists, a further nine of whom were wounded. The column then proceeded to Concord, but the powder was gone. As Pitcairn wondered what to do next, the local militias bore down from the entire neighbourhood, roused by news of the morning's 'massacre'. The Redcoats were obliged to abandon Concord and began their march back to Boston, running the gauntlet of militiamen sniping at them from copses and hedgerows along the way. They were only saved from annihilation by the arrival of a relief column accompanied by a force of colonial Tory volunteers, and struggled back to Boston bloodied and humiliated.

The Continental Congress, which convened at Philadelphia in May 1775, mobilized all the militias, yet few people on either side of the Atlantic believed that there should be a war. When news of Lexington reached London, a subscription was started for the benefit of 'the widows and orphans of our beloved American fellow-subjects inhumanly murdered by the King's troops'.[17] Whig politicians took the side of the rebels, and street orators denounced Parliament and the government. 'The Bostonians are now the favourites of all the people of good hearts and weak heads in the kingdom', as one observer noted.[18]

When Paul Revere galloped into Lexington at midnight on 18 April 1775, he shouted: 'The Regulars are coming out!' People sometimes referred to the troops as 'Redcoats', sometimes as 'Ministry Troops', and later as 'King's Men' – but never as 'the English'. And more than one rebel prepared to defend his homestead with the words: 'An Englishman's home is his castle!'[19] As the New Englanders bore down on Pitcairn's men at Concord's North Bridge, their fifer played a march called 'The White Cockade' because it was a Jacobite march guaranteed to annoy the Redcoats. Yet as soon as news of Lexington and Concord reached him, the famed Jacobite Alan Macdonald and his wife Flora – she who had helped Bonnie Prince Charlie escape to France after Culloden – began assembling an army of 1,500 highlanders in North Carolina to fight for King George.[20]

The man placed in command of the Continental forces, George Washington, nicely reflects the ambiguities of the situation. He was an ambitious and energetic Virginian country gentleman who had applied his talents and connections to furthering his ascent in the world. This involved the acquisition of large expanses of land and the assumption of a position within the ruling oligarchy of Virginia. He calculated wisely, manoeuvred with skill, and did not turn his nose up at string-pulling in the pursuit of wealth and status. He ended up with nearly 100,000 acres, progressing from burgess to judge, and from captain to lieutenant-colonel and command of the Virginia Regiment. He distinguished himself in action against the French and their Indian allies in 1755 and his reputation soared locally. He sought to seal this with royal approval, and petitioned for a regular commission in the British army. When this was rejected, he took it as a snub.

Like other colonial country gentlemen, Washington lived stylishly on the profits of his tobacco-crop. But in the second half of the eighteenth century the price of tobacco began to slide, while that of carriages, clothes, silverware, china, servants' liveries, and all the other finished goods which could only be imported from England began to rise. On the other hand, laws made at Westminster for the protection of Indian land stood in the way of his plans for expanding his estate. Washington's attitude towards the metropolis began to sour, and by the late 1770s he was turning into a republican. But these were not convictions reached at once or inspired by the reading of Voltaire, and they did not alter the fact that Washington was culturally an Englishman. And every evening he and his officers loyally toasted the king at dinner in camp.

While the hostilities deepened the divide and created martyrs to be honoured and victims to be avenged, they also produced a resurgence of loyalist feeling in the colonies. There were plenty of those whose interests were closely tied to British rule. These 'Tories' were not only wealthy landowners and magistrates; the arguments cut across families, and there were many interests at stake. The unassimilated Dutch, Germans and French Huguenots feared that independence would lead to cultural and political ascendancy by the dominant English element. The same was true of the Scots, while the Indians and the blacks were preponderantly 'Tory'.

The Continental Congress spent the next year trying to bring about honourable reconciliation. But in the spring of 1776 the political agitator Thomas Paine, newly arrived from England, published a pamphlet entitled *Common Sense*, in which he argued against the British constitution and the principle of monarchy, and strongly put the case that the only alternative to total submission was independence. It was one of those instances of a book finding its time. His vigorous and intransigent view of the situation concentrated minds and persuaded many of the necessity of separating from the mother country. The Westminster government continued to aggravate the situation by haughty mismanagement, and on 4 July 1776 the Congress passed a Declaration of Independence from Britain.

This was a constitutionally dubious act with no real democratic basis. Only one in five of the inhabitants of the colonies was in any sense active in the cause of independence, and there were at least 500,000 declared loyalists (out of a total population of 2,500,000) at the beginning of the war. Coercion and bullying of loyalists turned into legal persecution after the Declaration of Independence. Committees of Public Safety established themselves in New York, New Jersey, Pennsylvania and elsewhere, passing sentences in kangaroo courts. Passive loyalists were deprived of their civil rights. They were prohibited from collecting debts, buying or selling land, or, in some cases, practising their professions. Loyalists who spoke out or published their opinions could be fined, imprisoned and disfranchised. Those considered to be dangerous were imprisoned, ill-treated or exiled. With time, confiscation of property became general. In outlying or frontier areas, lynch law replaced such niceties. Even so, large numbers flocked to serve in loyalist units. Rebel slave-owners took preventive measures, locking up their slaves and even deporting them from the vicinity of loyalist areas or British garrisons. But the blacks nevertheless rowed out to British ships, joined loyalist or British forces, and fought with enthusiasm against the rebels. Many English officers declined to accept commands in the American colonies, and some resigned their commissions rather than fight in what they saw as a civil war.[21]

That was not how the intellectuals of Europe saw it. With few exceptions, they saw it as the birth of a new community, a nation they called 'the Americans', and they represented this in the image of their most cherished dreams. Paris theatres staged plays showing families leading an idyllic life in Virginia, with masters and servants praying in unison, blacks and whites singing together of liberty as they toil. In countless books and pamphlets the colonial legislators featured as latter-day Spartans, debating the future of their nation in the natural informality of sylvan glades. The militiamen were glorified as spiritual heirs of Cincinnatus, leaving the plough in order to attend to the salvation of the community.

'The cause of America is in a great measure the cause of all mankind,' Thomas Paine had written in the introduction to *Common Sense*, adding that it was 'the concern of every man to whom nature hath given the power of feeling'.[22] But he was primarily thinking of rights; others saw the events in a more metaphysical light. 'The independence of the Anglo-Americans is the event most likely to accelerate the revolution which will bring happiness to earth,' opined one French commentator. 'It is in the breast of this nascent Republic that lie the true treasures that will enrich the world.'[23] 'This will be the century of America,' declared King Gustavus of Sweden.[24] In Russia, the poet Alexander Nikolayevich Radishchev composed an ode to universal Freedom, and from Buda Janos Zinner wrote to Franklin with the assurance that he viewed him 'and all the chiefs of your new republic as angels sent by Heaven to guide and comfort the human race'.[25] Nowhere was this rhapsodical tendency more pronounced than in France, which was experiencing an orgasm of vicarious self-fulfilment. 'The Americans appeared to be doing no more than carrying out what our writers had conceived,' as Alexis de Tocqueville put it, 'they were giving the substance of truth to what we were dreaming.'[26]

'There is a hundred times more enthusiasm for this revolution in any café in Paris than there is in all the United States together,' reported a baffled Louis du Portail, a colonel of engineers who had spent over a year in North America, on his return to France in the autumn of 1777.[27] This enthusiasm was forcing the hand of a reticent French government, and when the rebels' victory over the rash General Burgoyne at Saratoga on 17 October 1777 showed that they meant business, Louis XVI and Turgot gave way. In February 1778 France signed a treaty of alliance with the American States. Young men rushed to enlist, not just to have a go at the British, but also to assert the intellectual supremacy of Enlightenment France.

Suitably, the venerable Voltaire arrived in Paris to take a valedictory bow. His house was besieged by throngs of admirers. At the opera his bust was brought on stage and crowned with laurels while incense was burned before it. Wherever he went, people gathered round the old seer, falling on their knees, touching his clothes, and even tearing pieces off to keep as relics. At the Académie Française Benjamin Franklin brought his little grandson to the old man. Voltaire extended his hand over the child's head, murmuring the words, 'God . . . Liberty . . .', and all those around them burst into tears while the sage of the old world and the apostle of the new embraced. 'It was', in the words of one contemporary, 'the apotheosis of a still living demigod.'[28]

This epiphanous atmosphere did not seem out of place. Many believed that something in the nature of a miracle was taking place, that a whole society was throwing off not only the shackles of monarchical denomination but also the cultural and spiritual taints of the old world, that it was reinventing itself as an entirely new kind of human polity. It seemed to be on the point of bringing about the chiliastic dream of a utopian state on earth, to make up for the paradise which the children of the Enlightenment no longer believed in.

3

Articles of Faith

The search for a heaven on earth had been on for some time, but it had mostly taken a literary form, and the second half of the century saw an avalanche in the utopian genre. There were primitivist utopias based on the Garden of Eden, on Arcadia, on the Golden Age and on the noble savage myth; there were utopias founded on faith in science and progress; there were highly organized statist utopias and anarchic ones; there were agrarian utopias and urban utopias; there were utopias set in 'Austral lands', on the Barbary Coast, up the Andes, on the moon, under the sea and underground. And whatever their tenor or setting, they all offered a vision of perpetual peace and abundance of the necessities of life, of the rule of reason and virtue, and above all, of happiness.

The quest for happiness also inspired a number of constitutional blueprints that were supposedly 'scientific', but in effect had more of the manse than the laboratory about them. They mostly envisaged 'organic' communities in which property was held in common and work was fun. Only Jean-Jacques Rousseau assiduously strove to relate his flights of fancy to the real world, animated by a passionate conviction that if people could be brought together in a new form of social organization, both spiritual and organic, they would incarnate the perfect prelapsarian condition of man. It was in large measure Rousseau's thoughts which inspired the European presumption of an ideal polity coming into being in North America. But they had been concentrated by two earlier rebellions nearer home, in Corsica and Poland.

The island of Corsica had been under Genoese domination for centuries, but from the 1720s it was in a state of intermittent revolt. In 1755 Antonio Filippo Pasquale Paoli, son of an exiled Corsican rebel and himself an officer in the Neapolitan army, sailed to his native island, ousted the Genoese colonial forces and was proclaimed '*Général de la Nation Corse*'. He was challenged by Corsican opponents backed by Genoa, and had to contract an alliance with France in order to maintain himself on the island. The only other potential ally was Catherine II of Russia, who was looking for a convenient naval base in the Mediterranean.

Paoli had been well educated in Naples, studying under the eminent political economist Antonio Genovesi, and between bouts of fighting he demonstrated remarkable qualities as a ruler. He convoked a parliament, the *consulta*, which voted a constitution on 18 November 1755. While this gave him virtually dictatorial powers, it also allowed him to introduce an element of stability and order. He abolished oppressive feudal rights, banned the *vendetta*, and implemented a programme of smallholding cultivation according to the most modern theories. James Boswell, who visited Corsica during Paoli's rule, was deeply impressed, and on his return to England attempted to raise funds for the general. He also, less felicitously, composed an anonymously printed panegyric, to the 'immortal man'.

Realizing that it could not recapture the island, Genoa decided to sell its interest and signed Corsica over to France in 1767. A force of 25,000 French troops moved in to take over the new colony. Paoli resisted this, but after some initial successes, he was decisively defeated at Ponte-Nuovo in 1769, and forced to withdraw to the mountains. Among the faithful remnants of his army and administration was his secretary Carlo Buonaparte and his wife, pregnant with a child who would be christened Napoleone. In June 1769 Paoli and the remaining four hundred of his followers embarked on British ships, and found haven in London, where George III granted the general a pension. Frederick II of Prussia sent him a sword, inscribed '*Pugne pro Patria*', and Catherine II of Russia, who was at that moment engaged in imposing colonial rule on Poland, a gracious invitation to visit her in St Petersburg.

In Corsica, Rousseau believed he had found a society untainted by the original sin of civilization. In his *Projet de constitution pour la Corse*, written in 1765, he suggested ways of keeping it so. 'I do not want to give you artificial and systematic laws, invented by man; only to bring you back under the unique laws of nature and order, which command to the heart and do not tyrannize the free will,' he cajoled them. But the enterprise demanded an act of will, summed up in the oath to be taken simultaneously by the whole nation: 'In the name of Almighty God and on the Holy Gospels, by this irrevocable and sacred oath I unite myself in body, in goods, in will and in my whole potential to the Corsican Nation, in such a way that I myself and everything that belongs to me shall belong to it without redemption. I swear to live and to die for it, to observe all its laws and to obey its legitimate leaders and magistrates in everything that is in conformity with the law.' Commitment to the nation dictated the class system within it. Rousseau envisaged *citoyens* as full citizens eligible for all offices, with two probationary classes below them, *patriotes* and *aspirans*.[1]

The Corsicans had also attracted the attention of the Abbé de Mably, just as he was completing his most famous work, *Des droits et devoirs du Citoyen*. He cited them as an example of the way in which war and revolution regenerate nations, by awakening talents and steeling virtues. Rousseau had written of societies reinvigorating themselves through conflict and suffering in *Du Contrat Social* and the idea that it was necessary to suffer in order to create was beginning to gain acceptance. In the next century it would become the metaphysical basis of the Romantic movement, and a canon of all modern ideas of creativity. These notions derive from the Catholic doctrine of sacrifice, which demands the immolation not of animals or third parties, but of the self. But their application to civil societies was a novel development, as was the attribution to them of organic and physical nature, including that essential element, blood.

Until now, nations had been defined variously by language, history or constitution. In grand historical painting and cartoons alike, they were represented by armorial devices, allegorical animals and objects, or by their monarch. Only Britain was regularly represented by the female figure of Britannia, which stood for people, land and constitution, a symbol devoid of any human attributes beyond its shape. That was changing. The nation was coming to be seen as a sentient humanoid entity. 'We have laid ourselves over the body of the motherland in order to revive her, just as the prophet Elijah laid himself on the body of the son of the Sunamite, eye on eye and mouth on mouth,' Paoli explained to Boswell. 'She is beginning to regain a little of life and a little warmth, and I hope that she will soon recover entirely her vigour and her health.'[2] Diderot would have none of such biblical imagery, but his recipe was essentially the same, and he held that 'a nation can only regenerate itself in a bath of blood'.[3]

There had been nothing unusual about the transaction between Genoa and France that put paid to Corsican hopes of independence. Such procedures were an accepted part of the diplomatic process. Entire provinces and small countries regularly changed hands, sometimes as a result of trade-offs at the conclusion of wars fought thousands of miles away, of which their inhabitants were not even aware. But the extinction of Corsican independence caused widespread repugnance. It was perceived as an insult to humanity by people as diverse as Rousseau and Edmund Burke, and as far away as the English colonies of North America, where associations such as 'The Knights of Corsica' founded in New York in 1770 sprang up to express indignation and sympathy. Most of thinking Europe was profoundly upset. As the nation began to be perceived in more human terms, so reactions to its rape grew more sentimental. And an even more emotional response was elicited a couple of years later by a similar diplomatic transaction carried out on the territory of another nation fighting for its independence, the Poles.

Once one of the greatest states in Europe, the Polish Commonwealth had been in relentless decline since the mid-seventeenth century and had effectively lost its sovereignty. Attempts at reviving the moribund structure met with opposition from the neighbouring powers of Russia, Austria and Prussia, for whom a powerless buffer state was convenient. They also came up against apparently bottomless depths of obscurantism and suspicion among the petty nobility, which made up the country's electorate.

It was a section of this petty nobility, the *szlachta*, led by a clutch of equally obtuse magnates, that launched an insurrection in 1768 in the form of the Confederation of Bar. It began as a rebellion against King Stanisław Augustus and his reforming policies, but it quickly shifted its principal sights on to Russia, whose troops were stationed in Poland. Russia had backed the election of the king but, ironically, by this stage also opposed most of his enlightened policies. France backed the rebels, mainly in order to embarrass Russia, sending military advisers and money. But these could not affect the outcome. After five years of sporadic fighting the rebellion was crushed. The international crisis it had helped to provoke was defused in 1772 by Poland's three neighbours helping themselves to slices of her territory in an act known as the first partition of Poland. This was denounced by one French diplomat as '*nationicide*'.[4]

The Confederation of Bar was a curious phenomenon. It based its view of itself on an imagined ideal past, when the Poles were supposedly all brave and uncorrupted Sarmatians. Nostalgia for lost virtues fused with opposition to the king's attempts to modernize the country; the defence of noble privilege was confused with republican mythology; Catholic devotionalism mixed up with tribal instincts. With its luridly expressed rejection of the alleged corruption of the Warsaw court, the movement set itself up as the defender of the nation's honour, its morals, its very soul. Its first marshal, Józef Pułaski, set the tone in a speech at Bar on 30 June 1768. 'We are to die so that the motherland may live; for while we live the motherland is dying,' he began, and carried on in much the same pathological vein.[5] This was something more than the accepted notion of '*dulce et decorum est pro patria mori*'; it actually demanded death as the price of the nation's life which, in this case, had little to do with actual political liberty. The Barians entertained a mythopoeic conviction that their ancestors, the legendary Sarmatians, had lived in a kind of ideal republican anarchy. It was this state of being, this Eden, they were dying to recover. These and other sentiments were echoed in an abundant crop of political poetry, woven on a loom of Catholic mysticism.

In line with the Enlightenment's usual obloquy of all things Christian, Voltaire condemned the rebels as grotesque religious fanatics, but for once he did not go unchallenged. Few people had any idea of what the struggle was really about, but they were learning to sentimentalize politics. And as soon as people began to talk in terms of a nation struggling for its existence, sympathy veered to the side of the confederates. Rousseau met one of the few intelligent members of the Confederation, its agent in Paris Count Michał Wielhorski, who gave him his views on the form of government appropriate to Poland.

Rousseau seized on these as a pretext for a theoretical discourse, actually a kind of utopian fantasy on the subject of nationhood. His *Considérations sur le gouvernement de Pologne* celebrates the form of the Confederation as a 'political masterpiece', allowing as it did a group of public-spirited men to stand up in the name of the nation and to assert its sovereignty by virtue of their will. He extolled the act of fighting for liberty as something great in itself. Realizing that the Confederation would probably be crushed, Rousseau urged the Poles to 'grasp the opportunity given by the present event to raise souls to the tone of the souls of antiquity'. But they must look to Moses as well as to the state-builders of Greece and Rome, for there was more to a nation than just a state. 'The laws of Solon, of Numa, of Lycurgus are dead while the even older laws of Moses still live,' he reminded them. 'Athens, Sparta, Rome have perished and have left no children on earth. Zion, while destroyed, did not lose its children . . . They no longer have leaders and yet they are a people, they no longer have a country and yet they are citizens.'[6] This asserted the primacy of the nation over the state and the geographical motherland, and suggested a role for it akin to that of a religious brotherhood. The title of 'citizen', which designated members of this community was, by inference, the most honourable a man could bear.

Rousseau himself had been born a citizen, of the Republic of Geneva, but this was not the traditional Spartan republic defying the corruptions of the outside world that he would have wished for. The country of William Tell figures in the imagination of the western world as the land of the free. But by the middle of the eighteenth century many of the hard-won codes of civic rights had atrophied into one group's instrument for dominating others. The venerable republic had become the fief of a small circle of patrician families, an aristocracy that dared not speak its name. They had excluded anyone who was not of their group from sitting on the *Petit Conseil*, and this ruled through an army of petty officials answerable to nobody else. To the outsider, it looked a model of equality, because the sumptuary laws forbade the wearing of rich clothes and jewellery, the excessive decoration of residences, and the use of elegant carriages. But in effect the republic had become a tyrannical oligarchy. Alone of all the governments of Europe, it immediately decreed that *Du Contrat Social* be lacerated and burned, which it was on 19 June 1762, and that Rousseau be banished. The *bourgeois* of the city, led by François de Luc (dubbed by Voltaire 'the Paoli of Geneva'), were behind Rousseau, but while they challenged the oligarchy of the patricians, they themselves vigorously resisted the pretensions of the lower orders.

It was in Zurich that the revival of Swiss ideals was launched, with the foundation of the Helvetisch-Vaterlandische Gesellschaft and of a chair of patriotic history and politics. The pastor and mystic Johann Kaspar Lavater published a collection of patriotic poetry enjoining young men to spend their evenings singing the praises of their fatherland and young women to choose patriots as husbands. Lavater's younger colleague Johann Heinrich Pestalozzi founded a school, and while it failed in 1780, his ideas lived on. That same year Pestalozzi published a book of aphorisms and reflections, and, in 1781, a novel entitled *Leonard and Gertrude.* The action of this political parable is set in a village, where most of the peasants and the bailiff are corrupt, devious, stupid and usually drunk. Gertrude, a model wife in every respect, reforms her husband, brings up her own children and those of others, and gradually redeems the whole community. At her instigation a village school is established, which brings about the 'regeneration' of the village, and ultimately of the state.[7] Another friend of Lavater, the Zurich-born painter Johann Heinrich Füssli, promoted similar ideas in a political 'catechism' published in 1775, which opens with a discussion on happiness and ends with the assertion that the highest form of civic life was 'a true patriot'.[8]

This is one of the earliest instances of a civic 'catechism', meant to enshrine political expediency with all the force of religious dogma. The very word 'catechism', which conjured up everything that Enlightenment man found most offensive in organized religion, was just beginning a new political career. So were the words 'citizen' and 'patriot', which acquired a fresh varnish of public spirit and commitment. Dr Johnson's oft-quoted jibe that 'Patriotism is the last refuge of the scoundrel' was made at a time when the word still designated, somewhat pejoratively, a radical purporting to stand up in defence of particular interests against his king. From there it came to denote those who put their country first. And, if there were true patriots, there were also 'false patriots'. For, if service to the common good had become an article of faith, then failure to serve or even lack of conviction was surely a dereliction.

The notion of the patriot-in-arms had assumed many of the characteristics of the chivalrous knight devoted to the service of his king and his faith, pledged to fight in the name of good against evil. Intensity of belief and dedication to the cause were everything. In his *Hymn to the Love of the Motherland*, written after the first partition of Poland, Bishop Ignacy Krasicki, a Voltairian and no friend of the confederates, extolled the 'delights' of suffering and dying in the cause. Paoli had pointed out that 'a martyr's crown awaited any Corsican who died for his country', a proposition that would have elicited amused surprise a few decades earlier. And if there was death and martyrdom, then there must be eternal life for the true patriot. One of the most interesting of the many texts begotten during the Confederation of Bar are the 'prophecies' of a Capuchin priest, which held out a vision of expiation through suffering and promised resurrection.[9]

Just as the questing knight could seek his grail anywhere, it did not matter where the modern patriot fought for the cause, as the cause was universal. Without being quite aware of what he was doing, Lafayette had set the tone. 'The moment I heard of America I loved her,' he wrote, quite untruthfully, to President Laurens in September 1778. 'The moment I knew she was fighting for freedom, I burnt with the desire of bleeding for her.'[10] On 9 September 1777, three days after his twentieth birthday, Lafayette had his baptism of fire at the Battle of Brandywine, in which he was wounded in the leg. Although it was only a flesh wound, it laid him up for some time, and he employed this to write elegant letters home telling of how he had bled in the cause of liberty.

The first foreign volunteers to muster in the American cause were French. A handful were private individuals in search of glory such as the flamboyant Comte Armand de la Rouërie, a Breton nobleman who rounded off a stormy youth in Paris involving passionate affairs with actresses, duels and even a spell in a Trappist monastery by coming over to America and making a fine reputation for himself as a dashing and gifted soldier under the name of 'Colonel Armand'. Next came a number of officers, who went to America with the approval of the French government in order to observe and report, as well as to help the rebels. They were followed by the men despatched by Broglie, mostly professional soldiers with no prospects at home. A good example of these was the Bavarian Johann Kalb. He had served in German and French ranks, receiving his baptism of fire at Fontenoy and becoming a lieutenant-colonel at the end of the Seven Years War. He would die in action at Camden on 15 August 1781, while covering General Gates's retreat.

Throughout 1777 and the early part of 1778 dozens of young French noblemen made the passage to the new world, some having resigned commissions or other posts. They were joined by men from virtually every country in Europe. From faraway Livonia came Baron Gustavus Heinrich von Wetter-Rosenthal, who served as 'Lieutenant John Rose'. From Germany came Frederick William Augustus Baron von Steuben, whose command of the English language was so poor that he even had to swear at his men through an interpreter, but who nevertheless instructed Washington's army in close-order drill and the use of the bayonet. From Hungary came Colonel Mihaly Kovacs, a fine cavalry commander who was killed at Charleston in May 1779.

The greatest number of volunteers came from Poland – an estimated six hundred, mostly former confederates who had been obliged to give substance to Rousseau's vision of a stateless nation. Although they were mostly officers, and generally desperate men, they were of limited value on account of the language barrier. One exception was Kazimierz Pułaski, son of the first confederate marshal. 'I long to die for such a true cause; I wish to expire on the bed of glory; I wish to perish at my post,' he wrote to Franklin as he sailed from France in June 1777.[11] Shortly after his arrival Pułaski found himself in command of a company of Poles at Brandywine, and four days later he was commissioned general in the cavalry of the Continental Army. He had been one of the best confederate commanders, making deep raids that proved highly effective against regular Russian troops, and he now formed up the first large unit of cavalry for the rebels. It was while leading it at the Siege of Savannah that he was killed.

The only foreign volunteer whose fame was to run close to that of Lafayette was the Pole Tadeusz Kościuszko. A professional soldier who came to America in order to gain experience, he served with the rank of general throughout the war. He embraced the most radical aspects of the cause he was fighting for and became an armed prophet of the cult of liberty. He was a brilliant engineer, and one of the few foreigners who actually contributed to the victory. For, whatever the moral boost they might have lent the revolt, all the knights errant could not make up for the one thing that was needed – namely the military and naval support of a European power.

In the summer of 1778 a fleet under Admiral d'Éstaing sailed from France to bring assistance to the colonists, while the army massed for an invasion of England. Among the soldiers concentrated at the encampments in Normandy were veterans of other French interventions. One was Colonel Charles François Dumouriez, who had only two wounds fewer than his twenty-four years of age by the end of the Seven Years War. He had then offered his services to Paoli in Corsica, but, having been turned down, took part instead in the French intervention that ousted him. In 1770, he had been sent to Poland as senior adviser to the Confederation of Bar. There were several others who had fought in Poland, including General Charles de Vioménil, and many who had taken part in the stifling of Corsican liberty. One of these was Armand de Gontaut-Biron, Duc de Lauzun, the Peter Pan and darling of the ladies at Versailles. He had enjoyed himself in Corsica, where he took his mistress into action with him. In 1778 he had sailed off at the head of a mixed corps of three hundred Poles, Hungarians, Germans and Irishmen to capture the English settlements in Senegal, and had returned just in time to join the troops in Normandy in September 1779. He had his own invasion plans, involving not England but Ireland. 'I will tell you in confidence,' he wrote to George Washington, 'that the project closest to my heart is that of making her free and independent like America; I have made some secret relations there. May God help us to succeed and may the era of liberty begin at last for the happiness of the world.'[12]

Rather than invade England, the French decided to send a small force under General de Rochambeau to America instead. The moment this became known, there was a scramble to be transferred to one of the regiments which were to go. Every young man in France wanted to fight. The Comte de Ségur, who had hoped to leave for America with Lafayette three years before, was desperate to discover that his regiment would not be going. He pestered every person of influence, including Marie Antoinette herself, to have himself gazetted to another. This was a war such people felt they just could not afford to miss.

With France's entry into the American war in February 1778, and even more so with that of her ally Spain in April 1779, it became a European war, or, if one prefers, a world war. This was compounded in 1780 when the Dutch Republic also declared against Britain. In these circumstances, continued possession of the colonies became a matter of minor importance to the British, who had far greater interests at stake. The critical moment came at Yorktown in 1781, where the Continental Army and its French allies had bottled up General Cornwallis. Lafayette distinguished himself in a brave frontal assault on one of the British redoubts, but it was hardly a blood-bath. British losses during the three-day battle were 156 killed and 326 wounded, the American and French losses 85 killed and 199 wounded.[13] Yet this battle proved decisive.

The American war was lost by the British rather than won by the colonists. It was lost on account of the terrain. It was also lost due to European diplomacy. And it was to a large extent lost because the issues and the motivations had been so unaccountable and, to the British, baffling. After Cornwallis's surrender at Yorktown, his troops marched out, having laid down their arms, with their colours cased as a sign of total defeat. Appropriately, their band played a march entitled 'The World Turned Upside Down'.

In Europe, the success of the Franco-colonial forces and Britain's evacuation of the thirteen colonies was acclaimed rather as a setting to rights. A sense of inevitability, of the hand of Providence, was widely felt to have attended it. It seemed a clear-cut case of the virtuous and the inspired triumphing over all the odds. It also seemed to hold out boundless promise. 'I saw at that moment that the Revolution in America signalled the beginning of a new political era, that this revolution would necessarily determine an important progress in world civilization, and that before long, it would cause great changes in the social order which then existed in Europe,' wrote Claude-Henri de Rouvroy, Comte de Saint-Simon, an officer of the Royal-Gatinais infantry who had fought at Yorktown aged only twenty.[14] This resounding language cannot be dismissed as the blusterings of a self-important youth. 'Perhaps, I do not go too far when I say that, next to the introduction of christianity among mankind, the American revolution may prove the most important step in the progressive course of human improvement,' wrote the Welsh philosopher Richard Price, foreseeing a new age when lambs would lie down with leopards.[15] 'Since the discovery of Columbus, there has been no event of equal importance to the human race,' concurred the French minister Turgot.[16] The message of the American Revolution, as read by countless Europeans, was that human communities could control their own destinies, that if they were morally healthy they needed only to will it in order to be free. And many were stirred by the example of America to regain their lost rights and prove their national manhood.

On 8 April 1782, six months after the Battle of Yorktown, revolution rocked the Republic of Geneva. After a night of confusion, during which the watch was overawed, the arsenal seized, and much gunpowder expended with little loss of life on either side, the fifteen members of the Petit Conseil gave in and handed over power to the rebels. Only one of these, Jean-Pierre Mara (brother of the future French demagogue), could be described as a radical. The others were people such as Étienne Clavière, the celebrated Dr Tronchin, Jacques Antoine du Roveray and Francis d'Ivernois, all respectable members of old Genevan families – albeit ones that had been elbowed aside. Predictably enough, very little in the way of reform or social enfranchisement followed the rebels' assumption of power, and the 'revolution' could soon be seen for what it was – a takeover by a rival patrician faction.

But while she ranted about liberty in America, France could not countenance even a shade of this in Geneva. The French Foreign Minister, the Comte de Vergennes, delivered a sharp protest and withdrew his diplomatic representative. He enlisted the support of the cantons of Berne and Zurich, as well as of the kingdom of Sardinia (whose mainland province of Savoy touched Genevan territory), and began massing his forces. In June French troops commanded by the Marquis de Jaucourt, an erstwhile defender of confederate freedoms in Poland, began to close in on the republic.

On 12 June, the French publicist Jean-Pierre Brissot arrived in the beleaguered city to witness and weep over the extinction of its liberty. Tronchin had already been dubbed the Genevan Franklin, and Roveray and d'Ivernois were vying for the mantle of Washington. 'We are ready to let ourselves be buried under the ruins of our liberties,' Clavière wrote to Vergennes. 'And you may treat these liberties as no more than fanciful dreams, but, my dear Count, these dreams are our dreams.'[17] The same dreams did not fire the majority of the citizens, and the leaders' nerve began to snap as French troops took up their positions. Jaucourt waited as the whole revolt imploded, and, after twenty-one ringleaders nominated by him had been expelled and sent into exile, he graciously accepted the city's capitulation on generous terms.

Such a result was only to be expected. It was not possible to make a credible stand without the commitment of the majority of the population, who were not prepared to risk life and limb for the sake of a few musty rights. Disaffected tribunes could hector and rant, but words would not rally the masses, as earlier, similarly inspired events in Ireland confirmed.

Like the Americans, the half-a-million strong English Ascendancy in Ireland were brought up entirely as products of English culture and within the English parliamentary tradition. Like the Americans, they were governed from the metropolis, which gave rise to the same misunderstandings and the same stirrings of libertarian thought. The Scots Presbyterian dissenters, settled mostly in Ulster and numbering nearly a million, identified strongly with the Americans; in the words of one contemporary, they were 'Lovers of Liberty, and almost republicans from religion, from education and from early habits'.[18] Their sympathy was strengthened, just as the defiance of their American cousins had been, by Westminster's lifting a few of the disabilities suffered by Catholics in Ireland. The three million Catholics enjoyed no political rights and kept out of the argument.

In April 1778 the Scottish-born American naval officer John Paul Jones sailed up to Belfast in the USS *Ranger*, discharged a broadside and departed, leaving a keen awareness of the defenceless state of Ireland. The threat of invasion by America's new ally, France, suddenly loomed large. As there were few British troops on the island, the propertied classes began forming militias. The government gave its approval and a supply of arms. By the end of the following year there were 40,000 Irish Volunteers. By the end of 1780 there were 80,000, under the command of the Earl of Charlemont. Catholics were excluded, but some nevertheless contributed financially.

When people come together in large numbers they become aware of their strength, and the Irish Volunteers were no exception. Their musters and drills were occasions for social junketing, but also for discussion and debate, and what emerged from these was a growing sympathy for the American cause, followed, inevitably, by some mimicry. A meeting of representatives of the Irish Volunteers at Dungannon on 15 February 1782 formulated a set of demands to be transmitted to Westminster. The principal one was for the lifting of all restrictions on trade, but there was also a demand for greater autonomy and for the partial removal of Catholic disabilities. 'Ireland is now a nation!' the patriot leader Henry Grattan exclaimed when the demands were granted on 22 February.[19] 'Grattan's Parliament', as it became known, settled down to govern this new nation, with misplaced complacency.

'The Revolution of 1782', wrote a law-student called Theobald Wolfe Tone, who had wanted to go and fight against the American rebels in 1780, 'was a Revolution which enabled Irishmen to sell at a much higher price their honour, their integrity, the interests of their country; it was a Revolution which ... left three fourths of our countrymen slaves as it found them.'[20] Instead of going home quietly, as Grattan and Charlemont had hoped, large numbers of Volunteers continued to meet and make further demands, notably for Catholic emancipation. In 1783 they even attempted something in the nature of a coup. They were outfaced and forced to retire, but consoled themselves with much steamy rhetoric.

At the same time a similarly confused attempt at national regeneration through a dusting-down of ancient rights and a return to spiritual purity had been taking place in the Dutch Republic of the United Provinces, once one of the most admired states in Europe. Defiantly Protestant, it had forged its national identity in long wars against Catholic Spain. Its citizens enjoyed rights and liberties that were the envy of Europe. Its political system had helped it to take a commercial and industrial lead, and by the end of the seventeenth century it was, on a per capita basis, the richest state in Europe, the home of philosophers, inventors and artists of the highest calibre. Renowned for its religious and political toleration, it was the printing-house of thinking Europe. Yet the Enlightenment, for which it was seemingly such a perfect model and most of whose seminal texts were printed here, had little impact. Rousseau's *Du Contrat Social*, published in Amsterdam in 1762, was not brought out in Dutch until 1788.

The Republic had begun to atrophy in the first decades of the eighteenth century. The social cohesion of this city-based democracy evaporated, with the very rich continuing to grow richer, and the numbers of the poor increasing. Public office was restricted to a small group of patricians, contempt for whom was expressed by the name under which this regime was to go down in history – as the *pruikentijd*, 'the time of the periwigs'. The pathetic and ridiculous Stadholder William V was a good focus for this discontent, and his court was popularly pictured as a den of iniquity and corruption.

There was much sympathy for the Corsicans and then the Poles as they stood up and fought for their freedoms, and several Dutchmen went off to fight for the American rebels. 'In America, a holy sun has risen,' declared one Dutch preacher. 'America can teach us how to fight against the degeneration of our national character; the debasement of its soul, the corruption of its will to resist . . . how to throttle tyranny and how to restore to health the all but moribund corpse of freedom.'[21] The anti-Stadholder opposition, which had taken the name of Patriots, made the American slogans their own. Supporting the Americans allowed them to undermine the Stadholder through his principal ally, England, and to bring that alliance to an end. When war broke out between England and Holland towards the end of 1780, the Patriots adopted the black cockade of the Americans, and in September 1781 Baron Joan Derk van der Capellen published a pamphlet calling the people to stand up in defence of their birthright as descendants of the 'free Batavians'.

There was much debate on what this alleged prelapsarian Batavian republic had actually been like, spawning an imagery of Spartan virtue and the notion of a covenant with God. As in America, there was a strong religious movement running alongside the Patriot revolt. The established

Reformed Church was perceived as having slipped into Babylonian degradation and came under attack in much the same way, and for much the same reasons, as the Anglican Church was reviled by the American colonists. The moral revulsion felt at the fashionable flauntings and the excesses of the rich was more potent than any social discontent felt by the poor. And the mobilization of popular support for the Patriot cause was most easily achieved by the absorption of popular religion. In a Patriot catechism entitled *Instruction in the Pure Sentiments of True Netherlanders*, van der Capellen is described as 'the true Son of Liberty, conceived from the spirit of the Patriots, born to the Virgin of Freedom; by Prince William wounded, died and buried and on the Third Day risen to a Heavenly Glory, whereon he now sits at the Right Hand of the Fathers of the Nation'.[22]

The success of the American rebels, sealed by the Treaty of Versailles in 1783, suggested to the Patriots that God was on the side of the righteous and the bold, and they revived the traditional city militias in the form of the Free Corps. In June 1785 thousands of volunteers from all over the Netherlands assembled at Utrecht to swear an 'Act of Association', in which they promised to defend their freedoms 'to the last drop of blood' and to strive for the regeneration of their republic. A few weeks later, they passed a resolution, the 'Leiden Draft', which declared liberty to be an 'inalienable right' of every citizen. It also made the point that 'the Sovereign is no other than the vote of the people', which was a direct provocation to the Stadholder, who was the sovereign.[23] But the Patriots were few in number, and the poorer sections of the population were loyal to the Stadholder. They had no stomach for the sort of terror that might have engaged the people in their cause, and were not prepared to spill enough blood to sanctify it.

The Patriots looked for support to France, which prevaricated. The Comte de Maillebois was allowed to raise a Legion that would go and fight for the Patriot cause. Young men who had failed to make it to America flocked to his standard in search of glory. Typical was Jacques Étienne Macdonald, son of a Jacobite from the Hebridean island of South Uist, who enlisted with Maillebois in 1785, aged twenty. He had been intended for the priesthood, but his first reading of Homer had suggested another role as Achilles. As well as the dreams in his head, he carried a marshal's baton in his knapsack as he marched off to Nijmegen with the Legion. In 1785 France despatched a number of artillerymen and engineers to help the Patriots, and even considered a seaborne relief of Amsterdam by Lafayette and a small force from Dunkirk. But she had no intention of going to war in the Patriot cause, and England urged Prussia to call her bluff. In September 1787 Prussian troops under the Duke of Brunswick invaded the Dutch Republic, and only a month later the Stadholder was reinstated in The Hague. Resistance melted away rapidly. A couple of thousand Patriots went into exile, mostly in France.

'It was only aristocracy against aristocracy,' the Duke of Brunswick later explained. 'The interests of the people were so little the object that there was never any question of forming a good national representation, the only true foundation of all free government.'[24] Much the same was true of Poland, where another ferment instigated by 'Patriots' determined to revive ancient glories began to bubble and bluster.

After the defeat of the Confederation of Bar and the partition of 1772, Poland had become a virtual colony of Russia, with its king and institutions directed from the Russian Embassy in Warsaw. But far from stagnating like the Netherlands, the country was undergoing a cultural renaissance. This involved the celebration of national myths and imagined Sarmatian virtues. History was delved into and reinvented, and a bright future was extrapolated from the treasures it yielded. A younger generation of politically articulate noblemen were no longer content to follow the king's policy of rebuilding the country economically without rousing its powerful neighbours. They wanted action and they wanted control. Towards the end of 1787 this rowdy opposition took from the Dutch the name of 'Patriots', and began to clamour for reform and independence. Russia was occupied with war against Turkey, and therefore temporarily powerless. Prussia was actively encouraging the Patriots, hoping to be able to fish in the muddied waters. By the summer of 1788 the political climate in Poland was, in the words of the Papal Nuncio at Warsaw, in a state of '*orgasmo*'.[25] But no climax came. When the parliament, the Sejm, met in October 1788, reform was talked of, but more time was spent striking attitudes than in real political work. The Patriots peppered their speeches with references to Washington, Franklin and Jefferson, and their most prominent leader, the young aristocrat Ignacy Potocki, was dubbed 'the Polish Lafayette'; they believed that they only had to make a serious act of will in order to achieve their aims.

Rousseau had identified the driving force in all political activity as something he called 'the imagination'. This was what he believed 'transported' people out of themselves and empowered them to act on behalf of others. The events in the Netherlands, in Switzerland and in Poland were instances of imagination run wild, but not quite in the sense he meant. The protagonists in these events were inspired more by blind faith in the power of their own will, and this was the enduring legacy of the American revolution.

4
FALSE GODS

The American paragon on which so many European hopes were being founded fell some way short of the imagined ideal. The seven years of fighting for independence were instrumental in forging a sense of solidarity and giving the rebels a collective identity. They also helped to purge the colonies of active loyalists, many of whom were killed, and a further 80,000 of whom emigrated. But that still left a considerable proportion of the population out of sympathy with the state of affairs in 1783. The unassimilated communities of Germans, Swiss, Dutch and Finns, and the religious settlements of Quakers, Shakers, Dunkers, Menonites, Schwenkfelders and others carried on much as before – oblivious to government and resistant to national inclusion. The settlers of what later became Kentucky and Tennessee debated the possibility of switching to Spanish sovereignty. In 1784 the western counties of North Carolina attempted to go their own way. Three years later the Wyoming Valley tried to secede from Pennsylvania. There was opposition, rioting and even revolt against the Congress, just as there had been against Westminster. One reason was that the tax burden had increased dramatically. In the last years of British rule, the colonies enjoyed lower taxation than any people in the Western world except for the Poles. By the late 1780s the Massachusetts per capita tax burden of one shilling had gone up to eighteen shillings; the rise in Virginia was from five pence to ten shillings.[1] And it is worth remembering that tax was what had sparked off the revolution in the first place.

The war had also given rise to division and grievances of every kind, leaving in its wake the desire for revenge and in some areas, such as the back country of the Carolinas, long-standing feuds. To Hector St John Crevecoeur, who believed that the American colonies had been 'the best society now existing in the world', the revolution was a catastrophe.[2] Aside from the suffering and devastation it had caused, it also brought to an end the state of innocence in which they had existed for so long. His sentiments were echoed by many of those who had been most active in creating the climate of revolt. Brought up in a religious tradition, and often trained for the ministry, the writers of this generation believed in their calling. In his poem *The Prospect of Peace*, started in 1778, Joel Barlow had a vision of America's poets leading her to become the seat of culture and spirituality, and the incarnation of a 'great moral sense'. But no 'moral sense' was in evidence after 1783. Carpet-baggers who had done well in the revolutionary turmoil aped the old loyalist upper class, and even those who had fought for the cause revealed distressing old-fashioned addictions. The Congress was prevailed upon to institute a decoration, the Order of the Cincinnati, in recognition of services rendered in the cause. This was a blatant attempt to import the vanities of European court hierarchy, rejection of which lay at the very basis of the revolution. Barlow felt so out of place in the new America that he settled in France.

In 1788 the Congress produced a constitution for the new country which, after a number of suggestions such as 'Alleghenia', 'Fredonia' and 'Columbia', was named the United States of America. The constitution was a remarkable document based on a blend of idealism and pragmatism that ensured a greater degree of consensus than had been there in 1776, and as a result the new state gained consistency. But it was not that of a nation as envisaged by Rousseau. It had nothing of the humanoid nature of his ideal society or of the spiritual communion on which it should be founded. 'Man must have an idol,' declared Judge Addison of Pennsylvania in 1791. 'And our political idol ought to be our constitution and laws. They, like the ark of the covenant among the Jews, ought to be sacred from all profane touch.'[3] The American state itself, not some spiritually regenerate and therefore divine people, was to be the validating element, the godhead.

In the 1770s British cartoonists often represented the cause of the rebellious colonists by an anthropomorphic figure of 'America', and some American publicists followed suit. But once the colonies had won independence, this image gave way to an array of more symbolic devices, dominated by the heraldic eagle, and the only human figure among them was that of Miss Liberty. But she was often featured in attendance to another deity, which should have been quite out of place in a society rejecting European servility.

As early as 1776 places began to be named after George Washington. Within a couple of years the Continental Navy, the navies of the individual states and the fleet of privateers included no fewer than fifteen vessels named *George Washington*. Soon after that, people began to be baptized with 'Washington' in lieu of a Christian name. In 1778 an almanac called Washington 'Father of His Country', and the usage caught on. Popular songs featured verses such as 'God save Great Washington', and even referred to him as 'god-like Washington'. In 1779 people began to observe his birthday as a holiday; popular prints and naive paintings of him hung in every home. In Alexandria, Virginia, the owner of the Royal George tavern painted out one George and painted in the other. When pulling down the statue of the king in 1776, the New Yorkers had left the plinth, and on this, in 1792, they erected one of Washington.[4]

Just as starry-eyed Western intellectuals in the twentieth century would transfer to the Soviet Union all their own fantasies of the ideal state, so the idealists of late eighteenth-century Europe doted on the American Eden. They ignored not only the materialism, the religious bigotry and the institution of slavery it rested on, but also the real ideological bases of the new state. Viewed through variously tinted filters, the American model seemed to bear out the feasibility of the *philosophes*' arcadian/biblical vision of the nation as a family coming together under the divine laws of nature.

As in the twentieth century, it was French intellectuals who gushed most profusely. They shamelessly invented whatever suited their argument and retailed utter rubbish to readers too avid for affecting images to bother about their veracity. 'The day when Washington resigned his command in the Hall of Congress, a Crown set with jewels had been placed on the Book of the Constitutions,' fabulized one. 'Suddenly Washington seized the crown, broke it, and threw it in pieces before the assembled people. How petty does the ambitious Caesar seem before this Hero of America!'[5] The peddlars of lowbrow literature joined in, setting their tear-jerking tales in the colonies. Jean-Pierre Brissot, who had founded the Société Gallo-Americaine, sailed to America in 1788 with the intention of writing a history of the country, and went about heaping indiscriminate praise on everything and everybody to a grotesque degree. His book was a curious mixture of practical information and religiosity, even mysticism. 'The potato is indeed the nourishment of the man who aspires, who knows how to be free,' he would announce sententiously.[6] In defence of the cult of Washington, he declared that new societies need civic saints. The Marquis de Chastellux, who knew America well, unwisely tempered the general enthusiasm and pointed out some of the exaggerations. This earned him a furious rebuke from Brissot. 'You wish, sir, to destroy this enchantment! Cruel man! Even if it were an illusion, would you still dissipate it?'[7]

A good example of the volitional myopia affecting the French is furnished by Ségur, who had disembarked on the banks of the Delaware in May 1781 to join Rochambeau's army. He found the countryside beautiful. The houses appeared more comfortable, the clothes more elegant, the manners more attractive, the parties more fun, and the women prettier than in the old world. He was full of praise for their unaffected simplicity and clear-cut morality. 'It is with infinite regret that I leave a land where people are, naturally and effortlessly, what they should be everywhere, sincere and free,' he wrote as he prepared to sail from America a couple of years later. His way back to France lay via the French colony of Saint-Domingue, and he decided to take the opportunity to visit a plantation he happened to own on the island. He was enchanted by the place and moved by the apparent joy with which his five hundred slaves greeted their unknown master. He gave them a day off work and generously paid for a feast. With deep *sensibilité* Ségur watched his grateful slaves as they danced for him, and his companion Alexandre Berthier sketched the touching scene.[8]

France, godmother of the Enlightenment and midwife of American liberty, had herself given birth to children who were politically illiterate. Not only could Ségur and Berthier, intelligent men who were to become an important diplomat and a Marshal of France respectively, not tell the difference between liberty and slavery. Most of France's élite had mislaid the connection between thought and reality. An otherwise intelligent lawyer by the name of Maximilien de Robespierre could, in 1786, when all were agreed that the peasant's plight was desperate, sit down and compose an atrocious poem containing the lines: 'How rich, how happy is he who lives in poverty! He lives his days in wisdom, and sleeps in peace. Only he can be really happy, only he is so always!'[9]

Few in France denied that at least some of the burdens should be lifted from the shoulders of the peasants. The majority accepted that someone like Lieutenant Berthier should not be prevented from rising above the rank of captain because he was not of noble birth. Lawyers themselves believed the legal system should be reformed, and even most of the clergy accepted that the Church could not continue in its present constitution. Yet nothing was done. Like Rousseau, who flooded the presses with precepts for the improvement of mankind but dumped his unwanted bastards without a thought for their future, the French displayed a curious inability to translate inspiration into deed.

Lafayette had dashed back to France immediately after the British surrender at Yorktown, and thereby single-handedly harvested all the admiration. The queen danced with him at Versailles, and he was crowned with laurels by the leading actress in his box at the theatre. He was referred to as '*Scipion l'Américain*'. He had the hall of his *hôtel particulier* redecorated; the wall on the left was dominated by a painting representing the voting of the Declaration of the Rights of Man in America, the opposite wall was left blank in pointed anticipation of a French equivalent.[10] But little came of all this posturing. Lafayette was a knight errant with a bottomless capacity to serve; he was no reformer. The French nobility, cut out of any serious participation in government for generations, were not up to the political challenge facing them.

This was all the stranger as the French continued to dominate the political discourse and France remained the cynosure of intellectual Europe. Paris was more truly cosmopolitan than any city had been since Rome in its imperial heyday. It was the hostelry of the Western world, attracting guests like a powerful magnet, and when they left it to return to their native lands, they commonly felt a despondency verging on despair. Those who had never been there both envied and resented the French, who regarded themselves as the premier nation, head and shoulders above any other. This exclusive sense of superiority annoyed many, but it was particularly offensive to the Germans.

While a collection of rebels in North America had managed to acquire the full benefits of sovereign statehood, the largest and one of the most creative peoples in Europe had no national or political identity of its own. It was divided up into three hundred states and another fifteen hundred minor units, together making up the Holy Roman Empire of the German Nation. And when a German travelled for more than three hours in any direction, he was likely to find himself in 'an island of different customs, dialects and manners'. When Goethe arrived in Leipzig from Frankfurt, he was laughed at for his outlandishness.[11] This state of affairs impeded not only economic but also intellectual life, as tolls, tariffs and censors challenged the circulation of books at every turn in the road.

The lack of a national homeland did not worry most Germans as such. They assuaged their sense of national insignificance by likening the Holy Roman Empire to the Hellenic world, in which many small states had made up one great culture. Cities such as Dresden and Weimar, universities such as those of Jena and Tübingen seemed to bear this out. This vision allowed them to rise above petty national ambitions. But such cosmopolitanism was difficult to sustain, particularly as most German thinkers were crushed by an overwhelming inferiority complex vis-à-vis France.

The cultural and spiritual dominance of France had begun with the disappearance of Latin as the language of European thought and its replacement by French. The language had, in the words of Voltaire, made more conquests than Charlemagne, and even Frederick of Prussia quipped that German was a language fit only for addressing soldiers and horses. This had allowed the French to arrogate to themselves the role of successors to the ancient Romans, and their culture of the seventeenth and eighteenth centuries reflects this. The kings of France had also assumed the title of Most Christian Majesty, and with it the mantle of Christian Rome. The Protestant Germans were excluded from this French-Catholic Roman legacy by language and the Reformation.

They were also disadvantaged by social factors. Intellectually eminent as they may have been, the German writers were of humble origin and lived quiet lives in provincial cities. As there was no political or cultural capital, they did not have a German intellectual agora of their own. And most could not afford to go to Paris. The few that did were not socially elevated or urbane enough to gain *entrée* to the aristocratic salons where the French *philosophes* held sway, and felt ill at ease in the French capital. As a result, the German writers of the eighteenth century mostly felt a degree of alienation from the mainstream culture of the age.

They drew some comfort from religion. The Pietist doctrines widespread in Germany were easier to accommodate with the spirit of the age than Catholicism, and as a result there was not the same flight from belief as in France. This was reflected in the German Enlightenment, the *Aufklärung*, which was more intense and more moral in its preoccupations than the French equivalent. The *philosophe* who had the greatest influence in Germany was Rousseau, whom Kant described as 'a Newton of the moral world' and Herder as 'saint and prophet'.[12]

The Germans also sought comfort in a sense of their own intrinsic worth, which involved establishing a separate identity. Some contrasted 'the simple, good, reasonable, staunch, modest, diligent, robust, persevering' Germans with 'the all too polished, too frivolous, too refined, too gallant, too facetious Gauls'.[13] A demand made itself felt for a distinctive 'German national spirit', for German heroes, German novels and anything else that could be construed as culturally German. The young Goethe spent hours contemplating the great minister of Strasbourg, surveying it in various lights. 'This is German architecture, our architecture! Something of which the Italian cannot boast, far less the Frenchman!' he exclaimed in conclusion.[14] He had never been to France or Italy, and he had little understanding of the medieval world or its artistic heritage. But many Germans enthusiastically claimed this 'Gothic' style, which the French *philosophes* equated with barbarism, as something they could rally to. 'True art is to be discovered rather among the pointed vaults and ornate edifices of medieval Germany than under Mediterranean skies,' asserted Wilhelm Heinrich Wackenroder.[15]

The search for 'Germandom' went deeper than books, artefacts and styles of architecture. It was a search for a state of being as much as anything else, and it was carried on with an intensity that appears laughable at a distance. In Darmstadt, the young Goethe joined a 'Community of Saints', as they called themselves, whose purpose was to indulge in adulation of the poet Klopstock, and lead their life in a series of exaggerated gestures. In Göttingen, there was a group calling itself *Hügel und Hain*, literally 'hill and coppice', who met by moonlight, dressed in fanciful robes, bedecked with oak-leaf garlands, in a quest for the supposed purity of earlier days and the essence of Germanic culture.[16] This quest led the Germans to embrace, with greater enthusiasm than one would have thought possible, the concoctions of a Scottish fraud.

A Scotsman by the name of James Macpherson was making a living in Edinburgh in the 1750s by producing translations of ancient Gaelic poetry which he claimed to have discovered while travelling around the highlands and islands of Scotland. In 1761 he published *Fingal, An Ancient Epic Poem in Six Books, together with several other Poems composed by Ossian, the Son of Fingal.* The work was an instant success, and he followed it up with *The*

Works of Ossian in 1765. The authenticity of these texts, supposedly originating in the third century, was questioned by Dr Johnson, who challenged him to produce the originals. Macpherson challenged Johnson to a duel, but never produced any originals. He did not need to: the public wanted to believe in the authenticity of the texts, and the forgeries developed a life of their own.

The works of Ossian are couched in a language redolent of bardic antiquity and rendered in a measured rhythmic prose. The stories they tell are Homeric in their simplicity, and unmistakably eighteenth-century in their sentimentality. But it is the setting that is so striking. The scenery is wild and romantic, the mountains are shrouded in mist, streams rush through gloomy valleys, the sea storms at the mouth of caves, wind blows through the dishevelled tresses of the white-bosomed heroines and the flaming manes of their valorous deliverers. This fitted in with a fashion for gloom and horror, fostered by prints of wanderers among ruins and young men brooding in graveyards, and by an interminable poem by Edward Young, *Night Thoughts*, which, bafflingly, sold like hot cakes all over Europe. But the success of Ossian had deeper roots in the utopian subtext of the poems, which Macpherson himself spells out in a preface written in 1773.

'The nobler passions of the mind never shoot forth more free and unrestrained than in the times we call barbarous,' he writes. 'That irregular manner of life, and those manly pursuits from which barbarity takes its name, are highly favourable to a strength of mind unknown in polished times. In advanced society the characters of men are more uniform and disguised. The human passions lie in some degree concealed behind forms, and artificial manners; and the powers of the soul, without an opportunity of exerting them, lose their vigour. The times of regular government, and polished manners, are therefore to be wished for by the feeble and weak in mind. An unsettled state, and those convulsions which attend it, is the proper field for an exalted character, and the exertion of great parts.'[17]

Ossian enjoyed extravagant success all over Europe. People called their children after Macpherson's Caledonian heroines, pilgrims went in search of Fingal's Cave, and the poems inspired a generation with boundless dreams. They were the favourite reading, in Italian, of the young Napoleon Bonaparte. But it was in Germany that they had the most profound effect. There was hardly a German writer, from Goethe onwards, who did not fall under the spell of Ossian. For the German reading public and particularly for the frustrated young, Ossian opened up new possibilities to the imagination. Ossian had drawn attention away from the classical world, which, with its Mediterranean and Latin associations, seemed to exclude the Germans, and back to the misty north. Ossian had made wind and rain sexy. Here was an area that the French and the Italians could not lay claim to. The gloom and the sublimation, as well as the relentless lack of humour of the texts, suited the German temper of the times perfectly. The whole Ossian phenomenon also suited arguably the most influential German of his age, Johann Gottfried Herder.

Herder was a Lutheran pastor in the Baltic port of Riga, then in the Duchy of Kurland, a vassal province of the Polish Commonwealth. His hobby was the study of the folklore of the Baltic peoples among whom he lived, and this led him on to speculate about the role of language in defining culture. He was fascinated by its organic development over time, its relation to place, its mysterious rules and harmonies. His book on the origins of language, published in 1772, was a vindication of its primacy as a cultural medium.

Herder believed that people thought as they spoke. It followed that people of one tongue thought and behaved differently from those of another. He therefore divided people into linguistic units, which he defined with the word *Volk*. A *Volk* was not based on racial grounds. It was a partnership linking a group of contemporaries living in a given place into a great cultural dialogue with their forebears and, by implication, with later generations. As a result, every existing nation was a unique compound of blood, soil, environment, experience and destiny. Central to this vision was the sense that every *Volk* was engaged on some great trek towards self-realization. This led him to view history itself as a continuous process in which nations struggled to achieve self-fulfilment. All the bardic Caledonian stuff in Ossian was grist to Herder's mill. Even when, much later, he realized that Ossian was a hoax, he continued to cling to all that it had inspired in his own thinking. The world conjured by Ossian was 'a new miraculous region', and it was German because, according to Herder, it was a region of the German mind.[18] What he and others were searching for, indeed, seeking to invent, was a spiritual *patrie*, a sort of church, to which to belong.

The population of the German lands had doubled over the course of the century, giving forth an overabundance of young men with nothing to do and little to believe in. It was their longing for life and action that gave rise to something one can call a movement or just a mood, known as the Sturm und Drang, 'stress and strain'. This was essentially an emotional revolt against all rational and moral constraints. The tenor of the passions evoked is well rendered by a description of the first night of Schiller's play *The Robbers* in 1781: 'The theatre was like a lunatic asylum, with rolling eyes, clenched fists, hoarse uproar among the audience. Strangers fell sobbing into each other's arms, women tottered, half-fainting, to the door.'[19]

Among the many strands that made up the Sturm und Drang were a rejection of Enlightenment disciplines, a revolt against the constraints of the archaic constitutional arrangements in Germany, and the instinct to stake out a cultural territory that could transcend these. In 1773 Herder published *Von deutscher Art und Kunst*, with contributions by Goethe on Gothic architecture and Justus Moser on the historical predestination of the German nation. These ideas of a nation in the mind were taken up with piety by Klopstock and the Göttinger Hainbund group. The works of Christoph Wieland, judged to be too French and too courtly, were ceremonially burned in Göttingen in 1773. 'Court manners' had, according to Herder, spoilt the French language, driving out its true 'genius', 'truth' and 'strength'. Determined that the same fate should not befall German, he called for a 'limited nationalism' to defend German literary culture.[20] In the following year Klopstock declared that the time had come for the Germans to reassume control over their own culture. As an instrument for this, he suggested the creation of a nationwide alliance of intellectuals, a *Gelehrtenrepublik*, for which he drew up elaborate tables of ranks, procedures and rules. The first steps in this reassumption of 'control' were to be a rediscovery of the nation's heroic past, which Klopstock promptly set about glorifying in his *Hermann* trilogy, and a return to the true values and culture of the *Volk* through the study of peasant lore. Here he was connecting with the universal crypto-religious conviction of corruption in high places and purity among the humble.

Whatever significance may be attached to the Sturm und Drang, and whatever its origins or causes, one thing is known – it took its name from the title of a play written in 1776 by a law student called Friedrich Maximilian Klinger. It is a fatuous play, with a plot involving a feud between English families in the American colonies, set against the background of the rebellion. 'Hurrah for the tumult and uproar, when the senses reel like a vane in the storm!' runs the opening line.[21]

German reactions to the American war were similar to those elsewhere in Europe, even if they were less marked. Kant supported the Americans, as they seemed to be putting into practice his doctrine that a people has an innate capacity for creating its own moral world. Klopstock wrote an ode and termed the revolution 'the dawn of a great day to come'. He was sent a cane made in Boston, which he would invite visitors to his house to kiss as though it were a fragment of the true cross.[22] The leading writers echoed these sentiments, and Franklin, whose persona was so congenial to German *Gemütlichkeit*, was the recipient of endless paeans.

These enthusiastic German reactions were accompanied by a gloomy conviction that what the Americans were doing could not be achieved in Germany, which was felt to be irredeemably ensnared in a web of corruptions endemic to the old continent. 'Thine example calls out loud to the Nations: Free is, who free would be, and is worthy to be!' wrote one professor in an incontinent poem published in the *Berliner Monatsschrift* in 1783. But he hears 'the clank of chains' in his ears, 'reminding me, poor me, that I am a German'.[23]

One way in which the Germans attempted to rise above the terrible predicament of being German was through the rediscovery and appropriation of the Hellenic world. This was started by Johann Joachim Winckelmann, the son of a cobbler from Stendal. Winckelmann studied theology at Halle, and science and medicine at Jena, only to become a village teacher. He improved his situation by becoming librarian to an aristocrat and then to a cardinal, finally converting to Roman Catholicism in order to get a job in Rome. He was drawn to the art of the ancients by the sight of a few cameos and casts in German collections, and in 1755 he published his first thoughts on the subject. In Rome, and later on the sites of Herculaneum and Paestum, he was able to study original works more extensively. He published several other treatises and, in 1764, *A History of Art among the Ancients*, which became a classic text. He was honoured by Maria Theresa and Frederick II, who offered him the post of royal librarian, but he did not enjoy fame for long. In 1768 he was murdered by a rent-boy in Trieste.

The neoclassical revival affected most European societies. The ruins of Greece were seen as vestiges of a lost Arcadia, and when visiting Athens in 1784 the French Abbé Delille knelt on the steps of the Parthenon and embraced its columns, his eyes filled with tears. But with the Germans it was different. The idea of ancient Greece came to obsess the German imagination, and evoked a sometimes frantic desire for spiritual emulation. For Winckelmann, beauty was a moral quality. The ability to see and feel it was the mark of the superior nature of man – the aesthetic equivalent of the Christian concept of the soul. He saw in ancient Greece a civilization which had attained aesthetic perfection. Its study was therefore a form of moral education.

Goethe began his with a pilgrimage to Rome in September 1786. As soon as he crossed the Alps he began to feel curiously at home. 'I enjoy everything as if I had been born and bred here and had just returned from a whaling expedition to Greenland.' He now realized that all his life he had been 'suffering under an unfriendly sky' and complained that all Germans were unjustly 'chained to the north'. The initial revelation was aesthetic. In Venice, one of his first stops in Italy, Goethe was shown some fragments from a Greek temple, and he was overwhelmed by a violent reaction against his former Gothic predilections. 'From this, thank heavens, I have rid myself forever!' he exclaimed. The second stage of the Roman revelation was more spiritual. 'When I arrived in Italy I felt reborn,' he wrote after a year in the country, 'now I feel re-educated.'[24] Goethe applied himself with fervour to the understanding of classical art. He would contemplate or 'read' a piece of sculpture with deferential intensity until he felt he really comprehended it. Reaching such a level of heightened appreciation was like entering a state of holiness, and could only be achieved by lengthy veneration and pious study. Goethe's Italian journey was nothing less than a religious experience, the recognition of art as an agent of moral salvation.

Friedrich Schiller was also a practitioner of this faith. In his *Aesthetic Letters*, published in 1795, he would argue that the ancients had lived in greater harmony with themselves and their environment, and were therefore better men. 'Who among the moderns could step forth, man against man, and strive with an Athenian for the prize of higher humanity?' he demanded.[25] Although this harmony ultimately resided in nature itself, he believed that beauty was the key, the element that could reconcile all the existential problems of mankind. Viewed through this prism, ancient Greece assumed the guise of a lost Eden.

Perhaps the most traumatized by this vision of Greece was the poet Friedrich Hölderlin, a delicate, unquiet youth. As a student, he formed a *Dichterbund*, or poetic brotherhood, for the purpose of reciting poetry with his friends Friedrich Wilhelm Schelling and Georg Wilhem Hegel.

He hated the Germans for not being what he felt they should be and, like Winckelmann, saw in ancient Greece the only possibility of salvation, 'the holy shrine of youthful humanity'.[26] As for Winckelmann, ancient Greece for Hölderlin was a state of being rather than a place in time. And in the end he began to pray for a kind of Second Coming of ancient Greece to redeem the world.

Hölderlin suffered from depression and schizophrenia. While working as tutor to a family in southern France in 1802 he disappeared, after learning of the death of his beloved. He was found wandering around the park of a French château addressing the statues of Greek gods in their language. The gamekeeper was about to eject him when the *châtelain* appeared. He could see that the young man was no ordinary vagrant. 'Are you a Greek?' asked the concerned count. 'No, on the contrary, I am a German,' answered the distraught poet.[27] To be Greek was to be in a state of grace, to be German was to be unredeemed.

Much of European society was gripped by spasms of self-hatred and angst in the closing decades of the eighteenth century. The optimism of the early Enlightenment had evaporated. Reason had turned out to be just as baffling as the Old Testament, providing no final answers, only two sides to every question. Science had not prevented earthquakes or famines, delivered perfect health, or done anything but raise more questions about the nature and existence of the universe. The comfortable faith in Providence had not stood the test of time. Countless political theories and systems, not put into practice, had withered on the branch like unpicked fruit. The cult of reason had been succeeded by a greater interest in emotion, intuitive intelligence and in man himself. But this created new problems. Sensibility, which had replaced moral discipline as a guide to distinguishing right from wrong, had slipped into sentimentality. The interest in man and his emotions had engendered a search for happiness and emotional fulfilment that was both irrepressible and doomed to frustration.

The contradictions of the age of Enlightenment were coming home to roost, creating an uncertainty and a feeling of doom that went beyond politics. Many came to believe that the old world was simply past making a fresh start, being inveterately corrupt. Established religion had been so intensively mocked by the likes of Voltaire for so long that there could be no return to religious piety – even to admit belief was a sort of social solecism. As Tocqueville points out, the aristocracy actually 'turned impiety into a kind of pastime in their life of idleness'.[28] And other classes took the tone from them. At a dinner party in 1788 one of the guests told the *philosophe* La Harpe that his hairdresser had, between clouds of powder, announced: 'You see, sir, while I may only be a miserable fellow, I'm no more religious than the next man.' It was a way of establishing his credentials.[29] But the religious urge remained. And, bereft of the dogmatic framework of the Church's teaching, it left society ridiculously prone to any mystical nonsense on offer.

One of the first beneficiaries of this was Freemasonry, which had ramified far and wide throughout Europe and North America. This secret brotherhood dedicated to spreading the rule of reason and working for the good of humanity was the formal church of the great congregation that vaguely worshipped anything from 'Nature' to the 'Supreme Being'. Although Freemasons mostly met to listen to lectures or just talk, often about nothing very challenging, there was also much ritual involved. This became increasingly melodramatic, with initiation ceremonies usually involving the whole panoply of gothick props such as daggers, hoods, blood and fire. The appeal was enormous. There were 104 lodges in France in 1772, 198 by 1776, and a staggering 629 by 1789. Their membership included virtually every grandee, writer, artist, lawyer, soldier or other professional in the country, as well as notable foreigners such as Franklin and Jefferson – some 30,000 people.[30]

It was in Germany that Freemasonry was taken most seriously, overlapping as it did with genuine religious trends that aimed to return to some kind of more essential early Christianity on the one hand, and with earnest attempts to give the Enlightenment a mystical basis on the other. This led to tremendous frontier wars between lodges, followed by conferences and conventicles intended to reach agreement. It also provided the background for the birth of one of the most absurd movements of all, whose pale but sinister shadow would continue to send shivers up spines for generations.

In 1776 Adam Weishaupt, professor of Canon Law and Natural Law at the university of Ingolstadt in Bavaria, started a student society called the Order of Perfectibles – such bodies pullulated in German universities, and their names were often far more fantastic. In 1778 he changed the name to the Order of the Illuminati and reorganized it, introducing grades, codes, pass words and signs. Bavaria was referred to as 'Greece', Munich was 'Athens', and Weishaupt was 'Spartacus'. He ran the Order through an Aeropagus of five members. As is usual with bodies that indulge in elaborate definition of form and ritual, the Order of the Illuminati was somewhat lacking in substance. But in Frankfurt in 1780, it recruited a man who would take it on further, Baron Adolf Franz von Knigge. He assumed the name 'Philo' and began to transform the Illuminati. He taught that the existence of political states destroyed the natural harmony of life on earth, and that they must eventually be abolished. The political establishment was to be replaced by a universal exchange of goodness, a sort of early Christian way of life based on equality and liberty. Astonishingly, this creed attracted several hundred supporters. The Order's influence crept along the masonic network, in Germany and Austria, then on to Bohemia and Hungary, reaching beyond that into some French and Italian cities. It made some noteworthy recruits, including Mozart, Goethe, Schiller, Herder and a number of statesmen. More and more rituals were devised, and new grades were instituted, including 'grand magus' and 'Man-King'. In 1785 the Order was suppressed by the Elector of Bavaria, on the grounds that it was undermining the state. The public was treated to spine-chilling exposes of the heinous aims of the sect in a spate of strident pamphlets.

One thing that could not be banned, or even stemmed, was the ovine rush to find a new belief-system. People sought either a purer and more essential form of Christianity, or some cosmic system of absolute truth from which all religions purportedly descended. They followed a variety of teachers, such as the mysterious Martines de Pasquallys, who started up a fellowship of the 'Elect Cohens' and wrote a treatise on 'reintegration'. He preached a perverted form of Christian dogma, with frequent recourse to the symbolism of numbers, and asserted, amongst other things, that the Earth is triangular in shape. Another whose teachings drew in seekers after truth was the mystic philosopher Emanuel Swedenborg. Swedenborgian societies sprang up in many countries in the 1780s, including one in Moscow whose members called themselves 'children of the New Jerusalem', and one in Berlin some of whose members claimed to witness people rising from the dead in large numbers.[31] Some flocked to rosicrucianism or theosophy, or to one of the many other sects that sprang up, almost in proportion as Catholic monastic orders were dissolved in the name of Enlightenment.

Those seeking the elixir of life, the secret of the alchemists, the kabbalistic key or some such panacea were drawn into alchemy, hermeticism, necromancy, cosmosophy, chiromancy and a whole gamut of sorcery. There was much juggling with magic numbers, deciphering of the Bible with the use of equations, substituting of values and numbers for musical notes or colours, developing theories from the alleged 'moral planes' in the structure of the Pyramids and like nonsense. Occultism rubbed shoulders with pseudo-science, dressed up in the fashion of the day – be it Gothic, Hellenic or Oriental. This was a rich hunting-ground for charlatans such as the Sicilian Giuseppe Balsamo, alias Count Cagliostro, who ranged across Europe making and losing fortunes, bedding the most desirable and befuddling the most respected, flogging love-philtres and elixirs of eternal youth. Barely more reputable was the Austrian doctor Friedrich Anton Mesmer, whose theory of 'animal magnetism' and claims of healing powers thralled fashionable Paris. People as self-regarding as Lafayette sat for hours in bubbling vats filled with dubious chemicals, holding hands in a dimmed interior with plenty of mirrors and soft music, while Mesmer drifted about dressed as a children's-party magician, waving a wand over his victims.

Those who scoffed at religious ritual and the supposedly irrational beliefs it celebrated, led by the denouncer of superstition Voltaire and the self-proclaimed 'mortal hater of Nonsense, Foppery, Formality and endless ceremony' Benjamin Franklin, fell over themselves to join masonic lodges, so they could dress up and utter mumbo-jumbo in an atmosphere that made the most baroque Catholic ritual look dour by comparison.[32] Casanova and Cagliostro were only the most famous of an army of frauds who preyed on people too scientific and sophisticated to believe in God and His miracles, but gullible enough to hand over any amount of money to some joker who offered an elixir of youth or promised immortality.

It was in this climate that France drifted towards a new attempt at reform, dictated by widespread popular unrest and above all fiscal chaos. Disastrous harvests only aggravated the endemic poverty of a large part of the population. The rigid social system was barring the aspirations of officers, lawyers, doctors and merchants alike. And the French state, indebted to the hilt, was insolvent. The challenge was beyond the Assembly of Notables, which met in February 1787. It passed some useful measures, but it had neither the terms of reference nor the power to do anything radical. And, with discontent spilling over into rioting in various parts of the country, public opinion demanded more than tinkering. In the following year the king convoked the Estates General, which was an admission of the exceptional nature of the situation. The whole political nation was being involved in what would have to be a major work of restructuring.

The eyes of the world were fixed on Paris as the Estates General met, on 5 May 1789. But it quickly became obvious that there was something fundamentally wrong with the institution itself. Not only was it unrepresentative, it distinguished qualitatively between the nobles and clergy on the one hand and the non-noble Third Estate on the other. This went against the grain of everything that had been said and written over the past decades, and was perceived as being morally unacceptable. On 10 June the deputies representing the Third Estate, mostly ambitious young lawyers, invited those of the clergy and of the nobility to meet for the process of verifying the mandates. On 17 June the three estates declared themselves to be a National Assembly, and, three days after that, finding themselves locked out of their regular meeting-place on the king's orders, set themselves up in the covered tennis court nearby, where they swore a solemn oath not to separate until they had rebuilt the state on a sound basis. They were overwhelmed by a sense of occasion, and instead of concentrating on specific problems, they hailed the New Jerusalem that they felt sure lay just over the horizon. In word and print, they went on about 'the public good', the 'sacred cause of liberty', about blood, self-immolation and, endlessly, about regeneration.

It was, in the words of Tocqueville, 'a time of the young, of enthusiasm, of pride, of generous and sincere passions'.[33] But these chivalrous instincts remained curiously jejune. The deputies were no longer concerned with merely civil liberties. They wanted a complete change. But they had no idea of how to bring one about. That was what made the events of 14 July 1789 so significant.

5
Civil Rites

On the afternoon of 12 July 1789, when news arrived from Versailles that Louis XVI had dismissed the reforming minister Jacques Necker, the republican agitator Camille Desmoulins leapt on to a café table at the Palais-Royal and shouted, '*Aux armes!*' A crowd formed, and, after listening to some fiery oratory, moved off in procession to rouse the city. They carried busts of Necker and the Duc d'Orléans, and pinned green ribbons or sprigs to their hats – green, the colour of hope in Christian tradition, was also associated with the 'natural'. After a day of disturbances and a bungled attempt on 13 July to restore order with troops, large mobs intent primarily on finding mythical grain stores took over the streets. On the morning of 14 July they went in search of arms, and this led them to the Invalides, which they ransacked. They helped themselves to 30,000 muskets and a few pieces of artillery. But these were useless without powder, and that had been moved for safe-keeping to the Bastille a few days before. To the Bastille they therefore went.

After much inconclusive parleying, the crowd's patience snapped, one of their number cut the ropes holding up the drawbridge and it swarmed into the courtyard. By this time the assailants had been reinforced by numbers of soldiers. The governor, the Marquis de Launay, tried to surrender, but despite his efforts to hand the fortress over, they insisted on capturing it. He was then led away to the Hôtel de Ville, where he was murdered. His head was hacked off and impaled on a pike to be paraded around the city.

The Bastille had been built in the Middle Ages as a military defence, and since the seventeenth century it had served as a prison. Most of the detainees were sent there under a *lettre de cachet*, that is to say by order of the king and without trial. In the eighteenth century they included some clergy suspected of heresy, a few writers accused of publishing seditious literature, and, most commonly, aristocratic delinquents of one sort or another. A typical internee was the Marquis de Sade, who had been transferred to the madhouse of Charenton some ten days previously. When the Bastille's cell doors were thrown open on 14 July 1789, no more than seven prisoners emerged. Four of them were judicially convicted forgers. Two were lunatics, one of whom believed he was Julius Caesar, and they soon found themselves locked up again at Charenton. The seventh was the Comte de Solages, whose sexual depravity had so alarmed his family that they procured his incarceration.

The all but redundant fortress had long been earmarked for demolition. The area it occupied was to be turned into a pleasant open space, surrounded by a colonnade and embellished with a monument whose inscription would read: 'Louis XVI, Restorer of Public Freedom'. In political terms, the storming of the Bastille was therefore the battering down of an open door. Yet Lafayette sent the key of the fortress to George Washington, with a note in which he explained that 'this is a tribute that I owe you, as a son to his adoptive father, as an aide de camp to his general, as a missionary of liberty to his patriarch'.[1] It was all in the imagination. The Bastille's physical bulk represented all that was backward. Its role as destination for those restrained under a *lettre de cachet* stood for everything that was arbitrary about the French monarchy. Thomas Paine characteristically labelled it 'the high altar and castle of despotism'.[2] Many who had passed through it wrote memoirs in which they demonized it, sometimes falsifying the conditions under which they were kept, and the subject was exploited in literature to lurid effect. The public had a dread vision of dark dungeons into which people were cast and forgotten about, and in the days after its fall, this mythology was enriched by countless horrible 'discoveries' as the building was ransacked.

The news of its fall had an electrifying effect and, in the words of Mary Wollstonecraft, 'all the passions and prejudices of Europe were instantly set afloat'.[3] Writers and poets of every nationality glorified the event. The Duke of Brunswick, who had just put down the Patriot revolt in the Netherlands, applauded it. A sense of relief surged through Europe. 'Although the Bastille had certainly not been a threat of any sort to any inhabitant of Petersburg,' wrote Ségur, now French ambassador there, 'I find it difficult to express the enthusiasm aroused among the shop-keepers, merchants, townsfolk and some young people of a higher class by the fall of this state prison and this first triumph of a stormy liberty. Frenchmen, Russians, Danes, Germans, Englishmen, Dutchmen, all were exchanging congratulations and embraces in the streets, as though they had been delivered from some excessively heavy chain that had been weighing down on them.'[4]

Over the past decade, the popular imagination had been gripped by the imagery of liberation, renewal and regeneration. If 1776 had been, for progressive Europeans, a clarion-call heralding the advent of a new age, news of the Bastille's fall announced its dawning. The event was described in the first printed account as '*L'Oeuvre des Sept Jours*', suggesting analogy with God's Creation. The revolutionary priest Claude Fauchet saw it as the Second Coming. 'The day of Revelation has dawned,' he preached, prophesying 'the regeneration of human nature and a new life of the nations'.[5]

The storming of the Bastille transformed more than the political situation in France. While the Deputies had been agonizing in the National Assembly over the shape of things to come, the people had, so it seemed, suddenly asserted the fraternity that had been declared in the Versailles tennis court but had remained no more than a pious wish. The regenerate French nation had announced its entry on to the world stage by storming the citadel of the forces of darkness. With remarkable spontaneity, French society began to reinvent itself as an ideal nation of the kind the *philosophes* had dreamed of.

Some ten days before the fall of the Bastille, the Marquis de Mirabeau suggested to the National Assembly that the city of Paris raise a civic guard, and after the expulsion of the royal troops from the capital, the existence of such a force for law and order became essential. The electors of Paris therefore created, on 13 July, the Gardes Nationales. Being made up of voting citizens, this conformed to the fashionable model of the American militias and their inspirations in antiquity. As the only visible incarnation of the national will apart from the Assembly, it quickly came to represent the nation itself, and every town began to recruit its own force.

The National Guard was placed under the command of the Marquis de La Salle and adopted a green cockade. But someone pointed out that green was the livery colour of the arch-conservative youngest brother of the king, the Comte d'Artois, so they exchanged it for a cockade in the colours of the city of Paris, blue and red. The following day Lafayette, who saw himself as a sort of godfather to the newborn nation, turned up in Paris and managed to get himself appointed commander of the National Guard. He immediately implemented a few changes meant to make it more than just a bunch of pike-wielding grocers, one of which was to add the traditional white cockade of France to theirs, turning it into a tricolour of blue, white and red.

On 17 July Louis XVI drove into Paris without pomp, virtually unattended and simply dressed. He came to the Hôtel de Ville to meet the representatives of the Paris Commune, who proffered him one of the tricolor cockades. He received it with '*sensibilité*' and pinned it to his hat. When he had gone, the representatives voted to erect a statue to him on the site of the Bastille, whose demolition had begun. Without a vote, and without a decree, the tricolor cockade was adopted overnight as the emblem of the nation – to be sported even by the monarch, who had never worn any emblem other than a crown on his head.

People of every condition made their act of adhesion to the new nation. After the château-burnings and disturbances known as the *Grande Peur* that swept the countryside in the following weeks, a few nobles in the Assembly decided that the peasants should be placated by the abolition of some of their burdens. As the Assembly had no power to legislate on this, it was agreed that the Duc d'Aiguillon, one of the greatest landowners in the country, would propose that the nobility take the initiative by voluntarily commuting all manorial dues. On the evening of 4 August the duke did so. Lafayette's brother-in-law, the Vicomte de Noailles, leapfrogged him with the suggestion that all remaining traces of serfdom be abolished. This triggered an extravagant auction of altruism, as deputies bested each other to renounce something. Hunting rights, tithes and manorial jurisdiction, local privileges, court pensions, hereditary offices were all cast on to the bonfire of noble vanity, while the deputies, 'drunk with patriotism', embraced one another and wept.

Gestures and symbols were coming to dominate politics. Public life was cluttered with more or less formal emblems and shibboleths defining and characterizing the regenerate nation. The first and most ubiquitous was the tricolor, which everyone had to wear as a sign of communion with fellow citizens. The cock of the ancient Gauls replaced the fleur-de-lys, but the female figure in classical dress representing liberty became the dominant image of the new state. The pike, which had played a major part in the events surrounding the fall of the Bastille, and on which severed heads were regularly paraded about the streets, became a symbol of the true patriot-at-arms. The bundle of sticks, or Roman *fasces*, was used to signify the coming together of the French nation in one body.

The nation came together most commonly round another potent new symbol, the tree of liberty. In May 1790 Father Norbert Pressac, *curé* of Saint-Gaudens in the Poitou, had a young oak planted in the village square which he blessed as a symbol of the new life of the French nation. As a priest, he would have been aware of the rich web of association linking the primordial cults of the tree as a symbol of fecundity and renewal with the medieval European maypole, itself possibly related to the Egyptian worship of the phallus of Osiris, and the *lignum vitae*, the cross of Golgotha. The American colonists had turned their maypoles into political symbols by posting manifestos and flying the flag from them. In 1789 French peasants had begun putting up liberty poles, draped in the tricolor, to which they attached anything they deemed to possess significance, from tablets inscribed with the Rights of Man to agricultural implements and broken symbols of feudal power.[6]

One of the more interesting symbols that accompanied the rebirth of the French nation was the red cap of liberty, the *bonnet rouge*, which topped every flag-pole and liberty tree, capped every representation of liberty or the *patrie*, crowned milestones and anything else that lent itself, was carried on the end of the pike, painted on banners, worn on the breast as a decoration and on the head as a declaration. The origins of the cap lie in antiquity. Roman slaves were not allowed to cover their heads, and when a slave was freed, he would be ceremonially coiffed with a cap by his master. Thus the cap became a symbol of the recovery of freedom, and there was a legend that the whole population of Rome donned one when Nero died. The Roman version of the cap was a somewhat ungainly object shaped like the top two-thirds of an egg. The artists of eighteenth-century France, who had introduced it into their depictions of classical scenes, modelled theirs on the more shapely Phrygian caps to be seen in ancient representations of Paris and Ganymede. It was this version that was adopted as the symbol of the nation's liberation. It was treated with requisite piety, and in some revolutionary clubs people donned it in order to speak, just as a Catholic bishop puts on a mitre to give the blessing.[7]

There had been many spontaneous festivals held around the country to mark the triumph of the nation over the forces of darkness, and as the anniversary of the storming of the Bastille drew near, the idea of a country-wide commemoration suggested itself. But the great celebration proposed by the mayor of Paris, Sylvain Bailly, for 14 July 1790 was to be much more than a commemoration. It was to be a kind of Rousseauist troth-pledging, at which the nation would come together and symbolically constitute itself as a body, simultaneously paying homage to itself as such – the first of many acts of political onanism. Bailly suggested that the solemnity should take the form of a 'National Federation', with delegations from every corner of France meeting in Paris while those from surrounding villages congregated in every provincial town. Lafayette steered the whole exercise into the military sphere, substituting companies of National Guards from every part of the country for civilian delegates.

The capital was to be decked out in a fitting manner to greet those making their long pilgrimage. Half the population of Paris spent three days in the pouring rain putting up triumphant arches and decorations. The Champ-de-Mars was transformed into a vast elliptical arena surrounded by grass banks on which seats were erected for spectators. At the end nearest the École Militaire there was a stand draped in the tricolor for the members of the Assembly and important guests. At the opposite end, nearest the River Seine, was the entrance, through a triple triumphal arch in the Roman style. Between the two stood a podium with a throne for the king and seats for the royal family, and, towering above everything else, a great square plinth with steps on all four sides, on which stood an altar.

The morning of 14 July was wetter than ever, and the feet of 300,000 Parisians soon turned the Champ-de-Mars into a quagmire. This did not make the event any easier to manage, but good humour triumphed. As they waited in the rain, people made jokes about being baptized in the national rain, and groups from different parts of the country showed off regional dances to each other.

The king and queen arrived at noon, but it took a long time for them to be settled into their stand. Then came a march-past by 50,000 National Guards. It was not until four in the afternoon that the Bishop of Autun, Charles Maurice de Talleyrand-Périgord, attended by four hundred priests wearing the tricolor, began to celebrate mass. The altar at which he officiated was not a traditional liturgical *mensa*, but a circular neoclassical affair redolent of burnt offerings in ancient Rome. It was not the altar of

God, on which sacrifice was offered up to the Almighty, it was the *autel de la patrie*, on which citizens pledged their devotion to the motherland.

Lafayette was much in evidence all day on his white charger, and when the mass was over, he took centre stage. As if by a miracle, the weather cleared and the sun came out, bathing the whole scene in a soft luminous aura. While trumpets blared, Lafayette ascended the steps of the altar. As he began to swear loyalty to the king, the nation and the law, he drew his sword with a flourish and laid it on the altar. Fifty thousand National Guardsmen then repeated the same oath, followed by the king. Next came the singing of the *Te Deum* specially composed by François Gossec, during which people of all stations embraced tearfully in a hundred thousand acts of national fraternity. Lafayette was carried by the crowd to his white horse, on which he majestically left the field, with people kissing his hands and his clothes.

It had been a remarkable day. And the long march home was every bit as remarkable. The *Fédérés*, as those who had taken part were known, returned from Paris covered in medals, ribbons and diplomas attesting to their presence on the great day, as though they were pilgrims returning from some holy shrine. The journey home took longer than the march up to Paris, because it was incumbent on the *Fédérés* to bestow the blessing of their presence on every township they passed through. They had to recount their experiences in detail, show their mementoes and present their banner for all to kiss. This banner was so charged with significance that a ceremony not unlike that of the veneration of the Blessed Sacrament was enacted before it as it was escorted to its resting-place for the night – in the house of the most deserving local. When the *Fédérés* finally reached their home town, there would be a ceremonial distribution of the sacred bric-à-brac they had brought back, and pieces of this, along with the banner, were paraded, endlessly, around the locality.[8]

The Fête de la Fédération represented a reconciliation of all the people living in France, and their betrothal as one nation. It mimicked Rousseau's vision of the Corsicans coming together to found their nation through a common pledge. The festival was also a recognition that the Marquis de Lafayette and the humblest peasant in France were brothers, both as members of a biological family and through the ideological kinship represented by the oath. At the same time, the celebration exposed a new reality. It showed how far the concept of nationhood had altered from the

Enlightenment vision of a congeries living in consensus to something far more metaphysical, and inherently divine.

This was also reflected in the way the representatives of the nation proceeded. This 'inviolable priesthood of national policy', as Mirabeau once called the National Assembly, set about furbishing the terrestrial environment to suit the new incarnation.[9] They began with a physical redefinition of the land, dividing up the country into evenly balanced *départements*, each named after a river or other topographical feature. This destroyed the feudal vestiges inherent in the old provinces, and created an ambience redolent of the utopias sketched out by various *philosophes* over the previous decades.

Next came the standardization of the tools of intercourse between all Frenchmen. The plethora of different systems of weights and measures in operation in the country, leading to confusion and giving rise to abuse, cried out for rationalization. But the Assembly was not content merely to simplify or standardize. The age of reason and of the rule of nature demanded something altogether grander and more harmonious. The result was the metre, based on a one-ten-millionth fraction of the arc of the earth's meridian running through Paris. Area and volume were to be achieved by squaring and cubing the metre, and weight determined by units of a cubic decimetre of water.

The technical elegance of this achievement paled before the ultimate parameter – the definition of a new epoch in time. For if there had been something in the nature of a new incarnation, it was unseemly to continue numbering the years from the first one. On 2 January 1792 the National Assembly decreed that 'all public, civil, judicial and diplomatic documents will henceforth be inscribed with the date of the era of liberty'. This was originally assumed to have begun in 1789. But when the legislators began to implement their idea, there arose a degree of uncertainty as to when the actual '*moment sacré*' had occurred. The Assembly changed its mind several times before fixing on the foundation of the French Republic in 1792. This digging up and shifting of chronological milestones brought into question the validity of keeping the first day of January as the beginning of the year. The obvious New Year's Day for some was 14 July; others favoured a connection with the burgeoning of spring – someone suggested 1 April.[10]

But rearranging the timing of the world was no joke. In the autumn of 1792 the Convention, which had succeeded the National Assembly, nominated a committee with the brief of inventing an entirely new calendar. Its chairman, Gilbert Romme, a former tutor who dabbled in mathematics, was a provincial with a chip on his shoulder, and he savoured his new sense of power. 'Time is opening a new book of history,' he explained, 'and in its march, majestic and simple as equality itself, it must use a new stylus with which to engrave the annals of the regenerate France.' His calendar reflected the fashions of the age. His year opened on the Autumn equinox, 22 September, which happened, by a happy coincidence, to be the anniversary of the proclamation of the Republic.[11]

Romme's year consisted of twelve months of thirty days each, divided into three decades, leaving a set of five days at the end of the year. Each day had ten hours, with minutes and seconds in multiples of ten. This tied in with the metric system, and deferred to the higher wisdom of nature – man had been meant to count in tens, since he had been created with ten fingers. On 6 October 1793 the calendar became law and a decimal clock was installed in the Convention. It was a fitting monument to the 'systems' and utopias of the past half-century.

'He who would dare to undertake to establish a nation would have to feel himself capable of altering, so to speak, human nature, to transform each individual, who by his very nature is a unique and perfect whole, into a mere part of a greater whole, from which this individual would in a sense receive his life and his being,' Rousseau had written.[12] He understood that any polity, however logical, simple, elegant, poetic or modern, would be inadequate to replace the layered sacrality of something like the Crown of France and the whole theological and mythical charge of the Catholic Church. Human emotions needed something richer to feed on than a mere 'system' if they were to be engaged. And engaged they must be, for if one removed religious control of social behaviour and the monarch's role as ultimate arbiter, the very fount-head of civil sanction would dry up. Something had to be put in their place. The question was ultimately how to induce people to be good in a godless society.

As it was the people themselves who gave the state its legitimacy, it was they who had to be invested with divinity. The monarch would be replaced by a disembodied sovereign in the shape of the nation, which all citizens must be taught to 'adore'. 'It is education that must give to the souls of men the national form, and so direct their thoughts and their tastes, that they will be patriotic by inclination, by passion, by necessity,' Rousseau explained.[13] This education included not only teaching but also sports and public ceremonies designed to inculcate the desired values. 'From the excitement caused by this common emulation will be born that patriotic intoxication which alone can elevate men above themselves, and without which liberty is no more than an empty word and legislation but an illusion.'[14]

A precondition of this was the total elimination of Christianity. Being a sentimental person, Rousseau could not remain entirely unmoved by what he saw as the 'sublime' core of Christianity. But the existence of a morally independent religion alongside the civil institutions was bound to be destructive. 'Far from binding the hearts of the citizens to the state, it detaches them from it, as from all earthly things,' he writes: 'I can think of nothing more contrary to the social spirit.'[15] It forced on people 'two sets of laws, two leaders, two motherlands', subjecting them to 'contradictory duties' and preventing them from being 'both devout practitioners and good citizens'. Christianity demanded self-denial and submission, but only to God, and not to any creation of Man's. A Christian's soul could not be fused with the 'collective soul' of the nation, challenging the very basis of Rousseau's proposition. His assertion that 'a man is virtuous when his particular will is in accordance in every respect with the general will', was heresy in Christian terms, according to which virtue consists in doing the will of God.[16] There was no room for someone whose ultimate loyalty was to God in Rousseau's model, which substituted the nation for God.

The National Assembly's attitude to the Catholic Church and its hierarchy reflected this thinking. The holocaust of 4 August 1789 saw the end not only of all feudal rights, but also of ecclesiastical prerogatives. Tithes and other rights pertaining to parishes, bishoprics and religious foundations were abolished at a stroke. Unlike their lay counterparts, parish priests did not enjoy alternative means of subsistence. Accordingly, on 2 November the Assembly voted to sell off the entire estate of the Church, and to use the proceeds to pay the clergy a salary. In February 1790 the Assembly decreed the invalidity of monastic vows, thereby abolishing religious orders. It then replaced the 135 bishops with 85, one for each *département*, and provided one *curé* for every 6,000 inhabitants. Bishops were henceforth to be elected (by an electorate including non-believers, Protestants and Jews) without reference to Rome. On 26 November the

Assembly decreed that all priests must swear an oath of loyalty to the constitution, effectively turning them into salaried state functionaries. This process did not go according to plan; nearly half of the clergy refused to swear, so they were dismissed and later deported. The next measure deprived the clergy of their social function as keepers of the civil registers; it was now the state that would conduct marriages and implement divorces.

Many observers noted pseudo-religious tendencies in the revolution that was taking place. Burke was struck by its dogmatic, almost theological aspects, while Paine saw it as part of 'a general reformation'. The social economist Arthur Young sensed a mounting paranoia as he travelled around France in 1790. People talked hysterically of plots and saw a counter-revolutionary in every stranger. They seemed to crave crisis and blood. Anyone whose tricolor cockade had fallen off his hat was arrested and had to look to his life. Thomas Paine himself was almost lynched outside the Tuileries for not wearing one. According to Tocqueville, the revolution 'became a sort of new religion itself, an imperfect religion it is true, without a God, without ritual and without an afterlife'.[17] On these last three counts, he is mistaken. The spontaneous piety of the people of France supplied all three.

The theology may have been shaky, but the new religion did have a god. That god was the sovereign nation, whose service was the highest calling, as countless revolutionary 'catechisms' pointed out. The nation was sometimes confused with the *patrie*, which was not so much God as the Faith itself, that which one loved and died for. The tricolor stood in relation to this as the cross does to Christianity, with people kneeling before it, and an insult to it was described as 'sacrilege'. Both *patrie* and nation were anthropomorphic divinities, whose 'dignity' was often 'outraged', and their 'purity' 'insulted'. So was *Liberté*, always referred to as divine, and often as 'chaste daughter of the heavens', which was sometimes substituted for Christ and sometimes for the Virgin Mary in the many parodical prayers of the time. The unfolding story of the revolution was 'the Gospel of the day'.

The pseudo-religious rhetoric came naturally, deriving as it did from the Catholic upbringing which most Frenchmen had received and from the eighteenth-century literature of sentimental redemption. The word 'sacred' peppered every speech and written text. Public buildings of every sort were referred to as 'sanctuaries', since they were inhabited by 'sacred liberty'. The faithful were described as 'apostles', and there was much talk of 'revolutionary virtue', and of 'revolutionary purity', which could only be some kind of perversion of the Catholic 'state of grace'.

A mongrel liturgy combining Catholic reflexes with scraps garnered from Graeco-Roman antiquity had begun to evolve from the day of the Tennis-court Oath. The *Pater Noster*, the *Credo* and other prayers were rewritten, with the new deities and virtues substituted for the originals. The *Marseillaise* was officially described as 'the *Te Deum* of the Republic'. The sign of the cross was made 'in the name of Liberty, Equality and Fraternity' or, to honour martyrs of the revolution, 'in the name of Marat, Lepeletier and Bara' or some other revolutionary trinity.

Soon after the fall of the Bastille, altars of the *patrie* were erected in order to underline the need to offer up sacrifice to it. They replaced the altars of Christianity as surely as the maypoles and liberty trees replaced village crucifixes. The altars were adorned with busts of the luminaries of the new faith – Voltaire, Rousseau, Franklin and Brutus were the most common, though there were occasional appearances by others, from Algernon Sydney to Mirabeau – and with tablets inscribed with the Rights of Man. Other ritual objects came into being at the whim of the crowd whenever it gathered for some festivity or other. Relics of the new faith – stones from the Bastille, blood-soaked fragments of clothing, arms that had been carried in some sacred cause – proliferated, eliciting as much veneration as any Catholic relics.

The enthusiasm with which the public joined in the various festivals should surprise nobody. There had been a staggering number of high days and holidays celebrated under the *ancien régime*, particularly in rural areas. Aside from the main holy days of the religious calendar, these included patronal feasts, rogations, seasonal festivals, votive rituals, agricultural rites, guild or corporation feasts and anniversaries. They involved masses, venerations of the Blessed Sacrament or particular relics, processions, blessings and other rites, and usually elided with more profane festivities which were often characterized by a primitive vigour and a tribal possession of the village or town space. As the Catholic element was drained out of these rites, the paraphernalia of the national cult flooded in, to be venerated and borne in procession with as much fervour as relics or statues of saints in the past. The ritual parading of severed heads of various enemies of the revolution fitted into this context, as did the politically-inspired ritual commination of people, tendencies and ideas, and effigy-burning.

The first canonization in the new faith occurred when news of the death of Benjamin Franklin reached Paris at the beginning of June 1790. Ceremonies of commemoration were held by clubs, associations and local government bodies, with panegyrics, speeches and rituals. Typical was that held by Les Amis de la Révolution et de l'Humanité at the Café Procope on 14 June. The room was hung entirely in black and on a pedestal stood a bust of the man himself, crowned with oak leaves. The pedestal was inscribed with the single latin word *Vir.* Either side of the bust stood cypress trees, and beneath it a serpent devouring its tail, masonic hieroglyph for immortality. After a number of speeches before the bust, there was a symbolic distribution of bread to the people, a curious form of communion. The Assembly decreed three days of official mourning, and a portrait of the new saint was hung on the wall. Eighteen months later, on 12 February 1792, the Jacobin Club held a ceremony to inaugurate the busts of Voltaire, Rousseau, Franklin and Mirabeau – who had died in the interim. The hymn sung on this occasion named them as 'gods'.[18]

On 4 April 1791, the Assembly decreed that the Church of St Geneviève was to become the resting-place for those who had rendered exceptional services to humanity. Later the same day, Mirabeau was laid to rest there, after interminable funeral rites. The architect Quatremère de Quincy turned the church – built to give thanks for the restoration to health of Louis XV – into 'a visible Elysium', cutting off the two towers and removing statuary, altars and other ornaments. He was determined that nothing should distract from the new 'religion' whose saints it was henceforth to celebrate. In July 1791, the remains of Voltaire were translated to the Panthéon, as it became known.

The prophets and patriarchs were soon succeeded by the martyrs of the new faith. First came Louis-Michel Lepeletier de Saint-Fargeau, a former marquis and a deputy to the Convention, murdered by a royalist the day after he had voted for the death of Louis XVI. His half-naked and bloodstained body was paraded around Paris for all to see before being laid to rest at the Panthéon. Jacques-Louis David painted an icon of him, which was duly hung in the Chamber. Then came Jean Paul Marat, assassinated by Charlotte Corday. His martyrdom was rendered by David in one of his most famous paintings, and that too came to grace the Chamber. The body itself lay in state until it stank, and was the object of elaborate rites. 'Jesus is a prophet, Marat is God', was but one of the slogans in evidence.[19]

Tocqueville was profoundly mistaken when he described the religion of the revolution as having no afterlife. Diderot, while raging against stupid people, priests, tyrants and other assorted aggravators of the philosopher's lot, had taken comfort in the idea of posthumous vindication. 'O Posterity, holy and sacred! Support of the oppressed and unhappy, thou who art just, thou who art incorruptible, thou who will revenge the good man and unmask the hypocrite, consoling and certain idea, do not abandon me!' he wailed. 'Posterity is for the philosopher what the other world is for the religious,' he added, just in case there should be any doubt.[20] His fellow *philosophe* and prominent revolutionary Condorcet viewed posterity as the collective spirit of future humanity. But Robespierre saw it as something more active and altogether greater when making the following speech in the Jacobin Club: 'O posterity, sweet and tender hope of humanity, thou art not a stranger to us; it is for thee that we brave all the blows of tyranny; it is thy happiness which is the price of our painful struggles: often discouraged by the obstacles that surround us, we feel the need of thy consolations; it is to thee that we confide the task of completing our labours, and the destiny of all the unborn generations of men! . . . Make haste, O posterity, to bring to pass the hour of equality, of justice, of happiness!' In his theology, posterity had not only elbowed God out of the judgement seat but taken His place as redeemer.[21]

In 1793 France was invaded, her armies were defeated, a royalist insurrection broke out in the Vendée, Toulon was in the hands of royalists, there were risings in Lyon, Bordeaux, Toulouse, Marseille and Normandy. The Republic faced extinction, and its preservation warranted extreme measures. In July a Committee for Public Safety (the French word, *salut*, actually means 'salvation') was established, and it immediately adopted an attitude and an imagery of extreme ideological fervour. Its practical need to eliminate enemies and cow the population was dressed up as a process of purification, from which the nation would emerge as the embodiment of good, set to triumph over the forces of evil in the shape of the monarchical world.

Condorcet saw Robespierre as a priest *manqué*, and there was certainly something sacerdotal about his sense of vocation. Others referred to him as 'the Messiah of the People', gracing his acolyte, Louis Saint-Just, with the title of his St John the Baptist. Their dedication to the cause was not in question. Robespierre really believed in the possibility of the whole nation achieving a state of exalted grace that would turn the revolution into an orgasm of perfection, and he did not stint himself. 'O sublime people! receive the sacrifice of my entire being,' he begged, 'happy is he who is born in your midst! happier still he who is able to die for your happiness!'[22] But if Robespierre had the nature of a priest, he had the heart of a lawyer. He controlled the fire in his thoughts with a cold, intransigent rationale, barely concealing his distaste for the spontaneous and the popular. He determined to mould the beliefs of the French nation, aided by a team of like-minded souls, including Saint-Just, the future arch-policeman Joseph Fouché and David, the original agitprop artist.

Their first venture in this direction was the Festival of the Republic, held on 10 August 1793. It was dreamed up by David and proposed in a document of astonishing lyricism. The people of France were to wake before dawn and come together as the sun rose, so that the rebirth of the nation would be illuminated by its first rays. The ceremony began at the site of the Bastille, where a Fountain of Regeneration had been erected in the shape of a huge statue of Nature, a nude female figure in the Egyptian style from whose copious teats gushed two streams of crystal clear water. Representatives of all the *départements* passed round a cup filled from this divine source and drank deep of the life-giving draught. The procession then moved off across Paris, pausing at five 'stations', each with its own liturgy. At the Place de la Révolution a pyre with thrones, crowns and other trappings of despotism was ignited and three thousand birds were released, each with a tricolor ribbon round its neck bearing the glad news of the national gospel. The last station was at the Champ-de-Mars, where, after the appropriate rites had been performed, the people settled down to a fraternal picnic.

This consecration of the nation was linked to the ultimate desecration of the defunct monarchy. The Abbey of Saint-Denis just north of the capital, founded by the eponymous first bishop of Paris and patron of France, had been the mausoleum of her kings since the sixth century. On 1 August 1793, the Convention decreed the destruction of the royal tombs. The task was far more complicated than imagined, and took months of hard work by large gangs of labourers supplemented by soldiers. It was nothing short of an act of exorcism, with the mortal remains being boiled, burned and ground up before being buried in quicklime. An analogous process of extirpation was taking place in the provinces, under the direction of special commissioners sent out by the Convention as 'apostles' of the revolution.

The Fête de la Raison, held in churches all over the country on 10

November 1793, took the whole process one step further, by invading the sacred spaces with the new rite. In the Cathedral of Notre-Dame an actress dressed as the Goddess of Reason and enthroned on the main altar presided over the proceedings, while other actresses performed an act symbolizing the birth of Reason, chanting an adaptation by Gossec of the anthem *O Salutaris Hostia*.

Robespierre and his associates sought to impose their own Jesuitical version of Rousseau's nation-building precepts on the people of France. They came up with a number of educational and civic projects of stunning humourlessness designed to control and direct even the most intimate human activities. The exemplar was a Sparta seen through the idealized prism of the writings of the *philosophes* and canvases of David. Every citizen must devote himself to the nation. 'Each of us is responsible to the nation for the talents he has received from nature', in the words of David, parodying Christ's parable of the talents.[23] He must be prepared to sacrifice himself, his wife, his children and anything he holds dear for the common good without demur or even question. Sentimentality, which had been such a weapon in discrediting the *ancien régime*, was now declared a dangerous indulgence which could lead patriots into the 'false sensibility' of compassion. This was the logic of Torquemada. It needed the sanction of a god, and Robespierre invented one.

On 7 May 1794, the Convention decreed that 'The French people recognizes the Supreme Being and the immortality of the soul'.[24] This permitted Robespierre to frame his levers of political control in pseudo-religious ritual and observance, and to anchor the functions of the state in the new temples of the nation. The new cult had defined ceremonies, with celebrants and congregation. Significantly, the Festival of the Supreme Being held in the gardens of the Tuileries on 8 June 1794 featured at its core an artificial mountain. This symbolized first and foremost the political Mountain – the Deputies of the National Assembly had divided into the moderate Girondins, the more violent Club des Amis de la Constitution, otherwise known as 'Jacobins', and the most radical group, who sat in the high seats at the back, known as La Montagne. When this last group came to power, their party was referred to as 'the Holy Mountain', and it figured in all revolutionary iconography. But on this occasion, the mountain erected in the Tuileries gardens was even more loaded with symbolism, and at a crucial moment in the ceremonies it was clearly meant to suggest Mount Sinai.

The *philosophes* had raged against the Church hierarchy's determination to force others towards salvation, but their pupils quickly succumbed to the same coercive impulse – and the new religion was as fond of the *auto-da-fé* as the old. People suspected of 'fanaticism', as Christianity was referred to, were ordered to kneel before a bust of Marat or some other revolutionary symbol. As in all fundamentalist sects, moderation, the sign of lukewarm faith, was considered to be as heinous as any sin it might lead to. Political life became a series of purges, confessions, denunciations, purifications and excommunications, to which nobody was immune.

The hysterical nature of the fight against the civil heresy of moderation shines through in the language used by Marc-Antoine Jullien, a representative of the people sent out to restore the authority of the Convention in north-western France, in a sermon to the Jacobin Club of La Rochelle in February 1794. He castigates the 'involuntary tendency by which the purest patriot is led on to moderation and weakness'. Vigilance is everything, and 'the popular societies, though repeatedly purged, still need regeneration'. 'But do not suppose that [the moderates] attack our sternness of character directly,' he warns. 'If they did, they would be like a wave breaking impotently on a rock. Do not think that they make open war on the patriots. They lack the manly courage for such a conflict. They kill us with caresses.' Like some early Dominican preacher, Jullien alerts his flock to the perils of 'honeyed politeness' and dangerous female temptresses. 'You must flee from them as you flee from roses that cannot be touched without exposure to the thorns. You must fear an agreeable contagion, the more dangerous because it is hidden. The serpent glides among the flowers.'[25]

The cult of the Supreme Being failed to catch on. It failed because it did not strike a chord in the essentially Christian psychological make-up of Frenchmen of the time. The cult of the nation was another story. With its application of Christian principles and forms of worship to man, and by extension to the great human collective that was the nation and the Eden-substitute that was the *patrie*, it held immediate, profound and universal appeal. Anthropomorphically visualized as a universal ideal female, the nation kindled desire for selfless sacrifice in its cause, and that was the great strength of the French revolution. 'Since it appeared to be more concerned with the regeneration of the human race than with reforming France, it aroused feelings that no political revolutions had hitherto managed to inspire,' explained Tocqueville. 'It inspired proselytism and gave birth to the *propagande,*' he continued, and, 'like Islam, flooded the whole world with its soldiers, its apostles and its martyrs'.[26]

6

Holy War

On 14 July 1792, the third anniversary of the fall of the Bastille, Europe was poised on the cusp of two political eras. The most offensive aspects of the *ancien régime* had been swept away in France and, to a lesser extent, in other places, at no great cost to political stability. The optimism of 1789 had not died away, faith in the triumph of reasonableness and humanity was still strong. 'There never was a time in the history of this country,' asserted William Pitt in his budget speech on 17 February 1792, 'when, from the situation in Europe, we might more reasonably expect fifteen years of peace, than we may at the present moment.'[1] There was no apparent threat from across the Channel. Louis XVI had become 'king of the French' and 'father of his country', modelling himself on his pragmatic and legendarily popular forebear Henri IV. Everything was done to forget that he had only recently tried to run away from his people and, stopped at Varennes, been brought back to Paris an actual prisoner. He and his consort Marie Antoinette presided over the anniversary celebrations on the Champ-de-Mars, with Lafayette in attendance just as at the Fête de la Fédération, held in the same place exactly two years before. Everything was as it should be, except that missing from the attendance was a detachment of several hundred Marseillais National Guards, still on the march from the south, singing a catchy new song composed by Rouget de Lisle for the Armée du Rhin a couple of months before.

The anniversary was also officially celebrated in Belfast, where the proceedings were barely coherent. The parade was opened by some dragoons, followed by the flags of 'the Five Free Nations': Ireland, the

United States, France, Poland and Great Britain, and a portrait of Benjamin Franklin. Next came a brigade of Irish Volunteers, followed by the artillery of the Belfast Blues. The centrepiece of the procession was a great standard, fixed on a cart drawn by four horses, a kind of carnival float. One side bore a representation of 'the Releasement of the Prisoners from the Bastille', the other a depiction of Hibernia in shackles being offered a statue of liberty by an Irish Volunteer. The standard was escorted by a second brigade of Volunteers, and the procession was closed by a portrait of Mirabeau with the inscription: 'Our Gallic brother was born in 1789. We are still in embryo.' In the evening there was a banquet. Wolfe Tone thumped his glass on the table so hard after every toast that he broke it. The first toast had been 'The King of Ireland' – George III was still for the Irish, as he had been for the Americans, 'the best of kings'.[2]

In Poland on the same day, that other 'good king' who modelled himself on Henri IV, Stanisław Augustus, was reviewing his Guards outside Warsaw. It was the pivotal moment of his reign. He had weathered the patriotic storm that began in 1788, and by the autumn of 1790 he was being referred to even by radicals as 'the heart in the body of the nation'. Thanks to this he was able to impose his own ideas on the commission nominated by the Sejm to produce a new constitution. This was passed on 3 May 1791, to universal chants of 'The King with the Nation, the Nation with the King'. The constitution was not particularly radical in itself, but it was designed to create a new nation in place of the old noble Commonwealth. The Empress Catherine II could not countenance this change, which threatened her own absolutist regime by implication, and Russian troops were on the move. The Polish army scored two minor victories, the first won by the king's nephew Prince Józef Poniatowski, the other by General Tadeusz Kościuszko. But the Poles could not hope to win the war against their powerful neighbour. Stanisław had written to Catherine suggesting they negotiate a settlement, and was awaiting her reply.

At Frankfurt-am-Main that very same 14 July 1792, Marie Antoinette's nephew Francis II was being crowned Holy Roman Emperor in 'one of the most grandiose and most magnificent spectacles it was possible to witness', in the words of Count Klemens von Metternich, who had assisted at the coronation of Leopold II only two years before. The seventeen-year-old had drunk in the splendour, reflecting that the ancient traditions on which it was founded offered a comfortingly solid bulwark against the sort of disintegration and mob rule he had recently witnessed across the border in French Strasbourg, where he had been pursuing his studies. It was only later that he saw his mistake. 'I was sleeping beside a volcano, without a thought for the lava that would pour out of it,' he recalled.[3]

The volcano erupted soon after. Less than a month after all the celebrations, the French monarchy had fallen, and six months later the king was executed. Within the month too, Poland had been overwhelmed by the Russian armies; the constitution was abolished and one of the old kingdoms of Europe extinguished. Within two years, Wolfe Tone would no longer be toasting the king, but plotting sedition. He would later go on to raise the standard of rebellion in Ireland, wearing the uniform of revolutionary France. Francis's was to be the last coronation of a Holy Roman Emperor. And the song of the Marseillais National Guards would resound across Europe from Lisbon to Moscow over the next two decades, leaving the Continent irreversibly altered.

Louis XVI's youngest brother, the Comte d'Artois, had seen the implications at once and left France two days after the fall of the Bastille. Catherine had also sensed them. She had stamped her foot with rage as she read of the 'horrors' being perpetrated in Paris. Her correspondent, the *philosophe* Baron Melchior Grimm, confirmed her in her views. 'If the French delirium is not properly repressed, it may be more or less fatal to the heart of Europe,' he warned, 'for the pestilential air must inevitably ravage and destroy everything it approaches.'[4] Gustavus III of Sweden agreed. 'The news from France has horrified me so much that I could not get to sleep last night until 4 o'clock,' he wrote to Baron Armfeld on 19 August 1789. 'What horrible people! they are the orang-outangs of Europe.'[5] He applied himself to forming a league of princes against the revolutionary threat, but he found little support for the idea; few had grasped the full implications of the birth of the new nation on 14 July 1789. These were to become apparent two years later.

On 20 June 1792 a large crowd from the poorest *faubourgs* of Paris came to plant a liberty tree in the gardens of the Tuileries and read to the National Assembly one of the innumerable petitions which made its life such hell. By sheer weight of numbers, the crowd pushed through the gates of the royal palace and came face to face with Louis XVI in one of the upstairs salons, where the defenceless monarch had to endure the abuse of the mob. Pistols and drawn sabres were waved in his face, and he was threatened with death. More significantly, he was made to don a red cap and drink the health of the nation – and thereby to acknowledge its sovereignty. By acquiescing, he toasted himself off the throne.

A week later Lafayette attempted something in the nature of a coup in order to restore the authority of the Crown but was unsuccessful. By the end of July Paris had become impossible to control, and in this climate of lawlessness the Jacobins prepared their revolution. On the night of 9 August the tocsin began to toll as armed gangs assembled all over the capital. By morning, a sea of people was converging on the Tuileries, where the royal family waited, defended only by the faithful regiment of Swiss Guards. At the last moment they were persuaded to take refuge in the building of the National Assembly, which probably saved their lives. The mob stormed the Tuileries and proceeded to slaughter every Swiss they could find. In their fury, they mutilated the corpses, cutting off genitalia and stuffing them into mouths or feeding them to dogs. Pieces of the red uniforms of the Swiss were carried about as trophies by the heroes of that day.

In the early stages of the revolution, a red flag was used as a warning that martial law was in operation: when it was hung out, people knew they might be fired on. On 10 August 1792, a Jacobin ringleader marching on the Tuileries had procured a red flag and written on it in black letters: 'Martial Law of the Sovereign People against Rebellion by the Executive Power' ('the Executive Power' was the role ascribed to the king in the new constitution). Later that day the red flag floated over the Tuileries.

A few weeks later, in September, the mob invaded the prisons of Paris and spent two days butchering all the inmates. When reproached for permitting these acts of savagery, the revolutionary leader Georges Danton replied that they had been necessary in order to put 'a river of blood' between the volunteers who would be called upon to defend the revolutionary *patrie* and those who would attempt to stifle it.[6] They certainly stamped the mark of Cain on the revolution and bound the French people into a bloody complicity that set them apart. There was a logic in Danton's words, for a contest had begun that was unlike any other war fought on the Continent for centuries. It was a contest between two incompatible and mutually exclusive views of how human society was to be organized – essentially a contest for the soul of Europe.

Back in May 1790 the Assembly had been obliged to address itself to the question of whether to honour France's old alliance with Spain and back that country in the confrontation with England over Nootka Sound. The Deputies did not like the idea of war because it would be expensive, and feared that a victory would increase the king's prestige. They also felt that the new France should make some kind of moral statement.

The Enlightenment had been essentially cosmopolitan in nature. Its arguments were developed across frontiers and applied to humanity as a whole. 'If I knew of something that would be useful to my country but also ruinous for another,' Montesquieu had written in his *Cahiers*, 'I would not propose it to my prince, because I am a man before being a Frenchman, or rather because I am a man by nature and a Frenchman only by accident.'[7] The Scottish philosopher David Hume had been of the same mind. 'Not only as a man, but as a BRITISH subject, I pray for the flourishing commerce of GERMANY, SPAIN, ITALY, and even FRANCE itself,' he had written.[8] Every political system propounded over the past decades assumed that its imposition would usher in an eternity of peace. With the people in power there could be no more war, since only wicked monarchs made war.

The attitude in which the Assembly had contemplated the possibility of war in May 1790 was therefore predictably pacifist. 'Following principles very different from those which have brought about the misfortunes of peoples, the French nation, content to be free, does not wish to engage herself in any war and wishes to live with all peoples in that brotherhood ordained by nature,' declared Robespierre. The Assembly's decree, dated 22 May 1790, stated categorically that 'the French nation renounces the undertaking of any war with a view to making conquests and will never use her forces against the liberty of any people'.[9]

They were as good as their word, even overscrupulous. Soon after the fall of the Bastille, delegates from Corsica had begged the Assembly for incorporation into France (it was only in French possession because of a deal made between France and its previous colonial master, Genoa). The Assembly debated the issue thoroughly before voting its assent. On 3 April 1790 Pasquale Paoli arrived in Paris from his exile in London, to be greeted by Lafayette and the National Assembly, whose president hailed him as 'hero and martyr of liberty'. On 14 July 1790 he sailed for Corsica, where he fell on his knees and kissed the ground. At his side was the son of his erstwhile secretary, the young lieutenant Napoleon Bonaparte.

The Assembly was even more scrupulous in other cases. The Papal fief of Avignon, whose people had voted to fuse with France on 11 June 1790, was kept waiting until September 1791 before the Assembly finally agreed. In May 1791 a delegation of Dutchmen appealing for French intervention were put off, and Alsace, which voted to become part of France, was only admitted after much hesitation. All these niceties could not hide the obvious, namely that events taking place in France were an example to other peoples and a provocation to their rulers. As the American minister in Paris, Gouverneur Morris, commented, 'the Declaration of the Rights of Man produces the effect of Joshua's trumpets'.[10]

On the evening of 19 June 1790, a body consisting of representatives of twenty-one nations had presented itself before the National Assembly to ask permission to join in the celebrations of 14 July. It was led by Anacharsis Cloots, one of the more colourful figures on the Parisian scene. Born in Cleves to one of Frederick of Prussia's councillors and christened Jean-Baptiste, Cloots had moved to Paris, where he amused himself publishing anti-religious tracts. In 1789 he came out as a militant revolutionary and changed his name. As his new patron he chose Anacharsis, a son of Scythian nomads who had absorbed the learning of Greece and been the first foreigner to be granted Athenian citizenship in the sixth century BC, and who had gone on to spread the political culture of his adopted land to other peoples. Cloots was supported by a costumed cast, with an 'Arab' on his right and a 'Chaldean' on his left. He read out an address to the Assembly, which he termed 'the Oecumenical Council of Reason', asking for permission to take part in the Fête de la Fédération. 'The trumpets which proclaimed the resurrection of a great people echoed to the four corners of the world,' he ranted. 'The Fête of the Fédération will be the fête of the human race.'[11]

In these circumstances, the Assembly's rejection of war was disingenuous. Even the pacifist Robespierre admitted that 'it is from France that the liberty and happiness of the world must originate'.[12] That was a challenge, if not a declaration of war, on every throne in Europe. Brissot declared that he 'cannot be at ease until Europe, and all of Europe, is in flames', and dreamed of 'a universal crusade for liberty'.[13]

On 20 April 1792 France declared war on 'the king of Bohemia and Hungary' (Francis had not yet been crowned Emperor). It was meant as a defensive measure, but it was ineluctably the start of a general European war. In an address to the French people, the Convention explained that it had heard the voice of the *patrie* crying out. 'Go, and make me free; assure my future happiness, even at the expense of my present tranquillity,' the motherland had demanded. 'If, in order for me to cease being a slave it is necessary to conquer the whole of Europe, make me fight against it.'[14]

By then, France already had what was beginning to look like an international army. In April 1792 a Belgian Legion was formed out of the 1,500 mainly Liégois patriots who had taken refuge on French soil after the failure of their rising against Habsburg rule. In July 1792 a Batavian Legion was formed from the Dutch refugees in France, most of whom had been living there since 1787. Another body, originally termed the Prussian, then the Vandal and finally the Germanic Legion, was raised at the instigation of Cloots. A few weeks later, on 8 August 1792, an Allobrogian Legion was formed out of Swiss, Savoyard and Piedmontese revolutionaries. Although the majority were Swiss, it was not called the Swiss Legion because this brought to mind the Guards who had been massacred at the Tuileries for their devotion to the monarchy. There was even an English Legion, under the command of John Oswald.[15]

When Austrian troops crossed the frontier into northern France, the first unit they encountered was some Irish cavalry commanded by General James O'Moran. He was one of the many Irishmen who had traditionally taken service with His Most Christian Majesty. In 1791 many of them followed the emigrés and continued to serve the monarchist cause. For others like O'Moran, the brotherhood of man was beginning to pull more strongly than the old religious affiliations. The French force closest to the border was a division of 4,000 men based at Lille under the command of General Theobald Dillon, a native of Dublin and an experienced soldier who had distinguished himself in America.

Dillon's attempt to bar the Austrian advance at Tournai turned into an ignominious rout as his troops fled back to Lille and hacked him to pieces. Further French resistance in the north proved hardly more effective, and the Austrians advanced in relaxed manner. On 19 August, a combined force of French emigrés, Prussians, Austrians, Hessians and other imperial troops, led by the Duke of Brunswick and under the overall command of the king of Prussia, crossed into France from the east. On 3 September the garrison of Verdun surrendered with hardly a shot fired, and the fortress's unfortunate commander, Colonel Beaurepaire, committed suicide.

The combined force advanced with confidence, expecting to march to Paris without hindrance. But after a daring flanking move General Charles Dumouriez barred its way in the forest of the Argonne. The Duke of

Brunswick turned the French position and forced Dumouriez to fall back, this time on Saint-Menehould, where he was joined on 19 September by General Kellermann with the Armée du Centre. Brunswick again tried to outflank the French, but they had taken up strong positions on the heights of Valmy between the village of that name and a prominent windmill. He would have to dislodge them before he could move on. Although his troops were not in a good position to give battle, it was assumed that the French army, supposedly demoralized and deprived of its best officers by the revolution, would scatter at sight of the Prussian grenadiers.

As the morning mist cleared on 20 September the Prussian artillery opened up on the French positions. The French lines did not flinch, and only wavered slightly when a Prussian shell hit a French artillery caisson, causing a gigantic explosion. And the French artillery fired back with regularity and precision. The cannonade lasted for four hours, during which the French infantry on the ridge and the Prussian grenadiers below them, both just out of range of each other's guns, eyed each other without much enthusiasm.

Watching them, and taking a keen interest in the proceedings, was Johann Wolfgang Goethe, who rode about the battlefield dressed in an unsoldierly brown riding-coat, making detailed observations on the behaviour of soldiers under fire, the sound of flying cannon-balls and the effects of heat on colour. He had come in the suite of his master, the Duke of Saxe-Weimer, who was personally leading his regiment of Life Guards.

In the early afternoon the Prussian grenadiers attacked. The going was hard and their heart was not in it. After a few hundred yards they stopped, hesitated, and then began to fall back. On the heights of Valmy, Kellermann raised his tricorn on the end of his sword and shouted '*Vive la Nation!*' He was answered by frantic cheering, followed by a blood-curdling rendering of '*Ça ira!*' and the song that had come to be known as the hymn of the Marseillais. But that was as far as the heroics went. The Duke of Brunswick realized he could not win easily and, reluctant to risk his reputation, broke off the engagement. But the French did not counter-attack.

In order to show that he had not lost, Brunswick ordered his army to occupy the field of battle. There they duly camped, getting cold and wet in the cause of preserving their honour. After ten days they began a retreat that gradually turned into a débâcle which cost far more in casualties and equipment than the battle itself. The losses on 20 September had been only 184 dead and wounded on the Prussian side and 150 killed and 260 wounded on the French – out of a total of some 70,000 men massed on the field of battle.[16] The engagement hardly warrants the prestigious designation of battle. It was more akin to two mongrels meeting on the edge of their patches, sniffing each other and then backing off, with much face-saving raising of hackles and spraying of lamp-posts. Yet the very name 'Valmy' quickly assumed an extraordinary significance.

'Here and now a new epoch in world history is beginning,' Goethe said to one of the officers with whom he huddled for warmth on the heath below the heights of Valmy after the battle.[17] The German poet Ludwig Tieck, who was still studying theology at Göttingen, never forgave fate for not allowing him to have been in Dumouriez's ranks at this 'French Thermopylae', as he referred to it.[18] Four decades later, the French poet Chateaubriand, on his way from Metz to Châlons, made a detour to avoid the heights of Valmy. 'I was afraid I might stumble on a crown there,' he explained.[19]

The crown he alluded to was the Crown of France, abolished the day after the battle, but retrieved nearly forty years later by someone who had been present at Valmy, and whose claim was based largely on this presence: among the officers on Kellermann's staff was a newly-promoted eighteen-year-old lieutenant-general by the name of Louis Philippe, Duc de Chartres, future king of the French. Five days earlier, on 15 September, his father, the Duc d'Orléans, had changed his name to citizen Philippe Égalité. Chartres's colleague at Valmy, General Alexandre Berthier, was a veteran of the American war, as was Colonel Alexandre de Beauharnais, father of Eugène and Hortense, who was also on Kellermann's staff. Dumouriez himself had fought in America, as well as in Corsica and Poland. Among the officers on his staff was the young Macdonald who had marched off to uphold Dutch liberties in 1787. And there were plenty of other interesting people in the French ranks at Valmy on that day. They included General Arthur Dillon, kinsman of the commander murdered at Lille, himself a veteran of the American war and a Deputy to the French National Assembly; General Isidore Lynch, another Irishman, who had served on Rochambeau's staff in America, now commanding part of the French infantry; General John Key Eustace, a New Yorker; and General Francisco de Miranda, a Venezuelan who was dreaming of wider horizons. A similar pattern obtained throughout the French army. James Bartholomew Blackwell from County Clare had taken part in the storming of the Bastille, and would distinguish himself as captain of hussars at Jemappes, along with one of his subalterns, a lieutenant by the name of Joachim Murat. One of the Confederation of Bar's leading soldiers and a friend of Pułaski, Józef Miączyński, was now a French general and commanded the garrison of Sedan.

The international nature of this army is significant. These men were not there to defend some tribal patch, but the motherland of regenerate humanity. The French nation had come to be seen as *La Grande Nation*, the epic nation representing all. Men from every land effortlessly fell in with her sons, who had themselves shed all other loyalties in her defence. In the front rank stood Lafayette and other scions of the French nobility, mostly veterans of America, such as Armand de Gontaut-Biron, Duc de Lauzun, who had renounced all to become Citoyen-Général Biron and command the Armée du Rhin, or the literary Marquis de Custine, who turned into a ruthlessly efficient general.

The élan of 1792 appeared to be unstoppable. After the victories of Valmy on 20 September 1792 and Jemappes on 5 November, the French army under Dumouriez forged ahead into Belgium. On 21 October Custine captured Mainz and reached Frankfurt. In the south, the French invaded Savoy and marched into Nice. 'Custine and Dumouriez, at the head of troops that know the value of victory, seem to be inflamed with a kind of zeal like that of Omar,' reported a British diplomat, 'and hitherto they have preached this new species of Mahometanism with a degree of success equal to that of the Arabian.'[20] Drunk on the heady sensation of victory, the Convention threw its pacifist principles and all caution to the winds, and on 19 November issued a decree offering support to all nations fighting for their freedom. On 1 February 1793 it declared war on England and the United Provinces, and on 9 March on Spain.

But at home, the Convention was making war on its own. Lafayette, the symbol of 1776 and 1789, had been declared a traitor. Soon after his attempt to save the monarchy, at the end of July 1792, his position became untenable and he fled rather than face the guillotine. Many more of those who epitomized the noble impulse of the young revolution would follow, particularly when bad news from the front began to feed the obsession with traitors in Paris. In April 1793 Dumouriez, who had led the advance into Holland, was defeated at Neerwinden. Guessing what fate awaited him, he chose to cross the Austrian lines, accompanied by the Duc de Chartres. Miranda, Miączyński and others in his army were arrested and tried, and over the next months Custine, Lauzun, Arthur Dillon and others who did not move fast enough would suffer the guillotine. Pasquale Paoli was declared a traitor to the French Republic, outlawed and forced to call on the protection of Admiral Hood, who occupied Corsica and sent him off to a second exile in London.

The time for France to carry the message of liberty all over Europe had not come. The country was in a mess, politically and economically, and in no condition to conduct large-scale military operations. The sense of failure engendered xenophobia, and foreigners were guillotined or expelled, destroying the internationalism at the core of the revolution. The foreign legions were disbanded. But the rest of Europe still saw France as the motherland of liberty and therefore the source of endless promise or danger.

Outside observers were for the most part at a loss as to what to make of events in France. They could not understand the processes at work or distinguish real signs of danger. Incomprehension breeds fear, and their worst fears were fed with misinformation of every kind. As if the events taking place were not gory enough, rumour and the reactionary press regaled the public with lurid reports of bloody excesses and even cannibalism on the part of the sansculottes. The source of the most fearsome ideas and doctrines appeared to be the Jacobin Club, where people openly discussed the unthinkable. The word 'Jacobin', used as a blanket term by conservatives, quickly acquired a demonic resonance. And the Jacobins were usually described as a 'sect', which added a whiff of the occult to their already sulphurous image.

Not surprisingly, it was the Catholic clergy who first began to examine the ideas emanating from the Jacobin Club and to trace their pedigree. The Abbé Barruel, a former Jesuit who had in 1781 published a book criticizing the works of the Enlightenment, branded the revolution as the consequence of 'philosophism'. In 1792 he took refuge in England, where he developed his great conspiracy theory. This was published in 1797 as *Mémoires pour servir a l'histoire du Jacobinisme.* It claimed that a sect numbering 300,000 adepts had been at work for twenty years. 'The sect first announced itself in America, with the first elements of its code of equality, liberty and sovereignty of the people,' he explained.[21]

From this it was but one short step to re-examining all movements spawned by the Enlightenment, most notably Freemasonry and its offshoot the Illuminati. It was not difficult to demonstrate that many of those in favour of the revolution had been members, and to point to contacts between known Illuminati and prominent French revolutionaries. To conservatives throughout Europe, it appeared that the sect had not been stamped out at all – it had merely gone underground, where it could do far greater harm. What kind of harm was chillingly suggested in a flutter of pamphlets. The climate was conducive to panic, and, this being an age that delighted in association and in mystification, there was no shortage of conspiracy theories. The assassination of King Gustavus III of Sweden at a masked ball on 16 March 1792 was seen as the work of the Freemasons, Illuminati and others allegedly committed to the overthrow of kings. By the beginning of 1792 Catherine II was convinced that unspecified Jacobins were plotting to murder her as well.[22] When the Duke of Brunswick, known to be the head of the German Masons of Strict Observance, withdrew after Valmy without much of a fight, some jumped to conclusions. There was a theory that while awaiting execution in 1314 (on the site of the Bastille as it happened), the last Grand Master of the Order of Knights Templar had founded four masonic lodges vowed to exterminate the Bourbons and all other kings who had helped to destroy the Order. When Louis XVI was executed, many saw this as part of a 'Templar revenge'.

The partisans of the *ancien régime* focused their anxieties on subversion. They convinced themselves of the existence of something they called '*la propagande*', a sort of Holy Office for the Propagation of the Jacobin Faith. This was supposedly orchestrating an international plot to overthrow the European order. Blood-curdling intentions were ascribed to it, and its existence and activities were reported in the most unlikely places with a hysterical mixture of horror and glee.

French people were regarded with universal suspicion. As the fount of fashion and taste, France had for decades been exporting tradesmen, valets, wig-makers, hairdressers, dancing-masters and tutors. In 1789 they naturally formed revolutionary clubs in their places of residence, and the radicalism of these followed that of the Jacobins in Paris. Host countries clamped down on this kind of activity and restricted the movements of foreigners. But French emigrés kept arriving in neighbouring countries, beginning with diehard supporters of the *ancien régime*, who were not unwelcome. The second wave was made up mostly of priests who had refused to swear the civic oath, many of whom were otherwise in sympathy with the events of 1789. The next waves consisted of constitutional monarchists, the very people who had made the revolution in the first place, followed by more revolutionary elements. Whatever their political affiliation, they were all children of the Enlightenment, and they all carried the taint of French political culture into the societies in which they took refuge. The local authorities saw their nefarious influence everywhere. In England, the Methodists were accused of being surrogate Jacobins. In the Spanish colonies of New Granada and New Spain, dozens of Frenchmen were rounded up and shipped to prison in Cadiz. The British were seeking out 'Jacobins' at the Cape of Good Hope, and there was panic when frontier Boers set up 'republics' at Graaff Reinet and Swellendam, though these were hardly revolutionary. The cabinets of Europe were more concerned than the Ottoman Porte when they got wind of the existence of Jacobin Clubs at Smyrna and Aleppo. News that Tippoo Sahib had planted a liberty tree in India brought some out in a sweat. The Grand Conspiracy, a Devil-substitute for an age that was too grown-up to believe in the horned version, had been born.

'There is something *satanic* about the French Revolution that distinguishes it from everything we have known, and perhaps from everything we will ever witness,' wrote Joseph de Maistre, whose *Considérations sur la France*, published in London in 1797, painted a blood-drenched picture of events.[23] 'We cannot, if we would, delude ourselves about the true state of this dreadful contest,' Edmund Burke declared after hostilities had broken out with France in 1793. '*It is a religious war.*'[24]

The fight was waged nowhere as frantically as in matters of form and appearance. In February 1795 two young Polish princes on their way to St Petersburg to pay their respects to Catherine II were stopped in the small Lithuanian town of Grodno and told to remain there until their hair had grown to a respectable length. Their 'Roman' haircuts would not be tolerated at the imperial court, where they would be seen as a declaration of Jacobin convictions; they could not make their appearance until they could tie their hair back with a bow and powder it. When the king of Naples saw some young men wearing no powder in their hair at the opera one night, he left immediately, ordering the building to be surrounded by troops. This exercise yielded a catch of seven Neapolitan noblemen, who were incarcerated in Fort St Elmo and on the following morning despatched to serve in the ranks of a regiment in Sicily.

The stiffening of hostility in European cabinets towards any hint of liberal convictions had the effect of polarizing people and forcing them to take issue. Not for or against France, or even for or against the revolution, but rather the vision of a new existence it held out to people of all lands. Those entranced by this vision were not discouraged by failure. The international coalition's assault on France, the subjugation of Belgium and the rape of Poland were powerful images of insult to, and defilement of, the sacred body of the nation. Such images only encouraged the faithful. 'These cruelties and these fears do us honour,' wrote Lafayette from a Prussian dungeon in March 1793, adding that he welcomed what he believed to be his impending martyrdom, trusting that it would win hearts to the cause of France. 'These people must think they are holding the devil himself in gaol,' he added, commenting on his treatment.[25]

In the summer of 1792 Lafayette had crossed the Austrian lines with a group of fellow officers to avoid being summoned to Paris and condemned at the bar of the Assembly, like so many of his comrades-in-arms. He had deserted, but he did not see it as such. He believed that the France he adored had been abducted by a gang of immoral politicians. It was them he was deserting, not his country, and he was a patriot, not a traitor. He was utterly taken aback when the Austrians and Prussians to whom he gave himself up asked him to hand over the money – they having assumed that he would take the army funds with him when deserting. When they asked him to disclose everything he knew about the French army's strength and dispositions, he responded with sincere indignation.

Baffled by his sense of honour, resentful of his aristocratic manner and fearful of his worldwide reputation, the allies resolved to make him suffer. The Prussians took charge and locked him in a damp underground cell in Magdeburg, measuring five-and-a-half paces by three, where he was miserably fed and not allowed out for exercise. He was not permitted to send or receive letters, even to or from his wife. His companions fared no better, and only the kindness of some of the gaolers allowed him news of his friend Alexandre de Lameth, who had crossed the lines with him and was now dying a few yards away from a combination of ill-health and old wounds received at Yorktown.

In January 1794 he was moved to the fortress of Neisse, where the prisoners were allowed some contact, but in the autumn he was handed over to the Austrians, who confined him in the grim castle of Olmütz. Here he was put in a cell below the level of the moat and not allowed out.

He was hermetically sealed off from the outside world, and the gaolers were forbidden to use his name, as though the Habsburg monarchy wanted to will him out of existence. Pressure from America and from sympathizers in England forced them to relent and to allow him guarded walks in the open. But a failed escape attempt, organized by local sympathizers, resulted in his being condemned to solitary confinement, and his health and hopes plummeted. In October 1795, to his intense joy, his wife Adrienne and his two daughters, who had survived the Terror and escaped from France, managed to obtain permission to share his captivity. In the event, this only meant that they were allowed to spend a few minutes together every day in order to gulp down some of the vile prison food. Adrienne soon fell ill herself, and no amount of pleading by highly placed people could soften the Habsburg heart. It was not until the Austrian armies had been soundly beaten in Italy by General Bonaparte in 1797 and the Emperor had to sue for peace, that negotiations for Lafayette's release could begin.

In spite of all the precautions taken to prevent it, Lafayette did manage to send a few letters during his incarceration. His reputation was such that he could count on finding friends even among the gaolers and the local doctors called in to see him from time to time. His letters were written on paper smuggled in or torn out of a book a visitor might happen to have with him. Lafayette's toothpick stood in for a pen, and the ink was made from soot mixed with vinegar or blood. One of his first letters, written in March 1793 to his old friend the Princesse d'Hennin who had managed to emigrate to London, conveys all his despair at his entombment and his terrible anxieties concerning Adrienne and his daughters, trapped in France by the Terror – his son George Washington Lafayette was with his godfather at Mount Vernon. Yet he still finds space to fret about the fate of the slaves he had freed on an estate he owned on Cayenne when, as with all emigrés' property, it would have been confiscated by the government.

'The cause of the people is no less sacred to me than it was; I would still give my blood for it, drop by drop; I would reproach myself for every moment of my life which was not exclusively devoted to this cause,' he wrote from Magdeburg on 22 June 1793. As he scratched away with his grimy toothpick, racked by ill-health, he was tortured in equal measure by the knowledge that the cause had been perverted by the likes of Robespierre and by the thought of his friend Lameth dying in an airless cell nearby. But nothing could shake his faith. 'I admit, my dear princess, to being in the throes of the most violent of passions; that liberty which received my first vows and which has so tossed about my life, is here the constant object of my solitary meditations,' he wrote. 'It is what one of our friends used to call my holy madness; and, whether a miracle draws me out of here or I have to present myself on a scaffold, liberty and equality will be my first and my last words . . .'[26]

7
Dying to be Free

The spread of 'French ideas' was to some extent an illusion entertained by their opponents. But reality tempered neither the fears of the conservatives nor the aspirations of those who dreamed of a better world. The former saw revolution where there were only harmless local aspirations. The latter looked for salvation in every upheaval. The over-reaction of both camps meant that embers of latent disaffection were fanned into flames of revolt, and occasionally into national conflagrations. And local malcontents could now feed on the hope of French support, particularly after the French victories at Valmy and Jemappes, and Dumouriez's subsequent advance into Belgium in 1792.

Most of Belgium, known as the Austrian Netherlands, had no practical grounds for discontent, as the country was prospering to an unprecedented degree under a generally benign regime. There was nevertheless a bedrock of resentment against imperial rule. The revolt of the American colonies had elicited sympathy and helped to awaken a spirit of resistance, while the revolt in the neighbouring Dutch Republic encouraged defiance. This came to the fore when the emperor Joseph II began implementing reforms. He was a tireless organizer inspired by the precepts of the Enlightenment, overly fond of tidying and rationalizing. He moved his attentions from province to province, leaving behind stacks of new laws and swarms of officious bureaucrats to put them into effect. The Josephine reforms were on the whole concordant with the wishes of progressive Belgians. But they cut across ancient rights and local privileges, and offended religious susceptibilities. '*Peuple Belgique, suivez l'Amérique,*' urged a popular ditty of the 1780s, and the *Manifeste de Flandres*, issued in 1787 and copied, almost verbatim in parts, from the American Declaration of Independence, invoked the right of the people to declare the province an independent state. But this elicited scant enthusiasm, and with the collapse of the Dutch revolt the local patriots had to lie low.

The revolution in France gave them new heart, and in August 1789 there was a rising in Liège. The ruling bishop was expelled, and on 18 August the 'Liégeois nation' abolished the existing constitution. The excitement spread, on a diet of pamphlets with titles such as *Commandements de notre Mère la Patrie à chaque fidèle citoyen*. In October insurrection shook Ghent and in December the patriots of Brussels rose against the Austrian garrison. On 11 January 1790 the Austrian Netherlands proclaimed their independence as the 'United States of Belgium'. The first edition of the new *Journal de Bruxelles* was dedicated to the *patrie*, and implored this 'idol of great souls' to inspire the love of heroes. The patriot General Van der Meersch had become '*le Washington Belgique*', while the advocate Henri van der Noot was referred to as '*le Franklin des Belges*'.[1] But there was no base of either national or revolutionary sentiment strong enough to build on, and little effective resistance when the Austrians reoccupied the province. Following the French victories of 1792, Dumouriez expelled them once again. On 1 February 1793 France invaded the United Provinces, supported by a handful of emigré Dutch Patriots, but her forces were defeated at Neerwinden. The French mounted a more vigorous offensive the following year, and on 22 July they were in Antwerp. Utrecht was taken on 17 January 1795, and two days later the Patriots took control in Amsterdam. William V had sailed into exile in England the previous night, and within days the whole country was in Patriot hands. But as they busied themselves planting liberty trees, their future was being decided in Paris. In May 1795 a Batavian Republic was established, at the cost of an indemnity of 100 million guilders, a huge loan to France at a trifling rate of interest and the cession to France of Maastricht, Venlo and Dutch Flanders. There was also an official pillage of the Stadholder's art collection. Belgium hardly did better. The Patriots were kept well away from power, and in October 1795 the whole country was annexed to France.

Switzerland also found itself being used as a pawn and a testing-ground, with the French encouraging local revolutions which were then abandoned to their fate. But neither revolutionaries nor reactionaries heeded these examples, and the pattern was replicated elsewhere. The greatest casualty of the ideological struggle taking place was Poland.

Catherine II had invaded in 1792 because she regarded Warsaw as 'a brazier of Jacobinism'.[2] In April 1793 she initiated a second partition and imposed a puppet government backed by Russian troops on the small remaining rump of Poland. There was a fierce clamp-down on every manifestation of liberalism, and the private papers of individuals were studied with a zeal redolent of the Inquisition. Anyone who had a hand in the constitution of 3 May 1791 was singled out. At the very least they had their estates confiscated and were stripped of rank. Every citizen was invited to sign his approval of the government imposed by Catherine, which contained an abjuration of the ideals of the past four years. Recusants were punished in ways that effectively barred them from public life.

The leading Patriots had taken refuge in Saxony, Poland's only neutral neighbour. They included 'the Polish Lafayette' Ignacy Potocki and the radical ex-priest Hugo Kołłątaj. They had hoped that the king would manage to reach a compromise with Catherine and safeguard elements of the 3 May constitution. But as they watched Catherine's depredations in Poland they became increasingly exasperated. They began to plan a national uprising, and for the necessary financial and military support they looked to France. They declared openly against monarchy, and rewrote King Stanisław's role in the passing of the constitution as that of a villain. The best Polish military commander available was Prince Józef Poniatowski, but he was the king's nephew. He was also a realist who knew that the 1792 war had been unwinnable. Instead, the emigrés put their trust in Kościuszko. His American credentials were impeccable, he was an honorary citizen of the French Republic, and he was insistent that the Poles could have won in 1792. His arguments, based on the American experience, were utterly erroneous in the context of Poland, but they sounded good. The example of Valmy had restored faith in the poetic myth that a free nation in arms was invincible.

It had also established France as the champion of the cause of universal liberation. 'Now in the whole of Europe there are only two parties: France for the freedom of peoples against all the rulers, and all the monarchs against France for despotism and old traditions', wrote Kołłątaj.[3] Many Poles had emigrated to Paris. One of them, Wojciech Turski, a kind of slavonic Cloots, renamed himself 'Albert le Sarmate' and besieged the Convention. He had translated Rousseau into Polish, and some of it had clearly rubbed off. 'O French, first nation in the world, we are your pupils,' he addressed it on 30 December 1792. While invoking the protection of a deity he called 'the God of Nations', he elevated the French to the rank of protector and arbiter.[4] In February 1793, Kościuszko himself went to Paris in quest of French support. His road lay through Brussels, at this stage occupied by the French. When he reached the city he naturally called on the commander of the occupying French forces, who happened to be his old companion-in-arms from America, General Dumouriez. The hero of Valmy had also fought for the Confederation of Bar. It was natural for Kościuszko to give him sight of the plans for the insurrection in Poland. He was not to know that less than a month later, Dumouriez would defect to the Austrians, and that he would need to trade every piece of intelligence he possessed in order to ensure that he was not clapped in irons like Lafayette.

From Paris, Kościuszko went to Kraków where, on 24 March 1794, he solemnly read out an Act of National Insurrection. He then marched out of the city at the head of an army of regular regiments supplemented by battalions of scythe-waving peasants. On 4 April these played an important part in his victory at Racławice over the Russian General Tormasov, whose artillery they cut up nicely. Kościuszko donned the white peasant coat that served as their uniform, and henceforth wore it ostentatiously as a sign of his democratic principles.

On the morning of 17 April the populace of Warsaw rose, and after two days of street-fighting the Russians evacuated the city with heavy losses. On 22 April King Stanisław announced his adherence to the insurrection. He had long known of the conspiracy and had vehemently advised against the enterprise, which he saw as hopeless and bound to end in the annihilation of Poland. But he determined to ride the storm, hoping with time to gain control of it. On 24 April a Jacobin Club was founded, and its members suggested hanging the king straight away, in order to commit themselves and the nation to a life-and-death struggle. Stanisław struck the right attitudes, donated money and plate to the cause, and even turned up to help dig defensive earthworks. But the Jacobins spread rumours of his plans to escape, and nearly succeeded in murdering him during one of his afternoon rides, which they had tried to turn into a replica of Louis XVI's flight to Varennes. At Kołłątaj's behest the Supreme National Council issued a proclamation telling people to beware of 'false patriots'. 'Baubles offered by unclean hands are not fit to be laid on the altar of the motherland', it ran, a clear reference to the king's gift of all his jewellery to the national cause the previous day.[5]

The Polish revolution was a confused affair. Kościuszko was a sincere and naive liberal. His popularity was enormous, and, like Washington, he quickly came to be seen as 'father of the country'. In dozens of popular prints he was represented as a crusader brandishing his sword in a gesture of dedication rather than defiance. In countless verses he was dubbed 'Saviour' and 'Champion of Humanity', while one poem urged him to succour the 'swooning' motherland and restore her to health, to banish vice and to make the trees flower.[6] Such imputed powers notwithstanding, Kościuszko was not really up to the job in hand. His populism sat uneasily with his fondness for the king, and his only real strategy was faith in the power of the will to be free. The insurrection's only chance of success lay in a rising of the entire population. On 7 May Kościuszko issued a manifesto which announced the abolition of serfdom and promised land to those who fought for their country, but the response was desultory.

After some initial success, the insurrection began to flag. Kościuszko was defeated and taken prisoner at the Battle of Maciejowice on 10 October 1794. On the morning of 4 November the Russians broke through the defences of Warsaw and proceeded to put the suburb of Praga to the sword. Some 20,000 people lost their lives in a frenzied butchery that even shocked many Russian officers. The remains of the Polish army evacuated the capital, leaving the king to make peace with the victorious General Suvorov. One of the more energetic Polish generals, Jan Henryk Dąbrowski, wanted to gather together as many of the remnants as possible and make an armed dash for France, but he was overruled, and the Poles capitulated.

Liberal Europe lamented. Samuel Taylor Coleridge wrote of 'murdered Hope' in a sonnet bewailing Kościuszko's defeat. The figure of the Polish patriot hovered beside that of Washington as paragon of Spartan virtue in the public imagination. The heroic aspect of the Polish struggle against overwhelming odds, the touching imagery of peasant volunteers defending their motherland armed only with the tools of their toil, and finally the horrible massacre of Praga added to a picture of martyred innocence. The Scots poet Thomas Campbell summed up the universal reaction to the Polish freedom fighter's capture:

Hope, for a season, bade the world farewell,
And Freedom shriek'd – as Kościuszko fell!

Poland's three neighbours decided that the only way of dealing with the infection that had gained hold in their part of Europe was amputation. In 1795 they carried out a final partition of the country, which was wiped off the map altogether. This extraordinary act liquidated a state that had existed for eight centuries and, in an attempt to stamp out the very memory of Poland, even prohibited the use of its name. In so doing, it threw out a challenge rich in consequences.

The human fabric of the nation could not be willed out of existence, and it protested vigorously. 'The nation is formed through the law of nature alone', ran the manifesto of the Society of Polish Republicans, founded in exile. 'Government stems from the will of the nation. The nation stands before all things and is the source of all things. Its will is always law. Above it and before it is but the law of nature alone. By virtue of its very existence, the nation is all things that it may be. The nation cannot surrender its rights to a tyrant.'[7]

Rousseau's fantasies had been prophetic. The Poles had become a nation without a state, and, repeating the history of the Jews, they were henceforth to carry their Polishness with them. 'Poland is wherever people are fighting for liberty', according to Józef Sułkowski, a radical young aristocrat who had escaped to Paris.[8] Within two years, while the diplomatists of the three partitioning powers were still bickering over how to apportion the debts of the state they had annihilated, there would be Polish units fighting alongside the armies of revolutionary France. They marched to a song whose first line affirmed: 'Poland has not perished while still we live'.

In the past, if a rebellion was put down, that was the end of that. Now there was life after death. In fact, there was no real death while the divine love of the nation filled the breasts of young patriots. If anything, an injustice on this scale inflicted on a nation could only galvanize and spur it on to struggle for the resurrection of the state. Causes began to feed off defeat. 'If the Poles are to become capable of effective resistance, they must first learn to be free, and in order to become free, they must learn to die,' theorized Sułkowski in a plan submitted to the French Directory in 1795.[9] And there was no easy way round learning to die, as the Hungarians were about to discover.

*

The kingdom of Hungary was a Habsburg dominion with a population of 9.5 million, of whom no more than 40 per cent were Magyars. The remainder was made up of Romanians, Slovaks, Croats, Serbs and other minorities. The social culture of the kingdom was nevertheless epitomized by the dominant Hungarian nobility, which had absorbed the elites of the other minorities. Like its counterpart in Poland, this nobility was the political nation.

The country prospered throughout the eighteenth century, but from the 1760s onwards it autonomy was steadily eroded by regulation from Vienna. This gradual process escalated into a frantic rush with the accession of Joseph II. No friend of the nobility or the clergy, and determined to rationalize his multi-ethnic domains, he pried into every sphere, issuing no fewer than six thousand edicts governing religious life and its practice alone. Joseph refused to be crowned king of Hungary in order to avoid the oath to respect the privileges of the nobles, and on 13 April 1784 his soldiers removed the crown of St Stephen, symbol of Hungarian statehood, from its traditional place of keeping in Pressburg, and conveyed it to a museum in Vienna. In the same year Joseph made what was probably his greatest mistake. Inspired by the spirit of modernity, he decided that the official language of the Empire, Latin, needed replacing by a living one, and to do so he naturally enough chose German.

For some time, traditionalists had been alarmed by the tendency among young nobles to leave their homes, jettisoning the manners and customs of their forefathers, along with language. Janos Ribinyi, a teacher at Sopron, tried to persuade his readers to cultivate the mother tongue, pointing out that failure to do so was to 'sin against the fatherland, against the Magyar name, against ourselves, and against our ancestors'.[10] Another partisan of the language voiced the fear that if they let it go, 'the Hungarian fatherland would be deprived of its independence and the nation would lose its nationality'.[11] He also advocated the wearing of the old Hungarian costume, as linguistic defiance dovetailed with the traditional distrust of all innovation and resistance to Josephine reforms. Plain-speaking and old-fashioned backwoods manners were held up as the height of 'old virtues'. 'I write because I cannot live without writing for a happy future, for the twentieth and twenty-first centuries, for the time when a Hungarian will be a real Hungarian or will not exist any more,' wrote Mihály Czokonai, an admirer of Rousseau who followed the calling of the writer with dedication and asceticism.[12]

A linguistic and literary revival was launched by György Bessenyei, assisted by Ferenc Kazinczy and József Hajnoczy. On 1 January 1780 *Magyar Hirmondo*, the first Hungarian-language paper, began publication. It dwelt at length on the past glories of the Hungarians, their alleged descent from Attila the Hun, their heroic role in the struggle with Tatar and Turk, and supported the preservation or revival of ancient traditions. As elsewhere, this came into conflict with historical reality. By the early eighteenth century there was much scholarly evidence disproving the Hungarians' Scythian-Hunnish origins, and attesting to their Finno-Ugrian descent. In 1769 the savant Janos Sajnovics went to Lapland to study the linguistic connections, and in the following year he published his findings in a work that all but proved this. It was rejected by the Magyar nobility, even the enlightened ones such as Baron Lorinc Orczy, who disdained 'a kinship smelling of fish-oil'.[13] They could not imagine building a future that was not based on a heroic past.

All this scratching about for past glories in the clutter of the national attic yielded a panoply of ancient rights to be revindicated. 'Since America became a free society after shaking the English yoke off her neck, all nations are yearning for the same golden liberties,' wrote the *Magyar Kurir*, which had taken over from the *Hirmondo*, on 27 May 1789.[14] The Hungarians began to protest not only against the Josephine reforms, but over other issues as well, and the old imperial chancellor Prince Kaunitz grew alarmed. With a war on the southern front with Turkey and the Austrian Netherlands in revolt, the international situation was anything but encouraging, and he persuaded Joseph to give way. On 28 January 1790, Joseph II decreed the return of the crown of St Stephen and revoked virtually all the reforms of the past ten years. This climb-down was greeted with jubilation, surpassed only by the indecent rejoicing at news of the emperor's death a few weeks later.

The nobles saw a chance of breaking out of the constraints of Vienna's centralizing administration, and dreamed of an independent kingdom of Hungary. Although the majority were interested primarily in the re-establishment of the undisputed hegemony of their own caste, they took care to disguise this. Through every available means, including the extensive masonic network, they courted the non-noble classes and even dangled vague promises before the mistrustful peasants. On 6 June 1790 the Hungarian parliament, the Diet, was convened in Buda, the first time it had met there since the sixteenth century. A noble national guard, the *banderia*, was formed. The Hungarian regiments of the imperial army were called on to transfer their loyalty from the Habsburgs to the Hungarian Diet. This was dominated by the progressive nobles, led by Count Ferenc Széchényi, who had spent time in the rebelling Austrian Netherlands in 1787 and then in England, and it included people such as Count Mihaly Sztáray and Count Janos Fekete, who renounced their titles of nobility. Sztaray drew up a 'citizens' oath', which he saw as a means of uniting the nation. But this was not going to be easy. They briefly managed to engage the support of the traditionalist gentry and the aristocracy, as well as representatives of a new radical intelligentsia made up of lawyers, teachers and other educated non-nobles. But the irreconcilable principles of these groups could not be held together for long. To make matters worse, some of the nobles of other nationalities began to stir uneasily.

The Slovak and Croat nobility felt it belonged to the *Natio Hungarica* and demonstrated solidarity with their Magyar brothers. But they had been growing more conscious of their origins. So had the national groups who had never felt any kinship with the Hungarian nobility, not having one of their own. In 1780 Juraj Papanek had published a history of the Slovaks, and in the following year Samuil Micu-Kleim completed his history of the Dacian-Rumanians, staking out their respective claims to nationhood. When the Hungarian Diet began to call for a Hungarian state ruled by the Hungarian nobility and using Hungarian as its official language, some of these groups began to feel the chill. While the Diet met in Buda, an Illyrian National Congress professed loyalty to the new emperor Leopold and called for the establishment of a separate province of Serbia within the Empire.

Leopold let the Hungarians bluster while he extricated himself from other crises, and then moved in troops. The Diet's truculence collapsed, and demands were cut down to include no more than some local autonomy and the teaching of Hungarian in schools. A compromise was struck in September, the *banderia* was dissolved and on 15 November 1790 Leopold swore in his coronation oath that 'Hungary together with her annexed territories is independent and should be governed and administered according to her own laws and customs and not as other provinces are.'[15] Few in Hungary were ready to fight for more than this.

Leopold's death in the same year nevertheless encouraged a small group of Hungarian Jacobins to act. Chief among these was Ignac Martinovics. Born in Pest of Croat origin, he had a chequered career, first as a Franciscan friar, then as professor of chemistry. In 1782 he toured Europe in the company of the future Polish Lafayette Ignacy Potocki, and later attempted to fly from Lemberg to Vienna in a hot-air balloon of his own design. He held the post of court chemist under Leopold II, and was a member of his secret police, a curious role for a freethinker, a devotee of Rousseau and Paine, and a pantheist who believed in a universe governed by material forces. In May 1794 he set up not one but two secret societies, each with its own catechism. On 23 July 1794 he and seventy-five members of the conspiracy were arrested. The authorities held a series of show trials, designed to make the flesh of conservatives creep and the hearts of would-be revolutionaries quail. Martinovics confirmed that he had intended to overthrow the Habsburg dynasty and set up a republic in Hungary. Others confessed to more or less heinous crimes, and the trials ended with draconian sentences. On 20 May 1795 Martinovics and four others were executed, on 4 June the sentence was carried out on two more, and the rest were commuted to imprisonment.

Martinovics was a harmless intriguer, and the others were a pathetic assortment. One exception was Ferenc Szentmarjay, who had translated Rousseau's *Du Contrat Social*, owned a real French tricolour cockade, which he made visitors kneel down to kiss, and who died singing the *Marseillaise*. These people could not have made a revolution if they had tried, and they represented nothing but themselves. But their trial and executions wrote another chapter in the Gospel of the nation, and added seven martyrs, known henceforth as 'the men of 1795', to the cause of Hungarian liberty, a cause that had not existed before Joseph II had embarked on his reforms.

The part of Europe that weathered the ideological storm of the 1790s with the least damage was the British Isles. That this should have been so was by no means evident in 1789. If the miseries of the toiling poor were not as terrible as those experienced by their French cousins, they were more capable of giving expression to them. And if the system itself was not as full of absurdities as the *ancien régime* in France, it contained quite enough perversity to arouse the reforming rage of intelligent men. The American war had generated criticism of the British political structure, and there had been enough agitation at the time to warrant predictions of 'a second Runnymede'. But the Gordon riots of June 1780, which caused much damage and frightened everyone, made reform seem less attractive, and the radicals lost ground.

News of the revolution in France had a profound effect on all sections of British society – 'the inert were roused, and lively natures rapt away!' in the words of William Wordsworth.[16] There was tremendous enthusiasm for what was seen as a modern equivalent of the 'Glorious Revolution' of 1688. Dr Joseph Priestley welcomed 'a totally new era in the history of mankind'.[17] Events in France gave new vigour to the latent campaign for constitutional reform, and societies dedicated to this sprang up in many cities; these corresponded with the French revolutionary clubs, and sent delegates to the National Assembly with addresses of congratulation and offers of support. Mass meetings were held, liberty trees were planted, seditious sentiments were uttered and there were calls for the people to be armed. In 1792 the invasion of France by the Austrian and Prussian armies roused pro-French sentiment and Catherine's attack on Poland turned this into a generalized anti-monarchist feeling. There were collections of money to help equip the French and Polish defenders of liberty.

The September massacres and the execution of Louis XVI in January 1793 shocked public opinion. But when Britain went to war with France a few weeks later, the country was far from united and many, even among the propertied classes, believed the war to be unjust. Yet while there was resentment among the lower orders at inequality of rights and property, there was not the same climate of class war as in France. Nor was there the same millenarian afflatus. The agitation in England concerned parliamentary reform, universal suffrage, and down-to-earth matters such as the harshness of the penal system and the price of bread. Even Paine, who was trying to rouse the masses, was calling not for national regeneration, but for a progressive income tax and the confiscation of excessive wealth. Only a few marginal groups caught the religious spirit of the times.

One such were the poets, whose reactions were as emotionally and spiritually charged as those of any Frenchman. Wordsworth's *Prelude* memorably conjures their 'pleasant exercise of hope and joy'. 'Bliss was it in that dawn to be alive, / But to be young was very heaven!' he recollects, adding that France appeared to the English as 'a country in romance', promising a new age. 'A visionary world seemed to open up on those who were just entering it', in the words of his fellow poet Robert Southey.[18] None was more excited by this prospect than William Blake, always fascinated by the sublime, the mysterious and the inexpressible. 'Rouze up, O Young Men of the New Age', he called. In his poem *The*

French Revolution, written in 1791, he reproduces all the style statements of the French children of Rousseau – nobles casting aside privilege, priests taking up the plough, soldiers throwing down their muskets – but gives the whole picture a characteristically English religious tint. The poet who came closest to the European spirit was Southey, in his *Joan of Arc*, an epic poem written by the 18-year-old in Brixton during the summer of 1793. The St Joan of this poem is a noble savage and a child of Rousseau. The English claims to France are represented as being perfectly valid, but only according to the arid principles of legitimacy, and they violate the natural wishes of the French nation, which are morally paramount.

In the spring of 1794 Coleridge went to Oxford to see his old school-friend Robert Allen, and there he met Southey. They talked of their frustrations and of better worlds. Their admiration for the revolution in France was evaporating, and they began to dream of seeking out a 'pure' corner of the world where they could bring about the longed-for state of being. 'What I dared not expect from constitutions of governments and whole nations I hoped from religion and a small company of chosen individuals, and formed a plan, as harmless as it was extravagant, of trying the experiment of human perfectibility on the banks of the Susquehannah; where our little society, in its second generation, was to have combined the innocence of the Patriarchal Age, with the knowledge and general refinements of European culture,' Coleridge later wrote.[19]

Many aristocratic French emigrés had already settled in the United States, where they attempted to recreate the life depicted in Bernardin de Saint-Pierre's *Paul et Virginie*, a best-seller published in 1787. America was, as the poet James Montgomery put it in *The Wanderer in Switzerland*, a land 'where tyrant never trod, where a slave was never known' (*pace* half-a-million blacks), and several English novelists, such as Thomas Holcroft and Robert Bage took up the theme of utopian resettlement. But Coleridge and his friends never followed through their plan. To the lasting benefit of future generations, they sought freedom and spiritual solace within themselves instead.

It was at its fringes that Britain was most receptive to the bacillus of revolutionary regeneration, and it would not have required a particularly sporting man to put money on the kingdom falling apart before 1800. There were grounds for discontent and historical grudges aplenty in Ireland, in Scotland, and even in Wales.

The half-million people inhabiting Wales lived in a world of their own, their relations with the rest of Britain conducted through an old Welsh gentry that had assimilated enough to be able to hold their own in the parliamentary market-place of Westminster. But the old way of life of Catholic Wales had begun to disappear as the eighteenth century progressed, edged out by a Protestant British culture. The native legal system was abolished and the language expunged from the administration. There was a steady drain of the educated to London, leaving the traditional landed squire increasingly stranded in his mountain fastness with his vast repertory of aurally-transmitted Welsh poetry, and his perfectly remembered and frequently recited thousand-year genealogy. Lower down the social scale, Methodism helped to stamp out the singing and dancing that had traditionally acted as conduit for Welsh culture.[20]

In the second half of the eighteenth century the population began to grow, under the influence of improvements in agriculture, the development of coal-mining and the opening of ironworks. One consequence was the emergence of an educated class outside the gentry which took a keen interest in the outside world. In London, where he had moved, Richard Price was one of the leaders of pro-American opinion in the 1770s, while the Presbyterian Minister David Williams corresponded with Franklin and wrote pamphlets that were read by Voltaire. He was later invited to France by the Assembly to advise on aspects of the new French constitution. Sympathy for the French Revolution in Wales was expressed in meetings, tuneful renderings of *Ça ira* and even riots. The French believed the grievances to be deeper than they were, and landed troops in South Wales in February 1797. The operation was a fiasco, and the French had to take to their ships. The Welsh were not ready, and much of their energy was absorbed elsewhere.

The latter part of the century had witnessed a resurgence of interest in the country's past, and the foundation of the London Welsh society, the Cymmrodorion, devoted to the purification of the language and the revival of atrophied traditions. William Owen, one of those engaged on this task, believed that Welsh was the *ur*-language, descended from Sanskrit. Such claims to international primacy were a hallmark of struggling nationalisms, as was the recourse to fraud, in this case the confections of the 'Bard of Liberty'.

Born in the Vale of Glamorgan in 1747, Edward Williams was a stonemason by trade. But he had another life as the poet Iolo Morganwg, and his real talent lay in forging reams of bardic verse, often under the influence of laudanum. He also invented traditions by the batch. He claimed that the ancient bards of Wales were not like other poets, but a kind of spiritual élite, both prophets and prelates, the mouthpieces of the nation. Other writers had likened the ancient Welsh bards to the Druids whom Julius Caesar had identified as the spiritual backbone of the Gauls and Britons. It was Morganwg who forged the missing links. He represented Druidism, which had survived only in Wales, as the original 'natural religion' which Rousseau had been looking for all his life.

A curious mixture of French-inspired utopianism and Dissenter millenarianism combined to turn this Celtic twilight zone into a national dream. The 'National Eisteddfod' was 'revived' in 1789, but being no more than a cultural festival it was not good enough for Iolo. He founded the Gorsedd, the Order of Bards of the Island of Britain, allegedly dating from Arthurian times. It was a kind of Druidical Freemasonry, complete with robes, ranks and rites. Its first meeting was held, somewhat improbably, on Primrose Hill in London on the summer solstice of 1792. The Gorsedd never grew into what it was supposed to be – a religious government for Wales. This was partly because many of those who might have supported it abandoned the attempt of creating utopia at home, and went to seek it across the ocean.

A hazy legend held that Prince Madoc had sailed across the Atlantic in the twelfth century and settled in America. It was elaborated in the sixteenth century in order to reinforce British imperial claims in the new world against those of Spain. This legend was taken up by William Jones, a country healer and schoolteacher who wrote a history of the Welsh, depicting them as victims of English persecution. In 1791 he announced that a tribe of Welsh-speaking Red Indians had been discovered on the banks of the Missouri. He called on the Welsh nation to quit the Egyptian bondage of life in Britain, and to join their lost brothers in a better world. This call struck a chord with Jacobins and Dissenters alike, and people all over Wales began to dream of a Welsh Zion on the Missouri.

In 1792 John Evans, a 22-year-old Methodist from South Wales, borrowed the passage money and sailed for America, driven by a sense of mission to find his long-lost brothers. He ranged all over Kentucky and Ohio, and wound up in Spanish Louisiana. From there he set off once more, and narrowly escaped death at the hands of Indians. Back in St Louis, he was gaoled as a spy by the Spaniards. After his release, he went up the Missouri once again, and spent a year living with the Mandan Indians, whom he took to be the lost brothers of the Welsh nation. After having finally to admit his error, he wound up in New Orleans, where he died of drink before his thirtieth birthday.

Another who dedicated himself to the quest was the Baptist minister Morgan John Rhys. This self-appointed Welsh Moses set sail from Liverpool on 1 August 1794 with a band of followers. He led them across Tennessee and beyond. Everywhere he went, he talked to the Indians, noting down sounds and words, desperately seeking traces of Welsh. After many disappointments, he gathered together all the lost Welsh emigrants he met along the way and set up his own satellite of Welshdom on the Susquehanna river, which he called Beula. But it began to fall apart soon after its foundation, along with the first tentative dreams of a new Welsh nationhood.

Across the water in Ireland, the French Revolution had a galvanic effect and, as elsewhere in Europe, made people take up positions. The centre of radical activity was Belfast where, as Wolfe Tone noted in his often ludicrous diary in April 1790, Paine's *Rights of Man* was 'the Khoran'. At a meeting of the Northern Whig Club in the same month, which included members of the aristocracy such as Robert Stewart (later Lord Castlereagh), toasts were drunk to 'Our Sovereign Lord the People' and 'A speedy establishment of Gallic Liberty'.[21] And it was in Belfast that, on 14 October 1791, the Society of United Irishmen was founded. A few weeks later a Dublin branch was formed, by Napper Tandy, William Drennan, Hamilton Rowan and Simon Butler. Other branches sprang up in the provinces over the next months. The society's badge was the Irish harp surmounted by a cap of liberty, supported by the motto: 'It is new strung and shall be heard'. The oath sworn by members was predictably picturesque. 'What have you got in your hand? A green bough. Where did it first grow? In America. Where did it bud? In France. Where are you going to plant it? In the crown of Great Britain.'[22] But there was nothing predictable about their political agenda.

The United Irishmen were a collection of liberals who resented the corrupt administration and the anomalies of the links with England more than they favoured any genuine promotion of the well-being of Ireland's poor Catholics. They hardly noticed that the huge peasant population existed in a condition of cruel subjection and misery. Although he was more inclined than others to include them in his political schemes, Tone himself admitted in 1791 that he was not personally acquainted with a single Catholic.[23] Neither he nor the other principal figures could have rustled up a genuine grievance between them. They saw an imperfect world and dreamed of changing it, by any means that suggested themselves. Tone admitted to having 'a romantic spirit', and this was shared by Edward Fitzgerald, another good example of the quite illogical and often contradictory trajectory made by the lives of so many of the early 'national' heroes of Ireland.

Lord Edward Fitzgerald's origins could hardly have been more aristocratic. His father was the Duke of Leinster, his mother a daughter of the Duke of Richmond. She had attempted to engage Rousseau as tutor to her children, and failing that, they were brought up according to his *Émile*. Lord Edward joined the army in 1779, aged sixteen, and served with distinction in America against the rebels. He was severely wounded at the Battle of Eutaw Springs, and his life was saved by a black man called Tony Small, whom he kept by his side to the end of his days. Back in Ireland in 1783, he entered the Irish parliament, where he sided with Henry Grattan. In 1787 he was spurned in love, and joined a regiment serving in New Brunswick. In 1789 he crossed a large part of uncharted Canada, making friends with Indians on the way, and, after a long stay at Detroit with the Bear tribe of Hurons, he made his way down the Mississippi to New Orleans. From there he sailed back to England, where he entered parliament and gave himself over to the pleasures of the capital. He was close to Charles James Fox and Richard Brinsley Sheridan, with whose wife he enjoyed a particular intimacy. He was the epitome of radical chic.

In October 1792 Lord Edward went to Paris, where he took lodgings with Thomas Paine and other anglophone visitors. At a banquet held there on 18 October he raised his glass to the abolition of hereditary honours and titles, and solemnly renounced his own. He had in the meantime fallen in love again. The girl, whom he first saw at the opera, was called – after the heroine of Richardson's novel – Pamela. She was the protégée of Madame de Genlis, governess to the children of Philippe Égalité, *ci-devant* Duc d'Orléans. Pamela was officially an orphan, but the whole of Paris was convinced that she was the daughter of the duke and Madame de Genlis. In a heroic gesture that flouted convention while assuring him prominence in society, Fitzgerald married Pamela, on 27

December, with Orléans' son the Duc de Chartres, Valmy's king-in-waiting, as witness.

In January 1793 the couple were back in Ireland, where Fitzgerald entered parliament, into which he imported the sulphur of the French Convention. He also fell in with Hamilton Rowan and other United Irishmen, who were gradually drifting from a position of disgruntled loyalism towards one of outright rebellion. The outbreak of war between England and France in February 1793 drew a line, and people had to choose which side they stood on. The choice was not difficult for people like Hamilton, Tone or Fitzgerald. They began plotting a rising in Ireland, to be supported by a French landing. But their conspiracy was carefully monitored by London through a web of spies. Realizing that he was about to be arrested, Hamilton Rowan slipped out of Ireland in a small boat in May 1794 and went to Paris. As it approached the French port of Roscoff, the craft was fired on by a shore battery despite frantic signals of friendship. With great presence of mind Hamilton Rowan went below and snatched up a crew member's red nightcap, which he stuck on a boathook and raised aloft. The battery fell silent and the refugees sailed in under the emblem of liberty. But Rowan was nevertheless cast into gaol as a spy. There he would probably have perished, were it not for a passing doctor who got news of his predicament to Paris and procured his liberation.

Rowan arrived in Paris just in time to have one audience with Robespierre before his fall, and set about plotting an invasion of Ireland with his successors. In a memorandum which reveals all the muddle and the double standards, as well as the overweening self-esteem, swirling around in his head, he proposed that the expedition should consist of 30,000 French troops, to be put ashore in three places. The landing should be accompanied by a proclamation granting the gentry's land to the peasants. 'Hamilton Rowan, that illustrious martyr to liberty, would lead the Wexford army,' the memorandum went on; 'his manifesto would infallibly stir the people of Dublin, whose idol he is; he is moreover the most striking patriot in Ireland; the veneration of the Irish for him is such that if they had the idea of giving themselves a king the majority of votes would combine in favour of Hamilton Rowan.'[24]

The French had no intention of establishing the Rowan dynasty in Ireland, and they dragged their feet. Disillusioned with France, Rowan decided to try his fortunes in America. But his experiences there were to prove no happier. He found the Americans rude, grasping and materialistic. Soon after landing in the new world, at Philadelphia in August 1795, Rowan had come across his old friend Wolfe Tone, who had also just got off a boat. He had been implicated in the same plot as Rowan but, after confessing everything, had been let off with a caution, provided he left the country. He naturally chose the United States, and he embarked with his family at Belfast in June 1795. After clearing the banks of Newfoundland and nearly at their journey's end, they were intercepted by a British frigate, HMS *Thetis*. Her captain, Sir Alexander Cochrane, sent his nephew Lord Thomas Cochrane aboard to press some fifty of the emigrants. He would have pressed Tone into service as a common British seaman had it not been for the entreaties of Mrs Tone, which finally caused him to relent.

Tone was relieved to set foot on American soil but he did not, any more than Rowan, like what he found. 'They seem a selfish, churlish, unsocial race, totally absorbed in making money; a mongrel breed, half-English, half-Dutch, with the worst qualities of both countries,' he wrote to a friend. He settled in Princeton, but remained restless. He was filled with dread at the prospect of his beloved nine-year-old daughter having to marry some American 'clown', even declaring that he would rather see her dead.[25] Whether it was to avoid this prospect or because of his devotion to the cause of liberty and equality is difficult to say, but on 1 January 1796 Tone sailed from New York for Le Havre.

After the conviction of Tone and Rowan in 1794, most of the United Irishmen went underground. As they did so they came into contact with and in many cases were subsumed by another movement that had started up in the late 1780s – Defenderism. The Defenders were a Catholic secret society whose radicalism came second to their profoundly sectarian outlook, which grew out of conflict with Protestant gangs in rural areas, notably the newly-formed Orange Order. The Defenders had been captivated by the imagery of the French Revolution, as their oath demonstrates. 'Are you consecrated? – I am – To what? – To the National Convention – to quell all nations – to dethrone all Kings, and plant the Tree of Liberty in our Irish land – whilst the French Defenders will protect our cause, and the Irish Defenders will pull down the British laws . . .'[26] There was a nice confusion here with the traditional role of France as the avenger champion of Catholicism. Some variants of the oath foresaw the planting not of the tree of liberty but of 'the true religion that was lost at the Reformation', and finished with the question and answer: 'Who sent you? – Simon Peter, the head of the Church'.[27]

The Irish Insurrection Act of 1796 mobilized the forces of law and order, but it was by no means certain that the militia would follow orders blindly. Many of the United Irishmen were confident that it would come out on their side if it came to open conflict. At the same time, many United Irishmen were themselves unsure of where they stood in the complex patchwork of loyalties covering the island. Yet the plotters were ludicrously sanguine about the numbers they believed would support a rebellion.

Wolfe Tone was more successful in France than Rowan had been. In February 1796 he held discussions with Lazare Carnot and General Hoche which culminated in a plan to invade Ireland. Tone was given a rank in the French army, and was 'as pleased as a little boy in his first breeches' when he donned his regimentals. 'Walked about Paris to show myself. Huzza! Citoyen Wolfe Tonee, Chef de Brigade in the service of the Republic.'[28] On 15 December 1796 the expedition sailed from Brest. It consisted of some 14,000 men under the command of Hoche. But the fleet of forty-three vessels was separated by bad weather shortly after leaving port, and less than half of the ships, with only 6,500 men and without Hoche, reached the landing-point at Bantry Bay. Tone, who was with this force, hung about waiting for Hoche's arrival, but not one local insurgent came forward during the week that the French ships rode at anchor in Bantry Bay before giving up and sailing home.

Undeterred, Wolfe Tone planned another invasion of Ireland, in collusion with Edward Fitzgerald. This time it was the Dutch fleet that would ferry the expedition, and Batavian troops that were to be landed. In July 1797 Tone embarked on Admiral de Winter's flagship, but in August the operation was called off and in October the Dutch fleet was wiped out in the Battle of Camperdown. The French Directory then began forming the Army of England under General Desaix. He was quickly succeeded by General Bonaparte, who engaged Paine to organize a revolution to coincide with a landing on the south coast of England, which was a more appealing prospect to the French than Ireland.

The Supreme Executive of the United Irishmen was riddled with informers, and in March 1798 the British authorities in Dublin Castle arrested most of the Executive, including Fitzgerald, and declared martial law. They also embarked on a country-wide operation to seek out and confiscate arms. This was accompanied by the use of terror, and culminated in a spontaneous and unco-ordinated rising in the Dublin area at the end of May. Just as this was brought under control, the south of the country rose, and a republic was proclaimed at Wexford. The rebels were defeated at Vinegar Hill and Wexford was retaken, but by then a new French invasion force was on its way.

The first wave, consisting of 1,000 French troops under General Humbert, landed at Killala in the north-west on 23 August and routed a small English force at Castlebar. The slogan 'France and the Virgin Mary' brought out a number of local volunteers, but they proved useless from a military point of view. On 8 September General Humbert, with only 850 French troops, came up against 5,000 British at Ballinamuck, and after a half-hour's fight he surrendered. The rebels supporting Humbert were mostly slaughtered by loyalist militia as they attempted to melt away into the countryside.

At the beginning of August the Viceroy, General Cornwallis, had declared an amnesty, and the rising, already defeated in the main, had begun to peter out. But the French plans took no account of this, and a second landing was made by Napper Tandy on the coast of Donegal. He hoisted the Irish flag and issued proclamations, but nobody rose in response. He consoled himself with drink while waiting for the expected volunteers, and in the end had to be carried aboard his vessel and back to sea. Meanwhile Wolfe Tone himself had sailed with a larger French force under General Hardy, but they were intercepted by a British squadron. After four hours' combat the ship carrying Tone struck its colours, and he was taken prisoner.

It was a pathetic but perhaps appropriate end to the muddled projects of these would-be heroes. Fitzgerald had been seized in Dublin, and died in June of the wound he received while resisting arrest. Tone, who pleaded to be shot as a French officer, was brought back to Dublin and condemned to hang. On the eve of execution he cut his windpipe with a pocket-knife. The wound was sewn up, but he died after a week of agony, on 19 November 1798. He was just one of some 30,000 who had suffered a more or less unpleasant death, only a fraction of them in battle.

The rising had been an explosion of confused and often conflicting motives and aims. The rural masses were easily goaded into revolt by a mixture of sectarian slogans and the desire for revenge. But their real grievance was that of poverty and hunger, and there was little community of interest between them and the rebel leaders. These had started out as Irish Volunteers professing loyalty to King George III, some had moved on to become radicals, some of whom went on to join the United Irishmen. Not all of them were prepared to fight alongside the French against their loyalist brothers. All too many withdrew from the revolt they had helped to incite when they saw the houses of the gentry in flames. Even radical patriots such as Daniel O'Connell were not behind the rebellion.

This had not been the birth of a nation in any sense, and the most tangible consequence was the Union with Britain in 1800. The episode nevertheless transformed the Irish scene and set the stage for the emergence of modern Irish nationalism. It helped to divide the complex and layered mix of ethnic, religious and social differences into two more or less distinct camps for the first time. And although the Catholic camp was soundly beaten and condemned to subservience, it had acquired that first and most important element in any cause – a legend, endowed with a hagiography of martyrs. They were all, as it happens, Protestant sons of the Ascendancy.

8
La Grande Nation

'You are, amongst the nations, what Hercules was amongst the heroes,' Robespierre assured his countrymen. 'Nature has made you sturdy and powerful; your strength matches your virtue and your cause is that of the gods themselves.'[1] France was unique in her destiny, she was *La Grande Nation*, and all interests were necessarily subordinate to hers. Her service was the highest calling, since it naturally benefited mankind. General Bonaparte's 'victory-banner' of 1797 proudly announced: 'Liberty bestowed upon the people of Bologna, Ferrara, Modena, Massa-Carrara, Romagna, Lombardy, Brescia, Bergamo, Mantua, Cremona, part of the Veronese, Chiavenna, Bormio, the Valtelline, the people of Genoa, the Imperial Fiefs, the people of the Departments of Corcyra, of the Aegean Sea, and of Ithaca.'[2] It is reminiscent of the declarations made by Spanish conquistadors, as they laid claim to vast provinces in the name of King Philip and the True Faith from some Caribbean beachhead.

The belief-system regnant in Paris at the time was imposed indiscriminately. Wherever the French armies went in the 1790s they chased the ruling class from their palaces and their offices, dissolved religious orders and confiscated their estates, and set up institutions modelled on those of France. Of the twenty-nine constitutions adopted in Europe in the decade between 1791 and 1802, all but three (one Polish, two Swiss) were a consequence of French military intervention. In effect, the period between Valmy and Waterloo witnessed a semi-conscious attempt to assert France as the modern Rome and to impose her civilization on the Continent. In trying to re-establish the Roman Empire with his own coronation in 1804, his dissolution of the Holy Roman Empire two years later and his imposition of the Code Napoléon over the Continent, Napoleon was merely building on this.

The process was accompanied by rapine and pillage. One of the novelties of the mobile volunteer armies of revolutionary France was that they were sent out on campaign without even basic provisions, and therefore foraged for food wherever they could. The quartermasters paid for this, if at all, in largely worthless paper bills. Behind the armies, specially appointed *agences d'évacuation* and later *commissions des sciences et des arts* put method into the looting of works of art, books, manuscripts, models, scientific instruments and drawings, collections of anything from herbs to minerals, and even machinery. This spoliation was entirely in tune with the Roman concept of continuous enrichment of the imperial metropolis, a process justified by its being the capital of the universe, from which benefits flowed back equally to all the provinces.

The manipulation of the 'liberated' territories for the benefit of France was shameless. In the Netherlands, France meddled without regard for Dutch interests. Bonaparte wanted it to be no more than a satellite, and in September 1801 imposed a constitution which reversed that of 1798. The Batavian Republic was turned into the Batavian Commonwealth. In June 1805 Louis Bonaparte was forced on the Dutch as king, and the Commonwealth became the kingdom of Holland. But the new king took his job seriously and, much to the alarm of his brother, became something of a model ruler, popular with his subjects. In 1808 Napoleon tried to dislodge him by offering him the throne of Spain instead. Louis refused, professing his loyalty to the Dutch people, so Napoleon invaded. Louis took refuge in Bohemia while Holland was incorporated into France as seven additional *départements*. The country was repeatedly sucked dry of cash and squeezed for recruits, and did not recover its independence until the Napoleonic system in Europe collapsed at the end of 1813.

Similar techniques were applied in Switzerland, where France felt a God-given right to exert her influence. In February 1798 General Brune recommended turning it into three republics, for which he suggested names redolent of the mood of the day: 'Helvétie', 'Rhodanie' (after the Latin for the River Rhône), and 'Tellegovie' (in honour of William Tell). But in the end the whole country was included in one Helvetic Republic. The Swiss cross was abolished, along with the heraldic flags of the cities and cantons which were replaced with a tricolor of green, red and yellow.

'*Burger*' replaced '*Herr*' as the form of address, and a tree of liberty crowned with a red bonnet was planted in every village. As an afterthought, the red bonnet was replaced by the green hat of William Tell. It was only in 1803 that the Helvetic cross was brought back, but it would be some time before Switzerland recovered its stability.

Such a foreign policy might have been expected to put people off everything France stood for, and in some cases it did. In Spain, the French incursion of 1793 provoked a popular crusade in defence of the faith and the throne. Elsewhere reactions were more mixed. But wherever the French penetrated, they contributed to the evolution of national consciousness. In the case of Italy, for example, they provided the catalyst for the process that was to culminate in the creation of an entirely new nation.

Since the fall of the Roman Empire, the geographical area of Italy had the most fragmented political history of any part of Europe, at times resembling a chessboard on which foreign powers played out their games. At the outbreak of the French Revolution there were eleven states in Italy: the kingdom of Naples and Sicily, ruled by a Spanish Bourbon dynasty; the kingdom of Sardinia, ruled by the house of Savoy; the Papal States; the republics of Venice, Genoa, and Lucca; the Duchy of Milan, ruled from Vienna; the Grand Duchy of Tuscany, ruled by a Habsburg prince; the Duchies of Parma, Modena and Massa, ruled by other branches of the houses of Bourbon and Habsburg; not to mention the tiny Republic of San Marino and a number of smaller enclaves. The various political units had widely discrepant systems of government, and they were cut off from each other by the lack of roads or navigable rivers, by a plethora of tariff barriers, and by language. The range of dialects was such that nobody could hope to make himself understood outside his own region.

Only a sprinkling of academics and antiquaries kept a dialogue going between the cities in which they lived. Being widely read abroad, they made an exceptional contribution to the European Enlightenment but passed unnoticed by the mass of their countrymen. Antonio Genovesi, for whom Charles III of Naples created the first university chair of political economy in Europe in 1754, used his lectures to suggest standardization and indeed unification, referring to 'our common mother Italy'.[3] But very few of his listeners had any sense of an Italian nationality. An interesting exception in this respect was Giambattista Vico, born in Naples in 1668, the son of a poor bookseller. He started out as a poet but turned his mind to greater things, and in 1725 published *Scienza Nuova*, a treatise on the history of humanity. His view of the universe was anthropocentric and he extended human nature to communities, persuaded as he was of the 'humanity of nations'. He believed the division of humanity into nations was ordained by God, and anticipated Herder in his vision of them evolving and struggling like so many individuals seeking self-fulfilment. Each nation had its specific character and even its soul. And the primary manifestation of nationhood was, for Genovesi, language.[4] A sort of linguistic purity committee, the *crusca*, had been set up in an attempt to standardize a national literary language, but it could not agree on which dialect to favour, and there were perennial calls for a return to Latin.

The Piedmontese nobleman Count Vittorio Alfieri, who was to become a celebrated poet and dramatist, grew up without being able to speak Tuscan, the only one of the dialects regarded as a proper language. And although he had literary tastes, he did not begin to read Dante, Ariosto and Tasso until the age of twenty-seven. He only learned to appreciate Italy and her culture while staying in England, whither he had been drawn by his love of thoroughbred horses. In 1786, after two long tours of Europe, he settled in Paris in order to be with his mistress, the Countess of Albany, widow of Charles Edward Stuart, Bonnie Prince Charlie. In 1789 he was absorbed in printing an edition of his works, but the outbreak of the revolution jolted him out of his habitual introspection. This tall, thin and somewhat farouche redhead who rarely shed his corrosive melancholy was moved to pen ecstatic dithyrambs. His fellow poet Ippolito Pindemonte, also staying in Paris, contributed a paean to France, calling upon Italy to emulate her sister. In Italy itself, Pindemonte's brother Giovanni wrote a poem in celebration, in which he conjured up a vision of resurrection, and in the larger cities young men responded with excitement to reports of the events taking place in France. Some formed secret societies with dramatic names and discussed the precepts of liberty and fraternity.

Alfieri's enthusiasm quickly gave way to irritation with the French, whom he henceforth referred to as 'gibbering monkeys'.[5] He left Paris in 1792, taking the Countess of Albany with him, and settled in Florence. There he began penning his *Misogallo*, a collection of violent diatribes in prose and verse against the French and all their works, which he published in 1799, the year they marched into Florence. A passionate libertarian, he had become convinced that personal freedom could only exist in a state of national liberty, and he began to entertain visions of a regenerate Italy. The dedications of his plays, which enjoyed huge popularity at this time, are telling. *Timoleone* is dedicated to Pasquale Paoli, *Bruto Primo* to Washington, and *Bruto Secondo* to the Italian people of the Future, to whom Alfieri appeared to ascribe some kind of national mission.[6] In the French, he saw the ideal unifying enemy. 'For you, O Italy, hatred of the French, under whatever standard or mask they present themselves, must be the single and fundamental basis of your political existence,' he wrote in the *Misogallo*. His anti-French feelings were shared by the majority of educated Italians but not by those dreaming of a resurgent Italy, most of whom realized that the French intrusion on to the Italian scene represented their only chance.

More characteristic in this respect was Filippo Antonio Buonarotti of Pisa, a descendant of the painter Michelangelo. A freethinker and a radical, he had long been suspect to the Tuscan authorities for possessing French books, and when he began writing enthusiastic articles about the French Revolution in the Florentine *Gazzetta universale*, he came under threat of arrest so he fled to Corsica, just in time to welcome back Pasquale Paoli on his return from exile in England in June 1790.

Like Rousseau before him, Buonarotti was delighted by the Corsican pattern of social organization, and he began to dream of imposing a similarly egalitarian system on the Italian mainland. In the meantime, he helped implement French revolutionary laws on the island, in the teeth of considerable opposition from the Corsicans. He later tried to foist a constitution, which turned out to be very close to Rousseau's nation-building project for Corsica, on the neighbouring island of Sardinia. But the Sardinians did not wish to become a nation. After this failure, he headed for Paris. There, he fell in with Saint-Just and Robespierre and at the end of 1793 he was appointed *Commissaire Éxécutif* in Corsica. On the way there he received news that the island had been taken by the British so he decided to instead follow the French Army which was invading Piedmont. On 22 April 1794 he was named French commissioner for the captured province of Oneglia. In this tiny place, where he was joined by republicans and malcontents from every part of the peninsula, Buonarotti began to build up a pan-Italian conspiratorial network.

He soon fell foul of local interests, and was arrested, sent back to Paris and cast into the prison of Plessis. There, Buonarotti met his soul mate,

Britannia defends Corsica from France; a classical example of national anthropomorphism.

A cartoon of 1775 showing America having tea forced down her throat and being outraged by the British government, while Britannia herself weeps. Nobody was being forced to drink tea, and the idea of a continent's skirts being looked up by a lecherous British minister, offensive though it is, seems a poor motive for war.

The death of General Montgomery in the attack on the British garrison of Quebec in December 1775 is presented here in the artistic convention of martyrdom.

General Warren offering his life to the cause of outraged America at Bunker Hill, in a pose usually associated in art with the depiction of crusaders.

FIRST in WAR,
FIRST in PEACE,
&
FIRST in the HEARTS
OF HIS
COUNTRYMEN.

Washington crowned by a grateful Miss Liberty, representing the spirit of the new nation. The liberty tree in the background is topped by the red cap popularized by the French Revolution.

Washington's spiritual son Lafayette gallantly leading the French Nation out of the tomb and crushing the monsters of despotism that oppressed her.

Lafayette taking the oath to the nation and the constitution at the altar of the *Patrie* during the Fête de la Fédération, 14 July 1790. The crucifix bears no figure of Christ, but instead a serpent, masonic symbol of eternity, and is dominated by the new emblem of the tricolor.

An allegory of 1792 illustrating the religion of the *Patrie*, to which mothers must offer their children, ladies their jewels, and young men their lives.

The Auto-da-fé on the Champ de Mars on 14 July 1792 commemorating the fall of the Bastille, in which symbols of the *ancien régime* were offered up in a ritual holocaust.

The Declaration of the Rights of Man, presented on this painted board in the traditional guise of the Mosaic Tablets of the Law.

Given their unique status as representatives of the people, the deputies to the Convention could not, according to the painter Jaques-Louis David, be allowed to wear any old clothes. This design for a costume produced by the artist in 1794 nicely jumbles pseudo-Roman garb with a *konfederatka* cap, made fashionable by the Polish insurrection of that year.

The beatification of Marat, one of the first to suffer martyrdom for his devotion to the French people.

The apotheosis of Marat, borne up to heaven after his death by the French Republic, who points to the building of the Panthéon, where his earthly remains will lie.

The *Patrie*, satisfied with the sacrifices he has made on her behalf, crowns the patriot with laurels, while the arts prepare to immortalize his virtue. A French engraving of 1792.

The exemplary patriot, vanquished but righteous. Tadeusz Kościuszko in London after his release from Russian captivity in 1797, painted by Richard Cosway.

Gracchus (formerly François) Babeuf. Babeuf's Corsica had been the poor villages of his native Picardy, where the peasants still operated an archaic system of strip-farming. During the five months of their imprisonment, the two worked out their political recipe, published by Babeuf at the end of 1795 as *The Plebeian Manifesto*. It was the first real communist manifesto, calling for the abolition of private property and stipulating that anyone who worked hard or tried to improve himself must be repressed as 'a social scourge'.[7] In 1796 Babeuf began planning an insurrection in Paris, but it was the means rather than the desired ends that are the most significant. They were quite novel, and derived from Buonarotti's experiences. He rejected the widespread belief, based primarily on the American paragon, that revolutions could be carried out through spontaneous popular effort when inspired by the justice of its cause. This, Buonarotti realized, was out of the question in the Italian peninsula, where the people did not care a hoot for any cause. So, if a revolution was to succeed, it would have to be implemented over their heads, and possibly even against their will, by a group of dedicated conspirators taking control of the levers of power. This they proposed to do by the gradual infiltration of the army, police and administration.

For his part, Buonarotti concentrated on enlisting the motley crowd of Italian patriots who had taken refuge in France, and who were to accompany the French army poised to invade the Austrian possessions in northern Italy. But only a couple of weeks later the French Directory uncovered Babeuf's conspiracy. Babeuf and one of his accomplices were executed, the rest were given varying terms of imprisonment. This put an end to Buonarotti's plans. But the model he had created, which enabled small and weak cells to subvert strong governments, was to shape most of European conspiratorial activity over the next century and keep the forces of the status quo in a state of permanent panic alert. Buonarotti was the godfather of all secret societies, and they would play an exceptional role in the history of Italy over the next decades.

In May 1796 General Bonaparte routed the Austrians at the Battle of Lodi, and over the next months he pushed them out of northern Italy while local radicals set up republics in his wake. But neither France nor Bonaparte was interested in world conflagration. By the Treaty of Campo Formio in October 1797, Bonaparte ceded Venice, which the local revolutionaries had liberated at the instigation of the French, to Austria. Adding insult to injury, he removed the bronze horses that adorned the roof of St Mark's basilica, and brought them to Paris so that they could 'rest at last upon free soil'.[8]

Bonaparte admitted no limits to his power while in command of the army in Italy, and he treated the locality in which he was operating as an adjunct to his military arrangements. He granted constitutions, set up representative bodies and created new political units entirely at his own convenience, taking little account of local feeling. He established a Lombard republics, then refashioned it as the Cispadane and Transpadane republic, and, a few months later, as the Cisalpine Republic. When a group of Lombard patriots came to ask if they could form a legion to defend the liberated province, he assented. But he was not prepared to let them fight under the flag of France, so he gave them an amended tricolor, in which he replaced the blue with a band of green. After Bonaparte's return to France, other French commanders followed his example. In 1798 the Pope was ousted and a Roman Republic created, and at the beginning of 1799 General Championnet occupied Naples and proclaimed a Parthenopean Republic.

Galling as this hubristic behaviour was to people like Alfieri, it contributed more to the cause of Italy's unification than all the patriots put together. Virtually everything the French did advanced the cause of Italy's unification in one way or another. They overthrew the foreign rulers and reduced the temporal power of the Church. By the beginning of 1799 the whole peninsula was under French control, and every part of the country save Venice had some kind of bicameral representative body. These bodies and the administrations they commanded needed to be staffed, and this gave rise to a new administrative class. Bonaparte set up armed forces in every political unit he created. Formed up on French republican lines, these were citizen armies drawing in men from all walks of life. As promotion was on merit, they were an important tool for the social advance of the able from the lower orders, and a breeding-ground for patriots.

In his 'Notes of Advice to the Cisalpine Patriots', the French representative of the people, Jullien, produced a set of guidelines for them. 'Oppose priestly mummeries with national festivals that appeal to the eyes and the imagination,' recommends Note 26. Note 27 urges them to 'give institutions to the people to regenerate them; create a new man.[9] Multiply civic ceremonies having a moral aim, such as marriages, adoptions, schools or gymnasia, prize distributions, military exercises, races, games, and mass meetings.' The more enlightened of the existing priests were to be used to bring about change, by associating the words 'religion' and 'patrie'. The French imported the revolutionary passion for association and talk, and political clubs sprang up like weeds after rain wherever they passed. They were mainly Jacobin in inspiration, and they aped the style of their model. Discussions were emotional, with much wailing over the shackled motherland and veneration of France, 'the apostle of nations'.[10] In July 1798, a huge crowd was gathered before an 'Altar of Liberty' in Rome. A heap of cardinals' hats, titles of nobility, papal insignia and the minutes of the Inquisition was stacked up in front of this, and ceremoniously ignited. One man broke a crucifix and threw it on the pyre, and then proceeded to 'de-baptize' himself by washing his hair.[11]

Not all Italian patriots approved of such excesses, but whatever they thought of France, they could not do without her support. This was confirmed when, in the summer of 1799, the Bourbon King Ferdinand and his British allies regained possession of Naples, and the Austrian and Russian armies reoccupied the north. Many leading Italian patriots had to take refuge in France, and it was only when, in 1800, Bonaparte swept into Italy once again, defeating the Austro-Russian forces at Marengo and eventually clearing the entire peninsula of France's enemies, that they were able to return.

This time, Bonaparte ordered things differently. He was no longer a revolutionary general but First Consul. A significant part of the 'liberated' territory was incorporated into France proper. The rest of northern Italy was lumped together into the Italian Republic which in 1805 became the kingdom of Italy, with Bonaparte, or the Emperor Napoleon as he became, as king. In the following year his brother Joseph became king of Naples, a throne which he relinquished two years later in favour of Joachim Murat, in order to ascend that of Spain. For the first time since the fall of the Roman Empire all the inhabitants of the peninsula were subject to the same legal system. They were also linked by a new network of good roads and posting stations, and these roads opened channels of communication, facilitating the dissemination of ideas.

The seeds sown by Buonarotti were fertilized by a renewal of masonic activity which came in on the tail of the French army, many of whose officers belonged to the movement. This produced a veritable explosion of more or less secret societies throughout the peninsula. Some were founded to promote the aims of the French Revolution, some to resist them. Others strove to resist French influence while promoting the cause of pan-Italian revolution. Such was the 'Black League', under Count Alessandro Savioli of Bologna, which later became known as the Raggi or 'Société des Rayons'. The Raggi changed their name in 1802 to Astronomia Platonica, but were often also referred to as the Centri. They were supposedly governed by a 'Solar Circle' presiding over two 'hemispheres', one at Milan the other at Bologna.

The most interesting of the societies was the Adelfi, whose members all took the name 'Emilio' in recognition of the influence of Rousseau on their outlook. It was founded by Buonarotti to promote revolution, and it seems to have grown out of a sub-masonic network of French officers opposed to Napoleon calling themselves Les Philadelphes, which probably had Babouvist roots. But it is dangerous to try to be precise about these societies, as they mutated, died and revived with baffling facility. Much of the information on them comes from agents and informers who often fleshed out their lack of factual intelligence with rumour or even fantasy. But their existence testifies to an unprecedented ferment.

The confusion of Italian reactions to the French occupation is captured in the life of the poet Ugo Foscolo. Born on the Ionian island of Zante, then a British protectorate, of a Venetian father and a Greek mother, he only learnt to speak and read Italian in the early 1790s, when he went to live in Venice. Appalled at the treaty of Campo Formio, Foscolo nevertheless saw in Bonaparte the only chance for the Italians to break free of Austrian domination. In 1797 he wrote a poem entitled *Bonaparte liberatore*, which glorifies him as an invincible leader, a 'God', whose triumph will see the sun of Italy rise again. In the following year, Foscolo took service in the French army, became an officer, and fought in the Battle of the Trebbia and the siege of Genoa, where he was wounded. Convinced that Bonaparte held the key to Italian independence, he clung to his star and even found himself in the Pas-de-Calais in 1800 preparing to invade England.

His novel *Le Ultime Lettere di Jacopo Ortis*, written in the late 1790s, is a sentimental story, but underlying it is the secondary theme of a doomed passion for a lost motherland, for which the lover pines more than for his mistress. And why a country should be loved by its children he went on to illustrate in his greatest work, the long poem *Dei Sepolcri*. In 1805 the

French passed an edict to the effect that cemeteries should henceforth be sited outside city boundaries, and that no more corpses were to be buried in churches and vaults. This caused Foscolo to reflect on the relationship of the living to the dead, and on the need for the living to be in touch with their past through the graves of previous generations. Like Herder, he pointed to a continuity, both cultural and moral, that bound nation to soil and ensured its continued development.

The themes treated by Foscolo were picked up by Vincenzo Cuoco, a Neapolitan lawyer who defined the problems facing those who longed to create a nation in Italy. He had taken part in the Neapolitan rising of 1799 that culminated in the establishment of the Parthenopean Republic, and had watched with dismay its demise only six months later. He had been forced to take refuge in France, and after the Battle of Marengo settled in Milan, where he published an account of the events of 1799. A sober realist, he had no illusions about the reasons for the failure of the revolution. 'Amongst our patriots, many had the republic on their lips, many had it in their heads, but few had it in their hearts,' he wrote.[12]

Cuoco also realized that the majority of the population were at the very best indifferent to the enthusiasm of the patriotic intellectuals. He concluded that the only way forward was to educate people and form them into patriots. Like Rousseau and Pestalozzi, he saw patriotism as the basis of all public life. People had to love their country in order to work and die for it, and without that commitment there could be no real national community.

From Milan, Cuoco began to put his views across in the *Giornale Italiano*. This also provided a diet with which to feed the sense of national pride required to motivate further effort. The paper reclaimed past glories and achievements for the Italian cause, reminding its readers that it had been Italians who had discovered America and China, and listing Italian achievements in the arts and sciences. In 1804 he published a novel, *Platone in Italia*, in which he glorified the Italian motherland, and purloined the entire Etruscan as well as the Greek heritage on its behalf. Back in Naples in 1807, where he was employed in Murat's administration, he laid the plans for a programme of national education.

French intervention in Italy was not limited in its effects to that region, but had an impact on areas further east. In 1797 Bonaparte had penetrated as far as Laibach and Klagenfurt, deep into an area where a great many rival ambitions crossed. These were the historic marchlands of Austria, fought over for centuries by Christians and Turks. They were also the approaches to Greece, a territory of the mind as well as of the globe, which gave title to imperial dreams and access to Constantinople, itself the gateway to eastern dominion.

In the eighteenth century, the whole of what is now Greece and most of the Balkans were ruled by Ottoman Turkey. Between the 1760s and 1792, Turkish dominion was undermined by two long wars with Russia. In 1769 a Russian force landed in the Morea and raised a minor rebellion there, only to abandon the rebels to a gory fate. But most of the action took place away from Greek soil, much of it at sea. The Empress Catherine's motives for waging war in the area were reinforced by the usual Enlightenment contempt for the Turks and adulation of ancient Greece. An ideological spur was provided by the old Muscovite claim to the legacy of Constantinople.

The tsars of Muscovy were descended from a daughter of the last Paleologue emperor of Constantinople, and Peter the Great had inserted 'King of Greece' among his titles. If Russia were the centre of the Orthodox Church, then she ought to rule over all believers, including the Serbians and the Greeks. By the treaty of Kutchuk Kainardji, which ended the first of her Turkish wars in 1774, Catherine was granted a vague protectorate over all Orthodox subjects of the Ottoman Empire. While she enforced control over the Orthodox Church in Russia and subscribed to views that could hardly be termed religious, she found it both convenient and exciting to champion religion in support of what was in effect a crusade to liberate the Balkans and the Peloponnese.

There was little evidence that the population of these areas had any desire to be liberated. Conditions under Turkish rule were not desperate for most of the 1.5 million Greeks. The Ottoman authorities practised a policy of unbenign neglect, and in the Peloponnese, Greek notables governed their own localities on behalf of the Turks. Across the isthmus in Attica and Acarnania, the Armatoli, a Greek police licensed by the Turks, ruled their manors like medieval robber barons. The only part of the country that was run directly by a Turk, Ali Pasha of Janina, was also the least lawless. In spite of the severe poll tax and the dress restrictions applying to Christians, the Greeks on the whole enjoyed greater freedoms than some occupied European peoples. The Turks were nevertheless unpredictable to the point of capriciousness, and occasionally resorted to savagery.

There were a few who dreamed of a better future for Greece. One was Adamantios Korais of Smyrna, who had gone to Paris to study medicine, stayed on through the whole revolution and become an established figure in French intellectual life. Rhigas Velestinlis, a poet who lived in Vienna, was a vigorous champion of the demotic language spoken by ordinary Greeks. He wrote a handbook of physics for the Greeks and produced a monumental atlas of Hellas. The periodical *Ephimeris*, which began publication in December 1790, fed Greeks in and outside the country with news of events taking place in France throughout the following decade. A Jacobin Club was established by some Frenchmen on the island of Corfu in 1793, and it busied itself with talk of Greek liberation. By then, Greeks in Vienna and Marseille had drawn up a map of 'Greater Greece' and composed a 'Hymn of Liberty'. The whole area began to come to life with the fall-out from events taking place elsewhere.

The collapse of the 1794 insurrection in Poland was followed by an exodus of patriots eager to avoid a spell in Siberia, and several thousand of these crossed into the safety of Ottoman dominions. With the semi-official support of the Turkish authorities, Colonel Joachim Denisko began concentrating them near Jassy in what was then Turkish Wallachia. He appealed for French help, and while France could not spare any military assistance, she did send an agent who was to facilitate co-operation between the Poles and their Turkish hosts, and to direct the Poles away from their plan to attack Russia towards an anti-Austrian stance.

Another Pole was concentrating a force outside Bucharest, and he too applied for French assistance. The French responded by sending Wojciech Turski, alias 'Albert le Sarmate', to Constantinople to co-ordinate these initiatives. There he found a Polish Committee which helped him to unite all the men into a Legion of the Danube, numbering nearly 2,000 by the end of 1795, uniformed with a Polish cap and a French cockade. The legion took part in only one military action, an incursion into Austrian-held Bukovina in 1797, before it was disbanded.

Another Polish group, based in Venice, had been trying to organize an armed force in Italy since the beginning of 1795. In October 1796 the French Directory agreed to allow the Polish emigrés to form up a legion as part of the army of the Cisalpine Republic. General Jan Henryk Dąbrowski was sent to Milan, where in January 1797 the agreement was finalized. The Poles would wear Polish uniforms and use Polish words of command but sport a French cockade and Italian epaulettes, inscribed with the motto '*gli uomini liberi sono fratelli*'. By the end of April there were over 5,000 men under arms, either emigrés or prisoners and deserters from the Austrian army drafted against their will in Austria's Polish province of Galicia.

Dąbrowski's plan was to march up through Croatia and Hungary into Galicia, while the Legion of the Danube made a raid through Bukovina. Its marching song, which would become the national anthem, predicted Dąbrowski's march from Italy into Poland. One of the verses has an old man in Poland shedding tears of joy as he and his daughter catch the distant sound of the legionaries' drums. In April 1797 the Poles were beating these drums at the Leoben Pass and preparing to march when Bonaparte changed his plans.

The French victories in northern Italy had aroused hopes all over south-central Europe, and particularly in Greece. The Bey of Maina, Zanettos Gregorakis, sent his son to Bonaparte's camp at Milan in the spring of 1797, offering to place his ports at the disposal of the French if they would support his independence from Turkish rule. Greeks from all over the country met in the Peloponnese to plan an insurrection and appealed to the French for assistance. In Paris, Adamantios Korais asked Thomas Jefferson for advice on the constitution of a future Greek state. From Vienna, Rhigas Velestinlis published a revolutionary proclamation, including a list of the rights of man and a French-style constitution.

Rhigas, a colourful character who paraded about in an ancient Greek helmet, was nothing if not ambitious in his designs, and his proclamation was addressed to 'the Inhabitants of Rumeli, Asia Minor, the Archipelago, Moldavia and Wallachia'. He envisaged a Hellenic republic not defined by any ethnic considerations. The flag of the new republic was to be a horizontal tricolor featuring red for the imperial purple and the sovereignty of the Greek people, white for the innocence and purity of the cause, and black symbolizing death in the service of the motherland. The flag was to be adorned with the club of Hercules surmounted by three crosses. 'The dress of the Greek soldier is heroic,' he explained as he detailed the colour and design of this too.[13] But the Austrians arrested Rhigas and turned him over to the Turks, who garroted him and several of his compatriots in 1798.

The treaty of Leoben, signed in 1797, ceded the Ionian Islands to

France, which occupied them that summer. The French began planting liberty trees and conducted a ceremonial burning of the books of Ionian nobility. The local nobles cast their title deeds and even their wigs on the flames in an act of expiation. Bonaparte recruited some klephts into an 'Ionian Legion'. He also sent envoys into the Morea to 'spread the seeds of real liberty, to make the children of Greece worthy of their ancestors and of the great nation that has begun to shatter their chains'. Characteristically, Bonaparte wanted to bring every possible pot to the boil while he decided in which one he would cook his dinner. While instructing his envoys, a couple of Mainotes born in Corsica, to incite the Greeks to a state of readiness, he told them that 'the time has not yet come' for anything more.

Bonaparte's envoys were well-chosen from an ideological standpoint. Asked by a Greek girl what religion he practised, one of them answered: 'I follow that of our forefathers, the religion of nature.' When asked whether he did not recognize any saints, he answered: 'I know four: Sparta, Athens, Thebes and France.'[14] They duly set their compatriots dreaming the impossible. 'Heavens above! what a new dawn shines over Greece!' exclaimed one old man. The Pasha of Janina proudly sported a tricolor cockade and Mainote women were reported to be praying to icons of Bonaparte alongside those of the Virgin. Their prayers were more nearly answered than anyone might have expected – and from the most unlikely quarter.

The Polish Legion had continued to grow. By the summer of 1797 it had reached over 7,000 men and was divided into two separate units, under Generals Kniaziewicz and Wielhorski, the son of the Confederate of Bar who had inspired Rousseau's *Considérations*. The Poles distinguished themselves at the capture of Rome and during the subsequent invasion of Naples. But they suffered during the French débâcle in Italy in 1799, and when the Cisalpine Republic ceased to exist their remnants washed up in southern France.

Kościuszko, who had been appointed nominal commander, had asked the Directory to collect all the Poles into one contingent and use them in northern Europe, but he was brushed off. Some 9,000 were reorganized as the Italic Legion and sent back to the peninsula under Dąbrowski. The rest were deployed in the north under Kniaziewicz, and fought at the Battle of Hohenlinden as the Legion of the Danube. But the Peace of Lunéville, signed on 26 January 1801, put an end to all the dreams of marching back to Poland. The French decided to disband the legions and turn them into three blandly-named *demi-brigades étrangères* of the French army.

As he contemplated the possible destruction of his force, Dąbrowski planned a better future for it. He decided to take them across the sea to Greece. 'There, uniting two unhappy nations deprived of their motherland, he wanted to found a new nation, called Greeko-Poland', in the words of one of his companions-in-arms. Dąbrowski had apparently been in touch with interested parties in Greece and had procured ships. He was ready to move when the French grew suspicious of his confabulations and quickened the pace of the dispersal of the Legions.[15]

The Greek Orthodox hierarchy was profoundly conservative and therefore preferred the spiritual certainties of the Turkish status quo to the unknown perils of French intervention. In a 'Paternal Exhortation' delivered in 1798, Patriarch Anthimos warned against the wiles of the devil who 'had devised in the present century another artifice and pre-eminent deception, namely the much-vaunted system of liberty'. 'Everywhere this illusory system of the diabolical one has led to poverty, murder, damage, rapine, complete ungodliness, spiritual destruction and vain repentance,' he continued, citing the examples of Italy and Venice.[16] And the majority of his countrymen doubtless agreed. For all the verbiage, it is doubtful whether many Greeks had any real sense of a national cause. But the Poles would still have fared better there than where they did end up.

The Caribbean island of Hispaniola was divided into the Spanish colony of Santo Domingo and the French Saint-Domingue. The Spanish half was a sleepy backwater, but Saint-Domingue was France's prime colony. It produced sugar, cotton, cocoa and indigo, and was the greatest market for the European slave trade. By 1789 it supplied two-thirds of France's overseas trade. The colony was worked by more than half-a-million slaves, the majority of whom had been born in Africa. They were subject to Le Code Noir, decreed by Louis XIV, which regulated their status and the punishments to be meted out to them. Also meticulously regulated was the status of the 128 different permutations of racial mixture on the island. But for present purposes only, four elements in the population need be considered. The *grands blancs* were the rich white planters, many of them born in France and some of them absentees, who despised everyone else more or less equally. The *petits blancs* were whites with little or no land, who hated the *grands blancs* about as much as they did the mulattos, and the mulattos reserved only contempt for the blacks. The climate of mutual hatred was so heavy that even the pure blacks born on the island despised the 'congos' who had come from Africa. And hatred meant cruelty – of a degree difficult to grasp.

The whites and many of the mulattos of Saint-Domingue were in close touch with France. The *grands blancs* wanted to take advantage of the political crisis there in order to gain greater autonomy. They resented the metropolitan government's tendency to meddle, and there was always the fear that it might emancipate the mulattos or even the blacks. In Paris, they lobbied opinion in the Assembly through the Club Massiac, named after one of their plantations. News of the fall of the Bastille opened up new possibilities. 'The intoxication of enthusiasm was carried to delirious lengths,' wrote a witness. 'Without distinction of class or colour, without looking into the gulf that was opening up for the future, everyone took fire in the name of liberty and equality; everyone embraced with transport the hope of a rebirth.'[17] Every group thought their own lot would improve, without taking account of the others. The whites formed a national guard, and set up local assemblies. On 25 March 1790 delegates from these met in the General Assembly of Saint-Domingue and the rivalry began. The *grands blancs* sported a red cockade, took the name of Patriots, and called for secession from France, while the *petits blancs* brandished white cockades and made great show of loyalty to the king.

In Paris, the two mulattos Julien Raimond and Vincent Ogé pleaded before the National Assembly to be given full rights, but there was little enthusiasm for their demands. Ogé went to England, where he was given funds by British abolitionists, and on 21 October 1791 he landed in Saint-Domingue with a supply of arms purchased in America. He gathered some 200 other mulattos and marched on Cap-Français, but his force was defeated and he himself was captured. His arms, legs, wrists, knees and elbows were cracked before he was broken slowly on the wheel. His execution was the signal for a general massacre of mulattos by the *petits blancs*. The French military governor, Thomas-Antoine de Mauduit, attempted to restore order. But his troops were no longer reliable, and the two fresh regiments sent out from France to reinforce him promptly joined the *petits blancs* and tore the unfortunate governor himself to pieces. But while the *petits blancs* celebrated their triumph, their enemies were massing against them.

In August 1791 a group of slaves lead by Boukman had started a rebellion which quickly embraced the plantations of the northern plain. Slave rebellions were nothing new. They tended to flare up with the ferocity of a brush fire, only to be put down with unspeakable savagery. But this one was different. It was more widespread than most. It grew in intensity rather than burning itself out in a few weeks. And it had a political slogan, somewhat incoherent it is true, but strongly voiced nevertheless. The rebels marched under a banner depicting a white baby impaled on a spear, and their battle-cry was '*Vive le Roi et l'Ancien Régime*'. While Boukman rampaged around the northern plain, a mulatto revolt aimed principally at the *petits blancs* erupted in the west of the colony. It managed to gain the support of some free blacks and, most importantly, of the *grands blancs* of the area.

During a debate on the situation in Saint-Domingue on 24 March 1792, the National Assembly decided to grant rights to 'people of colour'. But it did not specify which ones, and confirmed the continuation of slavery. It followed this up by despatching 6,000 fresh troops to the colony under the command of three commissioners headed by Léger Félicité Sonthonax. A friend of Brissot and Condorcet, he was no supporter of slavery. But there was little he could do in view of the kaleidoscopic revolutions of alliances between the various groups in response to every measure suggested. And anything he could suggest was ultimately irrelevant in the face of the gradual but relentless emergence of the black cause, and a real leader – Toussaint L'Ouverture.

Toussaint's father had been an African chieftain before being enslaved and shipped to Saint-Domingue. The planter who bought him recognized this and granted him special status within the plantation. He became a Catholic, married and produced eight children, the first of which he christened Toussaint. An old slave who had once worked for a priest taught the boy to read and write. When Toussaint grew up, he served first as coachman, and then as steward of the livestock on the plantation. This privileged position enabled Toussaint to educate himself further. Shortly after the outbreak of Boukman's rebellion, in September 1791, Toussaint joined the rebels. His superior intelligence soon told, and he became a valued counsellor and eventually undisputed leader. He trained the men to fight properly and, by declaring the outright abolition of slavery, gave the rebellion a real base. He also changed his surname from Breda (the name of the estate on which he was born) to 'L'Ouverture' to designate a dawning. When Sonthonax arrived with the fresh troops in the summer of 1792, Toussaint stood off, and in the new year he withdrew across the mountains into the Spanish colony of Santo Domingo. The Spanish, whose mother country had been invaded by revolutionary France, were happy to accept his offer of friendship.

On 29 August 1793 Sonthonax announced the abolition of slavery on his own initiative. This only helped to rally the whites and the mulattos, while the planters of the south placed themselves under the protection of George III of England. Sonthonax persevered. In January 1794 he despatched three deputies to the Convention: Bellay, a black former slave; Millas, a mullato; and Dufay, a *petit blanc*. They were greeted in the Convention on 3 February with high-blown speeches and histrionic gestures; the French Deputies fainted, wept and embraced in an orgy of self-esteem. Bellay made a rousing speech the following day demanding the formal abolition of slavery, and the Chamber passed the motion by acclamation. This paved the way for reconciliation between Toussaint and France. On 27 July 1794 he had a meeting with General de Laveaux, the new governor of the colony, and agreed to rejoin the service of France. Laveaux realized that he did not have much choice and placed his confidence in Toussaint, naming him assistant governor and later commander-in-chief. 'The Black Spartacus', as he called Toussaint, repaid this trust, and together they set about bringing peace back to the colony. But the atmosphere remained tense. The blacks, and Toussaint himself, could not rid themselves of the suspicion that France would restore slavery given the chance.

In September 1794 the British landed in the south and west of the island. Toussaint's efforts to dislodge them over the next years were vitiated by indiscipline and divisions in his own forces. Subordinates such as Jean Jacques Dessalines and Jean-François Christophe remained a law unto themselves. The British commander, Sir Thomas Maitland, was always looking to take advantage of the divisions within the French colony. In April 1798, he invited Toussaint to an interview, embraced him cordially to show that he had nothing against blacks, and showered him with honours. He suggested that Toussaint become king of Saint-Domingue under British protection. While Toussaint rejected the offer, he used the

British presence as an element in the complex power struggle going on in the colony.

Laveaux trusted Toussaint, but other French officials did not. Operating on the age-old principle of divide and rule, they took every opportunity – and there were plenty – to rouse latent animosities between the blacks and other groups, notably the mulattos. These had now emerged as the only force to rival the blacks, principally because of the talents of their leader, André Rigaud. Educated in Bordeaux, he had joined the French colours as a volunteer to fight in America in 1778, and had seen active service under Washington. In the best traditions of the island, Rigaud hated blacks and whites more or less equally, and was always open to suggestions of an alliance with one group to do down the other.

The realm of possibilities for this was expanded with the arrival, in 1798, of General de Hédouville as the new governor. He had a formidable reputation as the pacifier of the Vendée and had clearly been despatched in order to reassert France's control over the colony. He lost no time in inciting Rigaud against Toussaint, and his intrigues produced the desired result of a civil war and, in the end, the unwonted consequence of the French forces themselves being defeated. Hédouville was obliged to evacuate the island with the remnants, and when, on 1 August 1800, Toussaint finally crushed Rigaud, the black leader was undisputed master of what had become, de facto, an independent country. Not content to let matters rest there, Toussaint crossed the mountains into Santo Domingo, defeated the Spanish and united the whole island.

Toussaint was an exceptional character. He remained a devout Catholic, and seems to have carried with him none of the visceral hatreds that were the norm in the colony, rarely lapsing into brutality. Under his rule a measure of peace and order returned to Saint-Domingue. He was aware of his superiority and proud of his origins. He was prone to vanity, and his success and position naturally bred arrogance and a certain amount of ceremonial posturing. Yet he never let himself be trapped by flattery. If Toussaint had a weakness, it was a degree of naivety. After making himself master of the island, he wrote a letter to the First Consul professing his loyalty to France and enclosing a draft constitution from the colony. A more experienced man would have realized that the language of equals in which it was couched would strike the recipient as insolent. A less naive man would not have sent a copy of the constitution drafted by a rebellious black to the most prolific lawgiver since the days of the Roman Empire.

Bonaparte had no use for colonies that did not produce large quantities of income, and he believed that slavery was more cost-efficient than any of the alternatives. His wife Josephine was a planter's daughter from Martinique and her relatives owned property on Saint-Domingue. She corresponded with Toussaint and took a kindly interest in his son Isaac and stepson Placide, both at school in Paris. But this was probably an insurance policy and would not have affected her inherited prejudices. When General Vincent handed the First Consul a copy of Toussaint's constitution for the island, the Corsican exploded. 'I will not rest until I have torn the epaulettes off every nigger in the colonies!' was his response.[18]

He was as good as his word. On 14 December 1801, the first of eighty-six ships under Admirals Villaret Joyeuse and Latouche-Treville sailed from France, carrying an army of 20,000 French troops under the command of Bonaparte's brother-in-law, General Charles Victor Leclerc. With the expedition went Leclerc's wife, the stunning Pauline, and with Pauline went a vast wardrobe, a warehouse of furniture, paintings and household effects, a full complement of servants and an orchestra. Also on board were Toussaint's son and stepson, and his old enemy the mulatto leader André Rigaud. One of Leclerc's principal commanders was Donatien de Rochambeau, son of the French commander in America, who had himself fought as a colonel in the American war.

The fleet appeared off Le Cap on 29 January 1802, and on 2 February Rochambeau came ashore with the first contingent. Resistance was fierce, but Le Cap fell, followed by Port-au-Prince and other coastal towns. Toussaint's leadership was not equal to the situation, and he had no strategy, political or military. He capitulated to Leclerc, followed by Christophe, Dessalines and the other generals, who were accepted into French service, and soon the island was under French control.

Toussaint had been allowed to go home, but as soon as Leclerc felt strong enough, he had him seized along with his family and taken on board a French ship. Once they had him safely aboard, the French began to treat Toussaint with unwarranted brutality, to the extent of separating him from his family for the entire Atlantic crossing. He saw his wife and children only fleetingly on the quayside at Brest, before being bundled into a carriage and taken to the grim prison of Fort-de-Joux in the Jura Mountains. Upon arrival there, he was stripped of his uniform and robbed of most of his belongings, even his watch. He was given no adequate clothing to protect him from the cold climate and consistently underfed.

Despite repeated appeals to the First Consul by many distinguished people, Toussaint L'Ouverture, one of the few people who knew what the word freedom actually meant, was starved to death in the motherland of liberty and fraternity. He died on 7 April 1803. But his cause did not die with him.

'Never will the French Nation give chains to men whom it has once recognized as free', ran Bonaparte's original instructions to Leclerc early in 1802. By June he had restored not only the institution of slavery, but the trade as well, and ordered the disfranchisement of the mulattos throughout the French colonies. Only Saint-Domingue was temporarily exempted from this. In July Leclerc received orders to restore slavery as soon as practicable, at the same time as the news that reinforcements were on their way.[19]

These reinforcements turned out to be none other than the remnants of the Legion of the Danube, now incorporated into the French army and given the name of 113 Demi-Brigade, although they were allowed to wear out their Polish uniforms. The convoy came in sight of Cap-Français on 2 September 1802 and sailed straight into a hideous trap.

Word of the reimposition of slavery in Martinique and elsewhere had reached Saint-Domingue, and in August 1802 an uprising broke out against the French. In September, the yellow fever which was a constant threat to the French troops exploded into an epidemic, killing as many as a hundred men a day. Black units began to go over to the rebels, led by their black officers. At a meeting in Arcahaie, the rebels elected Dessalines as their leader. The table at which they were sitting was draped with the French tricolor. Dessalines tore it into three strips, discarded the hated white, and joined together the other two, which he waved over his head. Later that day his wife's goddaughter sewed them together, horizontally, with the blue above the red.

With all the blacks of the colony united against them, the position of the French was untenable. Men were dying fast from the fever – of the 2,750 Poles who disembarked in September 1802 less than 400 remained alive in January 1803. At that very moment 2,851 men of the second Polish Legion, those whom Dąbrowski had dreamed of taking to Greece, were being forcibly embarked at Genoa. They landed at Tiburon in the south of the island to relieve Les Cayes, and most of them died too. Altogether some 25,000 of the troops brought over from France in various stages perished, including their commander, Leclerc, who succumbed to the fever. Yet his wife Pauline partied and revelled throughout with epic hedonism.

Rochambeau, who succeeded Leclerc in command, fought on doggedly. But his policy of slaughtering blacks and mulattos wholesale was ultimately counter-productive. To make matters worse, the British were blockading the island, so supplies were not coming through. After trying to negotiate some kind of a compromise with Dessalines, he had to give in. On 29 November 1803 he put the remnants of his forces and as many civilians as he could accommodate aboard his remaining ships, and surrendered to the British fleet blockading the island.

Despite the efforts of a few men such as Brissot, Sonthonax and Laveaux, France's policy towards the colony had always been one of total domination, and had never wavered in its preference for slavery. The French Republic expended vast resources on trying to restore the *ancien régime* in the colony – enough in soldiers and equipment to liberate Poland or Ireland twice over. It had dragged the sacred words and emblems of liberty and fraternity through labyrinths of hypocrisy and rivers of blood. And yet the creed itself had been spread. In January 1804 the former French colony of Saint-Domingue became an independent state, the Republic of Haiti. In July, Jean Jacques Dessalines heard that Bonaparte had been offered the imperial crown. Not to be outdone, he drew up a petition from his generals asking him to assume the purple, to which he graciously assented, and, beating Napoleon to it, was anointed and crowned Emperor under the name Jean Jacques I on 8 October. Presumably in order to annoy Napoleon further, he aped George III, going about in an approximation of the Windsor uniform. Dessalines had never liked whites, and the following year he decreed and carried out a massacre of all whites in the colony – except for the Poles.

The first Pole to set foot on the island (and to die of yellow fever) had been General Władysław Jabłonowski, who, though born in Gdańsk, had been a classmate of Napoleon Bonaparte and the future Marshal Davout at the French military college at Brienne. Although he was a Polish nobleman, he was illegitimate and was in fact half black. None of the other Poles shared this advantage, yet they were quickly identified by the blacks as being different from the French. They wore a different uniform and most of them spoke no French. Their heart was clearly not in the war, and they appear to have shown reluctance in carrying out massacres of black prisoners.

Because of this, and because one of Dessalines's educated friends explained to him that the Poles were an oppressed nation fighting for their liberty, the future emperor took an indulgent view. Unlike their French fellows, Polish captives were not necessarily sawn in half or roasted on a spit. They were often spared altogether, and some volunteered to fight for black freedom. Dessalines had a small personal bodyguard made up of them, and when he later formed an elite personal guard, he called them 'the Black Poles'. When the French evacuated the island, some of the surviving Poles went with them and eventually got back to France. Others ended up on British prison hulks, some five hundred were pressed into British service, and three officers became successful privateers. But at least four hundred chose to become citizens of Haiti, a right uniquely extended to them by Dessalines.

The emperor Jean Jacques was assassinated in October 1806, two years after his coronation. He was succeeded by Henry Christophe, but this caused a split; the country was divided into the state of Haiti under Christophe and the Republic of Haiti under President Alexandre Pétion. Christophe eventually decreed himself King Henry I. He created a court of princes, dukes, marquises and counts, designing an elaborate ceremonial uniform for each rank, and instituted the Order of St Henry. He was attended by an élite corps of cadets called the Royal Bons Bons, and by a detachment of Royal Amazons, staffed by fifty interestingly uniformed young women wielding bows and arrows.

None of this was very edifying. But the fact remains that this island, the first part of the new world to be ruled by Europeans, had become the first independent state in the western hemisphere after the United States, and the first to be ruled by black men. This went against the wishes of every power in the area; the Americans were no happier to see slaves getting assertive than the planters of the Club Massiac. But the real achievement was the breakthrough that had taken place in the attitudes of the blacks themselves. They had dared to dream the impossible and reached out not just for freedom from slavery. They had assumed nationhood and invented a *patrie* in Haiti. Without this they would have been dispersed and crushed, as so many black revolts would continue to be elsewhere in the Americas. Whether he realized it or not, Jean Jacques Dessalines was ruling over a nation created along the lines and conforming to most of the precepts laid down by his namesake Rousseau, even though he himself was more influenced by Napoleon Bonaparte.

9
Un Pueblo Americano

Spanish America, or American Spain as one ought perhaps to refer to it before the 1820s, does not lend itself easily to generalization. It was a vast and variegated region, stretching from California in the north down to the southern tip of Chile, from the Pacific coast of the Americas in the west to the panhandle of Florida and the Caribbean islands of Cuba and Hispaniola. The area was inhabited by indigenous 'Indians' of varying ethnicity and culture. It also had a large population of black people of African origin, nearly all of them slaves. The white colonial population was more uniform in origin than that of the English colonies of North America, but it was far more divided.

There was a fundamental conflict between those born in the new world, the *criollos* or Creoles, and those who came out from Spain, known as *peninsulares*. The new arrivals tended to think of themselves as superior to the locals, but some were poor and came in quest of fortune, while many of the Creoles were rich. So while each despised the other at heart, there was an element of mutual envy. This intricate situation was further complicated by the fact that unlike the North American colonials, the Spaniards, usually those at the bottom of the social scale, miscegenated with the Indians and the blacks. This produced a large population of *mestizos*, who had varying admixtures of white and Indian or black blood, or both.

Even the grandest Creole families had some Indian and or African blood, reinforcing a Spanish American concept that the sap of the new world rises into its conquerors, and the conquering whites are themselves enslaved by the land. This added an edge of anti-colonial resentment to the feelings of these colonial masters towards their peninsular brethren, giving rise to continuous vacillation between Spanish patriotism and incipient rebelliousness. There was a long tradition, beginning with Cortés, Pizarro and Aguirre, of insubordination to Madrid, and glory in Spanish America always seemed to begin with an act of rebellion.

The Spanish possessions in the new world were divided up into the Viceroyalty of New Spain, including California, Mexico, Florida, Guatemala and the Caribbean islands; the Viceroyalty of New Granada, including all of what is now Colombia, Ecuador, Venezuela and Bolivia; the Viceroyalty of Peru, comprising Peru and Chile; and the Viceroyalty of La Plata, including most of present-day Argentina, Paraguay and Uruguay. The Spaniards had transported to the new world their own forms of local administration, setting up *cabildos* or regional parliaments made up of elected councillors, functionaries and local notables. Their role was to administer the municipalities, but they lacked authority and could be overruled. Essentially, the whole area was ruled directly from the metropolis, by viceroys and captains-general appointed by the king and usually sent out from Madrid.

There were exceptions. Ambrose O'Higgins was born in 1712 at Summerhill, County Meath, into the family of a poor peasant farmer. An uncle who had entered the priesthood in Spain paid for the boy to be brought over to Cadiz and educated there. The young man then set off for the new world in search of fortune. He joined the army in Peru, reached the rank of colonel, and the king bestowed upon him the title of Count of Ballenar. In 1788 he was appointed Captain-General of Chile and his title was upped to that of Marquis of Osorno. In 1796 he was made Viceroy of Peru. But such exceptions only prove the rule, for O'Higgins was not a Creole.

Spanish America in the eighteenth century was a prosperous and pacific world undisturbed by the wars that swept across Europe. It was in better shape economically than the metropolis, and dotted with attractive towns adorned with fine architecture. Lima and Mexico City had good universities, and every major town had its societies and masonic lodges which encouraged everything from advances in agriculture to political discussion. Mexico City and Caracas stood out as social and cultural centres, and all who visited them were struck by their beauty, wealth and civilization. The Creoles had a generally high standard of living, the mestizos were no better or worse off than the mass of non-noble people in most Western countries, while the blacks and the Indians were not in a position to make their feelings known, except through the odd rebellion, always quickly contained and savagely repressed.

In contrast to North America, where blacks and Indians did not figure, there really was something approaching a society in the Spanish American world, held together by, amongst other things, allegiance to the Crown of Spain and the Catholic faith. The sacred calendar, adapted to suit local conditions and incorporate elements of native religions, set the rhythm of life and brought the entire population together on numerous feasts, each with its set of rituals in which everyone could share, providing a common platform for all of Spanish American life.

The Declaration of Independence by the English colonists in North America and the subsequent war appeared to hold some relevance for the Spanish colonies. But if the spirit of revolt was there, the motivations and priorities were utterly different. The conspirators who held meetings in Mexico City in 1765 with the aim of establishing an independent state were hardly in the Washingtonian mould; they agreed that whoever came up with the best plan would be made a duke. At San Luis Potosí in New Spain a movement for independence in the early 1770s was motivated by the desire not to lose the Jesuits, whom Spain had already banned.[1]

If the North American rebellion had demonstrated anything, it had shown that the kind of force which a distant metropolitan power could bring to bear was not great enough to crush a determined armed effort. And it did not take a genius to see that a declining Spain would be even less able to exert such force than economically and militarily rampant Britain. To the Creoles, the American example suggested a new degree of impunity. For outsiders, it opened up the possibility of rich pickings, to an extent which alarmed the United States. 'Those countries cannot be in better hands,' Jefferson averred in 1786. 'My fear is that [the Spaniards] are too feeble to hold them till our population can be sufficiently advanced to gain it from them piece by piece.'[2]

Within the Spanish colonies themselves, neither the American war nor the revolution in France created anything one might describe as a ferment. There was enthusiasm for the French Revolution among some Creoles, and the clandestine publication in 1794 of a Spanish version of the *Declaration of the Rights of Man* by Antonio Nariño caused a stir. In Potosí the governor was alarmed to discover that people had been drinking toasts to the revolution. But the enthusiasm of the Creoles was tempered by their disapproval of the anti-religious bent of the French Revolutionaries and Nariño, a convinced Catholic, tied in the rights of man with the writings of St Thomas Aquinas.

In February 1795 there was a rising in New Granada engineered by three Spaniards who had been exiled from Spain for their conspiratorial activities, Picornell, Andres and Cortés. The rising was nipped in the bud and the three leaders imprisoned at La Guaira. They escaped and made their way to Guadeloupe, where Picornell issued another Spanish version of the *Rights of Man*. They, and a number of French refugees from Trinidad, recently taken by the British, continued to conspire. By July 1797 when it was uncovered, the conspiracy in Venezuela was far more widespread than any previous one, ramifying through sections of the Creole and the mestizo population. The battle-cry was to be '*Viva el Pueblo Americano!*' Two conspirators arrested in Caracas, Manuel Gual and José España, had been agitating for an independent state embracing the whole of Spanish America and also talked of an 'American people'. The German naturalist and geographer Alexander von Humboldt, who began his voyage of exploration in South America in 1799, thought this new sense of identity significant enough to record. 'These natives prefer the name of Americans to that of Creoles,' he wrote. 'Since the peace of Versailles, and particularly since 1789, one often hears them say with pride: "I am not a *Spaniard*, I am an *American*." '[3]

Whatever they meant by this, it was not what the North American colonists had meant when they made their declarations, for hardly anyone in Spanish America wished for a break with the Spanish monarchy. Nor was there any kind of revolution implicit in Spanish American society; there were only the quintessentially Spanish American instincts for rebellion. It was disgruntled Creole noblemen who would bring about independence, the first of whom was Francisco Antonio Gabriel de Miranda.

Miranda was a Venezuelan with an exceptionally large chip on his shoulder. His father, who came from an old family of Basque origin settled for centuries in the Canary Islands, had emigrated to Venezuela and made a fortune. But he made the mistake of considering himself to be as good as the local Creole nobility. They challenged his right to wear the uniform of a local militia in which only noblemen could be officers, which led to court cases and rivers of bad blood. In 1772, when Francisco was twenty years old, his father finally obtained from Madrid the coveted certificate attesting the age-old nobility of the Mirandas.

By that time, Francisco was himself an officer in the Spanish army. He had studied law and philosophy at the university of Caracas, followed by a stint at Mexico, and had then completed his education in Madrid. In 1772 he joined the army, and in 1774 he fought under O'Reilly at Algiers, then at the Siege of Melilla. In 1780 he was sent out as a captain in the Regiment of Aragon to take part in the American war against the British at the side of Spain's French ally. He participated in the Siege of Pensacola by a Franco-Spanish-American force, and was promoted to the rank of lieutenant-colonel after its fall in 1781. He commanded a joint expedition with which he took the Caribbean island of Providence, and in 1782 captured the Bahamas from the British. While in Jamaica, where he was sent to parley with the British on the exchange of prisoners, he indulged in a little business speculation involving two shiploads of black slaves. He was denounced for smuggling, and on 23 December 1783 he was stripped of his rank, fined and sentenced to ten years' imprisonment in the fortress of Oran. Miranda may have been suspected of treasonable activity. In February 1782 he had exchanged some equivocal letters with a Colonel Juan Vicente de Bolívar and two other Caracas noblemen, who professed, among other things, a desire 'to shed the last drop of our blood in noble and great things'. Exactly what was being contemplated is difficult to tell. Anything was possible in the strange twilight of loyalties through which the Spanish Americans perceived their relationship with Spain.[4] Imprisonment was not a fate Miranda was going to accept, and, as he was in the United States at the time, all he had to do was to avoid Spanish jurisdiction.

Miranda's incipient Creole quarrel with the Spanish mother-country was pushed over the brink by the sentence against him, which insulted his sense of honour. At Philadelphia, where he met Washington, John Quincy Adams, Thomas Paine and Alexander Hamilton, Miranda broached the question of liberating South America from the Spanish yoke. While they listened with varying degrees of interest, none of them showed much enthusiasm for the cause. This may have been because they saw through him. He was well built and quite handsome, with fiery eyes, and he expatiated with gusto on his chosen subject. 'A learned man and a flaming son of Liberty' is how Ezra Stiles, the president of Yale College, described him.[5] But the touchy nobleman had a particular view of liberty. He was disgusted by the sessions of Congress he attended in Philadelphia, which he referred to as an assembly of tailors and blacksmiths. 'I recollect very distinctly the two topics of his conversation,' recorded James Lloyd, who saw Miranda in Boston. 'The one, doubtless his darling theme, was the prospect of revolutionizing the Spanish provinces of South America; the other, an expression of his disgust at the degree of liberty possessed by the People of this Country.'[6] It may have been this, or perhaps envy, that dictated an unexpectedly harsh assessment of Washington. Miranda sarcastically referred to him as 'the Idol', taking every opportunity to belittle his military and political achievement and averring that his reputation was 'a usurpation as capricious as it was unjust'.[7]

When he realized he was getting nowhere with the Americans, Miranda sailed for England. He arrived there in 1784 and began laying proposals before Prime Minister William Pitt for a British-supported 'liberation' of New Spain. While he treated Miranda's suggestions with interest, Pitt was non-committal, so the would-be liberator decided to move on. He went to Berlin, where Frederick the Great allowed him to inspect the Prussian army, and where he came across a number of acquaintances from America, including Lafayette. Lafayette was interested in the idea of liberating the Spanish colonies and wanted to take part in any venture Miranda might be contemplating. But Miranda, who probably guessed that Lafayette would steal the show, declined to discuss the matter further.

From Berlin, Miranda went to Vienna and then on to Hungary, Milan, Rome and Naples. He visited Greece, Egypt, Asia Minor, Constantinople and the Crimea. In 1787 he went north, to Kiev. He told the king of Poland that he intended to become the George Washington of Venezuela, but then fell in with one of the greatest tyrants of the age: he managed to charm Catherine II, who gave him a pension and the rank of colonel, and he hung about the court, calling himself Count Miranda. From Russia he went to Stockholm, where he met King Gustavus III, and on to Denmark, Germany, Switzerland and Holland, before returning to London in June 1789.

The umbrageous Creole had gained in knowledge and experience by this long trip. He had met half-a-dozen monarchs, conversed with Haydn, visited Raynal and Lavater, on whom he made an extraordinary impression, and made a pilgrimage to the spot where William Tell had allegedly shot the tyrant Gessler. He had learned how to flatter tyrants and how to project an image of himself as a devotee of the principles of liberty. His arrival in London was interestingly timed. The course of events in France opened up possibilities for discussion if not action, and Miranda easily fitted into radical coteries, keeping company with Charles James Fox, William Wilberforce, Joseph Priestley and Jeremy Bentham. In 1790, when war with Spain loomed, William Pitt reconsidered his plans. But the matter was soon dropped, and Miranda once again found himself at a loose end, although he remained in contact with the British ministry, which paid him the occasional allowance. In December 1790 he crossed over to France in order to breathe the air of liberty.

In September 1792 Miranda was given the rank of adjutant-general (under the false impression that he had held it in the American army) and sent to take command of a division under Dumouriez. He distinguished himself in several skirmishes and was at Valmy on 20 September. A couple of weeks later he was promoted and sent to liberate the city of Lille. He missed the battle of Jemappes, but afterwards took command of the army of Belgium, at the head of which he besieged and captured Antwerp.

Brissot, who had founded the Société des Amis des Noirs back in 1787 and had been agitating for the liberation of slaves in the French colonies, suggested sending Miranda to Saint-Domingue to take over as commissioner. 'Miranda will soon silence the miserable quarrels of the colonies,' wrote Brissot, 'he will quickly bring the troublesome whites to reason, and he will become the idol of the people of colour.'[8] Having pacified Saint-Domingue and created a French revolutionary base in the Caribbean, Miranda could then embark on the liberation of New Granada. Brissot failed to elicit enthusiasm for his plan in the Convention, so Miranda carried on liberating Belgium instead. At Neerwinden, his corps on the left wing was the first to give way. After blaming the defeat on him, Dumouriez fled abroad, and Miranda was convoked to the bar of the Convention in order to justify himself against allegations of treason. He was acquitted on all counts and released. But instead of lying low, he got involved in French politics, and suffered two more spells of imprisonment before he came to the conclusion that there was no future for him or his plans in France.

There was not much of a future for them anywhere at this stage. Like some eccentric inventor with an ambitious project, he was picked up, toyed with and dropped by potential patrons with a capriciousness that would have put off a less determined man. He even made overtures to the Spanish First Minister Floridablanca, offering to sort out the whole misunderstanding privately in half an hour, 'chair to chair'.[9] But he never stopped dreaming and plotting. A number of Spanish American malcontents met regularly at Miranda's lodgings in Grafton Street in London, which was also the headquarters of a Masonic Lodge named after the Inca hero Lautaro. They adopted the sonorous name of 'Commissioners of the Junta of Deputies of the Towns and Provinces of Southern America' and issued a manifesto on 22 December 1797. This declared that the provinces of Spanish America had 'unanimously decided to proclaim their independence'. A convention was signed empowering Miranda to purchase in England arms for 25,000 men (the document stipulated 'Roman' swords and 'Macedonian' pikes), to enter into agreements with the British and American governments, and to assume supreme command of military operations.[10]

Miranda began to badger Pitt once more, suggesting risings in Spanish America promoted jointly by Britain and the United States, and even sketched out a form of government for the liberated colonies. He proposed a constitutional monarchy to cover the whole area, ruled over by a monarch with the title of Inca from a capital to be called Colombo.[11] Whether Miranda saw himself as assuming that title is hard to fathom, like much of his thinking. He was out of touch with life in Spanish America, which he had not set foot in for over a quarter of a century. The same was true of most of the other emigrés he mixed with in London. The young Bernardo O'Higgins, son of the Viceroy of Peru, who had been sent to school in Richmond outside London, was now taking lessons in arithmetic and algebra from Miranda before returning home to Lima. 'See, my Lord, the sad remains of my countryman Lautaro,' O'Higgins once presented himself to Miranda, 'in my bosom burns the same spirit which then freed my country Arauco from her oppressors.'[12] Quite how a Spaniard of Irish descent, and the son of a colonial viceroy at that, could see himself as the reincarnation of an Araucanian Indian who had led a rebellion against the Spanish invader does not bear thinking about. But then Miranda sounded more like a member of the French Convention than an aspiring Inca. 'Love your country! Cherish this feeling always; strengthen it in every possible way, for only if it endures and prospers will you act rightly,' he lectured the young O'Higgins in a valedictory letter. 'I would add that the obstacles impeding your service to your country are so many, so formidable, and so insuperable, that only the most ardent love for your homeland can sustain you in your striving towards happiness . . .'[13]

Dispirited by the lack of interest shown by the British, Miranda once again decided to try his luck in France, and he arrived in Paris in November 1800. His relations with the First Consul were not good. 'That man has a sacred fire in his soul,' Bonaparte is reported to have said after meeting Miranda for the first time, but he also believed him to be a British spy.[14] Miranda was arrested in March 1801, imprisoned, and eventually expelled from France. With Spain now an ally of France, it suited the British government to encourage diversions in the Spanish colonies. In London Miranda saw a great deal of a naval captain of some military distinction and dubious financial instincts by the name of Sir Home Riggs Popham, who was keen to take a British force on an invasion of New Granada, or alternatively Buenos Aires. But the British ministry was wary of direct involvement and did not wish to get landed with an unruly foreign colonial empire. One solution, put forward by Lord Castlereagh, was to make Louis Philippe, Duc d'Orléans, king, and to give him Miranda and Dumouriez, now living in England, as aides.[15]

In the event, Miranda was given the sum of £6,000 by the British government with which to go to the United States and there raise an invasion force. He arrived in New York on 4 November 1805, at what seemed like a propitious moment. The recent acquisition of Louisiana, ceded in 1801 by Spain to France and subsequently sold by France to the United States, had whetted the appetite for expansion. Miranda had a meeting with former Vice-President Aaron Burr, who was planning to invade Mexico, but they remained suspicious of each other. On 6 December he called on President Thomas Jefferson, before making the regulation pilgrimage to Washington's tomb. The meeting was not necessarily significant, but it did give Miranda an aura of official approval, and this facilitated recruitment and arms purchases.

On 26 January 1806 a frigate, the *Leander*, slipped its moorings in New York with a couple of hundred paladins of liberty on board. Once out on the open sea, it hoisted a red, blue and yellow tricolor, which was to be the flag of 'Colombia'. On the quarter-deck stood Miranda, dressed in his French general's uniform, surrounded by his officers. These included several Frenchmen, some Irish, and a handful of Poles, one of whom, Filip Maurycy Marcinkowski, a 21-year-old who had reached the rank of sub-lieutenant in the Royal Navy (he had been on Nelson's *Victory* at Trafalgar), was to play a prominent part in the struggle for independence.

Their first stop was Haiti, the island Miranda was supposed to have liberated more than a decade before. Here, he acquired two schooners and filled them with more volunteers. Thus reinforced, Miranda sailed for his native land. He made for Puerto Cabello, but was challenged by a Spanish man-of-war. As the invasion force tried to evade it, one of the schooners ran aground, and Miranda left that and the other schooner, which had gone to its assistance, at the mercy of the Spanish ship. After an unequal struggle, both were captured, along with sixty men, who were taken ashore. Ten of them were condemned to hang, and the rest given long sentences. In a ceremony before the executions in Puerto Cabello, the public hangman burned Miranda's proclamation, his portrait and the 'Colombian' tricolor.

A few months later Miranda was back, and this time he succeeded in landing. He captured a small fort outside the town of Coro and then occupied the town itself. He issued a proclamation bristling with fine phrases about the public good, and promulgated a raft of administrative measures. All males between the ages of sixteen and fifty-five were summoned to join the colours, and everyone was to wear the national cockade on their hats. But these rousing measures failed to stir the population. On 13 August 1806, a mere ten days after landing in New Granada, Miranda re-embarked and sailed away.

'The Spaniards would have nothing to say to us,' noted James Biggs, an ardent American republican who had risked everything to bring liberty to the oppressed colonies. 'They had no thoughts of accepting our proffer of liberty; and we could not oblige them to take it.' The *cabildo* of Caracas branded Miranda an 'abominable monster'. Juan Vicente Bolívar, son of one of the Caracas Creoles who, twenty-four years earlier, had promised to follow him to the 'last drop of blood' now marched in the ranks of the local militia 'against the traitor Miranda'.[16] On the other hand, an agent working for the British reported in October that 'Miranda has the secret and warm support of every respectable Creole in the province', so it would be wrong to make hasty judgements. The motives of all concerned were unfailingly dubious. Perhaps the most apposite assessment is that of the disappointed Biggs. 'I reflect that amidst all their alleged grievances, they have great wealth and prosperity,' he wrote, 'and whatever they suffer, they have in general no pain from the consciousness of oppression.'[17] In the following year a French naturalist travelling in the area found a grocer in Cumaná making paper bags out of the Rousseauist and Painite literature distributed by Miranda.[18] Not for nothing has South America been called the graveyard of ideals.

Miranda returned to London, where he continued to bombard people in high places with new projects. One person who was unexpectedly receptive was General Sir Arthur Wellesley. The future Duke of Wellington saw in Spanish America a field for his talents and rich rewards for his country at a time when British armies had been banished from the European mainland by Napoleon's triumph over the Third Coalition at the Battle of Austerlitz. Wellesley had assembled an army of 13,000 men in Ireland who were ready to sail from Cork in July 1807. Miranda advised a landing in New Granada, while Wellington himself favoured Mexico. But while plans were easy to make, the imponderables of such an invasion were highlighted by British failures in another part of the Spanish new world.

In June 1806 Sir Home Riggs Popham, who had for some time been dreaming of leading such an invasion, seized his chance. Earlier that year he had taken part in the British occupation of the Cape of Good Hope, and on the return journey diverted his squadron and the 1,400 troops under General William Carr Beresford. Instead of taking them home, he crossed the Atlantic and sailed into the River Plate. On 27 June Beresford led his men ashore and occupied Buenos Aires, which had been abandoned in haste by the Spanish viceroy. But the British triumph was short-lived. The local Creoles were made of sterner stuff than the viceroy, and had no intention of submitting. On 12 August Beresford was obliged to capitulate, and the British fell back on Montevideo. A year later, in July 1807, 8,000 men under General Whitelock repeated the attempt to take Buenos Aires, but were forced to surrender after suffering heavy losses. Perhaps Wellington would have fared better, but his talents were never put to this test. In the event, his force sailed not for the colonies, but for Spain itself.

Wellington confessed that he 'never had a more difficult business' to face than when he prepared to break the news of the change of plan to Miranda, who was 'loud and angry' with him.[19] As it happened, he need not have been, for the future of New Granada and the other colonies was to be decided not in South America, but in Spain. The humiliating débâcle of the British landings in Buenos Aires, no less than that of Miranda's attempts in New Granada, demonstrated that however disgruntled the

Creoles might be with the Spanish metropolis, they were fundamentally attached to it. Indeed, the first steps in the process of separation from Spain were promoted by Spanish patriotism in the face of foreign aggression, and supported by traditional religious feeling and loyalty to the Bourbon dynasty. For it was Bourbon Spain that was now exposed to the mixed benefits of liberation.

The Bourbons had taken over the Habsburg dominions in the Iberian peninsula (there was no actual state called Spain, which was merely a geographical expression) only a hundred years earlier, but they had gained the hearts of the people. The French Revolution elicited enthusiasm among a small group of literary radicals, but even these were put off by the execution of Louis XVI. Opinion was unanimous during the war against revolutionary France in 1793. This was not a glorious affair, and the general relief at the conclusion of peace in 1795 seemed to justify the bestowal on the chief negotiator, Manuel Godoy, of the title 'Prince of the Peace'. But Godoy, a handsome guardsman who held sway over the heart of the queen, and through her ruled the well-meaning Charles IV, was not popular. In 1796 he took Spain to war with England, which resulted in the Royal Navy cutting off all trade between Spain and her colonies. Combined with a famine and an outbreak of yellow fever, this brought the country to its knees. Nevertheless, in 1801 Godoy was appointed *generalisimo* of the Spanish armies and admiral of the navy, arousing further resentment. This coalesced around the figure of the heir to the throne, Ferdinand, Prince of the Asturias, dubbed *el Deseado*, 'the Desired One', by his supporters.

In July 1807, with the approval of Charles IV, Napoleon despatched 50,000 men across Spain under Marshal Junot in order to occupy Portugal and close the port of Lisbon to British shipping. The job was quickly done. Resistance was minimal, and the Portuguese royal family fled to their colony in Brazil. French troops lingered in Spain and Portugal, and early in 1808 Napoleon sent Joachim Murat with more men to Madrid, to act as his lieutenant in the peninsula. The approach of French troops gave rise to rumours that the queen and Godoy were intending to seize power, alternatively that the Spanish royal family were intending to take ship for the new world, like the Portuguese.

On the evening of 17 March 1808, a mob gathered outside the royal palace at Aranjuez, where the royal family were wintering, and demanded the death of Godoy. They then stormed Godoy's residence, while the

Prince of the Peace cowered, hidden in a roll of matting. This episode, known as the Tumult of Aranjuez, and probably staged by Ferdinand and his supporters, resulted in the dismissal of Godoy. Having tasted power, the rabble continued to intimidate the king, who abdicated two days later in favour of his son, 'the Desired One'. The prince's arrival in Madrid to take up the reins of power as Ferdinand VII turned the rioting into wild rejoicing, which spread throughout the country in a curious case of collective hysteria, as everyone gave in to a happy belief that their troubles were at an end.

Once out of danger, Charles IV had second thoughts and appealed to Napoleon to reinstate him. The Emperor responded by summoning him and his son to a meeting in Bayonne, just over the border in France. There, he forced both to abdicate in favour of his own brother, Joseph Bonaparte, who became the first actual king of Spain. The departure of the royal family had prompted a revolt against Murat in Madrid on 2 May, and news of the deposition of Ferdinand caused outrage throughout the country. Local committees of notables, *juntas*, began to organize armed resistance to the French in the name of 'the Desired One'. On 19 July the troops of the Junta of Seville defeated a French force under General Dupont at Bailén. Wellesley landed the army that was to have liberated New Granada in Portugal instead and defeated Marshal Junot at Vimieiro. Sir John Moore landed another army in north-western Spain. King Joseph had to evacuate Madrid and fall back on France. On 22 November, the Central Junta, which had established itself in Seville, issued a royal order in which it proclaimed Spain to be the liberator of Europe.

Napoleon responded by invading at the head of 150,000 troops, but while he could defeat any force the Spaniards could field, he could not pacify the country. The motives for the great patriotic surge that swept the land remain as mysterious as Goya's ambivalent representations of it. At first, it was directed as much against the nobles as against the French, but the juntas reasserted control, with the aid of the clergy. The parish priests and friars who enjoyed a close relationship with the common people had harnessed their influence to the cause of Ferdinand, calling for a crusade to oust the impious French. The regular forces at the disposal of the Junta were supplemented by fiercely patriotic local militias led by firebrands such as the student Francisco Xavier Mina in Navarra, the doctor Juan Paladea, appropriately known as '*el medico*', in La Mancha, the friar Sapia in the province of Soria, and others, who devised tactics appropriate to their own capabilities and the terrain they operated in which came to be known as *guerilla*, the little war.

The *guerilla* made life impossible for the French armies, and permitted Wellesley to begin the task of gradually edging them out of the peninsula. More importantly, it affected the political situation by involving the whole population. This became apparent when, in September 1810, the Regency summoned the Cortes at Cadiz. Conservatives saw the situation in terms of a war in defence of king, faith and country, but they lost ground to those who saw it as a national struggle for survival, a coming of age of more humble local elements which must be reflected in a constitution. The latter party won, and in 1812 the Cortes drew up and passed a 'sacred codex', in which what had been traditionally referred to as 'the Kingdom' was now 'the Nation', and which specifically enshrined the sovereignty of that nation. This constitution was to have a great future, not as a tool of government, but as a symbol of liberalism. And not, curiously enough, in the Spanish colonies.

There was outrage throughout Spanish America at the dethronement of the Bourbon dynasty. Regional *cabildos* spontaneously emulated the juntas in Spain and came out with declarations of loyalty to Ferdinand VII and the Catholic faith. Spanish soldiers were assaulted to cries of '*Viva el Rey!*' and in Quito a clutch of Creole marquises arrested the Spanish governor, with all the refinements of courtesy. The inhabitants of the colonies had never objected to being subjects of the king of Castille. Their only quarrel had been with the metropolitan government and its agents. Napoleon's imprisonment of Charles and Ferdinand neatly solved the implicit contradiction: the metropolitan government was now illegitimate, and could therefore be resisted openly by all true and loyal subjects of the king.

The acts of defiance began in 1809, with local juntas taking control from the Spanish administration in the name of Ferdinand in Quito, La Paz and Chiquisaca, and several minor revolts in the Andean region and La Plata, while an inchoate rebellion began in Mexico. The declarations of independence continued into the following year, with the deposition of the Captain-General of Venezuela and the proclamation of a junta on 19 April 1810, the seizure of power by a liberal junta in Buenos Aires on 25 May, a similar series of events in Santa Fé de Bogotá on 20 July and in Santiago de Chile on 18 September. There was nothing revolutionary about these events. The inflammatory speeches about 'the people' were predominantly being made by men who owned slaves and had no intention of allowing anyone outside their immediate circle to have any say in government. It is true that in some places the tax burden was lifted from the shoulders of the Indians and that in the summer of 1811 the Chilean congress abolished the slave trade. But as a rule, there was no rush to carry out liberal reforms. The revolutions were essentially to do with local autonomy.

The Cortés sitting at Cadiz failed to appreciate this. 'The general and extraordinary Cortes confirm the incontestable concept that the Spanish dominions of both hemispheres form one *single and identical Monarchy, one single and identical Nation and one single family*', ran a decree of 15 October 1810.[20] The former colonies were to be granted representation in the metropolitan legislature, in order to bind them more firmly into this family. The Cortes also enacted some reforms in the colonies, and allowed the Indians to own land.

This vision and these measures held little attraction for the colonials. 'With the monarchy dissolved and Spain lost, are we not in the condition of sons who become of age at the death of the father of the family?' demanded Camilo Torres, guiding spirit of the revolution in New Granada.[21] The local *cabildos* and juntas that came out in support of the true king against the usurping government of King Joseph tasted a power and authority they had never enjoyed before. As links with Spain came under discussion and local bodies took charge of affairs, there was an inevitable fragmentation that undermined the entire Spanish colonial system. The situation brought out all the contradictions and conflicts of loyalty inherent in the relationship between the metropolis and the colonies, the Crown and the people, the 'Spaniards' and the Creoles, the old world and the new. As viceroys fell and independence was declared, lines were drawn that zigzagged through society in the most baffling ways, with 'Spaniards' often on the side of autonomy and Creoles sometimes standing up for metropolitan government. In the absence of real issues, it could be dislike of a neighbour, umbrage at a slight from the junta or family ties that dictated where a man took up his position.

Mexico, or New Spain as it was officially termed, was a case in point. It had had its share of challenges to authority over the years but, as elsewhere, it was the Napoleonic intervention in Spain in 1808 that really upset the *status quo*. Beside the normal catalogue of colonial gripes, which included a particularly visceral hatred of the peninsulars, the underlying problem in Mexico was the land-hunger of the mestizos and the Indians, who were subject to a crippling poll tax. As in other colonies, the Indians were also obliged to work in the mines for no payment. Their plight had alarmed many, including the clergy, and it was a priest who led the first great rising.

Miguel Hidalgo, a poor, eccentric, even bumbling parish priest, was the rather improbable leader of a conspiracy professing loyalty to Ferdinand VII and advocating economic reforms and the abolition of slavery. His colleagues were mostly middle-class Creoles, and even included the *corregidor* of Querétaro. As their thinking was both confused and crafty, it is difficult to tell exactly how revolutionary the movement was. 'Since the natives are indifferent to the word liberty, it is necessary to make them believe that the rising is undertaken simply to favour King Ferdinand,' one of them wrote to Hidalgo on 31 August 1810.[22] In September 1810 Hidalgo launched his rebellion with the slogan: 'Long live Religion. Long Live our Most Holy Mother of Guadalupe. Long Live Ferdinand VII. Long Live America and death to bad government.' The mestizos and Indians who flocked to his banner simplified this to: 'Long Live Our Lady of Guadalupe! Death to the Spaniards!'[23] Thousands of them came forward, armed mainly with sticks and knives, fervently believing that once he heard their appeal, the good king would grant land and relief from taxation. But they were defeated, and Hidalgo was shot on 13 July 1811.

This was by no means the end of the rebellion. The leadership was taken over by José Maria Morelos, another village priest. Morelos had a more radical programme than his predecessor, including the confiscation of large estates and their division among the Indians and poor mestizos. He also wanted independence. In 1813 he convoked a congress at Chilpancingo, and, in a fog of verbiage about the sovereignty of the people and the supremacy of the Catholic faith, on 6 November this declared the independence of the colony. In October of the following year, the rebels held another congress, at Apatzingán, where they adopted a 'Constitutional Decree for the Liberty of Mexican America', which only narrowly escaped being renamed 'Anahuac'. But Morelos was captured soon afterwards and on 22 December 1815 he was stripped of his ecclesiastical robes and shot in the back as a heretic and a traitor to the king.

Morelos had wanted to bring about the equality of all citizens, based on the one criterion of their *not* being Spaniards. The Creole whose parents had been born in Spain was to be just as full an 'American' as the pure Indian or the black who had been born in Africa. At the Congress of Chilpancingo, Morelos had talked of avenging the crimes committed by the Spaniards against his nation, ignoring the fact that his own father was a Spaniard. He had described his cause, the cause of the '*patria*', as 'the true faith'.[24] Holy madness was spreading to the new world.

When Sir Home Riggs Popham weighed anchor off Buenos Aires in August 1806 after his failure to hold the city, he sailed home to face a court martial. But he also received the congratulations of the City of London, which presented him with a sword of honour – not for being a latter-day Lafayette, but for his endeavours to open up new markets.

The Viceroyalty of La Plata was the youngest of all the Spanish colonies, and it differed from the others in several ways. It was less densely populated and less stratified. Its huge estancias were run with the aid of relatively small numbers of mounted cattle-herds. The port of Buenos Aires relied on a large unskilled workforce, giving rise to a vigorous proletariat. All this made for less settled social patterns and extensive lawlessness. What social cohesion there was had evolved out of a continuous struggle against the trade restrictions imposed by the Spanish authorities. British merchants were continually trying to breach these in connivance with the locals, and the principal cause for discontent of the Argentine Creoles was not social, as in the other colonies, but economic. The resistance to the British invasion attempts had not been ideologically motivated. It was organized by the inhabitants of Buenos Aires in defence of their own property. Their success gave them not only a sense of pride and self-sufficiency, but also an edge over the Spanish authorities, which had fled at the approach of the British. These feelings were to manifest themselves when the Bourbons were deposed in Spain by Napoleon.

On 25 May 1810 a junta was formed in Buenos Aires in the name of Ferdinand VII. Its secretary was Mariano Moreno, a liberal patriot, known as 'the Jacobin of La Plata'. This label was not entirely appropriate, as he was highly religious and disapproving of everything that had taken place in France since 1789. But he was a passionate Rousseauist nation-builder, and in pursuit of this ideal he could be as ruthless as any Jacobin. 'The foundations of a new republic have never been cemented unless rigour and punishment were mingled with the blood of all citizens who might obstruct progress,' he wrote in a plan to be followed by the government.[25]

A certain amount of blood did flow in the civil war which broke out soon after.

'In the American provinces formerly subject to the Spanish Empire, a brilliant scene is opened at present,' wrote Bernardo Monteagudo. 'The valour, the resolution of the heroes, the enthusiasm of the ancient and modern republicans have been displayed gloriously for the cause of national liberty. The sword of expiring tyranny has immolated in some places many victims; but from their blood new heroes have arisen.'[26] The most prominent of these heroes were Manuel Belgrano, a schoolteacher turned soldier, and the young José de San Martin, recently returned from Europe.

Monteagudo dominated the assembly that convened in 1813 after the Argentinian separatists' victory over the royalists at Tucumán. He was a conventional Enlightenment soul who believed in the principles of 1789, and he helped to push through the resolution that effectively declared independence. The Inquisition was abolished, along with tithes, forced labour, judicial torture, royal symbols and titles of nobility. A new flag and national insignia were instituted: a sun, a red cap, a laurel wreath of victory, and two clasped hands.

Monteagudo believed in 'the sovereignty of the people', but felt that this was best exercised by a dictatorship, and he was nothing if not pragmatic. 'Your longed-for liberty cannot be decreed right away, as humanity and reason would wish,' his government bluntly told the slaves of Buenos Aires, 'because unfortunately it stands in opposition to the sacred right of individual liberty [of slaveholders in their property rights].'[27] Such contradictions, no less than the factionalism that surrounded the birth of the Argentine republic, sowed the seeds of endless internecine political feuding and civil war for generations to come.

One who tried to introduce some method into all this madness was Jeremy Bentham. He had heard wondrous tales of the beauty and riches of Spanish America, and imagined it to be the ideal setting for his utilitarian utopia. He approached the Spanish authorities with the suggestion that they send him out to the colonies as supreme lawgiver with carte blanche to implement his schemes. Failing to gain their interest, he then got in touch with Aaron Burr, who was planning to invade Mexico and make himself emperor. In 1808 Burr came to stay with Bentham to discuss the details, and promised to send for the lawgiver as soon as he was on his chimerical throne. But as time passed and Burr made no progress, Bentham switched his sights to New Granada and his cliency to Miranda, with whom he discussed constitutions and an educational system, to be run by Lady Hester Stanhope. For once, Miranda's dreams appeared to be less nebulous.

In June 1810, a young man by the name of Simón Bolívar walked into his rooms in Grafton Street and asked him to come and liberate their common motherland. The newcomer needed no introduction. He was the son of the Juan Vicente Bolívar who had written to Miranda in 1782 begging him to lead a 'great cause', and the brother of the Juan Vicente who had, only four years previously, branded Miranda a traitor. Simón's loyalties were no less volatile, and he was a far more complicated character.

Simón José Antonio de la Santisima Trinidad de Bolívar had been born in Caracas on 24 July 1783 into a distinguished family which had come out from Spain in 1588. They had grown in wealth and had been involved in local government in every generation, maintaining a position of influence in the colony. Like other Creoles, they married locally, and it is almost certain that Simón had black and Indian blood in his veins. In spite of their wealth, their slaves and their standing, they fitted the type of the disgruntled Creole, and Simón's mother had been desperately trying to obtain the title of count for him until her death, which occurred when he was only nine years old. Juan Vicente had preceded her to the grave six years previously, so little Simón was an orphan. As a result, he was more than usually influenced by one of his tutors, a freethinker by the name of Simón Carreno Rodriguez.

In January 1799 Simón Bolívar sailed for Spain, where he spent two years and married. In 1802 he brought his wife home to Venezuela, but in January of the following year she caught a fever and died. He went back to Spain and, in 1804, to Paris, where he met up with his former tutor, Rodriguez. Bolívar arrived in the French capital just in time for Napoleon's coronation as Emperor of the French, an event he watched with fascination. In March 1805 he set off on a tour with Rodriguez, and in Milan, he saw Napoleon crown himself king of Italy. 'I centred my attention on Napoleon and saw nothing but him out of that crowd of men,' he wrote. He travelled on to Rome under the spell of this vision and there, after considering what he had seen, he ascended the Monte Sacro, where he fell on his knees and swore an oath before Rodriguez to liberate South America.[28]

In June 1807 Bolívar was back in Venezuela, where he relapsed into the humdrum life of a wealthy Creole landowner. He took no part in the first moves towards autonomy or in the Congress that was being called in Caracas for the summer of 1810. Instead, he persuaded the junta to allow him to accompany Luis Lopez Mendez and Andrés Bello, who were going to London in the hope of enlisting British support. Once there, Bolívar had little difficulty in eclipsing the junta's envoys. He called on Miranda and on the Marquis of Wellesley, and took the time to meet William Wilberforce, who was given no inkling that the fiery young libertarian standing before him was the owner of slaves. On 14 July of that year the Caracas Congress made a commemorative gesture of abolishing the slave trade, but left the institution in place. The Venezuelan envoys gained the tacit support of Britain and while Mendez stayed on as unofficial ambassador, Bolívar went back to Venezuela, with Miranda.

Miranda's reception was mixed. Many young Creoles welcomed him as a revolutionary who would bring the spirit of 1792 and a hint of the guillotine to Caracas; his more conservative peers were wary. Having been away so long, he was little known outside a small circle. His reaction was to turn demagogue, organizing meetings and demonstrations. He was elected president of the Patriotic Society, founded in the previous year with the purpose of promoting trade and industry, and promptly turned it into a surrogate Jacobin Club. In the Congress, to which he was also elected, he began to raise the political temperature and to demand belligerent action against Spain. On 1 July 1811 the Congress passed a *Declaration of the Rights of the People*, guaranteeing their 'imprescriptible, inalienable and indivisible' sovereignty, and the individual's 'liberty, security, property, equality before the law', and, as a parting shot, 'happiness as the aim of society'.[29] Two days later, Miranda called for full independence, with Bolívar echoing his call the following day. On 4 July, with celebrations of the American anniversary raising hopes, they began to carry the Congress, and on 7 July the *Declaration of Independence of the American Confederation of Venezuela* was formally ratified.

It was not long before the new republic was behaving as such systems do. Protests were quelled with night arrest, prison and hanging after a peremptory judgement by the Patriotic Society, which sentenced people as 'traitors to the Fatherland'. Provincial towns revolted against the central government, provoking bloody reprisals. With no clear issues and no ideological base, the whole region fell prey to a series of minor conflicts of baffling intricacy, further weakening the hold of the Caracas government.

A force of 120 Spanish marines under the command of Don Domingo de Monteverde had landed at Coro in the summer of 1811 in order to re-establish the authority of the Cadiz *Cortes*. Numerous mestizos and blacks who feared the Creoles of Caracas rallied to the Spanish cause and swelled Monteverde's ranks. On 26 March 1812, Maundy Thursday, even the God they had been so careful not to offend turned against the Venezuelan separatists. An earthquake destroyed most of Caracas, killing thousands and prompting the assumption that it was divine retribution for the declaration of the republic, two years before, also on Maundy Thursday. The Congress persuaded the archbishop of Caracas to issue a theological refutation of this, but people were not convinced. And Monteverde was gaining ground.

On 23 April Miranda was proclaimed dictator, but there was little he could do to save the republic; morale was so low that recruits had to be brought to the colours in manacles. Miranda had put Bolívar in command at Puerto Cabello, the lifeline for Caracas, but Bolívar lost it to Monteverde on 5 July. He wrote Miranda an incoherent letter in which he scourged himself yet professed himself to be blameless, proclaimed his shame but declared his honour to have been saved. He then turned up in Caracas in a state of acute depression. Miranda himself had grown pessimistic, and the arrival of Bolívar did nothing to lift his spirits. He negotiated a capitulation with Monteverde, and made for La Guaira, where a British warship was waiting to take him to safety. Miranda's luggage was carried aboard, but Bolívar persuaded Miranda himself to spend the night ashore and embark in the morning. In the early hours, Miranda was dragged out of bed and taken to the town fortress, where he was locked up to await Monteverde. Two days later, Bolívar sailed for Curaçao, whence he intended to go to Spain to fight under Wellington against the French.

Bolívar's motives remain opaque. It has been alleged that he traduced his commander in order to rehabilitate himself with the Spaniards. If that was the case, then the ploy failed: when he reached Curaçao he learnt that Monteverde had confiscated all his property. His own explanation was that he had shopped Miranda for being a coward and capitulating to Monteverde. He accused him of having been too soft on the 'Spaniards', thereby weakening the republican cause. While such arguments might sound both spurious and irrelevant, they concealed within them the germs of a gradually maturing view of the prospects of revolution in Spanish America, to which both Miranda and Bolívar were contributing.

As Miranda sat in gaol in Puerto Cabello, where he had been taken from La Guaira, he came to the conclusion that there was no latent spirit of political revolt and no sense of nationhood in Venezuela, whatever people might say or write in moments of excitement. Creoles, mestizos and 'Spaniards' had changed sides in a kaleidoscopic tumble that defied analysis. And if allegiances were volatile, so were temperaments. However much he might have looked down on the French marquis, Miranda was cast in the mould of a Lafayette rather than that of a Robespierre, and he recoiled at the prospect of civil strife. 'God forbid that these beautiful countries become, as did St Domingue, a theatre of blood and of crime under the pretext of establishing liberty,' he had written back in 1798. 'Let them rather remain if necessary one century more under the barbarous and imbecile oppression of Spain.'[30]

Like Lafayette, he would pay a heavy price for having played with fire. From Puerto Cabello, he was taken to a prison in Puerto Rico, and then to one in Cadiz, which bore the name of La Carraca. A British naval officer who saw him there was shocked to find him fettered and chained to the wall of his damp cell. In this gloomy Bastille, whose name echoed that of his birthplace, Miranda died in 1816 – on 14 July.

Bolívar had arrived at some very different conclusions. He reckoned the leadership of the republic had failed because it had been too democratic, allowing people to change their allegiances, and condemned what he saw as its 'criminal clemency'.[31] After the passing of the 1812 Cadiz constitution the arguments for independence were less valid than before, and certainly not strong enough to warrant an internecine war. What was needed to galvanize people into one was something in the nature of the September massacres in Paris, something that would precipitate a life-and-death struggle.

Bolívar decided against going to Spain and instead crossed over to the Colombian port of Cartagena, still holding out against Monteverde and the Spanish loyalists. As he prepared to march on Caracas once more in March 1813, he proclaimed a new strategy. 'As this war has for its first and chief aim to destroy in Venezuela the accursed race of European Spaniards, including the Islanders, they must be debarred from joining the revolutionary force, however patriotic and sound they may seem, since not a single one must remain alive', ran the main argument. It certainly clarified the hitherto confused question of who was on which side. Antonio Briceño called on all slaves to rise up and murder their masters if these should be Spaniards, and when he took the town of San Cristóbal, he beheaded the only two 'Spaniards' he could find (both aged over eighty) and sent their heads to Bolívar. But Spanish America had a way of persisting in its confusions. The city of Mérida proclaimed its independence from Spain under the leadership of a Spaniard, Don Vicente Campo Elias, who was wont to say: 'I shall destroy all Spaniards and then shoot myself so that not a single man remain of this accursed race.'[32]

The introduction of the concept of race into the conflict seems absurd. The only difference on racial grounds between Bolívar and any Spaniard was the possible admixture of a drop of Indian and/or black blood several generations before. Santiago Marino, one of his associates and the leader of the republican invasion of the province of Cumaná, was actually of Irish descent. There was a considerable number of foreigners in prominent positions in the republican forces, including the Frenchman Pierre Labatut, commanding a division at Cartagena, and General Manuel de Serviez; Charles Louis Castelli, a Napoleonic officer; Louis Péru de Lacroix; the adventurer General Ducoudray-Holstein; the Poles Feliks Jastran and Filip Marcinkowski; and, most picturesque, 'Sir' Gregor McGregor, a former British army captain who had served under Miranda, upped himself to 'count' and married Bolívar's niece. Yet Bolívar found the racial concept useful. In a proclamation of 8 June 1813 he likened the Spaniards to wandering Jews, to be 'cast out and persecuted'. 'Our hatred shall be implacable and the war shall be to the death,' he declared a few days later.[33] On 6 August Bolívar entered Caracas at the head of an army of about 600 men, to be greeted by a dozen maidens draped in the national colours who crowned him with laurels and showered him with petals. One of his first acts was to order the wholesale slaughter of the Spaniards in the city.

Such actions made people sit up and take sides, and the conflict began to escalate in terms of brutality. A Spanish-born naval captain turned horse-trader by the name of José Tomás Boves who had been slighted by the republican government of 1812 and subsequently offered his services to Monteverde, formed up an army from the wild mounted cowherds of the plains, the *llaneros*, which quickly acquired the appellation of *La Legion Infernal*. An associate of his, Francisco Rosete, assembled a band of Indians and runaway slaves, which marched under the slogan of 'Long live Ferdinand VII' and massacred any white person they could find. In the first days of 1814 Rosete took the town of Ocumare, where the women were raped and three hundred people killed, after which their severed noses, ears, breasts and penises were nailed to the doors. When he heard of this, Bolívar ordered the massacre of some 1,200 Spaniards, who were shot or decapitated with machetes over a period of three days. 'You may judge for yourselves, without partiality,' Bolívar harangued the inhabitants of Caracas, 'whether I have not sacrificed my life, my being, every minute of my time in order to make a nation of you.'

Bolívar was thirty years old when he entered Caracas, and although he only had a few hundred men of dubious military worth under his command, he began behaving like his idol Napoleon. He assumed the role of dictator, and only as an afterthought prompted the *cabildo* of Caracas to appoint him, with the title of *El Libertador.* He invented a Napoleonic uniform for himself and instituted the Military Order of the Liberators as an equivalent to the Légion d'Honneur. But it was a little early for such gestures, and Bolívar's hero was now in trouble himself, following his disastrous invasion of Russia in 1812 and the defeat of his armies in Spain.

The Battle of Vitoria in 1813 heralded the end of the French presence in the peninsula, and in January 1814 the Cortes moved from Cadiz to the liberated capital. On 24 March 'the Desired one' Ferdinand VII, who had been released by his French gaolers, re-entered his kingdom. With the help of a group of reactionaries and the support of the masses marshalled by the clergy, he abolished the 1812 constitution. Spain returned to autocratic rule, with the Bourbons once again in the saddle. This concentrated the minds of many in the colonies, and gave heart to royalists, a feeling reinforced by Napoleon's abdication and exile to the island of Elba. Bolívar, who had been obliged to pull back from Caracas under pressure from the royalists and had tried to hold out in Cartagena, realized that the situation was hopeless, and on 9 May 1815 he sailed away to Jamaica aboard a British ship.

10
The World Spirit

If the French Revolution had profoundly shaken Europe, Napoleon Bonaparte had gone on to unsettle it in different ways. For the best part of twenty years he restlessly paced the stage, dominating the proceedings and allowing others a part only in relation to himself. He caught the popular imagination and exerted a fascination far beyond the reach of his power. To say that he appeared larger than life would be to understate. The vertiginous ascent of this wiry, unathletic youth was unprecedented and almost miraculous in a world of rigid hierarchies and frustrated ambitions. His achievement was grandiose, his style heroic. In his person and his epos he elided the grandly political with the intensely personal on a scale not seen since the days of Alexander the Great and, like that hero, suffused it all with an aura of divinity. To oppressed nationalists, impotent reformers and idle dreamers alike, he was an idol. To many he appeared as little short of a god.

He behaved as though he were acting out a preordained destiny. 'Why did Bonaparte spurn those beautiful armies of the Rhine, those eighty thousand well-armed and well-equipped men who were placed under the command of Jourdan and Moreau, and who would have been under his if he had wished, in favour of the twenty-five thousand naked and half-starved soldiers on the Genoese riviera?' mused Alexandre Dumas, whose father was one of their generals. 'It is because Italy is Italy, the land of rich memories . . . it is because he preferred to be Hannibal rather than Turenne or the Maréchal de Saxe.'[1]

Napoleon was also a brilliant propagandist. As early as 1796 he had produced news-sheets intended to shore up the morale of his troops and promote an epic image of himself. This was enhanced through some of the most successful heroic painting of all time. David's canvas of him crossing the Alps in 1796 likens him to Hannibal as well as providing one of the most exciting personal representations in European art. David's pupil Jean-Antoine Gros crossed the Alps with Napoleon and painted the unforgettable image of the young general clutching the tricolor on the bridge of Arcole. He later depicted him under the shadow of the Pyramids, metaphors for eternity, and visiting plague victims at Jaffa, where his own immunity and his gesture suggest both the royal touch and a Christ-like compassion. Dozens more canvases were produced over the years to provide a rich, symbol-laden iconography of the man's life. The vast painting commissioned from Anne Louis Girodet for the château of Malmaison, depicting Napoleon's generals being received in heaven by Ossian nicely scrambled conflicting visions of divinity.

The Bulletins of the *Grande Armée*, published regularly during campaigns, reported these in a way never known before in European history, so that they unfolded, act by act, like some epic of the gods. People grew accustomed to unprecedented achievements and came to expect transcendent actions. Few were surprised when Napoleon had himself crowned emperor, by the Pope no less. Nor did they laugh at the triumphal arches he built. On the Place Vendôme he erected a column of bronze made from 1,200 cannon captured at Austerlitz and placed himself, in Roman dress, where the Sun King Louis XIV had once stood. He created a new aristocracy and in 1805 instituted the order of the Légion d'Honneur, which, with its five grades, created a cross-sectional élite of the devoted and the brave.

Yet he allowed everyone to share in this glorious apogee, by somehow managing to represent himself as a man of the people, always on their side against kings, aristocrats and priests. This fantasy was kept going by his soldiers, to whom he was '*le petit caporal*'. They propagated stories of the emperor lending his coat to a frozen sentry or giving his flask to a wounded trooper. Through such gestures, fixed in the consciousness by popular prints, he asserted human solidarity and included them in his great march through history. Because he was himself of the people, and because he made his own person inextricable from the greatness and the glories of France, he had come to embody it. But he did not stand for France alone. The men he led were of many nations and creeds. They shouted '*Vive l'Empereur*!' not '*Vive la Nation*!' as they surged forward to die for the cause of the peoples against the kings.

In the memorable first sentence of *La Chartreuse de Parme*, Stendhal describes how on the day of Bonaparte's entry into Milan in 1796 a people learned that after so many centuries a successor to Caesar and Alexander had been found. With some poetic licence, he goes on to assert that a whole nation awoke and began to dream. This myth of Napoleon as catalyst, deliverer and saviour developed a life of its own as it was passed on, distorted and reinvented to serve as a vehicle for particular hopes and dreams. In Slovenia, the poet Valentin Vodnik visualized it in terms of the Sleeping Beauty. 'Napoleon has said: "Illyria awake!",' he told his countrymen, 'and she stirs, she sighs.'[2] In the Czech lands, peasants talked of him coming, flaming sword in hand, to smite the kings, lords and priests who oppressed them. In a bizarre transposition of hopes, it was sometimes the late emperor Joseph II (who had promoted the interests of the peasants against the lords and priests) who would reappear leading the French army, while some believed that Napoleon was none other than Joseph's avenging son. In Russia, the persecuted sect of Old Believers represented Napoleon as the Lion of the Valley of Jehoshaphat, come to overthrow the renegade tsar.[3]

This vision of Napoleon as some kind of avatar was not limited to superstitious peasants in far-flung regions. It pervaded many of the most sophisticated minds in Europe, which were not merely blinded by his éclat. A generation that was obsessed by the myths of Don Juan and Faust was spellbound by a man who seemed to have made some kind of pact with God or the Devil and openly challenged fate. Byron and other English poets were entranced, but it was the Germans who were the most deeply affected. Hölderlin's poem *Buonaparte* is characteristic in its fascination for a man who transcends all and cannot be contained even within the genius of poetic writing. Beethoven dedicated to him what is indisputably his most solemn, even religious, piano concerto. Heinrich Heine imagined Christ riding into Jerusalem on Palm Sunday as he watched Napoleon making his entry into Düsseldorf.[4] Many who plotted or merely dreamed of better times but could not identify the necessary catalyst viewed him as the 'providential man' who would initiate a new departure. To the philosopher Georg Wilhelm Friedrich Hegel, who saw him riding through the streets of Jena in 1806 on his way to annihilate the Prussian army, he was 'the world-spirit on horse-back'.

Wherever he went, Bonaparte let in a blast of fresh air and modernity, and nowhere did he have a more dramatic effect than on the fossilized German Empire. In 1801 Austria was forced to recognize the French Republic and her conquests in the Rhineland and Netherlands. This provided the impulse for a reorganization of the Empire. The ecclesiastical states were secularized and the imperial cities abolished. All over Germany ghettos were opened and Jews emancipated from legal constraints. In the following years the Code Napoléon, emblem of judicial modernity, was extended to large areas east of the Rhine. In 1806, after the successive defeat of the Austrian armies, came the next step.

On the morning of 6 August the grand Herald of the Reich rode through the streets of Vienna, resplendent in his ceremonial robes. At the Church of the Nine Choirs of Angels, he sounded a trumpet blast and then read out a proclamation from the Emperor Francis II to the effect that he had renounced his imperial title. At Napoleon's dictation, the Holy Roman Emperor Francis II had become the Emperor Francis I of Austria. As the herald trumpeted the Reich, and himself, out of history, people on the streets quipped that if he was not careful, the Emperor might end up as Francis 0.

Francis was not demoted further, but the transfer of sovereignty on that day was as drastic as that which had taken place on the Place de la Concorde on 21 January 1793. It did not entail decapitation, as the principal motive behind it was Napoleon's desire to steal the cloak of Charlemagne from the Habsburgs rather than replace them. But the thief left the door ajar for another sovereignty, that of the German nation. In the wake of the abolition of the Empire, a process known as 'mediatization' removed the prerogatives of hundreds of imperial counts and knights, whose erstwhile domains were fused into larger states. With them went thousands of borders, petty restrictions, and most of the archaisms that the writers of the Aufklärung and the generation of Sturm und Drang had inveighed against.

While there could not have been many intelligent Germans who did not approve of what Napoleon had done, it did beg many questions and touched some raw nerves. French influence and even interference following 1789 had been welcomed by progressive Germans. 'To become French is a greater benefaction than any German can understand who dreams of himself as a free man while the whip of the despot cracks behind him,' the poet Christian Friedrich Schubart had exclaimed after the incorporation of Alsace into France in 1791.[5] But such intellectual and emotional subjection to France could not last. The enthusiastic upheavals and dubious legal procedures of the French Revolution offended the Germans' respect for law, love of order and passion for rumination.

The area of Germany most immediately affected by events in France was the left bank of the Rhine, where a number of small states such as Cologne and Mainz typified all that was anachronistic about the Empire. The activities of the French over the border were viewed as somewhat un-German by the largely conservative press, but there was also a vibrant club of liberal 'patriots' in Mainz who were enthusiasts of the revolution. They included the Elector of Mainz's physician Georg Christian Wedekind and the peasant philosopher Adam Lux, a young man with long hair and beautiful eyes who dreamed of universal liberty. Appositely, he had written his doctoral thesis on the subject of 'Enthusiasm'. Another member of this group was Georg Forster, the original rootless internationalist. Born German of Scots descent, he was brought up in Poland, just outside Gdańsk. At the age of eighteen, he accompanied his father on a round-the-world voyage with Captain James Cook. He then worked as a teacher of natural sciences at Cassel, at the university of Wilno in Lithuania, and finally at Mainz.

In October 1792, when a French army under General Custine marched into Mainz, it was greeted rapturously by the likes of Forster and Wedekind. With Custine's encouragement, they set about introducing the revolutionary order into the city and the surrounding countryside. On 13 January 1793 Forster and Custine planted a liberty tree to mark the progress made. But Forster wanted to go further; he wanted the left bank of the Rhine to become part of the French Republic. Accordingly, in March 1793 he went to Paris with Adam Lux to beg the Convention the favour of allowing the First German Republic to incorporate with the French. This provoked indignation in other parts of Germany, and Forster's own father said that he ought to hang for it. Forster himself soon grew tired of the French, and even referred to the revolution as 'the excrement of humanity'.[6] Adam Lux was sent to the guillotine for standing up in defence of Charlotte Corday.

In his great work *On the Conflict of Faculties*, published in 1798, the ageing Kant maintained that however ghastly some of its manifestations, the French Revolution had been intrinsically moral, since every people had the right to create its own laws and its own morality. For Hegel, it represented the emancipation of the human mind; along with the introduction of Christianity and the Reformation, it was one of the great moments of breakthrough for humanity, a universal coming of age.[7] Kant's disciple Johann Gottlieb Fichte saw it in similar terms, declaring that 'henceforth the French Republic alone can be the country of the Just'.[8] But as the revolution progressed, the feeling grew in Germany that the French, with their habitual shallowness, had got it all wrong. They had allowed the pursuit of liberty to degenerate into mob rule and mass slaughter of innocent people, because they perceived liberty in mechanical terms. German thinkers were more interested in 'moral liberty', and many believed that it was the 'corrupt' nature of the French that had doomed the revolution to failure. Such conclusions allowed for a degree of smugness, suggesting as they did that the French Enlightenment, for all its brilliance, had been flawed, while German intellectual achievements had been more profound and more solid.[9]

Fichte identified Germany's uniqueness as lying in her essentially spiritual destiny. She would never stoop to conquer others, and while nations such as the French, the English or the Spanish scrambled for wealth and dominance, Germany's role was to uphold the finest values of humanity. Similar claims to a moral mission for Germany were made by Herder, Hölderlin, Schlegel and others. Goethe, who did not believe the Germans would ever make themselves into a nation, felt that they should concentrate on making themselves into freer human beings. Uppermost in his mind as he struggled back on the retreat from Valmy, riding in his duke's kitchen wagon, was not wounded national pride but disapproval of all the mess and waste involved. The strength of Germany was cultural and spiritual, and it was in these spheres that she should seek paramountcy. She must be the Greece to France's Rome.

Since there was no dominant metropolis in Germany, universities such as that of Jena were important political as well as literary centres. It was also in the universities that the Romantic movement burgeoned. In consequence, it not only influenced literature, but shaped the cast of mind of a whole generation, more so than in either France or England. Its roots lay in the Sturm und Drang period, and it coalesced in a group which met at the house of August Wilhelm Schlegel in Jena. These early Romantics, Ludwig Tieck, Wilhelm Friedrich Wackenroder, Friedrich Schelling, Friedrich Daniel Ernst Schleiermacher and Friedrich von Hardenberg, who wrote under the pseudonym 'Novalis', were known, appropriately, as the 'new sect'. They were certainly not Romantics in the affective sense, being more interested in form and aesthetics than in sentiment. Their yearning was not the craving for emotional fulfilment of the English or French Romantics. It was a search for a purer and more harmonious state of being. Whether they explored nature or the absolute, love or death, they were always looking for God. But their preoccupations were also inherently political; whether they drew their ideals from ancient Greece or early Christianity, they were still faced with the continuing problem of what to make of being German.

It was increasingly difficult for the German identity to find itself within what was no longer just French cultural hegemony, but a real *pax gallica* that was engulfing most of Europe. The Rhinelanders, whose homeland was transformed into the Cisrhenan Republic in 1797, had tried to be enthusiastic about it. The local patriot Joseph Görres personally planted the liberty tree in Coblenz and delivered a stirring paean to the French as the bringers of liberty. But the 'sister republic' was treated increasingly like a colony and a cantonment for French troops. These behaved as troops do, and the Rhinelanders grew disillusioned. The same was true elsewhere in Germany. The young writer Henri Beyle, a *Commissaire des Guerres* in Brunswick, introduced Parisian culture to the inhabitants, and showed his admiration for Germany by adding 'Stendhal' to his many pseudonyms in honour of Winckelmann's birthplace. But wherever the French went, organized looting followed; Germany seemed to be paying a high price for French culture. The concept of the Franco-German symbiosis as some kind of latter-day Graeco-Roman exchange began to look like a poor joke. 'We believed we were in Rome, but we found ourselves in Paris,' Görres conceded.[10]

It had been central to Herder's argument that each nation, by virtue of its innate character, had a special role to play in the greater process of history. One after another, nations ascended the world stage to fulfil their ordained purpose. The French were crowding the proscenium, but there was a growing conviction that Germany's time was coming, and her destiny was about to unfold. The Germans certainly seemed ready for it. The country was awash with under-employed young men, and since the days of the Sturm und Drang the concept of action, both as a revolt against stultifying rational forces and as a transcendent act of self-assertion, had become well established. Fichte equated virtually any action, provided it was bold and unfettered, with liberation.

The problem remained that the nation was still not properly constituted. Some defined it by language and culture, or, like Fichte, by a level of consciousness. The Germans were, according to him, more innately creative than other nations, being the only genuine people in Europe, an *Urvolk*, speaking the only authentic language, *Ursprache.* Others saw the nation as a kind of church, defined by the 'mission' of the German people. Adam Müller affirmed that this mission was to serve humanity with charity, and that any man who dedicated himself to this common purpose should be considered a German. In his lectures of 1806, Fichte made the connection between committed action and nationality. Those who stood up and demonstrated their vitality were part of the *Urvolk*, those who did not were un-German. Hegel saw the people as a spiritual organism, whose expression, the collective spirit or *Volksgeist*, was its validating religion.[11] The discussion mingled elements of theology, science and metaphysics to produce uplifting and philosophically challenging confusion.

But in the absence of clear geographical or political parameters, Germany's national existence was ultimately dependent on some variant of the racial concept. And this began to be stated with increasing assertiveness. 'In itself every nationality is a completely closed and rounded whole, a common tie of blood relationship unites all its members; all . . . must be of one mind and must stick together like one man', according to Joseph Görres, who had once been an enthusiastic internationalist. 'This instinctive urge that binds all members into a whole is the law of nature which takes preference over all artificial contracts . . . The voice of nature in ourselves warns us and points to the chasm between us and the alien.'[12]

The location and identification of this 'closed and rounded whole' involved not just defining German ethnicity, but also delving into the past in search of a typically German and organic national unit to set against the old rationalist French view of statehood based on natural law and the rights of man. The bible of this tendency was Tacitus's *Germania.* Placed in its own time, this book is as much about Rome as about Germanic tribes. It imagines the ultimate non-Rome, a place that had not been cleared and cultivated, and a people innocent of the arts of industry and leisure. The forest life it describes is the antithesis to the classical culture of Rome. It is also in some ways the original noble savage myth, representing everything that decadent Rome had lost; beneath Tacitus's contempt for the savage denizens of the forest lurks a vague fear that by gaining in civilization the Romans had forfeited certain rugged virtues.

The German nationalists picked up this theme, which mirrored their relation to French culture. Roma and Germania, the city and the forest, corruption and purity, could stand as paradigms for the present situation. The ancient Teutonic hero Arminius (Hermann) had led the revolt of the German tribes against Rome and defeated the legions in the Teutoburg Forest. His descendants who aspired to throw off the 'Roman' universalism of France could take heart.

Tacitus was also plundered to reinforce the image of a distinctive German nation with its own particular genius, its *Volkstum*. This entailed a great deal of dubious deduction and specious interpretation of the ancient text to support the metaphysical vision of the German people as blood, soil and soul. The historian Ernst Moritz Arndt, for instance, convinced himself that Tacitus 'realized how important it was for their [the Germans'] future greatness and majesty that they preserved the purity of their blood and resembled only themselves'.[13]

The very setting of Hermann's victory, the forest, became a subject of endless fascination. The oak tree was singled out as the symbol of the primeval Teutonic forest, and its legendary vitality gave rise to a real fetish. The fact that a gnarled old trunk can sprout into life with fresh foliage after appearing dead for years was surely a parable for Germany, which was burgeoning after centuries of political abeyance. Seen thus, the oak was the tabernacle of the nation's soul.

In their search for spiritual and aesthetic props, the early German Romantics reached back into history and rediscovered the Middle Ages, the 'beautiful, magnificent times, when Europe was a Christian land', in the words of Novalis. The Middle Ages predated the poisoned knowledge of the Enlightenment. They were a time of spiritual purity, an 'age of faith'. They were also a time when Germany had been dominant in Europe. The Gothic style, which reflected, in Goethe's words, 'the deepest feelings of truth and beauty of proportion, sprung from a plain and vigorous German soul', was the outward sign of that dominance.[14] The spirit of chivalry, which was the emanation of the cultural and spiritual unity of Europe in those days, was the expression of Germanness.

The search for the *Volkstum* also entailed the invention of a folkloric context, a culture supposedly latent in the souls of the masses, and Romantic poets were never happier than when engaged on such pursuits. Clemens Brentano and Achim von Arnim collected and published German folksongs. Joseph Görres produced two volumes of folk literature. Customs were rediscovered or invented, together with national dress, and folk wisdom was hailed as a direct emanation of the nation's genius. A style of behaviour came into fashion, supposedly modelled on the ancient customs of the Germans, but actually a concoction of pseudo-medieval notions of mettle-testing through duelling, physical self-assertion through acts of endurance, and the recreation of ancient jollity through over-eating, hard drinking and general rowdiness.

The process of national revival was given a jolt and a fillip by Napoleon's crushing defeat of the Prussians at the Battle of Jena in 1806. The humiliation of seeing the prestigious army created by the great Frederick trounced by the French led to painful self-appraisal and underlined the need for regeneration. But it also stung German pride and dispelled the last shreds of sympathy for France – and, with them, the universalist dreams of the previous decade.

The French became villains, and Napoleon himself was even portrayed as the Antichrist, a focus for the crusading struggle of deliverance that would regenerate Germany. Poets composed patriotic verse and anti-Napoleonic songs. Ludwig Jahn epitomized the curious mixture of paranoia, aggression and religious prudery that characterized this kind of nationalism. 'If you let your daughter learn French you might just as well teach her to become a whore', was one of his favourite asides.[15]

More methodical minds applied themselves to the nuts and bolts of nation-building. 'We must form men so that they can only will what we wish them to will,' Fichte declared.[16] Jahn wanted children to stop studying the history of the world, and to pore over that of Frederick the Great instead; he wanted the names of saints to be replaced in the calendar with those of Prussian generals, and feasts with commemorations of German victories. Lieutenant Boyen urged the improvement of the Prussian army through the abolition of private education and its replacement with a uniform school system leading to universal military service, which would link the army organically to the nation.[17]

The Prussian army was slow in rising to the occasion. Its defeat in 1806 only confirmed what a number of officers, such as Scharnhorst, Boyen and Gneisenau, had seen long before – that it was still an eighteenth-century army, lacking the kind of motivation that made the French victorious. August Neithardt von Gneisenau came from a family of lawyers and minor civil servants whose noble status had been invented by his father (the aristocratic-sounding Gerhard von Scharnhorst was a Hanoverian peasant's son). He had fought for the British in America, where he had first learned to appreciate the military superiority of inspired men fighting for their own country. The example of the French revolutionary and Napoleonic armies only confirmed this, and Gneisenau determined to reform the Prussian army.

An analogous wave of renewal swept through society. In 1808 the Tugendbund or League of Virtue, a society for the propagation of civic virtue, was formed in Königsberg and quickly ramified through Prussia. In 1809 Ludwig Jahn founded the more middle-class Deutsche Bund, based in Berlin. Joseph Görres demanded that all foreign elements be expunged from national life, so that essential German characteristics might flourish, and declared that no power on earth could stand in the way of a nation intent on defending its soul. 'That to which the Germans aspire will be granted to them, the day when, in their interior, they will have become worthy of it.'[18] Even the archetypically Enlightenment cosmopolitan Wilhelm von Humboldt was turning into a Prussian patriot. He was reorganizing the state education system at the time, and managed to transform it into a curiously spiritual one in which education and religion of state are inextricably intertwined.

But while the mood changed, reality had not. Germany was still divided and cowered under French hegemony. To the deep shame of much of her officer corps, Prussia was still an ally of France when Napoleon invaded Russia in 1812. Her forces, which did not take part in the march on Moscow, were to support the French and secure their flank in East Prussia. And it was when the frozen remnants were trudging back into Prussia and Poland that this support would have been most welcome. But it was precisely then that the Prussian military judged it safe to show their colours. General von Yorck, in command of 14,000 men in East Prussia, found himself in a pivotal position. With his support, Marshal Macdonald would be able to hold the line of the River Niemen and keep the Russians out of Poland; without it, he had no option but full retreat. The Prussian general had been in touch with the Russians for some time, through the intermediary of a young German officer in Russian service by the name of Carl von Clausewitz. On Christmas Day 1812 Yorck met the commander of the Russian advance guard and, by a convention he signed with them at Tauroggen, repudiated Prussia's alliance with France. It was an act of mutiny, the first in a series of acts by the German army to 'save' the fatherland against the orders of its political leaders. It was also the signal for all the nationalists to come out into the open.

The irascible Ernst Moritz Arndt was well to the fore. 'Oh men of Germany!' he exhorted, 'feel again your God, hear and fear the eternal, and you hear and fear also your *Volk*; you feel again in God the honour and dignity of your fathers, their glorious history rejuvenates itself again in you, their firm and gallant virtue reblossoms in you, the whole German Fatherland stands again before you in the august halo of past centuries ... One faith, one love, one courage, and one enthusiasm must gather again the whole German *Volk* in brotherly community ... Be Germans, be one, will to be one by love and loyalty, and no devil will vanquish you.'[19]

The king of Prussia did not feel quite brave enough to 'be German' yet. He ordered the arrest of Yorck, and then moved to Breslau, where he was out of reach of the French. In March 1813, when he saw that it was safe for him to jump on to the anti-Napoleonic bandwagon, Frederick William announced the formation of citizens' volunteer forces, the Landwehr and the Landsturm. On 17 March he issued a proclamation to the effect that his soldiers would 'fight for our independence and the honour of the *Volk*', and summoned every son of the fatherland to participate. 'My cause is the cause of my *Volk*,' he concluded, less than convincingly.[20] But nobody was looking too closely at anyone's motives in the general excitement. The cause of the German fatherland justified everything. 'Strike them dead!' Heinrich von Kleist had urged the soldiers setting off to war with the French. 'At the last judgement you will not be asked for your reasons!'[21]

The campaign of 1813, when the patched-up Napoleonic forces attempted to stand up to the combined armies of Russia, Prussia, Sweden and Austria, and finally succumbed at Leipzig, should, according to Chateaubriand, go down in history as 'the campaign of young Germany, of the poets'. That was certainly the perception. The by no means young Fichte finished his lecture on the subject of duty and announced to his students at Berlin that the course was suspended until they gained liberty or death. He marched out of the hall amid wild cheers, and led the students off to put their names down for the army. But whether large numbers of students did actually come forward is doubtful, judging by the figures for the most emblematic of all the volunteer formations.

Adolf Freiherr von Lützow organized a Free Corps to fight alongside the army. In order to underline its ideological pedigree, he designed a uniform that was supposedly based on 'old German' costume: a long green tunic and a great floppy hat. But the image of the unit was fixed for posterity by its most illustrious soldier, the young poet Theodor Körner, who had laid aside his pen to take up arms. Before being killed in action, which he very soon was, Körner managed to compose a number of poems which looked forward to death in the cause of Germany, representing the unity it brought to comrades killed together as 'nuptials' with their fatherland. It was all deeply morbid, but it hit the right note. The legend of the Lützow Corps as a body of self-immolatory poets and students entered German mythology. In fact, no more than 12 per cent of the Lützower ranks were made up of university or high school students, while the overwhelming majority were craftsmen and labourers.[22] But such details could not affect the progress of the ideological juggernaut, any more than the fact that much of the population were openly hostile to the 'liberators'.

The War of Liberation, *Freiheitskrieg*, was, above all, a war of purification and self-discovery. It did not stop with the expulsion of French forces from Germany in 1813. If anything, it was in the course of 1814, when Napoleon's forces were fighting for survival on French soil, that the War of Liberation really got going in Germany. All the societies and leagues that had grown out of the Tugendbund engaged in an orgasm of Teutomania, and the universities were in a state of patriotic inflammation. Students joined the gymnastic societies started by Ludwig Jahn, who had grown a Teutonic beard and wanted to start up an 'old German' language. They wore tunics of unbleached linen, floppy *altdeutsch* caps, which resembled a chef's hat that had failed to rise, and daggers in their belts. They addressed each other with purportedly medieval familiarity. Some made a great show of clean living and chastity, calling themselves *die Unbedingten*, the unbending. They went in for elaborate gymnastic displays in lieu of tournaments, and they spent a great deal of time singing their crude and inordinately bloodthirsty songs. Goethe, who as supervisor of Jena University was called upon to restrain some of their excesses, found the whole business foolish and very depressing. Hardly surprising: 'Give me a good gymnasts' song and you can have all of Fouqué and Goethe,' one of the students declared.[23]

But the War of Liberation was being waged no less vehemently at the cultural level. The poets were not squeamish when it came to singing of the national crusade, while the painters rallied to the cause in a memorable way. Caspar David Friedrich, who had already done so much to represent the symbolic German landscape as an object of worship through a series of paintings in which people are depicted contemplating its wonder like so many saints adoring the nativity in a medieval tryptich, now turned to glorifying the nation. He painted several representations of an imaginary tomb of Hermann, evocatively set among craggy boulders and fir trees. And he also produced various set-pieces representing the war. Other painters depicted groups of patriotic German volunteers going forth in their hats to free the fatherland. Joseph Görres led a movement demanding the completion of Cologne Cathedral as a sign of German regeneration. 'Long shall Germany live in shame and humiliation, a prey to inner conflict and alien arrogance, until her people return to the ideals from which they were seduced by selfish ambition, and until true religion and loyalty, unity of purpose and self-denial shall again render them capable of erecting such a building as this,' he wrote.[24]

Germaine de Staël, prominent writer and daughter of Jacques Necker, the minister whose dismissal triggered the French Revolution, had made two long voyages in Germany, in 1803 and 1807. She had met Goethe, Schiller and most of the other writers of the day, and was overwhelmed by them. She developed the highest admiration for the depth and spiritual qualities of German literature and the culture that underlay it, and she gave expression to this in her book *De l'Allemagne*. When the work went to print in Paris in 1810, the proofs were seized and destroyed on the orders of Napoleon. The emperor hated the author, a feeling that was heartily reciprocated, and had banished her from France. But it is not known whether this was his only reason for banning the book. His police chief, Fouché, gave a different reason when she protested. 'Your last work is not at all French,' he explained.[25]

Whether Napoleon really did despise the Germans or not is difficult to establish, but he certainly gave them that impression, and his effect on the country was catastrophic as a result. He incarnated the superiority of France and rammed it home with a series of victories that humiliated them from the military point of view as well. His behaviour awakened the most basic emotions, with disastrous consequences for the future. And equally disastrous consequences flowed from his very similar treatment of another great nation with profound problems of identity – the Russians.

With the active patronage of the Empress Catherine, Russian society had been far more exposed to the Enlightenment than, say, the Spanish or the Italians. By the 1780s, the works of the *philosophes* were widely available and being discussed in salons, societies for the propagation of learning, and the burgeoning masonic network. The poet Alexander Nikolayevich Radishchev wrote an ode on liberty in honour of the American revolution, looking forward to the day when its example might be followed in Russia. But that day was a long way off. All the dabbling with the Enlightenment in Russia took place within a framework of absolutism, in a slave-owning society in which, moreover, even the grandest aristocrat was not free in the western sense.[26]

The illusion of enlightenment did not survive the storming of the Bastille. The events provoked horror in court circles. They were discussed with greater interest and approval in some freethinking salons and even in parts of the press. But when, early in 1790, Radishchev published his *Journey from Petersburg to Moscow*, an imaginary trip made, as it were, by Sterne riding on the back of Raynal, which described Russian landowners as 'barbarians' and 'bloodsuckers', all hell broke loose. Catherine, who had prided herself on corresponding with Voltaire and Diderot, ordered the arrest of the author and the destruction of all copies of the work. In April 1790 she issued orders to halt the spread of the 'epidemic' of new ideas. In 1792, she called for a crusade against the French Revolution, and launched her own against the Polish constitution. In the same year, all booksellers in Moscow were arrested and their shops closed down for investigation. Secret societies were banned. Anti-Jacobin paranoia reached such levels that even being polite to a servant was suspect.

There was a long tradition of cultural xenophobia in Russia. Peter the Great's importation of European technology, manners and personnel had been resented, as was his transfer of the capital from old Russian Moscow to new cosmopolitan St Petersburg. Pique at the Germanic invasion of the military and political spheres was mirrored by suspicion of the French dominance in cultural matters. Foreign manners were associated with corruption and the abandonment of honest, true Russian values. But while writers strove to ridicule the slaves of French fashion, they were at a loss to supply an alternative cultural model. Educated Russians could read and write only in French.

The search for a national language that could serve as a literary instrument was complicated by arguments and the need to score points. The poet Mikhail Vasilyevich Lomonosov suggested taking Old Church Slavonic as the basis, on the grounds that it was ancient and religiously sanctioned, and therefore a worthy rival to Latin. The poet A. P. Sumarokov developed a theory that all root words are short; hence the Russian word for 'eye', *oko*, being shorter than the Latin *oculus*, Russian was a more ancient language than Latin.

This search for vindication through language was accompanied by a sentimental interest in the people, which began in the 1780s with the collecting of folk-songs and other lore. As elsewhere, the legacy of Ossian made itself felt, in the forgery of the supposedly ancient poem *The Lay of Igor's Host*, and a number of new tales set in a semi-legendary Russian past were composed. Collections of Russian antiquities of every kind were meant to provide the elements with which to piece together a past nobody had bothered to record. Attempts to produce a history of Russian ran into acrimonious disputes over rival theories as to the origins of the Russian people – talk of Varangian roots was unacceptable to those who rejected foreign cultural influence and swore by some deeper, more *ur*, Russian soul.

Given the fragility of this sense of identity, it is hardly surprising that Napoleon's invasion of 1812 was a traumatic experience for Russia. It did not have the liberating effect of French incursions elsewhere. His defeat of the Russian army, his occupation of Moscow, and, crowning insult, his destruction of this cradle of Russian statehood and culture, were deeply insulting. They provoked an explosion of patriotism of a kind nobody had felt before, followed by a sense of pride at having seen off the French threat. But they also deepened the cultural inferiority complex of Russian society.

The subsequent pursuit of the French and the Russian occupation of Paris was a triumph of sorts. Yet it left the Russians wanting. They did not win a single battle as resounding as Austerlitz or Jena. And the experience itself marked the soldiers deeply. Everywhere they went they saw ways of life that differed radically from their own. They observed that peasants in France and Germany lived in proper houses and ate well, and that even Prussian soldiers were treated in more human fashion than they were themselves. The experience was particularly disconcerting for the officers. Coming exclusively from the nobility, they had been brought up speaking French and reading the same literature as educated people in other countries. They could converse effortlessly with German and English allies as well as with French prisoners and civilians. Ostensibly, they were just like any of the Frenchmen, Britons and Germans they met, yet at every step they were made aware of profound differences. The experience left them with a sense of being somehow outside, almost unfit for participation in, European civilization. And that feeling would have dire consequences.

Equally fateful and culturally defining was the effect of Napoleon on Great Britain, which his threatening presence helped to save from internal strife, and which remoulded its identity and relationship to Europe for the nineteenth century largely in reaction to him and all he stood for.

Britain had come close to catastrophe in the 1790s. There was open sedition and plotting up and down the country, affecting the militias and even the regular armed forces, leading to the naval mutinies at Portsmouth and the Nore in the spring of 1797. Unrest in Wales and Ireland, and the French landings in those countries, exposed the British state's vulnerability to nationally-inspired revolt. There had also been stirrings of discontent in Scotland, whose union with England was not a hundred years old, and from where only fifty years earlier an army had marched right into the Midlands.

A society of United Scotsmen was founded to promote insurrection, culminating in a famous trial of alleged revolutionaries. One of the condemned, Thomas Muir, escaped from New South Wales, where he had been transported, and reached France via Vancouver, Mexico and Spain. In a memorandum submitted to Talleyrand in 1798, he claimed that 100,000 Scots patriots were waiting to rise up against British rule. Similar claims were made by another Scots exile in Paris, Dr Robert Watson, who maintained that 'descendants of the immortal Ossian' were preparing to reclaim a place for their country among the free nations.[27] Yet the French would see kilted soldiers wearing the cypher of King George marching down the streets of Paris before any Scot rose up against the English 'tyrants'. The reasons for this are difficult to fathom.

The western highlands and islands of Scotland had been settled by people from Ireland who, although they had originally sailed over from Scotland, were regarded as essentially alien by the lowland Scots. Their instrument was the harp, not the bagpipe, and they were identifiable by their Irish-style belted shirt or plaid. As the poorer people could not afford the trews that went with it, this often resembled a kind of skirt. It was an English officer in the 1730s who called this arrangement a 'kilt', and it was an English regimental tailor and a Mancunian cloth manufacturer who invented the modern version. In the aftermath of the 1745 Jacobite rebellion the highlanders were not allowed to carry weapons and wear kilts, trews, or any other kind of distinctive dress by which they could recognize each other. This had the immediate effect of lending significance to these rags, and, in the absence of the originals, it allowed artists to represent them in endless unrealistic and glamorous ways.

Macpherson's Ossianic industry placed the Scots centre-stage as far as the reading public of Europe was concerned, and they suddenly became a *Kulturvolk*; an endangered one at that. A Highland Society was founded in London in 1778 to preserve their feigned ancient traditions, and the act prohibiting the wearing of distinctive dress was repealed in 1782. But this did not presage a nationalist revival in Scotland. Highland regiments, of which a large number were raised over the next thirty years, were uniformed in kilts, of different colour patterns for each regiment, and it was the standardization implicit in this that created one of the most universally successful pseudo-traditions. But it was a quintessentially British tradition, forged on the battlefield and by association with the Crown.

The pseudo-national revivals in Scotland and Wales had been mirrored by revivals of provincial patriotism in England, but these were not a force for national cohesion. Those labelled 'patriots' in England tended to be sentimental poets who extolled the purity of the country over the corruptions of the court and the metropolis. William Blake wrote patriotically-inspired works, but his was a historical and religious patriotism harking back to the Jerusalem that England had supposedly once been. He did not even support the war with France. Thomas Chatterton did invent a whole corpus of supposedly fifteenth-century verse, and even some alleged to have been written before the Norman Conquest. But while it betrayed the poet's local patriotism and rejection of alien influences, it does not belong in the tradition of Macpherson or Morganwg. And the antiquarians who, like their Welsh and Scots counterparts, rooted about in old lore did so out of curiosity, not in search of weapons to use against their foes.

While no ethnically or spiritually inspired vehicle for the expression of Englishness emerged in this period, a new British sense of nationhood did evolve. And it was of a kind that could accommodate not only the discontented and mutinous in England, but patriotic Scots and Welshmen as well. Its most visible symbols were the army and the monarchy, both of which acquired a certain sanctity at this time.

The army had traditionally been represented as alien, disreputable and inefficient. The succession of victories during the Seven Years War had improved this image, and while this was dented by its brutality and incompetence in the unpopular American war, it recovered as soon as victories began to be scored against the old French enemy. The series of naval victories, culminating in the Battle of Trafalgar, validated the Union Jack that symbolized the fusion of nationalities and effaced memories of the mutinies – which had been largely inspired by United Irishmen pressed into the navy. Wellington's victories on land, won by Welsh, Irish and Scots as well as English regiments, vindicated a British army. They were all the more significant in that they were won against the inspired internationalist forces of *La Grande Nation*, led by a military genius, which had defeated every other army on the Continent.

The British army's glory was perpetuated in a new kind of iconography. Benjamin West's painting of General Wolfe expiring before Quebec at the moment of triumph, surrounded by faithful brothers-in-arms, was the first of many powerful icons. George III named West court painter and commissioned a series of canvases depicting England's past glories. Such paintings celebrated the British nation through its army and navy, which provided a new roll of saints and martyrs. The ultimate icon in this respect would be Arthur William Devis' *Death of Nelson*, painted in 1805. Nelson is represented as a Christ-like figure, swathed only in white cloths and enhanced with a halo cast by the lantern, breathing his last on the timbers of HMS *Victory*, surrounded by devoted disciples. The ship would become a national shrine, and many an artefact be made from its timbers and lovingly preserved.

King George had been impressed by the revolutionary festivals being staged in Paris, and in December 1797 he held a Naval Thanksgiving procession, in which ordinary tars took part. It was the first of many celebrations and commemorations which allowed the people to participate along with the king and the army. Eight years later, after Napoleon's coronation, George III held a splendid St George's Day installation of Knights of the Garter, more lavish than any before, designed to stress the antiquity of the institution. This was an oblique response to the usurped grandeur of Napoleon and his Légion d'Honneur. The 'Corsican upstart' was vilified and depicted in cartoons as the embodiment of thoroughly un-British tyranny, illegitimacy and vulgarity, and the British people no less than their king rejected and turned their noses up at him and his doings. George III's rebuilding work at Windsor was a similar assertion of ancient credentials, eliding with a process of reinventing the monarchy and forging ancient traditions. The process was riddled with nonsense and humbug, but it did strike a powerful, quasi-religious chord in the people.

Unlike its French counterpart, the British monarchy did not stand in contradiction to the people. Both deferred to a higher concept, represented by Britannia. When Nelson told his men before Trafalgar that England expected every man to do his duty, he was speaking in the name of a shared patrimony of land, people, culture and religion, not of the king or of some idealized redemptive *patrie.*

All of this set Great Britain apart from the other major European nations. The old religiously-inspired conviction of a chosen people fighting against Popish aggression was replaced by a more modern vision of an alternative destiny, sanctioned by the resounding triumph of British arms. This gave the British a sense of detached superiority in relation to the rest of the Continent, summed up in one word, 'Waterloo'.[28]

11

Golgotha

At about midday on 18 June 1815, the French writer René de Chateaubriand went for a walk in the countryside outside the city of Ghent, clutching a copy of Caesar's *Commentaries*. As he ambled along, absorbed by the book, he fancied he heard the rumble of distant thunder. He looked up at the sky, wondering whether to turn back, but as the one or two clouds looked unthreatening, he walked on. But when the wind suddenly changed direction, he heard the thunder again, more distinctly. After a while, he realized it was the sound of cannon. 'This great battle, still unnamed, whose echoes I heard at the foot of a solitary poplar,' he later wrote, 'was the Battle of Waterloo!'

Chateaubriand was profoundly and devoutly Catholic. He was also a confirmed monarchist. He hated Napoleon's illegitimate and violent regime. He despised the emperor for being a usurper, and for having murdered the Duc d'Enghien. He would never forgive him for ordering the death of his own cousin Armand. Chateaubriand was a minister in the service of King Louis XVIII, who had taken refuge in Ghent after being chased from Paris on Napoleon's return from Elba. Yet as he listened to the distant roar of the guns, he felt strangely moved, and found himself longing for Napoleon to defeat the British and their allies. 'At that moment the *patrie* took over my heart,' he recorded.[1] His reaction sums up the paradox that was to make France, and many other places, ungovernable over the next decades.

By any reckoning, the peace that descended upon Europe in 1815 brought relief to the overwhelming majority of the Continent's inhabitants, and it should have been greeted with universal joy. The wars had lasted, on and off, for nearly twenty-five years. Napoleon's cohorts operated over a wider area than any since the Mongols or the Romans before them, ranging from Lisbon to Moscow, and from the Baltic Sea to the Egyptian shore of the Mediterranean. It is true that this was not an age of total war, and that Napoleonic armies were less of a threat to the civilian population than those of the Thirty Years' War, let alone those of this century. The destruction was limited, and the effect on everyday life remarkably slight; ladies of rank continued to visit spas to take the waters, and British tourists travelled to Italy. Occasionally the outbreak of a new round of hostilities would force them to return by a different route. But for someone like Goethe, living at the very centre of Europe, the whole experience was more interesting than disruptive. In 1806, after the Battle of Jena, first Marshal Lannes, then Ney, then Augereau dropped in to see him on their way through. A few months before, it had been Madame de Staël, fleeing their advance. In 1809 Napoleon summoned Goethe into his presence at Erfurt. The master of Europe proceeded to tell the sixty-year-old author that *Werther* had been the favourite book of his youth, and awarded him the Légion d'Honneur. In 1812, as the defeated Napoleon, travelling incognito, stopped in Weimar, he did not fail to convey his compliments to the poet.

Nevertheless, three generations had grown up in a climate of war, whose fortunes touched every family at some point. For twenty-five years the Continent struggled to feed, clothe and equip huge armies, and its productive manpower was conscripted into them. This effort was paid for not in gold but in paper money, which was the most enduring legacy of the period. The French revolutionary government had brought in *assignats* in 1789; treasury bonds which were to be supported by the sale of the ecclesiastical estate. Within weeks, they were being used as currency, and fresh batches were printed to meet every emergency. By 1794, they were worth about a third of one per cent of their face value, and were declared valueless in 1797. The experience imbued the French with a distaste for paper currency still detectable today, but it did not put an end to the practice. Every European state printed paper currency during the Napoleonic Wars, and all of them, even the British one-pound note, rapidly depreciated in value. Labour, produce and goods were, in effect, stolen from the people of Europe on a grand scale.

Some areas did suffer severe depredations. In Spain, the fighting was exceptionally brutal and, on account of the *guerilla*, involved the whole population. Italy was robbed of a staggering part of her cultural heritage and taxed mercilessly by the French. Moscow was burned. Poland was treated as a free granary and a source of cannon-fodder. Even France was at the end of her tether. The country had been on a war footing since 1792, straining every resource to defend itself and then to impose hegemony over the Continent. In effect, no more than 7 per cent of the population was called up between 1800 and 1815, but the common perception was different. To contemporaries it appeared that as they reached the end of their schooldays, the entire male youth was pressed into the ranks. Respected writers such as Benjamin Constant had been fiercely denouncing Napoleon and his regime for years, and as his star waned after 1812, the grumbling became general. France longed for peace at any price. Yet far from ushering in an era of relief, contentment and new hope, the guns of Waterloo heralded a period of dissatisfaction and yearning. To many all over the Continent, they celebrated not a rebirth, but a multiple funeral.

The list of hopes buried in 1815 is long. For Voltairians as much as for followers of Rousseau, for German pietists as much as for English liberals, the dawn of 1789 had been a moment of boundless promise. This had become clouded for most of them at some stage of the morning, but most believed in the possibility of things coming right before the end of the day. When the curtain was drawn in 1815 they finally had to face up to the fact that it would not.

Some believed the French Revolution had not gone far enough. The alternative view was that the Enlightenment had been inherently flawed and the revolution its evil outcome. Some saw the revolution in apocalyptic terms, as an ordeal imposed by God to reawaken faith or as a punishment for the aberrations of the Enlightenment and the depravity of the *ancien régime*. Chateaubriand contributed *Le Génie du Christianisme*, an immensely influential book which vindicated Christianity and presented it in a way that appealed to modern intellectuals. His vision of a spiritually refreshed Catholicism emerging from the blood and suffering of revolution with a chivalric monarchism rising above the power struggles of the recent past, inspired most of the French Romantics. But submission to the will of God was no longer appealing to generations that had become used to the concept of the centrality of Man in the universe.

The demands of war and the consequences of blockade had forced parts of Europe to embark on an industrial revolution. This was invariably accompanied by appalling conditions and working practices, and both factory and mine produced deprivation and alienation of an order unknown to even the poorest peasants of the *ancien régime*. Nothing in the whole canon of Enlightenment thought had prepared anyone for this, and no amount of religious devotion could mitigate its horror. A few priests, most notably the Abbé Félicité de Lamennais, sought to adapt the Church into a more socially-oriented body, but got nowhere.

For many, the revolutionary and Napoleonic era had been heady times, giving rise to new aspirations, and at the same time making it appear not only possible but almost easy to realize them. Napoleon's own life was the ultimate paradigm of the man from nowhere whose only limits are set by his own genius and will. The endless need for heroism and self-sacrifice had provided the humble and uneducated with ample opportunity to achieve similar liberation. The system imposed in 1815, on the other hand, not only dispelled dreams and dashed hopes, it failed dismally to put in their place any kind of spiritual vision that might serve as an inspiration.

The regimes which imposed control over the Continent in 1815 officially involved Christianity as the basis of government and social organization. The Russian Tsar Alexander took things further. He had fallen under the influence of Baronness Julie von Krüdener, an adventuress from Riga who had suddenly found God and become convinced that she had been destined to save the world. In 1808 she had met the German pietist Johann Heinrich Jung-Stilling, who believed that a great man would emerge from the wastes of the north to overthrow the Antichrist Napoleon and usher in the millennium. She in turn decided that the Russians were a sacred race and Alexander the elect of God. On 4 June 1815 she marched into his headquarters at Heilbronn and proceeded to rant and pray for a full three hours, at the end of which the Tsar was a weeping wreck. She was with him when he entered Paris, holding prayer-meetings and seances.

On 10 September 1815 Alexander held a military review, over which the baroness presided like some divine envoy. After the parade, he declared that he loved all his enemies and meant to pray for the salvation of the world. He persuaded his fellow monarchs to invoke the sanction of Christ on the European order they had created at the Congress of Vienna. This they did by signing a declaration, known as the Holy Alliance, to the effect that they would base their actions 'upon the sublime truths which the Holy Religion of our Saviour teaches'. They solemnly declared 'their fixed resolution, both in the administration of their respective States, and in their political relations with every other government, to take for their sole guide the precepts of that Holy Religion, namely, the precepts of Justice, Christian Charity and Peace, which, far from being applicable only to private concerns, must have an immediate influence on the councils of Princes, and guide all their steps'.[2]

Metternich termed the declaration a 'high-sounding nothing', Castlereagh dismissed it as 'a piece of sublime mysticism and nonsense'.[3] But it was much more than that. It was, unwittingly, a challenge. It turned the peace treaty into an ideological orthodoxy, proclaiming to the world that all the hopes and desires which had agitated and inspired so many hundreds of thousands, if not millions, over the past few decades were excommunicate. Anyone who agreed with Voltaire or Rousseau, anyone who had fought for the independence of some duchy in Italy or a scrap of Poland, anyone who had doted on the brotherhood of man or indulged any of the other pipe-dreams of the period, was suspect. They were supposed to renounce those errors and embrace instead the Christian values proclaimed by the Holy Alliance, which determined not only to rule Europe, but to save it.

The monarchs who signed the declaration belied its intent. The settlement agreed at the Congress of Vienna was ostensibly based on the principle of legitimacy, but this was blatantly flouted. The republics of Venice and Genoa were not reinstated, the kingdom of Poland was not restored. They excommunicated the robber, but kept his spoils for themselves. They did not give back the Church's property where this was not convenient to them. The old aristocracy was not compensated, and the monarchs who ruled after 1815 pragmatically accepted a new elite born of the revolution and the Napoleonic epoch. While the Pope had not signed the Holy Alliance, the Church acquiesced in the new arrangements, and thereby allowed itself to become tainted by implication.

The Vienna settlement also created an entirely new array of wrongs. By obsessively pursuing and seeking to stamp out revolutionary tendencies, the statesmen behind it had blinded themselves to the national aspirations that either inspired or underlay those tendencies. They had redrawn frontiers and parcelled out territory in such a way as to wound those aspirations. Everywhere, they suppressed budding feelings and dreams of national fulfilment, which were growing into hallowed causes. By trampling on these, the Holy Alliance defined itself as the enemy. Standing on duty to defend it was the pursed figure of the Austrian chancellor Metternich, who saw revolution everywhere and marshalled inglorious armies of policemen and spies in mortal combat with it. The opposing ranks swelled with eager volunteers, people with no political agenda but a metaphysical sense of right and wrong. 'I have simplified my politics into a detestation of all existing governments,' declared Lord Byron. He saw the cause of oppressed nations as 'the very poetry of politics'.[4]

The nation uppermost in Byron's mind was Italy. In Italy more than anywhere else, the movers at the Congress of Vienna had intended to reintroduce the *status quo ante*. The only obstacle to this was Joachim Murat, still firmly ensconced on the throne of Naples in 1814. Britain, whose navy was the decisive factor in that theatre, was not averse to letting him stay on. But he dashed his own hopes. When news reached him of Napoleon's escape from Elba, he felt impelled to support the emperor and thought the time ripe to further an idea that had haunted him in the past. 'Providence calls on you at last to become a free nation,' he declared on 30 March 1815 in a proclamation to the inhabitants of the peninsula.[5] He then marched north. At Rimini he issued another proclamation reminding the Italians of their past glories and calling on them to unite under his banner. Rossini composed a hymn, beginning with the words: 'Arise, Italy, the time has now come!' Murat was dubbed *pater patriae*, but the time had not come: the numbers of those prepared to rise were small, and he was defeated at Tolentino on 3 May 1815, captured and shot.

Metternich could now do as he pleased. Italy was to be 'a combination of independent states, linked together by the same geographical expression'. Ten political units were revived along with the boundaries of 1789, with a few modifications. These involved the destruction of the two republics of Venice, incorporated into Austria, and Genoa, awarded to the king of Sardinia as a consolation for the cession of part of Savoy to France. The Republic of Lucca was remoulded as a duchy, leaving only tiny San Marino without a monarch. Ousted rulers were brought back and reinstated in pomp. The uncompromising Victor Emmanuel I of Savoy returned to his Sardinian-Piedmontese kingdom wearing a wig and knee-breeches. He went doggedly through the court almanac of 1798, reappointing every official who had held rank then. The rulers could count on Austria's military support, but they could also count on her nanny-like intervention if they started indulging liberals. Metternich even suggested 'a kind of central police to which all conspiracies, plots, and similar things could be reported'. The system was devised essentially to prevent any one unit in Italy becoming strong enough to challenge Austrian possessions, and to deny France any opening through which she might extend her influence in the peninsula.

This was to be achieved through Austria's presence in Lombardy and Venice, with its Habsburg-ruled outposts of Parma and Modena, Tuscany and Lucca. It was to be supported in the south by the Bourbon monarchy of Naples, now revived as the Kingdom of the Two Sicilies. Its king, Ferdinand I, formerly IV, was bound by treaty not to allow any change in his own dominions and to remain dependent on Austrian aid against all threats. In the north, the old kingdom of Sardinia, resurrected as the kingdom of Piedmont and reinforced with the addition of Genoa and its sea power, was to be Austria's obedient policeman. Its king, Victor Emmanuel I, was seen by Metternich as 'the vanguard for the defence of the peninsula, for the maintenance of a durable peace, and the overthrow of the spirit of Italian Jacobinism'.[6]

When Metternich spoke of 'the spirit of Italian Jacobinism', he meant the welter of conspiracy that had submerged the peninsula in the wake of the Napoleonic Wars. In 1809 Buonarotti had created an order, by the name of Mondo, to embrace the remains of the Adelfi, sometimes referred to as the Sublimi Maestri Perfetti. As with all secret societies, information on the history and development of this one remains patchy. There were five grades, each with its preparations and duties, and all members had to be senior Freemasons before they joined. Buonarotti theoretically controlled it through a 'Grand Firmament', but it is difficult to assess how far this control was exercised. Despite some reservations on the part of the leadership, Mondo coexisted and even co-operated with a far larger movement, one that was particularly characteristic of the age – the Carbonari.

The myths surrounding the origins of the Carbonari are legion. It has been variously maintained that they originated in England, Scotland, France, Germany and Switzerland; that they were founded by the Egyptian goddess Isis, Philomel of Thebes (who had resisted Philip of Macedon), the Roman god Mithras, the eleventh-century St Theobald, the Knights Templar, the French king François I, or just a German guild of charcoal-burners, as the name suggests. In effect, the Carbonari probably evolved from one of the offshoots of Freemasonry, like the Illuminati. But there also appears to have been a connection with the *compagnonnage* of the French charcoal-burners, something between a guild and a social club uniting people who, by the very nature of their trade, were scattered in remote places.

The Carbonari first appeared in Italy around 1808, and spread rapidly through the peninsula, reaching a vast membership, estimates of which vary between 300,000 and 642,000 'good cousins', divided up in Masonic-style lodges called *vendite*, each with its grand master. Although there was a degree of regional variation, their rites, ceremonies and catechisms generally conform to the same pattern. Initiation was carried out inside a *baracca* or hut in the middle of a wood (if such could not be located, a town house in a garden would be so denoted). The postulant would be left for a time in a 'grotto of reflection', after which he would be blindfolded and conducted into the interior of the *baracca*. Standing before the grand master, who was seated on a tree-trunk, he would give his name and other particulars, say that he had been in the forest collecting wood to kindle a fire, and declare that he had come to the good cousins to find truth and to learn to conquer his passions. After an exchange of mumbo-jumbo, he would be led, still blindfold, out into the 'forest' and made to stumble over obstacles placed in his path. This represented the weakness of mortals and the need for perseverance. He was then guided between flames symbolizing charity, which he must never allow to be extinguished in his breast. After this, he was led back into the baracca and made to kneel. Placing his hand on an axe, he would swear to keep the secret and never to deny assistance to his 'cousins'. Should he fail in this, his body would be chopped up and burned, the ashes scattered to the winds. He was then asked what he was seeking. 'Light!' he would reply. Only at this point was the blindfold removed. He was then made to swear further oaths, taught various signs and instructed in a number of 'mysteries'.

The Carbonaro 'catechisms' that have survived read like an amalgam of all the silliest precepts put forward by the *philosophes*, and property is referred to as 'an outrage against the rights of the human race'. But most of the material does not go beyond exhortation to what is in effect Christian virtue. The moral tone of the proceedings, set by incantations of 'Faith, Hope, Charity!', was highly uplifting, and in no way inimical to the prevailing religious or political climate. But initiation into the second grade, that of masters, turned these against each other in a manner that beautifully illustrates the confusion to which minds were prone at the time.

The ceremony took the form of the trial of Jesus, like the formal reading of the Passion on Palm Sunday – except that the man on trial was 'Jesus, Grand Master of the Universe', a perfect man who had tried to enlighten the poor and redeem them from slavery, and to enact the laws of nature; the charge against him was that of political sedition. For this he was arraigned by the forces of tyranny. They would enact the crowning with thorns, the flagellation, the bearing of the cross, stopping short of the actual crucifixion – to convince the candidate that if he made enough sacrifices for the cause, he too could expect to attain the blessed condition and triumph over death. The initiation of a Grand Elect Grand Master involved the postulant being 'crucified' between two others and branded on the left breast. As he pretended to expire, there would be a mock battle between some of his fellows dressed in Austrian uniforms and others in the guise of Carbonari. At this triumph over death, the initiand would be taken down from the cross, and his resurrection into the new grade would take place.

These rituals, as well as the patents, membership certificates and other material that has come down to us – all decorated with variable combinations of the cross, the crown of thorns, the sun, the moon, the cock, the fasces, the ladder, St Theobald, skulls, crossed bones, geometrical dividers, pentangles, triangles, and the odd papal tiara being struck by lightning – suggest that organized religion had somehow let these people down.

Just as for France, 1815 represented for Italy a burial of many dreams. In the introduction to the Fourth Canto of *Childe Harold*, written in 1818, Byron, who was sojourning in northern Italy, writes of the Italians' longing for 'the immortality of independence'. These were confused longings. Stendhal, who also spent a great deal of time in Italy, complained that the Italians did not understand their history, but acted like people trying to join in a game which everyone else was playing. Fabrice del Dongo, the protagonist of *La Chartreuse de Parme*, turns up at Waterloo in search of a transcendental experience, and spends the next months asking himself whether he had really participated in a Napoleonic battle. 'The whole Italian people is inwardly sick,' wrote another discerning traveller, Heinrich Heine, 'the suffering expression of the face of the Italians is especially noticeable when they are spoken to concerning the misfortunes of their country; and in Milan many occasions of this sort occurred. That is the most galling wound in the breast of the Italians; and they give a convulsive start if it is touched, however lightly.'[7]

It is in this context that the secret societies must be viewed. Membership gave a sense of action when none was possible, the rituals offered solace which an unsympathetic church could not provide. Indeed, the confraternity of members was nothing less than a community of the faithful – though the faith itself remained inchoate.

'The king vainly seeking his subjects in his people, the people vainly seeking their king in the monarchy, the French vainly seeking a motherland in France', is how the poet Alphonse de Lamartine represents the country into which Joan of Arc was born.[8] Yet one cannot help feeling that this poignant vision derived from his own experience of post-Napoleonic France.

When Louis XVIII arrived in Paris in 1814 in the baggage of the Russian army, he was surprisingly well received. 'The great majority of the population, even that of the surrounding countryside, came out to greet him with the most enthusiastic acclamations,' according to Marshal Macdonald. 'It was more than joy; there was almost a touch of ecstasy in this show of feeling.'[9] The king did not build on these sentiments, and his popularity plummeted.

It was probably his stubborn refusal to acknowledge what had taken place in France over the past quarter-century that offended most. He returned to Paris dressed as he had left it in 1789 – in breeches, stockings and peruke with pigtail. This was a gesture transcending fashion; Tsar Alexander wore trousers and had his hair cut in the 'Roman' style, as did Wellington. Louis banned the tricolor and introduced the old white cockade and the white flag of the Vendean rebels (which had never been the flag of France). 'Sire, the national cockade is today for you what the Mass was for Henry IV,' Marshal Oudinot pleaded.[10] But Louis would not listen. He also refused to allow anyone not born under the *ancien régime* to play a political role, by restricting the voting franchise to a minimum age of thirty, and eligibility for election to forty. This guaranteed a gerontocracy in politics and condemned young men to dangerous redundancy.

The king fled after a few months, as Napoleon escaped from Elba and marched on Paris. The emperor was welcomed ecstatically by the very people who had been glad to see the back of him only a few months before, and volunteers flocked to the colours with an enthusiasm not seen for years. When Louis XVIII re-entered Paris after the Battle of Waterloo, the reception was hostile. This did not bother him, as he was now firmly in control.

With Napoleon out of the way for good and Russian, German and British troops bivouacking on the streets of Paris, he feared no upheaval. And with the support of the Ultras, reactionaries determined to turn back the clock, he could dominate the elected chamber. Even with figures such as Lafayette at their head, the liberal elements could not mount an effective challenge. What opposition there was remained underground, concentrated in secret societies which included the remains of anti-Napoleonic Babouvist Philadelphes, pro-Napoleonic groups and a selection of obscure sub-masonic confraternities with ludicrous names which Buonarotti tried, unsuccessfully, to bring together from his base in Switzerland. The most active was the Loge des Amis de La Vérité, a masonic organization marked by religious mysticism whose membership included several well-known liberals such as Lafayette and Benjamin Constant. They planned an insurrection that was to break out in August 1820, but this was exposed before it could take place, and the organization was dissolved later that year. A plot to seize the fortress of Belfort and rouse the garrison was also forestalled and the conspirators rounded up. A march on Saumur failed to materialize, while a mutiny at La Rochelle was quickly contained. The trial of three sergeants at La Rochelle and their execution brought discredit to the government, but it did nothing for the opposition, which withered after 1821, thanks to the prevailing apathy. People read Walter Scott and gazed on paintings of medieval romance, which fitted the traditions of monarchy and the Catholic revival. Only a handful of artists, such as Lafayette's protégés David d'Angers and Ary Scheffer, who took an active part in the Belfort conspiracy, were in open revolt. But their numbers would grow, because Louis XVIII was spiritually out of touch with the majority of Frenchmen, and his behaviour offended their perception of themselves, which rested largely on the symbiosis that had arisen between army and nation.

Under the *ancien régime*, the nobility had traditionally considered the practice of arms as the most noble calling, but the virtues it bestowed upon them did not pertain to the common soldier, who was regarded as the lowest of the low, with good reason. 'One must not destroy a nation in order to form an army, and to remove all that is best in it would be to destroy it,' wrote the military reformer Saint-Germain in the 1770s. 'In the present state of things, armies can only be made up of the muck of nations and of all that is useless in society. It is then up to military discipline to purify this corrupted mass, to mould it and to render it serviceable'[11]

In his writings on Corsica and Poland, Rousseau had presented the defender of the motherland as the archetype of communal virtue. He suggested that military service was something every citizen should perform, in the interests not only of mutual defence, but of communal solidarity and personal integration. He identified willingness to fight with the right to national existence. The National Guard was, from the moment of its formation, the symbol of the new French nation. The volunteers of 1792 were represented as '*enfants de la patrie*', endowed with the innocence and purity of children, devoted to their mother. It was about this time that the expression 'baptism of fire' came into use to describe that holiest of all rites of passage. And the sanctity that came from defending the motherland did not evaporate once they crossed her frontiers. For they were engaged on more than the defence of France – they were bringing the message of the brotherhood of man to their fellows. These factors gave rise to an entirely new kind of *esprit de corps*. Before 1789, most soldiers dreamt only of getting back to their villages or finding some warm billet. The revolutionary and Napoleonic Wars created a race of soldiers who came to see the army as their family and their moral community, and to reject the peace and quiet of home.

Out of all this was born the cult of the faithful common soldier, the Napoleonic *grognard*. 'The most beautiful thing after inspiration, is devotion,' wrote Alfred de Vigny, 'after the poet comes the soldier.'[12] In March 1815 Alexandre Dumas, then aged 12, watched the Old Guard march through his village of Villers-Cotterets on its way to Waterloo. 'Oh! let us never forget these men marching with a firm step towards Waterloo, that is to say towards the tomb', he wrote. 'Here was devotion, here was courage, here was honour! here was the purest blood of France! here was twenty years of struggle against the whole of Europe; here was the Revolution, our mother; here was not the French nobility, but the nobility of the French people! [. . .] There was something not only sublime, but also religious, saintly, sacred, in these men who, condemned just as fatally and as irrevocably as any gladiator of antiquity, might have shouted: *Caesar, morituri te salutant!*'[13]

By disbanding the Old Guard, which epitomized everything that was finest about the past twenty-five years, Louis XVIII insulted not only the army but also the honour of his country. This was symptomatic of the whole Restoration regime. The governance of France was recast in an inglorious simulacrum of the *ancien régime* which was offensive to many sensitive people who had no particular liking for Napoleon or his cause. Noble instincts appeared to be out of date. Soldiers who had stuck to the emperor's cause were either shot, imprisoned or proscribed. The dashing, if stupid, Marshal Ney was executed for treason. Honourable patriots such as General Brune were assassinated – and his body was dragged out of its coffin and dishonoured. In the Midi, there were anti-Napoleonic witch-hunts. Less important officers, whose only sin was a refusal to recant their past, were penalized in minor ways, and many a hero was reduced to beggary.

Physical defeat and material failure were easily transformed into spiritual triumph in the Romantic imagination. The literature of the previous century had taught people to associate with great losers such as Prévost's des Grieux, Rousseau's Saint-Preux and Goethe's Werther, their status ennobled by an adaptation of the Christian concept of redemption through suffering and rebirth in death. In the early nineteenth century, the vanquished hero became as much of a cult figure as the unfulfilled genius. The grandeur and beauty of failure even came to make success vaguely suspect. When the heroes of France were being persecuted, happiness could appear an act of betrayal, or at least a sign of moral turpitude.

A refuge for Napoleonic soldiers, the Champ d'Asile, was established by General Lallemand in Texas, where they would supposedly live out their days surrounded by the atmosphere of a cantonment. Relatively few actually did go into exile. A vague but pervasive sense of exile was nevertheless felt by many who never left their native land. And this sense of alienation affected not only redundant soldiers.

The greatest casualties were to be found among the young men of the next generation. 'Conceived between two battles, brought up in schools to the roll of drums, thousands of children eyed each other with a serious look, while testing their puny muscles,' wrote Alfred de Musset. 'From time to time their bloodied fathers appeared, picked them up and pressed them against chests braided in gold, only to put them down and mount their horses once more.'[14] These young men were deprived of the chance to prove themselves, and they felt cheated. 'I belong to that generation, born with the century, nourished on the bulletins of the Emperor, which always had a naked sword before its eyes, and which came forward to seize it just at the moment when France was replacing it in the Bourbon scabbard,' wrote Alfred de Vigny, whose natural proclivities were royalist rather than Napoleonic.[15]

His colleague Musset pointed to the deeper causes of the malady. In his *Confession d'un Enfant du Siècle*, he describes a generation trapped in a limbo between two worlds. Old beliefs had been swept away, but nothing worthy of the name had been found to replace them. These young men had been born and bred to fight, but they had nothing to fight for. They felt robbed of greatness and demeaned by the new state of affairs. 'What is left for us to venerate?' Vigny asked rhetorically. 'In the universal shipwreck of faiths, what debris are there at which generous hands can clutch?'[16]

One piece of debris that floated to the surface was the memory of Napoleon. The emperor's dramatic fall made possible a new attitude towards him. While he was in power, he was a little too real, and occasionally too brutal. Once he had been chained, Prometheus-like, to his Atlantic rock, he could be safely admired. He was divested of responsibility for his own failure by the widespread conviction that his downfall had been 'bought' by small-minded, mercantile Britain. His fall made him fit the paradigm of the Romantic hero, whose divine spark leads him to rise above the herd and aspire to godlike status, and usually ends in nemesis. 'To fall back from Bonaparte and the Empire to that which followed them was to fall from reality into nothingness, from the summit of a mountain into a gulf,' declared Chateaubriand. 'Is not everything finished with Napoleon?' Hate the fallen tyrant as he might, he had to admit that there was poetry in him.[17]

Attempts by the Restoration regime to stamp out such feelings only made them stronger. In 1814 the statue on the Vendôme column was melted down to recast that of Henri IV removed from the Pont-Neuf during the revolution, but people still gathered in silence under the column on Napoleon's birthday. Many Frenchmen carried about in their heads a liturgical calendar whose feast-days were the birthdays of the emperor and the king of Rome, the anniversaries of the coronation, of the deaths of

Desaix and other heroes, and the great victories – Marengo, Austerlitz, Jena, Wagram, and the rest.

The Bourbon government prohibited references to Napoleon and pictorial representations of him and his reign. Writers resorted to allusion and symbol, or just referred to him as '*Lui*' or '*l'Homme*'. Fines and prison sentences were imposed, a long one for the writer who called him 'the son of Man', but more obscure euphemisms were easy to construct. Charlet's lithographs of grenadiers of the Old Guard were instantly recognizable, despite the absence of insignia on their uniforms. Particularly popular were those showing a wounded grenadier or lancer being helped by a comrade – they evoked fraternity and symbolized the nation in its moment of greatness and suffering.

In spite of the thousand miles of ocean separating him from France, Napoleon sensed what was going on in the minds of his former subjects. He instigated books, supposedly written by sympathetic British naval officers, which recorded his 'martyrdom' on St Helena and reflected on his virtues. He wrote memoirs in which he recounted his life and reign. And he dictated thoughts and reflections to his secretary, the Comte de Las Cases, who published them in 1823 as *Le Mémorial de Sainte-Hélène*. This extraordinary work reinvented Napoleon to suit the circumstances and created a legend that gripped the imagination of generations. It was the story of a man not like other men who had risen to the greatest heights attainable on earth, and then endured martyrdom so that his country might be redeemed.

These subliminal messages emanating from St Helena encouraged a consciousness of the Napoleonic age as a golden one. Old soldiers referred to the Empire in their memoirs as 'those wonderful times'. Men who had been conscripted against their will and forced to undergo the horrors of the Spanish campaign before being dragged all the way to Moscow and back, now sat around telling their tales of glory to anyone who cared to listen. The poet Pierre Jean de Béranger, who had wriggled out of military service under the empire and written at least one overtly critical poem in 1813, became the chief propagator of the myth of Napoleon as a champion of liberty and father of the people, gradually elevating him to a level of sainthood.

In his *Couplets sur la journée de Waterloo* Béranger suggested that the fall of Napoleon was a fall into a lesser state for humanity as a whole. But he held out a vision of resurrection. Napoleon had, after all, returned from the limbo of Elba, so surely he could be expected to return from the hell of St Helena. The French countryside perennially rippled with rumours of a landing at Bordeaux, or Toulon, of preparations being made in Italy or in Spain, where a great army was whispered to be massing. There were even rumours of his having raised armies of Americans and Turks.

Napoleon's superhuman nature, his divinity even, became accepted at some level of the French consciousness. Mementoes of every kind were brought out, shown and venerated as though they had been relics. An old woman made an altar around a glass he had drunk from during a short stop on the road. Pieces of a handkerchief, a crust of bread he had not finished eating, even a leaf torn from a tree under which he had stood or rested, were revered as holy relics. There was widespread refusal to believe news of his death in 1821, and rumours of his landing continued to affect rural France throughout the decade. A similar level of faith could be found in every place where Napoleon had brought hope, or just caught the popular imagination. A Polish memoirist recalls that one of the old friars at his school in Warsaw in the 1820s was convinced that Napoleon had merely 'eclipsed himself before the eyes of men, who could not bear the brilliance' but that he carried on ordering everything in the world, and would return one day to set things right.[18] In the 1850s a traveller in Greece came across a peasant who knew all about the death of Leonidas at Thermopylae, but felt sure that the other hero of the day, General Bonapartis, was immortal.[19] Travelling in Patagonia in the 1820s, the naturalist Alcide d'Orbigny encountered natives who wanted to touch him because he had seen 'the demi-god' Napoleon.[20]

The English writer William Hazlitt described Waterloo as 'the sacred triumph of kings over mankind'.[21] Some time later, Heinrich Heine called Waterloo the first station of the Cross. The battlefield drew visitors like no other before or since. Walter Scott travelled specially from Scotland to survey it. He trudged around the rutted field, still strewn with debris and stinking from shallow graves, and picked up souvenirs. When he stood where 'the man whose name had been the terror of Europe' had stood, he was overwhelmed by indescribable emotions.[22] With the exception of Walter Savage Landor, who wove a messianic myth around him, the British did not deify Napoleon, but they were fascinated, particularly by his youthful exploits. Byron wrote several poems on him and, in *Ode on Napoleon*, compared him unfavourably to 'the Cincinnatus of the West', George Washington. But he was also entranced, and visited the field of nemesis, in person and in the Third Canto of *Childe Harold*:

> *And Harold Stands upon this place of skulls,*
> *The grave of France, the deadly Waterloo!*

The Golgotha of French hopes did not presage the anticipated resurrection of Germany. In October 1814, on the anniversary of the Battle of Leipzig, bonfires had been lit on hills the length and breadth of Germany as witness to the new-found unity of the German nation. This great illumination was supposed not only to mark out territory, but also to proclaim the dawn of a new era for the German *Volk*. But those who lit the fires were to be grievously disappointed.

The Congress of Vienna, which had met in September, did nothing to satisfy the passions aroused in the *Freiheitskrieg*. It sanctioned the existing division of the German territories into a German Confederation of thirty-nine states with a common Diet presided over by Austria. This was supposed to replace the old Empire, and in order to suggest a continuity which nobody felt, the Diet was to meet at Frankfurt, where the emperors had traditionally been crowned. Austria had emerged from the revolutionary and Napoleonic era greatly weakened, while Prussia had been strengthened, notably with the Rhineland. This not only made what had been a north-eastern fringe state of Germany a more ubiquitous influence, it also established Prussia as the defender of the German lands against possible future French aggression.

Germany was, by and large, in far better shape than it had been in 1789. The absurd patchwork of a thousand sovereignties had been rationalized into a manageable thirty-nine, and communication between them was facilitated by the germs of a federal structure. But a great many people, particularly the young, were not happy. As Talleyrand reported from Vienna to Louis XVIII, the unification of Germany had become 'their cry, their doctrine, their religion, carried even to fanaticism'.[23]

For those who had dreamed since the 1790s of a new mission for Germany, a new German age, the 1815 settlement was an insult. The young men who had fought for the glory of Germany, and even those who had done no more than toast and sing of the great poetic epos they were living in the *Freiheitskrieg*, were faced with a boring, unhistorical reality, and the humdrum business of making a living. After the excitements of the past decade, this would not do. Liberals wrote of creating some kind of pan-

German union based on a universal legal system; the more radical began to dream of revolution.

University circles were particularly inflamed. New societies were formed, along a pattern thought up by a professor of history at the university of Jena. These *Burschenschaften*, as they were called, were less rowdy and more spiritual than the earlier associations of gymnasts. They were Christian, fervently nationalist, anti-French and hostile to the Jews, who were beginning to play a part in German intellectual life. They adopted the uniform of the Lützow Corps, complete with *altdeutsch* floppy hat. They wore beards and long hair. They carried daggers in their belts. They marched under a flag of black, red and gold, thought to have been the colours of the old German Empire. As faith in the future waned, faith in the past grew, and history supplied many of the comforts traditionally associated with religion. They sought refuge from a world drifting into an age of material progress in a comforting vision of a heroic Teutonic past. 'True to the poesy of their reverie, to the traditions of history, to the cult of the past, they made of an old castle, of an ancient forest, the preserving refuge of the *Burschenschaft*', as Chateaubriand admiringly put it.[24]

Less admiring was Stendhal, whose Gallic sense of the ridiculous never failed him. 'Yesterday I met a tall, handsome young man, German, rich, blond, an aristocrat,' he noted in his Italian travel journal in 1817. 'He talked to me with enthusiasm on the subject of ... a type of baggy pantaloon which they intend to introduce in Germany. If only they manage to institute a national costume, they believe, Europe will not hesitate to recognize their right to be a nation. Poor count! He attaches great weight to this pantaloon; he rates it far higher than twenty days such as Hohenlinden or Marengo. These poor Germans are dying to have some character.'[25]

On 18 October 1817, the fourth anniversary of the Battle of Leipzig, 468 members of the *Burschenschaften* from twelve universities met at the great medieval castle of the Wartburg, where Martin Luther had translated the Bible into German. In celebrating the tercentenary of Luther's launching of the Reformation and the anniversary of Leipzig, they were proclaiming their rejection of Rome as well as France. They were also following the Romantic urge to recover the authentic self from the contrived conventions within which it was supposedly trapped. In the figure of Martin Luther they identified one who had done just this.

The students processed into the Knights' Hall, where they listened to speeches by veterans of the war of liberation, sung hymns, recited prayers, took oaths and exchanged kisses. In the evening, they marched by torchlight to a nearby hill, on which they lit a great bonfire to commemorate the Battle of Leipzig. They then cast into the flames a number of books that calumnied Germany or otherwise incurred their displeasure – including the Code Napoléon – and various symbols of un-German repression that to their mind scarred the Prussian army, such as a Hessian soldier's wig and a corporal's baton. A group of students from Giessen wanted to march off to the battlefield of Leipzig and proclaim a republic there and then. 'Oh! my German people, raise yourself to the high moral dignity of humanity,' wailed a theology student by the name of Karl Ludwig Sand. 'German people, do not allow your sacred nature to be trodden underfoot.'[26]

It was a genuine yelp of pain. Sand's generation was emotionally and morally adrift. His near-contemporary Karl Immermann would describe their malaise as 'a desolate irresolution and perturbation, a ridiculous quest for security, a distractedness, a chasing after one knows not what, a fear of terrors that are the more uncanny for having no form! It is as if mankind, cast about in its boat on an overpowering sea, is suffering from a moral seasickness whose end can hardly be conceived.'[27] This predicament made them seek solace or oblivion elsewhere. Many were drawn towards the pure climate or the new world. The protagonists of several novels written at the time travel to America to fight for freedom, find oblivion or, most commonly, just to redeem themselves. Poems extolled the redemptive qualities of the land of freedom and hope, and in a novel published in 1815, Joseph von Eichendorff sends his hero off to America to find the spiritual strength to return and continue the struggle for Germany. 'From America the sun will illuminate and give life to a new Germany, and bring back seed and springtime to old Germany,' the poet Jean Paul Richter had written a couple of years earlier. In 1819 a Berlin university lecturer by the name of Karl Follen sketched his plan of founding a German republic in America. It was to be an ethical polity based partly on the writings of the Stoics and partly on Jacobin principles, and it would provide a model for the regeneration of the mother country.[28] But America was not the imagined panacea, as those who actually went there soon discovered. It was not even what it had been in the 1780s.

As soon as they had won their political independence from England, the Americans had begun to abandon their revolutionary rhetoric in favour of self-righteous conservatism. They remained steadfastly English in their attitudes and, having achieved their blessed republican state, paraded the same smugness of liberal superiority towards the rest of the world. 'Many hundred years must roll away before we shall be corrupted,' wrote John Adams to Thomas Jefferson in 1813. 'Our pure, virtuous, public-spirited, federative republic will last forever, govern the globe and introduce the perfection of man.'[29]

The conservatism of the Americans had been reinforced by the French Revolution, which the majority viewed with horror. Its excesses supplied the religious with powerful arguments with which to discredit the Enlightenment, and helped them to lead their brethren in the Second Great Awakening of the 1790s. They encouraged isolationism in those who dreamed of Rousseauist agrarian utopias no less than in those engaged on religious flight from the corruptions of the world. They allowed George Washington to cut the United States off from Europe's quarrels through his Proclamation of Neutrality in April 1793, and, in his Farewell Address of 17 September 1796, to cut his country off from the European revolutionary tradition as a whole, in what has been termed a second American declaration of independence. When, in 1802, Thomas Paine returned to America, he was vilified. Jefferson, who gave a dinner in his honour, was attacked for it. Thereafter he took his dinners at the Lovell's Hotel, where, according to one American, 'he dines at the public table, and, as a show, is as profitable to Lovell as an *Orang Outang*, for many strangers who come to the city feel a curiosity to see the creature'.[30]

The Americans worshipped their common political heritage in formulaic holidays such as the Fourth of July. In the 1790s they embarked on the building of a federal capital, the first in the Western world to be purpose-built. It was to be not only a political instrument of governance but also a shrine. But while they worshipped their state, the Americans did not feel a need to sacrifice themselves to it. One American lamented that they 'no longer treat liberty as lovers but as husbands'.[31] Those seeking salvation went to chapel or meeting-house; those more interested in adventure rode out not to fight for liberty in anyone's cause but to conquer Indian or, later, Mexican land. Only in the mid-1820s did a few bestir themselves to go and fight for Greek independence, and that was partly under the influence of Lafayette. The old warrior had come to his second homeland in 1824 at the invitation of President James Monroe. His progress round the country was an unprecedented affair, with thousands massing to meet him at every stage. He laid foundation-stones and unveiled monuments, he prostrated himself before the coffin of Washington and kissed it, while others prostrated themselves before him and kissed his hands and his clothes. But he went home, and the Americans got on with their lives.

In June 1782 the Congress had adopted the image of an eagle for its seal, and this became the emblem of the new nation. The eagle was usually set beside a young girl representing liberty, often in quite affectionate communion. As time passed, the figure of liberty was more often shown clutching a cornucopia than a pike, surrounded by bowls of fruit, sheaves of corn and agricultural implements. Miss Liberty was gradually replaced by Miss Plenty, republican virtue by capitalist well-being. While the poets lamented, the majority of Americans embraced the faith of peace and prosperity. European dreamers in search of the purity of the new world, such as the German Romantic poet Nikolaus Lenau, were horrified.

America could not help regenerate Germany, not in the way envisaged. There could be no escape for the Germans smarting under the perceived humiliation of seeing their country denied gratification in her lust for nationhood. The one-time Jacobin Joseph Görres believed that in 1815 German man had been condemned to slavery. 'He must never, at the risk of severe punishment, think of his country, which they have torn to shreds,' he wrote. 'He is allowed to ape all foreign follies, but when the young generation tried to bring back old German customs it was accused of Teutomania.'[32]

One of those making fun of the German nationalists was the minor dramatist August Friedrich von Kotzebue, a reactionary who was also an informer for the Tsar. On 23 March 1819, while he was going about his business in Mannheim, he was stabbed to death by the student Karl Ludwig Sand. The act provoked predictable outrage, and Sand was executed. But the young fanatic quickly became a martyr, and handkerchiefs dipped in his blood were torn into small pieces and passed around as relics.

Metternich called the principal rulers of Germany together and forced them to issue the so-called Karlsbad Decrees, by which the universities were brought under strict supervision, the student societies dissolved and the press muzzled. The decrees were hardly draconian and were sluggishly implemented, but they constituted a challenge. In the words of Görres, who had to flee the Rhineland and take refuge in Strasbourg, they ushered in a new epoch. It was a time of 'the breaking open of trunks and boxes, the going and coming of the gens d'armes and police agents ... the examinations and sealings of papers, arrests, and discharges from arrest' – in short, the era of the new Inquisition.[33]

The new order, as epitomized by Metternich's Austria, certainly shared characteristics with the Inquisition. It was more interested in sins of the spirit than acts of the body, in inferred heresy than venial transgression. It believed in prophylaxis. When one of his plays had been rejected, the Austrian dramatist Franz von Grillparzer confronted the censor, demanding to know which were the offending passages. The censor, all affability, said that there appeared to be nothing at all objectionable about the play, but then 'One never can tell'.[34] And the new Inquisition was just as implacable as the old. János Bacszany had been arrested on the flimsiest grounds in connection with the Hungarian Jacobin conspiracy of 1794. He was released in 1796, and settled in Vienna. He was there when the French occupied the city in 1809, and he helped Napoleon to pen a proclamation calling on the Hungarians to rise up and declare independence. Prudently, Bacszany moved to Paris in the wake of the French forces, and it was there that the Austrians caught up with him in 1814. He was dragged back and gaoled until his death in 1845.

In 1819 the king of Prussia erected a national monument to the War of Liberation on the Kreuzberg in Berlin. It was a fine Gothic affair designed by Karl Friedrich Schinkel, the only revolutionary element of which was its iron construction. This monument was supposed to set the seal on the whole episode. In 1807 the Crown Prince Ludwig of Bavaria had begun to dream of building a great national shrine, where Germans could come to find their true national spirit. But these dreams would not take substance until 1842, when Schinkel completed the Walhalla near Regensburg. Ernst von Blandel's statue of the ancient warrior Hermann, begun in 1819, would not be erected until 1875. German dreamers would in the meantime continue to meet in ruined castles and on the battlefield of Leipzig.

The Battle of Leipzig was not called 'the Battle of the Nations' for nothing. Many roads crossed at Leipzig. Wolfe Tone's son William, an officer of Chasseurs in Napoleon's army, won the cross of the Légion d'Honneur during the battle. General Donatien de Rochambeau, Knight of the Orders of St Louis and the Cincinnati, defender of American liberty and butcher of Saint-Domingue, was killed in it. So was Prince Józef

Poniatowski. It occurred when the Polish corps making up Napoleon's rearguard fell back on the River Elster only to find that their French comrades had blown the bridges. Dozens of representations of this episode were produced, in France, England, Germany and Austria, but the most emblematic and most frequently copied is the etching by Horace Vernet. It shows the wounded prince astride his white charger raising his eyes to heaven as the horse dives into the swirling current. 'God entrusted to me the honour of the Poles, to him I return it!' he is, apocryphally, supposed to have exclaimed at this moment.

The actual circumstances of the prince's death are somewhat different. He had been wounded four times during the three-day battle, and he was exhausted and feverish when his horse waded into the river and began to swim across. Just as it started to clamber up the opposite bank, he received the fatal bullet and fell back into the river. But such details are irrelevant. Poniatowski was universally admired, for his chivalry as much as his military talents. After the débâcle of 1812, he had been offered generous terms by the anti-Napoleonic coalition if he abandoned Napoleon and brought the Polish army over to their side. But he refused to desert his ally in the hour of need. Regardless of political sympathy, the whole of Europe wanted to see in the dashing Polish prince a latter-day Marcus Curtius, an unblemished hero leaping into the chasm to save the honour of his motherland. This icon perfectly conveyed the tragic yet magnificent end of the Poles' Napoleonic epos.

'The Poles are the only Europeans who can serve under the banners of Napoleon without blushing,' Madame de Staël had written a year before.[35] The Polish soldiers who were obliged to repress the blacks on Saint-Domingue and those who found themselves quelling bands of patriots in Spain might have demurred at this statement. What she meant was that they had not been given the chance to serve honourably under any other banner, and that while serving under Napoleon's they never ceased to fight for their own cause. Superimposed on the tricolor cockade they wore on their head-dress was the splayed knight's cross which had been the emblem of the Confederation of Bar. And the four-cornered *czapka* of the Napoleonic lancers was a stylized version of the *konfederatka*, the cap favoured by the Barians, and later taken up by the National Cavalry of 1791. Every Polish unit saw itself as a microcosm of the Polish nation.

Polish enthusiasm for Napoleon had always been qualified, and his abandonment of the cause of liberation in 1801 had further diminished it.

The grisly fate of the legions in Saint-Domingue killed it off altogether. The leading Polish statesman of the day, Prince Adam Czartoryski, advocated co-operation with Russia against Napoleon. A grateful Tsar Alexander would, the argument went, be inclined to grant Poland independence. But after the Battle of Jena in 1806 Napoleon's armies appeared on Polish territory. His defeat of the country's three oppressors could not but be agreeable to the Poles, and his next step was a challenge. If the Poles could show him that they were 'worthy of being a nation', he promised to give them a country. This could not fail to elicit enthusiasm. Young people flocked to the colours, burning to fight for the cause, and they did not analyse his motives. In 1807 he established a small Polish state, the Duchy of Warsaw, which he milked mercilessly for recruits and cash, and he ultimately dashed all the hopes he had aroused.

The majority of Poles had every reason to welcome the settlement of 1815. The kingdom of Poland that had been rubbed off the map twenty years before was back, albeit greatly reduced in size and ruled by the Tsar of Russia, as King Aleksander II. The ancient capital Kraków, disputed by all three neighbours, became a tiny independent republic. Large numbers of Poles were left stranded in Prussia, in Habsburg-ruled Galicia, and in the Western Gubernias of Russia. But now there was at least a Polish state, with one of the most liberal constitutions in Europe.

In his speech at the opening of the Sejm in 1818, Alexander intimated that he wanted to reunite all former Polish lands under his rule, which would have entailed detaching the Western Gubernias of Russia and adding them to the kingdom of Poland. But on the same occasion two years later he warned the Poles not to entertain ideas of autonomy. When some Deputies started insisting on the execution of certain constitutional rights, he closed down the session and threatened to abolish the constitution altogether. While still occasionally professing liberalism, he began to curtail freedoms and introduce repressive measures, bringing a number of Russians in to replace Poles in key jobs. However disappointing this might have been, it was a great deal more than any Pole could justifiably have hoped for after the catastrophe of the partitions.

But Napoleon had transformed Poland. 'What was this land before his eye came to look on it?' asked Kajetan Koźmian in a poem written in 1809.[36] He had awakened a society traumatized by the partitions, allowed it to share in his glory and set it dreaming. Napoleon had also given Polish heroism and gallantry the opportunity to shine on the world stage and wipe out the shame of the partitions. Between 1797 and 1815 over a quarter-of-a-million Poles had fought alongside the French in every campaign. The bravery, professionalism and loyalty of the Polish soldier earned the respect of the whole of Europe. Old Dąbrowski was still fighting at the gates of Paris in 1814, half of the troops that followed Napoleon to exile on the island of Elba were Polish Light-Horse, there were Polish units at Waterloo and among the last faithful battalions on the Loire, and a Pole sailed with him to St Helena. All of this and more was present in that image of Poniatowski leaping into the Elster, and that is why it hung in every patriotic Polish home. It was an icon representing not just the martyrdom of one of the nation's greatest saints. It also stood for a duty accomplished and a pledge redeemed.

It was an image of failure. But it was triumphantly one of greatness in failure. Literature had made failure morally superior, Napoleon had made it heroic. The print of Poniatowski at Leipzig, that battle where the soldiers of France and Poland stood alone against the nations of Europe, tied the Polish defeat to Napoleon's nemesis, and therefore to his enduring glory. This made the Napoleonic epos dangerously seductive to the Poles, and that is why a likeness of Napoleon also hung in every home.

The conviction, deeply held in France, that Napoleon's downfall had been 'bought', was shared by many Poles. This allowed generations of them to refuse to face up to unattractive realities. A world in which Poland could be partitioned and Napoleon defeated was not a world they wished to live in. Settling down to life at home after the wars, Aleksander Fredro found it painful, as one might find it to dwell on some intense love in the past, to talk of those days 'when a sea of hope and a drop of glory transformed life into the real life of the soul'.[37]

In 1815 a seventeen-year-old called Adam Mickiewicz went up to the university of Wilno in Lithuania. On the registration form, he put his name down as 'Adam Napoleon Mickiewicz'. His reason for giving himself this name was that he believed the sight of the *Grande Armée* marching through on its way to Moscow in 1812 had been his 'spiritual baptism'. There was nothing unusual about such an attitude. Ludwik Jabłonowski, who was only a few months old in 1812, cherished to the end of his life a strong memory of himself in the arms of a nanny in the doorway of a house as Napoleon rode by. 'Perhaps by some chance he cast a glance at me,' the baby later wrote, 'and with that glance took my spirit into a magnetic slavery, which lasts still and will endure to my death.'[38]

In adopting a new name at the start of his university life, the young Mickiewicz was entering an alternative world of the spirit. After a year of mathematics and natural science, he transferred to a course in literature, and began writing verse. In 1817, with a group of friends, he founded the Philomaths, an apolitical secret society dedicated to the propagation of knowledge. In the same year the students of Warsaw University founded one called Panta Koyna (Everything in Common) aimed, like the Philomaths, at reforming society through education. Both were inspired by the example of the *Burschenschaften*. In 1819 the Wilno society grew more political, with Mickiewicz stressing the need to 'implant a profound sense of nationhood' alongside the dissemination of knowledge. After graduating, he took a job as teacher in a school in Kowno, but he did not cease to play an active part in student life in Wilno. In 1820 he was involved with a new society, the Association of the Radiant, and later the same year helped to found the Philareths, which showed distinct affinities with the Masons and the Carbonari, to be succeeded in 1822 by the Philadelphians, which had a more active programme of proselytizing. But what such groups sought and what they taught had more to do with pseudo-religious self-fulfilment than politics.

In 1822 Mickiewicz published a volume of poetry, *Ballads and Romances*, which launched the Romantic movement in Polish literature. His literary pedigree was heavily marked by English and German Romantic authors, but his preoccupations were with history, nationality and the lore of the common people. Mickiewicz's next major poem told of a princess who sacrifices her life for her people in their struggle against the Teutonic Knights. It expressed sentiments that were beginning to stir in the breast of educated Polish youth, which insistently ignored the political benefits of the Vienna settlement and chose to see only a spiritual vale of tears. 'My very first impressions on growing out of childhood were caused by the dolorous state of the country, torn apart by three rapacious neighbours,' writes Natalia Kicka, a girl ten years younger than Mickiewicz. 'So from the very moment that I was in a position to consider my own thoughts and feelings, the love of our motherland embraced my heart with a ring of fire. In my sleep as in waking I heard the lament issuing from a million breasts, so it is no wonder that I fell so ardently in love with my motherland.'[39] The lament she heard was not that of the peasants caught in the trap of economic serfdom, but of well-born dreamers. Her generation had come to see the motherland not merely as a country to be regained, but as a paradise to be entered, and they avidly craved the struggle and the sacrifices that would have to be borne in order to achieve it. They were to be richly rewarded.

In January 1824 a group of schoolboys in Wilno plastered the walls of their school with patriotic declarations, and over a hundred of them were arraigned before a military court. Death sentences were meted out, but these were then commuted to floggings and service in the ranks of Russian regiments in far-flung provinces. The investigations had uncovered the various student networks, and in August 1824 Mickiewicz and twenty other Philomaths were condemned to internal exile. The following year Alexander would be succeeded by Nicholas I, who was to prove a worthy Nebuchadnezzar. 'Sometimes I see Nicholas as a tool chosen by Providence to enflame our love of motherland, and to deepen our faith and raise it to heights hitherto unattainable to us,' Natalia Kicka opined.[40]

12
Phantom Causes

The Romantic imagination soared above such earthy matters as practical assistance to the downtrodden and physical succour of the destitute. It flew to confront what it saw as more fundamental, spiritual wrongs. It was highly selective in seeking them out, guided by its sense of drama, pathos, heroism, Faustian destiny and not least of the picturesque. It identified causes where there were none, projecting its own aspirations on to societies which, viewed through a prism of ignorance and wishful thinking, appeared to fit the bill. Its quixotic instincts commanded action on behalf of such causes, and in the decade following the Napoleonic Wars this gave rise to a string of purposeless revolts and a chronicle of ludicrous errantry.

Nowhere was this more evident than in Spanish America, which seemed set, after the liberation of Spain from Napoleonic domination, to resume a degree of stability. A Spanish force of 10,000 men was assembled under the command of General Pablo Morillo, and on 15 February 1815 it sailed from Cadiz on forty-two transports escorted by eighteen warships, the largest armada ever to have sailed for the new world. On 16 April it appeared in the roads of Carupano, by May Morillo was in Caracas, and over the next year he recovered most of New Granada. A man of the people who had risen to prominence in the Peninsular War, Morillo was a national hero. He was greeted warmly wherever he went, by a population that longed for the peace and stability of the old days and cherished unjustifiably fond feelings for King Ferdinand. True to Bourbon reputation, this one-time darling of patriots and liberals had apparently learned nothing from experience. He failed to grasp that the relationship between the mother country and the colonies had been irreversibly altered, and over the next few years he and his officials did much to create disaffection with Spanish rule and a desire for autonomy. But this desire would have borne little fruit had it not been for outside factors.

British merchants, excluded from trading in the area by Spain, had always longed to penetrate what they imagined to be some kind of Eldorado. They assumed that independent states would open their markets and were therefore disposed to assist all independence-minded Creoles. Anti-Bourbon prejudice combined with liberal feeling to make the cause of Spanish America's 'liberation' popular in Britain. The government repeatedly stated its position as being one of strict non-intervention, but Royal Navy vessels in the area regularly assisted various 'patriots', under the general guise of looking after British trading interests. Much the same was true of the United States. This meant that the whole of Spanish America was wide open to anyone who wished to land there and live out their dreams.

The greatest beneficiary of this was the Liberator Bolívar, whose reputation as a dashing freedom fighter had unaccountably spread throughout the Western world. He had twice been rejected by a population who did not see themselves as a nation and wanted to be liberated only from the chaos and devastation caused by civil strife. But he was determined. 'Colombians prefer to descend to the eternal abysses rather than be Spaniards,' he thundered at one Spanish general who proposed conciliation, and he was prepared to drag the country down to hell if that was what it took.[1]

In the last days of 1815 he sailed to the Republic of Haiti, whose president, Alexandre Pétion, agreed to help him on condition that Bolívar committed himself to the liberation of slaves in Spanish America. Bolívar took command of the remnants of the Venezuelan patriot forces evacuated from Cartagena, which had sailed in on a flotilla of ten ships under the French corsair, Aury. Bolívar sacked Aury and replaced him with Pierre Louis Brion, a restless Dutchman from Curaçao. A number of other foreigners came forward to swell the Liberator's ranks and many Haitians also enlisted. Pétion gave Bolívar arms and money, as did various English merchants, and on 10 April 1816 Bolívar's force sailed. 'Admiral' Brion commanded the whole, 'attired in an English hussar jacket and scarlet pantaloons, with a broad stripe of gold lace down each side, a field marshal's uniform hat, with a very large Prussian plume, and an enormous pair of dragoon boots, with heavy gold spurs of a most inconvenient length', according to one eyewitness.[2] The expedition was a fiasco, as nobody in New Granada wanted to join the cause. 'Instead of contributing to the restoration of liberty they enlist of their own free will under the flag of the Spanish tyrants and most actively co-operate to our destruction,' Bolívar complained.[3] He sailed back to Haiti where, after declaring Pétion to be superior to Washington, 'a man rising above his country and his age', he begged him for further military aid.[4]

These were trying times for Pétion. Hardly had he furnished Bolívar with more men and arms, when another freedom fighter alighted on the shores of Haiti: the Spaniard Francisco Xavier Mina. As a student he had fought against the French in the siege of Saragossa in 1809, and gone on to become a daring guerilla leader. His loyalty to the liberal constitution of 1812 quickly landed him in trouble with the restored regime of Ferdinand VII, and he took refuge in England. There he engaged the support of a number of merchants for a plan to liberate Mexico. He arrived in Haiti accompanied by a small force of British and American followers, with enough money to raise and equip further volunteers. Having done so, he set sail and landed at Soto de la Marina in Mexico. After a few minor successes, Mina was captured and shot on 13 November 1817, while most of his foreign supporters fled to the United States.

Next came the Scots charlatan Gregor McGregor. He had fought on with surprising tenacity after the débâcle of Miranda's second expedition. Having been ousted from his command by local warlords, he raised another force and tried his hand in Panama. Failing to get a foothold here, he sailed off to Haiti, and thence to America, where he raised a force of 150 men with the intention of liberating Florida from the Spanish yoke. They landed on the island of Amelia off the Florida coast and declared it to be 'liberated'. But they were quickly robbed of their prize. Bolívar's erstwhile admiral, Aury, who had spent the intervening two years in piracy and attempts to invade Texas, now sailed in and captured Amelia from McGregor. Aury thereupon declared the independence of the Republic of Amelia. Early in 1818, he sailed to the island of Providence, intending to set up another republic there. As commander on Amelia, he left a newly-met Frenchman, Maurice Persat.

Persat was in every sense a product of the Napoleonic epos. He had fought his way up from the ranks in half-a-dozen campaigns and been personally decorated with the Légion d'Honneur by the emperor. He was at Waterloo as a captain of lancers, and would have fought to the bitter end on the Loire. In 1815 he was thinking of going to settle in the Champ d'Asile set up in Texas by General Lallemand. But then he read about Bolívar and, with a few comrades, decided to join him. At the port of Le Havre in the spring of 1817, he met a group of French officers returning from Venezuela whose accounts put Persat and his friends off the idea. But they sailed for the new world anyway, having got wind of an alleged plan by Joseph Bonaparte in New York to rescue Napoleon from St Helena. When they reached New York, it turned out that no such plan existed. With nothing better to do, in September 1817 Persat and his comrades sailed for Venezuela. In the Gulf of Mexico their ship found itself in the path of a hurricane, but Persat braved the elements by making the company sing the *Marseillaise* as it heaved and plunged. This act of faith saw them through, and after they emerged from the storm they fell in with Aury. Persat's command in Amelia was short-lived. On 22 December the US Army occupied the island. Persat then went to Haiti, where he raised a contingent of a couple of hundred men, mostly former Napoleonic soldiers, with a view to joining Bolívar at Angostura on the River Orinoco.

Bolívar had reached the mainland on the last day of 1816, but after another failed attempt to take Caracas, he retired eastwards to the province of Guyana. He was hampered at every step by the waywardness of the patriot leaders and the open rivalry of some, like Antonio Paez, chief of the plains horsemen. In the face of what was increasingly obviously a messy civil war, he decided to give himself greater legitimacy. He convoked a congress which met in February 1819 in the town of Angostura. While the whole exercise was primarily meant to bestow formal dictatorship on him, the Liberator could not resist the opportunity of describing the brave new nation he meant to create combining the best of Athens, Sparta and Rome, governed by 'a holy tribunal' to ensure the highest level of morality.[5] There was a way to go.

'On my arrival at Angostura, there were many more officers than soldiers,' recorded Persat, who joined Bolívar there in 1818, 'and what soldiers! unfortunate blacks who had only been given their freedom so they might be killed by the Spaniards or die of hunger and poverty, for the Republic had neither finances, nor quartermastership, nor uniform depot, so that many of these poor devils regretted their slavery.'[6] The place was full of Napoleonic officers, many of them disenchanted and on the point of leaving. Bolívar promised to give Persat and a former lancer of the Guard, a Pole by the name of Marzewski, regiments of their own, but after witnessing the quarrels of the commanders and seeing the patriots in action, the two men decided to quit. When Persat returned to Europe, he was reprimanded for airing negative views of Bolívar and his cause. European public opinion wanted to believe in the myth of valiant South Americans fighting for their freedom.[7] And there was no shortage of chivalrous souls longing to give their all to such a cause.

'In this country, it is only necessary to represent a nation fighting for liberty, to excite a generous sympathy,' wrote George Chesterton, a captain of horse recently discharged from the British army. He was walking down the Strand in London in 1817, dejectedly contemplating a dull future on some small estate in the country, when he bumped into a brother officer. 'Now, my boy,' exclaimed the latter, 'for South America, flags, banners, glory, and riches.' And he dragged him off to Grafton Street to see Luis Lopez Mendez, who had been instructed by Bolívar to form up and send over complete units.[8] Mendez had handed the task to a Colonel English, who proposed the formation of two regiments of hussars, two of lancers, one regiment of riflemen, and one of artillery.[9]

In May 1817 Gustavus Hippisley, a half-pay lieutenant, began organizing the 1st Venezuelan Hussars, of which he was to be colonel. They were fitted out in 'a dark green jacket, with scarlet collar, lapels and cuff; some figured gold lace round the collar and cuff, with an ornamented Austrian knot on the arm above; a laced girdle round the waist, and two small gold scaled epaulettes; dark green trowsers edged with similar gold lace down the sides.'[10] The 2nd 'Red' Hussars had even more gorgeous uniforms, and the lancers and artillery vied with each other. But the regimentals of Colonel Campbell's 1st Venezuelan Riflemen stole the show. Each regiment acquired a band and a banner inscribed with the motto '*morir o vencer*'.

A goodly proportion of these men joined up in order to escape some personal problem, or simply found peacetime irksome after the excitements of war. But most of them were 'dazzled by representations of immortal glory that awaited the liberators of millions of human beings, pining under the united influence of religious and political slavery', according to Chesterton, who cited examples of an officer actually selling his commission in the Guards in order to join up, and of another who spent £1,200 of his own money on fitting out a unit. The poet John Keats was among those stirred by the idea of going off to fight in Venezuela. 'Success to the enterprise of the Spanish South American patriots, and a glorious triumph to their cause, came from the mouth of nearly every Briton!' explains Hippisley.[11]

The first contingent, totalling nearly 900 men, set sail in five ships in December 1817, with bands blaring. One of the vessels foundered on the Ushant rocks, and the whole complement of the 1st Venezuelan Lancers, uniforms and all, went to the bottom. The rest sailed on, their enthusiasm gradually sapped by provisioning difficulties in the Azores and the monotony of the voyage. By the time they reached the West Indies, morale had sunk to dangerous levels. The rank-and-file began deserting, the officers quarrelled and duelled. They were kept hanging about at Margarita, losing men to disease and desertion, and the remaining 150 did not disembark on the Guyanan mainland until July 1818.

No preparations had been made to receive the arrivals. This was reflected in appalling physical conditions and lack of victuals. They were nevertheless supposed to parade solemnly around a liberty tree hurriedly transplanted to commemorate the eighth anniversary of the proclamation of Venezuela's independence. In the absence of the promised pay, the volunteers were soon selling off bits of their uniforms, which found a ready market among the local Napoleons. Colonel Macdonald was murdered for his. The soldiers' boots had fallen to pieces, and many were parading barefoot and half-naked. Their disgust at the way they were treated turned to contempt when they witnessed the cowardice of some of the patriot commanders, and to abhorrence when they saw prisoners being butchered in cold blood.

They were mostly unimpressed by the Liberator. With his large head and small spindly legs encased in tight breeches and huge boots, Bolívar did not cut a dashing figure. Within six months several British officers had left, including the enthusiastic Chesterton. Hippisley sold his cocked hat and feather to a delighted Bolívar before he went. Once back in London, Hippisley tried to have Mendez arrested, but no amount of detrimental reports could stop young men avid to shed their blood for Spanish America's liberty. Another 700 under a Colonel Elsam arrived before the end of 1818, along with some hussars from Belgium and a steady flow of individuals from virtually every country in Europe. A second contingent recruited by Colonel English, the 1,000-strong British Legion, landed on 14 July 1819, at the same time as a group of Hanoverians under Colonel

Johannes Uslar. Conditions at Angostura had gone from bad to worse; of the 700 that arrived with Elsam, 350 died from fever before they had a chance to fire a shot for liberty. Devoid of medical supplies, J. B. Siegert, chief surgeon to the British Legion, treated the fever with a concoction of local spices and herbs which, if it did little to help his patients, later made him a fortune and enlivened many a cocktail when marketed as 'Angostura Bitters'.

But there was no stemming the flow of volunteers. The irrepressible Gregor McGregor made his way to London, where he borrowed money from Mendez and began raising a 'Hibernia Regiment', very much in his own image, described as 'stuffed turkies' and 'walking wine vaults' by one newspaper.[12] McGregor sailed into Porto Bello with his men, captured the town, trampled the Spanish flag, designed the regalia for a new Order of the Knights of the Green Cross, and set about drinking and whoring. When the Spanish counter-attacked, he sailed away, leaving his Hibernians to face the music.

He was run close in fecklessness by John Devereux, the son of an Irishman executed for his part in the rebellion of 1798. After meeting Bolívar and receiving his approval, he returned to Ireland, where he began a profitable recruiting campaign by selling commissions to adventurous young men eager to fight for liberty. He so impressed Daniel O'Connell that the Irish patriot bought a commission for his own son, Morgan, aged fourteen. The 'Irish Friends of South American Independence' gave a banquet in his honour at which Ireland was urged to give her sons 'to unmanacle the slave, to unsceptre the despot, to erect an altar on the Inquisition's grave, to raise a people to the altitude of freedom'.[13]

Devereux sent out a total of 2,100 men, in two echelons. They landed on the island of Margarita, where 750 caught yellow fever and died. The remainder ran out of money and resorted to selling their kit, while some deserted and went off to the United States. Eventually, Devereux set sail himself. On arrival at Margarita, he came ashore arrayed in French field-marshal's uniform and mounted his horse for the triumphal ride into town. The animal, which had been confined on a heaving ship for the past two months, could not resist the lure of a muddy pond. Without pausing to throw its cavalier, the horse plunged in and began rolling around in the ooze. Nothing daunted, Devereux squelched into the banquet arranged in his honour and delivered a speech, lasting fully two hours, to the effect that he was personally ready to kill every Spaniard in

South America. He drew his sword for greater effect, but this startled more than it delighted his listeners, none of whom had a word of English.

Devereux, who styled himself 'the Lafayette of South America', never once came under fire, but he ended up being buried in the National Pantheon in Caracas. And even if the overwhelming majority of those he had sent off from Ireland never lifted a finger in the cause of liberty, there were enough brave and useful men among them to redeem the rest. One such was Francis Burdett O'Connor, brother of Fergus, who fought hard and long for liberty, and died a Bolivian general.

It is estimated that as many as 6,000 European volunteers passed through Bolívar's ranks. There were probably no more than about 1,200 in his army during any one campaign, and only a hard core of a few hundred stayed with him from beginning to end. But when one remembers that there were rarely more than about 3,000 men engaged on either side in any of the battles he fought, their contribution can be appreciated.[14] As a rule, the most committed were those who had come on their own, drawn by personal conviction. They included Frenchmen, such as Baron Bruix, a former page to Napoleon, and Charles Éloi Demarquet; Italians such as Agostino Codazzi, a Napoleonic artillery officer; the Swedish Count Frederick Adlercreutz, the German Baron Friedrich von Eben; and Poles such as Ludwik Flegel and Ferdynand Sierakowski. But even some of those from the units recruited by English turned out to be devoted to the cause, despite their appalling treatment. One such was Daniel Florence O'Leary, a cornet with Wilson's Red Hussars who later became Bolívar's aide-de-camp. And few could outdo Colonel James Rooke, who was put in command of all the Britons who had survived Angostura. When his arm was torn off by a cannon-ball, he picked it up and waved it in the air, shouting '*Viva la Patria!*' Asked which country he was referring to, England or Ireland? he answered: 'The one which is to give me burial.' He died of the wound a couple of days later.[15]

Such heroics seem grotesquely inappropriate to the circumstances. There was no *patria* on the South American continent. The sonorous slogan had been hijacked by a few ambitious men born of the Spanish American tradition of insubordination, spiritual heirs of Cortés and Pizarro. Their ultimate aims were hazy and confused – Bolívar swung between democratic principles and dreams of continental empire, as did his counterpart in La Plata, San Martin. Their immediate purpose was power. To achieve this they laboured the myth of a people groaning under

Spanish slavery and despotism. But their only hope of success lay in projecting a Napoleonic image, in presenting themselves as meteors to the tails of which men with similar dreams but lesser daring might hitch their hopes. This was why they aped Napoleon and why they sought their crossing of the Alps and their Marengo.

José de San Martin did not quite fit the pattern of the disgruntled Creole rebelling against the metropolis out of personal pique. While he was born in Uruguay, in 1778, both his parents were Spaniards; when he was only seven years old his father, an officer, was posted back to Spain and young José went to school in Madrid. From there, he went on to join the army. He fought against revolutionary France and against the British, and then alongside them in the Peninsular War. Having gained the rank of lieutenant-colonel, he decided to leave the Spanish service and go to the Americas. By early 1812 he was in Buenos Aires, where he offered his services to the junta. He formed up a corps of mounted grenadiers, which he led to victory over the royalists at Tucumán.

By 1815 the colony had asserted its independence but remained vulnerable. The base of Spanish power on the South American continent was in Peru, from which it spread southwards through Chile to the Viceroyalty of La Plata. The revolutionary movement in Chile had been defeated in 1814, and the patriot Bernardo O'Higgins was forced to seek refuge across the Andes in La Plata. It was here that he came across San Martin, who was based in the provincial capital of Mendoza. In San Martin's study, on the wall of which hung an engraving of Napoleon, they began to plot the truly Napoleonic enterprise of crossing the Andes.

San Martin assembled an army of some 4,000 men, half of them former slaves, with a 100-strong 'British Legion' composed of British and American expatriates. He had sent small forces over two of the possible Andes passes in order to confuse the Spaniards, before setting out in January 1817 with his main body of troops over the third. The crossing of the *cordillera* was a terrifying undertaking which could easily have turned into disaster. It was a feat of generalship on the part of San Martin and of endurance on the part of his men, and it firmly established his legend as a latter-day Hannibal.

Once over the Andes, San Martin defeated the royalists at Chacabuco on 12 February 1817 and entered Santiago. He re-established an independent government, presided over by O'Higgins, and in April 1818 defeated the remaining royalist forces at Maipú. But while Chile was almost free of royalist troops, royalist sentiment had not died, and there was no sense of Chilean nationhood to replace it. The moment he stopped fighting, San Martin's position grew shaky, as did that of Bolívar, who had decided to emulate him.

In May 1819 Bolívar marched out of Angostura with all the men he could muster, crossed the mountains and descended on New Granada, taking the Spanish forces from behind. It had been an even more perilous undertaking than San Martin's, a great achievement by any standards, and it had the desired effect of enhancing his standing at a stroke. In August he routed the Spanish forces at Boyacá. On 18 September he entered Santa Fé de Bogotá to a carefully stage-managed reception, preceded by his Grenadiers of the Guard and the English 'Albion' Legion. He went to the Cathedral to hear mass and the singing of a *Te Deum*, then he ascended a podium, from which he listened to a hymn sung in his honour while twenty maidens dressed in white brought forth a laurel crown, which they placed on his brow.

In December 1819 the Liberator was back in Angostura, where he proclaimed the birth of the Republic of Colombia, of which he was unanimously elected President. But Colombia was no more a *patria* than Chile, and it would fall apart from its own inertia. Neither San Martin in Chile nor Bolívar in New Granada was strong enough to impose his authority over a largely royalist population and rival patriot generals, let alone withstand determined opposition by Spain. But just as this was being prepared, Spain herself was plunged into chaos.

When 'the Desired One' had returned to Spain in March 1814, he was greeted deliriously by most of the population. Liberals were horrified at his abolition of the constitution of 1812 only two months later, but the clergy supported him and rallied the masses behind him. With remarkable vindictiveness, Ferdinand made war on anyone with a liberal record, and many were thrown into gaol, including renowned heroes of the war against the French. As a result, there was little in the way of an opposition in evidence.

In a situation where there were no legitimate channels of political dissent and not much in the way of civil institutions, and where secrecy was essential in order to evade the attentions of the dreaded Inquisition, the officer corps provided just about the only body capable of organizing protest. And they could call out troops to back this up. But since, for reasons of secrecy, those troops could not be prepared ideologically, they could not be used for much more than a show of strength. From these factors a new form of political action was born – the *pronunciamiento*.

A group of officers would decide to act in some cause. They would communicate with others through regimental and masonic channels in order to ensure as wide support as possible, and elaborate some kind of manifesto. They would then choose a day, draw up their troops, and read out the declaration. This act, known as the *grito*, was meant to initiate a revolution. But the fear of discovery was such that in most cases the *grito* was staged before arrangements with other military units and civilian sympathizers had been firmed up, and, as a result, it was all too often no more than a kind of suicidal demonstration. The first of these *pronunciamientos* came in 1814, when General Francisco Espoz y Mina attempted to rouse Pamplona, on the grounds that his army had been 'slighted'. He was obliged to take refuge in France, while his nephew sailed off to liberate Mexico. In 1815 General Juan Diez Porlier roused the garrison of La Coruña and got as far as Santiago de Compostela before his revolt fell apart. The 1817 revolts by Generals Lacy in Catalonia and Vidal in Valencia were even less successful.

In 1819 Ferdinand began concentrating forces at Cadiz, meaning to send them to South America. This was a dangerous policy in the circumstances. Large numbers of men with nothing better to do than exchange gripes were thrown together, and for once the other ranks were as discontented as the officers. Nobody, least of all common soldiers, wanted to be shipped across the ocean for an indeterminate period. Their commander, General Count O'Donnell de la Bisbal, attempted to use this discontent in order to force a constitution on the king, but he lost his nerve, and several liberal officers were arrested. The initiative was then seized by Colonel Antonio Quiroga and Major Rafael de Riego. On 1 January 1820, they made a *pronunciamiento* in favour of the constitution of 1812. While Quiroga held Cadiz, Riego marched through Andalucia. Other military mutinies took place in Pamplona, Barcelona and Saragossa, and King Ferdinand was obliged to give way. He was lumbered once again with the constitution of 1812, for which he had such a pronounced distaste and which liberals saw as a universal panacea. This constitution had begun to assume fetishistic properties quite out of proportion to its real significance. It was revered far beyond Spain, and only seven months later Ferdinand's cousin and namesake in Naples was landed with it too.

*

When Napoleon's troops had overrun the Italian mainland, King Ferdinand IV of Naples had taken refuge in Sicily, where he was protected by the Royal Navy. Under British pressure, in 1812 he had given the people of Sicily a constitution not unlike the Spanish one of the same year. Once back on his throne in Naples, Ferdinand repealed the Sicilian constitution. This gave the Carbonari and other malcontents a specific grievance to focus on, and the focus became sharper when, in January 1820, they heard of the events in Spain. The Neapolitan army was largely officered by men who had served in the Napoleonic Wars and remembered fondly the reign of Joachim Murat. They had been well treated by the returning Bourbon king but those of them with liberal instincts found the new regime oppressive, and the rest were just bored.

On 1 July 1820, the feast of St Theobald, patron of the Carbonari, Luigi Minichini, an unholy priest who was the grand master of the *vendita* in the village of Nola, raised the banner of revolt. He had persuaded Lieutenant Michele Morelli to join him with his disaffected squadron of cavalry, which was garrisoned there and unpaid. Mounted on a horse, with a musket slung across his shoulder, the priest led the rebels in a march on nearby Avellino. Having proclaimed his loyalty to 'Ferdinand the Constitutional King', Lieutenant Morelli handed over to his superior at Avellino who was nonplussed and appealed to his commanding officer, General Pepe, for instructions on how to react.

Guglielmo Pepe had an interesting past. At the age of sixteen he had joined the forces of the Parthenopean Republic, and he took refuge in France after its fall in 1799. He had served in the Italic Legion, but left this in order to plot, with other patriots, the overthrow of the Bourbons of Naples. He had enthusiastically enlisted in the Neapolitan army of Joachim Murat, in which he had risen to the rank of marshal. Although the returning Ferdinand had kept him in service, Pepe was naturally out of sympathy with the restored regime. When confronted with a half-hearted mutiny against it, he dithered.

One by one the units sent out against the rebels fell in with them, and so in the end, largely by default, did General Pepe. By this time other *vendite* had mobilized, and the troops were joined by large numbers of unruly Carbonari. On 6 July King Ferdinand caved in and accepted the constitution, but he declared his retirement from active political life, and appointed his son, Francesco Duke of Calabria, Vicar-General of the Kingdom. On 9 July the Vicar-General took the salute as the rebels marched into Naples. In the van rode Morelli, leading the 'Sacred Squadron' as his mangy mutineers had been dubbed. He was followed by the regular troops who had gone over to the side of the rebels, and then by some 6,000 barely armed Carbonari, led by the dubious priest and marching under the Carbonarist tricolor of red for the fire of charity, blue for the smoke of hope, and black for the charcoal that represented faith.

The leaderless revolution was soon drifting aimlessly. When those who had rebelled in its name actually acquainted themselves with it, the 'Sublime Spanish Constitution, palladium of human happiness and greatness,' turned out to be inadequate. The necessary modifications were made and a parliament was elected. But before this could open its deliberations in October 1820, the Sicilians rebelled, demanding their old constitution and autonomy from Naples. A large military force was despatched to Palermo to restore order, drawing all the best Neapolitan troops away from the mainland, where they would soon be badly needed.

Metternich had not been idle. As soon as the trouble started in Spain, he began to array all the forces of the *status quo* at the diplomatic level, in preparation for armed intervention. In November, a congress at Troppau issued a declaration condemning what had happened in Naples and convening a congress of crowned heads at Laibach for January 1821, to which King Ferdinand was invited. Once there, surrounded by friendly upholders of the *status quo*, Ferdinand was able to say what he could not say in Naples; namely that he would very much appreciate it if Austria sent in her troops to restore order in the Kingdom of the Two Sicilies.

The troops were already on the march. Metternich was keen to quell the Neapolitan revolt before it could spread, and he was well aware that others were plotting all over Italy. As soon as news that Austrian forces were on the move reached Naples, the militias which had been so quick to form up and parade began to dwindle. Those with money paid some beggar to take their place in the ranks, others made themselves scarce. The officers who had risen under Murat and made their peace with the Bourbon once already were not prepared to make a pointless stand this time round, and they too began to disperse their troops and prepare their excuses.

General Pepe made a principled decision to stand by the revolution. He was supported by the foreign volunteers who had homed in on Naples to join the rebels, including Maurice Persat, fresh from disturbances on the streets of Paris, and his friend from South America, Marzewski. There were a couple of dozen other Poles, including a Captain Szulc, who had been among the Light-Horsemen accompanying Napoleon to Elba, and some Frenchmen. Realizing that the general slide in morale would wash away his army completely if he did not take the initiative, Pepe marched out into the Papal States to meet the oncoming Austrian column. On 7 March 1821 he engaged it at Rieti, but his troops gave way under the first counter-attack, and he was routed. On 23 March the Austrians marched into Naples. The remaining stalwarts made a last stand at Messina under General Rossarol. A few who had played a major part in the revolution fled into exile, the rest made their peace with Ferdinand. Two men were executed, and a couple of dozen condemned to lengthy incarceration in the unspeakable conditions of the kingdom's prisons.

Just as the Neapolitan revolution was being mopped up, another erupted in Piedmont. A number of liberal noblemen in Turin had been plotting to force King Victor Emmanuel I to abdicate in favour of his 22-year-old nephew Charles Albert, Prince of Carignano, whom they knew to be a liberal and an Italian patriot. But on 10 March 1821 the Italian tricolor was hoisted and the Spanish constitution proclaimed in nearby Alessandria by a group of officers, led by Colonel Ansaldi and Lieutenant Carlo Bianco. The Prince of Carignano was alarmed at their radicalism, and began to waver in his convictions. Victor Emmanuel abdicated in favour of his brother Charles Felix, but as he was absent, the Prince of Carignano was appointed regent. The prince was a weak character, while the liberal noblemen surrounding him were certainly not ruthless enough to turn the revolt into a revolution. Typical of them was Count Santorre di Santa Rosa, who 'loved liberty, not only for its effects, but also as a sublime and poetical state of existence', in the words of one of his comrades. In 1814 he had decided not to fight for Murat, on the grounds that the 'majesty' of the Italian people would have been affronted were it to owe its freedom to a foreigner.[16]

When the Piedmontese army was defeated by the Austrians at Novara on 18 April 1821, Charles Albert stepped aside in favour of his uncle, Charles Felix, who rescinded all the reforms carried out in his name. Two of the leaders of the coup were shot; a few were given lengthy prison sentences. Those who managed to get away made for Spain, where the liberals were still holding on. Count Palma d'Ivrea joined the Madrid militia as a grenadier. Bianco became a volunteer in Catalonia. Count Giuseppe Pecchio's first act on entering Spain at Irún was to go and 'contemplate' the monument to the constitution. Such monuments had been erected in every town following the *pronunciamiento* of Riego and Quiroga. 'The constitution should be, like religion, an indestructible monument on which eyes and hearts should be constantly fixed,' he wrote. 'Wherever there is a cross, there should also be a monument to the constitution . . . twin signs of redemption.'[17]

When the Cortes had met in the spring of 1820, the moderate liberals, many of whom had been instrumental in passing the constitution of 1812 in the first place, realized that it was unworkable and required amendment. But they were hemmed in on one side by the radicals, the *exaltados*, for whom the 'sacred code' was indeed sacred, and on the other by the king and his *serviles*. In August 1820 Riego arrived in Madrid, raising the political temperature. He was the hero of the *exaltados*, and popular with the rabble, who processed through the streets singing the 'Hymn of Riego' and carried palm fronds as they bore his portrait around the city. When soldiers attempted to disperse one procession, they were attacked by a lady screaming: '*Profanators!* how dare you attack the idol of the nation?'[18] Riego proposed himself as dictator, but was brushed aside by the Cortes. He nevertheless continued to make trouble on the sidelines, and his influence was transmitted through a popular sub-masonic movement, the *Comuneros*, whose fantastic rites of initiation curdled the blood of moderates.

In the same month, revolution rocked neighbouring Portugal, whose post-Napoleonic history had been similar to that of Spain. On 24 August 1820 two colonels called out their troops in Oporto. They appealed to King João VI to come back from Brazil and give the country a constitution. In September Lisbon declared for the constitutionalists, and an assembly was summoned. A protracted discussion of aims then began, with some demanding the Spanish constitution, and others insisting on a more gradual approach.

These curiously purposeless revolts attracted ardent supporters from outside, and the Italians were not the only ones to fly to the aid of the Spanish liberals. The first to start pouring across the border were Frenchmen, mostly former Napoleonic soldiers, and the Spanish began forming them into a legion at Barcelona. They included many of the participants of the military conspiracies in France after 1815, such as Lieutenant Armand Carrel, Captain Nantil and Major Caron, who had led the Marseille plot. There was also a contingent of Frenchmen who had taken part in the Italian revolutions, including Maurice Persat and Augustin Toussaint Régis, a black soldier in Saint-Domingue who had fallen into British hands with Rochambeau, and then served under Napoleon until 1815. The French Legion, numbering over five hundred men dressed in a variety of Napoleonic uniforms dug up from the bottom of trunks, was commanded by Colonel Charles Fabvier. Six feet tall, Fabvier was the kind of splendid Napoleonic officer who stalks the pages of French nineteenth-century novels. A graduate of the École Polytéchnique, he served in the artillery from 1805, was awarded the commander's cross of the Légion d'Honneur and made a Baron of the Empire. After 1815 he lived on nostalgia until 1821, when he participated in the Belfort conspiracy.

There were plenty of other foreigners about, including, as usual, numerous Poles, among them Szulc, late of the Neapolitan revolution. There was also a very unusual Englishman, Sir Robert Wilson. A cavalryman who had fought with distinction against revolutionary France, he had been awarded the Order of Maria Theresa and made a baron by the Emperor Francis II. He had fought at Alexandria and at the Cape of Good Hope in 1806. During the Peninsular War, he had raised and commanded the Lusitanian Legion alongside the British. He had then been seconded to the Russian army, in whose ranks he had fought in 1812, and distinguished himself at the Battle of Leipzig in 1813. But in 1816, while in France with the British forces of occupation, he had chivalrously assisted the escape of a condemned Napoleonic officer, for which he was cashiered and imprisoned. This experience radicalized his outlook. In 1818 he was returned to Parliament in the Whig interest as the Member for Southwark. In 1822, when it began to look as though the Holy Alliance might be arming against the Spanish liberals, he went to Spain and offered his sword to the cause.

This had lost what little unity it had. The Cortes were in the grip of an *exaltado* majority. The king and all conservatives, including many moderates who had been pushed into the camp of reaction, stood back and now placed their hopes in foreign intervention, while a civil war began to rage in the countryside. Bands of conservatives, led by priests and styling themselves 'the Army of the Faith', hunted down local *Comuneros* and liberals. Their respective slogans, 'Long Live the Absolute King!' and 'Long live the Untouchable Constitution!' had a nicely theological ring to them.

Early in 1823 Russia, Prussia and Austria issued identical notes to the Spanish Cortés, demanding modifications to the constitution. This provoked uproar among the *exaltados*, who began to make declarations about the invincibility of armies made up of free men, quoting Thermopylae and Valmy. There had been a growing force of Spanish royalists gathering in the Pyrenees, and as French troops now started massing on the border the situation did indeed begin to resemble 1792. The difference lay in the attitude of the people. 'Nothing is more remarkable', reported the Marquess of Wellesley, 'than the apathy of the people who have taken neither side of the question but look on the quarrell as to be one between the army and the king.'[19] Radicals muttered about staging something in the nature of the September massacres in order to commit the people to the cause, but while mobs occasionally gathered in Madrid baying for someone's blood, there was no great patriotic surge.

The motivation of the other side was far stronger than that of the Austrians in 1792. France was desperate to prove her credentials as a partner for the Holy Alliance and to re-establish her position as a European power. She was also trying to exorcise her ghosts. Even though the majority of Frenchmen were welldisposed to the Spanish liberals and felt aversion at interfering, Lafayette and three other Deputies were the only ones to protest at the decision to intervene, staging a sit-in at the Chamber of Deputies. Another member of the Chamber, Chateaubriand, saw in the military intervention a chance to bridge the terrible gulfs dividing French society. 'If there is still something wanting to the complete reconciliation of the French, it will be accomplished under canvas,' he enthused. 'Companions in arms soon become friends, and all other memories lose themselves in a common glory. The king has entrusted the white banner with a generous faith to captains who made other colours triumph.'[20]

On 7 April 1823 a combined force of some 60,000 French troops and 35,000 Spanish royalists marched into Spain in order to deliver Ferdinand from the revolution. It was commanded by the royal Duc d'Angoulême, and was meant to reclaim the ground of military glory for the Bourbon cause. It had little difficulty in overcoming the resistance it encountered, facing its greatest test outside Bilbao in the shape of the French Legion. Fabvier had issued a proclamation to his invading compatriots, dated from 'the Headquarters of Free Men', calling on them to respect 'liberty, that noble emanation of the supreme being, which makes man both just and virtuous'. When the Legion came face to face with the advancing French, they unfurled the tricolor and intoned the *Marseillaise*, but a French officer with presence of mind unlimbered his guns and opened up with grapeshot, and the royal troops did their duty.[21]

On 23 May the French army entered Madrid. The *Cortes* had temporarily deposed King Ferdinand and set up a regency, which fell back on Seville and then Cadiz, taking the Desired One with it. Also evacuated, in order to avoid the possibility of profanation, were two urns containing ashes of heroes of the Dos de Mayo, the revolt against the French on 2 May 1808. But the contrast between 1808 and now was stark. Peasants in the countryside greeted the French with joy and the people of Madrid burned Riego in effigy. Riego himself, down to a couple of thousand men, was trying to fight a *guerrilla* in the mountains, but he was cornered and defeated. Those of his troops who avoided capture melted away, and he found himself attended only by three officers – one Spaniard, one Englishman and one Italian. He was captured after being betrayed by a farmer in whose house he had taken shelter.

The Duc d'Angoulême pursued the Spanish Regency to Cadiz, while other French columns mopped up. In the north-west, Quiroga was holding out with the help of the French Legion and a force Wilson had raised in Vigo. But after a heroic defence of La Coruña, during which he was seriously wounded, Wilson had to fall back and take refuge in Portugal.

The end could not long be delayed. The French forces were strong, and full of young aristocrats eager to show their mettle, among them the Prince of Carignano, doing his best to redeem his reputation in the eyes of the Holy Alliance. The final act came on 30 September with the storming of the Trocadero fortress by Angoulême's troops, which obliged the Regency to surrender.

On 13 November Ferdinand made his solemn re-entry into Madrid, on a classical triumphal chariot twenty-five feet high drawn by a hundred men dressed in green-and-pink livery, and surrounded by groups of dancers. His attitude had not been mollified by the events of the past three years, and the moment he was out of danger he began to take his revenge. The French, to whom many Spanish officers had surrendered on the promise of a pardon, attempted to restrain him, but in vain. He instituted draconian reprisals, knowing that the people were behind him. On 7 November Riego was dragged through the streets of Madrid in a basket tied to a donkey's tail and jeered by the crowd that had acclaimed him three years before. He was then hanged. 'The constitution of 1812', declared one liberal officer on surrendering to the French, 'was made entirely for the people, but they hated it.'[22]

Some Spanish patriots fell back on Portugal, where General Pepe, Persat and other members of the international brigade had also pitched up, hoping to fight on for the holy cause. But the course of the revolution did not run smooth there either. The Portuguese Assembly had met in January 1821 but soon got bogged down over whether sovereignty resided in the people or the nation. On 30 June it published a proposed constitution, and three days later King João VI finally returned from Brazil, where he had left his son Dom Pedro as regent. The constitution was an extremely progressive one, granting everyone equality before the law and abolishing all class privileges, and the king took some persuading before assenting. His younger son Dom Miguel recused, and rallied all those opposed to it in what was to be the start of a protracted civil and dynastic struggle.

The hopes of liberals throughout the Iberian peninsula were dashed for decades. But it mattered not in the eyes of such people as Pecchio, who had retreated to Portugal along with the other refugees from Spain. 'The constitutional idea seems to gain new strength since the constitution has been trampled underfoot,' the count wrote. 'Liberty dies, but it rises again,' he added, once he had reached London.[23] The poet Thomas Campbell, bard of lost causes, took a similar view. 'There is a victory in dying well / For Freedom, – and ye have not died in vain', he wrote in *Stanzas to the Memory of Spanish Patriots*, adding that 'the Patriot's blood's the seed of Freedom's tree'.

Most of the refugees from Spain and Italy washed up in England, where they were greeted with deceptive enthusiasm. When General Mina landed at Portsmouth, he was carried to his hotel in triumph. But he soon sank into oblivion. 'In 1823, London was peopled with exiles of every kind and every country,' writes Pecchio, 'constitutionalists who would have but one chamber, constitutionalists who wished for two; constitutionalists after the French model, after the Spanish, the American; generals, dismissed presidents of republics, presidents of parliaments dissolved at the point of the bayonet, presidents of cortes dispersed by the bomb-shell; the widow of the negro king Christophe, with the two princesses, her daughters, of the true royal blood, "black and all black"; the dethroned Emperor of Mexico; and whole swarms of journalists, poets and men of letters. London was the Elysium (a satirist would say, the Botany Bay) of illustrious men and would-be heroes.'[24] They were soon at one another's throats, accusing each other of incompetence and even treachery in the conduct of the late revolutions. But there was generosity too, and Persat remembers them pooling the charity they received to help the less fortunate.

The outbreak of the revolution in Spain had prevented the armada assembled at Cadiz from sailing, which gave Bolívar and San Martin a respite. It also weakened the forces of order in all the colonies, while the example of Riego beckoned to men of thwarted ambition. In Mexico, it brought out the Napoleonic streak in Augustín de Iturbide, a descendant of an ancient though impoverished noble family from Navarre whose father had emigrated. Augustín, who was two months younger than Bolívar, was described as 'a Spanish child' in his baptismal certificate, and nothing in his early life suggested a rebel. As soon as he was old enough to bear arms he joined the militia as an officer and at twenty-two he married the daughter of the local *intendiente*, also a Spaniard. During the fighting against the insurgents of Hidalgo and Morelos he had shown bravery and proved himself a good strategist. He was promoted to the rank of lieutenant-colonel in 1812, and later appointed *intendiente* of the province of Guanajuato. But Iturbide craved greater recognition, and felt that he should be given the Order of San Fernando at the very least. In 1816 he resigned in dudgeon.

The execution of Morelos had not brought peace to Mexico. The rebellion continued to simmer in various regions, and its new leader, Vicente Guerrero, was holding out in the south. In 1820, following the events in Spain, a royal pardon was extended to the rebels while the Spanish Cortes decided what reforms to introduce. But Guerrero and his dichards refused to be seduced by this and entrenched themselves in Acapulco. Iturbide was placed in command of the troops sent out against them. After consulting with other officers and talking to Guerrero, Iturbide worked out a compromise, which he published on 24 February 1821 at his headquarters in Iguala. The 'Iguala Plan' laid down the framework for a constitution, based on the maintenance of the position of the Church, the establishment of a direct relationship with the king of Spain, and equal rights for Spaniards and Creoles, asserting the separate status of the 'Mexican nation'.

On 2 March, Iturbide drew up his troops at Iguala. With one hand on the hilt of his sword and the other on the holy scriptures, he swore to uphold the independence of the 'Mexican Empire', to support the Catholic faith, and to keep the peace between Mexicans and Europeans. These he called the Three Guarantees. He also swore loyalty to King Ferdinand, conditional on the king accepting to abide by the decisions reached by the Cortes to be called in Mexico. He then tore off his royal insignia of rank.

One thing Iturbide could count on was the support of the Church. 'The war for our independence is a religious war,' declared a preacher in Guadalajara Cathedral. Soldiers leaving the royal colours to join Iturbide were decorated by nuns at the doors of convents with holy medals and scapularies, and blessed as though they were setting off on a crusade. It was the Bishop of Puebla who first dubbed Iturbide '*El Libertador*', and he egged him on in language that seemed neither appropriate nor strictly necessary. 'Yield with docility to the high purpose for which Divine Providence has designed you,' he exhorted.[25] The Iguala Plan did actually promise a way out of the by now compulsive pattern of rebellion and suppression. The US Consul in Mexico reported that the Iturbidista revolution was sweeping through the country in a spirit of 'brotherly love, patriotism, disinterestedness, truth, and good faith', and likened the Mexican leader to George Washington.[26]

Spain sent a new Captain-General in the person of Juan O'Donojù, a hero of the Peninsular War and a man of liberal views, for which he had suffered imprisonment in Spain after 1814. He met Iturbide and quickly assented to most of the Iguala Plan's stipulations. In September the two men rode into Mexico City together and on 28 September the Act of Independence of the Mexican Empire was signed by the Junta, which declared that the Mexican nation was emerging from the oppression under which it had been labouring for the past three hundred years. The Junta named a regency council of five people, with Iturbide presiding, while the king's assent was awaited.

The euphoria was general. Manuel de la Barceña, archdeacon of Valladolid Cathedral, compared the liberated Mexicans to the Israelites after the Red Sea crossing. 'You, my friend, will be our Washington,' wrote General Pedro Negrete to Iturbide, 'greater than all the conquerors in the world.'[27] This happy state of affairs was not to last. On 8 October O'Donojù died, removing the only bridge for reaching a compromise with Spain and at the time leaving a dangerous vacuum which beckoned to the 'Washington of Mexico'. In the absence of conciliatory gestures from Spain, on 27 October the independence of Mexico was solemnly proclaimed. The Regency Council announced that the national emblem would be an eagle wearing an imperial crown, and that the flag would be the tricolor of the Army of the Three Guarantees, green, white and red. On 24 February 1822, when the Sovereign Constituent Congress of Mexico met, Iturbide moved to take the central seat, but was directed to another. A Washington, let alone a Cincinnatus, he was certainly not. The figure reigning over his imagination was Napoleon.

On the evening of 18 May 1822 a crowd which gathered outside Iturbide's residence proclaimed him emperor. He made a great show of reticence, but the next day the Congress elected him to the purple, possibly under threat. On his way home, the horses were unharnessed from his carriage, which was then pulled by friars. Augustín, by Divine Providence and by the Congress of the Nation, First Constitutional Emperor of Mexico, took to the part. He established the Imperial Order of Guadalupe, whose knights were to wear cloaks and sombreros with tricolor plumes. For his coronation, he pillaged accounts and prints of Napoleon's for procedure and costume, and, after the president of the Congress had placed the crown on his brow, Iturbide personally crowned his consort. But the grumbling already audible during the coronation quickly turned into protest and conspiracy, and on 2 December 1822, General Santa Anna proclaimed the republic at Vera Cruz. The revolt spread quickly through the country, and on 19 March 1823, after failed attempts at negotiating a compromise, Iturbide abdicated and sailed off into exile.

His departure brought neither stability nor consistency to Mexico. As there was no sense of nation, once loyalty had been withdrawn from the Spanish Crown it could only be bestowed on an individual. And, as dozens of self-styled liberators and saviours were to discover over the next century, one man was as capable of engaging loyalty as the next. A liberator was only a liberator while he was engaged in the act of liberating, as San Martin was also finding out.

Although the Riego revolt in Spain meant that he was out of immediate danger, he could not hold on to Chile unless he controlled the crucial colony of Peru, still garrisoned with Spanish troops. While these were showing liberal tendencies in sympathy with their colleagues across the water, the Creole population of Peru was, as in Mexico, overwhelmingly anti-liberal and pro-royalist. But Peru could only be successfully attacked from the sea, and for this a navy was needed.

The oceans around South America had long attracted adventurous souls, particularly from Britain. One such was William Brown, a native of Ireland whose family had emigrated to the United States. He had worked his way up from cabin-boy to master of a merchant vessel, which was eventually captured by the French. He escaped from the fortress of Metz, and, after being recaptured, from that of Verdun. He bought a ship and began trading along the coast of South America, eventually settling in Buenos Aires. In 1814 he was given the rank of commodore and placed in command of the Argentine navy, such as it was. Over the next three years Brown cleared the continent's east coast of Spanish shipping, and then set out to do the same on the Pacific coast. Valparaíso, which had been liberated from the interior by San Martin and where the Chilean navy was being formed, swarmed with Britons, some six hundred of them, and in 1818 they were joined by Lord Thomas Cochrane.

Cochrane had entered the Royal Navy at the outbreak of war with France, but in 1798, two years after his brush with Wolfe Tone off Newfoundland and aged only twenty-three, he had been court-martialled for indiscipline. The presiding admiral, Earl St Vincent, described him as 'mad, romantic, money-getting, and not truth-telling'. It was a good description, but it left out that he was a brilliant sailor and daring to the point of recklessness. In 1800 he was given command of the brig HMS *Speedy* with orders to patrol Spain's Mediterranean coast. He took on ships with several times his own firepower, capturing one after another and earning himself more prize-money than anyone else in the history of the Royal Navy – £75,000 in 1805 alone. He made himself unpopular at home by denouncing abuses and by using his seat in Parliament, to which he got himself elected, to accuse superior officers of incompetence and cowardice. Not surprisingly, he incurred the disfavour of the sea lords, was denied a command and put on half-pay. His unruly life included arrest, escape from prison, an elopement to Gretna Green and a breath-taking Stock Exchange fraud in 1814 that resulted in his being cashiered and stripped of his knighthood. In 1817 he was approached by agents of the Chilean patriot government, and he leapt at the chance of fighting. On 28 November 1818 Cochrane hoisted his flag on the *O'Higgins*.[28]

The fleet sailed from Valparaiso on 20 August 1820, and Cochrane's habitual audacity served the cause well. On 5 November he sailed into the port of Callao under the nose of several coastal batteries and an entire Spanish squadron, and cut out its best ship, the *Esmeralda*. He made several such daring attacks, capturing the main Spanish naval base and defeating forces on land using his marines, led by William Miller, a Kentish man who had served under Wellington in the Peninsula.

Meanwhile San Martin invaded Peru overland, and in July 1821 he entered Lima. Here he proclaimed himself 'Protector of Peru' and instituted the Order of the Sun in imitation of the Légion d'Honneur. Although he was less fond of grand public occasions than Bolívar, preferring a more severe image, he was no less Napoleonic in his instincts. He relentlessly persecuted 'Spaniards' and royalists, confiscating their land and forcing them into exile. But only a year later he was ousted and forced to share their fate. He left for Chile, but could find no place for himself there or in Argentina, and ultimately settled for a life of exile in London. Aptly, the only thing he took with him from Peru was the banner of Pizarro.

His departure left the stage clear for the arch-rebel Bolívar, whose instinct for survival was as strong as his taste for glory. In June 1821 he had finally broken the back of the royalist forces in Venezuela at the Battle of Carabobo. How little it took can be gauged from the fact that the battle, which was won thanks to the Albion Legion and a battalion of volunteers commanded by the Pole Flegel, lasted only one hour and cost two hundred lives. Bolívar's entry into Caracas three days later was none the less splendid. Having reinforced his political position, he then turned his attention to the south, and, after defeating the royalists there, in June 1822 he marched into Quito. With the surrender to Antonio Paez of the last Spanish garrison in Venezuela, at Puerto Cabello, in the following year, Bolívar was able to move against Peru. His timing could not have been better.

The collapse of the Spanish revolution turned out to be a watershed in the history of South America. A few days after the French had delivered him from Cadiz, at the end of September 1823, King Ferdinand had rescinded all reforms introduced since 1820. As soon as the British Foreign Secretary George Canning heard of this, he appointed British consuls in all the successor states of former Spanish colonies of South America. In a message to the United States Congress on 3 December, President James Monroe declared the American continents, north and south, closed to European colonialism. This meant that, whatever might be the wishes of the populations of her colonies, Spanish tenure was necessarily limited. Since loyalists could not be assisted from Spain, any rebellion was bound to succeed in the end as the rebels could draw on all Spain's enemies throughout the continent. It gave those confronting the metropolitan power a sense of impunity. Oddly enough, the first consequence of this was the creation of the Empire of Brazil.

Dom Pedro, who repeatedly refused the Portuguese Assembly's summons to return to Lisbon, decided to go his own way. On 7 December 1822, when the last of many demands reached him, he drew his sword and exclaimed: 'The time has come. It is Independence or Death!' He designed an armband of yellow and green, with these words inscribed on it, and made preparations to resist any attempts to extinguish the flame of liberty in Brazil. He wrote to Cochrane, asking him to come and assist 'the Sacred Cause of this Hemisphere'. The diplomat who passed on the note added his own exhortation. 'Come, reborn Hercules, and with your honourable efforts help to tame the Hundred-Headed Hydra of a frightful Despotism,' he wrote, 'the Sacred Standard of Independence is unfurled from the Galapagos as far as the Cedar Isles of California!'[29] Cochrane, who had by then quarrelled with everyone in Peru, obliged. With his customary dash he decimated the Portuguese fleet, pursuing it all the way across the Atlantic back to Portugal. He amassed a deal of money and was created a tropical Marquis before falling out with the Brazilians and returning to England.

He had not been there long when, at the beginning of May 1824, he was contacted by ex-Emperor Augustín, with plans for a raid on San Juan de Ulúa followed by an invasion of Mexico. The former emperor had intended to end his days peacefully in Rome, but, refused right of sojourn there, he had ended up in London. He had little money and he was not looking forward to a life of exile. At the same time enticing news started reaching him from Mexico, where many felt genuine loyalty to him and others had been slighted by the new authorities. In April 1824 he discussed the situation with San Martin at a coffee-house in Regent Street. San Martin advised Iturbide that there was nothing to be gained by returning to Mexico, but Iturbide was by now set on going back, with or without Cochrane. On 11 May, having placed his son at Ampleforth College and his daughters at convents in France, he sailed from Southampton. The ex-emperor's entourage was hardly glittering. The small ship carried only himself, his pregnant wife with their two smallest children, Colonel

Charles Beneski, a veteran Polish lancer and now his aide-de-camp, and a handful of associates. The ship dropped anchor off Soto la Marina on the Mexican coast on 1 July, and the final act of the tragicomedy of Emperor Augustín I began.

On going shore, Colonel Beneski made contact with the local military intendant who gave the impression that he would support Iturbide, so on 17 July the latter also ventured ashore. No sooner had he set foot on Mexican soil than the intendant arrested him. He was handed over to the civil authorities at Padilla, who took the view that it was a clear case of rebellion, and passed sentence accordingly. Two days later, on 19 July 1824, the first emperor of Mexico was executed by firing squad at Padilla. This meant that there was only one Napoleon left on the continent still dreaming of imperial glories.

Bolívar had been growing increasingly megalomaniacal, never missing a chance to flex his power. He liked being carried about in adulation on the shoulders of crowds, and had a habit of venting his contempt by strutting up and down tables in the middle of a banquet, grinding plates and glasses under his boots. Innocent of any sense of ridicule, let alone modesty, he hung in the dining-room of his villa outside Bogotá a huge portrait of himself being crowned by two genii, with the inscription: 'Bolívar is the God of Colombia'. He took every opportunity to project a numinous image of predestination, and bestowed upon the late Miranda the title of 'The Precursor', thereby setting him up as a kind of John the Baptist to his own incarnation.

Bolívar was encouraged and supported in his self-glorification by an extraordinary woman who dominated the latter part of his life. Manuela Saenz was no conventional *femme fatale.* She was forty-five years old, five years older than Bolívar, when he first met her after his triumphal entry into Quito in 1822, with a stormy past that included two husbands, one Spanish, one British. But she had a strong character, which apparently complemented Bolívar's tendency to vacillate, and she spurred him on to further glory.

With Spain no longer able to support the royalists in Peru, Bolívar had no trouble in subverting that colony. In August 1824 he defeated one royalist army at Junín in a great clash of cavalry during which hardly a shot was fired. One of the few casualties was Captain Charles Sowerby, a Briton born in Bremen and therefore drafted into the *Grande Armée* with which he had marched to Moscow and back, before coming to fight for the independence of La Plata, then Chile and lastly Peru. The royalists were finally beaten in an even more phoney battle at Ayacucho in December, designed to save face for all concerned.

The South American continent was now free of Spanish rule. 'Caracas no longer exists,' Bolívar wrote in 1825 to an uncle who had expressed horror at the devastation wrought, 'but its ashes, its monuments, the land it stood on, have remained glowing with liberty and covered with the glory of martyrdom. This comfort compensates for all the losses.'[30] But it was cold comfort to the majority of the population. It is generally accepted that the former Spanish colonies never again achieved the wealth in which they had basked before 1810. Some maintain that they were also better governed, more lawful and more peaceful under Spanish rule than at any time since, and there is something to be said for this view.

Slavery was finally abolished in the former Spanish colonies in the late 1850s, but economic slavery remained endemic throughout the region. The manner in which independence and nationhood were forced upon these societies gave rise to systemic instability. The various Liberators could not count on devotion to a cause to animate their troops and supporters, as the cause was imaginary. Nor could they mobilize one whole section of the population on behalf of a specific interest for any length of time. And they certainly could not depend on colleagues, who were bound, sooner or later, to contest their authority. They therefore had to keep rearranging alliances and decapitating any faction that grew too strong. In order to enlist the loyalty and sympathy of the lower orders, they would make a point of drawing these into the army. But as such recruits became professionals, they cut their links with the classes they came from and grew into arrogant Praetorians who carried with them an element of incipient mutiny.

Bolívar himself experienced plots to topple him and rebellions against his regime, notably that of General Paez in 1826. In his search for stability, he increased his army to the ludicrous strength of 40,000. By this time he wielded more power than any Spanish viceroy had ever done, and this spawned a sycophantic and venal court which vied for the favour of Manuela Saenz, widely believed to be ruling from behind the throne. Bolívar continued to nurture a great Napoleonic dream of uniting the whole South American continent and having himself made president for life or alternatively crowned emperor. His plans were mercurial and hazy, and he lurched between Alexandrine ambition and miserable self-effacement. Before his death, on 17 December 1830, the Liberator voiced serious doubts as to whether the whole exercise had been worth while.

13
Glorious Exertions

One of the longest delayed reactions to the upheavals of the Napoleonic Wars was that which took place in Greece. The Ionian Islands had been occupied by France in 1797. In 1803 they were taken by Russia, but four years later they passed back to France, along with a strip of the Dalmatian coast. A Greek legion, the Chasseurs d'Orient, was formed up under Hadji Nicole Papas Oglu, and an Albanian regiment under Marco Botsaris. In October 1809, a small British force commanded by the adventurous Irishman Major Richard Church took possession of the islands in the name of Britain. No sooner had he landed than he began to recruit an auxiliary force among the ferocious klephts, with the help of a sheep-stealer by the name of Theodore Kolokotrones. The result was the Duke of York's Greek Light Infantry, which fought in several minor actions, before being disbanded in 1814. The islands remained under British protection, but Major Church went to Italy, where he took service with King Ferdinand of the Two Sicilies, and Kolokotrones went back to his sheep.

The French and British incursions served to open up what had hitherto been a closed area for all but the most adventurous travellers. Cultural tourists began to converge on Greece, drawn by the lure of ancient monuments. They took a dim view of the locals, who showed no reverence for the ruins and could not understand the classical Greek they themselves had so painstakingly learnt in the classroom. 'All came expecting to find the Peloponnesus filled with Plutarch's men', one pointed out, 'and all returned thinking the inhabitants of Newgate more moral.'[1] Those looking for spiritual roots were grievously disappointed. 'Well, Monsieur, I have seen Greece!' Chateaubriand wrote to a friend from Constantinople in 1806. 'I visited Sparta, Argos, Mycenae, Corinth, Athens; beautiful names, alas! nothing more . . . Never see Greece, Monsieur, except in Homer. It is the best way.'[2]

It seemed eminently more sensible to remove some of the better examples of Greek art and expose them where they would be properly appreciated. Lord Elgin had realized this and arranged for the Parthenon frieze to be shipped to England. In May 1820 the Comte de Marcellus sailed from Marseille on a French naval frigate for the island of Melos, where, the French ambassador at Constantinople had heard, a statue of Venus of great beauty had recently been found by a ploughing peasant. After much haggling and some intimidation, the statue was loaded on board in six pieces, and began its journey to the Louvre.

By then, attitudes had changed, largely as a result of Lord Byron's visit to Greece in 1809, whose fruits were the second canto of *Childe Harold*, published in 1812, *The Giaour* and *The Bride of Abydos* (1813), and *The Siege of Corinth* (1816). More interested in people than in stones, Byron concentrated on depicting the craggy nobility of the natives. He was also much affected by the notion of a once great people under alien oppression. The negative picture of the Turks and their culture – rococo Ottomania had given way to priggish neoclassical contempt – made the oppression all the crueller to the European imagination, in which the Turk combined lustfulness with barbarity. The educated European of 1800 was as disgusted by the idea of the 'terrible' Turk defiling Greece as his twelfth-century forebear had been at the idea of Saracens profanating the Holy Land. And just as the Holy Land called out to Christendom for vengeance and crusade, so the oppressed Greek land called out for liberation.

In *The Giaour*, Byron challenged the modern Greeks to rekindle the spirit of their forefathers and reclaim their motherland. He urged them to give their lives for a land that must always remain 'Freedom's home, or Glory's grave'. But the Greeks showed no signs of wishing to take his advice. Even Greek patriots favoured more pragmatic methods of promoting their cause. Adamantios Korais put his faith in a 'fermentation of minds' and a 'moral revolution' that were supposedly in progress, and believed that the Greeks must educate themselves before they could aspire to nationhood.[3]

Greek cultural revivalism centred on the Ionian Islands. In 1809 the local school in Corfu adopted the ancient name of the Academy of

Korkyra, dated its prospectus in the first year of the 647th Olympiad, and began bestowing crowns of laurel and olive as prizes. In 1811 Lord Frederick North, son of the Prime Minister who had lost England her American colonies, settled in Corfu. He was an early worshipper of Greece, having visited the country in 1791 and been received into the Orthodox Church. A few years later Lord Guilford, as he had become, founded a Greek university. He adopted a Socratic purple robe and around his head wore a velvet band embroidered with olive leaves and the owl of Athens, and made the teachers wear similar garb. But the number of Greeks who could read and write remained insignificant, stemming any cultural revival. And there was no sense of community between the inhabitants of Greece itself, let alone between them and the wealthy Greeks of Constantinople, Odessa and Alexandria.

The first step to changing this was the foundation in 1814, by a group of Greeks living in Odessa, of a pan-Greek association, the Philiki Hetairia. Its ultimate aim was the liberation of Greece and the restoration of a Greek Empire. More immediately it was concerned with the 'purification' of the Greek nation. With its four grades of mystery, it was marked by masonic ritual, with much talk of 'blood-brotherhood'. By 1821 the Hetairia had a total of 911 members.

In 1820 the *Hetairia* elected a new president, Count Alexandros Ypsilantis. He had served in the Russian imperial guard and lost an arm in battle in 1813, after which he became aide-de-camp to Tsar Alexander. In that same year of 1820, Ali Pasha of Janina, who in the past had been happy enough to oppress Greeks on behalf of his Turkish overlords, made a bid for autonomy. He pronounced himself a friend of the Greeks, joined the *Hetairia* and declared his independence from Turkey. The Turks responded by sending an army, which quickly got bogged down outside Janina. The time seemed ripe for action, and Ypsilantis assembled a force of some 4,500 men, mostly Greeks living in Russia and Albanians. On 6 March 1821, with a 'Sacred Company' in the van, he crossed the River Pruth into Turkish territory and summoned Greece to rise up against the Turks. The enterprise was hopelessly mismanaged and, his little force quickly defeated, Ypsilantis was obliged to flee to Austrian territory where he hoped to find asylum. Instead, he encountered the Austrian police. They clapped him in irons and confined him with quite unnecessary cruelty until his release, only months before his death in 1828.

Four weeks after the count's foray, on 2 April 1821, Archbishop Germanos, head of the *Hetairia* in the Morea, called for a general uprising, of which Ypsilantis's younger brother Demetrios took theoretical political control. Petros Mavromichales, Bey of Maina, attacked Kalamata and put its Muslim inhabitants to the sword. The former British officer Kolokotrones dealt similarly with Karytaina. Within a few weeks, some 20,000 Muslims had been massacred, and the Turks had been effectively wiped out in the Morea, hanging on only in a few towns such as Tripolitsa and Nauplia. The rebellion spread across the isthmus, and the Muslim inhabitants of Athens were blockaded on the acropolis.

The Turks had been unprepared for the rising, with their main forces bogged down fighting Ali Pasha, and the pacification of the Greeks would be no easy task. The terrain was mountainous and the coastline deeply indented, which hindered the operation of regular armies and large troop-carrying fleets, and favoured bands of fighters and the small Greek ships. The Turks would nevertheless have doused the rebellion and reimposed their rule without much trouble if it had just been a question of them and the Greeks.

'Let us recollect, brave and generous Greeks, the liberty of the classic land of Greece; the battles of Marathon and Thermopylae, let us combat upon the tombs of our ancestors who, to leave us free, fought and died,' Ypsilantis wrote in his declaration of 24 February 1821. 'The blood of our tyrants is dear to the shades of the Theban Epaminondas, and of the Athenian Thasybulus who conquered and destroyed the thirty tyrants' – and so on.[4] This high-sounding stuff was not aimed at his countrymen, most of whom had not the faintest idea who Epaminondas was. It was meant for the intellectuals of the Western world, to whom Petros Mavromichales also addressed a harangue. 'We are unanimously resolved on Liberty or Death,' he wrote. 'Thus determined, we earnestly invite the united aid of all civilized nations to promote the attainment of our holy and legitimate purpose, the recovery of our rights, and the revival of our unhappy nation. With every right does Hellas, our mother, whence ye also, O Nations, have become enlightened, anxiously request your friendly assistance with money, arms, and counsel . . .'[5] If idle poets were going to bask in the reflected glory of ancient Greece and have the presumption to call on the present-day Greeks to rise up and risk their lives, then they could pay for it.

Mention of Greece touched a chord in every educated European. Since the Renaissance, the cultural legacy of the Graeco-Roman world had gradually displaced the increasingly unfashionable Christian heritage as the intellectual bond underlying the European common identity. 'We are all Greeks,' wrote Shelley in the preface to his poem *Hellas*. 'Our laws, our literature, our religion, our arts have their roots in Greece. But for Greece ... we might still have been savages and idolators.' The fact that, Greece or no Greece, the Romans had become savages and idolators, and that it was the Judaeo-Christian tradition that lay at the root of European beliefs, was conveniently ignored. The retreat from Christianity made faith in Greece a necessity for Western intellectuals.[6]

The image of Hellas at the mercy of the dreaded Ottoman aroused the deepest chivalric feelings. The rising of the oppressed galvanized liberal opinion. As it challenged the interests of nobody, the cause engaged the support of even the stuffiest bourgeois rentier. The most conservative statesmen, schooled in Hellenic culture, could not but see in the struggle a crusade for civilization against barbarism. Christians saw it as one against the infidel Turk, royalists as an evocation of the days of Saint Louis and Richard Lionheart. The events even held resonance for the new world. 'Since the days of the American war of independence, there has been no scene of exertion so pure and so glorious as this,' exclaimed the United States minister in Paris over dinner with Lafayette.[7]

From the start, reporting of the events in the European press contained oceans of wishful thinking, and every klepht bandit was Ulysses reincarnate. 'It is hardly possible to name a spot in the scene of action, without starting some beautiful spirit of antiquity,' effused one English newspaper in 1821. 'Here are victories at Samos, the birthplace of Pythagoras; at Rhodes, famous for its roses and accomplishments; at Cos, the birthplace of Apelles, Hippocrates, and Simonides. But to behave as the Greeks have done at Malvasia is to dispute the glory even with those older names.' What the Greeks actually did at Malvasia, in August 1821, was to promise the starving Turks besieged in the small town safe passage to Asia Minor if they surrendered, and massacre most of them when they did. The five hundred or so who survived were dumped on a deserted island and left to starve. And this was the least savage end to the many sieges of Turkish towns conducted that summer.[8]

But there were no European witnesses in Malvasia. Constantinople and Smyrna, on the other hand, had plenty of Europeans eager to report every Turkish atrocity, starting with the Turks' initial response to the rebellion, which had been to massacre Greeks living in Constantinople and to execute the Patriarch Gregorios. But it was the Turks' doings on the island of Chios that brought public opinion to the boil. The island was a notoriously happy place. Its Greek inhabitants were rich, mainly from the sale of the mastic crop, a sort of chewing gum, and uninterested in liberation. They lived in harmony with the Turks on the island, and were loyal to the Sultan. In March 1822 some jealous inhabitants of the poorer neighbouring island of Samos landed on Chios, burned a mosque or two and proclaimed independence. When a Turkish fleet hove to, the Samians murdered their Turkish prisoners and sailed back home, leaving the Chiotes to face the music. The Turks were in ugly mood when they landed. They massacred tens of thousands, and took 40,000 Greeks away as slaves.

Turkish violence was noted and reported, because people wanted to hear about it, and Greek bandits were turned into legend for the same reason. Kolokotrones was represented as a noble savage; Odysseus, who had changed his name from the more prosaic Androutzos, was depicted in heroic guise; Botsaris was a latter-day Leonidas. A whole mythology was woven around the figure of Bobolina, an Albanian woman who fitted out three ships and sailed about meting destruction to any encountered Turks. She was represented in popular prints produced in various parts of Europe as a kind of Greek Joan of Arc on board her corvette, the *Agamemnon*. Greece itself, depicted as a woman in chains, epitomized the enormity of the situation.

All this acted like a bugle-call to would-be crusaders throughout the Western world. It sounded particularly loud to the Germans, whose *engouement* with ancient Hellas was the most sickly. Ever since Hölderlin's *Hyperion*, published in 1797, in which a young Greek fights for the liberation of his country in a kind of extended act of love, the idea of such a crusade was inherently locked into Germany's quest for its own identity, its wish for self-fulfilment and regeneration. Hölderlin himself, prophetic as well as poetic, explained that he loved Greece 'as the moth loves the light', and that he sought 'the dangerous proximity' of the heroes of Greece. At universities all over Germany, Switzerland and Denmark, professors encouraged students to drop everything and set off on the great crusade. For political reasons, virtually the only place of embarkation for Greece was Marseille, and young men were soon trekking across Germany, some singly, some in groups, singing and praying, like so many medieval pilgrims. All the elements that had gone to make up the *Burschenschaften* resurfaced in this coming together of German youth. Some had fantastic romantic uniforms made for them before leaving home, others stripped their poor wardrobes of their most dashing offerings.

There were a few soldiers among the German volunteers, men with nothing to do and axes to grind. One such was General Count Karl Friedrich von Normann, a Württemberger who had fought for his monarch alongside the Austrians against the French, then alongside the French against the Russians in 1812, and who had been among those who in 1813 took the honour of Germany into their own hands by unilaterally discarding the French alliance. His monarch had not viewed this favourably, and the general had been cashiered. Normann had been looking for a chance to vindicate his honour and employ his military talents ever since. Others had their own fatalistic motives for joining the crusade. Baron Eduard von Rheineck was so cut up when he heard that the woman he loved was to marry another that after dancing with her one last time at a ball, he set off for Greece and oblivion. Paul Harro Harring, a poet and painter from the province of Schleswig, actually set out with the intention of getting himself killed. He was a fervent *Burschenschafter* and admirer of Karl Sand, whose portrait he had painted in heroic mode. He had had a dream in which he saw himself, dressed in liturgical vestments, being shot in the cause of liberty, and had inferred from it that 'the blood would be the fruit of freedom'. He got his mother to sew him a black uniform for the purpose.[9]

The Greek rising also elicited enthusiasm in America, where Ypsilantis was likened to Washington by Greek-quoting students, and a Philadelphia newspaper advocated the 'Romantic project' of sending an American fleet to help the Greeks.[10] Even poor, friendless Haiti rushed to the rescue. In 1821 a number of Greeks living in Paris wrote to Jean Pierre Boyer, Haiti's President, asking for help in the shape of arms and men. Boyer replied that he could not spare any men and had no arms, but sent a consignment of coffee harvested by free black hands, to be sold in aid of the Greek cause.[11]

The first on the scene were Piedmontese revolutionaries, whose rising was stamped out in the same month as the rebellion in Greece erupted, and Neapolitans dodging Metternich's police, such as General Rossarol. Within months they were joined by comrades who had gone on to fight in Spain. Count Santorre di Santa Rosa, one of the leaders of the Piedmontese insurrection, left his life of exile in Nottingham. 'His intense love of liberty was inflamed by a tincture of religious enthusiasm: he went to Greece with the courage and devotion of a true crusader', in the words of his fellow exile Giuseppe Pecchio. When Pecchio himself left for Greece, an English lady of his acquaintance presented him with a handsome edition of Byron's *Childe Harold* to take with him in lieu of a Bible.[12]

The Italians were followed by a mixed bag of foreigners, arriving as and when means permitted. Richard Church, who had been putting down peasant risings in Calabria for King Ferdinand, chartered a ship and set sail for Leghorn, meaning to pick up more volunteers for what he termed 'this holy war'. But he ran out of money, so he sold the vessel to Lord Guilford. He went to London in an effort to persuade the government to back the Greece cause, then returned to Naples to raise another force, and did not reach Greece until 1827. Thomas Gordon of Cairness, a Scot who had visited Greece as a youth, learned Greek and married a Greek-Albanian woman, was quicker.

News of the risings reached him in Scotland, but he made haste to Marseille, where he chartered a ship, loaded it up with six cannon, six hundred muskets, bayonets and ammunition, took on board a complement of volunteers, and set sail. He came ashore at Hydra on 1 September 1821. The reception was hardly what he and his companions had expected. The locals treated them with suspicion and charged exorbitant prices for food and lodging. One of Gordon's companions, Count Palma di Cesnola, a Piedmontese revolutionary and veteran of the Spanish and Portuguese revolts, was astonished to discover that the inhabitants of Hydra were quite contented under Turkish rule and felt 'no need' for any change.[13] Undaunted, Gordon marched on to Tripolitsa to join Demetrios Ypsilantis, who was in nominal control of a force of some 12,000 Greeks besieging the town. But the moment Ypsilantes left the camp to head off a Turkish force, Kolokotrones took command, stormed Tripolitsa and massacred 8,000 of the inhabitants. Gordon was so disgusted by this that he left, never to return to Greece.[14] His experience was not an isolated one.

The shock that faced European philhellenes on arrival in the fancied Arcadia was indescribable. 'As soon as the stranger puts his foot on the shore,' wrote Pecchio, 'his enthusiasm ceases, the enchantment disappears.'[15] They were lucky if that was all – the less fortunate were either robbed there and then or gradually by extortion. Many of the volunteers never saw a Turk, but went in frequent peril of their lives at the hands of those they had come to assist. Among the early arrivals was that old trouper Maurice Persat. In August 1821 at Marseille he bumped into Thomas Gordon, who took him and a group of his friends, including Marzewski, on board. It turned out that Gordon's dragoon regiment had been cut to pieces by Persat's lancers at Waterloo, but now they were united by the sacred cause. Persat's ardour received its first check with the sack of Tripolitsa. At Nauplia, he and his companions met the legendary Bobolina, who, thought Persat, resembled 'one of our filthy cheese-sellers from the Paris *Halles*'. For their reception, she had decorated her courtyard with three hundred heads of Turkish men, women and children killed at Tripolitsa. But it would take more than such sights to put him off. 'While despising the Greek bands and particularly their chiefs, I continued to see the beauty of their cause,' wrote Persat.[16] Most of those who had got this far persevered, including the Englishman H. W. Humphreys, who had set off to fight for the freedom of Italy, but having reached Naples after the revolution had been put down, had gone on to Greece with Gordon. Captain William Fenton, a Scot who had fought under Mina in Spain, had similarly drifted over to Greece.

Demetrios Ypsilantes formed up a separate regiment out of these Europeans under the command of the Piedmontese Colonel Dania, with the Germans and Swiss-Germans under General Normann. They wore a black uniform, the hat adorned with a skull and crossbones and the inscription 'Liberty or Death'. Being made up of half-a-dozen nationalities and mostly of officers, it was beset with problems. Their uniforms soon fell to pieces and further supplies failed to come through. There were no uniforms or arms for new arrivals, so supernumerary foreign volunteers formed themselves up into a 'Sacred Company', armed with whatever came to hand. The Greeks treated them with derision, while their illusions about the Greeks faded rapidly. Both sides had a point. To the Greeks, who were good at sniping from behind rocks, the volunteers' strutting heroics appeared laughable. To the volunteers, who had braved privation and dangers to come to the assistance of glorious Hellas, her sons' tactics appeared to fall short – particularly the klephts' habit of jumping up from behind their boulders while the Turks were reloading and making obscene gestures such as baring their bottoms.[17]

Humphreys thought the Greeks 'debased, degraded to the lowest pit of barbarism.'[18] Persat was finally disgusted by the show of cowardice, cunning and cruelty during the siege and fall of Nauplia. He decided to seek another cause, taking with him an eight-year-old Turkish girl he had saved from the massacre. He was lucky to get away with this. A Hungarian former officer in the French cavalry who stopped one of Kolokotrones' klephts from molesting a woman after the fall of Nauplia, was murdered that night. Another who saved lives at Nauplia was the captain of HMS *Cambrian*, Commodore William Gawen Rowan Hamilton, son of the Irish Volunteer, who rescued five hundred Turks aboard his ship. Hamilton nevertheless remained devoted to the Greek cause and went far beyond the bounds imposed by neutrality to help it over the next few years.

Persat had been wise to leave. In the spring of 1822 the foreign regiment, some 100 strong, was operating alongside the Greek forces under Alexander Mavrokordatos. On 16 July the Greeks wandered off, leaving the foreigners isolated at Peta. The Turks saw their chance and surrounded the regiment, which put up a heroic but pointless stand. The death toll was: 34 Germans, 12 Italians, 9 Poles, 6 French, 3 Swiss, 1 Dutch, 1 Hungarian, and a Napoleonic Mameluke. The couple of dozen who managed to extricate themselves from the fighting retreated to Missolonghi, where several more perished of wounds or fever. General Normann died a broken man in November, a few committed suicide, and one, a Swiss lieutenant from Zurich, went mad. He was chained up like a dog and fed by a Turkish slave-girl until he died, still howling uncontrollably.

The only Europeans who fared well in Greece were those who went native. This was not an easy thing to do, as the physical conditions of guerilla life in the Morea were rough. Frank Abney Hastings was one of the few who succeeded. Hastings was not, on the face of it, cut out to be a guerilla fighter. He took twelve volumes of Gibbon, the complete works of Shakespeare and a 52-volume set of Walter Scott with him wherever he went. He had been discharged from the Royal Navy for fighting a duel, and set off for Greece in March 1822, accompanied by George Jarvis, the son of an American diplomat. He quickly learned the language, took to native dress, and ended up a Greek general. Other successful 'natives' included Jarvis, who joined the Greek navy, the Poles Dąbrowski and Dzierzawski, and the French Marquis de Vilasse.

It was not a question of bravery, but of adaptability. Francis Lieber, who had fought in the Prussian ranks at Waterloo, aged fifteen, and been left for dead on the field of battle, was no coward. He had walked from

Dresden to Marseille and reached Greece early in 1822. But after two months he left, disgusted at the 'cowardice and incapacity' of the Greeks. The majority reacted in similar ways. Some made for the nearest port and gave their last pennies to be taken back whence they had come. Others were rescued from the inhospitable shore by British naval vessels. Many fell ill. Harro Harring was delirious when he was shipped to Italy. Suicides were not uncommon.

Those who did manage to get back to Marseille found the port full of fresh volunteers eagerly awaiting passage. They desperately tried to cure these of their misconceptions and warn them of the dangers. The volunteers listened to their tales with more or less indulgent disbelief, and sometimes insulted them for profaning the sacred cause. The whole philhellenic movement had gathered so much momentum that it was unstoppable, certainly by reality. Fantastical reports continued to appear in the London papers, one of them describing Lafayette leading a bayonet charge at Lepanto.[19]

By the spring of 1822 there were Hellenic committees in a dozen European cities, and over the next year these would multiply to include America. On 3 March 1823 a couple of dozen British philhellenes met at the Crown and Anchor in the Strand, where they launched an appeal for funds to help the Greeks. They would later help to raise a 'Greek loan' in the city of London, but their greatest contribution to the cause was something quite other.

Lord Byron was in Genoa, suffering from *ennui*. His major preoccupations were how to ditch his mistress and how to assure himself an acceptable lifestyle on his diminishing income. One solution was to emigrate to Venezuela – he felt sure that Bolívar would greet him with open arms. He was so taken by all he had heard of the South American hero that he had named his recently-built yacht after him. In April 1823 Byron was approached by the London Greek Committee. They figured that his presence in Greece, represented as a second 'pilgrimage', would glamorize the cause and help their fund-raising, but he understood that he was being asked to go and lead the struggle for liberation. He was interested, but he was torn. 'On Andes' and on Atlas' peaks unfurled, the self-same standard streams o'er either world,' he wrote, without much apparent excitement.[20] His mistress's brother, Count Pietro Gamba, thought they should go to defend the cause of liberty in Spain. It was then that the tearaway Edward Trelawney arrived and convinced Byron to go

The dream of Ossian, by Ingres. Variants of this dream inspired countless young men, including the young Bonaparte, to seek strength in the mists of the national past and to act out a higher destiny.

A reliquiary containing fragments of Napoleon's undergarments, discarded when he took his first bath on the retreat from Moscow, at the posting house in Łomża in December 1812, and piously preserved by his worshippers.

The father of the first black *Patrie*, Toussaint L'Ouverture.

The poet Theodor Körner, in dreamy profile on the left, and two of his comrades of the Lützow Freikorps (note the *altdeutsch* floppy hats) contemplate a heroic national future among the sacred German oaks.

This vision of Nelson, expiring Christ-like on the timbers of HMS *Victory* after a righteous triumph over the shameless usurping French, sums up much of what being British meant to his contemporaries.

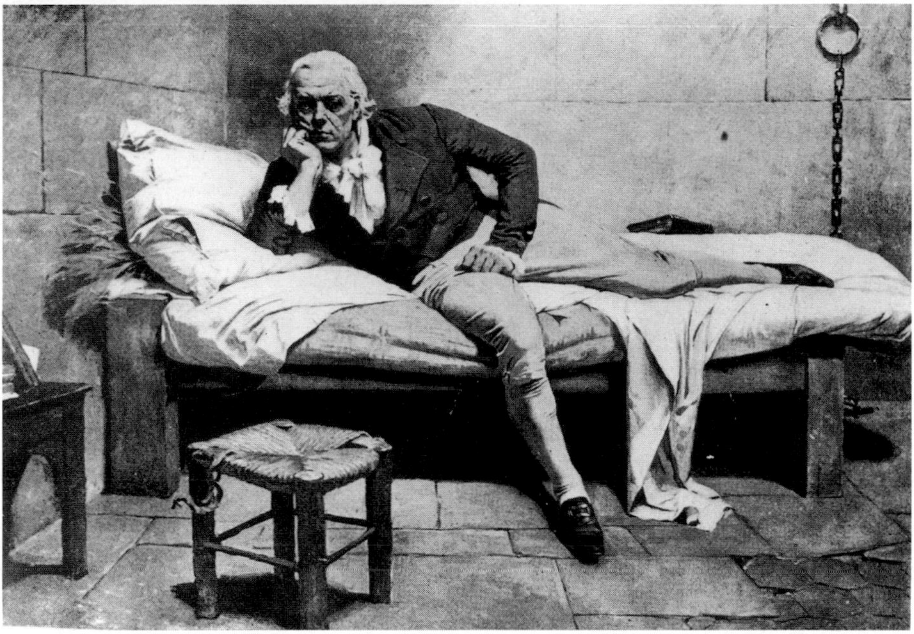

El Precursor, Francisco de Miranda, awaiting death in a Spanish gaol, having twice failed to convince his countrymen that they were a nation.

The Apotheosis of *El Libertador*, Simón Bolívar, who forced his countrymen to become a nation in spite of themselves.

The ultimate Romantic image of the anthropomorphic *Patrie*: Eugène Delacroix's *Greece Expiring on the Ruins of Missolonghi*, a challenge to all chivalrous souls.

The wildly misleading reports of the heroism of the Greek patriot Bobolina inspired young ladies all over Europe.

This engraving of 'the Wounded Patriot' was all that the West wanted to believe about the Greeks.

Richard Church, one of many Britons who went native in the Greek cause.

Lord Byron in his 'very magnifique' Greek costume.

One of the girls who read too much poetry and ran away from home to fight for a free Poland in 1830, Miss Tomaszewska was only 16 when she joined the colours.

Wishful thinking at its height: the Polish peasant shown brandishing the archetypal scythe and the national banner in a French engraving of 1830.

A French view of Poland's martyrdom, affirming that she will rise again.

A French painting depicting a wounded Polish soldier in the ruins of Warsaw tracing with his own blood the first line of the Song of the Legions, affirming that the nation lives on.

A German view of the Polish soldier leaving his country for a life of pilgrimage and exile.

An Italian patriot bids farewell to his native land as he wanders into exile.

Icon of the patriot in chains: Szymon Konarski in his death-cell.

Icon of the martyred patriot. Note the halo.

Reliquiary containing a twig from the place where the Bandiera brothers were shot in 1844.

to Greece. The poet had half-a-dozen extravagant uniforms run up, acquired two gilded helmets, ten swords and various other accoutrements. For practical as well as cosmetic reasons, he sold the *Bolívar* and chartered a clipper, the *Hercules*.

Byron came ashore at Missolonghi to gun salutes on 5 January 1825 resplendent in a scarlet uniform, and was given the title of *archistrategos*, but it did not confer any authority. The various Greek leaders, who had learned to impress their European admirers by dressing up in increasingly picturesque costumes, were vying for attention and support. News of the English lord's arrival and all the talk of a loan had whetted their appetites, and by the time Byron reached Missolonghi a full-scale civil war had broken out between the various Greek factions. Each one sought a British client, and they managed to transfer their differences to their allies. One faction promoted Odysseus. 'Is he not a noble fellow – a Bolívar? let's make a Washington of him; there are elements in him to form one,' gushed Trelawney.[21] Byron preferred Mavrokordatos, 'the only *Washington* or *Kosciuszko* kind of man amongst them'.[22]

Before long, however, Byron caught a malignant fever and on 19 April 1824 he died. The poor fellow would never know, commented the Duc d'Orléans, that he was dying so that one day people would be able to eat sauerkraut at the foot of the Acropolis. But most people saw the death in more poetic terms. 'He died for the Greeks like another Jesus . . .' wrote Alexandre Dumas.[23] Many believed, because they wished to, that he had died in battle.

The poet's tragic death had a shattering effect; in France alone, no fewer than fourteen books about him appeared in the next six months. Over a hundred volumes of philhellenic verse had been published, and books on every aspect of Greece and its cause poured from the presses. A committee bristling with writers and Napoleonic heroes, headed by Lafayette, collected money. It was the height of fashion in Paris to wear one's watch or locket on a blue-and-white ribbon, thereby indicating that one had donated the gold chain to the cause. Musicians of every kind contributed their offerings, and there were fund-raising concerts and recitals. Berlioz composed a *scena* entitled 'The Greek Revolution', while Rossini's opera *The Siege of Corinth* drew fervent audiences.

But it was the painters whose response proved most memorable. They found in the subject a wonderful opportunity to throw off all restraint, and to wallow in an exotic sphere of the imagination that nobody could question. The sumptuous ethnic dress, the background of blood and ruins, and the decadently priapic associations of the Turk, made the rape of virginal Greece excruciatingly exciting. The Salon of 1824 was dominated by Delacroix's *Massacre of Chios*, which sent shivers of vicarious horror and fascination down Parisian spines. Ary Scheffer contributed his no less prurient *The Souliote Women* and *The Defence of Missolonghi*. And in his *Greece expiring on the Ruins of Missolonghi* of 1826, Delacroix created the ultimate erotic icon of anthropomorphic nationalist desire.

The defence of Missolonghi in April 1826, in which the Greeks fought hard and some blew themselves up rather than surrender, was the one truly heroic episode of the war. The Turks' capture of the town was the result of the energetic direction of the war by Ibrahim Pacha, who had gradually pacified the islands, then, from his base at Navarino, begun recuperating the towns of the Peloponnese one after the other. This new threat, combined with the memory of Byron's fate, mobilized further waves of volunteers for the cause. Captain Jonathan Peckham Miller, who had abandoned a career in the US Army in order to go to university and study the classics, heard the call after a fire consumed the college and all his possessions in 1824. After a short time in Greece, he earned the reputation of a daredevil, unlike his compatriot William Townsend Washington, who claimed to be the son of the great George and got himself painted in Greek costume by Delacroix before coming to Greece, where he contributed only to the sum of intrigue before losing his life in a riot. In May 1825 Colonel Fabvier arrived with a party of battle-hardened freedom fighters from Portugal, including Regnault de St Jean d'Angély, who had been the last man decorated by Napoleon, on the field of Waterloo, and would become a marshal of France. Napoleon's nephew Paul Bonaparte offered his life to the Greek cause, but lost it three weeks after his arrival, when a servant cleaning his gun accidentally shot him. Adolph von Sass, a Swedish officer who had come out with the first wave of volunteers and gone home in disgust, now came back, only to be murdered by a Souliote ally.

Alongside the heroic crusaders came a more practical breed, armed with the full panoply of Benthamite schemes for self-improvement. Leicester Stanhope set about founding schools, hospitals and printing-presses. He was followed by utilitarians and missionaries of every kind determined to assist in the birth of a nation. Dr Samuel Grindley Howe, a 21-year-old medical graduate from Harvard, crossed in love and fired by Byron's example, borrowed the passage money and reached Greece in 1825. He learned Greek and went native, fighting bravely and later setting up farming communities and teaching Greek peasants how to build wheelbarrows.

Late in 1826 Lord Thomas Cochrane sailed on to the scene. Having fallen out with his Brazilian friends and returned to London the previous year, he was approached by the London Greek Committee. He insisted on being paid a great deal of money, even though he was keen to go and fight for the cause. He designed a blue and white flag with an owl at the centre, and looked forward to more derring-do, but he was to be disappointed. Whenever he managed to get within cannon-shot of a Turkish vessel, all his own ships would cut and run. He considered the Greeks under his command to be 'wild and frantic savages', and 'collectively the greatest cowards (not excepting the Brazilians)' he had ever encountered.[24] In 1827 he too abandoned the cause in disgust.

By then, most idealists had become disillusioned. The war had escalated and drawn in the interests of various European powers. In July 1827 Britain, France and Russia agreed to mediate in the conflict and sent a fleet which, three months later, inadvertently sank the entire Turkish fleet in the Bay of Navarino, and the following year Russia went to war with Turkey. In 1830 Greece was declared independent, and in February 1833 Otto I, son of the king of Bavaria, ascended the throne. Sauerkraut indeed.

A German Otto on the throne of Greece was a negation of the dreams that had made Catherine II of Russia christen her grandsons Alexander and Constantine. Her blatant desire to extend her dominion into the Balkans had so alarmed the European powers that Alexander realized he risked a general war if he made a move in that direction. That was why Ypsilantis's call for Russian intervention had gone unanswered. But it does not explain why, amongst the hundreds of young men of every nationality who went to fight for Greek independence, there was not a single Russian. This act can only be explained by the malaise affecting those in Russia who might have answered the call.

It was when the victorious Russian troops returned home at the end of 1814 that the problems started. At the most obvious level, there was the painful readjustment from excitement to boredom. 'Having returned to the fatherland, the armies – from general down to soldier – continually spoke of how good it was in foreign lands', according to a police report. It was now that the backwardness and the absurd nature of the Russian state hit them with full force. The administration was chaotic as well as corrupt. They were offended by the institution of serfdom, the 'degrading sale of men', and felt inspired 'to follow the appeals of Haiti and America'.[25] Worse than any of this was the absence of culture and a general spiritual deadness in society which Pushkin portrays so well in his poems of the time.

The returning heroes were also shocked by the lack of recognition for their services. They had become superfluous. Their sacrifices on the battlefield had not won them, as they would have done elsewhere, inclusion in the power processes of the state. Autocratic Russia expected its soldiers to fight, and when they were not fighting they were subjected to rigorous discipline and a gruelling routine of parades. When not engaged on either of these pursuits, they were to gamble, drink and whore, but under no circumstances occupy themselves with political matters, which belonged solely to the huge, stratified and tightly controlled civil service. The Tsar had noted with displeasure that in the course of their progress through Europe the troops had shed some of their servility. Even his favourite, the Semeonovsky Guards, which had fought with distinction from Moscow to Paris, had grown less stiffly formal. He therefore appointed an undistinguished martinet as colonel and instituted a regime of parades and flogging. These parades, which took place with astonishing frequency, in the presence of the Tsar or one of the Grand Dukes, were choreographed displays of power and control, ballets of submission designed to reduce the man in uniform to the level of automaton.

In 1811 Nikita Mikhailovich Muravyov, who had been reading too much Rousseau, started a society that was to regenerate mankind, and planned a utopian colony on Sakhalin Island. At Poltava in the Ukraine, Peter Borisov founded a 'Pythagorean Sect' and his brother planned to establish a Platonic republic. At about the same time, General Mikhail Orlov, who admired the German Tugendbund, formed a secret society in the army called the Order of Russian Knights. This was superseded by the Union of Salvation, which, two years later, turned into the Union of Welfare. These were not revolutionary societies. They were a response to the moral and systemic inadequacies of Russia as revealed by her defeat at the hands of Napoleon and her inability to open a new chapter after 1815. The constitution of the Union of Welfare, for instance, rambles on incontinently about bringing charity back into human relationships, and while it betrays the influence of Rousseau, it also quotes Saint Paul. Its aim was the welfare of society and, by extension, the restoration of Russia's moral greatness.

This was a period of unprecedented literary flowering in Russia, and its protagonists saw themselves as blazing a trail through a jungle of derivative verbiage, stale attitudes and institutionalized mediocrity. Leaving aside the purely political aspects of censorship, young writers found themselves up against a chillingly impervious establishment. The societies they formed, such as Kondrati Fyodorovich Ryleyev's Free Society of Lovers of Russian Literature; Arzamas, of which Pushkin was a leading light; the 'Green Lamp'; the Friendly Literary Society of Moscow and so on, could not avoid crossing over into politics in a situation where the state itself viewed all activity as political.

The cast of thought afflicting these people is nicely illustrated by a piece, entitled *A Dream*, written by Alexandr Dmitrievich Ulybyshev for his colleagues of the 'Green Lamp' around 1819. The person having the dream finds himself in a Petersburg that he cannot recognize; one of the imperial palaces has been converted into a pantheon for the great men of Russia, the Smolny Monastery has been replaced by a triumphal arch erected 'on the ruins of fanaticism', and so on. Seeing a crowd converging on a gigantic building, he follows it. 'Inside, a noble simplicity corresponded to the magnificence outside,' explains the dreamer. 'The interior of the cupola, supported by three rows of columns, represented the Heavens with their constellations. In the middle of the hall rose a white marble altar on which an eternal flame was burning.' He listens to a magnificent rendition of Haydn's *Creation*, after which a venerable old man addresses the congregation. He tells them that the poor are in need, and in minutes a vast amount of money is collected for them. The dreamer approaches the priestly figure, who becomes his mentor. Noticing that everyone is wearing the 'old Russian kaftan', the dreamer asks him when they gave up Western clothes. 'Since we have become a nation,' comes the answer. There follow pages about the need to recover ancient simplicity and to reject the false sophistry of foreigners.[26]

Levels of excitement rose perceptibly among members of these societies with news of Karl Sand's assassination of Kotzebue, of Bolívar's triumphs, of the risings in Italy and the Riego revolt in Spain. It was this last that held the greatest fascination, for most of the members of secret societies were officers, and the model of the *pronunciamiento* one of the few instruments open to them in the prevailing conditions of Russia.

In October 1820, the commander of the Semeonovsky regiment ordered the flogging of a number of soldiers who had been decorated with the St George Cross, Russia's highest military decoration. This broke an unwritten code, and the soldiers wrote a note of protest. Tsar Alexander, who heard of the incident while at the conference in Troppau, took it as a mutiny, a manifestation of the 'general mental infection' sweeping Europe. After being disciplined, the men of the Semeonovsky regiment were dispersed among other units in different parts of the Empire – a characteristically imbecilic way of dealing with infection, which demands isolation rather than dispersal over the widest possible area. The authorities were rattled. On 1 August 1822 all societies were banned. The university of St Petersburg was 'reorganized', and this was followed by waves of expulsions from the universities of Dorpat and Wilno. Russians were forbidden to attend German universities.

The Union of Welfare was now illegal, and its programme grew markedly more political as a result. In 1822 it split into a Northern Society in St Petersburg and a Southern Society based in the garrisons of the Ukraine. The leader of the latter was the 29-year-old Pavel Ivanovich Pestel. He had been educated in Germany and at the St Petersburg military academy, had been wounded at Borodino and distinguished himself in the campaigns of the next two years, becoming a full colonel in 1821. He was a convinced republican, in favour of emancipating the serfs, but he had no social programme or economic policy in place, and no shared platform with local dissidents.

The Society of United Slavs had been active in the Ukraine since 1823, when the Borisov brothers, founders of the 'Pythagorean Sect', joined forces with a number of Poles in the area. It had no programme, only a hazy set of philanthropic principles and a masonic oath brim full of love and liberation. While it rejected violent upheaval in favour of moral regeneration through a process of self-improvement, it had extensive contacts with the Poles, Ruthenes and other national groups. Pestel was categorical that all minorities in Russia, including the Jews, must either assimilate completely or face expulsion. He made a pragmatic exception of the Poles, whose right to independence he conceded, but only on condition that they introduce social equality and accept frontiers to suit 'Russia's convenience'. In 1823, negotiations were opened between the

Southern Society and delegates of the Polish Patriotic Society, but there was suspicion on both sides. Local Polish landowners such as Stanisław Worcell had been setting up regional branches in the Ukraine, and this annoyed the Russians, who felt it to be their preserve. Meetings were arranged, but no real community of interest emerged. The Russians wanted the Poles to stage a rising in Poland that would tie down Russian forces, and to infiltrate the mixed Russian and Polish army units. The Poles were wary of being used by the Russians for their own ends, while the Russians feared the Poles might take advantage of the situation to detach former Polish provinces from Russia.

The Northern Society was led by Nikita Muravyov, a younger man than Pestel. His plan for Russia envisaged a federal constitutional monarchy based partly on the American model. But his close associates included a number of desperadoes, such as Alexander Yakubovich, memorably described by a colleague as 'a storm in a glass of water'. A typical 'superfluous man', he had distinguished himself fighting in the Caucasus, where he had been sent as punishment for a duel, and now wanted to assassinate the emperor. Another who wanted to kill Alexander was Peter Kakhovsky, who had returned from a tour abroad in 1825 and, disgusted with the situation in Russia, decided to go and die for liberty in Greece. He was dissuaded from this course by Ryleyev, who urged him to join the Northern Society instead. Ryleyev was trying to put together a '*garde perdue*' of people prepared to act suicidally, and in Kakhovsky he had found the perfect man. 'What can be sweeter than death after feeling that one has contributed something to one's country?' Kakhovsky would write in his prison cell.[27]

These people were living out a fantasy of sorts and there was much posturing in their behaviour. The original literary depiction of a 'superfluous man', Pushkin's hero Eugene Onegin, has a portrait of Byron on the wall and a statuette of Napoleon on the desk of his study, and for his morning stroll he dons, fashionably, a 'Bolívar' hat. In Griboyedov's play *Woe from Wit*, Chatsky is recognizable as one not because of what he says, but because of the way he behaves. His rejection of certain rituals of politeness, his seriousness and air of morose condescension identify him as 'a dangerous man'. While these men talked of hope, they were deeply fatalistic and enjoyed contemplating daggers, skulls and death. They compensated for their alienation from formal society with a cult of fraternity. As Pushkin explains in the unfinished tenth book of *Eugene Onegin*, it had all started as idle chatter between the Château Lafitte and the Veuve Clicquot, and while the discussions grew more dangerous, the drinking and debauchery remained a part of the ritual, an affirmation of togetherness and otherness. They were condemned to immaturity by their upbringing and the system under which they were obliged to live, a system in which the state took responsibility for everything, including its subjects' consciences.

In March 1824 Pestel came to St Petersburg to confer with the leadership of the Northern Society, but their talks only brought out their divisions and lack of direction. All they could agree on was that they would warn each other if either society decided to act, and support the other when it did. With their groundless admiration for Riego, they never bothered to prepare their men to participate in a revolt or to enlist the support of other sections of society. 'Our revolution', Mikhail Pavlovich Bestuzhev explained to Borisov, 'will be similar to the Spanish Revolution of 1820; it will not cost a single drop of blood, for it will be executed by the army alone, without the assistance of the people.'[28] Nobody bothered to point out that Riego had failed.

On 19 November 1825 Alexander I died in Taganrog. His natural successor was his brother Constantine, and on 27 November, after news of the Tsar's death reached St Petersburg, the army and the civil service solemnly took the oath of allegiance to him. What nobody knew outside the imperial family was that Constantine, who had contracted a morganatic marriage, had renounced his claim to the throne in favour of the younger brother, Nicholas. Once this was made known, the date of 14 December was set for the army and civil service to take the oath to him instead.

Constantine was no liberal, but many in Russia fancied he might be. And he was, for no very good reason, popular in the army. These two pieces of flimsy ground, and the slight confusion caused by the need for a second oath-taking, were what the leaders of the Northern Society decided to build their hopes on. They made hasty preparations to act, and sent word to their colleagues in the Ukraine. They held a last meeting on 13 December, in an atmosphere of romantic delirium quite incompatible with the execution of any serious purpose. 'We are destined to die!' exclaimed Ryleyev, at his most poetic, to which Prince Alexander Odoyevsky added: 'We shall die, oh how gloriously we shall die!'[29] They then dispersed into the night.

Early next morning, Mikhail and Alexander Bestuzhev assembled their battalion of the Moskovsky regiment and explained to the soldiers that Grand Duke Constantine, to whom they had sworn allegiance, had been chained up in a dungeon, all because he had wanted to improve the lot of the common soldier. They then led the bewildered troops out to liberate him. They marched the battalion to Senate Square where, soon after 9 a.m., they were joined by units of the Marine Guards and Grenadiers, under Nicholas Bestuzhev. On his way, he had called in on Ryleyev, whom he had found togging up as a peasant, meaning to appear on the square in this guise to symbolize the union between army and people.

The situation was skirting the absurd. There were by now some three thousand troops formed up neatly in Senate Square, making up a sort of standing revolution. It was freezing cold, and nothing was happening. The spectacle drew large numbers of civilian onlookers. Every so often, one of the officers would shout 'Long live Constantine and the Constitution!' and the soldiers dutifully huzza'd what they took to be the imperial couple – none of them had the faintest idea of what a constitution might be, while the Russian word for it, *konstitutsya*, sounded to them like a lady's name. As time passed, other members of the Northern Society turned up and made a great show of revolutionary zeal, only to disappear again. Yakubovich, the desperado who had been talking of assassination, appeared holding his hat aloft on the end of his sabre. He hailed liberty and death, then, pleading a headache, went home. The two most senior conspirators on the spot, Prince Evgenyi Petrovich Obolensky and Nicholas Bestuzhev, tried to make one another take command. Colonel Bulatov, who was to be the right-hand man to the 'Dictator', turned up, had a look round, and then reported to military headquarters, where he took the oath to Nicholas. Of the 'Dictator' himself, there was no sign.

Prince Sergei Petrovich Trubetskoy had been chosen for this role because he was the most distinguished member of the Northern Society in the social sense. Although he was prone to the same emotions as his colleagues, he was a conservative at heart. He had prepared a proclamation which promised the abolition of serfdom and other liberal measures, but it was never read out. He feared upheaval and had hoped that matters would somehow be arranged with the consent of the new emperor. Instead of going to Senate Square to take command, he went to military headquarters and asked where he could take the oath to Nicholas, then took a cab and drove from one government office to another, protesting his innocence, after which he sought asylum at the Austrian Embassy.

In the course of the morning, most of the army and the civil service took the oath to the new emperor without demur, and the commander of the St Petersburg garrison, General Miloradovich, had no trouble in mustering a sufficient body of loyal troops to confront the mutineers on Senate Square, where Nicholas joined him. The Tsar sent Miloradovich to the mutineers with a summons to surrender. They shouted abuse at the general and, when he turned to ride back, shot and killed him. Nicholas sent another officer, who was also shot, then the Metropolitan Seraphim, and finally the Grand Duke Paul, who was nearly shot as well. His next move was to send a body of cavalry against the mutineers, which was a mistake. The horsemen could not charge properly on the icy cobbles, and when they found themselves forced to turn back, many horses slipped and ditched their riders. By the middle of the afternoon, fortune was beginning to swing to the side of the rebels. The crowd had swelled, and shouts hostile to Nicholas began to be heard. These became louder and more frequent, with the call for him to abdicate accompanied by flying stones and even a few shots.

Nicholas was finally spurred into action by one of his generals, and gave the order for the artillery to open up with canister shot. The mutineers had no option but to fall back, but as they began to retreat, they became mixed up with the fleeing crowd of civilians, and the whole seething mass was lacerated by the bursting shells. Many tried to escape by taking to the ice on the River Neva, but the artillery broke that up with cannon-balls, and they drowned. Nobody has been able to compute the death-toll of the Decembrist revolt with any accuracy.

While the Northern Society passed into history on Senate Square, their comrades in the south were doing nothing. By a curious coincidence, Pestel had been arrested on 13 December. His comrades were debating what to do about this when, on 23 December, they received news of the planned and, unbeknown to them, already quelled rising in St Petersburg. As it happened, the next in command after Pestel, Sergei Muravyov-Apostol, was away in Kiev, so they did not go into action at once. When they did, it was with more energy but even less sense of purpose than their northern colleagues. Muravyov-Apostol mustered some 800 men of the Chernigovsky regiment on 30 December. He marched about collecting other small units, but he lost as many men through desertion as he gained through adherence. On 31 December, he drew up his whole force before a church and read out his 'catechism', which explained to the soldiers that they were unhappy because the Tsars had been acting against the will of God, and that it was their duty to rise up and free themselves from this perverted rule. It is doubtful that he made himself understood. After he had finished, one soldier turned to his lieutenant and politely asked which Tsar it was they had just sworn an oath to. On 3 January they came up against a superior force, supported by artillery, and they were quickly routed.

There followed a massive rounding-up and meticulous interrogation of suspects. The investigation singled out some 300 who were disciplined, transferred to other regiments and kept under surveillance, 121 who were given sentences ranging from imprisonment in Siberia, through internal exile, to demotion and service in the ranks of a line regiment. Pestel, Ryleyev, Muravyov, Muravyov-Apostol and Mikhail Bestuzhev were condemned to death. They were hanged at dawn on 13 July 1826 in the Peter and Paul Fortress, in the presence of the garrison, drawn up in parade order. As though fate had wished to prove a point, three of the ropes broke, and the condemned men fell to the ground. 'They can't even hang a man properly in Russia!' snapped Muravyov as he waited for the executioner to prepare a new rope.[30]

The Decembrists accepted their fate with a passivity redolent of martyrdom. The survivors did not sit around going over their mistakes or wishing they had planned things otherwise. They appeared almost content to have played the role of precursors, of those whose sacrifice was necessary in order to show up the evil nature of the system. The priest officiating at the executions reported that the five had did like saints, and handed out effects taken from them as relics. As though sensing this, the authorities forbade those sent to Siberia to have their portraits sketched in any form – they might be used to make prints, which would become icons.

Alexander Herzen, a schoolboy of fourteen, watched as Nicholas celebrated his victory over the Decembrists at a special service of thanksgiving in the Moscow Kremlin, with the guards regiments kneeling in serried ranks. He was possessed by a violent hatred of that monarch and those guards. With his schoolfriend Nikolay Ogarev, he began to think only of joining in the struggle begun by the Decembrists, and the decision matured one day when they were out walking together on Sparrow Hills. 'The sun was setting, the cupolas glittered, the city lay stretched further than the eye could reach; a fresh breeze blew on our faces, we stood leaning against each other and, suddenly embracing, vowed in sight of all Moscow to sacrifice our lives to the struggle we had chosen,' writes Herzen. They made secret plans together and dreamed of changing the world, but their imagination was gripped by the fate of the Decembrists. 'It is a strange thing that almost all our day-dreams ended in Siberia or the scaffold and hardly ever in triumph,' he remembers.[31] This was not surprising. Nicholas never forgot the fear he had felt and never forgave the humiliation he had suffered at the very outset of his reign. He was to prove a worthy partner for Metternich.

By the end of the 1820s the Holy Alliance appeared to have triumphed over all the young enthusiasms of Europe. The budding hopes of national regeneration in the Italian and Iberian peninsulas had been effectively snuffed out. The mirage of a brave new dawn in South America had dissolved, the glorious promise of Greece had been collared by the powers, the fresh spark of new life in Russia had been no more than that. The policemen had the Continent under control. There was nowhere left for young Romantics to go and die for a cause, and they felt powerless to affect conditions in their own countries. All they could do was read the wonderful new literature and dream of more heroic times.

14
Glory Days

'People and poets are marching together,' wrote the French critic Charles Augustin Sainte-Beuve in 1830. 'Art is henceforth on a popular footing, in the arena with the masses.'[1] There was something in this. Never before or since had poetry been so widely and so urgently read, so taken to heart and so closely studied for hidden meaning. And it was not only in search of aesthetic or emotional uplift that people did so, for the poet had assumed a new role over the past two decades. Art was no longer an amenity but a great truth that had to be revealed to mankind, and the artist was one who had been called to interpret this truth, a kind of seer. In Russia, Pushkin solemnly declared the poet's status as prophet uttering the burning words of truth. The American Ralph Waldo Emerson saw poets as 'liberating gods' because they had achieved freedom themselves, and could therefore free others.[2] The pianist and composer Franz Liszt wanted to recapture the 'political, philosophical and religious power' that he believed music had in ancient times.[3] William Blake claimed that Jesus and his disciples were all artists, and that he himself was following Jesus through his art.[4] 'God was, perhaps, only the first poet of the universe,' Théophile Gauthier reflected.[5] By the 1820s artists regularly referred to their craft as a religion, and Victor Hugo represented himself alternately as Zoroaster, Moses and Christ, somewhere between prophet and God.

Social man's natural reaction to repression and censorship is to transfer his thoughts to a medium other than words or one in which words can have a double meaning. Parallel modes of expression, visual and aural, spring up to serve the need for communication, comprehensible to all yet difficult for the censor to nail down and condemn. The debate that should be conducted in the open with plain words is simply transferred to another forum, one far more dangerous for the authorities, as it denies them the possibility of any response but that of outright prohibition. Thus the arts followed the secret societies in becoming a political means of communication and the expression of a political faith. Heinrich Heine once declared that he did not mind whether he was remembered as a poet. 'But a sword should be laid on my bier, for I have been a steadfast soldier in the war of liberation of humanity,' he insisted.[6]

In the repressive climate of post-1815 Europe, poetry and music served this purpose best, particularly in forms where they came together. The *chansonnier* poets were powerful manipulators of public opinion in Restoration France, and the increasingly popular form of opera was to take this role further still. It became the platform not for disseminating information or views, but for generating mood and feeling, and a marshalling ground for their active expression. There was much that was ironic in this, since opera as an art form grew out of court masques and entertainments aimed at the glorification of the monarch.

The connection between opera and the court remained tight up to the revolution. After 1789 the relationship shifted to one with the Assembly and then the Convention. If anything, the art form became even more firmly bound to the state, whose glory it was now called upon to proclaim, without the niceties of allegory. Spectacle moved out of the theatre on to the street, in the many festivals and rituals of the revolutionary period. Napoleon did not need opera. With its stylish trappings, its cast of heroic thousands, its Faustian plot and, most of all, its Promethean hero, the Empire provided a grand opera in itself. After the Restoration, opera assumed the role of making up for the dreariness of life, providing escapist dreams and encouraging people to entertain their own. It reverted to the domain of the court in terms of control, but it had developed a nature of its own, and that nature was not royalist.

When Don Giovanni sings '*Viva la libertá!*' in Mozart's eponymous opera, he is dreaming of debauchery rather than revolution. But when the opera was staged in Vienna in 1788 the censors demanded that he sing '*Viva la societá!*' instead.[7] Their apprehension was prophetic: from the 1790s onwards, a remarkable proportion of operas dwelt on tyranny, imprisonment and escape, and by the 1820s most were fundamentally subversive. Many were set in historical context and drew their dramatic effect from the juxtaposition of personal revolt and national rebellion. Subjects such as the legend of William Tell or Tomasso Aniello's (Masaniello's) 1647 revolt in Naples combined grand national rhetoric and stirring choruses with intimate personal tragedy in a winning formula.

When faced with Daniel Auber's *La Muette de Portici*, one of many operas and plays on the subject of Masaniello's revolt, the French censors cut heavily, deleting lines such as '*le peuple est maître*' and '*Il faut armer le peuple*', but little good it did them. When, at the première in February 1828, the tenor Adolphe Nourrit, playing the part of Mansaniello in an open shirt, tricolor pantaloons and a red phrygian cap, intoned the refrain '*Amour sacré de la Patrie*', he brought the house down. What the censors had failed to notice, since the old anthem had been banned in 1815, but the audience *did* recognize immediately, was that the phrase came straight out of the *Marseillaise*.[8] There was, in fact, no way of making such an opera 'safe'. The more the authorities tried, the more it grew into a symbol of subversion and a clarion-call of revolt. Such symbols and calls played a vital part in what happened in the year 1830.

The first night of Victor Hugo's play *Hernani*, on 25 February 1830, set the tone for the new year. The play, which is about an outlaw struggling for love and liberation against fate and the Habsburg establishment, nicely encapsulated all the most fashionable themes. Its form also broke all the artistic conventions, and in the preface Hugo declared that the Romantic style was no more or less than liberalism in the arts. The theatre was the scene of a pitched battle between classicists and Romantics, an artistic dress rehearsal for what was to come in the political sphere.

The ineptitude of the opposition under the Restoration had given the Bourbons the impression that they were firmly in the saddle. Louis XVIII died peacefully in 1824 and was uneventfully succeeded by his brother, the Comte d'Artois, as Charles X. He began turning back the clock as soon as he ascended the throne, insisting on having himself crowned at Rheims in May 1825 with the full ceremonial of tradition. Meaning to strengthen the throne's position further, Charles X strove to undermine the principles of the *Charte* that had been the foundation of the Restoration. An economic depression in the years 1826–7 provoked unrest in various parts, and in November 1827 there was a rising in Paris. But the feelings that led to it were diffuse and vague. Among the young men on the barricades was Auguste Blanqui, who confessed to not knowing exactly what he was fighting for, even though this was to be the beginning of a long life dedicated to revolt. The rising was quickly quashed, but the emotions that underlay it were not so easily dealt with.

These had no leader to coalesce around, aside from the largely symbolic figure of Lafayette. He had been associated with every conspiracy since 1815, but did not lead any of them. Although he took pride in his revolutionary credentials and could not resist young enthusiasts, he had grown more practical with age and was now keener on constitutional reform. He nevertheless remained the most respected figure in French public life. His American trip of 1824 had enhanced his standing, and his agitation for the Greek cause had given him an opportunity to fly the flag of liberty. He was recognized as representing all that was finest in French political culture.

Frustrated by the Chamber of Deputies, Charles X decided to dissolve it and call an election in March 1830. This yielded an increased opposition. The king set his mind on a show of strength and on 26 July announced a set of emergency *ordonnances*, abrogating press freedom, dissolving the newly-elected Chamber and limiting the franchise for the next election. The following day barricades began to go up and people started looting gunsmiths' shops. The situation was serious but not critical, as the protesters had no leaders, no plan, and no particular idea of what they wanted. Nor were they representative of the population at large. The former Napoleonic marshal Marmont was in command of the 10,000 troops in the capital, and he should have been able to prevent the rising from gaining ground, but he received conflicting orders. The king intended to ride the storm but then changed his mind, by which time it was too late. After two days of confused fighting, Marmont's troops began to go over to the other side. By 29 July most of Paris was controlled by the insurgents, and the municipal committee in the Hôtel de Ville was behaving like a provisional government. Charles X fled abroad, as he had done on 16 July 1789.

This rising, unplanned and undirected, was motivated by a spectrum of grievances and desires, but frustration of one sort or another was probably the dominant motor during its three-day duration, which came to be called '*Les Trois Glorieuses*'. Some of the insurgents were poor and hungry, but poverty and hunger were noticeably absent from the slogans and banners. The most commonly heard shout was '*Vive la liberté!*', but its meaning depended very much on who was doing the shouting. There were those who wanted constitutional change, but most would have been hard put to it to define their demands. The cry of 'Smash the Romantics!' was more in evidence than any calls for bread or better working conditions.

The Romantics were out in force. Alexandre Dumas manned a barricade with the painter Paul Huet, a former *Carbonaro.* Franz Liszt was caught up in the excitement and roamed the streets encouraging the insurgents and meditating a Revolutionary Symphony. Stendhal stayed at home during the three days, engrossed in *Le Mémorial de Sainte-Hélène,* that bible of the cult of Napoleon. Dumas, who was helping to build a barricade on the Place de l'Odéon on the second day of the revolt, witnessed a scene that fully justified Stendhal's studies. As he and his companions toiled away, tearing up paving-stones and heaving furniture on to the barricade, the owner of a nearby riding-school rode up on a white horse, in a tightly buttoned coat and a black tricorn hat, and came to a halt, with one hand held behind his back. The resemblance to Napoleon was so striking that the whole crowd began to shout: '*Vive l'Empereur!*' An old woman fell to her knees, made the sign of the cross, and cried out: 'Oh! Jesus! that I should have been allowed to see him before I die! . . .'[9]

In the moral confusion, it was symbols and shibboleths that carried the day. Foremost among these was the *Marseillaise.* It was on the lips of the first confused crowds as they began to build their barricades, and the sound electrified the capital. When the tenor Nourrit sang it on the stage of the Opéra, a religious silence fell, and some went down on their knees. By popular demand, Nourrit would mount the stage in full National Guard uniform every evening for the next three months to sing the sacred hymn, holding a tricolor flag. For the composer Hector Berlioz, the hymn provided one of the great musical experiences of his life. He had been writing an orchestral cantata for the competition of the Institut de France when the revolution began. All through 28 July he worked feverishly at the score in the Palais Mazarin, while bullets and cannon-balls thudded against the walls and pattered over the roof. The following day, having finished the piece, he got hold of a pistol and joined 'the holly rabble' on the streets. At one point he came across a group of young men singing rousing battle-songs. A crowd gathered, and when Berlioz and the singers wanted to leave, they were pursued by thousands of frantic admirers. They were finally cornered in a cul-de-sac, and had no option but to continue singing. They ascended to a first-floor room and opened the windows so that they could be seen and heard by the crowd. They intoned the

Marseillaise. 'Almost at once the seething mass at our feet grew quiet and a holy stillness fell upon them,' recalls Berlioz. When it came to the chorus of '*Aux armes, citoyens!*' the multitude of men, women and children, 'hot from the barricades, their pulses still throbbing with the excitement of the recent struggle', gave voice, and Berlioz sank to the floor, overcome with emotion.[10]

The other defining symbol of *Les Trois Glorieuses* was the tricolor, also banned in 1814. Dumas was crossing a bridge on 28 July when he suddenly saw it flying over Notre Dame. 'I leaned over the parapet, my arms outstretched, my eyes fixed and bathed in tears.'[11] And it was the tricolor that was to decide the outcome of the revolution. The instincts driving the insurgents on to the barricades, and those that made the royal troops waver and then go over to the other side, were emotional and spiritual rather than political. Those July days were not born of any deep sense of injustice and they were not about bringing in a new social order. They were a rejection of the Bourbon restoration and an attempt to regain the spirit of 1789. They were a reaffirmation of the primacy of the nation, which had been ignored and insulted by the Bourbons.

On 29 July, when the fighting was pretty well over, Lafayette set out for the Hôtel de Ville, cheered by the population. He was the one man everyone could fall in behind. But he was not a man who could wield power. No one understood this better than the only member of the French royal family still in Paris, the Duc d'Orléans. Louis Philippe d'Orléans had been crafting his image carefully, gradually manoeuvring himself into the position of being both the acceptable face of royalty and the representative of the spirit of 1792. He cultivated artists and heaped patronage and flattery on popular writers, who served him well. In 1824 he sponsored a great exhibition of contemporary French painting at the Palais-Royal, which, incidentally, featured two great canvases by Vernet depicting him at Valmy and Jemappes.

The duke kept out of sight during the July Days, using Béranger and Ary Scheffer to put forward his name and sound out opinion on his behalf. He had the support of many constitutional liberals, and of what might be described as the business interest. As soon as it became apparent that the cause of Charles X was dead, people opposed to a republic began to look to Orléans as the lesser of two evils. It was only then that he sidled into the limelight. On 30 July a delegation from the moderates in the Chamber of Deputies invited Orléans to become 'Lieutenant of the Kingdom', and the following day he went to the Hôtel de Ville, where Lafayette was doing his best to contain the more radical elements.

As Orléans stood on the balcony of the Hôtel de Ville with Lafayette, facing a sullen crowd, he had the brilliant idea of seizing a huge tricolor flag and brandishing it while he embraced the general. Its folds framed the figures of Lafayette and the duke, brushing their faces, and the crowd erupted into a frenzy of enthusiastic applause. Orléans was the hero of the hour, and a couple of days later he had been acclaimed Louis Philippe, King of the French. It was his reward for intelligent observation. He knew the power of the tricolor and its importance for ordinary Frenchmen. When an officer serving with the French forces in Algeria gave his soldiers the news of *Les Trois Glorieuses*, explaining that the hated Bourbons had fallen, and that their new king was a constitutional monarch who had fought at Valmy, they were unmoved. 'It was only when they learned that the tricolor had replaced the white standard that these good men gave vent to their joy,' he writes.[12]

Joy was the prevalent emotion in France at the end of July 1830. 'As soon as the heat of combat had died down,' noted the legitimist Comtesse de Boigne on 29 July, 'it became a city of brothers.'[13] The poor were still poor, the hungry still hungry, but they had been given back their dreams. A few days after the theatricals at the Hôtel de Ville, Eugène Pottier, a minor composer best known for writing the *Internationale*, wrote a short poem which said it all:

Je vois déjà le drapeau tricolore
De mon pays emblème protecteur
Sur nos remparts qu'avec gloire il décore
Il est pour nous le signal du bonheur.[14]

This joy at the new dawn was not confined to France. Just as in 1789, a shudder of excitement ran through the Western world. 'It roused my utmost enthusiasm, and gave me, as it were, a new existence,' wrote John Stuart Mill, then twenty-four, who hastened to Paris, where he gazed rapt on Lafayette and other heroes of the July days.[15] Heinrich Heine, though older, reacted with lyricism to 'the thick packet of newspapers with the warm, glowing-hot news'. 'Each item was a sunbeam, wrapped in printed paper, and together they kindled my soul into a wild glow . . . Lafayette, the tricolor, the Marseillaise – it intoxicates me. Bold, ardent hopes spring up, like trees with golden fruit and branches that shoot up wildly till their leaves touch the clouds.'[16]

And there was the same quasi-religious reverence surrounding what had happened. A Belgian radical who was in Germany at the end of July recorded a scene in a Karlsruhe inn. 'We saw a group of Baden officers, sitting together at the table d'hôte, rise up suddenly in a respectful silence when one of them, opening a letter sent to him from Strasbourg, let a tricolor cockade drop out of the envelope.'[17] In an attempt to stop the spread of the infection, several German governments prohibited performances of operas such as *La Muette de Portici* and *Guilleaume Tell.*[18] They knew what they were doing: a performance of one of them was responsible for launching an insurrection that created a nation where people had least expected it – in Belgium.

The new kingdom of Holland created by the Congress of Vienna was a characteristic botch. It lumped together the predominantly Catholic Habsburg provinces of Flanders and Brabant with the Protestant Netherlands, creating a country which consisted of some two million Dutch and four million Belgians. 'The unification of Belgium and Holland fundamentally violated all the laws of affinity', in the words of one contemporary. 'Religion, manners and customs; history, industry and commerce, everything clashed in this monstrous association.'[19]

At the top of the social scale, there was resentment at the Dutch dominance of the officer corps in the army, further down there was discontent over the Calvinist grip on education, and at the base there was anger at what appeared to be unfair fiscal penalization of the more industrialized Belgian areas. This last was inflated by the bumpy process of industrialization in the fifteen years after 1815, which created troughs of unemployment and low wages. There had been a hard winter, followed by a drop in demand and massive lay-offs, resulting in widespread misery. The feelings bred by this were focused not on employers, but on machines and, to a certain extent, on the government that stood behind them, that of King William I of Holland.

Brussels ran London close in terms of providing haven for political refugees. The city was home to the arch-conspirator Buonarotti and the ageing former member of the revolutionary Convention Sieyès, to the regicide painter David and to countless exiles from Italy, Spain and Portugal. But there was no active group of local radicals. And there were no poets. When the exiles heard the news from Paris in July, most of them rushed to the French capital in order to breathe the air of revolution.

The news from Paris also set a few Belgian patriots dreaming. More importantly, it emboldened the by now desperate workers of the south, creating an atmosphere of unrest that suggested to officials the wisdom of cancelling the usual celebrations of the king's birthday on 25 August. But nobody thought of cancelling the Brussels première of Auber's opera *La Muette de Portici*, scheduled for the same evening at the Théâtre de la Monnaie. The house was packed, and every rebellious hothead in Brussels was in the audience. When the singer playing the part of Masaniello intoned *Amour Sacré de la Patrie*, they stood up as one and joined in, after which they burst into a rendering of the *Marseillaise*. They stormed out of the theatre and marched on the offices of the unpopular newspaper *Le National*, which they sacked. The owner's private house came next, followed by those of the chief of police and the minister of justice.

The *Garde Bourgeoise* failed to contain the situation, and what troops there were in the city judged it wise to retire. The poor scented their chance, and food shops were looted. After satisfying the first pangs of their hunger, labourers began to smash machinery and voice demands. This sobered up the middle-class patriots, who had been happily tearing down royal insignia and replacing them with a tricolor in the black, yellow and red of Brabant. The civic guard went into action, and by the end of the second day the capital was quiet.

There had also been rioting and a rash of machine-wrecking in other towns, notably in Verviers and Liège, where the French tricolor had been flown and the *Marseillaise* sung, and where shouts of '*Vive Napoléon!*' had been heard. But here, as in Brussels, the outbreaks were quickly brought under control by the propertied classes through the agency of the civic guard. By the end of August calm had settled on the country, and the only problem was that of what to do next. 'Few Belgians, beginning with the authors, or rather actors, of the insurrection, understood it', according to a contemporary observer, 'nobody, or nearly nobody, wanted a revolution.'[20] But that was soon to change.

On 31 August the king's son, the Prince of Orange, announced his intention of entering Brussels at the head of his troops and demanded that all tricolor flags and cockades be replaced with orange ones. This incensed the fortuitous patriots, and a few barricades went up in the city. The prince was in conciliatory mood, and the next day he rode in without an armed escort. The discussions he held with the provisional council turned mainly on the symbolic question of national colours, for, aside from a raft of petty local grievances, there was not much else at issue.

But the opposition to Dutch rule was coming together. On 2 September a contingent of a hundred young patriots from Liège marched into Brussels singing the *Marseillaise*, some of them wearing retrieved medals bearing the profile of Van der Noot, the 'Washington' of 1787. Emigrés returning from France joined Brussels lawyers, journalists, minor noblemen and former Napoleonic officers, all of whom felt a sense of thwarted ambition, in making patriotic noises. The middle classes, who had come out into the street as civic guards to restore order and guarantee their property, and having hijacked the popular unrest, had to harness it to a cause that would not threaten their own interests.

On 3 September, the word 'separation' was publicly uttered in Brussels, and a body of opinion rallied to the idea. The papers inveighed against a system that went 'against nature'. 'From now on everything will be Belgian in Belgium,' announced the *Journal de Verviers*. 'What immense consequences will flow from this one fact! What a future! What a magical and beneficent revolution!' All the anti-Dutch feelings came flooding out. 'Let us be ourselves, let us be Belgians,' urged *La Politique*, 'then we will have a motherland, a motherland that will no longer be a lie, a motherland that will not have been imposed by a congress, but one which lives in our hearts.'[21]

Although he was not averse to some concessions, King William decided to negotiate from a position of strength, and he set his younger son, Frederick, the task of reoccupying Brussels with 10,000 picked soldiers. This was a mistake. The approach of the royal troops only galvanized the radicals. On the night of 19 September crowds led by Charles Rogier and a detachment of Liégeois volunteers gathered in the city centre. They levelled accusations of treachery at the middle-class Committee of Safety, and shots were exchanged. By morning most of the civic guards had been disarmed, and the rest joined the mob. Moderates left Brussels or skulked behind shuttered windows, while a provisional government was established. Detachments of armed volunteers roamed the streets singing *La Brabançonne*, the Belgian *Marseillaise*.

On 21 September the first skirmishes with royal troops took place outside the city, and although few people fell and no advantage was gained by either party, both sides drew confidence from them. The royal troops took their time to prepare their next move. The defenders, mainly journeymen and artisans, with a sprinkling of middle-class youth and former Napoleonic soldiers, topped up with a complement of foreigners, were no match for regular troops. But their baptism of fire gave them heart.

Prince Frederick launched his attack on 23 September, and the main column of royal troops marched into the outskirts. The population was mostly passive, some people cheered, and in one instance at least, they dismantled a barricade to let the troops pass. But a less cordial reception met some cavalry that had ridden into the narrow streets of one of the poorer quarters, and it had to retreat before a hail of cooking pots and other projectiles. The main column was engaged in the city's principal park by the most spirited of the insurgents, volunteers from Liège and Louvain. The troops made slow progress for the rest of that day and the whole of the next. By the evening of 24 September the insurgents had been reinforced by volunteers from the countryside, and by some civic guards. They had also acquired leaders.

One was Anne François Mellinet, a French colonel who had fought at Waterloo and been exiled in 1816. He had settled in Brussels, where he shared lodgings with the painter David. He now assumed command of the insurgent positions in the Place Royale. 'He was dressed in a great blue riding coat belted at the waist with a sash of monstrous proportions', according to a witness. 'A large Turkish sabre and a great tricorn hat crowned by an immense cockade completed this hybrid costume of a representative of the people, in which two generations met without becoming one.'[22] An intermediate generation was represented by General Giovanni Durando, a Piedmontese officer who had taken part in the revolt of 1821 and then moved on to fight for liberty in Portugal before settling into Belgian exile.

Another old hand was Don Juan van Halen, a Spaniard descended from a Walloon family. He had fought in the Spanish navy at Trafalgar and been wounded on the streets of Madrid on 2 May 1808, the Dos de Mayo, and had subsequently captured three fortresses from the French. Like so many other heroes, he was shabbily treated by Ferdinand VII, fell in with other disaffected officers and joined a masonic lodge. He was arrested in 1815, handed over to the Inquisition and tortured. Friends helped him escape from a dungeon in Madrid, and he made his way to London. Having no means of subsistence, he volunteered for service in Russia, and was commissioned as a major of cavalry in 1819. He served under General

Yermolov on the Caucasian front, and then in Georgia, Ossetia and Karabakh. When he heard news of the Riego rising in Spain, he asked the Tsar for a discharge – for which he was cashiered by the disgusted Alexander and escorted to the frontier as a criminal. Back in Madrid, he married Carmen Quiroga, sister of one of the leaders of the rising, and fought bravely against the French under General Mina. After the fall of Barcelona he fled, and eventually settled in the Netherlands. On the evening of 24 September he was made commander of the insurgent forces in Brussels.

Notwithstanding the presence of these and other doughty fighters, the insurgents were in a parlous situation by the evening of 26 September. The royal troops were making heavy weather of the assault, but they did have numbers and guns, while the insurgents could never muster more than about a thousand men at any one time, and, heroics aside, pretty indifferent soldiers at that. They spent that night digging in and reinforcing the weakest points in preparation for a final, and, as they believed, fatal, assault. But as the morning mist lifted, it revealed deserted enemy positions.

Prince Frederick had lost no more than 108 dead and 620 wounded, while insurgent casualties had reached 430 dead and 1,200 wounded.[23] Had he driven home his attack, he would undoubtedly have crushed the insurgents. But he was put off by the prospect of having to capture the city block by block, and so he decided to withdraw. This was seen as a tremendous victory for the people of Brussels, and the ease with which it had been achieved went to their heads. The news brought out the whole country in revolt, and Belgian soldiers began to desert from the Dutch army.

The Belgian War of Independence had begun. Yet there was no political leadership, no army and no cause – beyond the worn slogan of 'Liberty or Death!' None of this seemed to matter. Before the end of September, the throne of Belgium was offered to Lafayette, and over the next months the most bewildering cast of other candidates was put forward, including Eugène de Beauharnais's son, the duke of Leuchtenberg; Louis Philippe's second son, the Duc de Nemours; Prince Adam Czartoryski; Archduke Charles of Austria; and, improbably, Count Stanisław Rzewuski, a debonair Polish nobleman who happened to have made a lot of friends while travelling in Belgium a few years earlier.

There was nothing about this array, or indeed about the chosen candidate, Prince Leopold of Saxe-Coburg-Gotha, to suggest a glorious cause.

But this did not prevent people from flocking to its defence. By the end of September 1830 there had already been Spaniards and Portuguese, as well as Poles, Frenchmen and Germans in evidence in the insurgent ranks. And more converged on the scene in the ensuing weeks. On 1 October came ninety men styling themselves the Légion Belge de Paris, followed by the Légion Gallo-Belge and the Belge-Parisienne. On 4 October it was the turn of the Regiment des Tirailleurs Parisiens, led by the Vicomte Adolphe de Pontécoulant, a French nobleman who had fought in the Napoleonic Wars, in Brazil, and on the Paris barricades in July before rushing to support the cause of liberty in Brussels. Others came off their own bat, like the two Americans Arthur and Augustus Beaumont, who had gone to Paris after the July days, joined the National Guard, and now marched into Brussels 'in order to depose the King, by the Grace of God, imposed on the Belgians by order of the despots of Vienna'. They expressed the desire 'to give back to Lafayette that part of the debt which every American owes to that Patriarch of Liberty, and that every friend of the rights of man can only acquit by doing all he can for the same cause, which is the benefaction of the whole human race'.[24]

The cause fared less well in Spain, where, notwithstanding the involvement of a major poet, it collapsed into tragic chaos. This was not altogether surprising, as the Spanish exiles, based mostly in London, had developed serious differences of opinion, which not only set them at each other's throats, but also helped the Spanish government to infiltrate their circles.

One of the exiles, the firebrand General Torrijos, managed to engage the enthusiasm of a couple of Cambridge undergraduates, John Sterling and Richard Trench, a typical believer without a cause. They were members of the Cambridge Conversazione Society, a kind of ideological soul-brotherhood popularly known as 'the Apostles', which included Alfred Tennyson and Arthur Hallam, and they drew these into various plans to assist the Spanish exiles in liberating their country. Sterling's cousin Robert Boyd suddenly came into a considerable inheritance, and Sterling persuaded him to devote this to the cause. A ship was bought, arms and supplies accumulated, and a complement of volunteers assembled.

General Francisco Espoz y Mina, hero of the *guerilla* and then of 1823, had been violently opposed to Torrijos's plans, but when he heard of the events in France, he decided the time was right. He left his English refuge and turned up in Paris, where he was warmly greeted by Lafayette. King Louis Philippe made fulsome promises, so Mina assembled a small force of Spanish liberals in the Pyrenees. It was there that Tennyson and Hallam went, bearing messages that were supposed to help co-ordinate the actions of the various patriot leaders. But they did not like what they found in the Spanish camp and soon returned to England.

Torrijos's expedition was dealt a blow when his plans were uncovered and the British authorities impounded the ship and its cargo just as it was about to weigh anchor. He managed to get away and borrow money from Lafayette in Paris, and most of his comrades, including Trench, Boyd and other Apostles reassembled at Gibraltar. While Mina's attempt across the Pyrenees petered out for lack of French support, the Torrijos initiative degenerated into a number of futile attempts to raise a revolt by landing on the south coast of Spain and ended when they were all captured and shot on the beach.

Things went only slightly better in Italy, where news of *Les Trois Glorieuses* also elicited much excitement. Plans were made for a rising in Piedmont. Carlo Bianco, who had just published a three-volume handbook on national insurrection, got together with Buonarotti in Paris to further this. At Marseille General Pepe assembled some 1,000 men and was planning to embark for Sicily, where he hoped to start a revolution. In January 1831 Francesco Salfi founded the Giunta Liberatrice Italiana, without much tangible effect.

There were risings in Parma, in Modena, and in the Papal States. The risings, which began in February 1831, were muddled affairs conducted by handfuls of squabbling intellectuals and exalted young noblemen. Typical was the conspiracy hatched by Count Guglielmo Libri and others, who intended to corner Grand Duke Leopold of Tuscany at a masked ball and force him to sign a petition, on the basis of which they would bring in a constitution. It was a fiasco, and they all fled abroad, Libri going on to become a celebrated scientist and legendary book thief in Paris.

The risings attracted the usual clutch of disaffected knights errant in search of a cause, including Louis-Napoleon Bonaparte, son of Louis, erstwhile king of Holland. The future emperor had earlier wanted to go and fight for Greece, but had not been permitted to. With his younger brother in tow, he reached the rebels' camp at Spoleto in March 1831. He managed to take part in a skirmish with Papal troops before being told by the rebels that his presence in their ranks was a political embarrassment for them. He decided to go and fight for Poland's freedom instead, but then his brother died of measles, and, discouraged by this, he went home. In Bologna a rising by local Carbonari managed to maintain itself for a few months, under the command of General Józef Grabiński, a veteran of the Kościuszko rising of 1794 and the Polish Legions. But Austrian troops had the situation under control throughout the peninsula within months. They hanged a brace of liberals in Modena including Ciro Menotti, but most of the troublemakers obligingly escaped, swelling the numbers of exiles carrying on their political arguments in various European cities. Pope Gregory XVI published an encyclical, *Mirari vos*, which condemned the entire liberal movement, and that was that.

The main body of Napoleon's Polish troops had been turned into the army of the new kingdom of Poland in 1814, and it was not long before they began to feel disaffected. Junior officers, all of whom had tasted at least some action and excitement in the Napoleonic Wars, now faced a future of garrison duty with sluggish promotion. They were mercilessly drilled by the Tsar's brother Grand Duke Constantine, who was also commander-in-chief of the Polish army. But the soldiers Constantine played with and insulted were veterans and heroes, not afraid to remind him of the fact. On being sworn at on the parade-ground for supposedly marching out of step, one general answered: 'I would remind Your Imperial Highness that it was nevertheless with this step that I marched into Moscow in 1812.' Not surprisingly, Constantine loathed these officers and enjoyed persecuting them. He could spot a missing button a hundred yards off in the street, and that could land a senior officer in the guardroom for days. Some were driven to suicide, others left the army, but most of the younger ones had nowhere to go and suffered in silence.

In 1819 Major Walerian Łukasiński of the 4th Infantry founded an organization called the National Freemasonry, a pseudo-masonic society dedicated to the defence of Polish nationhood. Initiation ceremonies were conducted by flickering candlelight, over a table covered in blue cloth, on which lay a copy of the constitution of 3 May 1791, a sword and a hammer. In 1820 another society, the Union of Free Poles, was started in Warsaw with the aim of preparing for insurrection. In the same year an Association of Templars was founded in the Ukraine by an officer who, having been captured in Spain, had spent several years as a prisoner in Scotland, where he had become a high-ranking Freemason. Yet another secret society, the Scythemen, had sprung up in western Poland. There were also Carbonarist groups active in Warsaw, Kalisz and Wilno in Lithuania, made up of officers who had served in Italy, and in 1820 they entertained a plan to form up a legion to go and fight for General Pepe in Naples.

In 1821 Łukasiński, who had adopted the pseudonym 'Lycurgus', negotiated a fusion of all these groups into the Patriotic Society, whose aim was the achievement of independence for Poland. Grand Duke Constantine soon came to hear rumours of plots, and in 1821 he interrogated Łukasiński. The major admitted to the defunct National Freemasonry, but said nothing of ongoing movements. He was transferred from active service to the reserve and kept under observation. The following year he was arrested, and further arrests were made at the universities of Warsaw and Wilno. After much inconclusive questioning, in 1824 Łukasiński was sentenced to nine years' incarceration in a military fortress.

The Decembrist revolt had elicited two abortive military demonstrations, in Wilno and Brańsk. This had shaken the guardians of order, and all possible contacts between the Russian mutineers and Polish sympathizers were meticulously followed up. In the Western Gubernias, where no more than an administrative decree was required to condemn someone, this served as an excuse to round up all Poles with a displeasing attitude and send them off to exile in Siberia. In the kingdom of Poland, it led to the arrest of leading members of the Patriotic Society, who were put on trial in 1828. There was not much of a case to answer, and the court dismissed most of the charges, imposing the lightest possible sentences. Tsar Nicholas demanded sterner punishments, and thereby provoked conflict with the Polish Sejm.

The arrest of the leading members of the Patriotic Society left it in the hands of frustrated subalterns. They had waited patiently in the hope that a Polish Riego would call them out one day, but by the end of the 1820s they had come to realize that no senior officer would do any such thing. In December 1828 the 31-year-old lieutenant Piotr Wysocki brought together a group of fellow subalterns and suggested they start preparing a national rising. They tried to gain the support of other members of the Patriotic Society, and cast about for a leader, but failed on both counts. When they asked Kościuszko's erstwhile aide-de-camp Julian Niemcewicz to be their nominal leader, he was horrified and told them to grow up.[25] Faced with such lack of enthusiasm, they began to think of forcing the issue. They even considered assassinating Nicholas and the entire imperial family when he came to Warsaw to be crowned as king of Poland in 1829.

They were not the only ones to have thought of this. A Warsaw student called Wincenty Smagłowski had hatched an altogether more imaginative plan and he enlisted a group of fellow students, with much oath-taking by torchlight in darkened chambers, as accomplices. They would steal into the throne-room of Warsaw Castle and hide behind the arras until the imperial family arrived for the coronation. They would then leap out and arrest them all, forcing Nicholas to renounce his claim to the Polish throne in favour of Napoleon's son, the Duke of Reichstadt. Only after the young duke had been released by the Austrians, brought to Warsaw and crowned Napoleon I of Poland, would Nicholas and his family be released.[26]

In the first half of 1830 Wysocki and his associates opted for an insurrection in the Decembrist style, based on officers calling out their troops at a given moment. During the summer manoeuvres they spread their network to include some two hundred officers, and then began to recruit civilians. The task was made easier by the news of the July revolution in Paris, and, later, by that of the rising in Brussels. Nicholas seemed prepared to help the king of Holland suppress the Belgian revolution, and France was arming with the intention of defending it. Newspapers in Paris were calling on people to revive 'the spirit of Jemappes', and there was much talk of a new war of the peoples. 'The revolution can only defend itself by attacking,' wrote Armand Carrel in *Le National*, 'that was the instinctive cry of France in 1792, and this time too our only hope lies in striking the first blows.'[27] Louis Philippe's constitutional monarchy suggested parallels with 1791, and in St Petersburg there were those who felt that a timely intervention might save years of warfare. Nicholas therefore ordered the mobilization of the Russian and Polish armies in mid-November, with a view to sending them to Belgium.

The plotters, led by Wysocki and another second lieutenant, Józef Zaliwski, found themselves being precipitated by events. The police had got wind of their conspiracy. A handful were arrested at the beginning of November, and the remainder were only one step ahead of the sleuths, leaving Wysocki and Zaliwski little room for manoeuvre. On 19 November they attempted to enlist the support of the radical historian Joachim Lelewel, but he put them off. The conspirators were getting desperate, and, leader or no leader, they decided to strike on the night of 29 November.

The signal for the outbreak was not picked up by most of the conspirators, so they all went into action at different times. The first were a group of officer cadets, civilians and a poet, who stormed the Belvedere Palace, residence of Grand Duke Constantine, intending to assassinate him. But they made so much noise that he had time to hide in a servant's bedroom while they killed a few of his aides, and he was later rescued by a regiment of Russian dragoons. These were supposed to have been bottled up in their barracks by Wysocki and his infantry cadets, but they made such a heroic frontal attack on the barracks that while they annihilated one regiment, they allowed two others to get away by the back gate.

In the city centre another group of rebels stormed the Arsenal and armed a crowd of civilians. Several other units marched out of barracks and took up positions at strategic points, cutting communication between the various Russian forces stationed in the capital. By midnight, most of the city was in Polish hands. But as no Russian units had been disarmed or surrounded, they managed to withdraw with the Grand Duke to a position just outside the city. More ominously, in most parts of the city shutters were firmly closed and doors battened in response to the insurgents' call to arms. They roamed the streets, challenging people to join them. General Maurycy Hauke, forebear of the present Prince of Wales, had been an aide to Dąbrowski in 1794 and fought in the Legions, but he was now acting minister for war, and as such unpopular with junior officers, and when he refused to join them, they killed him. One highly popular general was offered the chance of leading the rising, but when he refused he too was killed. Another was murdered in a case of mistaken identity. One group of insurgents stormed into the Variety Theatre, where they stopped the performance and arrested all the Russian officers in the audience. Sitting in the front row was the most popular soldier in Poland, General Józef Chłopicki. The insurgents begged him to lead the rising. 'Leave me alone,' he replied, getting up and yawning, 'I'm going home to bed.' As he left the theatre, he muttered: 'The half-wits have started a riot which they will come to pay for dearly.'[28]

In the early hours of 30 November, Prince Adam Czartoryski and the Administrative Council of the kingdom met in order to bring the situation under control. They prevailed upon Chłopicki to assume command,

and co-opted respected figures such as Julian Niemcewicz and Stanisław Węgrzecki, who had been mayor of Warsaw during the 1794 insurrection. But none of them had the slightest intention of emulating Kościuszko's ill-fated rising. 'Look, there's the Polish Cincinnatus, a new Washington,' people exclaimed as they saw Chłopicki, still in civilian clothes, surrounded by a bevy of officers.[29] He was actually mobilizing a national guard of property-owners and organizing the reclamation of the arms taken from the Arsenal by the populace. And while people spilled out into the streets sporting the French tricolor or Polish white-and-crimson cockades, the Council was composing letters to the Tsar in an attempt to patch up the situation.

While the overwhelming majority of the population had no wish to start a war with Russia and all the most capable men in the country did not believe in such a cause, the Poles did have a real chance of winning one. Instead of negotiating with the Grand Duke, they could easily have captured him and his small Russian force. The Polish army was an élite officered by men who had fought under the greatest generals in Europe, and its regular strength could immediately be swelled by 100,000 reserves before mass recruitment was even contemplated. With determined leadership, it could have seen off any Russian force. But nobody stepped forward.

Chłopicki, who reluctantly assumed the function of dictator on 5 December, was a man of uncommon military experience. He had volunteered in 1788 to fight under Potyomkin against the Turks and taken part in the storming of Ochakov. In 1792 he had fought under Poniatowski against the Russians, then been forcibly pressed into a Russian regiment. He had deserted from this and escaped to Poland in 1794 to join Kościuszko's insurrection, fleeing westwards after its collapse and ending up in Milan in 1797 as a captain in the Polish Legion. He had fought throughout the Italian campaigns, distinguishing himself at the siege of Gaeta in 1799, and was highly prized by his French superiors. Between 1808 and 1812 he commanded the Legion of the Vistula in Spain, becoming a general and a baron of the Empire in 1809. He rendered his last service to Napoleon at Borodino, where he was gravely wounded.

In 1814 Chłopicki was made a full general in the new army of the kingdom of Poland, but in 1817, after a shouting-match with Grand Duke Constantine on the parade-ground, he resigned and retreated into a morose retirement. He was certainly a clever and brave soldier, magnificent under fire, but he had no wish to embark on what he considered an illegitimate war, and saw himself as a temporary caretaker for the legal ruler, Nicholas, to whom the Administrative Council despatched a delegation on 10 December in the hope of avoiding further unpleasantness. Nicholas retorted that he would have no dealings with rebels and demanded immediate unconditional surrender.

The Patriotic Society, under the presidency of Joachim Lelewel, had assumed the role of a kind of Jacobin Club, pressing for radical measures and galvanizing the populace through the words of its finest orator, the writer and critic Maurycy Mochnacki. This Polish Sainte-Beuve had been an ardent partisan of the Romantic movement in literature. He had condemned classicism for being the style of the grave-diggers of Poland in the previous century, and called for a fresh one in which the covenant of the new nation could be written. His message had been taken up by the younger generation. 'Under the banner of Romanticism, which broke down old laws in the arts, in philosophy, which called out for unlimited freedom of thought, we called for a political revolution,' wrote Józefat Bolesław Ostrowski.[30] 'We have improvised the most beautiful of poems – a National insurrection,' declared Mochnacki. All the poets in the capital, and there were many, penned rousing verses and songs inciting the nation to do battle, with Juliusz Słowacki, who had spent his adolescence 'dreaming of the many heroes of the new Greek uprising' and weeping bitter tears over the news of Byron's death, in the forefront.[31]

When, on 18 January 1831, a final rebuff arrived from St Petersburg and Chłopicki resigned his dictatorship, declaring he would not fight against his lawful sovereign, the moderates were left powerless. On the evening of 25 January, after long and heated discussion, the Sejm passed an act dethroning Nicholas as king of Poland. On 7 February the Polish army marched out of Warsaw. Seven days later, General Józef Dwernicki defeated a Russian corps at Stoczek, and this was followed by further Polish victories at Wawer and Grochów. On 31 March the Poles won a resounding victory at Dębe Wielkie, and another on 10 April at Iganie. The first Russian success did not come until 26 May, at Ostrołęka, but this was a Pyrrhic victory, with losses that even Russia could ill afford. The Poles had contested every inch of ground, and a brilliant artillery commander, Józef Bem, had decimated entire Russian infantry columns by galloping up close, unlimbering his guns and delivering several salvoes of grapeshot, then retreating before Russian cavalry could get at him.

After Ostrołęka the Russians found themselves in difficulties, particularly as the cholera epidemic that swept Europe that year took hold in the dirty conditions of the Russian camp, carrying away the commander General Dibich himself.

None of the Polish successes was followed up properly, however. After Iganie the Poles failed to seize the Russian supply depot, which lay defenceless before them, and other opportunities to destroy the main Russian force operating in Poland were bungled. This was principally the result of poor co-operation. Bred in Napoleonic ranks, then treated like lackeys and denied responsibility under Constantine, the Polish generals needed a strong leader. The new commander-in-chief, General Jan Skrzynecki, was a fine tactician as well as a dashing soldier, but he was no leader.

The Polish forces were dispersed and squandered on operations such as General Antoni Giełgud's foray into Lithuania in support of local insurgents, some 8,000 of whom were fighting a *guerilla*. They included a number of women, the best known of whom was the 25-year-old Countess Emilia Plater. Brought up on Scott, Byron and Mickiewicz, with pictures of Joan of Arc and Bobolina hanging above her bed, she could not resist the call. She was a fine horsewoman and served in various partisan detachments before joining up with Giełgud's corps. Her death from an infection not long after was universally represented as having occurred in battle, and she joined the heroines of her youth as a subject for poems and prints.

Giełgud failed to score a single success, and, cornered by the Russians, crossed into Prussia with 7,000 men in July, while a part of his army made a dash back to Warsaw under Colonel Henryk Dembiński. By then, the Russians had effectively encircled the capital, and the area controlled by the insurgents was shrinking. On 11 August, Dembiński was promoted to commander-in-chief, but he was no more effective in this role than his predecessors.

Although many advantages had been thrown away and much ground lost, there was still a chance of defeating the Russians. But the political leadership, which had never been enthusiastic, wanted to minimize the blood-letting while it sought other means to resolve the situation. After Nicholas refused to negotiate, Czartoryski and other moderates had turned their attention to gaining foreign support or, at least, mediation. The more radical elements in Poland had also counted on international support, but of a different kind. 'Our revolution should be the revolution of nations,' declared the Polish press to the world at large. 'The whole of Europe, the entire world should support it . . . Nations of the world! See how sacred is our cause. Support it for your own sakes.'[32] In January 1831, a great procession took place in Warsaw, led by students released from prison by the insurrection. They bore a black coffin adorned with a laurel wreath entwined with a tricolor ribbon, and, behind it, five shields bearing the names of the hanged Decembrists. The banner carried by the volunteers of the National Guard who marched out of Warsaw to face the Russian troops bore the inscription: 'For Our Freedom and Yours'.

Their idealism could hardly have been more misplaced. In Russia, the poets were not marching with the people, but with the Tsar. 'The war which is about to begin will be a war of extermination, or at least it should be,' wrote Alexander Pushkin to a friend in December 1830. Patriotism could work in many ways. Students at Moscow University rejoiced at news of Polish victories and Alexander Herzen hung a print of Kościuszko on his wall. Pushkin defended his view vigorously against more liberal souls, such as Prince Peter Viazemsky. 'From a poetic point of view this is all very fine,' he wrote to Viazemsky in June 1831, 'but it is nevertheless essential that the Poles should be smothered.'[33]

In England, several poets wrote verses in honour of the Poles, and Thomas Campbell founded a powerful lobby in the Literary Society of the Friends of Poland. The Polish cause was espoused by the radicals, who were looking for an issue over which to denounce the Holy Alliance. Enthusiasm for Greece demanded a classical education, so that had been largely an upper-class cause. Poland was more accessible, and support for it was strong in manufacturing cities such as Birmingham, Manchester, Glasgow, Hull and Newcastle. Reform and Poland were tied together in the eyes of the radicals, who held that all the ills suffered by England since 1792 were the result of the partitions and the consequent rise in power of despotic states such as Russia, Prussia and Austria. An article in the *Westminster Review* of January 1831 carried this argument to the point of parody. 'If the Russians are driven over the Niemen, we shall have the Ballot; if they cross the Dnieper, we shall be rid of the Corn Laws; and if the Poles can get Smolensko we too in our taxes shall get back to the ground of 1686,' it proclaimed. 'Poland had its liberation to win, and so have we. We have both fallen among thieves; and we cannot do better than carry on the contest in concert.'[34] Similar sentiments were voiced at the other end of Europe, in Hungary, where a young lawyer by the name of Lajos Kossuth declared that 'the cause of the Poles is the cause of Europe and I can boldly affirm that whoever does not honour the Poles . . . does not love his own motherland.'[35]

The news from Poland was having much the same effect on young people as the news from America had half a century earlier. Although only eleven years old, the future Chartist leader Ernest Jones ran away from home and was found wandering in the Black Forest on his way to fight for Poland. For the young Richard Wagner, it was a continuation of the French revolution of July. 'The victories which the Poles obtained for a short period during May 1831 aroused my enthusiastic admiration: it seemed to me as though the world had, by some miracle, been created anew,' he wrote. 'As a contrast to this, the news of the battle of Ostroleka made it appear as if the end of the world had come.'[36] There were many young Germans among those who went to Poland as volunteers. Other nationalists represented were the Swiss and the Italians. Many more were preparing to go, but, like a group of young Bostonians, could not overcome the physical difficulties of getting there. Two Russians who had fought in Colombia turned up in Paris with a letter of recommendation from General Paez, and there was a Major Cochrane recommended by 'the Lafayette of Colombia' Devereux.[37]

The insurrectionary government had written to the real Lafayette, asking him to accept the title of 'First Grenadier of the Polish National Guard'. In his letter of acceptance, he expressed regret that he could not take his place in the ranks and the hope that other Frenchmen would. Those who did were mainly junior officers, and the most famous, Girolamo Ramorino, was an adventurer. Born in Genoa around 1790, he encouraged the rumour that he was the natural son of Marshal Lannes. He served in the French army, being discharged in 1816 with the rank of captain. He took part in the Piedmontese rising of 1821, after which he returned to a life of petty commerce in France, finally becoming bankrupt in 1829. The Polish rising was a godsend, and Ramorino dashed off to Warsaw, where he managed to persuade the military authorities that he had been a colonel in the French army. He was duly given the same rank, and, after distinguishing himself at the Battle of Wawer in April, promoted to general. Consistently shy of engaging with the enemy, he repeatedly marched away from the action or failed to make appointed rendezvous, which allowed more than one Russian corps to escape from a trap. His behaviour began to look more like treachery than incompetence, but his gift for self-promotion meant that he had a consistently favourable press and was not dismissed, with fatal results.

Shouts of '*Vive la Pologne!*' had been heard on the barricades of Paris during the July Days, long before the Poles had stirred, and news of the November Rising elicited demonstrations all over France. Whenever there was news of a Polish victory, there were heady shows of jubilation, often leading to disorder, but the angry mobs that rampaged through various cities at the news of the defeat of Ostrołęka made the French police pray for Polish triumphs.[38] *La Varsovienne*, a song composed by Casimir Delavigne, was all the rage, and pro-Polish feeling made itself felt in dozens of poems.

Lafayette moved heaven and earth to make France go to war in support of Poland, but he could not move Louis Philippe. He formed a committee to help the Poles, with the participation of Victor Hugo and a string of artists and heroes. It collected some half-a-million francs over the next months, much of it in small donations sent by Napoleonic veterans. Lafayette also persuaded Fenimore Cooper to establish a committee of support in the United States, which transferred the money it collected through Paris. Some of these funds went on the purchase of arms, whose despatch was a difficult undertaking.

On 9 July an American brig chartered for the purpose, loaded to the gunwales with arms purchased in Birmingham, set sail from the Port of London. On board was a small band of Poles under the Napoleonic veteran Jan Jerzmanowski. They made for Połąga in Lithuania, where they hoped to meet up with General Giełgud's corps. But as they entered the port, they learned of his defeat and forced refuge in East Prussia. Miraculously, they managed to sail away without being caught by the Russian navy.

Time had begun to run out for the Poles. A large Russian army under General Paskievich had circled Warsaw and launched a massive attack on the capital from the west. The defence was heroic but uncoordinated. Lieutenant Konstanty Ordon, the last officer left on his redoubt, blew up several hundred Russians when they swarmed over it – yet he himself miraculously survived. This spirit was not emulated at the top, and on 7 September a capitulation was arranged, allowing the remains of the army to evacuate Warsaw eastwards while the Russians marched in from the west. There were still substantial Polish forces in the field, but their commanders could not agree on what to do next. In the south, Ramorino's corps was cut off and on 18 September crossed the border into Galicia, where it was disarmed by the Austrians. Other units were surrounded one by one and forced to choose the lesser evil of surrendering to the Prussians rather than the Russians. The insurrection petered out as aimlessly as it had begun.

When news of the fall of Warsaw reached Paris, it was kept quiet for two days while the authorities called in troops and made preparations for meeting the inevitable reaction. When it leaked out on 16 September, large crowds gathered. The Foreign Ministry was attacked and its windows were smashed before troops restored order. The following day the National Guard was out in force, but so was the mob. The Palais-Royal was attacked, the Foreign Minister General Sebastiani almost lynched, armourers' shops were broken into and barricades thrown up. On 18 September the situation was brought under control. With troops bivouacking on the boulevards, the crowd could not force its way across the city, and a couple of cavalry charges dispersed the most threatening clusters. Large numbers of rioters were arrested, including a high proportion of Italians and Spaniards. By the following day, despite some minor disturbances, it was evident that the crisis was past. It had all ended, as it had begun, with three days of street-fighting in Paris.

15
Apostles and Martyrs

'No, Poland has not perished yet,' Heinrich Heine wrote in 1831, echoing the first line of the song of the Legions. 'Her real existence has in no sense ended with her political substance. Like Israel after the fall of Jerusalem, so perhaps after the fall of Warsaw Poland will arise, called to the highest destiny.' Thomas Campbell pictured the defeat as 'Polonia's Golgotha'. 'Sleep, O Poland, sleep peacefully in what others call your tomb, which I know to be your cradle,' prayed the Abbé Félicité de Lamennais.[1] These were prophetic utterings, for something called the Polish Question had come into being. Some 55,000 Polish troops and 6,000 civilians refused to surrender to the Russians, initiating a great exodus that was to weigh heavily on the course of European history.

Many of the soldiers had only one thought – to continue the struggle for independence. General Józef Bem ensured that the troops which had crossed into East Prussia under his command remained together in disciplined units. He was thinking of creating a Polish legion under the aegis of Prussia, which might one day need to go to war with Russia. The circumstances looked propitious. The whole of Germany was in an uproar of sympathy for the defeated Poles, giving rise to a batch of poetry, the *Polenlieder.* The defeated soldiers were greeted with open arms wherever they went. But the Prussian military authorities had a different agenda. They tried to separate the officers from the men, and to persuade the latter to return to Poland. Some were rounded up and put on ships bound for America. Others were forced over the border, into the hands of waiting

Russian troops. And one company that refused was mown down by Prussian infantry.

General Bem and Prince Czartoryski, now in Paris, sounded out the French government on the possibility of forming up a legion in French service. When that plan fell through, Bem looked to Belgium. In July 1831 Leopold of Saxe-Coburg had made his solemn entry into Brussels as king of the Belgians, but King William of Holland had refused to accept the new situation and invaded. Leopold needed men, particularly experienced officers, and the fall of Warsaw the following month suggested where he could find them. The Poles had already been identified as exemplars by the Brabantine patriots as they prepared to defend their new-born *patrie*. 'Like the Poles, we should not bind ourselves to long fusillades, to protracted discharges of artillery, but go straight for the enemy with blades and bayonets,' urged *Le Courier* of 1 July.[2] Leopold originally wanted a Polish legion of 2,000 cavalry and 600 artillery, but changed his mind and only took some sixty Polish senior officers into his service. After considering Generals Lamarque, Guilleminot and Robert Wilson for the post of commander-in-chief, Leopold chose Skrzynecki.

Bem entertained the idea of a legion in Portugal, then one in Egypt. But while it was easy to find positions for experienced officers, the diplomatic niceties involved in creating an autonomous force with its own flag and language of command were an insuperable obstacle. Gradually, the rank and file melted away, while the officers found themselves jobs, sometimes in the oddest places. A committee for the emancipation of the Jews, founded in Paris by Lafayette, had come to believe that one way of helping their co-religionists in Egypt and Syria to emancipate themselves was to get Polish officers to form them up into military units. General Dwernicki assumed control of this implausible scheme, and in 1833 a group of officers was sent to the Middle East, under the leadership of General Henryk Dembiński. They included Major Bartłomiej Beniowski. Born in 1800 into a wealthy Jewish family in Grodno, Beniowski had gone to war in the Russian army in 1830, as a staff surgeon. He had taken the first opportunity to change sides, and become an officer of Polish lancers. On his arrival in Paris in 1831 he had applied to join the French army, but, on being refused, decided to give the Jewish cause a try. His efforts in Syria and Egypt were not crowned with success, and he was soon back in Paris, where all emigrés seemed to wash up after each failed venture.

As it became clear that attempts to maintain a Polish armed force abroad were coming to nothing, common soldiers accepted the amnesty promised by Tsar Nicholas and drifted back to Poland. Many officers who had not been politically implicated also took advantage of this, particularly where they had a family and a farm back home. This left a hard core of some 8,000 emigrés committed to carrying on the struggle from Paris, London and the other cities they settled in.

In Britain, Parliament annually voted a sum of £10,000 from which exiled Polish soldiers were to be paid a monthly allowance, distributed by the Literary Society of Friends of Poland. No restrictions were placed on their movements, and they duly took their place among the cohorts of Italian, Spanish and French exiles in the major cities. The French were less accommodating, unsurprisingly since they had to deal with a far greater number of exiles – up to 5,000 at one stage. Louis Philippe, already regarded with disapproval by Metternich and Nicholas, had no wish to harbour thousands of their deadliest enemies. Moreover, the exiles were prime revolutionary material, naturally drawn into the French political scene. But strength of feeling in France was such that he could not refuse them entry. That they had a second *patrie* in France, for which they or their fathers had fought under Napoleon, was a cliché not to be challenged. One poem which appeared in print at the time proposed setting up a 'holy enclave' in which the Poles would be sheltered, to be paid for by cutting their uniforms into small pieces and auctioning them as relics.[3] In the event, the Poles were packed off to depots at Avignon and Besançon, where they lived on soldier's rations. Only senior officers, political figures and those with private funds were allowed to take up residence in Paris and other major towns, subject to police supervision and restrictions on their movements.

It was nevertheless Paris that became the centre of emigré life, for it was there that the leaders congregated, along with artists, such as the poets Adam Mickiewicz and Juliusz Słowacki, and the composer Fryderyk Chopin. Paris was where all the different threads came together. The solemnity commemorating the first anniversary of the November Night was held at the house of Lafayette, where over two hundred Poles squeezed in to hear words of comfort and encouragement from the patriarch of liberty. Czartoryski had decided to call the Sejm into being in Paris, hoping that this would provide leadership for the future. It was not until January 1833 that a quorum of elected deputies assembled, and began quarrelling. The emigrés quickly divided into two main camps, whose views of the past differed fundamentally and whose visions for the future were irreconcilable.

The conservatives, led by Czartoryski, took it for granted that nothing could be achieved for Poland without the support of the liberal powers, and therefore worked on public opinion and governmental circles in England and France. A nerve centre was established in Paris, with branches in London and Constantinople and agents in key cities, an extended political lobby which functioned with remarkable efficiency until the mid-1860s. The other group, which took the name of Polish Democratic Society, brought together those who believed that the rising had failed because it had been carried out by a noble minority of the nation in its own interests. The leadership of the society, *Centralizacja*, literally 'the centralization', was based at Versailles. It published far-reaching programmes of social reform, including the emancipation of the peasants and abolition of all privilege. But all the emigrés, of whatever political affiliation, were marked by the same emotional and spiritual malaise.

St Augustine had represented Christians as pilgrims, alien to this world because they sought another. Schiller described Romantic poets as 'exiles pining for a homeland', and all those touched by the sensibility of the Romantic movement to some extent saw themselves as outcasts from Arcadia. At some level, they rejected the world, with its conventions, its material values and its moral constraints. The Polish exiles, who were themselves rejected by the political and social arrangement of the world, were obliged to live their lives on another, moral plane. That is why, instead of analysing the true causes of the failure of the November Rising, the Polish emigrés immediately began to formulate moral explanations.

Those on the left quickly came up with theirs: the Poles had failed because they were a rotten, class-ridden, materialistic society incapable of real self-sacrifice. This provided an argument for rejecting the whole social and political culture of the old Polish state. 'Poland perished through egoism', in the words of Stanisław Worcell, 'and she can only rise again through self-sacrifice.'[4] Worcell was born a wealthy nobleman in the Ukraine where he had conspired with the United Slavs and the Decembrists. He had fought in a detachment of partisan cavalry in 1831, and subsequently been elected to the Sejm, where he demanded the emancipation of the peasants. He could only continue as a democrat, and therefore in his own eyes as a real Pole, by rejecting his noble origins, and by atoning for them.

Whatever their degree of piety, the emigrés were strongly wedded to a Catholic frame of reference, and they naturally pondered the implications of every situation in religious terms. When things went wrong, they could not help seeing it in terms of God having abandoned them. And if a catastrophe had been visited upon them, it was because God meant to test them, for He never acted in vain. From there, it was a short step to the conclusion that there must be a providential purpose to the failure of the November Rising – it was all part of a divine plan to compel the Poles to examine their moral position, steel themselves and grow stronger.

In December 1831 a group of democrats issued a proclamation in which they blamed the failure of the insurrection on the lack of total faith in success, echoing Kościuszko's assertion that all the Poles needed to do in order to win was to believe in themselves. The realities of an unwinnable war were eclipsed by the image of the peasant scythemen's victory over Russian artillery at Racławice, an image redolent of Rousseauist belief in the power of conviction. Being the most primitive weapon of all, the scythe required the greatest commitment on the part of the soldier. It was also the harvester's tool, suggesting a Cincinnatus-like notion of ploughshares reluctantly turned into swords. Only the common people, inspired by their faith in the cause, could triumph over soulless military power. In a book written in 1800 and reprinted in 1832, Kościuszko had gone on to argue that the scythe and the bayonet were better weapons than rifles and cannons because they forced people to place greater faith in their own strength.

The writers of the Left argued that the November Rising had been a predestined cataclysm which, like 1789 in France, had given birth to a new nation. The defining *moment sacré* had been the night of 29 November 1830. The poet Stefan Garczyński actually likened it to Christmas Eve, and he spoke for many. 'What would I not give in order to be able to live through just one more such moment,' prayed one who had rampaged over the streets of Warsaw as a twenty-year-old student on that night, from his exile in south-western France many years later.[5] It was another poet, Adam Mickiewicz, who wrote the gospels of this new incarnation, turning the spiritual fantasies of a handful of soldiers and intellectuals into the articles of faith that built a modern nation.

Mickiewicz had established his reputation as Poland's foremost lyric poet in the 1820s, and enhanced his political credentials by his exile in Russia, where he met several prominent Decembrists and grew close to Pushkin. In 1829 Mickiewicz received permission to go to Germany to take the waters. He met Mendelssohn and Hegel in Berlin, Metternich in Marienbad, and August Schlegel in Bonn, and attended Goethe's eightieth birthday party in Weimar. Goethe kissed him on the forehead, gave him the quill with which he had worked on *Faust*, and commissioned a portrait of him for his collection. Mickiewicz then went to Italy where, apart from a *de rigueur* trip to Switzerland (Chillon and Altdorf, with Byron and Schiller's *Wilhelm Tell* in his hand), he spent the next year-and-a-half. It was in Rome that news of the November Rising reached him. He set off for Poland, but his attempts to cross the border were foiled by cossack patrols, and he was obliged to watch the débâcle from Dresden.

In this tranquil Saxon city he was gripped by inspiration and wrote frantically in fits lasting up to three days, without pausing to eat or sleep. The fruit was the third part of a long poetic drama entitled *Forefathers' Eve*, which can only be described as a national passion play. Mickiewicz had also seen the significance of the holy night, and he likened all monarchs, and Nicholas in particular, to Herod – their sense of guilty foreboding led them to massacre the youth of nations. The drama describes the transformation through suffering of the young poet and lover, Konrad, into a warrior-poet. He is a parable for Poland as a whole, but he is also something more. 'My soul has now entered the motherland, and with my body I have taken her soul: I and the motherland are one,' he declares after having endured torture. 'My name is Million, because I love and suffer for millions . . . I feel the sufferings of the whole nation as a mother feels the pain of the fruit within her womb.'

In Paris in 1832 Mickiewicz published a short work entitled *Books of the Polish Nation and of the Pilgrimage of Poland*. It was quickly translated into several languages and caused a sensation. It is a bizarre work, couched in biblical prose, giving a moral account of Polish history. After an Edenic period, lovingly described, comes the eighteenth century, a time when 'nations were spoiled, so much so that among them there was left only one man, both citizen and soldier' – a reference to Lafayette. The 'Satanic Trinity' of Catherine of Russia, Frederick of Prussia and Maria Theresa of Austria decided to murder Poland, because Poland was Liberty. They crucified the innocent nation while degenerate France played the role of Pilate. But that was not to be the end of it. 'For the Polish nation did not die; its body lies in the tomb, while its soul has left the earth, that is public life, and visited the abyss, that is the private life of peoples suffering slavery at home and in exile, in order to witness their suffering. And on the third day the soul will re-enter the body, and the nation will rise from the dead and will liberate all the peoples of Europe from slavery.' In a paraphrase of the Christian Creed, Liberty will then ascend the throne in the capital of the world, and judge the nations, ushering in the age of peace.

So the Polish nation was now in Limbo, and all it had to do in order to bring about its own resurrection and that of all grieving peoples was to cleanse and redeem itself through a process of expiation which Mickiewicz saw as its 'pilgrimage'. This was to be a kind of forty days in the wilderness. The pilgrims must fast and pray on the anniversaries of the battles of Wawer and Grochów, reciting litanies to the 30,000 dead of the Confederation of Bar and the 20,000 martyrs of Praga; they must observe their ancient customs and wear national dress. One is reminded of Rousseau's admonitions in his *Considérations sur le Gouvernement de Pologne.*

Rousseau would have been proud of this generation. As one freedom fighter writes in his memoirs: 'Only he loves Poland with his heart and his soul, only he is a true son of his Motherland who has cast aside all lures and desires, all bad habits, prejudice and passions, and been reborn in the pure faith, he who, having recognized the reasons for our defeats and failures through his own judgement and conviction, brings his whole love, his whole – not just partial, but whole – conviction, his courage and his endurance, and lays them on the altar of the purely national future.'[6] He had taken part in the November Rising and a conspiratorial fiasco in 1833, for which he was rewarded with fifteen years in the Spielberg and Küfstein prisons. Yet decades later he still believed that the November Rising had 'called Poland to a new life' and brought her 'salvation' closer by a hundred years. Such feelings were shared by tens of thousands, given expression by countless poets and artists, and understood by all the literate classes.

Most of Mickiewicz's countrymen read his works and wept over them. They identified with them and learned them by heart. They did not follow the precepts laid down in them, nor did they really believe in this gospel in any literal sense. These works were a let-out, an excuse even, rather than a guiding rule. But they did provide an underlying ethical explanation of a state of affairs that was otherwise intolerable to the defeated patriots. It was an explanation that made moral sense and was accepted at the subconscious level. It was a spiritual and psychological lifeline that kept them from sinking into a Slough of Despond. It made misfortune not only bearable, but desirable.

And it was by no means an expression of uniquely Polish sensibility. The cast of mind that underlay it was common to most of Europe, as can be gauged from the incidence of images of ashes bursting into flame, of phoenixes, of seeds buried underground giving forth new shoots, of subterranean regions viewed as dungeon, tomb and cradle in the Romantic poetry of every country, and the ubiquitous theme of self-immolation. It was a faith shared by all who worshipped the nation and could find no place for themselves in Metternich's Europe. And if its gospels had been written by Mickiewicz, its first theological texts were formulated by Mazzini.

Giuseppe Mazzini was born in French-ruled Genoa in 1805, the son of a university professor. Ten years later, Genoa was incorporated into the kingdom of Piedmont by the Congress of Vienna. The young man studied law, but showed a greater appetite for literature, which he devoured, consuming not only all the Italian authors, but also the French and the English, of whom he was particularly fond. He was enamoured of Scott, whose every novel he read, and adored Byron. Neglecting his legal career, he devoted his time to literary criticism. He also joined the Carbonari, some time around 1829, in the fervent desire to fight oppression and bring about the rule of justice. The following year he was denounced by a colleague and imprisoned. But he was released for lack of evidence, just in time to take part in an abortive invasion of Corsica, after which, forced to remain in exile, he fixed his abode at Marseille. This gave him, like the many other exiles, plenty of time to ponder the condition of his homeland.

The events of 1831 had revealed, possibly even more glaringly than those of 1820–1, that Italy really was only a geographical expression. None of the revolts since 1815 had evoked any echoes of solidarity elsewhere in the peninsula. The notion of Italian community was still an entirely cultural one, generated by literature and the arts. Propagating it as a political concept was not easy. Censorship was only a small part of the problem. Less than a quarter of the population could read, but even those who could were not always able to read things written by authors from a different province. The only vehicle through which ideas could be transmitted and emotions stirred was the theatre and particularly opera, which enjoyed great popularity. Mazzini appreciated this, calling Meyerbeer 'the prophet of the music with a mission, the music standing immediately below religion'.[7] The censors were formidable, but people read into themes or phrases whatever they wished, and the music caressed their fondest dreams or excited their most belligerent passions. 'If I have ever seen human madness, it was certainly during a performance of *Crociato in Egitto*,' noted Heinrich Heine in Genoa. Yet there is nothing in Meyerbeer's opera, first staged in 1824, that a censor could have quarrelled with.[8] And the feelings behind the 'madness' did not go deep. The overwhelming majority of ordinary people in the peninsula accepted their rulers and the situation with equanimity.

There were exceptions. 'When I awoke first to consciousness, I also awoke to love of country,' wrote the young aristocrat Felice Orsini, 'my life belonged to Italy, and she might claim it at any moment.'[9] But people like him were few and far between. They had no support among the masses, and they did not actively seek it. The poet Ugo Foscolo had gone so far as to declare that the common people were too mean to take part in such an elevated endeavour as the regeneration of Italy.[10] More to the point, they were afraid of stirring up the peasants, knowing them to be even more antagonistic towards liberals than towards the Austrians. The majority of liberals belonged to the nobility or the propertied classes, and it was they, not the reigning king or duke, that the peasant identified with oppression. And the patriots were not interested in improving his lot as such.

Mazzini was convinced that any improvement in the social and political conditions in the peninsula was not just bound up with, but utterly dependent on, the achievement of unity. 'The question of Italy is not one of more or less personal security or administrative improvement in one or another corner of our country; it is a question of *nationality*; a question of independence, liberty, and unity for the *whole* of Italy; a question of a common bond, of a common flag, of a common life and law for the twenty-five millions of men belonging – between the Alps and the sea – to the same race, tradition, and aspiration.'[11]

In his youthful enthusiasm, Mazzini thought that if one of the rulers in Italy were to give the lead, he might sweep the others along with him in asserting the independence of the peninsula. Piedmont was the strongest of the states, and when the reigning king died in 1831, Mazzini saw a window of opportunity opening. The new king was Charles Albert, the same who had shown liberal tendencies as regent in 1821 and then had to expiate them by fighting the constitutionalists in Spain. Mazzini wrote an open letter to him. 'Place yourself at the head of the Nation, write upon your banner: Union, Liberty, Independence,' he exhorted the king. 'Proclaim the sanctity of ideas, declare yourself the champion of the People, the regenerator of Italy. Free Italy from the Barbarians! Build up her future! Give your name to a Century! Become the Napoleon of Italian Liberty! It is a general belief that kings have nothing in common with Humanity, and History confirms that belief. Disprove it! Act so that beneath the names of Washington and Kosciuszko – citizens born – shall be written: "There is a name greater than these, there is a throne built by twenty millions of free men; on its base is inscribed: TO CHARLES ALBERT BORN A KING, ITALY REBORN BY HIM".'[12]

Charles Albert was a vaguely mystical dreamer who fancied himself as a soldier, and he had certainly entertained liberal thoughts in his youth. But he was a Hamletic figure. A devout Catholic, he was under the influence of the Church. He had been given a humiliating lesson by Metternich in 1821, and was not inclined to repeat it. Any appeal to his better nature was bound to sting his conscience and his smarting pride. He responded to Mazzini's missive with ill-concealed irritation, and ordered repressive measures against all conspirators to be stepped up.

Mazzini was not put off. From his base in Marseille he began corresponding with every like-minded Italian he could locate. His eloquence and his total devotion to the cause quickly singled him out. So did his ideas. He dismissed all movements and doctrines based on the concept of rights, which he saw as promoting the interests of the individual at the expense of the collective. To him, rights were the product of a materialistic view of the world. In place of rights, Mazzini put duty to the community, or rather the nation, which was both the basis of human life and the vehicle for salvation. 'Nationality is belief in a common origin and end,' he wrote, conjuring up the image of a kind of church, whose faith, nationalism, was 'the gospel of the brotherhood of all the men of a nation'. Duty towards the nation was the expression of a deeper belief. 'The mere *conviction* does not suffice to begin a struggle,' he explained; 'that must break forth as the manifestation of a *faith*.'[13] The religious language was not accidental. 'Religion and politics are inseparable,' he wrote elsewhere.

'Without religion, political science can create only despotism or anarchy.'[14]

In July 1831 Mazzini brought together more than thirty other patriots and founded an organization by the name of Giovine Italia, Young Italy. This was a new departure, radically different from the Carbonari and other sects. For one, it had no rituals. It was a regular society, with annual subscriptions and a definite goal – the attainment of equality and social democracy through the unification of Italy. But it was also a movement, an 'apostolate' calling its members to a life of privation and self-sacrifice in the cause. 'Tomorrow, victory will crown your crusading banner,' Mazzini exhorted his followers. 'Onward in faith, and fear not.'[15]

Metternich had given one hostage to fortune. By appointing Austria the policeman of the whole peninsula (with the aim of excluding the French from it once and for all), the Congress of Vienna had inadvertently helped to unite Italian patriots on one point at least: they all had the same enemy to define themselves against. And Austria behaved with grotesque heavy-handedness, fully earning the epithets of 'Vandals', 'Huns' and 'Barbarians' by which her representatives were referred to. They viewed with horror any but the most conformist conduct. This was the Italy of Stendhal's *La Chartreuse de Parme*. In the novel, Fabrice del Dongo is advised that the only way he can rehabilitate himself in the eyes of the regime is by going to Mass, taking a sensible (not too pious) confessor, shunning the company of anyone considered to be intelligent, avoiding cafés, reading no newspapers aside from the official court gazette and no books published after 1720 (with the possible exception of Walter Scott), and taking a well-born and respectable mistress.

The Austrian police saw danger lurking everywhere, and overreacted in a way that offended Italian sensibilities and created mortal enemies. Silly young noblemen and rich brats who sang a patriotic song or shouted a slogan while in their cups at one of the fashionable cafés of Milan were whisked off to some gloomy northern fortress. They were usually condemned to a regime known as *carcere duro*, which entailed solitary confinement, permanently chained by ankles and wrists, with a quite unnecessary metal ring round the waist for good measure. Sometimes they were chained to the wall as well. The prisoner slept on bare planks. He was given bread and water, with a ration of bread steeped in hot water with some tallow in it every other day. There were thirteen inspection visits by the guard in twenty-four hours. Any misbehaviour was punished with flogging on the *cavaletto* – a bench eight feet long on which the prisoner was held down by a kind of vice, with manacles for the wrists and ankles – which sometimes resulted in the prisoner's death.

Anyone who had been put through this ordeal was consecrated to the cause for life and became an exemplar to others. Upon his release from the Moravian fortress of Spielberg in 1827, Count Arese commissioned the artist Francesco Hayez to paint his portrait. The painting, which depicts the young aristocrat chained up in a gloomy cell, conveys the same message as any saintly martyrdom in a baroque altarpiece. The fate of the poet Silvio Pellico was even more emblematic. Born in 1789, he wrote a tragedy on a theme from Ossian at the age of ten. An acquaintance of Madame de Staël, August Friedrich Schlegel and Byron, Pellico was the soul of a patriotic literary group in Milan. This coterie could not have produced the smallest tremor in the Austrian edifice of state, however much they might have wished to. In 1820 he was nevertheless arrested, along with Count Oroboni and Federico Confalonieri, an emissary of Buonarotti, condemned to death, reprieved, and sentenced to ten years in the Spielberg. When he emerged in 1832, he published the memoirs of his life in prison. A devout Catholic, he offered up his sufferings, and the writing is subdued rather than rebellious in tone. But it was a terrible indictment of Austria and became the first great book of Italian martyrology.

The roll of martyrs was rapidly built up through the 1830s as a result of a string of unsuccessful conspiracies and risings, each giving forth its crop of victims. At a distance, they appear ludicrous, and sometimes outright comic, but the blundering brutality of the existing regimes sanctified them by ensuring that they had tragic conclusions. And that was in line with Mazzini's aims. 'Ideas ripen quickly when nourished by the blood of martyrs,' he pointed out.[16]

This kind of thinking also animated the Poles, who were developing a pathology of martyrdom. During the 1820s the Polish Romantics had been gripped by the doom-laden heroics of the Confederation of Bar. 'This Confederation was like the call of a mother who wishes to test the love of her children,' explained one writer, for it was in order to die or to suffer in captivity, not to triumph, that they had come forward to fight. In the Romantic imagination, the thousands of prisoners sent to Siberia became 'a monastic, fraternal, religious community', taking upon themselves the burden of the sins of the whole nation, and they did so gladly, seeing the long road as a pilgrimage towards their own perfection as well as redemption for the nation.[17] The place of degradation or execution assumed the sanctity of Golgotha, and by the same token became a place of spiritual rebirth. This was why Mickiewicz referred to Bar as the Bethlehem of the creed of the nation.

He suggested that a book of martyrs be compiled, recounting the lives and sufferings of all those who had died for the motherland, as an example and encouragement to others. In his poem *To a Polish Mother*, he advised mothers to give their sons chains to play with instead of toys, so that they should feel no fear at the sight of the instruments of their martyrdom in the future. He need not have bothered. 'In my youthful imagination, I considered it to be the height of happiness to become a martyr,' wrote one patriot. 'I would look with real envy on others as they were locked up, feeling it almost a personal shortcoming that, on account of my youth, I was not considered worthy of sharing that fate with the others.'[18] He never made Siberia, and had to make do with fifteen years in the Spielberg. But the severity of the sentence was not the most important element.

The most severe conditions obtained in the iron-ore mines of Siberia, where prisoners were chained to their barrow all day long and to the wall at night. They were underfed and worked to exhaustion. Any misdemeanour was punished with ritual floggings: the prisoner had to run the gauntlet between two files of soldiers for as long as it took for the 1,000 blows to be delivered. When he was too weak to walk, he would be attached to a specially designed barrow, on which he would be dragged along until the sentence had been carried out, even if he was already dead.

Most of the sentences handed out were less gory, consisting of internal exile, confinement, or service in the ranks on the Circassian front. But they all reflected the same inhumanity. For having taken part in the November Rising, Prince Roman Sanguszko was sentenced to exile in Siberia, with a personal notation by the Tsar that he must go there not in the usual carriage but on foot, chained to a gang of common criminals. He fell dangerously ill along the road and his life was only saved by the intervention of passing Russian travellers. When he finally reached Tobolsk, his sentence was amended, and he was assigned to serve as a common soldier in a regiment stationed near by. After two years, he was transferred to the Caucasus, where he was wounded, fell ill, and lost his hearing. Living alongside Russian common soldiers was no holiday, conditions were appalling, and discipline was draconian. Some 9,000 Polish officers were degraded in this way after the November Rising, and the majority of them were either killed in the savage warfare against the hill tribes or died of disease. Many committed suicide. A few deserted and joined the Chechens or Circassians. Sanguszko, who came from an ancient family of royal Russian descent, was helped through by some of the officers he served under, who did what they could to ease his lot. In 1836 he was even allowed to go and convalesce in the relative comfort of the small town of Pyatigorsk, where he consoled himself by reading Silvio Pellico's prison memoirs.

The only way the prisoners could avoid being broken by the experience was by delving deeper into the comforts of martyrology. The dissident Russian student Alexander Herzen felt strangely elated after his arrest in December 1834, which he referred to as his 'consecration'. 'I am reading with delight *The Lives of the Saints*,' he wrote from gaol, 'there you have examples of self-sacrifice, there you have men!' Others talked of their first interrogation as their 'noviciate'.[19] Herzen was sentenced to exile in the Ural region, and during his time there he noticed that prisoners sought the strength to survive in spiritual resources that often verged on the morbid. In Perm, he made friends with a Pole, and when a change of sentence forced them to part, Herzen gave him a shirt-stud as a memento, whereupon the other rummaged in his bundle and offered Herzen a few links of the first chain he had worn, as the most precious thing he possessed.

A degree of holiness enveloped the implements and the scenes of martyrdom. The Russians spoke with veneration of the Peter and Paul Fortress and the Schlüsselburg; the Italians, Hungarians and Poles of Küfstein and the Spielberg; to the Sicilians, the Vicaria prison in Palermo was 'the place where one received the baptism of patriotic regeneration'.[20] In the iconography of the day, the cells of these prisons, many of which were actual monastic cells, since a large proportion of the political prisons were located in former monasteries, were represented in the convention of 'mystic chapels'.

Those denied the chance of martyrdom could achieve sanctity by other means. Like any faith, this one had its contemplative and penitent orders, as well as its soldier-monks who went on crusade. In August 1834 a group of emigrés in London founded the London Commune of the Polish People, a kind of social organization modelled on what they believed to be ancient Slavic patterns. These had been invented by the left-wing historian Joachim Lelewel, whose theory of history was that in Slav cultures life had in ancient times been organized on organic lines, giving rise to an idyllic rural democracy. An important element in this fiction was that there had been no private ownership of land. This model, which he held up as being superior to anything devised in Western Europe, had, according to him, been perverted by the nobility, who had garnered all the power and taken possession of the land. The London Commune, which was influenced by Buonarotti and Babeuf as much as by Lelewel, professed the principle that 'property is at the centre of all the evil which oppresses mankind at present'. Like Babeuf, its members entertained the dream of a political Second Coming. 'The French revolution at the end of the last century was the John the Baptist of the new faith and till now the Christ has not appeared,' they claimed. 'This Christ will not be an individual man but some great nation which, having assimilated everything truly good in the achievements of all its predecessors, and having created from this an ordered whole, will bring to humanity a new social faith. Why should not Slavdom be this Christ of the new faith?'[21]

The London Commune was given a unique chance to put its beliefs into practice in 1834, when a consignment of Polish soldiers being deported to America by the Prussian government jumped ship at Portsmouth. Some two hundred of them were accommodated by the British government in disused barracks at Portsea, whither members of the London Commune hastened. They took the soldiers under their wing, and taught them to read and write. They established a commune at Portsea, where a number of the officers and gentlemen from the London group went to live. After a lengthy noviciate, on 6 November 1835, the officers were duly 'raised to the people'. Another commune was established on the island of Jersey, where penitent nobles could steel themselves for the next crusade.

Just as Christians see themselves as 'brothers in Christ', so believers in the cause called themselves and each other 'brothers in the nation' or 'brothers in the people'. General Antonio Paez referred to the Poles as 'our brothers in Liberty'.[22] When Worcell first met Mazzini, at the graveside of another emigré in London, the two instantly recognized their kinship. When, in 1832, he met Buonarotti, Worcell experienced 'a feeling of religious emotion' that reminded him of the blind faith in God that had made his childhood so happy. A cornerstone of this vision of communal salvation through self-sacrifice was a transcendent love between peoples. 'Do not covet your neighbour's country,' wrote one Polish emigré in his *Commandments of the Fatherland*. 'You will love the Fatherland and freedom with all your heart and all your strength, and you will strive as if for yourself so that all nations shall become free.'[23] This sense of mutual love brought together Russians and Poles, Italians and

Frenchmen, and even, briefly, affected the self-obsessed Germans.

German responses to the revolutions of 1830 had not been dramatic. There were disturbances in the Rhineland, where people began wearing French tricolor cockades, and riots in industrial areas, where Luddites broke up machinery. It was tame stuff on the whole, with much flag-waving and declarations of solidarity. Fairly typical were the political activities of the seventeen-year-old Richard Wagner, who marched to the city gaol in Leipzig with his fellow students to demand the release of political prisoners. They then went to a well-known brothel in order to flush out establishment figures whom they assumed would be patronizing it. When a constitution was conceded and the king's nephew Prince Friedrich was appointed regent, Wagner duly composed a piece entitled *Friedrich und Freiheit*. The local radicals followed the vicissitudes of the Polish rising closely, and Wagner was out on the street with the others in January 1832 to hail the first echelon of soldiers marching into exile. He took an active part in fund-raising for them and was inspired, at a great banquet of solidarity, to write the overture *Polonia*.

Such disturbances gave rise to fear of greater violence, which strengthened the hand of constitutionalists all over the country. In Brunswick, a group of liberal notables used the discontent to negotiate the deposition of Duke Carl and the succession of his brother William, who brought in a constitution in 1832. In Hesse-Kassel, the Elector William II was also forced to accept a progressive constitution. A three-day revolt by the students of Göttingen University culminated in Hanover being granted a constitution. Reforms of one sort or another were forced on Saxony, Baden, Württemberg and Bavaria over the two years after 1830. Non-violent piecemeal reform was the order of the day. Reacting against the godlessness of the Enlightenment and the revolutionary period, the later German Romantics had sought refuge in a vision of a society inspired and governed by Christian principles. The French historian Edgar Quinet, an enthusiastic Germanophile who had settled there in the 1820s, called Germany 'the land of the soul and of hope, where under the oaks of Arminius, the pure spring of moral duty gushes forth and where sooner or later the neighbouring peoples will come to quench their thirst'.[24] Others identified the law itself as the basis for social organization, relegating the concept of the nation to second place. The emotional antics of the *Burschenschafter* had ceased by 1820, and those young men still desperate to suffer for the nation did so for Greece during the 1820s.

A series of academic conferences, launched in 1822 and aimed at creating a pan-German intellectual space, soon became, in the words of the founder Lorenz Oken, 'the spiritual symbol of the unity of the German people'.[25] The meetings, which brought together hundreds of people, were occasions for jollity of a characteristically German kind, with much spiritual bonding, but that was as far as it went. Middle-class practicality seemed to be in the ascendant. It was generally felt that measures such as the establishment of the Zollverein customs union in 1834 would do more for the unification of the German lands than all the floppy hats and beards. The king of Saxony called the railways, which began to be built in various parts of the country after 1835, 'one of the best ways of consolidating a truly German outlook', and every town craved one 'out of a sense of patriotism' as much as for economic reasons.[26] But the events of 1830 had stirred up deeper longings than these in the souls of German liberals.

In January 1832 the journalist Johann Georg August Wirth established the Pressverein, with the aim of disseminating liberal ideas. One of its first actions was to organize a great festival, set in the picturesque ruins of the castle of Hambach in the Hardt mountains. On 27 May 1832 over 20,000 people congregated at the castle to open the proceedings. They marched behind the black, red and gold flag, inscribed with the words '*Deutschlands Wiedergeburt*', 'Germany's regeneration', and included many old *Burschenschafter* as well as younger students from all over Germany. They sported oak leaves and ribbons in the Lützower colours, and there was no lack of maidens clad in white shifts and crowned with garlands. Wirth lectured them, proclaiming the need for education, which would provide the *Volk* with the weapons necessary to achieve unification and freedom. But while German national unity was the key theme in the proceedings, the spirit was not exclusive.

There were French and Swiss students, Polish emigrés, and representatives of half-a-dozen other nations. Harro Harring was there, his belt flush with pistols and daggers, writing odes to suffering nations. He also composed a paean to Lord Goderich, the British Colonial Secretary who had just put forward a scheme for the universal abolition of slavery, in which he referred to him as 'Man and Christ' and linked the causes of Greece and Poland with the recent slave rebellion in Jamaica.[27] A message of solidarity from the *Centralizacja* was read out, the *Marseillaise* was sung and airs from Rossini's *Masaniello* and *Guilleaume Tell* were played, while speeches were made about the overthrow of tyrants and the freedom of nations. 'As soon as German popular sovereignty is given its legitimate place there will be the closest federation of peoples', ran one, 'because the people love where kings hate, the people defend where kings persecute, the people do not grudge brother nations what is most precious to themselves and which they seek to acquire with their life-blood – freedom, enlightenment, nationhood and popular sovereignty. The German people therefore does not grudge its brothers in Poland, Hungary, Italy and Spain these great, invaluable benefits . . . Three cheers for the united free states of Germany! Three cheers for federated, republican Europe!'[28]

This was a challenge to everything Metternich stood for, and he responded as he had done to the murder of Kotzebue, pressing the German Diet to reassert the laws on censorship and to ban the flying of unauthorized flags, wearing of cockades, planting trees of liberty and holding gatherings. The military restored order and the ringleaders of the Hambach festival were sent to prison. Over the next months reaction set in, leading to the reversal of the liberal reforms carried out since 1830.

There was some protest but little resistance. The only attempt at armed demonstration took place in Frankfurt in April 1833, when a group of students and emigré Polish soldiers attempted to seize the guardhouse where some political prisoners were being held. They were counting on a degree of popular participation and on the arrival of a 'Sacred Company' of Poles from the Besançon depot, on the march under Colonel Oborski and the Piedmontese exile General Antonioni. Predictably, these got delayed en route and most of them eventually wound up in Switzerland. Attempts to raise the local population failed dismally, and the rebels were rounded up by the civic guard after an hour or so.

The ease with which that crisis had been contained did not reassure the authorities, and in June 1833 the German Confederation formed a Central Bureau of Political Investigation. This seemed to be warranted by a never-ending trickle of rumours of plots, all of which had to be taken seriously, however ineffectual those that actually come to fruition. Typical was the *Centralizacja*'s attempt to revive insurrection in Galicia earlier that year. Captain Zaliwski, who had played a prominent part on the November Night, was in overall command, and he set off from France followed by hundreds of others, travelling in twos and threes. On arrival, they found themselves less welcome than they had anticipated, and went into action with a few bands of poorly armed men. Most were quickly rounded up and sentenced to death, with commutation to twenty years' imprisonment in the fortress of Küfstein.

Equally ill-starred was a planned coup by officers in Turin. Twelve were executed, 100 were imprisoned, and dozens escaped abroad. Mazzini himself was sentenced to death in absentia, and, at the request of the Piedmontese authorities, expelled from France. He took refuge in Geneva, where he began to hatch plans for a mutiny in the Piedmontese navy and a simultaneous land invasion from Savoy. The naval mutiny was a wash-out. One of the most ardent plotters, Giuseppe Garibaldi, who had only been a member of Young Italy for a year, narrowly escaped with his life, and fled to Brazil. The land invasion was an even greater shambles.

It was to be carried out by Italians supplemented by contingents of Poles, Germans and Swiss, who began arriving in Switzerland towards the end of 1833. Within a couple of months, a force of some seven hundred had assembled, including the Polish company which had been diverted from Frankfurt, veterans of the 1820s risings in Italy and Spain such as Antonioni and Carlo Bianco, and free spirits like Harro Harring. Some of them were patently mad, others were swept along by a desire for heroics, while Harring's Polish commander was mostly drunk. But they were in earnest. 'We wanted to seal with our blood the statutes of a new alliance; to awaken the youth of Europe and all the peoples by our deeds; to shake all the thrones by our death; to regenerate Europe with the last groans of the expiring sacred phalanx,' affirmed Harring.[29]

Any chance of success the scheme might have had was blown away by the choice of commander. General Ramorino, who had demonstrated his incompetence in Poland, had turned up in Switzerland and presented himself to Mazzini. Mazzini was so impressed by the general's fanfaronade that, overruling the violent protests of the Poles present, he appointed him to lead the invasion. The results were predictably chaotic. One force, consisting of some four hundred of the most experienced men, was supposed to sail round and land in Piedmontese territory on the coast of Lake Geneva. But the authorities had got wind of the plan, and the invaders arrived to find a military reception committee lining the shore. They sailed up and down looking for alternative landing places until forced to give up, having run out of food, water and patience. The main column marched out bravely on 1 February 1834. Harro Harring, whose thoughts as he marched through the night dwelt on Ossian and on a Greek bandit he had fought alongside in 1822, planted a liberty tree in Annemasse, the first town they came to in Piedmontese territory. There followed some pointless marches and counter-marches, after which Ramorino led them back across the border and vanished. The volunteers trudged back, amid mutual recrimination. But for real believers, there was no such thing as failure. 'We have lived only for the salvation of humankind!' concluded Harro Harring. 'We have sacrificed the goods and pleasures of this world for the sake of suffering humanity! We will not turn back in the way we have chosen! We shall seal our deed with our blood, with our death! We will know how to die for the good of humanity – with a sword in our hand or on the scaffold! Amen.'[30] Back at his base in Carouge, Mazzini must have been animated by the same spirit as he changed the passwords. The new ones were: 'Martyrdom – Resurrection'.[31]

The failure nevertheless shook Mazzini, who blamed himself for encouraging people to risk their lives. He withdrew to reconsider his policy. As he was in hiding and saw nobody, his only relief was reading, and his constant companions were Homer, Ossian and Lamartine. After this period of introspection he emerged with a firmer sense of mission, underpinned by an increasingly religious commitment. 'Ours was not a sect but a religion of patriotism,' he later explained. 'Sects may die under violence; religions may not.'[32]

The majority of Italians already had a religion. And there were those who believed that Italy could only be politically reconstituted under the protectorate of the Pope. Mazzini was an enemy of the Catholic Church, 'not in the name of philosophic rationalism but in that of a new mysticism which claims to be more in conformity with the humaner spirit of the Gospels'. In his eyes, the Church had failed humanity. Like so many of his contemporaries, he believed he had found the essence of the faith itself. He saw his mission as 'the rebuilding of Humanity, a new age, an age built on Faith . . . a moral unity, the Catholicism of Humanity.'[33]

Humanity was not limited to one people, and there was nothing chauvinistic about Mazzini. His nationalism was not intended to create worship of the nation in rivalry with others, but rather to create a church through which all of mankind, represented in its nations, could achieve mutual harmony. Indeed, the fulfilment of each nation could only take place with the accord of others. Each nation had its part to play in this act of universal salvation, its own special mission, and that salvation depended on each one doing its bit. He sometimes represented humanity as an army on the march, with the nations making up its various divisions. There was no room for egoism here. As he meditated on the distant promise of universal salvation, Mazzini even contemplated the possibility that one day the nation might become redundant.

In Berne on 15 April 1834 Mazzini and seventeen others, including Swiss, Germans and Poles, created a nationalist international called Young Europe. A year later, there were 86 clubs of Young Italy, 260 of Young Switzerland, 50 of Young Poland, 14 of Young Germany and 14 of Young France. They would be joined in time by others, including a Young Ukraine, Young Tyrol, Young Argentina, Young Austria and Young Bohemia. A Young Ireland also came into existence, under the influence of Thomas Davis and others grouped round the *Nation* newspaper. But Mazzini dismissed the movement as bogus, and his reasons are revealing. Although Davis used to sign himself 'the Celt', he and most of his associates came from outside the Celtic tradition and did not speak the vernacular. They and other champions of Ireland such as Daniel O'Connell were not devotees of the cult of the nation; they fashioned bardic mythologies and Celtic warrior traditions to set against the satanic and materialistic English oppressor, but they were fighting for the rights of a disfranchised and dispossessed section of the population of the British Isles. 'I sympathize enormously with Ireland,' wrote Mazzini, 'but not so much with O'Connell and his way of dealing with the question.'[34] For Mazzini, the politics of rights and constitutional reform were anathema. 'Without Nationality neither liberty nor equality is possible – and we believe in the holy *Fatherland*, that is the cradle of nationality, the altar and patrimony of the individuals that compose each people,' he explained in the essay *Faith and the Future*.[35]

Humanity needed neither the sophistry of rights nor the help of any Catholic god. 'That which Christ did Humanity can do,' Mazzini asserted brazenly. And he felt no doubt that it was to be Italy's special mission to act as that Christ-substitute. Italy had already, he argued, twice acted as the torch-bearer of a new order: in the days of the Roman Empire, and with the advent of Christianity. It was now time for her to rise again to this great task. 'From your cross of misfortune and persecution announce the whole faith of the Age,' he exhorted his followers.[36] Italy, the 'people-messiah', was predestined to lead the crusade on behalf of enslaved humanity throughout Europe. 'There flashed upon me, as a star in my soul, an immense hope,' he exclaimed: 'Italy reborn, at one bound the missionary to Humanity of a Faith in Progress and in Fraternity more vast than that of old.'[37]

Implausible as they appeared to most people, such beliefs fired the initiated with a catechumen zeal. 'Your life is a romance from beginning to end,' exclaimed an exasperated Austrian officer interrogating young Felice Orsini, 'this love of country becomes a religious monomania with you Italians.'[38] The number of believers was still pathetically small. But the cult fed off itself and grew steadily, aided by Austrian repression, as ever greater numbers of liberals from every part of the peninsula were obliged to take refuge in the same French towns, in Switzerland and in London. Here they at last met each other and began to collaborate, bringing into being the first pan-Italian leadership and a country-wide network of communication. Their writings, which were clandestinely disseminated throughout the peninsula in the periodical *Giovine Italia*, gradually created a web of sympathizers.

They communicated and plotted with the aid of invisible ink, codes, false-bottomed trunks, and all the paraphernalia of espionage. Obliged even in Switzerland to hide his whereabouts, Mazzini developed a mastery of disguise and dissimulation that foiled all attempts to catch him. In their determination to keep ahead of any plot, the police of every state in Europe maintained a look-out for correspondence between exiles, and hired armies of spies and informers. In order to enhance their own importance and justify their salaries, the informers and the police tended to exaggerate the significance of the activities they monitored, and the *agents provocateurs* they employed often created rumours of conspiracy, generating panic and paranoia among the defenders of the *status quo*. All the old insecurities that had fed the blind fear of the Illuminati and other 'sects' resurfaced. A beleaguered establishment lived in fear of imagined groups of desperate men roaming the Continent looking to assassinate kings and ministers, of a threatening, unquantifiable, crepuscular underworld vowed to the annihilation of the *status quo*.

Metternich took this seriously: by 1847 the treasury of the kingdom of Austria was spending 1,131,000 florins on the police, compared with 37,000 florins on education. Metternich created a special Italian department within the police, with a permanent staff of eighty people, to monitor the activities of the conspirators. He described the secret societies as 'a real power, all the more dangerous as it works in the dark, undermining all parts of the social body, and depositing everywhere the seeds of a moral gangrene which is not slow to develop and increase'.[39]

The actual effects of the plotting were negligible. Most of the planned risings never took place, and most of those that did quickly lurched into fiasco. The Calabrian rising of 1844 was typical. It was organized by the brothers Attilio and Emilio Bandiera, sons of a Venetian who was an admiral in Austrian service. They themselves were officers in the same navy, but they became obsessed with the idea of Italian independence. They wrote to Mazzini to tell him of their hopes and their plans, but their correspondence was intercepted by the police. They landed in Calabria with a small band of desperadoes, and knelt to kiss the ground. By this stage they new they had been betrayed, but it mattered not to them. 'Italy will never live until Italians learn to die,' one of them asserted.[40] The local insurgents they were to meet up with never showed up, and they were easily rounded up by the local gendarmes. Three weeks later they were shot at Cosenza. Mazzini published a sonorous funeral oration, suggesting that their death had brought Italy closer to 'a moral priesthood among the people of Europe'.[41] The two became 'the martyrs of Cosenza'. The bullets with which they were shot were retrieved, and passed around to be kissed and venerated by the faithful.

The generation brought up on the literature and art of the Romantics abhorred inactivity and routine; they demanded bursts of action and craved danger, they relished the mysterious, the hidden, the forbidden. Action in this sense was a sublimation of love, and was indulged in with the requisite passion and the same relish for the hopeless, the unrequited and the fatal, which translated into politics as a capacity to luxuriate in the poignancies of failure and defeat. The Romantic *Sehnsucht* was an infinite and permanently dissatisfied longing for nirvana, for the ultimate experience, for that which could only find resolution in death – than which there could be no greater liberation.

The conspirators went in for increasingly colourful initiation ceremonies, with hooded cloaks, daggers, skulls and other props. The language was highly religious, with baptisms and anointings, descents into the grave and resurrections to a new life. Many took new names, like monks on joining an Order, to denote both the beginning of a new life and the renunciation of old ties. 'He who sacrifices his life for his brothers can never commit sin, but always fulfils the law of Christ', runs a characteristic line from one of the Polish 'catechisms'.[42]

Those who had tasted the sweetness of risking their lives in the elusive cause of national liberty became addicted, and leapt at every chance, adopting foreign causes or inventing them when there were none of their own to hand. That is why one Polish veteran of 1831, Mikołaj Szulczewski, led a detachment of 177 men over the American border into Canada in November 1838, meaning to liberate it from the British yoke, and gladly accepted the noose about his neck when he was defeated. It is why Harro Harring was trying to start a Young America in New York in 1843, with aims it would have been difficult to divine.

In places such as Poland, where there were plenty of social ills to address, the conspirators mostly acted out their own fantasies and satisfied their own metaphysical needs. The Association of the Polish Nation, formed in 1836 by, amongst others, Gustaw Ehrenberg, a natural son of Alexander I, had as its aim to 'rejuvenate the Polish nation' and 'wipe away the tears of suffering humanity'.[43] But there is no evidence that any of them contemplated practical help for the downtrodden, and the misfortunes of the peasants do not figure in their grandiose plans. Conspiracy seemed to justify itself, and even where there was a specific aim, it was the means and the sanctification they brought, not the end, that drew people.

In 1835 Szymon Konarski founded the Association of the Polish People, an altogether more serious organization calling for the emancipation of the peasants, with the motto 'by the people for the people'. He had fought in the November Rising, and had then taken part in revolutionary activity in Belgium and France, and in Mazzini's Savoy fiasco, before returning home. He operated in the Western Gubernias of Russia, drawing some three thousand people into the conspiracy over the next two years. He was arrested in Wilno in May 1838, and another one thousand people were interrogated. His public shooting in 1839 marked the end of years of painstaking efforts. But instead of being seen as a setback for the cause, it went down as a great day in the martyrological calendar. 'I saw it! O blessed moment!' wrote one member of the crowd that had been encouraged to attend by the Russian authorities. 'I see you walking up to the stake! I see you standing before the stake, like a second Christ on the Cross! Man above others! Konarski! Great martyr in the cause of humanity!'[44] The peasants he had sought to help were forgotten, but his death encouraged more young men to embrace the destiny of martyrdom.

16
Resurrection of the Spirit

On 9 August 1830 the youngest of the generals at Valmy became king of the French. He was not actually crowned. The ceremony, devoid of any religious elements, took place in the Chamber of Deputies in the presence of the representatives of the people and some eighty members of the Chamber of Peers, all dressed in normal city clothes. The diplomatic corps and the Church hierarchy were not in attendance. There was no music. Louis Philippe d'Orléans entered dressed in general's uniform, accompanied by his two eldest sons, the dukes of Chartres and Nemours, also in uniform. All three wore the sash of the Légion d'Honneur and no other decorations. They walked in and sat down on three stools in the middle of the Chamber. The president of the Chamber, Casimir Périer, read out the declaration framing the new monarchy and its conditions, which Louis Philippe swore to observe, in a pregnant phrase which took God as witness and acknowledged the sovereignty of the French nation. He was then acclaimed Louis Philippe I, King of the French, and four marshals handed him the attributes of monarchy: Macdonald the crown, Oudinot the sceptre, Mortier the sword, and Molitor the hand of justice. The new king then sat down on the throne, stripped of the fleur-de-lys and flanked by two large tricolors. After making a short speech promising to observe the law and promote the happiness of the people of France, he rode home, escorted only by his two sons, shaking hands along the way with people on the street.

This ceremony would have been approved of by Voltaire (who had patted him on the cheek when he was a child), but it did nothing for the sensibility of the 1830s. Rejecting both the Bourbon lily and the Napoleonic eagle, Louis Philippe selected the Gallic Cock as the finial on the standards of the National Guard. It was a sensible and pacific gesture that would have endeared him to the *philosophes*, but not one calculated to enthuse the Romantics. The new regime was rationalistic, secular and bourgeois. The only moral imperative thrown out by the king was that people should get on and grow rich. Such capitalist values at the top and the single-minded pursuit of material wealth by the majority of the population created a climate of selfishness that repelled the Romantics. In countless works they lavished contempt and condemnation upon it. Stendhal's hero Julien Sorel sees life as a lonely Napoleonic struggle against the overbearing forces of restraint and the corruption of its values. Musset's *Chatterton*, written in 1835, woven around the death of the English poet, is little more than a miracle play in which capitalist society takes the place of the devil. Alexandre Dumas summed up these feelings when he called Louis Philippe's 'the least poetic of all the thrones on earth'.[1]

While the new king looked bravely into a future that seemed to lie with materialistic solutions and with people moving, as Engels put it, 'from utopia to science', people actually kept drifting back to utopia.. And it was not just the poets. Even in Britain, where pragmatic utilitarianism held out the promise of steady improvement, young men such as John Stuart Mill were fired by a longing for more inspirational doctrines, and combined the missionary emotionalism of the Evangelical tradition with the spiritual questing of the Romantic movement. Robert Owen, archetype of the early capitalist factory owner, sought to create utopia among the smoking stacks, and at New Harmony in the United States, he attempted to establish an alternative society dedicated to achieving happiness for its inhabitants. But it was France that yielded the most varied and the most comprehensive schemes for salvation.

Henri de Rouvroy, Comte de Saint-Simon, descendant of Charlemagne and companion-in-arms of Lafayette, was an unusual product of the Enlightenment in that he combined its early obsession with science with its later cult of emotion. This resulted in a Romantic passion for all things scientific and in particular for canals – which he wanted to build across the isthmus of Panama and through Suez. 'The philosophy of the last century', he wrote, 'was revolutionary: that of the nineteenth century must be organizational.'[2] In line with this, he devised a system for the administration and social arrangement of the world based entirely on productivity. But he himself drifted into Romantic mysticism, and came up with a new religion, '*le Nouveau Christianisme*'. His disciples took this further and developed a faith in a female messiah from the east, which gave particular relevance to the concept of piercing the membrane of Suez as mystic marriage between Europe and the Orient.

The Saint-Simonians were succeeded by a movement founded by Charles Fourier, a seedy, obscure travelling salesman. This pedantic, routine-bound, bachelor denizen of grubby boarding-houses believed he was the messiah. 'I alone shall have confounded twenty centuries of political imbecility and it is to me alone that present and future generations will owe the initiative of their boundless happiness,' he modestly acknowledged. 'I came to dissipate political and moral darkness, and upon the ruins of uncertain sciences I erect the theory of universal harmony.'[3] Similar dreams were entertained by Étienne Cabet, who styled himself 'the apostle of sacred equality', and wanted everyone to live in exactly the same way, eating and dressing alike. In 1838 he wrote a utopia entitled *Voyage en Icarie*, which described a kind of theocratic communist state in which virtue had become effortless.

Although these religions eventually marginalized themselves out of existence, they attracted broad interest and the meetings of the Saint-Simonians and Fourierists were attended by the intellectual élite of Paris, with many leading poets, painters and musicians taking part. One of Saint-Simon's secretaries was Auguste Comte, who went on to found his own religion of Positivism, which had a worldwide following. After Fourier's death, his disciple Victor Considérant carried on his ideas, exerting an influence as far afield as Russia and the United States. Every socialist, from Pierre Leroux to Proudhon and Marx, took something from them.

And if these religions at least pretended to some more or less 'scientific' basis, there were plenty of others that did not. Antoine de la Salle and Pierre-Hyacinthe Azais held out the promise of salvation through their 'universal system'. A man by the name of Gannot founded a religion he called *Évadisme* (an anagram of Adam and Eve), a bizarre concoction of Zoroastrian myths and pseudo-Celtic tradition mixed on a bed of Christianity. Being the essence of both manhood and womanhood, and therefore both mother and father to mankind, *Mater* and *Pater*, he designated himself by the formal title of *Le Mapah*, and wrote a letter to the Pope dismissing him. The *Mapah* lived in a garret on the Ile St Louis, from which he bombarded the royal family and prominent politicians with letters instructing them how to run things, and where his disciples came to visit him. He was fond of uttering gnomic statements, such as '*Dieu, c'est le peuple!*', which his disciple Caillaux noted down avidly and published in an 'Ark of the New Covenant'.[4]

A more sinister and pervasive cult was that of the dead emperor. In October 1830, Victor Hugo wrote a poem entitled *Ode à la colonne*, which contains the line: 'We, who never had you as our master, worship you as God.' With the fall of the Bourbon monarchy in 1830 the ban on writing about Napoleon was lifted, and the emperor became a favourite subject for historians, novelists and poets. Dumas, Balzac and others mined the literary potential of the Napoleonic epos, conveying a roseate vision of happier times. Consciously or not, they also spread the notion of the emperor's immortality. In a poem entitled *Il n'est pas mort!*, Béranger begged God to give him back to France. 'My God, without him, I cannot believe in you', the poem ends.[5] The faith in the emperor's resurrection was transmitted in various subliminal ways, found graphic expression in popular prints, and was unequivocally enshrined in a monument in the small town of Fixin in Burgundy, commissioned from the sculptor Georges Rudé, representing a dead eagle on a rock, on which Napoleon, his eyes still closed, is parting his shroud and rising to life.

By the 1840s there was a minor literary-philosophical industry dedicated to distilling the essential genius of Napoleon and his significance for the world. In *Le Secret Politique de Napoléon* and its sequel *Le Faux Napoléonisme*, the mystic philosopher Hoene-Wronski set out to discover what lifted the emperor above the other great men of history. Napoleon, according to Hoene-Wronski, was the divine agent who had created the first real nation by inspiring the French people. He was the providential man, leading humanity to its moral goal.

A more interested champion of the emperor was Louis-Napoleon Bonaparte. The death of Napoleon's son, the Duke of Reichstadt, in 1832 cleared the way for his more ambitious cousin, who was determined to make a political career out of his uncle's legacy. 'The Emperor should be seen as the messiah of new ideas,' he claimed in *L'Idée Napoléonienne*, written in London in 1840. 'Great men have this in common with the Divinity that they never die entirely,' he wrote, juxtaposing his uncle with Moses, Mahomet, Julius Caesar and Charlemagne. 'Their spirit survives them, and the Napoleonic idea has sprung from the tomb of St Helena just as the teaching of the Gospel arose triumphant over the passion of Calvary.'[6] Such notions found resonance with those – and there were plenty – who longed for a transcendental hero who might save the world.

But while these religions appeared for a time to supersede the cult of the nation, this turned out to be no more than an eclipse. Faith in *La Grande Nation* was resilient. It held deeper and more universal appeal than the pseudo-scientific pipe-dreams, and it could accommodate the cult of Napoleon. It came to life again, under the influence of a new generation of theologians, the first of whom, appropriately, was a priest, the Abbé de Lamennais.

Originally devoted to the idea of reconquering France for the Catholic faith, Lamennais realized that the resumption by the Church of a sort of patched-up business as usual in 1815 was not going to re-spiritualize a society shaken by the sophistry of the Enlightenment and devastated by the revolution. His *Éssai sur l'Indifference*, published in 1823, caused a sensation throughout Europe. It reclaimed Catholicism from its *ancien-régime* context, by rejecting both the rationalist arguments of the *philosophes* and strict adherence to revealed dogma. He saw man as the conduit for God, and based his view of Christianity on the presence of God in every man. He thought that the revolution might have been willed by God, in order to punish and to test, and it followed from here that the people, the principal actor in those events, were God's chosen instrument. The people thus assumed a sacrosanct quality, and came to take the place of the Church.

In 1831 Lamennais met Mickiewicz, and they struck up an immediate rapport. When Lamennais read Mickiewicz's *Books of the Polish Nation* he pronounced it the most beautiful book he had ever known and likened it to the Gospels. It awakened feelings that inspired his own *Paroles d'un Croyant*, published in 1834.[7] This extraordinary work, with its apocalyptic vision of a world gone wrong groaning in a spiritual version of the Babylonian Captivity, held out a promise of global salvation through humanity itself. It had an enormous impact – it was said that the typesetters were reduced to tears as they worked on the proofs – comparable, according to the English radical W. J. Linton, only to that of Paine's *Common Sense*.[8] It also earned the condemnation of the Pope and led to Lamennais leaving the Church of Rome.

'The cause of the people is the holy cause, the cause of God,' he wrote, and he transferred his worship to the people, constituted as nations.[9] These nations were emanations of God and, like Christ, they had a redemptive role to fulfil. 'It is a martyr-nation,' he wrote in an essay on Poland. 'In its body a holy mystery is being accomplished . . . It has been delivered for a time to the powers of evil, so that, tempered in its suffering like steel in the waters of a torrent, it will become the sword that will vanquish the evil genius of humanity . . . Blessed, forever blessed the nation which, having suffered with constancy on behalf of all nations, has been judged worthy of vanquishing on their behalf!'[10]

But it did not come naturally to the sons of *La Grande Nation* to hand over the torch of redemption to other peoples. On 29 January 1832, the Saint-Simonian newspaper *Le Globe* announced France's unique claim to universal reverence. 'France has drunk of the revolutionary chalice; she drained it at once; France was crucified', it ran. 'France became the Christ of the nations.' The socialist Pierre Leroux, who edited *Le Globe*, saw France as 'a nation-religion' on account of her universal mission.[11]

It was Lamennais who laid down the canon of the relationship between the people, the *patrie* and other nations. 'The motherland is the common mother, the unity within which isolated individuals penetrate and become enmeshed,' he wrote, 'it is the holy name that expresses the voluntary fusion of all interests into one interest, of all lives into one lasting and perpetual life.' The basis of the *patrie* must be love rather than the law, for sacrifice and devotion can only stem from love. The love of the *patrie* should come before love of family, but the love of humanity as a whole before the love of *patrie*.[12] This universal motherland was France. She now needed to be saved from the state of paralysis into which she had fallen and reinstated as more than a cult, as the religion for all humanity. The high priest of this new religion was the historian Jules Michelet.

This was the great age of the historian, his status enhanced to that of seer, since he was writing the *res gestae* of the nation. 'It is from you that I shall ask for help, my noble country,' Michelet wrote in his journal on 6 August 1831, 'you must take the place of the God who escapes us, that you may fill within us the immeasurable abyss which extinct Christianity has left there.'[13] Armed with this faith in France, Michelet set about constructing a religion around it. He had read Herder and translated Vico's *Scienza Nuova*, so it is not surprising that he re-interpreted the whole of history as the spiritual evolution of the French people. Gradually, down the ages, France becomes a 'moral being', until finally 'a magnificent mystery opens: the great soul of France'.[14]

One of the key figures in this process is Joan of Arc, whom Michelet represents as being inspired not by God but by the love of France. As the author wrestles with the Christian imagery that he both rejects and uses, she emerges both as a kind of medieval French Virgin Mary, giving birth to the redeemer-nation, and as a messiah in her own right. This theme was picked up by Lamartine, who also appreciated the need to re-spiritualize political life. His book on Joan of Arc is a hagiographic fairy-tale, drifting from the historical to the supernatural, from the religious to the political, confusing and compounding all goodness with and into love of country, and all evil into political rejection of it. The thatched cottage in which the girl was born was France's stable of Bethlehem. 'The force of her national feeling is her greatest revelation,' asserts Lamartine. 'Her triumph attests to the energy of that virtue in her. Her mission is no more than the explosion of that patriotic faith into her life; she lives by it and dies of it, and she ascends to victory and to heaven on the double flame of her enthusiasm and the stake at which she was burned. Angel, woman, people, virgin, soldier, martyr, she is the emblem on the banner of the troops, the image of France made human through beauty, saved by the sword, surviving martyrdom, and deified through the holy faith in the *patrie*.'[15]

For most of the French intellectuals of the 1830s and 1840s, the revolution was not the crowning of the Enlightenment, but a divine revelation of one sort or another. Some saw it as the dawn of a new faith, others as a kind of second Reformation. Edgar Quinet suggested that it fulfilled the old faith. 'Christianity remains locked away in tombs up to the time of the French Revolution, when we can say that it revives, takes shape, is touched and felt for the first time in the hands of non-believers, in institutions and in the living law,' he wrote in 1845.[16] Michelet went further. He saw the revolution as a Second Coming, the birth of a new God, '*le Dieu de 1789*' – France. He likened the royal tennis court at Versailles, where the famous oath was sworn, to the stable at Bethlehem, and represented it as the crib of the new faith.

In 1838 Michelet was installed in the chair of '*Histoire et Morale*' at the Collège de France, and he envisaged his role as that of a kind of high pontiff of the national faith. In 1840 he was joined at the same institution by Mickiewicz, who was to reveal the mysteries of Slav civilization, and in 1842 by Quinet, who was to lecture on southern Europe. Together, they began to proclaim truths that had more to do with their spiritual convictions than literature or history.

In 1846 Michelet began a course on the subject of nationality. It was based on the principle that neither a monarchy nor the Church, which was the enemy of national individualism, could represent the nation, which derived only from the people. His thoughts on this he collected in a work whose title, *Le Peuple*, is misleading. 'The people' had replaced the noble savage as the object of sentimentality, of social guilt and of numerous fantasies and self-projections. But this did not equate with any real desire to help them in practical ways. Michelet saw the people as a mystic entity which, having cast aside king and pope, could at last spread the real gospel of humanity.

'Rome is nowhere but here,' he wrote, explaining that Rome had led a primitive world, that medieval monarchy had governed the era of uncertainty, and that France was to be the 'pontiff' of the age of light. France carried through the mission of Rome and of Christianity. Where Christ could only promise happiness in another world, France brought fraternity and equality to this one. 'The day France remembers that she was and must be the salvation of the human race, when she gathers her children about her and teaches them France as faith and religion, that day she will once again be alive, and as firm as the earth itself,' he declared.

Every child should be brought up to worship God in the Universe and God in the *patrie*. 'First the *Patrie* as dogma and principle. Then the *Patrie* as legend: our two redemptions, through the holy maid of Orléans, through the Revolution, the elan of 1792, the miracles of the new banner, our young generals, admired and mourned by the enemy, the purity of Marceau, the magnanimity of Hoche, the glory of Arcole and Austerlitz, Caesar and the Second Caesar, in whose person our greatest kings are reborn greater still ... Above that even the glory of our sovereign assemblies, the peaceful and truly human genius of 1789, when France offered to all with such good will freedom and peace ... Finally, above all else, as supreme lesson the immense talent for devotion, for self-sacrifice that our fathers showed, and how often France has given her life for the sake of the world ... Child, may this be your highest Gospel.'[17]

One great advantage of the gospel according to Michelet was that while he represented the peasants as embodying the ageless spirit of the people and of France, the new faith was open to all. Even an aristocrat could become a member of the Church of France provided that he believed sincerely and did penance for past attitudes. But this church needed its devils as much as any other, elements to unite against. Michelet and his colleagues were children of the Romantic age as well as of centuries of Christianity. An intense dislike of trade, of every activity that is not purely productive, of money and the logic it imposes as well as the corrupting influence it exerts, pervades their writings. This half-sentimental, half-religious legacy was also handed down to Socialism, in which it still perennially surfaces. Another legacy of these influences was modern French anti-Semitism, based on a vision of the Jew as an agent of materialism and corrupter of the Children of France. And as for Britain, that epitome of the grocer mentality, that shamelessly successful and supposedly materialistic nation, she was simply the Antichrist, or, as Michelet put it, 'the Anti-France'.

That France was paramount was an article of faith. Michelet strongly asserted the principle of the diversity of nations and of their interdependence, following the Mazzinian vision of a family of different characters, all complementing each other. 'When one of them is eclipsed for a while, the whole world is sick in all its nations,' he writes. But that did not apparently entail equality. France was 'henceforth the pilot of the vessel of humanity'.[18] 'Only France has the right to project herself as a model,' he affirmed elsewhere, 'because no people has merged its own interest and destiny with that of humanity more than she.' Victor Hugo was in no doubt about this when he came to write *La Légende des Siècles*. He glorifies 'France, summit of nations', explaining that she gave birth to the Revolution, which in turn gave birth to the peoples.[19]

This kind of thing did not always sit comfortably with the canons of other national churches. Under the influence of Mickiewicz, most Poles accepted the primacy of France, and subsumed their own messianic mission within it. Heine felt that the French fought for all, 'even when they fight out of vanity, egoism or folly'.[20] But Mazzini was becoming so obsessed with his own nation as to begin to sound exclusive. 'It is in Italian nationality that are based all the hopes of religion as well as the civil and universal hopes of the world, Italy is the chosen people, the model people, the initiating people, the Israel of the modern age,' he wrote in Lausanne in 1846.[21] But this kind of religious emulation was as nothing to the reactions provoked in German national sensibilities by French claims to leadership.

'The day will come', one of the speakers at the Hambach Festival had comforted his fellows, 'when sublime Germania shall stand on the bronze pedestal of liberty and justice, bearing in one hand the torch of enlightenment, which shall throw the beam of civilization into the remotest corners of the earth, and in the other the arbiter's balance. The people will beg her to settle their disputes; those very people who now show us that might is right, and kick us with the jackboot of scornful contempt.'[22] These Germans felt as oppressed as the Poles or the Italians. But since they were not actually being oppressed by any other power or people, they had to blame their discontent on some foreign other, one who made them feel inadequate. That other could only be France: the old complexes of the eighteenth century and the antipathies of the Napoleonic period simmered below the surface.

In 1840 the French government of Thiers, isolated and humiliated by foreign policy reversals, tried to save face with rhetoric about 'France's natural frontiers' and the spirit of 1792, backed up with ubiquitous singing of the *Marseillaise.* This provoked an outburst of nationwide hysteria in Germany. Belligerent statements were made and sabres rattled. Nikolaus Becker wrote the *Rheinlied*, which lays claim to the 'German Rhine', and Max Schneckenberger contributed the patriotic song *Die Wacht am Rhein.* There were appeals for the unification of the country in the hour of need, and much unpleasant comment on the French and their manners.

Various people did their best to calm the situation, including Lamartine, who wrote a pacific poem referring to the Rhine as the Nile of the West, from which all nations should drink, and which should wash away all 'challenges and ambitions'. But his efforts were undermined by his colleague Musset, who weighed in with an insultingly dismissive poem ridiculing Becker's *Rheinlied* and pointing out that the Germans could sing as much as they liked, but would never efface the marks left by the hooves of French cavalry, drenched in the blood of defeated Teutons. The tumult did eventually die down, but attitudes had soured.

In 1842 Richard Wagner, returning home from Paris, experienced something he had never felt before. 'For the first time I saw the Rhine,' he writes, 'my eyes filled with tears and I swore that I would, although only a poor artist, devote my life to the service of my German fatherland.'[23] Until then, he had been of the same mind as his countryman Heine, who detested the backwardness and provincialism of Germany. Heine had also ridiculed Becker's lofty phrases about the purity of the Rhine, reminding him how many times victorious French soldiers had urinated in it. In his long poem *Deutschland*, written after a trip to Germany in 1843, Heine asks Hammonia, the goddess of Hamburg, to reveal to him the country's future. Obliging, she leads him to a chair in the corner of the room and lifts the seat:

What I saw, I will not betray,
for I promised never to tell it.
But seeing was only half the tale–
Ye gods! if you could smell it!...[24]

The Germanophile Quinet had moved back to France in 1837. 'The Germans, awakened by their poets, have lately made themselves the object of a self-worship which will lead to their destruction,' he wrote.[25] In their longing to be a nation, the German intellectuals had made the *Volk* the basis for their ideology of unification, rejecting both geographical and state-based visions of a future homeland. This made them inward-looking and increasingly resentful of external influences: 'foreign ideas' appeared to them as some kind of a threat; those filtering in from Paris through the writings of people such as the emigré Heine were, in the late 1830s, being branded as 'Jewish ideas'. As early as 1816 Jakob Friedrich Vries had published *On the Threat Presented by the Jews to the Wellbeing and Character of the Germans*.

This was something the messianic nationalisms of the Poles and Italians had avoided, and it raised questions about the possibility of ever achieving the kind of international solidarity they were dreaming of. 'A drama will be enacted in Germany compared with which the French Revolution will seem like a harmless idyll,' wrote Heine in a moment of foreboding. 'Christianity may have restrained the martial ardour of the Teutons for a time, but it did not destroy it; now that the restraining talisman, the cross, has rotted away, the old frenzied madness will break out again.'[26]

Such a view was not warranted by the German emigrés living in Paris and London. In 1836 a large number of those in Paris formed the Bund der Gerechten, the League of the Just. Although their aim was to free Germany from the multiple subjection in which she found herself, they saw this enterprise as one to be undertaken together with other nations, and as part of the liberation of all. And they gladly accepted the primacy of France. 'France represents alone in Europe the pure and unalterable principle of human liberty,' wrote the German political reformer Arnold Ruge in 1844. 'This nation fulfils a mission of cosmopolitanism.'[27]

The Germans did nevertheless have a great deal to answer for, if only indirectly. By their example and their challenge, they inspired a number of national movements in central and eastern Europe as exclusive and as prone to defensive hysteria as their own.

In his *Ideas for the Philosophy of the History of Mankind*, published in 1784, Herder applied the noble savage myth locally. In the music and poetry of the Slavs, which he collected assiduously, he detected an innate genius and a transcendent morality. From this, he extrapolated that the apparently supine and incult Slav peoples of east central Europe had a glorious destiny, and would be the spiritual leaders of Europe in the next century.

There was one problem here. The only Slav nation that generally spoke and wrote in its own language were the Poles. In all other cases the educated élites had transferred to Latin, German or French, while the uneducated could neither read nor write. Their only cultural heritage was a ballast of tribal lore transmitted orally from generation to generation. The songs and poems that delighted Herder so much were almost entirely unknown and incomprehensible to the literate classes.

Vernacular cultures of one sort or another were among the subjects explored in the Enlightenment, and the vogue for Ossian was a typical consequence. It was in this spirit that a chair of Czech language and literature was endowed at the university of Vienna in 1775. In Bohemia, the Enlightenment's stirring of such issues awakened a novel sense of national consciousness among the nobility and educated classes. This was ruffled into resentment when, as in Hungary, the Emperor Joseph II refused to have himself crowned king of Bohemia and forbade the use of Czech in schools, insisting on German as the language of the Empire. In 1792, he sugared the pill of his centralizing reforms by establishing a chair of Czech language and literature in Prague. The educated classes of Bohemia were ignorant of both, and the first professor made his inaugural address, on the usefulness, importance and beauty of the Czech language, in German.

A Patriotic Theatre was founded in Prague in order to produce plays in the vernacular, but it shut down after four years. Several societies devoted to the resuscitation of past glories sprang up in the 1780 and 1790s. Ancient annals and manuscripts were snatched from their state of dusty repose and published. The Scientific Society of Prague sent a professor to Sweden to study manuscripts removed during the Thirty Years War, and another to

Moscow to scour seminal texts and compare early verse. But all this antiquarian ferreting could not make people in drawing rooms converse in Czech or young men and women write their love-letters in the language.[28]

This began to change in the 1820s, again under the influence of the Germans. It was during his studies at the University of Jena that Jan Kollár tasted what he called 'the bitter and agonizing fruit from the tree of nationality'.[29] The words he used are not out of place, for one of his teachers was Vries, who had identified a Jewish threat to German culture. The examples of the *Burschenschaften* and the sense of elation he had experienced at the Wartburg Festival remained with Kollár as he returned to Prague in 1819. The other image that stayed with him was that of his native country's historical eclipse. 'I see her in tears, that land which, once the cradle of my nation, is today its tomb,' he wrote. He began writing poetry which fuses the sentimental with the patriotic, so much so that in the whole considerable body of his work there is no expression of love that is not aimed at the motherland. His best-known work, the sonnet sequence *The Daughter of Slava*, published in 1824, is a bugle-call for Czech national revival and emancipation from the influence of Germany.[30]

He admitted that the Slavs had got there a bit late, but their day would come, in the next century when 'everywhere like a mighty flood the Slavs will extend their limits; the language which the Germans wrongly consider a mere speech of slaves will resound in palaces and even in the mouth of its rivals. The sciences will flow through Slav channels; our people' dress, their manners and their song will be fashionable on the Seine and on the Elbe.' Like Herder, he identified the special contribution of the Slavs as being 'humanitarianism', a spiritual superiority which naturally dictated a messianic role to them.[31]

Poets and intellectuals came forward to join him in the 'holy war', as they referred to the process of rebuilding a Czech culture. They felt themselves to be members of a 'church', and saw the second and third decades of the century as a period of 'resurrection'. 'Oh Lord, give a new birth to the nation buried alive!' wailed one.[32] Pavel Josef Šafařik, a poet who had also studied in Germany and attended the Wartburg Festival, was a major contributor to the archaeological struggle to assert Czech national self-respect in the face of German cultural hegemony. This went a long way further than poetic outpourings, and concerned recreating Czech history.

The process got under way in the 1820s, with the work of the historian František Palacký. 'My life and my soul, and every moment of my life will be devoted to the motherland and to the nation,' he wrote in his journal, and he was as good as his word. In his writings, he made of the fifteenth-century heretic Jan Hus a pivotal figure in European thought. He presented the doings of the Czechs in such ways that Bohemia could be seen to have been, in the days of Hus, the initiator of progressive and liberal ideas and therefore the forerunner of the Enlightenment and European progress. In this context, Germany's role in European culture dwindled in a way that made every Czech patriot's heart swell.[33] It swelled even further when the Czechs found their Macpherson.

Mystifications were an integral part of national revivalist activity. Kollár incorporated work of his own in anthologies of ancient folk songs, Ladislav Čelakovský invented a Czech female poet of the past and retailed a delighted public with the works of this 'Bohemian Sappho'. But the poet Vaclav Hanka went further. He had been inspired by German Romanticism while studying in Vienna, and wrote much undistinguished lyric poetry. On returning to Prague, he met Palacký and was fired by his enthusiasm for the past. He was given the post of archivist at the Museum of Bohemia, where he began rummaging among old manuscripts. He started by rescuing fragments of archaic Czech verse and collating them into a corpus of work, which involved a certain degree of imaginative patching and pasting. One thing led to another, and eventually to outright forgery. In 1818 he published *The Judgement of Libuša*, alleged to be a thirteenth-century Czech epic. Like Ossian, it was translated into a dozen languages and widely admired, while Czech patriots read it over and over, learning great chunks by heart and quoting them at the slightest opportunity.

Kollár and Šafařik were both Slovaks, but they had allowed themselves to be carried along by the dominant Czech influence. The next generation were not so easily led. In 1836 Slovak students held a festival in the ruins of the castle at Devin where the glorious ruler of Moravia, Duke Svatopluk, had lived. Slovak patriots had already begun to disinter their own antiquities and study their language. They came to the conclusion that their own Tatra Mountains were the real cradle of Slavdom, and that theirs was the purest of all the Slav languages. By the late 1830s the Czechs and Slovaks were at loggerheads over these and other claims. But however acrimonious their quarrels sometimes grew, there was nothing dangerous about them;

the fraction of the population involved was microscopic. What was more alarming was the need felt by some Czech nationalists for a deeper and wider Slav base from which to defy the perceived threat of Germandom. 'Scattered Slavs, let us be a united whole, and no longer mere fragments,' Kollár pleaded. 'Let us be all or naught.'[34]

Such sentiments struck chords in other small Slav nations. In 1842, Šafařik published a book which included a map showing the extent of territories settled by the various Slav nations and giving population figures. 'When I bought a copy of this map, the local patriots and even the non-patriots almost tore it out of my hands,' wrote Stanko Vraz from Zagreb. 'All of them cannot get over the fact that the Slav nation is spread so far. The map arouses more patriots than a whole literature could do.'[35]

The Balkans were beginning to stir. The Croats had taken advantage of the Napoleonic occupation of their lands to publish a grammar and a few literary texts, and the poet Valentin Vodnik wrote some odes evoking past glories. The interest in the region of powers as different as Britain, France and Russia caused locals to take a different view of their place in the world. In the early 1830s the journalist Ljudevit Gaj started an Illyrian movement with the aim of bringing about the unification of the southern Slav peoples.

The Serb revolt of 1804 had been a simple affair of the oppressed rising up against the depredations of the Janissaries stationed in Belgrade, but the subsequent fighting and Turkish reprisals had created their own epos. When peace came in 1826, under the terms of the Convention of Ackerman, which made Russia the protector of the Serbs' rights to autonomy within the Ottoman Empire, the concept of Serb nationhood and its membership of the Slav community were established. The poet Vuk Karadžić, who called the Serbs 'the greatest people on the planet', underpinned the budding nation's self-esteem by describing a culture 5,000 years old and claiming that Jesus Christ and His apostles had been Serbs.[36]

Such claims were by no means unique, and a similarly missionary nationalism had flourished in the Ukraine, originally through the Society of United Slavs founded by the Borisov brothers in 1823, with which the Decembrists and the Polish Patriotic Society had co-operated. Peter Borisov had drawn up a catechism which demanded the unification of all Slavs, hitherto divided only by ignorance. The emblem of the society was an octagon to represent eight Slav nations (Russians, Poles, Slovaks, Czechs, Serbo-Croats, Bulgars, Lusatians, Slovenes) and four anchors to represent four Slav seas (Black, White, Dalmatian, Arctic). Each member had to swear that he would overcome 1,000 deaths and 1,000 obstacles for the sake of Slav unity.

The Ukrainian cause was later taken up by the Brotherhood of Cyril and Methodius, named after the saints who brought Christianity to the Slav lands, founded in Kiev around 1840 by Vassily Bilozerski and Mikola Kostomarov. Its most famous member was the poet Taras Shevchenko. Born in 1814 into a peasant family south of Kiev, Shevchenko had been a house serf and accompanied his master to St Petersburg, where he managed to buy his freedom with the help of friends who had spotted his talent. He published his first poems amid derision from Russians who dismissed Ukrainian as a mere dialect. These were mostly heroic verses about the cossack past, in which there is much drinking, dancing, singing, fighting, killing, looting and raping, with a fair amount of weeping over the cruelties of fate. Shevchenko was prey to a kind of self-hating xenophobia, often reproaching Ukrainians for being too 'Russian' or too 'Polish'. He lamented the fraternal struggles of the Poles and cossacks, and expressed the longing to see a hero rise up who would unite the Slavs against foreigners. But it was Kostomarov who formulated the true aims of the Brotherhood, and his thinking was strongly marked by the works of Mickiewicz, the historical writings of Lelewel and the example of the Polish communes of penitents at Portsea and on the island of Jersey.

Kostomarov's *The Books of the Birth of the Ukrainian People* was modelled on Mickiewicz's similarly titled work. Its theme was that the Slavs had received Christianity as a holy destiny, but had failed to fulfil God's divine purpose on earth – or at least Russia and Poland had, leaving only the Ukraine, suffering, devastated but still pure and unbending. The Ukraine had brought about the brotherhood of man in the form of the cossack way of life and defended Christendom from the infidel Turk. And for this, according to Kostomarov, she had been crucified by her sister Slav nations. 'Ukraine is lying in the grave, but she has not died,' he wrote. 'And her voice, calling on all Slavs to liberty and brotherhood, resounded throughout the Slav world.' Eventually, her voice would be heard, and then Slavdom would triumph.[37]

In an 'Appeal to the Russians and the Poles', the Brotherhood called on these nations to cast off their hierarchical social patterns and return to Slavic simplicity. 'Russian and Polish Brothers! It is the Ukraine that calls to you, your poor sister, which you divided up and destroyed, and which does not remember evil, sympathizes with your misfortunes and is ready to shed her blood for your liberty.'[38] Kiev, where the Brotherhood were based, had been the capital of ancient Rus, and they saw it as the future capital of a kind of United States of Slavdom, modelled on the USA. 'We were not able to precisely draw the map of where our planned federation of states was to arise, and we left the final picture to history,' wrote Kostomarov.[39] History is still at it.

The universalist spirit of the Pan-Slav dream resonated powerfully in some quarters. Mickiewicz opened his first lecture at the Collège de France with words taken from the Czech poet Šafařik. 'All the peoples have had their say,' he quoted, 'now, Slavs, it is our turn to speak.'[40] This essentially Herderian view of nations succeeding each other on the world stage was here linked to a fundamental conviction that no one Slav nation could or should achieve this without the others. This sense of solidarity is evident in the way the Polish emigrés never failed to commemorate the Decembrist Rising. On one such occasion, in London in 1841, the main speaker was a Haitian, Dr Linstant. He was amazed to find Poles commemorating Russian martyrs. 'What has happened to national frontiers and hatreds, where is the memory of old injustices and murders destroying the unity of the human family?' he asked. 'We see men united by love, by love for the common cause, by the reverence for the sacred martyrs, symbolizing this cause. Their graves become an altar around which representatives of all mankind gathered together to receive the Holy Communion of freedom.'[41] Russian emigrés reciprocated by attending Polish commemorations of the November Rising, but they were in an uncomfortable situation. Russia was the only Slav nation not ruled by a foreign power, and therefore the one in the best position to deliver and lead her sister nations. But Russia was herself oppressing Slav nations, and had a different vision of her leading role.

If the Decembrists had not shown much in the way of solidarity with other nations, their spiritual heirs were more politically aware. Groups of students at the University of Moscow rejoiced at the news from Paris in July 1830 and wept at that from Warsaw in September 1831. They wore berets *à la* Karl Sand and discussed liberation through spiritual perfectibility. But most of them were arrested during a clamp-down in 1834 and sent to prison or internal exile. And they represented only an insignificant minority.

The majority of Russians reacted to the cultural and economic challenge of the West with xenophobic defensiveness. In the late 1820s Pushkin noted that people were talking of going back to their roots, literary and otherwise. Rather than accept a role as relative latecomers to European civilization, they sought to place themselves in a unique (and superior) position outside it. Like the Germans before them, the Russians hid their sense of inferiority by staking a claim to be the *Urvolk*, the most genuine people, spiritually closest to the roots of mankind. They invented a *Volkstum* for Russia, translated as *narodnost*, a compendium of conservative nonsense and religious exaltation supposedly emanating from the soul of the uniquely 'holy' Russia.

In 1832 the Minister of Education Count Sergei Uvarov submitted a report to Tsar Nicholas I in which he held up *narodnost* as 'the last anchor of our salvation and the most secure guarantee of the strength and greatness of our fatherland'.[42] The Tsar took his point, and *narodnost* was introduced into schools and universities through subjects such as history, literature, geography and philology. This stagnant and oppressive self-image crept in everywhere, marking even the most unpolitical literature with a stamp of alarmist jingoism. Not surprisingly, it was to resurface a century later, under Stalin, as a foil against 'rootless cosmopolitanism' in art.

Narodnost was underpinned by an imagined ideal Russian past, an Elysian condition. The writer Konstantin Sergeyevich Aksakov, who, according to one contemporary, 'wore a dress so national that the peasants in the streets took him for a Persian', built on this.[43] He developed a theory that in the West states had been founded by tyrants, while in Russia authority was willed into being by the people. 'Therefore at the basis of Western states lie violence, slavery and enmity,' he wrote. 'At the basis of the Russian state lie goodwill, freedom and peace.'[44] In the circumstances, it was highly tactless of Pyotr Yakovlevich Chaadayev to publish a comprehensive attack on everything the Russian state stood for, in his *Letter* of 1836. He maintained that Russia had contributed nothing to civilization except autocracy and serfdom, and he inveighed against what he termed 'the imbecilic contemplation of [Russia's] imaginary perfections'.[45] In doing so, he committed the cardinal sin of questioning the Emperor's new clothes. He was declared insane and confined. As the poet Tyutchev put it, one could not assess Russia, or love her, only believe in her.

It was a belief that could only be sustained by the invocation of an imaginary threat. From the early 1840s the Slavophiles propagated the twin notions of a great Western conspiracy to crush Russia and of a noxious Western 'disease' threatening to undermine her spiritual health. This paranoid vision demanded action, and the response was a dream of empire. The historian Mikhail Pogodin argued that if they were united under one sceptre, the Slavs could conquer the world, while Tyutchev dreamed of a Russia 'from the Nile to the Neva, from the Elbe to China, from the Volga to the Euphrates, from the Ganges to the Danube'.[46] The Czechs and the Serbs appeared amenable, but the Poles treacherously resisted this vision. To Tyutchev it was no coincidence that the Poles enjoyed the sympathy of that liberal West which looked down on Russia: 'Only our Judas is honoured by their kiss.'[47]

If a Slav sea were to start surging from the Neva to the Nile, one nation that would be washed away entirely was the Hungarians. Their country had fallen behind the rest of Europe in terms of economic development, and the old Magyar virtues that had seen them through the vicissitudes of past centuries were worthless in the face of new realities. These fears were reflected in the literature of the time, which sought to strengthen the Magyars' sense of nationhood.

In this spirit, the poet Ferenc Kölcsey wrote a long poem entitled *Hymn*, which provides a biblical view of the country's past, detailing the Tatar invasions and other disasters with almost morbid relish. In *The Flight of Zalan*, written in 1825, Kölcsey's colleague Mihály Vörosmarty contributed the national epic, the missing *Chanson de Roland* or *Niebelungenlied*. The old Jacobin poet Ferenc Kazinczy, who had been influenced by Herder and adopted his concept of the genius of language, started the process of reforming and purifying the vernacular. This began to take over as the medium of culture, of learning, and, finally, of all public transaction. As the language evolved, it inspired more writers, who supplied the myths and imagery that would transform the inchoate love of traditional values into modern Hungarian nationalism.

A more practical framework for the development of national identity was provided by a number of magnates, and principally by the remarkable Count István Széchenyi. Born in 1791, he had served with distinction in the Austrian army, fought at Leipzig in 1813 and been present at the Congress of Vienna. This and his extensive travels gave him a wide range of experience. He wrote his diary in German, with occasional lapses into English or French, displaying a cosmopolitan spirit that was soon to prove outdated. In his travels, it was England that had engaged his admiration, and he determined to introduce the English mix of liberalism and economic progress into his homeland. In 1825 he offered one year's revenue from his estates to establish a Hungarian Academy of Sciences, provoking others to make generous donations. He moved on to found discussion clubs, silkworm farms, rolling mills, shipyards, steamboat companies, and just about anything else feasible, culminating in the construction of the first permanent bridge over the Danube linking the cities of Buda and Pest.

Széchenyi represented a class which had always aspired to rule in Hungary with minimal interference from Vienna, and whose interests had never included the extension of political rights to the lower orders. In the past, this gave Vienna an advantage. Whenever the Hungarians grew truculent in their demands, Vienna would raise the peasant question and the nobles would fall silent. Such a relationship could not go on. In Vienna, Metternich was growing tired of the continual demands of the Hungarians, as well as their political waywardness. The Diet that met at Pressburg in 1832 and sat for the next four years was dominated by radical patriots such as the poet Kölcsey and Baron Miklós Wesselényi, and particularly by a non-participating delegate, Lajos Kossuth.

Born in 1802, the son of a landless nobleman, Kossuth had followed his father into the legal profession. In 1824 he had attempted to enter the civil service, but had to settle instead for a minor job in the provinces, where he relieved his boredom by taking up the pen. He made some adaptations of French and German plays, and wrote treatises on the French Revolution. He was influenced by German historians and adopted what he saw as a philosophical and pragmatic view of history. In 1830 Kossuth went into local politics, demonstrating a talent for leadership and organization. But this did not make him popular, and it was largely thanks to this that he was sent to the Diet in 1832. Nobles unable to attend themselves had the right to delegate an observer, and those of Zemplen county nominated Kossuth. Such a deputy had no voice and no vote, but this was not going to stop the ambitious young lawyer.

Kossuth began reporting the debates of the Diet in the form of letters, which were copied and widely circulated. Since he not only selected what to report, but added his own gloss, Kossuth quickly became an influential figure. The Diet achieved little: the burdens of the peasants were eased slightly, the privileges of the nobility were eroded, and Hungarian was made the official language in courts of law. But Kossuth enhanced its significance by weaving in a nationalist subtext. When, in February 1835, the Diet was dissolved for being unruly, he turned his last editorial into a manifesto. 'Our hand trembles as we take up the pen to set down our report of today's session,' he wrote. 'Our heart is filled with courage and anger, and in our present temper the sword would be more fitting in our clenched fist than the quavering pen.' He went on to hint that if the Austrians wanted a showdown, they would get war. 'But one cry forces itself from our throat, a cry which repeats itself as often as we try to utter any other sound: "Hungary awake!" '[48]

He seized every opportunity offered by Austrian repression to bring about a confrontation. When the poet László Lovassy was arrested, charged with uttering seditious thoughts and hiding Polish refugees in 1831, Kossuth sprang to his defence, giving the trial blanket publicity. When Lovassy was sentenced to ten years in the Spielberg, Kossuth hailed him as the first martyr of the Hungarian cause.

In 1837 Kossuth himself was arrested, along with Wesselényi and others, and charged with treason. He was sentenced to four years' imprisonment in Buda Castle, which he put to good use learning English. On his release, he founded a new paper, *Pesti Hírlap*, which became the vehicle for his nationalist views. These came under attack by Széchényi, who published a book in which he warned that they would lead to civil divisions and even strife. He had a point. The kingdom of Hungary was home to many peoples. As a boy, Kossuth spoke Hungarian to this father, German to his mother and Slovak to the servants and people in the street. Ethnic Hungarians, who numbered some five-and-a-half million, made up 40 per cent of the population, and intensive Magyarization was bound to alienate the non-Hungarian minorities, the Romanians, Slovaks, Serbs and Croats. Kossuth did not accept that these minorities had any real claim to nationhood, except in the case of the Croats, for whom he had some sympathy. The others, he believed, should assimilate into the Magyar nation.[49]

In 1844 Hungarian finally became the official language in every sphere of life throughout the kingdom, crowning a half-century of efforts. In that same year *Pesti Hírlap* was closed down, so Kossuth turned his attention, like Széchényi before him, to the modernization and development of the country. He was less knowledgeable and less practical than Széchényi in this area, but he succeeded in making the industrialization of the country appear patriotic and exciting, and thereby stole some of Széchényi's supporters for the nationalist cause.

This was being built up by every possible means, with old traditions being dusted down and new ones invented. In 1839 a group of Magyar nobles invited Franz Liszt to give some recitals in Hungary. Though born there, he had left as a boy of eleven to pursue his dizzying career as a virtuoso pianist. He had never been back and spoke not a word of the language. It mattered not. He drove into the country in a convoy of carriages full of aristocrats, progressing triumphantly through Pressburg to Pest, giving recitals that turned into ceremonies of national devotion, mobbed by hysterical crowds of students which he addressed from balconies. A spurious genealogy was concocted, and Liszt spent a fortune on a sumptuous Magyar noble's costume. A group of aristocrats petitioned the emperor to have a title bestowed upon him, and presented the pianist with a magnificent jewelled sabre. By this act he was dubbed in the national cause. But it was a defensive and narrowly-perceived cause, lacking the universalist faith that gave those of Italy and Poland their resilience.

Few things gave Metternich so many sleepless nights as something he called 'polonism'. Although he coined the word with the Poles in mind, he used it as a blanket term for the whole gangrenous *internationale* of bards and braves threatening his pan-European monarchical order with the promise of universal redemption through the apotheosis of the nations. Unlike the essentially egocentric national creeds of many central European nations, which could be kept in check by permutations of the policy of divide and rule, 'polonism' was unstoppable on account of its peripatetic nature and universalist appeal.

This phenomenon had nothing to do with the great nineteenth-century hobby of national heritage construction. This was the age of revival, Gothic or otherwise, of collecting, of excavation, and of invention. Professors applied themselves to the task of furbishing their country with every conceivable kind of historical and cultural credential, often without a thought for academic integrity. Artists harnessed their talents to the cause of glorifying the national past, present and future, with a dedication that often undermined the artistic value of their work. Those who failed to devote themselves and their art to the cause were castigated for it. Chopin was reproached by various of his countrymen, for not writing a great national opera. The best work of the Czech Romantic movement, Karel Hynek Macha's *Maj*, was given a poor reception when it first appeared in 1836, being seen as insufficiently patriotic.

Countries untouched by the revolutionary and Napoleonic upheavals and not threatened by the presence of powerful neighbours tended to approach the issue with less passion and urgency than others, but the urge to seek roots was universal. It is noteworthy that hardly any of the writers and artists of the day, with the notable exception of Victor Hugo, saw fit to dwell on the miseries of the industrial poor and the underprivileged, except as a sentimental device. Yet the call of the nation in distress was answered generously.

In Scandinavia, the Gotiska Forbundet, or Gothic Society, founded in 1811, revindicated the moral supremacy of ancient Scandinavians, while Carl Jonas Love Almqvist of Upsala dreamed of a national utopia. Nordic mythology was dredged up and used to great effect by Romantic nationalists, with Adam Oehlenschlager contributing a Nordic epic. The Danish historian Laurits Englestoft, who had been much impressed during his travels in revolutionary France, tried to regenerate his nation by composing civic catechisms and planning festivals. There is no evidence that this changed outlooks or stirred passions, although these were briefly aroused when the Swiss launched an attack on Danish mythology. The land of William Tell, which laboured its legends and imported real and invented rituals such as *Festspiels* and archery contests, refused to countenance the appearance of a learned pamphlet which argued (probably correctly) that the Tell legend was actually Danish in origin: the pamphlet was condemned and ceremonially burnt in the canton of Uri.

Many Italians laboured for decades in an attempt to net the cultural heritage of the Etruscans for themselves, and in 1840 Angelo Mazzoldi outdid them all with his theory that Italy was a relict of ancient Atlantis, which had sunk into the sea somewhere between Rome and Sardinia. By a similar sleight of hand, Vincenzo Gioberti swiped the whole of Hellenic culture for the Italian nation.

And it was not only the marginal nations that invented and appropriated: the British also built up a national heritage and paid unselfconscious homage to it. The Scots read their Scott and their Burns, they tartanized themselves and elevated the haggis. In Wales, Owain Glyndwr was reinvented as a national hero and stone circles were erected as part of the quest for Druidical roots; cremation was re-introduced and Lady Llanover turned an outdated English fashion that had survived in the valleys into a national costume.

The Italians, feeling more threatened, were more concerned with stirring the masses than the Welsh and the Danes. Painters such as Francesco Hayez produced canvases representing historical events in allegorical or emblematic ways, subliminally introducing into the national consciousness a vision of a fair, virginal Italia being abused by foreign barbarians or degenerates. Poets and novelists such as Alessandro Manzoni promoted similar images and begged the same reactions. In the opera house, composers such as Verdi played on the emotions with patriotic themes: in *Nabucco* (1838) he introduced the harrowing chorus *Va pensiero*, which laments the lost motherland, and in *I Lombardi* the highly charged *O Signor che dal tetto natio*, in which the crusaders assembled in Milan look forward to the holy war in a just cause.

It was this longing for the holy war of redemption that differentiated the religious nationalism of the Romantics from the fantasies of the heritage-hunters, for it was driven by the desire for salvation. And although it took its inspiration from the nation it was a desire for universal salvation. While it doted, to a pathological degree, on the concept of the nation as human organism, this brand of nationalism was actually drifting away from anything that could be termed political nationalism. It was coming to resemble an international movement of the emotionally dispossessed, and, as in the 1790s, it pinned its hopes on France.

Even under the un-poetic regime of Louis Philippe, Paris was closely bound up with the enthusiasms of contemporary humanity, and pilgrims of every nation entered it with reverence, as men used to enter Jerusalem and Rome. The foremost upholder of the image of France as *La Grande Nation* or, as he sometimes referred to her, the 'arch-nation', was Mickiewicz. He maintained that France possessed more of the 'sacred fire' than any other nation, and that she had therefore been called upon to usher in the 'new age'.

But Mickiewicz's promotion of France as the saviour of the world was becoming increasingly detached from France itself, and confused with the poet's long-standing quest for a 'man of destiny' and his lifelong fascination with the figure of Napoleon. At the same time, under the influence of the charlatan Andrzej Towiański, he developed a conviction that the mission of redeeming humanity originally entrusted by God to the Jews had been passed on, through a symbiosis of the two nations, to the Poles, and thus to the Slavs. His messianism was growing more international as he drifted away from terrestrial concepts of the motherland. For him, as for his brother-poets Juliusz Słowacki and Zygmunt Krasiński, 'Poland' was no longer just a place, or even a nation, but a state of mind, and that was what Metternich meant by 'polonism'.

Mickiewicz's second series of lectures at the Collège de France, which began in December 1841, rapidly turned into a socio-political and artistic happening. As a piece of performance art, they were unbeatable, with the bard declaiming barely comprehensible improvizations to rapt adepts and swooning ladies. He represented Slav literature in spiritual terms, and wove God, Napoleon, the Slavs, the Jews and the people of France together into one godhead. 'Our actions are religious-political,' he wrote to a fellow poet, describing the 'church' he and Towianski had founded, 'our tone is Christo-Napoleonic.'[50]

Mickiewicz was coming to see the nation more as a means of salvation, a conduit. Using the word to signify 'chosen', he maintained that there were three 'Israelite' nations through which humanity could be redeemed: the Jews, the French and the Slavs. He told his compatriots that they must learn to love Russia. In the summer of 1842 he spent two days on the battlefield of Waterloo, praying to the spirit of the emperor to strengthen him, and organized a vigil in the Paris synagogue on the anniversary of the destruction of the Temple in Jerusalem. In his lecture of 21 May 1844, entitled 'The *Ecce Homo* of our age', Mickiewicz challenged the genius of France to reveal itself and lead the nations.[51]

17
On the Threshold of Paradise

On 1 January 1848 King Louis Philippe told a foreign diplomat that 'two things are from now on impossible in France: revolution and war'.[1] In a sense that he did not intend, he was right. The great revolution that was meant to consummate the work of 1789 would abort itself, while the great war for the liberation of nations would never be declared. In effect, 1848 was to see the death of the ideals of 1789. They were drowned beneath the waves of two new forces: a Darwinian nationalism based on the right of the strongest, and a materialistic socialism that would, in time, enslave half of the world. The supposed solidarity of monarchs based on the Holy Alliance of 1815 did fall apart, it is true, giving way to shameless rivalry between crowned heads, but so did the solidarity of peoples, giving way to a far more savage rivalry of nations.

It was not supposed to be like that. 'This time, it was not just a question of bringing about the triumph of one side; people wanted to found a social science, a philosophy, I could almost say a religion, capable of being mastered and followed by all men,' wrote Tocqueville.[2] At Mâcon a few months earlier, Lamartine had called publicly for 'a revolution of contempt' to be levelled at the whole existing political and social order.[3] In the first days of 1848 Louis Antoine Garnier-Pagès announced that 'the hour of liberty and independence will strike for all the peoples of Europe, even for the peoples of Russia, who also have their day of deliverance marked in the Book of God,' and prophesied that there would be no more wars, as there would be no more division between weak and strong.[4] It was time for all the dreaming and plotting that had been going on since 1815 to come to fruition. 'It's here on earth, not in a fantastic heaven, that the life of the spirit will be realized,' declared the former priest, Ernest Renan.[5]

One could cite many more such statements of conviction, but they all come from people belonging to a restricted social group unrepresentative of society as a whole – contempt is not an emotion felt by starving workers, but by affronted idealists. Much the same went for all the complaints about the tastelessness and lack of spiritual depth made against the regime. Certainly, the poor and the oppressed wanted to see the kingdom of heaven descend to earth, but they saw it in terms of shorter working hours and cheap food rather than in a new politics of morality.

Defenders of the *status quo* feared that the 1815 settlement was decayed beyond repair, and agonized over the impending upheaval in an incontinent rhetoric of disease, earthquake, sweeping tides, straining dams and dark abysses. Yet the 1840s had been a relatively peaceful decade, with little in the way of social or industrial unrest. There had been nothing to compare with the regular disturbances of the 1830s. There had been an economic depression and a food crisis between 1845 and 1847, but conditions had improved rapidly in the second half of that year. There were, to be sure, starving workers and peasants aplenty, but it was not they who were behind the revolutions of 1848. Nor indeed were the revolutionary leaders, radicals, poets and dreamers who had been talking of little else for the past decade-and-a-half. For, while the talking went on, the drive for action had withered. Only the Italians and the Poles were actively plotting violent upheaval in any numbers, and their hopes looked distinctly forlorn by the end of 1847.

There had been a revival of activity on the part of the Polish Democratic Society in the mid-1840s, this time led by sanguine activists in the lands of partitioned Poland, not by the emigrés. The two centres were the Prussian-held city of Poznań and the city-republic of Kraków, which was closely connected with the Austrian Polish province of Galicia. These two cities featured as the starting-points for a new country-wide insurrection conjured up rather than planned by an irrepressible though unstable character who was asserting his claim to leadership – Ludwik Mierosławski.

Mierosławski was a fine-looking young man with blond hair and a heroic attitude. Born in 1814, the son of a Napoleonic officer and a French girl, he had taken part in the November Rising as a boy, and dreamed of leading armies ever since. In the meantime, he adhered to the Democratic Society, which he referred to sometimes as a 'church militant', sometimes as a 'crusading order'. He spoke in fiery tones of grandiose plans that could not fail, and carried people along by his self-assurance. He saw violent struggle against oppression as his element. He was convinced that too much peace was corrupting the nation. He believed that 'the surgery of a rising' was needed if the younger generation were not to go soft.[6]

In 1845 Mierosławski got together with the 23-year-old Edward Dembowski, and planned simultaneous risings to take place in Poznania and Galicia. Once these had been recaptured from the Prussians and the Austrians respectively, they could be used as a base for ejecting the Russians from the rest of Poland. The provisional government was to be headed by the Poznanian Karol Libelt, and the rising was to begin on the night of 21 February 1846. Mazzini was asked to stir up diversionary unrest in Italy to keep the Austrians busy, and a column of Frenchmen and Poles was to march through Switzerland into Italy with the same purpose. The enterprise collapsed when Libelt, Mierosławski and the other Poznanian leaders were rounded up by the Prussian police. On hearing the news, some conspirators wanted to countermand the rising, others to hasten it. As a result, a rash of premature outbreaks took place. On 18 February, Austrian troops marched into Kraków and began arresting conspirators in Galicia. The plotters in Kraków decided to rise anyway, and issued a manifesto of far-reaching social reform. 'The free nations of the world are calling upon us, urging us not to abandon the basis of our national existence', it ran. 'God himself summons us, He who will one day call us to account. There are twenty million of us. Let us rise up at the same moment like one man, and no power on earth will overwhelm us. Then we shall enjoy a freedom the like of which has never been seen on earth.'[7]

On 27 February 1846 Dembowski, in peasant costume and clutching a crucifix, led a procession through the surrounding countryside rallying the peasants. The exercise failed to elicit much enthusiasm, but as it trudged back towards Kraków, the procession was set upon by Austrian troops supported by scythe-waving peasants who had been offered money to massacre 'wicked revolutionaries' and enemies of the 'good emperor'. Dembowski was bludgeoned to death. Soon afterwards, the Republic of Kraków was annexed by Austria. Astonishingly, in these histrionic shambles Karl Marx identified the first democratic revolution of modern history.

What was certainly new was a perfidious Austrian policy of incitement, with officials offering money for 'insurgents' brought in dead or alive – having previously spread rumours that the Polish gentry had summoned French colonial troops, and that hordes of black men were about to swarm over the Carpathians and murder and then eat the peasants. The exercise culminated in the massacre of over 2,000 minor gentry, students and other suspects by peasants eager to demonstrate their loyalty to the emperor. This came as a terrible shock to the patriots. The peasants responded with apathy to all their blandishments, but sprang to the support of 'their emperor' with enthusiasm. This cooled the ardour of many a patriot. And the spectre of peasants marching on manors also haunted gentlemen-plotters in other Habsburg dominions such as Hungary and Italy, where recent developments were anything but encouraging to patriots.

In June 1846, a new Pope was elected, taking the name of Pius IX. Pio Nono, as he was known in Italy, caused controversy from the very beginning of his pontificate, by releasing political prisoners and implementing reforms. Wishful thinkers anticipated him. Angelo Brunetti, a golden-haired son of the streets of Rome, nicknamed 'Ciceruacchio' for his eloquence, started up a veritable cult of the Pope, imputing all sorts of liberal intentions to him. Others assumed that the Pontiff was responding to the call of Vincenzo Gioberti, who had published a book in 1843 proposing the redemption of Italy under the leadership of Rome.

Reforms were also introduced in Piedmont and Tuscany, which formed a customs union with the Papal States. Grand Duke Leopold of Tuscany similarly found himself cast in the role of reforming sovereign, and pressure grew on other rulers in the peninsula to follow suit. Metternich was alarmed. He forced extra treaties on Parma and Modena, and strengthened the Austrian garrison in Ferrara in order to overawe the Pope. But Pius protested, and his voice carried, for hundreds of volunteers were drifting towards Rome. Generals Durando, Skrzynecki, Bem and Ramorino offered their swords, while foreign artists and expatriates in Rome enthusiastically enlisted in the Civic Guard. Metternich had to back down.

Mazzini was anxious. National awareness was still limited to a small number of zealots. With the standard of living gradually edging upwards throughout the peninsula, the self-immolation required by the national faith appeared increasingly out of place. Agricultural societies, schools, children's homes, savings banks and other institutions able to help the poorest were taking effect. Land reclamation and improvement were making their mark, while the spread of railways favoured the development of agriculture-based industries. Patriots such as Carlo Cattaneo were putting progress above unification, and in 1847 a Piedmontese periodical, *Il Risorgimento*, began propounding a programme of practical regeneration.

This was all the more alarming to crusaders like Mazzini because it seemed to be part of a general trend in Europe. In Switzerland, the divisions between two groups of cantons, exploited by Metternich for reactionary reasons and fuelled by French-inspired liberals and revolutionaries, had been resolved with a minimum of upheaval after a short civil war. That the Confederation came into being in 1847 was a victory for pragmatic liberalism rather than inspired nationalism. Rumblings of discontent in Belgium had died out. In Britain, the social unrest of 1839 had given way to legalistic and constitutional action by the Chartists. In Ireland, Daniel O'Connell's calling-off the planned mass meeting at Clontarf in 1843 marked a retreat from confrontation. In Hungary, nationalist aspirations seemed to be contained by the regular constitutional channels. For those who craved upheaval and cataclysm, things were not looking good. The cause of nations was beginning to be superseded.

After a meeting of protest at the Austrian annexation of Kraków, the People's International League was founded. On 29 November 1847 1,500 Frenchmen, Poles, Germans, Italians, Swiss, Spaniards, Englishmen, Irishmen and Americans met in the rue St-Honoré in one of the largest of the traditional commemorations of the November Rising, and there was much enthusiasm for a great union of free peoples. But on the same day, in London, Karl Marx spoke in a different spirit at the meeting of the Fraternal Democrats. In the same month the first Communist Congress was held in London, and Karl Marx and Friedrich Engels were commissioned to prepare a manifesto.

In the event, Mazzini's anxiety was premature. There was enough local disaffection to cause incidents, and enough determination on the part of Metternich to ensure that these blew up into confrontations. The Milanese, for instance, had decided in November 1847 to stop smoking in order to deprive the Austrian treasury of the high excise levied on cigars. Anyone seen smoking was browbeaten into stopping, and on 2 January 1848 an Austrian captain had his cigar knocked from his mouth. The Austrian commander Field-Marshal Radetzky promptly issued all ranks with cigars and sent them out into the streets, ordering them to smoke. As thousands of soldiers poured out of their barracks puffing away at cigars, they were hissed, jeered and then assaulted, and in the street-fights that followed several lost their lives and hundreds were wounded.

While the political fragmentation of the Italian peninsula was a hurdle in the way of pan-Italian nationalism, it did lend far greater significance to local unrest; reported in Venice or Naples, the Milanese incidents sounded heroic. It also meant that while order might be restored in one place, there was always another in which the situation was ready to combust. Just as Milan calmed down, a revolution broke out in Palermo on 12 January 1848.

This was a confused and confusing affair, and it set the tone, no less than the style, for much of the revolutionary activity throughout Europe over the next two years. It was, as usual, initiated by followers of Mazzini, but in other respects it was a local revolt. Many of those taking part were little more than bandits intent on looting. But they were picturesque. Steel engravings depicting flamboyant Sicilian freedom fighters flooded the market, lending an illusion of relevance to many a Romantic opera, and launching a fashion for the 'Calabrian' look. Radical students all over Europe donned conical hats with feathers, high boots and cloaks.

While the Sicilian revolution, and the revolt that erupted in Naples a couple of weeks later in sympathy, lent grist to the mill of those conservatives who were prophesying doom and destruction, it carried little significance in the Continental context. It was no more likely to initiate an avalanche than the Neapolitan revolution of 1820. The numbers in favour of upheaval were insignificant, there were few potential leaders, and no plans. Some radicals in Denmark demanded a constitution, but nobody paid much attention. In Paris, Tocqueville made a fine speech in the Chamber of Deputies warning that a storm was brewing, but only hindsight made it notable. What took place a month later happened almost by accident.

On 21 February the conservative government of François Guizot refused permission for the last in a series of public banquets held by radicals in order to air the grievances of the working classes. The organizers accepted this decision, but a group of students did not. The following day they assembled at the Panthéon and marched by a roundabout route taking in the poorest areas of Paris, so that by the time they reached the Palais Bourbon, seat of the National Assembly, they had snowballed into a huge crowd. The police did their best to disperse it, but barricades began going up in various quarters. The National Guard was carried out and troops went into action. A few of the barricades were taken and dismantled, after which the troops retired for the night. The persistent drizzle acted as a dampener on spirits, and there was none of the fire and passion of the July Days of 1830. But on the morning of 23 February there were fresh demonstrations, leading to clashes with troops. More barricades went up, and the red flag appeared on one in the rue Montmartre.

What rattled the ageing Louis Philippe and stopped him from responding with firmness was that National Guardsmen from the poorer sections were joining the insurgents, and only those from the wealthier *quartiers* were standing by him. He therefore dismissed Guizot and promised a measure of reform. This defused the situation, and by the evening of 23 February the streets were full of celebration, some of it admittedly a little rowdy. On the Boulevard des Capucines there was an altercation between troops and a group of civilians, during which tempers frayed. A random shot was taken by the troops as a signal to open fire. The result was a heap of corpses, which were duly arrayed on a wagon and paraded around the city by torchlight. More barricades went up, and by the morning of 24 February the revolution had started in earnest.

Louis Philippe tried to restore order through a combination of military force and another change of government, but soon realized that it was too late. He abdicated in favour of his grandson, the Comte de Paris, and left the Tuileries, which were promptly sacked. But the Comte de Paris was not to reign. In the Chamber of Deputies, Lamartine declared himself in favour of 'that sublime mystery of universal sovereignty', a republic.

The throne was taken from the Tuileries and borne in procession to the Place de la Bastille. There, at the foot of the column erected by its late occupant to commemorate the events of 14 July 1789, it was placed on a stack of faggots and burned. That evening at the Comédie Française, the renowned actress Rachel came on to an empty stage, dressed in a simple white tunic of Roman cut, carrying a tricolor. She began reciting the words of the *Marseillaise*, slowly and quietly at first, mounting to a tremendous crescendo, a veritable delirium of patriotic declamation, only to kneel, enfolded in the tricolor, and deliver the line '*amour sacré de la patrie*' with hushed reverence. The national liturgy was back, and the *Marseillaise* had been declared, in the words of one journalist, the *Pater Noster* of France.[8] 'Paris has risen from the tomb, radiant as a new Christ,' wrote one of the popular *chansonniers*.[9]

But there was something routine in all this. 'People were trying to warm themselves with the passions of their fathers, without succeeding,' as Tocqueville put it, 'they imitated their gestures and their poses as they had seen done in the theatre, without managing to reproduce their enthusiasm or feel their fury.'[10] This was evident to the English Chartist

W. J. Linton, who had come over with a delegation to express solidarity with the French working classes shortly after the February days. 'Already it was plain', he writes, 'that French policy was separated from the nascent republican hopes of revolutionary Europe.'[11]

The battle-cry most frequently on the lips of the insurgents on the Paris barricades had been '*Vive la Pologne!*' This did not signify that the liberation of Poland was one of their principal objectives; it was an element of the liturgy. It did nevertheless express a universal desire to see Poland freed, as part of a general reordering. 'The Republic has been proclaimed! we shall be happy now!' exclaims the working-class hero Dussardier in Flaubert's *L'Éducation Sentimentale* as he comes off the barricades. 'I overheard some journalists saying that Poland and Italy would be freed! No more kings! you realize! The whole world free! the whole world free!' The logic that suggested a republic in 1848 demanded the invocation of the spirit of 1792 and a crusade for the liberation of nations. Many felt that the promise of 1830 had died precisely because France had failed to rise to the occasion in this respect. All over Europe, radicals anticipated and conservatives feared that France would make war over Poland, foment revolution in Germany, and go to the assistance of the Italians.

But Lamartine, who had taken the portfolio of foreign affairs, immediately wrote to all the chancelleries of Europe explaining that although France had repudiated the spirit of the treaties of 1815, she had no intention of supporting any claims by captive nations that might disturb the peace. 'He bored us in verse and betrayed us in prose', as Heinrich Heine put it.[12]

Before the dust of the February Days had settled, groups of foreign exiles began to besiege Lamartine's office, asking for arms and financial assistance. Among the first were the Poles, who were subjected to a priggish lecture on the niceties of international law and the policy of non-intervention. Then came some Italians and Savoyards. They were warned that French troops would be posted along the border to prevent them from invading Savoy. Then came Belgians. These were allowed to form up a corps of 2,000 men, and were even provided with rail transport – the only problem being that the trains did not take them to the border, but right into Belgium, where they were surrounded by troops on arrival. The only group who had any luck at this stage were the German exiles.

Conditions in Germany were in many ways more conducive to revolution than they had been in France. Population growth had outstripped food production during the 1840s. There was a downturn in the economic cycle in 1846–7, boosting the numbers of unemployed. Potato blight and crop failures further aggravated the situation, resulting in rises of up to 400 per cent in food prices. There were riots in Berlin and Hamburg, while large numbers of wandering poor and restless mobs in cities created a sense of threat and instability. Food prices came down and the situation stabilized towards the end of 1847, but this was not the end of the problem.

With its numerous universities, Germany produced a surfeit of educated people, with too many graduates chasing too few jobs. 'In Germany, the intellectual proletariat is the real, fighting church of the fourth estate,' wrote the German conservative Wilhelm Riehl, listing 'civil servants, schoolmasters, perennial students of theology, starving academic instructors, literati, journalists, artists of all kinds ranging downwards from the travelling virtuosi to the itinerant comedians, organ-grinders and vaudeville singers', and concluding that 'Germany produces more mental product than she can use or pay for'.[13] This redundant 'mental product' was an unstable element, and when news of the risings in Sicily and then France reached Germany, it was at the forefront of a wave of demonstrations, strikes and attacks on authority that swept through the whole country. Liberal concessions were exacted in Württemberg, Baden, Saxony and other states. In Bavaria a combination of outrage at the king's patronage of the Irish dancer Lola Montez, and liberal pressure, brought about his abdication. In Berlin, events took a more drastic turn.

On 10 March large demonstrations ignited a fuse that led to the Prussian army opening fire on an unarmed crowd a week later. The populace was aroused and fierce street-battles ensued. After a few hours of blood-letting, King Frederick William IV ordered his troops to leave the city and agreed to the formation of a liberal ministry. The Polish prisoners of 1846 were released from the Moabit gaol. In heroic pose and crowned with laurels, Mierosławski and his colleagues were drawn around the city on open carriages in a carnival triumph. When the convoy reached the royal palace, the king, no doubt grinding his teeth, came out on to the balcony to salute the exultant rebels. A civil guard was formed, and the king was henceforth attended in his palace by a cohort of students dressed in a medieval Teutonic version of the Calabrian look.

Independently of the revolutions taking place in various parts of the country, the Diet of the German Confederation passed a number of reforms in the first months of 1848. On 3 March, for instance, it voted to allow individual states to repeal the laws imposed by Metternich in 1819, and a few days later it adopted the black, red and gold colours. On 5 March some fifty liberals met at Heidelberg and called for an all-German parliament, and the Diet decided to summon it straight away in provisional form.

All of this upset the system built up by Metternich, but the Austrian chancellor was in no position to protest. As he had made Austria into the policeman of Italy, trouble in any part of the peninsula had an immediate impact in Vienna and evoked echoes in other Habsburg dominions. Within a month of the insurrection in Palermo, tracts supporting it were being distributed in the streets of Prague. News of events in Paris and Berlin raised hopes there further. A group of Bohemian radicals organized a rally on 11 March that turned into a mass meeting formulating demands for national autonomy. A delegation was despatched to Vienna, and patriots began enlisting in the St Wenceslas Militia. The Hungarians were not far behind. Nationalists were well represented in the Hungarian Diet which met at Pressburg towards the end of November 1847. The run-up to the elections had been unusually agitated, with the anti-Habsburg opposition campaigning on brazenly nationalist grounds. People paraded in colourful Hungarian costumes, with grand ladies dressed as peasant women in diamonds and poets decked out like cattle drovers from the *Puszta*. News of the February Revolution in Paris reached Pressburg on 1 March 1848 and two days later Lajos Kossuth made a thundering speech demanding total reform of the Habsburg monarchy. On 13 March revolution broke out in Vienna, sparked partly by his speech, and the great Metternich, linchpin of the Congress System, was swept from office.

On 14 March the Hungarian Diet agreed to demand constitutional autonomy for Hungary. That evening there were torchlight processions around Pressburg, and when Kossuth appeared on the balcony he was greeted as 'the Liberator of Hungary'. The aristocrats who had hitherto eyed him with a mixture of disdain and alarm, were swept along. The following day a delegation drawn from both Chambers climbed aboard a steamer, the *Bela*, and paddled up the Danube. When, a couple of hours later, the Hungarian noblemen, with their gem-studded sabres and fur caps adorned with egret feathers, hove in sight of Vienna, they were dubbed 'the Argonauts' by the Austrian press. Crowds lined the streets as they began their stately progress to the imperial chancellery to lodge their petition. People cheered and wept by turns, women surged forward to kiss Kossuth's cloak, and students unharnessed the horses from his carriage so that they could pull it themselves. Again and again he was obliged to stop and talk to the crowd.

Kossuth was forty-six years old and physically unimpressive. But the moment he began speaking he would summon up enormous energy, and his eloquence never failed to carry his audience. He was also a tough negotiator, as the following day, spent bargaining with the emperor, demonstrated. The emperor acceded to virtually every demand the Hungarian Diet had made. The Argonauts climbed back aboard the *Bela* and steamed off. On stepping ashore at Pressburg, Kossuth fell to his knees and hailed his free motherland. The following day, in a replay of the French Assembly's Fourth of August, the Diet voted to abolish feudal dues and the clergy gave up its right to tithes. The revolutionary government was made up exclusively of nobles, and included the most illustrious names, such as Széchenyi, Esterhazy, Batthyányi and Teleki. These were not the only parallels with the French revolution.

The city of Pest boasted its own equivalent of the Palais-Royal, in the rather less glamorous shape of the Café Pilvax, a favoured venue for officers, students and restless spirits. The Pilvax's Camille Desmoulins was a 24-year-old poet, Sándor Petöfi. The son of a village innkeeper, he had run away from home at the age of sixteen to join a troupe of strolling players. Although he did not stay with them for long, he remained something of a wanderer, always at odds with his environment. This prickly rose began writing lyrical poetry, and in 1846 joined with other poets to found a 'Young Hungary'. 'In our days God has ordered poets to be the fiery pillars and so to lead the wandering people into Canaan's promised land,' he wrote.[14] In 1847 Petöfi put himself forward for election to the Diet. He was laughed out of court and even threatened with violence, but this apparent rejection by the people did not sour his attitude to them. 'Blessed be the name of the People, now and for ever,' he chanted in his non-election address.[15]

The February Revolution in Paris thrilled Petöfi and his friends, and news of the 13 March revolution in Vienna spurred them into action. On the morning of 15 March, Petöfi and his brother-poet Mór Jókai came to the Café Pilvax, which was crowded with young hotheads. Petöfi mounted a table and drew from his pocket the fruit of a sleepless night, a poem entitled 'Magyar Arise!' which he proceeded to read. As the great work was inaudible to the crowd that had gathered in the pouring rain outside the Pilvax, the poet led the swelling mob off to the square in front of the National Museum, where he recited it once more and addressed the crowd, or rather a sea of umbrellas. With Petöfi in the lead, the mob then marched off to a printing-shop, where the poet tossed the manuscript to the compositors. It was set within minutes, and the thousands of copies dashed off the presses were distributed to the crowd. This had now swelled to impressive dimensions; it crossed Széchenyi's bridge into Buda, where it 'stormed' the castle, releasing one solitary political prisoner, who was now paraded like a trophy of war. The next stop was the National Theatre, where Rosa Laborfalvy, the heartthrob of the season, embraced Jókai and Petöfi, to the delight of the crowd. By the evening, they had seized arms and formed into National Guard units, and barricades were being put up all over the city – nobody could say against whom. God had spoken through the people, according to a contemporary press account. 'What other nations had achieved with the sword, this nation had obtained with its bare hands, only by the flame of its holy enthusiasm.'[16]

Kossuth made use of the disturbances in Pest for his own ends. In normal circumstances, Vienna would have threatened the Hungarian nobles with the spectre of a loyalist peasant rising against them, similar to that they had provoked against the Poles in Galicia in 1846. But Kossuth now held up a far more alarming scenario – that of a radical revolt in Hungary led by rootless revolutionaries. The Diet therefore had no trouble in gaining acceptance of a new constitution for the kingdom of Hungary, giving it wide-ranging autonomy under the Habsburg Crown, and the Hungarian nobility ultimate control within a more liberal system. The radicals had been outmanoeuvred, and Petöfi retired to write his last important poem, *The Apostle.* The poet-hero knows he was placed on Earth to redeem his people and his country, but the people do not understand him, and they follow their oppressors, the priests and the tyrants, in condemning him. When, having assassinated the king, he stands on the scaffold before a crowd that fails to recognize its saviour, he lets out a desperate cry:

> *'Was it not enough to crucify Christ,*
> *Must you crucify all redeemers?'*[17]

Throughout the spring of 1848, events unfolded all over Europe in a manner that suggested the realization of their wildest dreams to the liberators, and the ultimate nightmare to supporters of the post-1815 *status quo*. Not for nothing was it dubbed 'the Springtime of the Peoples'. The length and breadth of Europe, poets and demagogues ranted from balconies to crowds assembled in streets and squares, calling for a new crusade just as preachers had once done from pulpits all over Christendom. Every week brought news of barricades going up and charters being granted, of gaols broken open and tricolors hoisted. Even from the usually unruffled Scandinavia came reports of flag-waving and chanting crowds. There was a patriotic banquet in Stockholm, and radicals took their seats in the government of Denmark. Harro Harring was whipping up rebellion in Friesland and later came up with a visionary scheme of creating a Greater Scandinavia. Nobody understood what he was talking about, but the local peasants and fishermen were much taken with his stylish black uniform, the naval cutlass at his side, the dagger and pistols tucked into his belt, and his South American felt hat with the black cockade and gold star of Young Europe. In England, the Chartists were marshalling their forces for a decisive confrontation. In March there was a revolution in Madrid – not much of a revolution, it is true, as its start was delayed by the principal plotters taking too long over their lunch. Some six hundred leaderless insurgents went into the streets and were easily dispersed by the forces of order. But other risings followed, in Barcelona, and again in Madrid.

In effect, many of the revolts were as fortuitous as the February Days in Paris, and were endemic to the way civil order was enforced. There was not time to analyse the underlying strength of every movement and judge the seriousness of every eruption, so the merest pustule had to be treated by the authorities as potentially volcanic. In the confusion, and given the sheer pace of events during the spring of 1848, it was possible to think that the whole structure of the Continent was about to fall apart.

European governments of the 1840s were not equipped to deal with civil unrest; police forces were small and unarmed, briefed only to round up burglars and drunks, with no back-up of any sort. Whenever a riot began, they lost control and retired from the scene. The government could then only call out troops, but by the time these materialized the crowd had usually swollen and, feeling the self-assurance born of its quick triumph over the police, begun to formulate political demands. Such situations always seemed to produce a holiday atmosphere, with women and children joining the crowd. The troops that would arrive on the scene were not trained for crowd control, and they were led by officers who despised all civilians. One stray shot or a shower of stones would usually provoke a shoot-out, resulting in casualties among innocent bystanders, which outraged even conservative opinion, and undermined the position of the government at the moment when the barricades were going up.

The grievances voiced on the streets of Madrid, London and Copenhagen could be defused or accommodated by some fiscal or social tinkering. Those voiced in Palermo, Prague or Poznań could not, any more than those in Buda, Bologna or Berlin, because they emanated from states of mind that aspired to national orgasm. And as the revolutionaries sought to build their respective heavenly kingdoms, they came up against the imperial structures erected in another age. It was with the aim of dealing with this problem that the liberals at Heidelberg had called for an all-German parliament.

On 31 March, the 574 delegates to the preliminary *Vorparlament* met at Frankfurt, in the great hall where the Holy Roman Emperors had been crowned. They were thrown into confusion at the start by two delegates from Baden, Friedrich Hecker and Gustav Struve, who demanded the immediate declaration of a German republic. When the other delegates demurred, they called for an insurrection. Hecker was one of the most popular men in Germany at the time. Tall, handsome and impulsive, he had been the leader of the liberals in Baden for many years. He enhanced his political profile by adopting his own version of the Calabrian look, going about in a blue blouse, thigh-high boots, cloak and plumed conical hat, with a sabre and a couple of pistols tucked into his belt. Struve could not have been more different. A small man, ascetic and intellectually tortured, he was the kind of person who tried to order everything. Believing in the pseudo-science of phrenology, he even chose a wife without the bump of passion. At one stage he devised a calendar, the adoption of which would turn Germans into greater people. Every day was to be given over to meditation on the life and deeds of leaders such as Lafayette and Washington, while every tenth day would be devoted to the study of monsters such as Metternich and Nicholas I.

This improbable pair proclaimed a republic in Constance and offered an 'amnesty' to all rulers willing to go quietly. They marched north, expecting tens of thousands to answer their call, but only a few responded. Characteristically, the most eager were a cohort of Germans in Paris, led by Georg Herwegh. The son of a Stuttgart restaurateur, he had deserted during his national service in order to escape a court martial, and taken refuge in Switzerland. There, he published an anthology of vigorous denunciatory verse, whose lack of intellectual depth was made up for by its youthful anger, directed with the precision of a scattergun at any institution that came to mind. The 'songbird of war', as Herwegh was dubbed, became immensely popular – not with the authorities in Germany, or indeed Switzerland, which he was obliged to quit in 1843.

Luckily for him, Herwegh had married Emma Siegmund, the daughter of a wealthy Berlin entrepreneur, and when the couple moved to Paris the following year, they were able to avoid the penury that made the lives of most emigrés in that expensive metropolis such a misery. The Herweghs took their place in the literary firmament of the French capital, and it was to them that the German democrats in Paris looked in 1848. Herwegh organized a demonstration to affirm the brotherhood of the French and German nations, and called on the French revolutionaries to hand over their weapons to their German comrades so that they could go and do likewise in their native land. He formed up a legion, the French government contributed to its travel costs, and Emma supplemented this by selling her silver, for they had to be properly kitted out. She had a martial riding-habit run up in the national colours of black, red, and gold, while Herwegh opted for the Calabrian look. The 800 legionaries set forth at the end of March, cheered on their way by enthusiastic crowds. In the towns and villages they passed through people gave them food and drink, often refusing payment. On 25 April the German Legion crossed the Rhine, but they were too late.

Regular troops from Hesse and Baden had been despatched against Hecker and Struve, whose forces were routed. Struve was captured, and Hecker was forced to flee to Switzerland. When Herwegh's men, who had marched unsuspecting into Baden, heard of Hecker's defeat, they turned towards the Swiss border. But they were overtaken and forced to make a stand at Dossenbach on 27 April. Herwegh had told them that brother Germans would not dare to fire on them, but he was wrong. Some fifty of the legionaries were killed, a large number surrendered, the rest fled. Among the latter group were the Herweghs themselves. The 'songbird of war' hid in a ditch and, after shedding his operatic uniform and shaving off his martial beard, he and Emma made a dash for Switzerland.

With these theatricals behind it, the *Vorparlament* finished its preparatory work. Elections were held – under wildly varying franchises – in every state of the Confederation, and on 18 May the Deputies to the German

National Assembly met at Frankfurt. Having gathered under the portraits of the emperors in the coronation hall, they marched in solemn procession to the Paulskirche, whose size would permit the debates to be held in full view of the press and spectators. The great rotunda, adorned with a huge painting of 'Germania', was already packed when the procession entered.

The first act of the parliament was to elect a president, which proved easy. Heinrich von Gagern was the undisputed choice. Just old enough to have fought at Waterloo, a *Burschenschafter* in his student days, and a moderate liberal, he was gentle and conciliatory, qualities that would be much in demand over the next weeks. The assembly included more than a hundred university professors, two hundred lawyers, and dozens of others with intellectual and oratorical pretensions. There was a predictable glut of verbiage as they unleashed their lecturing and courtroom skills.

The principal task facing the Assembly was to draw up a constitution that would bind together and embody the sovereignty of the German people. But this people was ruled by a bevy of sovereign princes. And that was not the only circle they would have to square, for some of those princes also ruled over subjects who were not German at all. The most obvious example was the emperor of Austria, the majority of whose lands lay outside the German Confederation. The king of Prussia ruled over two provinces – Poznania and West Prussia – that did not belong to the Confederation and were populated with Poles. And some German lands were ruled by foreign princes.

The two provinces of Schleswig and Holstein were ruled by the king of Denmark, but while they were legally inseparable, Holstein also belonged to the German Confederation. They were governed by the Salic Law, which meant that their sovereign must be male, and as the male line of the royal house of Denmark was on the point of extinction, their future was in doubt. Although the provinces were ethnically mixed, German nationalists hoped to use the impending constitutional crisis in order to disengage both duchies from Denmark and join them to Germany. But on 21 March Denmark annexed Schleswig outright. The German population in the south of the province rebelled. The Danes sent in troops, and the German Schleswigers sought the support of their brothers in Germany. These responded with generosity, calling for national solidarity and petitioning the king of Prussia to fly to the aid of his oppressed compatriots. But the king had quite enough to worry about at home.

When the Polish prisoners freshly sprung from the Moabit gaol by the insurgents were drawn around Berlin on 20 March. Mierosławski brandished a German tricolor as a sign of his commitment to the solidarity of peoples, while Berliners waved the Polish white-and-red colours. For these Prussians, whose country had only fifty years previously swallowed up a large slice of Poland, this was a gesture of remarkable generosity, as well as a pledge of their democratic intentions. The citizens of the colonial power were affirming the national rights of the colony. It was common to see the cockades of the two nations side by side on the same hat, and the climate of brotherhood was, according to one German source, 'idyllic'. It had the consistency of an intoxicating dream, and it could not last.[18]

The Poles in the colonized province of Poznania had sprung into action on hearing news of the disturbances in Berlin, but they found the local Germans, many of them recent settlers, a good deal less friendly. This was hardly surprising. The Berlin government had announced that a 'national reorganization' would be implemented in Poznania, allowing the Poles their own schools and cultural institutions. But the National Committee set up by local Poles was already several steps ahead. They wanted independence, and they saw Poznania as a base from which the rest of the Polish lands could be liberated. They began recruiting an armed force, and homing emigrés converged on the area. Among them was a sprinkling of foreign volunteers, including the Russian revolutionary Mikhail Alexandrovich Bakunin, who set off from Paris at the end of March.

For once, Polish and German interests coincided, as they faced a common enemy. By the end of March, Russia was the only power on the Continent untouched by revolt, and Nicholas I the only upholder of the Holy Alliance left. He did not blink, and told the nations to 'tremble'. It was widely believed that he would send his armies into Prussia and Austria in order to defeat the revolutionaries and rescue the beleaguered monarchs. On the day after his release from the Moabit gaol, Libelt published a proclamation in Berlin linking the two feelings uppermost in the minds of most Germans at that moment. 'You feel that the time has come to expiate the fatal deed of Poland's partition, and to safeguard a free Germany by raising the bulwark of an independent Poland against the onset of the Asiatics,' he summed up.[19] On 4 April the *Vorparlament* had decreed that 'the German Union proclaims the partition of Poland to be a shameful injustice, and considers it the sacred duty of the German peoples to do their utmost to achieve her reconstitution'. And on 6 May the new

Austrian government echoed: 'Free Austria will bring freedom to Poland, and with the support of Europe, will not hesitate to fight Russia in order to realize so high an ideal.'[20]

Russian forces in Poland only stood at about 25,000 men, and Field-Marshal Paskievich was preparing to evacuate the province if the Poles marched in from Poznania, as his position would be untenable. Prince Czartoryski, who had come from Paris and was greeted in Germany as a future king for Poland, was hoping to gain the military support of Prussia in the forthcoming campaign, just to be on the safe side. But the Berlin government could not consider going to war with Russia without securing an ally, and the only possible one was France. Lamartine emphatically ruled out anything that might involve France in war. Without an ally, and undermined by King Frederick William, who was Nicholas's brother-in-law, the Berlin government could do nothing for Poland.

As the possibility of common action receded, the mutual interests evaporated. Even the limited aim of 'national reorganization' was pared down, under pressure from Germans in Poznania. The Poles in the province had few options; they lacked leaders with authority, and their policy veered erratically between conciliation and confrontation. The poet Juliusz Słowacki had also come from Paris in the middle of April, by which time confrontation with the Prussian authorities was looking increasingly likely. On 27 April he attended a meeting of the National Committee, where the options were being discussed. When the members began evaluating the military possibilities, he stood up and, emaciated with consumption as he was, began to harangue them. 'You think that it is still, as it used to be, a question of cannons, regiments, officers?' he preached. All they needed to do was walk up to the fortress of Poznań and demand the keys – the German troops would hand them over. 'I tell you that the new age has dawned, the age of holy anarchy . . .' Some knelt as they drank in this visionary nonsense.[21]

Two days later the Prussian army moved. The Polish forces consisted of some 10,000 volunteers, whose organization and armament would have warmed Słowacki's heart. Gentlemen had fowling-pieces, while the peasant volunteers had only scythes. For once in his life Mierosławski proved effective. He managed to win two pitched battles against the Prussian army, and was only defeated when caught in open country under a heavy artillery bombardment. The defeat was of no consequence to Słowacki. The 'people' had fought valiantly, demonstrating that they bore within themselves the germ of the new era. The insurgent forces then laid down their arms or melted away, many of them to Galicia where an analogous situation had developed, thanks to the chaos in Vienna.

The Austrian administration in Galicia had avoided confrontation but worked consistently to undermine the Poles. At Czartoryski's behest, the Polish landowners were planning to emancipate the peasants, by cancelling all labour rents and donating tenanted land. This was meant to prevent the Austrians from repeating the jacquerie of 1846, and to win the peasants to the national cause. Having got wind of this, the Austrians rushed through an emancipation decree two days before the Polish measure was to come into force. On 25 April, Austrian troops successfully nipped in the bud a fresh rising in Kraków, by bombarding the city. But there was not much the local authorities could do when the centre could not hold. On 15 May, following demonstrations and riots in Vienna, the emperor gave in to demands for universal suffrage. Three days later he fled his capital and set up court at Innsbrück, while a Committee for Public Safety was formed in Vienna. The students, as usual, took centre stage, forming an Academic Legion, with the by now customary extravagant uniform.

By the end of May liberals and nationalists were triumphant in every corner of the Empire. Hungary was behaving like an autonomous state, and Italy looked as though it had finally slipped out from under Habsburg tutelage. The Sicilian revolt had forced the king of Naples to grant a constitution, and in February the rulers of Piedmont and Tuscany had done likewise, followed in March by the Pope. On 18 March the Milanese rose against the 12,000-strong Austrian garrison, and after five days' fighting, the '*Cinque Giornate*', expelled it from the city. The same happened in Venice, where the young lawyer Daniele Manin declared the rebirth of the Republic, while the rulers of Parma and Modena fled their states.

There was something unreal about the ease with which all this was achieved, and the sense of make-believe was reinforced by the theatricality of the events. In Milan, it had been a performance of Verdi's *Nabucco* that had sparked off the first riots in the spring of 1847. Verdi himself, growing daily more aware of his role, made two pilgrimages – to the house of William Tell and to the field of Waterloo. In London, where he went for a performance of one of his works, he met Mazzini, who begged him to compose an Italian *Marseillaise*. Following the 'cigar wars', the Austrian authorities in Milan had banned the audience at the opera from wearing tricolor bouquets, so everyone stayed away. Forced to attend, they appeared dressed in black. Performances were interrupted by shouting and the singing of patriotic songs, and the demonstration that began the *Cinque Giornate* was made up of people spilling out of the theatre. In Genoa, the troubles began with the appearance on stage of forty-eight dancers wrapped in the tricolor and singing '*Fratelli d'Italia*'.

At the end of March, King Charles Albert of Piedmont went to war with Austria in support of the newly liberated provinces of Lombardy and Venetia. Tuscany came in on the side of Piedmont, as did an unwilling King Ferdinand of Naples. Mass demonstrations outside his palace called on him to send troops into Lombardy in support of the Milanese. The beautiful exile Princess Cristina Belgiojoso, the last love of Lafayette, turned up in Naples offering herself as a guide to any who might wish to volunteer. A swarm of eager young men followed her. 'War against Austria was holy and necessary,' in the words of one Neapolitan.[22] The king placed 14,000 men under the command of General Pepe, back from twenty-seven years of exile to have another go at the Austrians.

All the usual suspects were joining in. Mickiewicz was in Rome, imploring the Pope to decree a new crusade for the freedom of all nations. As much to get rid of him as anything else, the Pontiff authorized the poet to form a legion, and on 11 April 1848 Mickiewicz marched out at the head of a couple of dozen men, including one Napoleonic officer and ten artists studying in Rome. They wore a vaguely Polish style of uniform, with a crimson *konfederatka*, and a large white cross on their left breast. They were greeted with veneration in the villages and towns they passed through, being seen as crusaders sent forth by the Pope. It was, in the words of one of them, 'a triumphal progress of pilgrim Knights'.[23] In Milan, Mickiewicz received a visit from Mazzini, who assured him of 'the fraternity of our aims, hopes and faith in a religious crusade for humanity and my motherland'.[24] At Genoa, Poles of the Czartoryski camp were forming a legion intended to absorb all Slavs identified among Austrian prisoners of war. It was to march under a flag bearing the colours of the rainbow with the inscription 'Slav Brotherhood'.[25] Some Croat prisoners did join up rather than languish in captivity. But the Czech prisoners, who were also keen on joining, would only do so on condition that the Croats, whom they loathed and feared, were excluded. On 1 June a column of 150 Poles from Paris crossed the Alps and joined Mickiewicz's legion. While the poet hastened back to Paris to raise funds, the legion was sent to the Front and fought, at Lonato, under the command of General Giovanni Durando, a veteran of 1821 in Piedmont, of Belgium and Portugal, who had given up his command of the Pope's troops when the pontiff had refused to go to war. 'I feel that I am something halfway between a knight and a monk, which is what I have always dreamed of', one of the volunteers wrote to a friend.[26]

The sense of elation was contagious. For the first time, national sentiment seemed to affect more than just a few intellectuals and romantic aristocrats. 'Words cannot indicate the emotions we felt at hearing many humble people shouting: "*Viva Italia"!* We are Italians!"' wrote the Neapolitan Luigi Settembrini. 'That word "Italy", which had at first been uttered by a few and in secret, which had been heard by only a handful, and which had been the last sacred word uttered by so many honourable men as they died – to hear it now uttered and shouted by the people made me feel a tingling run down my spine and through my body, and constrained me to tears . . .'[27]

But such appearances were deceptive. When Ferdinand of Naples recovered his nerve and recalled the troops he had despatched under Pepe, most of them were delighted to go home. Only a handful followed their general across the Po to fight for Italy. The people of the Romagna would not rise, because their dislike of the Romans prevented them from following their example; most of the Veneto sided with the Austrians against Venice itself; Sicilians fought Neapolitans; the Tuscans would not co-operate with the Romans; and everywhere, except in Sicily, where they were resolutely for themselves, the peasants were overwhelmingly on the side of the Austrians. They regarded the risings in the cities as the sport of the rich, and showed no interest unless it were blanket disapproval. In Lombardy, they shouted '*Viva Radetzky!*' They regularly assisted Austrian troops against the Piedmontese enemy, and on the whole delighted in reporting fugitive patriots to the forces of order.

They were only reflecting the lack of unity at the top and the ambivalence of many of Italy's most prominent sons. The influential Massimo d'Azeglio was openly opposed to violence and to any idea of unification, knowing it to be of no interest to the majority of the population. Francesco Pellico, brother of the martyr Silvio, saw no point in a homeland at all, arguing that Catholicism provided every Italian with a *patria* of the soul. Even those not opposed to unification relentlessly put their own province first. Mazzini, who arrived in Italy at the beginning of April, was appalled by what he saw as the selfishness of the political élite. As he subordinated everything to the prime aim of national unification, he was prepared to make an alliance with the Devil himself in order to forward that cause. He had tried to do so with the Pope, whom he begged in September 1847 to unite Italy under his own leadership. When the Pope proved reluctant, Mazzini switched his sights to Charles Albert of Piedmont, who looked like having the best chance of defeating Austria. But this antagonized many, particularly in Milan, where it was feared that Charles Albert would do no more than annex the province of Lombardy. The Lombard patriot Carlo Cattaneo actually declared that if he had to choose between being ruled by Austria or by Piedmont, he would choose Austria. The Tuscans were also fearful of Charles Albert's ambitions, as were republican patriots all over Italy. Charles Albert did nothing to allay these fears. Convinced that the rest of Europe would only tolerate his acquisitions if he kept a staunchly conservative political profile, he was determined to avoid any connections with republicans. He saw the cause of Italy, if at all, as that of the House of Savoy and the kingdom of Piedmont. When, in July, Radetzky defeated the Piedmontese at Custozza, the loose skein of common interest binding Italian patriots began to unravel. Charles Albert signed an armistice, returning to Austria all his gains in Lombardy and elsewhere, and the revolutionary movements in the various cities and provinces began to cave in one after the other.

The ability of the Austrian state to survive in the teeth of revolution at home and national challenges in every province implicitly contradicted all the assertions of nationalist and revolutionary theoreticians. A more flabby monarchy and a more intrigue-riven court would be hard to identify. It provided no leadership for an army which was composed of men belonging to the very captive nations that were in revolt. Yet it was in large measure these weaknesses that proved to be the strengths of the bizarre state. The emperor had given way to every show of force and granted every constitution presented to him with the requisite degree of threat, decamping from Vienna with his court in order to avoid unpleasantness. Such an ability to yield under pressure without breaking endowed the system with the resilience of a slug. The advantages inherent in such a response are clearly apparent in the way the Czechs and other Slav peoples were foiled, and gradually turned into allies of the monarchy.

Czech national aspirations had never been visceral. They had grown up out of a genuine interest in the past, out of cultural insecurity, and out of the spirit of the age. These had all been satisfied with a certain amount of fossicking about in the detritus of past glories and a little judicious forgery. The numbers stirred by these arcane emotions were anyway extremely small. When the leaders of the national movement assembled on 11 March at the St Wenceslas Baths in Prague to greet the dawn of liberty, one of them remarked that if the roof were to cave in, that would be the end of Czech nationalism.[28] But that was to change as a result of the constitutional tussle with Vienna and, most of all, as a result of what was happening at the German Assembly in Frankfurt.

The Assembly invited the provinces of Bohemia and Moravia to send delegates, but the Czech majority of the population declined. They had been granted extensive concessions, and had formed a National Committee, in effect a government of their own. They would rather have regional autonomy under Habsburg rule than become an ethnic minority in a united Germany. The Frankfurt Assembly sent out a delegation, one of whose members explained to the Czechs that they need fear nothing, since the Germans understood freedom better than anyone. 'We want to take you Bohemians in our arms,' explained one of the delegates. 'Yes – and strangle us,' answered one of the Czechs. The Germans then threatened the recalcitrants with 'the sword'.[29] They whipped up hitherto dormant loyalties among the German minority in the two Czech provinces and a pan-German lobby in Vienna. A German from Moravia hysterically alerted the Frankfurt Assembly to the fact that he and his fellows faced 'total annihilation' by the Czechs.[30] The argument grew nasty. The Germans ridiculed the concept of Czech nationality and bullied its proponents. The Austrians attacked from the other side. 'Having learned everything that they know from the Germans, as a sign of gratitude they also imitate the Germans' latest follies,' sneered Franz von Grillparzer. 'Where does this outcry about nationality, this emphasis on an indigenous language and history come from but the German universities, where learned fools have provoked the spirit of a quiet, sensible nation to madness and crime? There is the cradle of your Slavomania and if the Bohemian declaims loudest against the German he is merely a German translated into Bohemian.'[31]

The Czech National Committee grew alarmed and called for a meeting of all Slav nations in the Habsburg dominions – Czechs, Slovaks, Poles,

Ruthenes, Serbs, Croats and Slovenes. Delegates converged on Prague at the end of May, and the Slav Congress opened on 2 June, amid fitting pageantry. Led by the Student Legion, the delegates, dressed in a riot of national costumes, many of them bogus, processed to the church of Tyn behind a 'Slav' tricolor of white, blue and red. The Slovak hymn '*Hej Slovan'*, was sung. Lime-tree branches were brandished to ward off German spirits – Kollár had established that if the Germans laid claim to the oak, the Slavs could arrogate the lime, the '*Slovanska Lipa*'. 'Lipa' also means 'humbug' in Polish, but that was the least of the misunderstandings that would come to light during the Congress.

Palacký opened the proceedings with a rousing speech in which he asserted that the Slavs had an innate understanding of freedom superior to that of other races, and that it was incumbent on them to spread light and liberty around the globe.[32] Šafařik, who spoke next, was intoxicated by the sheer might of the peoples represented at the Congress. 'Even the cosmic forces do not equal the strength of a great nation which has risen to its moral consciousness and in a just struggle defends its existence,' he assured his listeners.[33] Nobody doubted the solidarity of the peoples in question, and when the Pole Karol Libelt delivered the Congress's appeal to the nations of Europe, he spoke of 'hearts beating in unison and through the identity of spiritual interest'.[34] The following day the Poles denounced the Tsar as the enemy of all Slavs. They were backed by Bakunin who, having failed to get through to join the insurgents in Poznania, had fetched up in Prague. He called for the destruction of the Russian Empire, without which the Poles, Ukrainians and even the Russians themselves could not be free. He depicted Russia as an empire of death. This upset the Czechs, who liked the idea of a strong Slav state as a counterbalance to German power, and by the Serbs, who felt an historic kinship with the Russians and depended on their financial assistance. The southern Slavs denounced the Magyars as the greatest enemies of the Slav race, and reproached the Poles for supporting them, and so did the Slovaks. But the Poles and the Czechs taunted the Croats and Slovenes for being German poodles.

The arguments were cut short by Field-Marshal Windischgrätz, who used the excuse of a minor confrontation to bombard the city into submission, and the Congress into dispersing. Once the rhetoric had blown away, it was clear that the only effective strands of solidarity were those binding the smaller Slav peoples of the south and east, which felt threatened by Magyar nationalism, and to a lesser extent those of Bohemia and Moravia, which feared German hegemony. And when all was said and done, their best protection was the cloak of the Habsburg monarchy. These were rural nations, whose peasants were more conservative than their nobles, so they found it easy to accept this reactionary solution.

Another nation that would seek liberation not through self-determination but through loyalism to the Habsburg monarchy were the Romanians. It was a Romanian, the historian Simion Bărnuţiu, who suggested that 1848 was not so much the 'Springtime of the Peoples' as a time of 'the resurrection of dead races', apparently without irony.[35] The process of Romanian exhumation had been going on in Transylvania since the 1780s, with the express intention of digging up an ancient Roman. The alphabet was changed from the cyrillic to the Latin, and the first published grammar firmly related the language to Roman origins. But it was not until the 1830s that a group of politically active patriots came of age, including a poet, Andreiu Mureşanu, who sang of the greatness of the Romanian race. The patriots took the Italians and Poles as models, and a Young Romania came into being. A number of them went to Paris, where they worshipped at the feet of Michelet and Mickiewicz, and one, Nicolae Balcescu, founded the Fratia Brotherhood, which adopted a tricolor of red, yellow and blue. The Romanians in Paris were supported by Czartoryski, who promoted the idea of a 'Greater Dacia' which might one day become a useful anti-Russian ally.

After the February Days, a delegation of Romanians in Paris announced to Lamartine that Romania demanded the right to exist. In March there was a Romanian rising in Jassy, which was easily put down, and on 2 May the Transylvanian Romanians assembled in a field outside Blaj and called for greater recognition within the Habsburg Empire. In June their fellows in Turkish-ruled Wallachia rose under Balcescu, took Bucharest and passed a constitution, but they were quickly put down by the Turks. Only the 150-strong Bucharest fire brigade put up a stiff resistance. Those leaders who did not manage to get away were incarcerated on a hulk in the Danube. 'That boat, holy ark of a ship-wrecked people, contained its government, its literature, its soul and its thought, and, we hope, its future!' in the words of Michelet.[36] But the future looked bleak for Romania; the only hope of survival lay in a policy of loyalism to the Habsburgs, which was welcome to the latter as it sought to hem in Hungarian ambitions.[37]

A month after Windischgrätz bludgeoned the Czechs into submission in Prague, the 81-year-old Radetzky routed the Piedmontese army at Custozza. Johann Strauss composed the Radetzky March, while Grillparzer wrote a poem in honour of the old field-marshal. It contained the line '*in deinem Lager ist Österreich*', which translates as 'Austria lies in your camp', which proved to be more profoundly true than he could have imagined. The army, composed of every nationality in the Empire, confounded all the expectations of the devotees of nationality. It epitomized the unity of the Habsburg dominions, and proved the most vigorous defender of the monarchy. The Austrian army and the Habsburg monarchy were the fatherland of its soldiers, not some Romanian or Bohemian pipe-dream.

In August the imperial court felt secure enough to return to Vienna, which had calmed down. By then the bad dream of the 'Springtime of Nations' had been dispelled, and in most places the forces of reaction were mopping up for business as usual. The only person who had actually lost his throne was Louis Philippe, which, legitimists could argue, was a just desert. And the revolution that had ousted him and rocked the whole of Europe was not turning into the social upheaval which rulers had been dreading.

This became clear after the April elections in France. The new Chamber was not short of poets, with Victor Hugo and Béranger joining Lamartine on the benches. Among the other Deputies were Lamennais and Quinet. But the elections had returned a majority of moderate republicans and three times as many monarchists as radicals. This left the radicals with no option but to resort to force. On 15 May 100,000 Parisians staged a demonstration. They marched behind a Polish flag, their ostensible aim being to demand the declaration of war on Russia and Prussia if those two countries did not restore Poland instanter. But there was a hard core who wanted to overthrow the government and seize power. They overran the Hôtel de Ville and stormed the Palais Bourbon, calling for a new uprising. As they surged through the Chamber, pushing and jostling the terrified Deputies, one of the proletarians noticed the name 'Lafayette' over the seat occupied by George Washington Lafayette, and asked him whether he was the son of the famous general. On receiving an affirmative answer, the latter-day sansculotte exclaimed: 'Oh! Sir, what a pity that your daddy is dead! He would be so happy if he were here today!'[38]

It is doubtful whether the old paladin of liberty would have approved of the proceedings. But he would have seen the high point of the French

Revolution of 1848. Before the end of the day, the radicals were cornered by the National Guard and their leaders were arrested. The government solved the unemployment problem by drafting the able-bodied into a new auxiliary formation called the Gardes Mobiles. In June the Left staged a last attempt to wrench back control of the revolution. The National Guard, the Gardes Mobiles and regular troops launched a savage attack on the revolutionaries, which resulted in some 3,000 deaths. 'The Republic is fortunate,' Louis Philippe quipped bitterly from exile in England, 'she is allowed to order troops to fire on the people!'[39] Revolutionaries all over the Continent gasped with horror at this brutal negation of all their most dearly cherished convictions.

In England too the high point of upheaval had passed. The great Chartist demonstration of 10 April had failed to break out of the bounds of peaceful constitutional protest. The numbers had been there, but they did not use their force. 'My poor friends,' the composer Hector Berlioz, who was in London at the time, said to his English hosts, 'you know as much about starting a riot as the Italians about writing a symphony.'[40] And the denouement of the mounting crisis in Ireland had been a grotesque fiasco.

The potato blight had brought mass starvation, and by the middle of 1847 over 3 million people were surviving only on government handouts. There were outbreaks of violence and looting, to which the British government responded by imposing martial law. News of the February Revolution in Paris galvanized all those eager for action, and the Member of Parliament William Smith O'Brien went to Paris with a delegation to seek support from Lamartine. They were sent away with a few fine words, so they resolved to act alone. They were arrested and tried, but O'Brien was acquitted. In July 1848 he set up a 'War Directory', but the most he could manage was to whip up a crowd which threatened a group of fifty constables and forced them to take refuge in a stone farmhouse occupied by the widow McCormack. The battle of Mrs McCormack's cabbage-patch, as it went down in history, cost the lives of several Irishmen before ending in farce. O'Brien was condemned to be hanged and quartered, and grew very irate when the sentence was changed to transportation.

There was little to show for all the revolutionary activity of the spring of 1848. Where parliamentary bodies had been established they failed to live up to the hopes placed in them. The revolutions in Vienna had obtained the repeal of repressive legislation and the granting of the constitution. In May, further protest yielded universal suffrage and a single elected chamber. This new parliament, the Reichstag, which met in Vienna on 10 July, abolished the remains of feudalism throughout the Empire. But it lost momentum and shied away from further social reform, wasting a great deal of time in squabbling and windbaggery, paving the way for its own demise. The Frankfurt Assembly, paralysed by its own inconsistencies, proved an even greater disappointment.

There were two questions pivotal to the whole enterprise of the Assembly: that of consistency and that of dominant authority, and it failed to address either with honesty. It did not define the Germany it meant to represent because it could not bring itself to forfeit claims to alien territories such as Poznania and Bohemia. It failed to establish a legitimate authority in Germany because it slavishly threw itself at the feet of, first, the Austrian emperor and then of the Prussian king. The metaphysical audacity and the literary recklessness of its Deputies were born of books and lecture-halls. They blustered about renewal and liberty, but they were really looking for a master.

Contemplating the Germans in a state of revolutionary excitement, Alexander Herzen was reminded of 'the playfulness of a cow when that excellent and respectable animal, adorned with all the domestic virtues, takes to frisking and galloping in the meadow, and with a serious face kicks up her two hind legs or gallops sideways chasing her own tail'.[41] But there was nothing amusing about the conclusion of the Frankfurt Assembly's sally into liberalism.

Faced with the prospect of relinquishing territory, even the most liberal members of the Assembly drew back from their earlier enthusiasm. As the constitutional historian Professor Dahlmann put it, the Germans had found out that their thirst for freedom could only be satisfied by power.[42] They threw in their lot with autocratic princes in order to achieve it, and drew emotional compensation for the democratic dreams they had buried from myths of national destiny and German cultural superiority. Not for the last time, a desire for social and political reform by the middle classes was bought off with a dream of national greatness.

In July 1848 the German minority in Poznania demanded the province's incorporation into the Confederation. This embarrassed the liberals. But it was championed by Wilhelm Jordan, a left-wing Deputy from Prussia, who made one of those speeches that figure as milestones in European history. 'It is high time that we awaken from the romantic self-renunciation which made us admire all sorts of other nationalities while we ourselves languished in shameful bondage, trampled on by all the world; it is high time that we awaken to a healthy national egoism which, to put it frankly, places the welfare and honour of the fatherland above everything else,' he said. Egged on by enthusiastic applause, Jordan argued that the Slavs were an inferior race, and that the Poles were a nation 'of lesser cultural content' than the Germans. Having thus demoted them, he went on to suggest that it was Germany's mission to civilize the Poles. But that was not his clinching argument.[43]

'I admit without beating about the bush that our right is only the right of the stronger, the right of the conqueror,' Jordan declared defiantly. Another delegate ventured that 'self-preservation is the First Commandment of the political catechism'. 'I stand by the fatherland, by our Germany,' spelled out a delegate from Moravia, 'and that is to me *über alles*.'[44] By this stage, even polite liberals like Gagern had changed their tune. 'I believe that it is the role of the German people to be great, to be one of those who rule,' he stated.[45] After decades of agonizing rumination over their destined role in the scheme of things, they had found their mission.

However hysterical some of the claims made by Romantic nationalists of various kinds, their impulse was fundamentally a generous one. Mazzini's view of Italy's primacy was one in which her people were called upon to suffer the most. Polish messianism was essentially a vision of an association of spirits realizing a mission that would, in one way or another, redeem all of humanity. The spirit of devotion and self-sacrifice is reflected in the respective anthropomorphic representations of the nation: expiring Hellas, suffering Italia, abused Polonia. Even France's Marianne, who, as the icon of *La Grande Nation*, had to display a certain triumphant assertiveness, remained coyly feminine. The Germania that began to appear at this time was different – more of a helmeted Valkyrie demanding vengeance for past affronts.

Back in the spring, Richard Wagner had told a friend that the revolution had already taken place in the minds of men, and that 'the new Germany is ready, like a bronze statue which requires only a single blow from a hammer in order to emerge from its mould'.[46] In the event, what did emerge from that mould destroyed all the most dearly cherished dreams of the apostles of universal brotherhood. As they looked around Europe in the late summer of 1848, they could barely contain their despair. 'We stood on the threshold of paradise,' wrote the poet Ferdinand Freiligrath, '– but the gates were slammed in our faces.'[47]

18
Sustaining Legends

Although the hopes of most European liberals and nationalists had been dashed by the summer of 1848, that did not signify the end of the fighting. Dedicated crusaders ignore setbacks and pay no heed to writing on the wall; adversity only serves to steel their resolve and dark prospects cause them to reaffirm their faith. There would be another twelve months of largely pointless heroism and immolation, new pages would be inscribed in the gospel of the nations, and new champions would step forward to take up the challenge.

And it was in adversity that Italy's national cause gained its first credible victories, as well as a new breed of commanders, committed as none hitherto. One such was Daniele Manin, who led the revolt in Venice. Asked whether he wanted to become Doge, he grew angry. 'Doge?' he said. 'No. My aim is far higher. It is so high I hardly dare tell it to myself – Washington!'[1] It was such sentiments that would animate the long defence of the Republic of Venice against overwhelming Austrian forces. The other leader to emerge was Giuseppe Garibaldi, who more than any other came to epitomize the quixotic struggle for the mirage of Italian unity.

Garibaldi was born in Nice in 1807, then part of Napoleonic France. But in 1814 it was ceded to Piedmont and he became a subject of King Victor Emmanuel I. His first language was Ligurian, his second French. Only when he was grown up did he start to learn Italian. The son and grandson of sailors, he naturally went to sea, working his way up from cabin-boy to deck-hand. In Marseille he met Mazzini and joined Giovine

Italia. When, in 1833, Garibaldi was called up for his national service in the Piedmontese navy, he attempted and failed to start a mutiny, and fled to Brazil.

On his arrival in Rio de Janeiro, Garibaldi located a group of Italian exiles and joined the local branch of Giovine Italia. In a house over which flew the Italian tricolor, they planned the liberation of all the oppressed peoples of the world. An Italian merchant provided Garibaldi with a small boat, with which he made a living trading up and down the coast, and in 1836 he wrote to Mazzini asking for authorization to wage war in the name of Italy on shipping flying the Austrian and Piedmontese flags. In the interim, he devoted himself to the cause of Rio Grande do Sul, a province of Brazil which had seceded under the leadership of Benito Goncalves. Goncalves was a natural leader. He had a sense of theatre, and he enhanced his presence with colourful clothes, displays of horsemanship and occasional imperial gestures of generosity. Garibaldi was captivated by him, and, consciously or not, adopted some of his style. In May 1837 Garibaldi sailed out of the Rio Grande on a twenty-ton boat he had renamed the *Mazzini*, with the mission of preying on Brazilian shipping. He became the Robin Hood of the South Atlantic; ambushing merchantmen and playing cat-and-mouse with the warships of the Brazilian navy; he threw cargoes overboard and freed slaves but did not loot or relieve passengers of their valuables. As far as he was concerned, every one of his men who was killed or drowned was 'one more martyr to the cause of Italian liberty'.[2]

One day in 1839 as he stood on his deck in the roads of Laguna, Garibaldi saw through his telescope a woman walking along the street, and he was smitten. He followed her home and declared his love. Without a thought for her husband, she came aboard and sailed away with him. Anna Ribeiro da Silva, or Anita as she was popularly known, was probably of mixed Portuguese and Indian blood, and she was beautiful. She was also tough, sharing Garibaldi's life on the seas and joining in the fighting when the occasion demanded it. In 1840 she bore him a son, who was named Menotti, after a fallen Italian hero.

The war of liberation gradually disintegrated into banditry, and the disillusioned Garibaldi decided to abandon the cause. He moved south to Montevideo, the capital of Uruguay, which had itself recently seceded from Argentina, where he tried to make a living, first as a cattle drover, then by teaching, and finally as a commercial traveller in the textile trade.

But it quickly became apparent that he was not much good at anything other than sailing and fighting. Fortunately, he did not have to wait long for these to become highly prized qualities. Uruguay was plagued by splits and coups that ensured a rapid succession of presidents, and when, in 1842, General Rosas of Argentina intervened in support of one deposed president, Garibaldi naturally volunteered to help his rival, who was deemed to be resisting the forces of oppression. He was given the rank of colonel and despatched up the Paraná river in command of three ships and three hundred men. He was soon cornered by the superior Argentine fleet under Admiral Brown, late liberator of Peru, and defeated.

In 1843, when Montevideo itself was threatened by the Argentine forces, all the inhabitants were mobilized for its defence. The city had a colony of Italians, and Garibaldi was given the job of forming them up into a separate legion. A significant proportion deserted to the enemy at the earliest opportunity, but Garibaldi was determined to turn the rest into an exemplary fighting force. He was well aware of the importance of flags and uniforms, and he went in search of one for his men. This quest took him to a clothing company that made blood-red smocks for the abbatoirs of Buenos Aires, and which, cut off by war from its principal market, had a redundant consignment in stock. Garibaldi bought them at a knock-down price, and a legend was born.

Resplendent in their red smocks, made to look like tunics by the addition of a belt, marching under a black banner, to signify mourning for Italy, with a depiction of an erupting volcano, representing the power of the inner fires that burned below, the legion rose to the occasion, and was dubbed 'the Sacred Battalion' for its prowess. Garibaldi, who had learned much about warfare and leadership, became a prominent figure. He amassed a following, with a small core of compatriots as devoted to the cause of liberty as himself. One was Francesco Anzani, who had been exiled in 1821 and had fought in Greece, Spain and Portugal, then for the republicans in Brazil before meeting up with Garibaldi in Rio Grande do Sul. Another was Giacomo Medici, a Milanese who had fought for liberty in half-a-dozen theatres of war before reaching Montevideo by way of New York and joining Garibaldi's legion in 1846.

Garibaldi's fame had been carried all over Italy through Mazzini's enthusiastic articles in *L'Apostolato Popolare*, and elsewhere through a bad novel written by Harro Harring, who had encountered him in 1842. In 1846 Garibaldi wrote to Mazzini, offering to bring six hundred men of his legion over to start a revolt in Italy, and sent Medici over to plan it. In 1847 he wrote to Pope Pius IX, whom he called 'the political Messiah of Italy', offering to place himself and his legion at the pontiff's service, and he even approached the Grand Duke of Tuscany in the same vein. Determined 'to fight out the war of redemption on Italian soil', Garibaldi chartered a ship to take him and his men across the Atlantic. In the event, only about sixty men agreed to go with him, including two black slaves he had freed. They embarked on the aptly-named *Speranza*, which sailed from Montevideo on 15 April 1848, 'towards the fulfilment of the longing, the passion, of our whole life'.[3] Before sailing, they heard of the revolution that had broken out in Palermo. They were nevertheless sailing into the unknown, and they kept their spirits up by gathering in a circle on deck every evening to sing patriotic hymns.

It was only when they put in at a port in Spain to take on water that they heard the news of the risings in Milan and Venice, and of Piedmont's declaration of war. In a state of elation, Garibaldi sailed into his native city of Nice on 23 June, to be greeted as a returning hero. He went straight to Charles Albert's headquarters, where, to his astonishment, he was met with cool condescension and told to take himself elsewhere. Outraged, Garibaldi went to Milan, where Mazzini had preceded him. But here too he met with disappointment. He was welcomed rapturously on arrival, given the rank of general, and then left to fend for himself. Volunteers flocked to his side. To equip them, he raided the depots abandoned by the retreating Austrians, with the result that they marched out clad in uniforms improvised from the Austrians' white summer kit, looking, according to one of them, like a regiment of pastrycooks. They joined other volunteer units fighting alongside the Piedmontese army, including Mickiewicz's Poles, under the command of General Durando.

The rout of the Piedmontese forces at Custozza on 23 July was a blow, and the armistice signed by Charles Albert two weeks later left the volunteers redundant. The Polish legionaries entertained plans to take themselves off to Slovenia, so Garibaldi decided to fight on alone, conducting a *guerilla* in the Austrian rear. He was joined by Mazzini, clutching a musket and a flag bearing the inscription '*Dio e Popolo*', and by other volunteers who refused to accept the Piedmontese armistice. Suffering heavy casualties in daily struggles against overwhelming odds and lacking the most basic supplies, he was soon down to thirty men, so he took refuge over the Swiss border.

Things were looking decidedly grim. Most of the revolutionary activity in Europe had either been crushed or was fizzling out. Venice was still holding out under Manin, whose forces were commanded by General Pepe. Sicily remained in the hands of the revolutionaries, thanks more to the hopelessness of the Neapolitan regime than to the merits of its own forces. These were commanded by a succession of foreign officers, including the Napoleonic veteran General Trobriand and Ludwik Mierosławski, described by one of the local papers as 'this noble foreigner who has embraced the name and the cause of Sicily like a religion'.[4] But Mierosławski allowed himself to be outmanoeuvred by the Neapolitan troops and although he fought bravely and sustained a wound, he was replaced. He duly cast aspersions on the courage of the Sicilians under his command, and sailed away in a huff, pursued by accusations of treason.

Elsewhere on the peninsula, the speeches made from balconies enveloped in the tricolor were forgotten, the heroics of the various *giornate* were consigned to legend, and the preoccupations of everyday life were resumed. Throughout the autumn and winter of 1848 Mazzini and Garibaldi did everything to keep the cause of the nation alive against all the odds, much to the annoyance of most Italians. Verdi had at last produced the desired *Marseillaise* for Italy, in the form of *Suona la tromba*, but nobody would sing it.

The *Marseillaise* itself had been banned in France, where in the presidential elections held on 10 December 1848, Louis Napoleon, representing the party of law and order, obtained over five-and-a-half of the seven-and-a-half million votes cast. Lamartine received a pitiful 17,000. Nobody had much time for poets and visionaries any more, and the dreams of 1789 were out of place in the increasingly complex modern industrial society France had become.

From Switzerland, Garibaldi went to Nice, where he was elected to the Piedmontese parliament. But he was methodically sidelined. After his humiliating defeat at Custozza, Charles Albert had begun to rebuild his army in anticipation of an opportunity to get his own back. As commander-in-chief he engaged the Polish general Wojciech Chrzanowski, late of the Belgian army, and he took into service a number of other Polish, French and Hungarian officers. In January 1849 he signed an agreement with Prince Czartoryski on the formation of a Polish legion in Piedmontese service. This was meant to absorb Mickiewicz's men and all other Slav volunteers, but many declined to serve in it. The Italian volunteers were grouped into a division which, unbelievably, was given to General Ramorino to command. There was little promise for the likes of Garibaldi in these circumstances, particularly as the Piedmontese, from the king downwards, could not hide their contempt for his lowly origins.

He therefore gathered a force of seventy men and chartered a small vessel, intending to take them to Sicily, which was still in revolt. Halfway there, he changed his mind and went to Tuscany, where Domenico Guerrazzi, one of the founders of Giovine Italia, had ousted the Grand Duke. In Florence, Garibaldi came across Mazzini, who had been lured by similar hopes of continuing the struggle for a united Italy. But the Tuscan leaders wanted to be rid of Garibaldi as quickly as possible. They already had quite enough trouble with a couple of hundred of Mickiewicz's legionaries who had come from Lithuania, via the fighting in Poznania and Paris, brandishing a red banner inscribed with the words *Per la Vostra e la Nostra Libertate.* Guerrazzi suggested that he take himself off to Venice, so Garibaldi's handful of desperadoes set off over the snowbound Apennines, oblivious of hardship and privation. Hardly had they got across to Ravenna when Garibaldi heard a new call. This one came from Rome, where, on 15 November, the government of Pius IX had been overthrown. Unable to restore order, the Pope had fled to Gaeta in the kingdom of Naples, and called on Naples, Spain, France and Austria to come to his aid.

Garibaldi marched his legion back across the mountains. The force was now down to some 350 men, but they had been joined by two hundred lancers equipped and led by the Emilian nobleman Angelo de Masina, who had fought for liberty in 1831 and then in the Spanish civil war. When they arrived at Rieti in January 1849, Garibaldi got himself elected by that city to the Roman parliament, and went on alone, while his men rested. In Rome, he met with a by now familiar reception. A young artist, seeing him for the first time, thought he looked like Christ. 'I left my studio,' he wrote. 'I went after him; thousands did likewise. He only had to show himself. We all worshipped him; we could not help it.'[5] But while the crowds cheered Garibaldi to the heavens, the political leaders longed to see the back of him. In the parliament, he immediately began calling for the establishment of a republic, which embarrassed the other deputies, and his offers of bringing his legion into the city were politely eluded.

Rome was in a state of ferment. It had always had a large colony of foreign artists and writers, their hangers-on, and aristocratic dilettanti of one sort or another, tending by definition towards liberalism. From the accession of Pius IX, it had also drawn Italian radicals and liberals, who sat about in cafés rebuilding the world. Giuseppe Verdi was there, supervising a production of *La Battaglia di Legnano*, whose every performance was packed out. The libretto was based on the victory of the Lombard League over the Emperor Frederick Barbarossa in 1176, an event recently much represented in painters' oils. The opera's opening chorus of '*Viva l'Italia*' affirmed that a sacred pact bound all her sons together, and its final one confirmed that anyone dying for the cause would be counted among the elect. It was full of martial airs, trumpet-calls and vows of liberty or death.

On 9 February the Roman Republic was at last declared, to be governed by a triumvirate consisting of Count Aurelio Saffi, Carlo Armellini and Giuseppe Mazzini, who was expected soon. Garibaldi wrote to him, affirming that the Italian Legion, still at Rieti but now numbering over a thousand men, were his 'friends in the faith'.[6] They were now desperately needed. President Louis Napoleon Bonaparte of France, who was determined both to engage the support of French Catholics, and not to permit the Austrians to re-establish hegemony over the Italian peninsula by recapturing Rome for the Pope, had despatched an army under Marshal Oudinot. This landed at Civitavecchia on 25 April and began its march on Rome.

Two days later, the *garibaldini*, as everyone had come to refer Garibaldi's soldiers, entered the eternal city, causing astonishment as they made their way through the streets. Dirty, bearded and disreputable-looking, they were dressed in the remains of their blue Piedmontese uniforms, while those that had joined recently had done their best to make civilian clothes look martial. They wore broad-brimmed felt hats of various kinds, adorned with plumes, feathers or anything else that came to hand. They were armed with an assortment of muskets, shotguns and rifles, while some carried only lances, but most had a dagger in their belt. Some of the officers wore the distinctive red shirt. Only Masina's lancers, who liked to call themselves 'the Squadron of Death', cut a slightly more elegant figure, with their dark blue dolmans covered in black braid, red trousers and white cloaks with a black skull embroidered on the side of the hood. Garibaldi, sporting long blond hair down to his shoulders and a silky beard, never abandoned his uniform of white poncho, thrown back over his shoulder to reveal the red shirt underneath, and a great black felt hat adorned with ostrich feathers. Always at his side was the black orderly

Andrea Aguyár, who had followed him from South America.

Taking advantage of this diversion in Rome, and hoping that the presence of so many different armies in the peninsula might have shaken Austria's self-assurance, Charles Albert judged the time ripe for another thrust, hoping to salvage something from his earlier humiliation. He repudiated the armistice signed with Austria in August 1848 and sallied forth. His new Polish commander did no better than the previous one, and the Piedmontese forces were routed at Novara on 23 March 1849. Mickiewicz blamed the defeat on the general's 'lack of revolutionary faith'.[7] A more probable culprit was ill-will among the commanders. True to character, Ramorino had moved away from the action with his division of volunteers as soon as the Austrians attacked – but at least this time he was court-martialled and shot for it. Charles Albert had no option but to abdicate in favour of his son, Victor Emmanuel, who made his peace with Austria and abandoned the policy of aggrandizement for the time being. This in turn meant that all non-Piedmontese volunteers had to leave his territory. Not surprisingly, many of them headed for Rome.

The eternal city was drawing defenders from every quarter. They included Colonel Haug, late of the Vienna Academic Legion, the Swiss Gustav von Hofstetter, General Rybiński, last commander-in-chief of the November Rising, Colonel Aleksander Milbitz, a veteran of the same rising who had been supporting himself playing fiddle in a Paris orchestra, Major Gabriel Laviron and a group of Frenchmen. Two hundred men of the Polish Legion who had landed up in Tuscany, hoping to get to Hungary, made for Rome. 'These young men, brought up in the great school of national conspiracy, believed passionately in the resurrection of Poland, in the regeneration of the world through revolution, and in the oneness of our cause with that of the freedom of all nations', their commander explained.[8] The most striking among Rome's new defenders was Colonel Hugh Forbes. He was a 41-year-old former Coldstream Guards officer, endowed with private means and a detestable character. He had married an Italian and settled in Tuscany, become involved in revolutionary activity, and had already fought in Venice and Palermo in the past fourteen months. He stood out among the other volunteers in their grubby coarse clothes, by never appearing, in battle or anywhere else, dressed otherwise than in a fine white cotton suit and top hat.

Italians who came to the defence of Rome included the Neapolitan aristocrat Carlo Pisacane and others who had fought in various parts of the peninsula over the past fifteen months. Luciano Manara, a Milanese, marched in at the head of a brigade of 600 *bersaglieri*, made up of men who had fled Lombardy after the occupation of Milan by the Austrians. They had formed themselves into a unit in Piedmont, but could not remain there. They were monarchists and proudly wore the cross of Savoy on their belt-buckles. They disliked the idea of a republic and had little time for the likes of Mazzini and Garibaldi, but they too wanted to die for Italy.

That death, or at least defeat, awaited them could hardly be in doubt. 'There was the same superabundance of standards, of cockades, of badges of party that had characterized the last few months of Milan's liberty,' wrote Emilio Dandolo, an officer of the Lombard *bersaglieri*, 'the same clanking of swords along the public streets, and those various and varied uniforms of officers, not one matching with the other, but all seeming more suitable for the embellishment of the stage than for military service; those epaulettes thrown, as it were by chance, on the shoulders of men whose very faces seemed to declare their unfitness to wear them ... All this array of warriors in glittering helmets with double-barrelled guns and with belts full of daggers, reconciled us but little to the scanty numbers of real, well-drilled soldiers.'[9] The only professional soldiers at the disposal of the Roman Republic were the couple of thousand Papal troops who had decided to transfer their allegiance.

The defenders were no match for the large French army, sporting the most modern equipment, not to mention the lesser corps of Neapolitan troops advancing from the south, the Spanish army bearing down from the north-west and the Austrian forces moving in from the north-east. Mazzini nevertheless believed in victory. He convinced himself that the French would join forces with the Romans and lined the route of their advance with large posters quoting the article of the French constitution declaring that France would never make war on any other nation aspiring to freedom. When the first French prisoners were taken, he had them treated well and sent back to their camp, and he allowed himself to be taken in by a diplomatic mission that was nothing more than a smokescreen.

Garibaldi was no less sanguine. Not because he expected anything good from the French, whom he despised, but because he trusted in the invincibility of free men fired with the holy cause. And when the French launched their first attack, on the outlying *garibaldini* positions in the Pamphili Gardens on 30 April, he was apparently proved right. His volunteers counter-attacked the French regulars with such dash, that they inflicted heavy casualties and sent them reeling. The French, who had been told that Italians do not fight, were astonished.

Oudinot summoned the city to surrender, and gave it three days to do so. But before the cease-fire had run its course, on the night of 3 June the French launched a surprise attack. The *garibaldini* were thrown out of their forward post in the Villa Corsini. Garibaldi rallied them, and launched a series of frontal assaults at the by now entrenched enemy. A Roman military band played the *Marseillaise* relentlessly in an attempt to make the French soldiers reconsider, while wave after wave of volunteers went to their deaths. Hundreds of brave men were lost that day, including Masina of the lancers and Manara of the *bersaglieri*. But the slaughter only served to strengthen the cause.

The loss of the Villa Corsini, which occupied high ground outside the city walls, further reduced the already slim chances of holding out against the French, particularly as these had now brought heavy siege artillery into play. Yet the city hung on for another four weeks. This was achieved by a mere handful of defenders, few of them citizens of Rome. The population of the city, with the exception of the poor denizens of Trastevere, viewed the whole business as a tiresome inconvenience. Not only did few come forward to fight, it was difficult to get anyone to dig or repair the defences. Even the wounded were being tended by an assortment of foreign residents and grandees from other parts of Italy, marshalled by the inevitable Princess Belgiojoso.

Garibaldi was at his finest. Every morning as he went over the defences, he would pose in his red shirt and white poncho, taking an exaggeratedly long time to light his cigar, while the French sharpshooters tore the air around him. He had been seriously wounded and had seen many die. But nothing could dampen his ardour. 'These people are worthy of their past greatness,' he wrote to Anita on 21 June. Among his redshirts were a hundred fifteen-year-old boys who called themselves the Battaglione Speranza, and seemed to know no fear. 'Here they live, die and suffer amputation, all to the cry of "*Viva la Repubblica!*" One hour of our life in Rome is worth a century of ordinary existence.'[10] But while he savoured every minute, he appreciated that he and his men were in the wrong place.

Their peculiar talents were of no use behind ramparts and their elan was at a discount in what had become a siege of attrition. Garibaldi felt that they should be used to harry the French flanks, cut their lines of communication, and defeat smaller units. But the commander-in-chief, General Pietro Roselli, was a regular soldier who wanted to conduct the defence by the book. And Mazzini, who had pinned such hopes on the physical significance of Rome and having spent his life in exile, wanted to make the last stand there. He envisaged the Roman Republic going down in a blaze of glory, offering itself up as a holocaust to the cult of Italy.

It never came to that. The French launched their final assault on the night of 29 June. By the morning it had become clear that there was no way they could be dislodged from the foothold they had gained. Garibaldi stormed into the Assembly on the Capitol, covered in blood and dirt, to demand what it was going to do about it. Not many were prepared to go down the Mazzinian road, so it was just a question of terminating the existence of the Roman Republic in as seemly a manner as possible. This left Garibaldi free to act as he saw fit, and he had no second thoughts. 'Rome will be wherever we are', he exclaimed, intending to take the Republic with him.

That evening, he announced to the people assembled before the basilica of St Peter that he would carry on the fight, and offered a part in his crusade to anyone who wished to follow him. Like Christ addressing his apostles, he warned them that he could offer them only hardship and possibly death. Some 4,000 assembled at the Lateran on the evening of 2 July to follow him out of the city, many of them simply intending to seize this chance of getting out and making their way home. They began falling away soon after the column moved out.

Garibaldi marched south, in order to give the impression that he was making for the Pontine Marshes, and then turned north into the Abruzzi Mountains, and thus gave himself three days' lead on the pursuing French. At Terni, he met up with Hugh Forbes and 900 soldiers who had also marched out of Rome. They went on together, dodging and feinting to throw the pursuing French and later the Austrians off their track. He intended to cross the peninsula in a northerly direction, hoping to reach Venice where Manin was still flying the flag. The march involved crossing mountains by seemingly impassable mule-tracks, doubling back in order to gain half a day on the pursuers, moving by night and lying low by day, sometimes with enemy forces operating within view. Things were not made any easier by the local population, which closed its doors and often assisted the enemy. Garibaldi, who did not himself know fear in the service of the cause, could not understand how they could put their own safety and that of their families first. Nor could he understand those who kept peeling off from his own force, even though it was becoming obvious that they would never make it to Venice. He never wavered in his resolve, even though his strength was being sapped by a festering stomach wound and anxiety over his wife, who was pregnant and seriously ill, but who categorically refused to be left behind.

On 31 July, unable to evade the surrounding Austrian forces any longer, Garibaldi led the remaining 1,500 of his men on to the territory of the tiny Republic of San Marino. That night, accompanied by two hundred of his faithful, he slipped between the Austrian units and forged on towards the Adriatic coast. At Cesenatico, they commandeered a flotilla of fishing boats and set sail for Venice. All but three of the craft were captured by the Austrian navy. Garibaldi sailed on as far as he could, and then came ashore, carrying the by now dying Anita. He had only one companion left with him. Just as the situation seemed hopeless, with Austrian soldiers about to bottle him up as he blundered through a coastal marsh, he was saved by a local landowner. The man, who happened to be a liberal and an admirer, led the three fugitives out of the trap and gave them shelter.

Relief came too late for Anita, who died in Garibaldi's arms. He could not even stay long enough to bury her, and was despatched, with his one remaining companion, through a network of patriots and sympathizers, right across the peninsula. They were spirited through the countryside under the noses of Austrian troops and peasants eager to claim the reward for Garibaldi's capture, and reached the Mediterranean coast at Portiglione, where a fishing boat waited to take them to Genoa. As the boat pulled away from the shore, Garibaldi stood up and waved to the four local patriots who had accompanied him on the last leg of the escape, and shouted '*Viva Italia!*'

Mazzini had slipped out of Rome with the help of the American consul and a sympathetic French captain, and he was soon back in Switzerland planning the next moves. The situation looked even grimmer than it had when he was last obliged to take refuge in Switzerland, a year earlier. As soon as things had quietened down, the rulers of the various German states began to reverse concessions made in the spring of 1848. In November, King Frederick William brought the army back into Berlin and

Schönen, Guten Morgen, Germania!, a German lithograph showing Germania pregnant with promise for the future, with a radiant Frankfurt in the distance.

Princess Cristina Belgiojoso, who abandoned the drawing-rooms of Paris to rouse the Neapolitans to arms.

One of the many proposals for a national costume which might help the Italians feel more like a nation, a lithograph of 1848.

Two of the ubiquitous Polish volunteers.

The glorious tragedy of Hungary in 1849.

Kossuth being welcomed by Mazzini on his arrival in London, as seen by an Italian patriotic paper. The caption assures the reader that with 'apostles' such as these, the nations need not fear for the future.

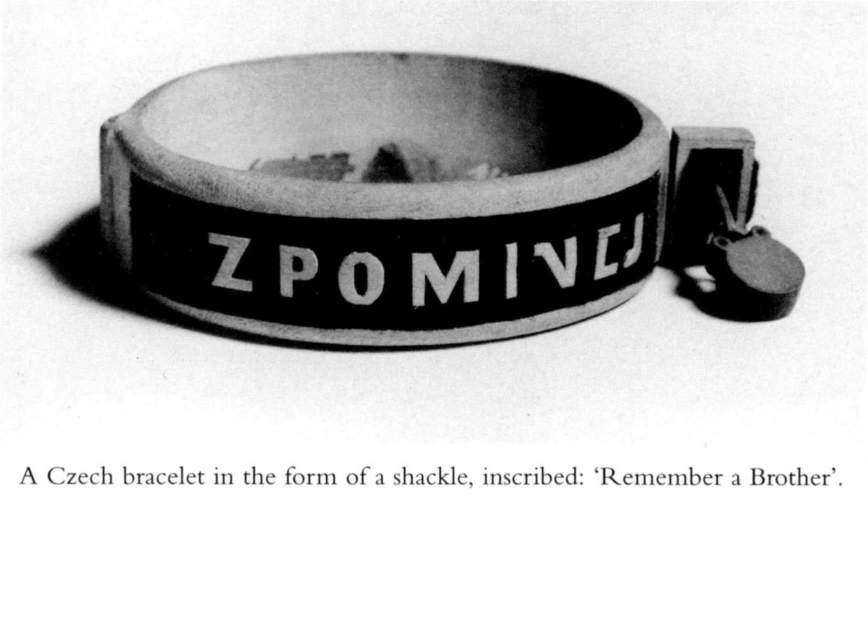

A Czech bracelet in the form of a shackle, inscribed: 'Remember a Brother'.

Garibaldi as Redeemer, complete with stigmata on his hand, calling the faithful to follow and blessing their sacrifices. A typical but vain attempt to stir ordinary people to stand up in the national cause.

L' anima di questo generoso vola al cielo dove è aspettata da tutti i Martiri che la precedettero morendo per l' Italia. Gloria immortale al Martire! Esecrazione a' suoi carnefici!

The execution of a patriot in Milan in 1851. The caption explains that his soul flies to heaven, where it is greeted by all the martyrs who have given their lives for Italy.

Polonia being manacled by the Russians in 1863.

This drawing of a last stand by insurgents in some Polish forest epitomizes how a generation of young men wanted to die.

This picture by Gustave Doré shows the French soldiers of 1870 marching past the shades of ancient Gauls and Napoleonic grenadiers to reconquer the Rhine from the Germans.

A defeated France obliged to sign the shameful peace ceding Alsace and Lorraine to Germany in 1870.

Such images of the motherland no longer held out the promise of redemption, they demanded vengeance.

disbanded the parliament. In March 1849 he felt strong enough to send troops in support of Frederick of Saxony, who wanted to abolish the constitution he had granted twelve months earlier.

Military resistance in Dresden was directed for the local revolutionaries by Wiktor Heltman and a couple of other Poles sent by the *Centralizacja*. Wagner and Bakunin were among those building barricades, and the famous soprano Wilhelmina Schröder-Devrient sang encouragement from a first-floor window. The Prussians attacked on 5 May, and after three days resistance broke down. Wagner fled to Weimar, where Franz Liszt gave him shelter; others made for Switzerland.

Next came the turn of Baden. As most of the Badenese officers remained loyal to the Grand Duke, they refused to take up arms against the approaching Prussians, whose assistance he had invoked. The soldiers elected a few non-commissioned officers to lead them, but there was a dearth of senior officers. The revolutionary authorities therefore sent for Mierosławski, who was in Paris nursing his Sicilian wound and salvaging his reputation. He duly turned up in June 1849, resplendent in bright red trousers and a blue coat heavily trimmed with gold braid. In his wake several other Poles materialized, including General Sznayde who had commanded the Bavarian revolutionaries at Ludwigshafen, and others who had fought in various parts of Germany. A group of fifty Poles and Frenchmen who had been on their way to Rome diverted to Baden instead, picking up a number of Swiss and Germans on the way. They arrived in time to fight at Durlach in June, but soon after that Mierosławski petulantly declared that neither the people nor the soldiers of Baden knew the meaning of liberty or what they were fighting for, and on 1 July, the day Rome surrendered to the French, he resigned his command and went back to Paris. The defence collapsed and most of the volunteers crossed into Switzerland. This was filling up with derelict fighters, who now had only two options left: Venice and Hungary.

Perhaps the most emblematic of all the risings of the 'Springtime of the Peoples' was the Hungarian struggle for independence. The image of the dashing Magyars fighting for freedom under the leadership of Lajos Kossuth eclipsed all others in the European mind's eye, eliciting immoderate enthusiasm in the most staid quarters. But while the image was true enough and the enthusiasm not misplaced, the Hungarian rising was not quite what it seemed.

When Kossuth had been elected to the Diet in 1847 his supporters marched to the polls waving flags and wearing feathers in the national colours of red, white and green. But in spite of the razzmatazz the turnout in his constituency was a pathetic 2,500 out of an eligible electorate of 14,000 – hardly an auspicious result, and certainly not one suggesting an overwhelming surge of national feeling.[11] Kossuth went to great pains to rally the people to the Hungarian cause, demanding total identification with it. But this proved self-defeating. As he strove to redefine the nation in strictly Magyar terms, it shrank; the other peoples within the kingdom of Hungary felt threatened and began to weave dreams of their own. The Slovaks, Slovenes, Romanians, Croats and Serbs, not to mention the Saxon minority, grew increasingly hostile to his aims. And it was this hostility that Vienna would tap in order to regain control of the kingdom and curtail the national aspirations of the Hungarians.

Back in March, Vienna had appointed a new *ban* or governor of Croatia, a province of the kingdom of Hungary. The man chosen was Josip Jelačić, a Croat colonel who enjoyed reading patriotic verse of his own composition to his troops and was as loyal to the Habsburgs as he was devoted to Croat nationhood. Having pacified the revolutionary movement at home, put down the nationalists in Prague and defeated the Italians at Custozza, Vienna was ready, by the end of the summer of 1848, to proceed with the recovery of Hungary. In September Jelačić crossed the Drava river at the head of a mixed force of 50,000 men, proclaiming that he was coming to Hungary to preserve the unity of the Habsburg monarchy. On 29 September a small Hungarian force stopped him in his tracks at Pákozd, but while this saved Hungary for the time being, it also revealed some of the problems inherent in the situation. The most important part in the battle had been played by artillery, and this was supplied on both sides by batteries of the very same unit, the 5th Prague regiment, made up entirely of Czechs.

When the Hungarians had wrested constitutional autonomy from Vienna in April 1848, they inherited those regiments of the Habsburg army that happened to be stationed in the kingdom of Hungary. Some of the soldiers were Hungarians, but many were not; they included Italians, Czechs, Poles, Slovaks, Austrians, Serbs, Romanians and Croats. They had no difficulty in accepting the authority of the new Hungarian government, as they did not have to abandon their allegiance to the Emperor, who was also king of Hungary. Even after the outbreak of hostilities, when they found themselves facing units of the same army across a battlefield, they were still obeying legal authorities and drawing their pay from 'His Majesty's Minister for War'. That was why units made up of Czech conscripts did not desert the Hungarian cause. But it was also why units made up of Hungarian conscripts serving in Italy, Galicia and Bohemia did not desert in order to join the Hungarian forces but continued to repress sister nations with aspirations similar to those of the Hungarians. To disentangle these knotted loyalties was not going to be easy.

Kossuth began recruiting a new national army, the *Honvéd*, 'defenders of the fatherland'. They had distinctive uniforms, but the rest of the Hungarian forces wore Austrian regimentals, which gave rise to chaos and provided a number of tragicomic moments as units obeyed bugle-calls or orders shouted by the other side. Windischgrätz ordered his troops to wear a white band around their shakos to facilitate identification. But identifying the true loyalties of the men and officers was to prove more difficult.

After his defeat at Pákozd, Jelačić turned west and made for the Austrian frontier, hoping to obtain reinforcements from Vienna. But when the Austrian government attempted to send units stationed in the capital to his aid, there were demonstrations of protest, and these sparked off a fresh revolution in the capital on 6 October 1848. The court fled to Olmütz, and revolutionaries from defeated outposts homed in on Vienna for another round. 'I saw beautiful people everywhere,' enthused Wagner, who had also turned up and delighted in the sight of the students in their 'old Germanic garb'. 'Ah, this richness, this life.'[12] General Bem, who had been in London trying to persuade the British government to back a rising in Poland, then leading the revolutionaries in Lemberg, was named commander of the Vienna Civil Guard and organized the city's defences. But these could not stand up to Windischgrätz, who stormed the city on 31 October at the head of 70,000 troops.

The Hungarians had missed their only chance by not moving swiftly and coming to the aid of the revolutionaries in Vienna. This hesitation can be explained by the situation in Hungary itself. As the conflict with Vienna developed from a constitutional tug-of-war into armed conflict, many Hungarians drew back, out of a mixture of loyalty to the Habsburg monarchy and cool realism. The resignation of Prime Minister Batthyányi meant that Kossuth was virtually a dictator, but this did not enable him to pursue his aims with as much determination as he would have wished. Kossuth's greatest problem was finding men who were competent without being disloyal, and persuading them to work together. To head the army, he appointed the 31-year-old Arthur Görgey, who was to prove himself a brilliant soldier but an awkward partner, and ultimately to seal his downfall.

In mid-December 1848 Windischgrätz marched into Hungary at the head of a force of 52,000 regulars. Görgey fell back, the Hungarian government withdrew its seat to Debrecen, and on 5 January 1849 the Austrians entered Budapest. Windischgrätz was not Jelačić, and some officers and whole units on the Hungarian side now transferred their allegiance to him. That he managed to carry on the war for another eight months was Kossuth's great achievement. The majority of the population did not want it. Kossuth travelled about the great plain of Hungary rallying the peasants, but while they came to revere him personally, they were not ready to be swept up in a cause of which they did not see the necessity. They gratefully accepted improvements in their condition, but did not see these as being linked to national independence. 'People are unspeakably tired of the war,' his friend Bertalan Szemere reported from the north in January, 'Liberty and Nationality are mere lyrics to them of which they understand nothing.'[13] Even allowing for some exaggeration, the picture was not a happy one. In spite of this, Kossuth managed to build up the *Honvéd* army to an overall strength of some 170,000 men, and, thanks to his tireless personal efforts, he fed, clothed and armed it from a small and under-industrialized geographical base.

One thing that Kossuth never managed to achieve was satisfactory control of military operations. At the beginning of January 1849 Görgey issued a manifesto to the effect that he no longer accepted Kossuth's authority, and from then on he cooperated with him or not according to his whim. Kossuth did not make matters any easier by appointing over Görgey's head a Pole who had offered his services, General Henryk Dembiński. This irritated not only Görgey but a number of other senior officers. It also internationalized the war, turning it into something more radical than an internal constitutional spat.

There had been a Polish Legion fighting in Hungary for months. It consisted of some 3,000 men under the command of Major Józef Wysocki, operating in the north-east of the country. By its side there was a company of Viennese students, dressed in black and sporting a death's-head on their caps. There was also an Italian Legion under Count Monti, and an assortment of volunteers, including the English General Richard Guyon. But putting a well-known international revolutionary in command of the main

Hungarian forces was a signal of a different order. It was a godsend to Habsburg propaganda, which could represent the rebellion as a part of the world revolution, and it made many of the regular Hungarian officers uneasy by the same token. It was also a military mistake, as Dembiński was not a good soldier. On 26 February he gave battle at Kapolna and mishandled every aspect of the operation. His officers refused to serve under him further, and he was forced to tender his resignation. He was given a minor command in the north, where he did little good but no harm.

An altogether different level of competence was displayed by another Polish volunteer, General Bem, whom Kossuth sent to Transylvania, where the position of the Hungarians was parlous. The imperial commander in Transylvania had rallied the local regular units, enticed the Romanian National Guards and other ethnic armed bands to follow him, and effectively reclaimed the province for the Habsburgs. Bem defeated the Austrian regulars and managed to detach some Romanians from the Habsburg camp by giving them to understand that they could expect fair treatment in an independent Hungary.

In the first days of April Görgey defeated Windischgrätz in a series of minor engagements. The old field-marshal was replaced by General Ludwig Welden, but this did not improve the position of the Austrians, who were pushed back along the whole front. Most of Hungary was freed, and on 23 April the *Honvéd* army re-entered Budapest, where only a small Austrian garrison remained ensconced in the fortress of Buda. Instead of pursuing the retreating Austrians towards Vienna, Görgey made the mistake of concentrating on dislodging this force. It was not until 21 May that Buda Castle was successfully stormed, and the wasted month put paid to any hopes of defeating the Austrians.

Any possibility of negotiating a settlement had been ruled out by Kossuth's declaration of Hungarian independence on 14 April 1849. The declaration was personally drafted by him in conscious imitation of the American model, but in true central-European style it had something of the history lesson about it. While it left the form of government open and did not establish a republic, it did dethrone the house of Habsburg. This made many professional officers, who could hitherto still claim that they had not betrayed their loyalty to the king of Hungary, resign from the army. Many noblemen, who were aware that historically both Hungary and their caste owed a great deal to the connection with the house of Austria, also now distanced themselves. In April Görgey had declared that the coming struggle 'would be fought by Europe as a whole for the sacred national rights of all peoples against tyranny'.[14] This was a challenge, and it was duly taken up.

From the very start of the Hungarian rebellion, Russia had offered her assistance and showed impatience to send an army into Hungary. Vienna had resisted this, both on account of the potentially provocative political implications, and because it would be humiliating to admit that Austria could not handle her own problems. In February 1849 the Austrian commander in Transylvania had called on his colleague across the border in Moldavia for help. A force of 6,000 Russians came to his aid, but they were defeated by Bem. In May, as the Hungarian rebellion began to take on an international dimension, Francis Joseph formally asked Tsar Nicholas for assistance 'in the holy struggle against anarchy'.

On 27 June, Kossuth, who had re-established his seat of government in Budapest, issued an internationalist manifesto. 'Awake, O peoples and nations of Europe!' he exhorted. 'Your freedom will be decided on the fields of Hungary.'[15] But everything he did was at variance with this ostensible internationalism. He reprimanded Bem for treating with the Romanians, and denounced the talks which his own agent in France, Count László Teleki, had entered into with Czartoryski with a view to gaining the support of the Slav minorities by offering them some form of autonomy in a federal Hungary. Kossuth accused Czartoryski of stirring up the southern Slavs against the Magyars. Instead of seeking their help, he persisted in trying to obtain support for the Hungarian cause from outside, offering the crown to the Bonaparte family in return for help from France, and trying to buy British support with the offer of a port on the Adriatic.[16] It was only at the very end of June 1849 that Kossuth declared himself in favour of allowing the minorities to use their own languages in schools and law courts. It was by then patently too late.

Command of the Austrian forces had been transferred to General Ludwig Haynau, a brutal individual with an unenviable reputation. He had distinguished himself at Custozza, and following that victory, had led the Austrian army back into Brescia. There, he ordered the flogging of all Italians who had demonstrated patriotic instincts, including women of noble birth. This had been made into a *cause célèbre* by the liberal press and earned him the sobriquet of 'The Hyena of Brescia'. The first thing he did on taking command of the forces in Hungary was to execute a few Hungarian prisoners. He then began a methodical reconquest of the country. With his 175,000 seasoned troops, he had the means, and used them efficiently. The Russian army which had marched into northern Hungary was superior in strength, numbering some 200,000, but it failed to play any serious part in the action. Either way, the Hungarians, with a total of some 170,000 men, possibly as many as half of them shut up in Komárom and other fortresses, were in no position to delay the inevitable. They were also bedevilled by personal rivalries.

Görgey continued to fight his own war, sometimes plotting to overthrow Kossuth, sometimes merely ignoring him. He was also conducting negotiations with the Russians. Kossuth wavered between the extremes of attempting to depose him on the one hand and making him supreme commander on the other. 'The state of morale in the army and the country reminds me of the state of affairs with us towards the end of 1831,' noted a newly arrived Polish colonel.[17] On 13 July Haynau retook Budapest, and Kossuth removed his government to Szeged. On 30 July he once again gave overall command of the army to Dembiński, who fell back on Temesvár, hoping to join forces with other Hungarian units. On 31 July Bem was routed by the Russians at Segesvár, where the poet Petöfi was last seen heroically brandishing a sword at charging cossacks – his body was never found.

On 9 August Bem reached Temesvár, where Haynau had just launched an attack on the main *Honvéd* force. Kossuth put Bem in command in lieu of Dembiński in the middle of the action, giving rise to predictable confusion. As he struggled to restore order and confidence, Bem had a horse killed under him and was himself wounded. The tactical situation was so bad that even his panache and popularity could not revive the flagging enthusiasm of the *honveds*, who broke and in many cases threw away their weapons.

The débâcle at Temesvár left a small force under General Klapka at Komárom, and another under Görgey at Arad. On 11 August, Kossuth resigned, leaving Görgey in sole command. The twelve remaining deputies of the National Assembly that had superseded the Diet met for the last time, to declare the war lost and the Assembly suspended, and to embrace tearfully before heading off into a life of exile. Kossuth shaved off his moustache and changed his hairstyle to avoid being recognized, and went off to Bem's camp. There he discharged all the Polish volunteers, who were led off into Serbia and thence into Turkish territory to avoid capture by the Austrians or the Russians.

On 13 August Görgey surrendered to the Russians at Világos in the belief that they would assure an amnesty for him and his 30,000 men. They certainly took his surrender in the most gentlemanly way, with full military honours. The *honveds* passed round their standards, which every man kissed, before burning them. That evening the Russian officers feasted and toasted their captives in the best traditions of chivalry and etiquette. But the next morning they marched them off to General Haynau's camp. Only Görgey himself was granted amnesty, at the personal request of the Tsar. Kossuth had crossed the Danube into Turkish territory at Orsova on 17 August, having buried the Crown of St Stephen on the banks of the river. 'My principles were those of George Washington,' he declared to the small band of Hungarians who had followed him, before taking leave of them to begin a life in the outside world more reminiscent of Lafayette.[18]

'The triumphant Imperial-Royal arms have smashed the thousand-headed hydra of the Hungarian revolution,' Haynau declared on 18 August 1849.[19] He was anticipating events a little, since a couple of fortresses held out for many more weeks, and the valiant General Klapka did not surrender Komárom until 5 October. It was only when the Hungarian tricolor was lowered over the ramparts of Komárom on that day that the 'Springtime of the Peoples' finally came to an end.

Austrian retribution in Hungary was swift and savage. Batthyányi was condemned to hang, but was shot after having attempted to cut his own throat. Fourteen generals were also shot, while hundreds of other officers were sentenced to death and reprieved. Even those who had abandoned the Hungarian cause in the autumn of 1848 were given brutal sentences. The Spielberg, Küfstein, Olmütz and other prisons were filled to bursting. And in countless acts of lawless sadism, Haynau's soldiers flogged men and women suspected of Magyar sympathies.

Those who had managed to cross the border into Turkish territory avoided these dangers, but their lot was hardly enviable. Thousands of fugitives found refuge in August 1849 at Vidin on the Danube, where the Turkish authorities allowed them to camp. Hungarians were outnumbered by Poles, Italians and other foreign volunteers, and each had a different set of possible places of asylum in mind. In the meantime they were obliged to wait, never free of the fear that the Turks might give in to Russian and Austrian pressure and extradite them. Conditions were far from good, and malarial fever carried off many an emaciated soldier. The Turks were in need of experienced officers, and made offers which were alluring to the men languishing in the vermin-infested camp at Vidin. The one drawback was that Ottoman service was conditional on embracing Islam. A number of them nevertheless opted for this way out, and Bem changed his faith and entered Ottoman service as General Murad Pasha. The refugee camp eventually was moved from Vidin to Sumla, while Kossuth and the more prominent leaders were moved to the Turkish mainland. The soldiers were gradually allowed to depart in batches, depending on which country would accept them.

In March 1851, one ship left Kutahya for Liverpool with 261 Poles on board, but was obliged to put in for repairs at a small port on the west coast of Ireland after a storm. The men were allowed to disembark in order to stretch their legs. The appearance of these strangers in their unfamiliar uniforms drew out the locals. There was much jabbering at cross-purposes until the name of Kossuth was uttered. Not only had everyone in Ireland heard of the Hungarian leader, it turned out that admiration for the Hungarians' struggle for freedom transcended all barriers. The local gentry reached into their cellars, and for a couple of days this small Irish coastal town saw English gentry, Irish peasants and the whole garrison of the local fort fraternizing with the Poles, drinking the health of the Hungarian hero. When the refugees reached Liverpool, the local population, mobilized by Chartists, found them food and shelter, and, with time, jobs.[20]

Kossuth himself was being cheered on the other side of the Atlantic. The United States Congress had voted to give him asylum and sent a warship to fetch him. In September 1851, the frigate USS *Mississippi* sailed into the Bosphorus, and raised the Hungarian tricolor as he stepped aboard. The *Mississippi* made a stop at Marseille, where thousands assembled on the quayside to greet the Hungarian heroes. But the ship was denied permission to dock, as President Bonaparte did not wish to offend the Austrian government; while Kossuth paced the deck of the *Mississippi* in the roads of Marseille, he was being hanged in effigy in Budapest. But the French people were more generous. Thousands came out in small boats to shake his hand or merely to gaze on him.

At Gibraltar, Kossuth transferred to an English steamer, as he wished to visit England before going on to the United States. He had many friends there, and he admired the country as a haven of liberalism. When his ship entered the Solent, it was met by a boat carrying the mayor of Southampton and Lord Dudley Stuart, bearing a letter of welcome from Lord Palmerston, the Foreign Secretary. Thousands of people on the quayside cheered as he came ashore, and he had to force his way through a huge crowd to a waiting carriage, decked out in the Hungarian colours. When this arrived at the town hall, a group of workmen carried him in on their shoulders. He made a speech from the balcony and then attended a banquet held in his honour.

Kossuth's progress up to London was unprecedented. Special trains were run for those wishing to see him along the way, and he received invitations from the mayors of cities through which he would pass. He also received more than three hundred from towns up and down the country inviting him to banquets and celebrations, and on 3 November the trades unions paraded before him in London. In Manchester, he was cheered by a crowd of half a million. Such demonstrations of public adulation could not fail to annoy some. Lord Palmerston's excessive cordiality to Kossuth and testy rebuff of formal Austrian complaints were taken badly by Queen Victoria, and the Foreign Secretary found himself obliged to offer his resignation.

The Hungarian hero's reception in the United States was even more rapturous. A thirty-one-gun salute greeted his ship as it berthed at Staten Island on 6 December 1851, and virtually every person of importance in New York came out to greet him. Chief Kagigahgabow of the Ojibbewaj Indians came to express his delight that the Hungarians had been upholding the ancient Indian cult of liberty, while the Venezuelan patriot General Paez welcomed him on behalf of the Spanish Americans. He was treated to parades of regiments that had fought in the American Revolution and of German gymnastic societies.

Many exiles who sought asylum in America were warmly received, and Hecker's arrival in the previous year had been like a scene from grand opera, but the reception accorded to 'the Magyar Demosthenes' was unique. He was accepted by all sections of the population as a symbol of undefined hopes and ideals. 'Kossuthism' gripped the nation like a frenzy. He visited city after city in a whirl of banquets, speeches, bands and flowers. Kossuth's portrait was everywhere, flanked by those of Washington and Lafayette. Buttons were torn off his coat to be treasured as relics, while he was showered with tokens of esteem. He saw in the new year as a guest of President Millard Fillmore at the White House, knelt in silent recollection at Washington's tomb, and on 7 January addressed Congress, an honour extended only to Lafayette before him.

But while this recognition of the Hungarian cause and the money which he was able to raise on its behalf were very welcome, Kossuth found himself in an uncomfortable position. He was approached by delegations of Indians and taken to meet groups of runaway slaves. The abolitionists tried to enlist his support, but he was wary of antagonizing the slave-owning states. He fell between two stools, earning the scorn of abolitionists and failing to convince the slaving interests, who began to undermine his reputation.

There were no gun salutes or cheering crowds when Kossuth and his party sailed from New York on 14 July 1852, bound for Southampton. Kossuth had originally intended to settle in the United States, but he realized that the enthusiasm of the Americans was superficial. The sheer remoteness of America made exile appear more final. Sándor Petőfi's colleague Frigyes Kerényi had tried to start afresh at New Buda (now Davis City) in Iowa, but fell prey to violent homesickness, which he poured out in despairing verse, and finally died in the wilderness on his way to Texas. Kossuth was determined to carry on the fight and return to his homeland one day, and the best base for this was now London.

19
Bearing Witness

Paris, for so long the kitchen in which recipes for universal salvation had been concocted and the base camp from which crusades had been launched, had been stained with the mark of Cain. The June days, when proletarian Gardes Mobiles had enthusiastically slaughtered patriots and revolutionaries, stuck in the memory of idealists as a grotesque insult to all their most cherished beliefs and hopes. On his return to Paris, Berlioz noted that even the Spirit of Liberty on top of the Bastille column had a bullet through her body.[1]

The political climate had altered radically, and the French government had begun to clamp down on dissent. People implicated in subversion were sent to penal colonies and foreign political emigrés were expelled. This did not apply to the harmless likes of José de San Martin, who was living out his old age outside Paris, passing the time with a little carpentry and playing with his granddaughters. Nor did it apply to those prepared to abandon political activity; Michelet, who could not bring himself to abandon his beloved France, exiled himself to the country. But in the prevailing climate, many who were allowed to live in France could not bear to stay there. Only the Poles clung to their illusions of France, while their special claim to French sympathy made them practically unexpellable.

London, which had been a haven for the defeated and the deposed for decades, now became the nerve-centre of subversion. The various shades of French politics were represented by Louis Blanc, the ascetic man of the masses, of whom it was said that 'a religious brain and an absence of sceptical misgivings encircled him with a Chinese Wall, over which not one new idea, one doubt could be flung'; and Alexandre Ledru-Rollin, the spiritual heir of 1793, living in a world of his own, committed to the holy faith of revolution.[2] The Italians were overshadowed by Mazzini, though not all subscribed to his views. An older exile was Antonio Panizzi, an active Carbonaro who had been obliged to flee Modena in 1821. He had settled into London as the Librarian of the British Museum and designer of its round Reading Room. The Germans included Arnold Ruge and the poet Ferdinand Freiligrath, as well as a great many humbler individuals split into a myriad political groupings. As they had few natural leaders but many professors, their arguments were not only intense but also exceedingly recondite. The Poles, who also had a marked propensity for dispute, included the veteran socialist Albert Darasz and Stanisław Worcell, who was also universally respected and generally regarded as a kind of saint. The Hungarians never strayed from their allegiance to Kossuth, who kept up a dignified sense of position, always surrounded by a small court of martial-looking colonels. His impressive manner of speech, his renowned charm, and his melancholy smile assured him the benevolence of all he met. There were also groups of Spaniards, Portuguese and Romanians bearing witness to their respective causes. The Greek word for 'witness' is *martyros*, and its modern homonym fairly renders their plight.

The most informed, as well as the most moving, picture of this is painted by the Russian exile Alexander Herzen. He had been in Rome when the republic had been declared, and arrived back in Paris just in time to witness the June days, during which he was arrested and nearly shot by the Gardes Mobiles. He was obliged to take refuge in Switzerland, but eventually decided on London, where he took a house in Euston Square which quickly became a port of call for exiles of every nation and political creed.

While the prominent ones could rely on a degree of benevolence and generosity on the part of British society, most of the rank and file were dependent for survival on government handouts or their own efforts. In some instances, Parliament had voted pensions for soldiers of defeated insurrectionary armies, but this did not cover the participants in obscure plots and risings. They had to subsist on their own talents or on remittances from home. Italians, Frenchmen and Germans could give tuition in their respective languages, but such a resource was not widely exploitable for a Magyar or a Serb.

This mass of human jetsam deposited on the shores of England by the ebb and flow of revolution and reaction led an aimless existence in the foggy murk of London, distinguishable by their outlandish beards, funny caps and exotic, though worn, clothes. They lived in dingy basements or draughty attics in Bloomsbury, Clerkenwell and Islington and congregated in the same cheap eating-houses in the back streets off Leicester Square, to discuss the same issues over and over again, and to affirm the same spiritual truths with greater conviction, and bitterness, with every passing year.

They were largely ignored by their British hosts, who knew little of their causes and cared less. The radical activists who had taken a keen interest in European liberation movements in the 1840s had drifted into isolationism. Only the old Chartist Julian Harney and the radical Joseph Cowen continued to support the exiles, morally and sometimes materially. These could only seek solace in solidarity, and in 1850 Mazzini attempted to construct a great international movement, aided by Harro Harring. A 'European Committee' was established, and Mazzini and Kossuth penned proclamations for each other to further Hungarian-Italian solidarity. The social revolutionaries formed a Revolutionary Commune, calling for a holy alliance of peoples in the spirit of 1792 in order to bring about a world republic. Herzen subsidized the Polish press in London, and established his own Russian one alongside it in Regent Street. But while they cooperated amicably at this level, the Poles and the Russians could not make common cause: the Poles looked only to the past, and the Russians only to the future.

In 1855, Herzen launched his periodical *The Polar Star*, to be superseded two years later by *The Bell*, on which he was assisted by his newly-arrived childhood friend Nikolay Ogaryov. Ogaryov was an adept in the old tradition. Having inherited an estate of 1,870 souls, he gave them his land. When, in Pyatigorsk, he came across one of the Decembrist exiles, he knelt before him and prayed that he too might receive the palm of martyrdom. There was little in the way of dissent in Russia, but many idealists had warmed to the distant murmurs reaching them from the West in 1848. But the failures of that year were followed by intensified repression in Russia. In April 1849 a secret discussion club inspired by Saint-Simon and Fourier, the Petrashevsky Circle, was swooped on, and twenty-one members, described in the verdict as 'a handful of nonentities, the majority of them young and immoral' was condemned to hang. The nonentities, who included the novelist Fyodor Dostoyevsky, were led out to execution and only reprieved on the scaffold. The bitterness of their experiences and the abeyance of hope drove Dostoyevsky's generation either into a spiritual quest for the Russian soul or into a more radical cult of violent political change, neither of them comprehensible to the beached patriots in London. And these were also troubled by other emigrés, such as Marx and Engels, who stood apart, condemning the devotees of the nation for following the wrong faith.

These gathered at the annual commemorations of various revolutions, whose dates had come to punctuate their calendar like so many religious festivals. The oldest was the rite of 29 November, commemorating the Polish rising of 1830. Typical was the meeting of 1855, attended by 1,500 people, with Worcell presiding. Representatives of half-a-dozen nations made speeches, regurgitating all the finest ideals and feelings in a pointless incantation. Herzen ended his speech with the plea for 'an independent Poland and a free Russia', which Worcell answered by embracing him and 'forgiving Russia in the name of Poland'. Another yearly event was the commemoration organized by the Poles since the 1830s in honour of the Russian Decembrists. The French revolution of 1848 was remembered on 24 February by the same crowd. There were also special gatherings whenever some member of the international confraternity of exiles passed through London.

In February 1854 Garibaldi turned up. He had sought refuge and a new life in New York, but quickly noticed that America 'is a land in which a man forgets his native country'. After a gloomy year recovering from his hardships, he resumed his old profession and went back to sea. The first ship he captained, the *Carmen*, transported guano under the Peruvian flag, and he plied the shipping lanes of the Pacific on her deck. In 1851 he made a detour to venerate a living relic. He landed at Payta near Guayaquil and called on Manuela Saenz. The formidable mistress of Bolívar was in poor health, so she lay on a sofa in a shuttered room. As Garibaldi was suffering from rheumatism, he lay down beside her, and thus they communed for several hours in the spirit of the dead Liberator. They parted with tears in their eyes and emotionally drained. As he recovered his strength in a daily battle with the elements, Garibaldi conceived a dream of getting all the exiled warriors to become sailors, and to form a fleet of merchant vessels manned by the initiated. 'That would be a floating emigration, unapproachable and independent, and ever ready to land on any shore,' he mused.[3]

In 1854 Garibaldi sailed into Newcastle to pick up a cargo of coal, and he was met by a delegation of working men, led by Joseph Cowen, who presented him with a sword of honour. On his way to deliver the coal, Garibaldi put in at the East India Docks in London, and his old comrade from Rome, Colonel Haug, came to have lunch on board with him, along with Mazzini and Herzen. Also present was Felice Orsini, who had just escaped from the fortress of San Giorgio in Mantua where he had been serving out a sentence of *carcere duro*. The following day Garibaldi attended a dinner given in his honour by the American Consul in London, a Mr Saunders. He had invited all the prominent exiles, including Herzen, Mazzini, Orsini, Ruge, Ledru-Rollin, Kossuth and Worcell, as well as the American Ambassador, who happened to be the future President James Buchanan, and the sympathetic Member of Parliament Sir Joshua Walmsley. The evening ended with everyone getting drunk on the Kentucky whiskey punch Saunders had mixed and Mrs Saunders strumming the *Marseillaise* on her guitar.

Such moments of gaiety were rare, and when Garibaldi put out to sea once more, the other exiles went back to the contemplation of the one terrible truth that faced them all. They had failed. Worse, they had been rejected by the very people they had set out to help. A great vision, born in the 1760s, was seeping away into the London fog. The urge for national liberation, so long assumed to be a natural instinct, intimately bound up with personal liberation and empowerment, appeared not to have fired the masses at all. Earlier failures had been put down to lack of education among the people and to their indoctrination by the civil and religious agencies of the *ancien régime*. But this argument was wearing thin. If anything, they had rallied against the revolution with some spontaneity.

In Poland, the insurgents had been massacred by their own people. In Italy they had met with scant support and often with hostility. The pattern had been the same everywhere: the people on whose behalf they fought had not supported them. Soldiers preferred to serve their royal masters rather than embrace the faith of national freedom. Despite all the appeals, only a couple of hundred Hungarians had defected from the Austrian ranks in Italy to join the Italian patriots. All the dreams of solidarity had been so much hot air. 'Conviction was not, courage failed, and truth was something to be doubted of,' wrote Elizabeth Barrett Browning in *Casa*

Guidi Windows, a poem about the dawn of freedom and its betrayal which she had witnessed in Florence in 1849. Those who had already abandoned the cause of nations for that of the people, viewed through the various socialist doctrines, were just as disillusioned. The masses had not responded to their slogans either. It had been the working-class Gardes Mobiles who had crushed revolution during the June days.

Faced with such total defeat of their most cherished hopes and beliefs, and condemned to inactivity, the emigrés became more politicized, formed splinter groups, and drifted into various brands of theoretical socialism. Most had come to question the wisdom of further action along traditional lines. Some made determined efforts to start a new life, by taking up a profession or interest that took their minds off the burning questions. The would-be leader of Jewish legions in Egypt Bartłomiej Beniowski, who had later been an energetic Chartist, invented a system for reforming the spelling of the English language, along with his *Anti-absurd or Phrenotypic Alphabet*. Others went off in quest of oblivion and a new life in America.

The stalwarts who remained true to their cause were Ledru-Rollin and Mazzini, the one sending emissaries to France charged with building up a conspiracy that could overthrow the hated Napoleon III, the other organizing risings in various parts of Italy. Ledru-Rollin's agents were quickly caught and faced a wasting end in the penal colonies of Lambessa or Cayenne, while Mazzini's apostles languished in Austrian or Papal dungeons. Victor Hugo, who spent his days lambasting the abhorred '*Napoléon le Petit*' from self-imposed exile in Jersey, tried to dissuade Mazzini from this course of action, without success. 'Mazzini, like a medieval monk, had a deep understanding of one side of life, but invented the others', according to Herzen; 'he lived a great deal in thought and passion, not in the everyday world.' Herzen admitted to being fascinated by this man who sat in his dank lodgings in Goodge Street, not far from where Miranda and others had plotted, a cigar eternally in his mouth, sending messages down the 'spiritual telegraph system' that linked him to the whole Italian peninsula. 'In this unyielding steadiness, in this faith which runs far ahead of facts, in this inexhaustible activity which failure only incites and provokes to fresh effort, there is something of grandeur, and, if you like, something of madness,' he wrote.[4]

There was much madness in some of the enterprises Mazzini planned. In 1853 he launched a rising in Milan, with an optimism that beggars belief. 'The entire surface of Europe, from Spain to our own land, from

Greece to holy Poland, is a volcanic crust, beneath which sleeps a lava which will burst forth in torrents at the upheaving of Italy,' he assured the men he was sending to their doom. 'Four years ago the insurrection of Sicily was followed by ten European revolutions; twenty European revolutions will follow yours. – All bound by one compact, all sworn to one fraternal aim. We have friends even in the ranks of the armies who rule us; there are entire peoples whose alarum-cry will answer yours.'[5] In the event, the plotters were undecided, and only half of the already inadequate number rose. They were quickly defeated by the Austrians, and, needless to say, there was no ripple of solidarity anywhere else in the peninsula, let alone across the surface of Europe.

The outbreak of the Crimean War in 1853 sent waves of excitement through communities of exiles. 'It looks as though the whole of Europe is gradually being drawn into a general war,' the poet Zygmunt Krasiński wrote to a friend at the end of October. 'There will be ruins aplenty, but our tomb will be broken open in the destruction.'[6] When Britain and France went to war the following year, the excitement reached fever pitch. Mazzini and Kossuth confabulated in St John's Wood on the possibilities for their respective countries. Worcell and Kossuth toured Britain agitating for the opening up of another front against Russia in Poland, while grizzled soldiers packed their knapsacks and polished up their old decorations.

In February 1855 Czartoryski negotiated the formation of a 15,000 strong Polish Legion under Turkish command to fight alongside the Franco-British forces in the Crimea, and veterans of every rising since 1815 began to enlist. Others plugged their own schemes. General Wysocki offered the throne of Poland to Prince Napoleon, 'Plon-Plon', if the French would land an expeditionary force in the Baltic. Mickiewicz sent Napoleon III plans drawn up by himself for a French landing at Riga, which, he assured, would provoke an insurrection throughout Lithuania. When this met with no response, the 57-year-old bard set sail for Istanbul. He arrived in September 1855 and joined his countrymen at the Legion's camp. He encouraged the soldiers and their commander, General Sadyk Pasha, alias Michał Czajkowski, with his conviction that the liberation of Poland was at hand. Soon, Mickiewicz developed a new idea – that of forming a Jewish armed force, the Hussars of Israel.

The idea was eagerly embraced by the poet's friend Armand Lévy, a French Jew who believed that the chance to die in battle would help to 'elevate' the spirit of the Jews as a nation. The Hussars of Israel would cement the common destiny of the two nations by liberating first Poland and then Palestine. Volunteers were found, and a fine uniform designed. But problems soon arose, not the least of them being that the Ottomans had no intention of raising a unit which would subvert one of their own provinces. It was while he was trying to overcome these difficulties that Mickiewicz died of cholera in a squalid room in Pera.

The Crimean War did have the consequence of creating a Romanian state. Otherwise it was a disappointment. It never spilled over into revolutionary activity. It was conducted clinically by governments and professional armies, far away from any place where the population could be drawn into the fray. There was no room here for poets or volunteers. Far from being allowed to form legions, Polish deserters from the Russian ranks were treated little better than criminals by the English and French. The nation was being squeezed out by the state, which requires obedient soldiers, not devoted patriots.

This reinforced the sense of redundancy felt by the exiles. Nobody seemed to want them any more. Their methods as well as their slogans appeared increasingly out of date. Some of the things they had fought for heroically on barricades and battlefields – civil liberties, representative government and national unification – were being brought in pragmatically by governments they despised. Most of the principles of 1789 had triumphed, but they had also been devalued in the process. Many liberals and less committed radicals lost confidence in their clear, uncompromising idealism, and had begun to imagine that pragmatism, if not outright cynicism, was the sensible way to get things done. The new concept of *realpolitik* appeared more sophisticated than the romantic intransigence it supplanted. This left the unbending ones truly beached.

These men's real lives had stopped at some point, at some moment of failure or catastrophe, and their minds remained fixed on that one point. Cut off from their natural, living environment, they were like plants regularly watered but deprived of real nourishment. They fed on an ever-diminishing set of memories and a dwindling circle of people, and remained stuck at the same point, like a clock that had not been wound. The only indication of the passage of time was in the lines on their faces and the elbows of their coats. Time passed, slowly since they had nothing to do, but inexorably all the same. By the mid 1850s men who had been so alive and dangerous only a few years before were withered and desiccated. They lived deprived of hope, in conditions that worsened daily.

They became poorer and hungrier, and they could only seek solace in their imaginations, which grew more tortured. They had to tie their present inglorious suffering into the cause, otherwise it had no point. But this became more difficult with every passing day. There was nothing for them to do battle with, and they had become irrelevant, though many of them were still quite young.

The willed consensus of the Romantic rebels began to splinter under the pressure of events. Heine, driven to despair by the inertia of the once idealized people and their maddening refusal to be saved along the lines imagined by the intellectuals, came round to Napoleon III. So did Panizzi. The socialist Louis Blanc found himself in a state of ideological and emotional disarray when Napoleon launched his adventure in Mexico, where the radical's natural sympathy for the Mexican patriots was pitted against the Frenchman's feelings for the beloved tricolor. Mickiewicz, who had been an early advocate of the Emperor, had horrified many by his faith in a man whom most regarded as a reactionary monster. But Mickiewicz would have been devastated had he known that during the Crimean War Mazzini was hoping Russia would triumph.

Now the emigrés came together only for each other's funerals. These were almost festive occasions, providing an excuse to gather, wave the flag and make speeches, to check on who was alive and who was not, to go over, yet again, the events that had brought them here. They gave each other strength to carry on, buoying up each other's faith. Funerals, which celebrate the passage to sainthood and the resurrection of the body, revived the faith in the Second Coming and the resurrection of Hungary, Poland or the French Republic. 'For me, you see,' one French exile told Herzen, 'the republic is not a form of government, it is a religion, and it will only come true when it has become one.'[7]

On a sunny springlike day in February 1857, 'the company of the wrecked' and their English friends gathered outside a small shabby house in Hunter Street, near Russell Square. A few days earlier, in a dingy ground-floor room, Stanisław Worcell had finally coughed out his life with the London smog in the arms of Mazzini. Herzen had hurried over as soon as he heard the news, and by the light of a guttering candle bade a last farewell to the wasted corpse of his friend. 'As afflicted as Job, he had fallen asleep with a smile on his lips, faith was still steady in his dimming eyes, closed by a fanatic like himself, Mazzini,' he recorded.[8] Mazzini, Ledru-Rollin and Herzen walked behind the coffin, which was carried by a group of Russians and Poles, to a grave that had been paid for by a sympathetic English Member of Parliament. This was inscribed with an epitaph, composed in Latin by Kossuth. They had buried an epoch.

Mazzini and his followers were still orchestrating risings, in the fervent belief that each new martyr contributed to ultimate victory. Only such a justification could have been invoked in defence of ventures such as the 1856 rising by Baron Francesco Bentivegna near Cefalu in Sicily, in which all the participants lost their lives, the attempted rising in Genoa in 1857, or the tragic self-immolatory expedition of Carlo Pisacane in the same year.

Pisacane was a Neapolitan aristocrat and former regular officer who had fought for the Roman Republic in 1849. He had published a book on the events of 1848–9 in Italy, and he had few illusions. 'Insurrections made by a few who attempt to raise the people in order to achieve a state of affairs that these very people do not understand, must fear defeat, their inevitable end,' he had concluded. Yet he insisted that 'poetry' must triumph over 'grammar'. In a political testament that reads like a suicide note, he argued that those devoted to the cause of Italy should pay less attention to success and concentrate more on the moral value of failure. There were the makings of a 'moral revolution' in the *mezzogiorno*, and it must be brought on, whatever the cost.[9]

On 25 June 1857 Pisacane, his Calabrian friend Giovanni Nicotera and two dozen others boarded the postal steamer *Cagliari* out of Genoa. They hijacked the vessel and made for a rendezvous at sea with the Sicilian Rosolino Pilo, who was to bring more men in another boat. They failed to make contact, and sailed on to the island of Ponza, where they attacked the Bourbon prison. They released the inmates, but were disappointed to find that the two hundred convicts far outnumbered any 'politicals', and that many of these were old men who had been banged up since 1820. Undaunted, Pisacane took the ex-prisoners, convicts and all, aboard the *Cagliari* and made for the mainland. They landed at Sapri and came ashore shouting '*Viva l'Italia!*', to be greeted by a few local liberals with cries of '*Viva Murat!*', soon followed by the forces of law and order, strongly backed up by bands of local peasants, who enthusiastically set about butchering the would-be liberators.

A more effective plot exploded, literally, in Paris on the night of 14 January 1858, as Napoleon III and the Empress Eugénie were driving to the opera. One of the items on the programme, fittingly enough, was an aria from *La Muette de Portici*. As the carriage drove up to the opera house, three bombs were hurled at it. Eight people were killed and 156 wounded, dozens of horses killed and the imperial carriage reduced to matchwood, but Napoleon and Eugénie emerged almost unscathed. The culprits were Mazzini's friend Felice Orsini and two accomplices. Orsini had been an official of the Roman Republic in 1849 and, after a spell in the Austrian gaol at Mantua, had been living in London. He was popular in England, having conducted a lecture tour and sold a large number of copies of his autobiographical book *The Austrian Dungeons in Italy*. The terrorists were swiftly arrested, tried and guillotined. But the outrage at their act had by then been assuaged by Orsini's fine bearing during the trial (which had caused some of the grandest ladies in Paris to fall in love with him and the empress herself to beg for his life to be spared), and by his open letter to Napoleon, printed in all the papers. This recited the wrongs suffered by his country and appealed to the emperor to win the gratitude of 25 million Italians by going to war in support of Italian liberty.

The French emperor often thought of Italy. It was the scene of his illustrious uncle's early triumphs, and it was a natural jousting-ground for France. Napoleon III liked to make connections with the heroic age, and it was he who had insisted on sending troops to Rome in 1849. They had remained there ever since, not only to protect the Pope, but also as a mark of France's determination to maintain her influence in the peninsula. The emperor was in dire need of a dose of *gloire* with which to illuminate his fustian image. After the attempt on his life by Orsini, he was also keen to see all Italian subversives put out of business once and for all. If something were to be achieved for France in Italy, it would have to be through the agency of Piedmont, and with the complicity of that kingdom's First Minister, Count Camillo di Cavour.

Cavour was forty-two years old when he became First Minister in 1852. He had served in the army and made his way in a number of professions, acquiring wide experience and a deep understanding of men. He was a non-revolutionary progressive, a royalist and a pragmatist who admired Britain, clever, energetic and devious. He made it his ambition to aggrandize Piedmont, necessarily at the expense of Austria, and he realized that he risked nothing: the Great Powers would never allow Austria to retaliate and reduce Piedmont. But he needed an ally, and only France could fulfil that need.

In July 1858 Napoleon III and Cavour got together incognito in the French town of Plombières. As they drove around in a closed carriage for the sake of privacy, they hatched a plan that would accommodate their respective fancies and fears. The French Empire and Piedmont would make war on Austria, and sweep her forces out of northern Italy. They would then make peace and carve up the spoils. Piedmont was to get the whole of Lombardy and, it was permitted to hope, Venetia and most of the Papal States. In return, it would hand over to France the province of Savoy and the city of Nice. In effect, Napoleon had no intention of allowing Piedmont to get anything other than Lombardy. Cavour was not being entirely frank with his French ally either. Suspecting Napoleon of double-dealing, he was planning to create a major crisis, from which France would be unable to back out, and one in which he would have the maximum number of options. This could best be achieved by the covert use of subversive elements, and Cavour turned to the most subversive of them all, Garibaldi.

In 1854 Garibaldi had bought himself a piece of the little Mediterranean island of Caprera, and began playing at Robinson Crusoe. With his own hands he cleared away the ubiquitous rocks, dug a well and built himself a house. He began to grow vegetables and some wheat, planted an orchard, and waged war on the wild goats after which the island had been named. He installed his three children and a housekeeper there, and employed a local peasant. But he went on doing all the hardest work himself, deriving childlike pleasure from this earthy existence. He was visited by a stream of old comrades-in-arms and English tourists, who would carry away shirts, locks of hair and even finger-nail parings as mementoes. He was also in receipt of a huge volume of letters from admirers all over the world, including marriage proposals mainly from English women. But he also kept up a more serious correspondence with associates in various countries, and devoured the press, looking out for any sign of an opportunity for action. In 1856 he went to England to confer with Panizzi, who was hatching a plan to release the political prisoners held in the island fortress of San Stefano. The librarian had collected considerable funds with which he intended to buy a boat that could sail to the island and liberate the prisoners. Garibaldi was the natural choice to lead the enterprise. But the ship was wrecked off Yarmouth and the plan abandoned.

Garibaldi was growing restive. He was 'terrified at the likely prospect of never again wielding a sword' for Italy. News reaching him on Caprera filled him with uncomprehending gloom. For him, Italy was 'the cult and religion of my entire life', and to fight for her was 'the Paradise of my belief'. He could not conceive of happiness while the motherland was enslaved. Yet most Italians, as far as he could see, cared little. 'The Italians of today think of the belly, not of the soul,' he complained.[10]

In August 1858, Cavour summoned Garibaldi to Turin and informed him of the planned war. He invited him to form up a volunteer force to fight alongside the Piedmontese army, promising to equip it and to allow it operational independence. Garibaldi came to life again at the exhilarating promise of action. He began to alert the old gang, and soon volunteers were trickling in from all parts of Italy and from abroad.

Leaving nothing to chance, Cavour also intended to unleash the Hungarian exiles on Austria, and made contact with Teleki and Klapka. They had been carrying on negotiations with Plon-Plon, who was possibly dreaming of a throne in Hungary. Kossuth had been summoned to Paris to see the emperor himself, but it is not known what was said. Kossuth then went to Italy, where he had an interview with Cavour on 14 July 1859, and on to Genoa, where Teleki and Klapka had established a Hungarian National Directorate and were recruiting volunteers. Cavour's real intentions remain opaque. He was preparing to send consignments of arms to Hungary and the Balkans, and at one stage even considered embroiling Britain in a conflict with Russia, Greece and the United States. In order to achieve what he called 'the expansion of Piedmont', he was prepared in his own words 'to set fire to the whole of Europe'.[11]

War was declared on 27 April 1859. French armies poured in to support the Piedmontese and quickly defeated the Austrians at the battles of Magenta and Solferino. The Piedmontese, who played only a minor part in the fighting, moved in to support risings which were now taking place in Modena, Tuscany, Parma and Romagna. Patriots rejoiced all over the peninsula. If Napoleon remained true to the cause, Giuseppe Verdi wrote to a friend in June, 'then I shall adore him as I adored Washington'.[12] But Napoleon III was no Washington. The course of events had alarmed other European powers, which he had no intention of antagonizing, so he decided to make peace. By the Treaty of Villafranca, on 8 July, Austria ceded Lombardy to France, which promptly handed it to Piedmont in exchange for Nice and Savoy. Cavour resigned in indignation at this high-handed and insulting treatment of his country, but he was soon back at his post.

Far greater was the indignation of Garibaldi. In March 1859 he had been named major-general and confirmed in command of a force to be known as the Cacciatori delle Alpi. It stood at a strength of about 3,500 men at the start of hostilities, mostly young Milanese noblemen, middle-class professionals and students who recited Tasso and Alfieri round the camp-fire. There was a sprinkling of old *garibaldini*, such as Giacomo Medici, who had fought in the red shirt on the pampas, Nino Bixio, and Garibaldi's son Menotti. There were other revolutionary veterans such as Enrico Cosenz, who had fought for Manin in Venice, and a number of foreigners. The Hungarian Colonel Istvan Türr had deserted from the Austrian army in Italy in 1848 and fought for the Italians. Konstanty Ordon, who had killed more Russians than any other by blowing up his Warsaw redoubt after its fall in 1831, had subsequently fought in half-a-dozen causes, most recently in Mickiewicz's Legion. An unlikely recruit was the Englishman Colonel John Peard. 'I have great respect for Italian independence', he answered someone who questioned his motives, 'but I am also very fond of shooting.' He accordingly brought his deer-stalking rifle, with which he inflicted much carnage in the Austrian ranks. He wore his well-cut sporting kit in the field, until he was warned that he ran the risk of being shot as a spy if captured. He then relented and donned the regimentals of the Duke of Cornwall's Rangers.[13]

The Cacciatori were fobbed off with old muskets, but this did not matter to Garibaldi, who believed that as long as the men had bayonets and faith in their cause, they would carry the day. They marched off to war singing a hymn which describes martyrs of the cause breaking out of their tombs to take up arms once more. Garibaldi had been given *carte blanche* as far as campaigning was concerned, and he therefore moved off smartly to get beyond possible recall. He crossed the southern tip of Lake Maggiore, and after brushing aside several small enemy units, took the city of Como on the flank of the main Austrian forces. Untrained as they were, his men fought like lions and pushed themselves to the limit. Their dedication to the cause was exemplary. 'Not a single complaint was heard among the wounded,' Garibaldi wrote, 'and if a cry found utterance while surgical operations were going on, it was that of *Viva l'Italia*!'[14] They were, in the words of one, 'living in a world of poetry'.[15]

'When Garibaldi passed through a village,' reported Giovanni Visconti

Venosta, Cavour's agent in the Valtelline, 'you would not have said he was a general, but the head of a new religion followed by a crowd of fanatics.'[16] This was in stark contrast to the reception accorded to the regular Piedmontese army, and it annoyed Cavour. On 13 June 1859, shortly after Garibaldi had entered Brescia amid scenes of wild excitement, he was ordered to march up into the Valtelline, where he was effectively put out of sight and out of mind. That was where the Treaty of Villafranca found him.

France's withdrawal from the war left a curious state of affairs in the peninsula. Piedmont had acquired Lombardy. The Austrian-protected regimes in Tuscany, Parma, Modena and Bologna had been toppled, and their successors, formed up in the Central League, demanded incorporation into Piedmont. Without her French ally, Piedmont felt too weak to acquiesce, and Cavour prevaricated. The leader of the new liberal regime in Tuscany, Baron Ricasoli, invited Garibaldi to leave the service of Victor Emmanuel and to take up that of the Central League. Garibaldi accepted, and reached Florence in August. Mazzini, who had himself arrived in Florence, could have told him that he would be disappointed, just as he had warned him that Piedmont would merely use him and then sideline him. Many of the Cacciatori had followed him, and from Bologna, where he made his headquarters, Garibaldi began planning an invasion of Rome. But when he went into action, Ricasoli grew alarmed at the possible consequences, and he was ordered to turn back. Garibaldi resigned his command and, refusing the high rank he was offered by Victor Emmanuel, went home to Caprera, where he hung up his sword and took up the spade. But he was not to enjoy peace for long.

In March 1860, plebiscites held in Tuscany and the other central states voted overwhelmingly to incorporate with Piedmont, creating the kingdom of Northern Italy. Cavour had done well by his king – but not, in Garibaldi's eyes, by Italy. Garibaldi wanted to sail to Nice and reclaim it from its new French masters. Mazzini, who had been plotting an invasion of Sicily for years, urged him to look south to the 'land of the Vespers'. Quantities of arms had been assembled by Mazzini's people at Malta and in Sicily itself, and plans for an expedition, to coincide with a rising on the island, were well advanced. Mazzini invited Garibaldi to take command, but Garibaldi hesitated.

On 4 April a rising did break out in Palermo. But the preparations had been known to the police, and as soon as the first group of seventeen rebels took to the streets they were confronted with troops. After a chaotically heroic defence of the convent in which they had barricaded themselves, the rising collapsed. When the news reached Genoa towards the end of May, Garibaldi decided that intervention was out of the question. Two days later, on 29 May, Garibaldi was handed an encouraging message from his man in Sicily, Rosolino Pilo, informing him that the insurrection was still going on. The message was almost certainly faked by those who wanted the expedition to go ahead, and it did the trick. Garibaldi decided to sail.

Preparations were put in hand, and the call went out for volunteers. Most of those who had joined up with the Cacciatori had been retained in Piedmontese service, and Garibaldi was not able to use them. But plenty of others came forward to take their places. Thus apart from a few old hands such as Bixio and Türr, the 1,089 who gathered at Genoa were all new volunteers. The 'Thousand', as the force has gone down in history, came mostly from the towns of northern Italy. Only a hundred or so came from Sicily and the south, and there were some thirty non-Italians. About half of the Thousand were under the age of twenty. There were 150 lawyers and 100 doctors, 100 merchants and 50 engineers. There were chemists and ships' captains, gentlemen of leisure, journalists, teachers and at least ten painters and sculptors. There were also some workers from the larger cities and a few vagabonds. The youngest was eleven years old, the eldest had served in the Napoleonic Wars.[17]

On the night of 5 May 1860 this company assembled in a secluded bay at Quarto, where they embarked on a flotilla of fishing boats which took them out to meet two steamers, the *Lombardo* and the *Piemonte*. These had actually been rented but, for form's sake, were stolen at night from the harbour at Genoa. Cavour, who was himself in two minds about letting Garibaldi loose in Sicily, could not afford to be seen to be abetting the adventure. Once they were out at sea, some fifty red shirts were distributed to the men, most of whom were dressed in old Piedmontese uniforms, and Garibaldi started composing marching-songs to tunes by Verdi. He read out a proclamation, in which he explained that 'the mission of this corps will be, as it has always been, based on complete self-sacrifice for the regeneration of the fatherland'.[18]

The north-western tip of Sicily was reached and an unopposed landing effected at Marsala. It was here that high-flown rhetoric came face to face with Sicilian reality. The natives showed no interest in the new arrivals, and attempts at winning them to the cause were hampered by the fact that they spoke what was virtually a different language. Garibaldi, who proclaimed himself Dictator of Sicily, would not let such details stand in his way. 'Liberty itself must sometimes be forced on the people for their future good', he had recently affirmed to an American acquaintance.[19] Things perked up when the Dictator abolished taxes on pasta and salt, and people began to respond to his cheers of '*Viva l'Italia*'. It mattered little that they answered '*Viva la Talia*', whom they assumed to be the Dictator's mistress. The important thing was that they cheered. After marching out of Marsala, Garibaldi met a band of armed peasants left over from a previous rebellion, and they joined him in his onward march. So did an enthusiastic Bourbon-hating friar, Fra' Pantaleo. The frocked figure of the friar riding beside the Dictator lent him, in the eyes of the peasants, the endorsement of the Church.

When news of Garibaldi's landing reached Palermo, a force of infantry was despatched to intercept him. It did so outside the village of Calatafimi. The Sicilians who had joined Garibaldi made for a nearby hill and settled down to watch the contest, occasionally cheering and firing into the air, but taking no part in it. Garibaldi's men showed remarkable mettle, repelling an attack by the Neapolitan regulars, and pursuing the retreating troops back up to their original positions on a hill. As they paused to regroup under cover of the walled terraces halfway up the hill, the volunteers' spirits began to flag. Even Bixio, who had been rallying the men fearlessly, wanted to fall back. But Garibaldi, who had come up to the front line, which crouched behind the low stone walls of the terraced hill, knew that if they fell back now it would be the end of his expedition. 'Here we shall make Italy – or die!' he angrily shouted at Bixio, and, leaping up, personally led the charge that overran the Bourbon positions.[20]

The engagement had not been decisive in any way. Garibaldi's losses of 30 dead and 150 wounded hardly suggest the kind of battle that decides the fate of a kingdom. Yet this paltry skirmish had violently tilted the scales. The upper ranks of the Bourbon army were filled by a flabby gerontocracy that ordered withdrawal whenever in doubt. And this is what they did now. The Sicilians who had watched the proceedings from their hillside were overawed. They had never even considered standing up to regular troops. Garibaldi's willingness to face soldiers and his ability to defeat them represented something in the nature of a miracle. With that miracle, Garibaldi had conquered Sicily.

The next day, as the Dictator pursued his march, peasants by the roadside dropped to their knees. It was already being whispered that he was invulnerable. The news flew from village to village that after Calatafimi Garibaldi had shaken his red shirt, whereupon one hundred and fifty bullets had cascaded from its folds. Ready to exploit any superstition, Garibaldi bowed to Fra' Pantaleo's wishes and allowed himself to be blessed by the friar as he knelt in church, clutching a crucifix. One of the priests from Calatafimi declared that it was Pius IX who was the Antichrist and Garibaldi the Messiah. From there, the march to Palermo became a triumphal progress.

Garibaldi overran the area round Palermo, while the 20,000 Bourbon troops squeezed themselves into unstrategic positions inside the town, and those outside it dispersed over the island. In the bay, a Neapolitan naval squadron rode at anchor, its heavy guns largely useless. Also in the bay were British, French and American warships. A couple of British naval officers who went for a drive outside the town actually stumbled on Garibaldi's headquarters and had lunch with him. The *Times* correspondent in Italy, a Hungarian by the name of Nandor Eber, also visited Garibaldi's camp, accompanied by two American officers from the USS *Iroquois*.

Garibaldi decided to fight his way through the strongly-held southern gate into the centre of the city, and hoped to take the defenders by surprise, attacking at night. But his Sicilian volunteers cancelled out any element of surprise by letting off all their blunderbusses while they were still far away and then running off. The *garibaldini* nevertheless stormed the defences, at considerable cost. The Hungarian Colonel Tuköry was killed, Nino Bixio was badly wounded in the chest, and so was Francesco Nullo from Bergamo, who was the first man into Palermo, closely followed by Garibaldi himself.

At first, the Palermitans hid behind their shuttered windows, but when they realized that all was safe they came out and fêted the 'liberators' with an enthusiasm bordering on frenzy. The Bourbon forces could think of nothing better than to bombard the city from the Castellammare fortress and from the sea, causing carnage among the population but little damage to the *garibaldini*. A determined attack could have crushed the revolt and captured Garibaldi, who was out of ammunition and had to cadge some powder from the captain of the American warship. But the old men in command had no will to fight. They made one attempt to dislodge the *garibaldini* from the city and then gave up. A truce was negotiated on board one of the Royal Navy ships. On 6 June, one month to the day from when the Thousand set sail, the Bourbon troops began to evacuate Palermo. Garibaldi then marched out to clear the island of the other Bourbon units. This involved fighting his fiercest battle so far, at Milazzo, but by the end of July the whole of Sicily was in Garibaldi's hands, and he was planning his next move.

On 9 June, a second batch of volunteers consisting of 2,500 men under the command of Medici arrived in Sicily aboard two steamers, the *Washington* and the *Franklin*. They included some 500 Hungarians, mainly veterans of 1848, who were formed into a Hungarian Legion, with two squadrons of hussars, under Colonel Türr, Adolf Mogyorody and Nandor Eber, who had put aside journalism. They were deeply committed, and some of them, like Gusztav Frigyesy, a veteran of the Cacciatori, would fight for Garibaldi again in 1861, in 1866 and 1867 (he would die in Milan in 1878, penniless and insane).

The next largest contingent was the British, which included John Peard; the erstwhile defender of the Roman Republic Hugh Forbes; and Colonel John Dunne, who had commanded Turkish levies during the Crimean War. Another 1,000 volunteers were embarking at Harwich under Captain William de Rohan, an American follower of Mazzini who had recently fought for Peruvian independence. In order to evade the provisions of the Foreign Enlistment Act, the expedition was described as an excursion to visit Mounts Etna and Vesuvius, armed for self-defence and uniformed for ease of recognition.[21]

The smaller French contingent was led by Lieutenant Paul de Flotte, a naval officer who had circumnavigated the globe twice by the age of twenty-three, then taken part in the 1848 revolution in Paris. Jean Philippe Bordone, a French officer and veteran of the Crimea and Italy, became Garibaldi's chief of engineers. Gustave Cluseret, also a former regular officer, had brought a group from the United States, where he had settled. Another French volunteer was the journalist and friend of Flaubert Maxime du Camp, who attached himself to the Hungarians. And three days after the fall of Palermo Garibaldi was joined by Alexandre Dumas. The novelist, whose father, a Napoleonic general, had been imprisoned by the Neapolitan Bourbons in 1799, wanted to kiss the ground as he came ashore in a 'free Sicily', but the state of the quayside put him off. He confessed that the sight of barricades made him feel young, and he emulated those who, after the fall of the Bastille, told hair-raising stories of its infernal workings. The Bourbon demonology was enriched with tales of gothic torture and cruelty, which would leaven his next novel, *La San Felice*. Dumas had arrived aboard his own yacht, a luxurious schooner whose crew included his mistress, dressed as an admiral, in which he followed Garibaldi's advance, playing a role somewhere between diplomacy and espionage.[22]

A more practical presence was that of Jessie White Mario, an Englishwoman married to a prominent follower of Mazzini, who had helped to prepare the Pisacane expedition and served time for it in a Piedmontese gaol. She was one of Garibaldi's most trusted associates, and became the Florence Nightingale of the Thousand. She had formed a committee in London to raise funds for the care of the sick, and not only set up and ran hospitals, but went out under fire to drag the wounded back to the dressing stations.

Among the other foreigners was a group of Germans from California. There were also Americans, some of them, like Lieutenant Frank Murray of Tennessee, Captain van Benthuysen of Louisiana and Colonel C. Hicks of Virginia, from the slave-owning southern states. There was the usual contingent of Poles, including General Aleksander Milbitz, who had led the Polish Legion during the defence of the Roman republic and then taken it off to join the Hungarian insurgents. They had got as far as Greece when the rising collapsed, but many had rejoined Milbitz in the Polish Legion in the Crimean War.

It is impossible to be specific about either the composition or the number of Garibaldi's forces. Both changed rapidly as new volunteers arrived and others were lost or went home. No proper lists were kept, and adherence was not formalized by any document, or even by uniform. Only a handful had been issued with red shirts, and the majority wore the clothes they arrived in. The volunteers who had come forward in Sicily were of marginal significance. Not only did their numbers fluctuate wildly, they were motivated by little more than a general excitement over the destruction of Bourbon rule. Once Sicily had been cleared of the resented Neapolitans, they either went home or reverted to banditry, without a thought for '*La Talia*'. But the original Thousand had been supplemented by the 2,500 under Medici, and by a further 6,000 at the beginning of August. This was more than enough for Garibaldi's style of warfare.

On the night of 18 August Garibaldi crossed the straits and landed in

Calabria, to a hostile reception from the local peasantry. Not only did none come forward to join up, they actually sniped at the *garibaldini* from behind rocks and even skirmished with them on occasion. But the Bourbon troops in Calabria were no better led than those in Sicily, and once he had brought over the rest of his men, Garibaldi was able to encircle them without difficulty at Reggio, where they surrendered. Further forces were picked off one by one, and on 30 August, a mere ten days after his landing in Calabria, the last Bourbon troops in the south surrendered. Garibaldi had taken to a small carriage and raced ahead of his army, greeted like a saviour and addressed on occasion as the 'Second Jesus Christ'. He was in a hurry to reach Naples and embark on the next stage of the enterprise, the invasion of the Papal States, before Cavour could prevent it. At one point he passed a column of 3,000 Bourbon troops, who did not even attempt to capture him. The theatrical had always played a part in the Italian struggle for liberation, but this situation was rapidly degenerating into farce.

The closest of his units, Türr's division, was 48 hours' march behind him. Ahead lay Naples, a huge city with a volatile population by no means entirely hostile to its Bourbon rulers. There was also a large regular army only waiting to be rallied. On 4 September King Francis II left Naples to join his main forces at Gaeta. Garibaldi, who had reached Salerno, received a telegram of welcome from the king's First Minister, addressed to the 'redeemer of Italy', and a communication from the city's mayor asking him to defer his entrance until triumphal arches had been erected.

Garibaldi would not wait. He went to the nearest railway station and boarded a special train, and in a fittingly ludicrous climax to the campaign, steamed into Naples, accompanied by a small staff and a horde of enthusiasts picked up along the way. Garibaldi made a triumphal progress across town in an open carriage, and the city went into carnival mode, the streets filled with cheering, dancing people celebrating day and night. A few days after entering Naples, Garibaldi went to the cathedral to pay his respects to the phial with the blood of St Januarius. Fra' Pantaleo mounted the pulpit and preached a sermon which represented Garibaldi as a man sent to redeem the world after Moses and Christ had failed.

A few days later Mazzini turned up, and the two men started planning a march on Rome, desperate not to lose momentum. They guessed that Cavour wanted to incorporate the Kingdom of the Two Sicilies into the realm of Victor Emmanuel and leave things at that for the time being.

Such an outcome might defer the realization of their dreams for decades, as well as putting paid to any hopes of a republican Italy. If Garibaldi could storm on and take Rome, and then push on to liberate Venice, Italy would have to unite, and the position of Cavour and his royal master would be a great deal weaker.

But before he could go anywhere, Garibaldi had to wipe out the remaining Bourbon forces and chase Francis II from the land. This would not be easy. The people of Naples continued to make merry, without much heed to what they were celebrating. They would stop passers-by and threaten with daggers and pistols any who did not shout '*Viva Garibaldi!*', but none of them could be induced to join up, let alone provide supplies or care for the wounded. For the overwhelming majority, the whole thing was an irrelevance. There had been plenty wrong with the Bourbon regime, but after a couple of weeks of Garibaldean rule there were rumblings of discontent. Naples had been subject to corrupt and inefficient rule since the days of the Norman kingdom, and its people were too wise to believe that a change of regime could alter that. The same people who had cheered Garibaldi were quite prepared to welcome back King Francis.

Such considerations had never stopped Garibaldi before, and he marched out to confront the Bourbon forces. The core of his army was made up of men who had thrown over everything for the cause and suffered for it. Whatever reason had led them to do so, they had to some extent fused their own identities into a collective sense of mission that made it easy for noblemen to live and fight beside men from the lowest orders of society. Something of the spirit of 1792 had been conjured. The fighting of the past months had hardened them and taught them a range of military skills that made them far superior, man for man, to any regular soldiers. But all these men were as nothing without Garibaldi himself, who validated their faith and their sacrifices, and it was his physical presence at the Battle of the Volturno on 1 October 1860 that won the day.

He kept a constant watch over every corner of the battlefield, taking advantage of the enemy's mistakes and personally leading most of the attacks. His seeming invulnerability lent credence to the notion, never far below the surface, of his divine nature, inspiring his own men to greater risks and making the enemy hesitate. To the astonishment of some, he shouted 'Victory!' at the moment when this seemed least likely. He was willing victory, and he obtained it. But the Bourbon forces lost fewer than 1,000 killed and wounded, with some 2,250 taken prisoner, and they trudged back into the formidable fortresses of Capua and Gaeta, from which only a large professional army with siege artillery could hope to dislodge them. Garibaldi had to give up his dreams of Rome.

In November 1860, after some tortuous negotiations, Garibaldi agreed to hand the Kingdom of the Two Sicilies over to Victor Emmanuel. A meaningless plebiscite had been held to legitimize this, while Francis II still reigned behind the walls of Gaeta. Garibaldi invited Victor Emmanuel to come to Naples, and the two met, on horseback at the head of their respective armies, the king scarcely able to conceal his distaste at having to receive a kingdom from the hands of a commoner. A few days later Garibaldi was brought a document naming him full general and the offer of a title and lands to go with it, but he screwed up the paper and threw it into the waste-basket. He boarded the *Washington* and sailed back to Caprera, where he put his horses out to grass and gave his Piedmontese general's uniform to one of his labourers. Garibaldi went to work on the land with the vehemence born of frustration, while the number of trippers coming to see this astonishing Cincinnatus rose sharply.

20

Keeping the Faith

In October 1861 Herzen received a letter from San Francisco. It was from Bakunin, who had just escaped from Siberia. 'Friends, I long to come to you with my whole heart, and as soon as I arrive I will set to work, I will take a job under you on the Polish Slavonic cause, which has been my *idée fixe* since 1846,' he effervesced.[1] The date he mentioned was significant. After upsetting some with his strong views at the Slav Congress in Prague in June 1848, he had moved on to Dresden, where he took an active part in the city's defence against the Prussian army. Unlike Wagner, who managed to slip out at the last moment, Bakunin was captured and condemned to death. The king of Saxony did not carry out the sentence, and handed him over to the Austrians instead. He spent a few months chained to the wall in Olmütz before Austria decided to oblige Russia by handing him over. At the frontier, his fetters were removed and returned to the Austrian officer in charge, who insisted they were crown property, and duly exchanged for Russian manacles. He was conducted to St Petersburg, where he was incarcerated in a dungeon of the Schlüsselburg fortress. In 1857 he was released from this and sent to Siberia. He managed to escape, reached the Amur river, and persuaded an American skipper to give him passage to Japan, whence he made for San Francisco.

Bakunin had not witnessed the worst failures of 1848 and missed out on the bitter contemplation of them, so he was still full of fire and energy. After so many years of imposed inactivity he was straining for action, and everything seemed straightforward to him. As soon as he reached London, he joined Herzen and Ogaryov for dinner and quizzed them eagerly about the political situation. 'Clouds are gathering, but we must hope that they will disperse,' Herzen replied to his enquiry about Poland.

'And in Italy?'

'All quiet.'

'And in Austria?'

'All quiet.'

'And in Turkey?'

'All quiet everywhere, and nothing in prospect.'

'Then what are we to do?' said Bakunin in amazement. 'Must we go to Persia or India to stir things up? It's enough to drive one mad; I cannot sit and do nothing.'[2]

Bakunin's was a heroic nature. Trapped inside the titanic body with its leonine head was an eternal student, lazy, nomadic, careless of money and possessions, fired by total childlike conviction. He was a magnificent rabble-rouser. Wherever he went, he identified the potential revolutionary forces, set them alight and fanned the flames. In London, where he found Russians, Poles, Czechs and Serbs, he began to forge a Slavic front. Making up for years of silence, he argued, lectured and shouted. He failed to see the essential differences between the causes of the various Slav nations, and he would not be put off. The fight must go on whatever the cost.

The only other person with a comparable single-minded dedication to action was Garibaldi, who also refused to face up to unwelcome realities. Instead of leading to the liberation of the whole peninsula, his heroics in Sicily and Naples had resulted in Victor Emmanuel being acclaimed king of Italy. Having been elected to the Italian parliament, he marched into the chamber in his red shirt, looking to some like a prophet, to others like a comedian. He regarded all politicians with the utmost scorn, and gave healthy vent to this feeling, calling for a march on Rome and protesting at the government's intention of disbanding the volunteers. When both demands were ignored, he unleashed a savage verbal attack on the whole political establishment and retired to Caprera. The *garibaldini* were duly disbanded, along with the 4,000 strong Hungarian Legion of Colonel Ihasz which had fought under Piedmontese command, and the various derelict Poles. The Italian authorities did allow the establishment of a Polish military training centre at Genoa, later moved to Cuneo. Here Mierosławski and Marian Langiewicz, an artillery officer who had sailed with the Thousand, trained up some two hundred officers over the next year-and-a-half. But there was little prospect of their skills being put to any use. The whole of Europe seemed to be settling into the kind of calm that Bakunin dreaded so much, and the pattern of life had changed, making it even more difficult for exiles to survive.

Some did the sensible thing and returned to civilian life. Others went off in search of alternative causes. A small group of *garibaldini* went off to fight in Greece at the end of 1860. Many more sailed for America, where the Civil War had broken out. A few saw a struggle for survival in the cause of the South. Wincenty Sulakowski, a veteran of the November Rising and the Hungarian war of 1848, formed up a Polish regiment that fought for the Confederacy. Another group of exiles made up a 'Garibaldi Legion' in Louisiana. But most rushed to serve the Union. Typical was Filip Figyelmessy, a dashing major in Kossuth's *Honvéd* cavalry, then commander of Garibaldi's hussar squadron in Sicily, who offered his sword to the Union in 1861 and served as a colonel in the US Cavalry. Gustave Cluseret, who had been with Garibaldi in Sicily, ended up as a general in McClellan's army. President Lincoln's call was answered by many old crusaders who had started a new life in the United States in the 1850s. They included an estimated eight hundred Hungarians, many of whom served in Colonel Frederick Utassy's 39th New York Volunteers, better known as the Garibaldi Guards. The regiment, which also had a mixed company of French, Spaniards, Italians and Swiss, wore *bersaglieri*-style uniforms with a plumed hat adorned with the initials GG. It marched under three flags – the Union, the Hungarian tricolor and Garibaldi's volcanic standard – and it fought at the first Battle of Bull Run, Harper's Ferry and Gettysburg. Other Hungarians joined the 8th New York Infantry, raised by Julius Stahel, a bookseller and friend of Petöfy who had fought in the *Honvéd* ranks. He distinguished himself at the First Bull Run and became a general in the army of the Potomac, going on to command a division at the Second Bull Run and an army corps in the advance down the Shenandoah Valley.

The Poles were mainly grouped in the 58th New York Infantry, also known as the Polish Legion, commanded by Włodzimierz Krzyżanowski, who had been with Mierosławski in Poznania in 1848. They fought at Cross Keys, the Second Bull Run and Gettysburg. Krzyżanowski too became a general of the Union Army, as did his countryman Józef Karge, another Poznanian soldier of 1848, who formed several cavalry regiments and led them in action, most notably at Gettysburg. Perhaps the most unexpected spectre of 1848 to reappear in the Union ranks was the flamboyant German republican Friedrich Hecker, last seen weeping over the shattered hopes of the aborted 'Springtime of the Peoples' in Strasbourg in 1848. He had settled in the United States and in 1861 helped to raise a regiment of volunteers, of which he became colonel.

One who never made it was Garibaldi himself. He had been delighted to receive a letter from Abraham Lincoln inviting him to come and take command of an army corps, and prepared to go. 'Your fame will be greater than Lafayette's,' wrote an enthusiastic American consul.[3] But before he set off, Garibaldi wrote to Lincoln demanding overall command of all the Union forces. He did not trust any politician, not even Lincoln, after whom he had named one of his sons. As no answer came, Garibaldi went back to plotting his own wars.

In April 1862 he was proposing to start a rising in Venice and assembled a force of volunteers under Francesco Nullo, a businessman from Begamo and veteran *garibaldino.* But the Italian government arrested them and put a stop to the enterprise. Desperate for action, Garibaldi then sailed for Palermo, where he was greeted deliriously. He toured the battlefields of 1860, attended by crowds of peasants kissing his hands and feet, and holding out their babies for him to bless. This adulation only served to highlight the underlying absurdity of Garibaldi's position. The peasants as a class worshipped him but resolutely ignored the message he preached. 'I do not know a single instance of one of its members being seen among the volunteers,' he admitted.[4] And it was not as though they were universally supine – as late as 1859 there were demonstrations of loyalty to the Austrians in places such as Parma and Modena, with thousands of peasants happily waving black and yellow flags.[5]

In an attempt to harness the pro-Garibaldi sentiment and channel it into support for the cause of Italy, his associates purloined elements of the Catholic Catechism that were ingrained in the peasant consciousness and tailored them to their own ends. One example is a cheap but decorative poster, produced in 1864, headed 'The Doctrine of Giuseppe Garibaldi'. This opens with the words: 'In the name of the Father of the Nation', shamelessly substituting Garibaldi for God, and the service of Italy for Catholic practice. The catechetical question of how many Garibaldis there are elicits the answer that there is only one Garibaldi, but that there are three distinct persons in him: 'The Father of the Nation, the Son of the People, and the Spirit of Liberty'. Garibaldi was, of course, made man in order to save Italy, and to remind her sons of the ten commandments, which are:

1. I am Giuseppe Garibaldi your General.
2. Thou shalt not be a soldier of the General's in vain.
3. Thou shalt remember to keep the National Feast-days.
4. Thou shalt honour thy Motherland.
5. Thou shalt not kill, except those who bear arms against Italy.
6. Thou shalt not fornicate, unless it be to harm the enemies of Italy.
7. Thou shalt not steal, other than St Peter's pence in order to use it for the redemption of Rome and Venice.
8. Thou shalt not bear false witness like the priests do in order to sustain their temporal power.
9. Thou shalt not wish to invade the motherland of others.
10. Thou shalt not dishonour thy Motherland.

The poster contains an 'Act of Faith' to be recited daily, as well as an act of contrition for those who have transgressed the commandments and offended the Father. There is also a travesty of the Lord's Prayer which contains such gems as 'Give us today our daily cartridges'.[6]

Only a man as humourless as Garibaldi could have gone along with something as dubious as this, or indeed continued to preach the cause as though it were an unquestionable truth. His speeches consisted of phrases that were by turns plaintive and aggressive, strung together like some litany, and they were delivered in clerical style. During an address at Marsala, where he called for the wicked French troops to be expelled from Rome, someone in the crowd shouted '*Roma o morte!*', 'Rome or death!' The following day, during a solemn Mass in the Cathedral, he ascended to the altar and made the whole congregation repeat the slogan, as a solemn pledge.

Sicily and the old Bourbon realm in the south were seething with discontent against the Italian government, which treated the whole area like a conquered colony rather than a liberated province of the common motherland. Garibaldi tapped this discontent to assemble a force of some 3,000 volunteers, with which he crossed the Straits of Messina and began a march on Rome. At first, the Italian troops in the area did nothing to hinder their progress, but when Napoleon III complained to the Italian government, they were ordered to intercept Garibaldi. On 29 August

1862, a battalion of *bersaglieri* caught up with him at Aspromonte and made to attack. After the first shots, Garibaldi stormed out in front of his lines, waving his arms and shouting for his men to hold their fire. But the regulars kept firing, and Garibaldi was hit in the thigh, and then a second time in the foot. The great red-shirted figure crumpled and fell, and his volunteers waved white kerchiefs frantically.

The thigh wound was of no consequence, but the bullet lodged in Garibaldi's foot proved impossible to extract, having wedged itself between a number of small bones. He was carried off on an improvised stretcher and, although he was in evident agony, he was locked up like a criminal. But the outside world came to his rescue. English sympathizers had a whip-round and raised 1,000 guineas to send the most eminent surgeon out to attend him, and over the next weeks no fewer than twenty-three surgeons from various countries came to give the benefit of their advice before the bullet was eventually removed. This, along with the holed boot and bloody sock, not to mention hundreds of squares of blood-stained bandage, became relics to be fought over and cherished. But while some were venerated with the same reverence as relics of earlier days, the exercise was now becoming confused at the edges with mere souvenir-hunting. As he struggled to revive something of the spirit of 1848, Garibaldi found himself being enveloped by cheap sensationalism, and he was increasingly the object of curiosity and indiscriminate hero-worship rather than an inspirational leader offering redemption through his sacrificial crusade. This meant that his public life was more and more prone to lurch into the realm of farce, as his visit to England in 1864 illustrates.

The motives for this visit remain obscure. He hobbled ashore at Southampton in civilian clothes, and only addressed a few words to the crowd on the quayside. But the next day he appeared clad in his red shirt and openly revelled in the ovations of the populace. He went to the Isle of Wight, where he planted a tree and recited Foscolo's *Dei Sepolcri* for Tennyson, and whither Mazzini and Lord Shaftesbury came to greet him. His arrival in London provoked scenes never witnessed before. Half-a-million people lined the route from Waterloo Station to the Duke of Sutherland's house, where he was to stay, and his carriage took six hours to cover the three miles. Over the next days the most distinguished people in the land came to pay homage to him and crowds besieged the house. The Duke's servants made a small fortune selling bottles of soap-suds from his wash-basin. Queen Victoria expressed shame at belonging to a nation that could behave with such indecorous infantilism. Her sentiments were echoed by Karl Marx, who thought the whole thing 'a miserable spectacle of imbecility'.[7] Garibaldi met all the exiles living in London, but the exchange of sonorous acts of faith in the future did little to lift spirits. While driving down to Chiswick to venerate Foscolo's tomb, Garibaldi confided in Panizzi that he had decided to curtail his trip, even though fifty towns and cities up and down the country were preparing banquets to mark the great progress he had been planning to make through the land.

He duly sailed back to Caprera, where he sat brooding over the unpropitious situation, mulling over in his mind every possible plan for landings in Venetia, Dalmatia, the Papal States and Sicily. It is difficult to assess whether this earnest giant ever had doubts. He himself was still fired by his mission – to fight for Italy until she emerged triumphant from the house of bondage. But now that the Bourbons had gone and the Austrians were on the run, now that Italian patriots no longer languished in dank dungeons, that mission had lost much of its earlier appeal. Younger intellectuals were cast in a different sensibility, and fewer of them fell prey to the sacred obsession with the nation. The masses, being mostly a great deal better off than they had been in the past, were even less interested in upheaval than before.

Yet outside his native land, Garibaldi remained an inspiration to all who aspired to raise themselves above some perceived state of subjection. He was, according to Herzen, 'the Uncrowned King of the Peoples, their enthusiastic hope, their living legend, their holy man – and this from the Ukraine and Serbia to Andalucia and Scotland, from South America to the northern of the United States'.[8] Bakunin confirmed that 'not a few peasants of Great and Little Russia awaited Garibaldi's coming', while in Warsaw in 1860 street-urchins taunted Russian soldiers and policemen that Garibaldi was about to come and deal with them.[9] And it was in Poland that the Garibaldean myth was to have the most tragic consequences.

The year 1855 was a watershed for the Poles; the abominable Nicholas died and the myth of Russian military invincibility was blown apart in the Crimea. In May 1856 the new Tsar, Alexander II, visited Warsaw and promised reforms. Martial law, which had been introduced in 1831, was suspended. Thousands of political convicts were released from Siberian captivity, and an amnesty was extended to emigrés who wished to return.

In 1857 the first Polish institution of higher education came into being since the closure of Warsaw University in 1831. In the same year the landowners were permitted to form an Agricultural Society, which became a kind of senate bringing together the most active members of the Polish aristocracy. This was of particular significance in view of the fact that the greatest single reform challenging the whole Russian Empire involved the peasantry.

The Polish lands within the Empire had been growing prosperous throughout the 1840s and 1850s, and the only segment of the population that did not share in this were the poorest peasants. Unlike the rest of the Empire, there was no serfdom in the former Polish lands. Landless peasants were nevertheless in a state of bondage, as the only way they could rent land was by paying for it with their labour. The fact that the lord of the manor was usually the local magistrate meant that they were often legally as well as financially subjected to the same master. It behove the Polish landed nobility to improve the lot of these people. Poland's Russian master was moving towards reform in this area, and it would be desirable for the Polish peasant to owe his future well-being to his countrymen rather than to a foreign despot – the Galician jacquerie of 1846 was but a decade past.

'No pipe-dreams please, gentlemen', the Tsar had warned while declaring his openness to reform. He was determined that the concessions he might make should not revive aspirations to Polish independence. The overwhelming majority of the population welcomed the improving economic and political conditions and was prepared to wait for further concessions that would, it was hoped, lead to a return to the kind of national autonomy existing before 1830. But they and the Tsar were fooling themselves. The lives of many revolved around dreams, and the poets kept alive the vision of revolt as the ultimate act of human expression, bringing sanctification through death. And a Napoleon on the French throne stirred all sorts of memories, while events in Italy suggested no end of possibilities.

Few of the exiles took advantage of the amnesty offered by the new Tsar, both for ideological reasons and because most of them had no life to go back to in Poland. They could conceive of no other return than an heroic march with weapons in their hands. The failure of the Crimean War to provoke a general conflagration had caused despondency, but the example of Garibaldi at the end of the decade revived their ardour. The exploits of the Thousand triumphantly reaffirmed the myth that with courage and faith everything was possible – all that was needed was a Polish Garibaldi. The chief beneficiary of the desire for one was Ludwik Mierosławski. In a pathological speech delivered on the anniversary of the November Rising in 1858 he had lambasted all those in Poland who believed in material progress and education as the way forward. The only fruit of such constructive policies was, according to him, a 'moral decay' which was seeping through the nation. He accused all conservatives of attempting to dull its instinct for freedom in their own interests. 'Nation, awake!' he exhorted on the same anniversary a year later, calling for young men from Poland to come and join him in Italy.[10]

His call did not go unanswered, for there was a hard core of dedicated patriots steeled through the trials of the past decades, whose upbringing seemed to be but a preparation for a life in the service of the cause. Generations whose fathers and grandfathers had fought and suffered experienced a sense of inadequacy if they too did not face up to the ultimate challenge. 'Each family must regularly offer a few sacrifices on the altar of the nation,' a young man wrote to his sister.[11] The second generation of Poland's Romantic poets were contributing shoals of verse expressing the longing to fight and die for the cause. In this poetry, spring was looked forward to not because it clothed nature in bloom, but because it was the time to fight. These patriots believed any outcome to be less important than the act of self-sacrifice that would redeem them and awaken the nation to a new life.

In February 1859 the poet Zygmunt Krasiński died in Paris. His body was brought to Warsaw on the way to its final resting place at his family estate, and this provided an opportunity for a public demonstration in his honour. Everyone felt so uplifted that some students arranged a Mass in memory of the three great poets of the Romantic era, Mickiewicz, Słowacki and Krasiński. As the crowds gathered, the Russian police prohibited the service. This had the effect of turning virtually any demonstration or commemoration into a patriotic act, and the students took up the challenge with relish. The thirtieth anniversary of the November Rising, on 29 November 1860, was the occasion for a huge street demonstration clearly aimed at provoking the police.

Determined to force them into violence, a group of activists consisting of students and junior army officers, who became known as the 'Reds', organized a demonstration on 25 February 1861 to commemorate the anniversary of the Battle of Grochów in 1831, the Poles' first victory in the November Rising. The crowd was dispersed by a charge of mounted police, but there were no casualties. Two days later, however, another demonstration did the trick. Those taking part wore 'national mourning' and carried holy pictures and a huge crucifix. When they refused to disperse, they were charged by cossacks laying about them with whips, and the holy objects were trampled and defiled in the process. The mood of the crowd turned to anger, and it surged forward, whereupon one section of Russian infantry opened fire, killing five civilians. The immediate reaction was to 'celebrate the wrong done to the nation', and the five corpses were duly borne in procession to a coffee-house in the centre of Warsaw, where they were laid in state. Conservative elements led by the Agricultural Society attempted to defuse the situation, and the Tsar ordered all Russian troops and police out of Warsaw, which was to be patrolled by special Polish constables nominated by a City Committee. But the Reds were determined that there should be no accommodation, and they did everything to undermine the position of the 'Whites' who were attempting to broker a compromise.

'They have reduced their whole political programme into one desire: they want to get themselves killed,' wrote one Warsaw lady to her brother in the country, commenting on the activities of the Reds.[12] There was much parading of provocative national symbols, singing of patriotic songs and attending of commemorative Masses. The Russian authorities could not countenance the increasingly provocative nature of these activities, and on 8 April troops were deployed again against a demonstration. A squadron of cossacks charged the crowd, followed by a battalion of infantry bludgeoning the demonstrators with the butts of their rifles, but, as one witness recorded, the demonstrators behaved 'like the early Christians in the circus', letting themselves be struck.[13] Eventually, the exasperated infantry opened fire. In an effort to avoid a parade of corpses as well as to conceal the large numbers of dead, the troops quickly gathered up the victims and buried them secretly that night. By common consent, patriotic Poles went into mourning. Grand ladies wore only jewellery made of jet or corundum, in the shape of chains and manacles, or representing crowns of thorns, crosses, martyrs' palms and anchors of hope.

Nation-worshippers in other countries looked on in vicarious ecstasy. 'It is with delight that one reimmerses oneself in the moral life of a nation which, oppressed and chained as it is, breathes only for liberty, right and sacrifice,' drooled Lamennais' friend Charles de Montalembert. 'Vanquished on the battlefield, it has found another arena, where the odious supremacy and the brutal infallibility of numbers are powerless, the arena on which one dies, on which martyrs serve in place of soldiers, on which it is no longer a question of victory or death, but on which victory is certain for those who know how to die.'[14] In London, Algernon Charles Swinburne wrote of 'the firewhite faith of Poland', while Bakunin revelled in the impending cataclysm, convinced that this was the one that would finally rock the empire of the Tsars.[15]

With no more than 45,000 troops in Poland itself, Russia was in a difficult position. The announcement of the emancipation of the serfs that year was causing rural unrest in various parts of the Empire, and events in Warsaw were having an effect in Russia. Demonstrations organized by Polish students in St Petersburg and Moscow were attended by their Russian colleagues in large numbers. On 15 March Herzen printed an article in which he spread the rumour that one Russian soldier had refused to fire on the crowds in Warsaw and had urged his comrades to do likewise. 'Even if you were to be punished for it by death', he had allegedly said, 'it will be a holy one, you will die as an offering of redemption, and your martyr's death will seal the indissoluble, free association of Poland and Russia, the beginning of a free association of all Slavs in one indivisible community.'[16]

As none of his conciliatory moves had any effect, the Tsar reimposed martial law. On 13 October 1861 Russian troops swarmed into Warsaw and set up camp on the principal squares, with field-guns unlimbered and ready to fire. All parks were closed, a curfew was imposed, national emblems were banned, as was the singing of songs. No more than two people could talk in a public place – three constituted an illegal gathering – and cossack patrols ranged the city enforcing the ban. That evening Russian troops surrounded three churches in which patriots had gathered to pray, and proceeded to drag them out. Women and children were sent home, the men marched off to the Citadel. The Polish hierarchy responded by closing all churches until the authorities agreed to respect the sanctity of holy places and the immunity of worshippers. The Protestant and Jewish religious leaders closed their places of worship in solidarity. Britain and France made indignant diplomatic noises, and Russia was isolated. The Tsar despatched his brother Constantine to restore order in Poland and the conservative Pole Aleksander Wielopolski was made effective head of the government. But even the conservative Whites distanced themselves from anything that could be construed as co-operation with Russia, so he had less and less room for manoeuvre.

The Reds had meanwhile turned the City Committee into the Central National Committee, in effect the cabinet of a country-wide underground government, and prepared for a large-scale rising to take place in the summer of 1862. The military leader of the Reds, Jarosław Dąbrowski, planned to take over the Warsaw Citadel and the vast fortress of Modlin to the north. The operation was to be carried out by Polish officers in the Russian army in connivance with Russian sympathizers and it would have placed the rebels in an extraordinarily strong position. The fortress of Modlin was virtually impregnable and contained enough military supplies to equip and sustain a major army. But while the plotters prepared, the Russians began reinforcing and redeploying their forces in Poland, which involved replacing some units and moving others, with the result that the conspiratorial networks were torn apart like a flimsy spider's web. On the faintest hint of a suspicion, the Russian police arrested a number of Polish officers, including Dąbrowski.

By the end of 1862 there were as many as 100,000 Russian troops in Poland, not counting fixed garrisons, military police and frontier companies. These troops, which were in the process of reorganization following the Crimean débâcle, were not in particularly good shape, and morale was low. In November a Russian officers' association issued a leaflet urging their fellows not to fight, and to march through Russia demanding freedom. It was couched in the same hallucinatory idiom as some of the Polish literature. 'Comrades!' it ran, 'We who are marching towards our death salute you. It depends on you whether it will be a real death or the beginning of a new life!'[17] But this did not signify that the Russian army would disobey orders, let alone that there was any plan afoot to help the Poles. And, after the collapse of the plan to take over Modlin and the Warsaw Citadel, there was no plan for action in Poland either, only the persistent vague longing for martyrdom. This might well have remained no more than a longing had it not been for a clumsy attempt by Wielopolski to crush the conspiracy in Warsaw.

The annual recruitment of men for the army, the *branka*, was one of the most dreaded aspects of Russian rule. Young men were conscripted for a period of ten years in theory, but usually fifteen to twenty-five years in practice, and sent off to serve in some far-flung outpost of the Russian Empire. The practice had been discontinued in 1855, but there was a new intake of some 30,000 men from Poland scheduled for 1863. Normally, most of these would have been chosen from unmarried peasants between the ages of twenty and thirty. But Wielopolski decided to focus the *branka* on Warsaw, where it would net the young intelligentsia, and most of the conspirators with it. Young men began to slip out of the city and make for the forests in order to avoid conscription, and, faced by possible extinction, the National Committee decided to launch an insurrection.

On the night of 22 January 1863 groups of Poles attacked seventeen Russian garrisons in various parts of the country. Most of the insurgents had left home at short notice, and they found themselves camping out without equipment or supplies in the polar conditions of a Polish January. 'It was as if the insurrection were an afternoon's hunting party, after which everyone would return home safe and sound,' reminisced one of the commanders.[18] Worse, they had no real plan. After the arrest of Dąbrowski, the military direction had fallen into the hands of people such as Zygmunt Padlewski, whose principal ambition was 'to become the Polish Washington', but whose undoubted bravery was not matched by any organizational skills or military experience.[19] As a result, the rising did not explode like a well-laid charge, it spluttered and flared like scattered powder.

On 26 January two delegates of the provisional government knocked on the door of a dingy little apartment in the rue Mouffetard in Paris, and offered their occupant, Ludwik Mierosławski, overall command. He rose to the occasion with his usual braggadocio, and followed through with his customary ineffectiveness. On 17 February he crossed the frontier from Prussian territory into Russian-occupied Poland, and was met by a hundred insurgents, most of them armed only with scythes. At their head, he gave heroic and doomed battle to a superior Russian force. He managed to evade capture and joined up with a slightly larger force of insurgents, which he led into another noble defeat, after which he was forced to take refuge behind the Prussian frontier. He had spent less than a week in Poland. He then went to Kraków, where he gathered another force, and marched into Poland once again, only to meet with much the same fortune as before.

Mierosławski's exploits were rivalled by those of Marian Langiewicz. A former lieutenant of Prussian artillery, he had fought at Garibaldi's side at Calatafimi, Palermo and Milazzo. After collecting a force of a couple of thousand men, armed for the most part with scythes and sticks, he led them successfully in a number of minor engagements in early February. Although his encounters with the Russians were hardly that, he reported them as decisive victories, and on 17 February he was promoted to general. Having managed to procure some rifles and knocked his men into shape, he spent the next weeks evading superior Russian forces and defending himself more or less successfully when cornered. The very fact that he was marching about the countryside at the head of a sizeable force of insurgents lent him credibility, and on 8 March he was nominated 'Dictator'. But on 19 March, while on his way to rally other detachments, Langiewicz was caught by Austrian gendarmes and imprisoned.

Perhaps the most interesting Polish commander to emerge was Józef Hauke, sometimes known by his conspiratorial alias of Bosak. He was the nephew of the general killed by the insurgents on the streets of Warsaw on the November Night. As a Russian count, he had been brought up under the wing of the Tsar, serving in the Corps des Pages and then the Hussars of the imperial guard. He had volunteered for active service in the Caucasus, and had been promoted to colonel and decorated twice for bravery in action against the tribesmen of Shamil. A visit to Poland awoke his patriotism, and he left the Russian army, married a Pole, and broke with the rest of his family (his first cousin, the morganatic wife of the Prince of Hesse, was made Countess Battenberg and was the progenitor of that family). By December 1863 Hauke had gathered a force of 4,500 men, and he dealt the Russians several painful blows.

But even good commanders could not make up for lack of proper troops, equipment and supplies. And the outlook of the insurgents prevented them from exploiting the one advantage they did possess – that of freedom fighters indistinguishable from civilians, and therefore impossible to track down. While they believed in improvization and the power of will, men like Mierosławski could only conceive of waging war by traditional tactics, facing the enemy out in the open; although he depended on civilians armed with scythes, he would not countenance a real undercover *guerilla*. The insurgents took an inordinate amount of time and trouble kitting themselves out in uniforms that constituted a statement of sorts. Nurtured on the Romantic literature of the past decades and its accompanying iconography, they were fired by the vision of a mounted warrior, embodying the fusion of spirit and nature, seeking ultimate liberation.

One reason partisan warfare could not be conducted in Poland was that the population was not uniformly behind the rising. Patterns varied, but most of the peasants were passive, and many denounced fugitives rather than hiding them. With time, many did begin to view the insurgents as being on their side, and an increasing number came forward to join the ranks in the later stages of the insurrection, but it was a far cry from the situation in Spain in 1808. The Jews, who were a feature of every Polish village, on the whole felt no loyalty to the Polish cause, and had no good reason to break their legal obligations to the Tsar by denying his troops the information they asked for. Only the Jewish intelligentsia of the larger cities made common cause with the Poles.

There was nevertheless no end to the supply of brave young men ready to pay the ultimate price. There were never more than about 20,000 fighters in the field at any given time, but successive waves of eager recruits stepped forward, and it is estimated that some 200,000 took part in the fighting over the eighteen months of the rising. They did so in the knowledge that there was no hope of success. 'Let us go and win freedom through our death, let us go and cover our death with fame!' runs a poem written by Felicjan Faleński on the night of 22 January 1863. 'Before the bullet pierces our breast, before a stream of blood bursts from our veins, we who go forth in quest of death salute thee, our Motherland!'[20]

The hopelessness of the Polish cause was not relieved by any realistic prospect of assistance from outside. Revolutionaries and nationalists of every hue greeted its outbreak with relish at the possibilities it seemed to herald. 'The era of revolution is once more fairly opened,' an excited Marx wrote to Engels in February.[21] Bakunin left London for Sweden, in order to be closer to the scene of the action; Mazzini called for an international crusade; Garibaldi declared it the cause of the whole of humanity and offered his services. His son Menotti began recruiting volunteers.

Francesco Nullo, who had taken part in the defence of Rome in 1849 in the ranks of Masina's lancers, served in Garibaldi's Cacciatori in 1859, led the attack on Palermo and been at Aspromonte, gathered together twenty-seven *garibaldini*, including eight Frenchmen and three Hungarians. They travelled through Trieste and Vienna to Kraków, where they unpacked their red shirts and joined a small force of Polish insurgents. On 5 May 1863, the anniversary of the embarkation of the Thousand at Quarto, they were surprised by a superior force of Russians near Olkusz. In the rout that followed, Nullo and most of his redshirts were killed. Other Italians arrived singly, along with many French volunteers, some of them former *garibaldini*. The most famous was François Rochebrune, who raised a regiment of dramatically uniformed 'Zouaves of Death'. There were also significant numbers of Czechs, Serbs and Slovaks, Scandinavians and Germans, but the largest contingent were Russian. But a few more men, however brave, were not going to make a significant difference. Nor were some of the romantic schemes to bring help to Poland.

One such was a marine operation prepared with the support of Herzen, Mazzini and Karl Marx. The SS *Ward-Jackson* was chartered in London, and loaded with arms and 145 volunteers under the command of Colonel Teofil Łapiński. An Austrian officer, he had fought in Hungary in 1848, after which he had enlisted in the Turkish army under the name Teffik Bey. In 1855, he had joined the Polish division in Turkey, and he later commanded a Polish unit fighting alongside the Circassian tribes against the Russians. After a brush with British customs, the *Ward-Jackson* sailed from Southend on 21 March 1863, bound for the coast of Lithuania. Bakunin was picked up at Helsingborg, but then the English captain got cold feet and put in at Copenhagen, where he and his crew deserted. A substitute crew was found, and the party sailed on to Malmö, where the ship was boarded by Swedish officials and the arms impounded. The members of the expedition began quarrelling amongst themselves, and a few went home, but in June Łapiński managed to obtain more arms and charter a smaller ship, which took them to the eastern Baltic. He attempted to land at Memel, but a storm blew up and twenty-four of the volunteers were drowned, including ten Frenchmen, four Italians and two Swiss.[22]

In his appeal on behalf of Poland, Mazzini called on all European patriots to extend the struggle to Venice, Hungary and the Balkans. He had visions of 'a general uproar from the Baltic to the Black Sea and the Adriatic'.[23] There was no shortage of eager trouble-makers, and no lack of crazy schemes. They included one devised by Prince 'Plon-Plon' to seize Odessa, and another, hatched by Wysocki and Klapka in Geneva, for a Polish-Hungarian landing in Moldavia from the Black Sea. Yet another was for Menotti Garibaldi to march into Poland through Romania, while one group of Poles urged Garibaldi to stage a march on Moscow starting from Venice. There was a plan to arm a number of ships and harry the Russian fleet on the Black Sea. The SS *Princess* was purchased in Newcastle, renamed after a hero of the 1794 insurrection, and despatched to Messina, where it was to be handed over to a Polish crew. This was to be commanded by 'Admiral' Andre Magnan, a French former slaver and adventurer. The ship was seized by the Spanish authorities at Malaga and confiscated. Only marginally more successful was an expedition mounted jointly by Czartoryski and a Circassian committee founded by the British Russophobe David Urquhart. They bought a ship, loaded it with six field-guns and a large quantity of rifles and ammunition, and despatched it, along with a detachment of seventeen Poles and a couple of Frenchmen, to the Black Sea. On reaching its destination, the detachment fought alongside the Circassian tribes for six months before being obliged to evacuate.

All this activity could not obscure the fact that the Poles were on their own. They had always talked a great deal of the possibility of French intervention on their behalf, but they thought of it rather as one thinks of divine intervention – to be devoutly prayed for rather than counted on. Had they ever paused to think seriously about the practicability of foreign intervention, or considered the feasibility of their schemes, or even honestly estimated the numbers of volunteers that would come forward when the hour struck, they would never have risen. But the tiny flicker of wishful thought they entertained that Napoleon III would send a *Grande Armée* to their aid or that Garibaldi would march in with ten thousand redshirts allowed them to make the great act of faith required in order to launch the insurrection.

It was only in the last phase of the rising, towards the end of autumn 1863, that the Romantic mood of profligate sacrifice gave way to a new realism and toughness, reflecting the attitude of a new breed of leader. On 17 October 1863 the supreme leadership was taken over by Romuald Traugutt, and everything about the occasion and the man marked a distinct break with past tradition. Although a poet was present, there was no darkened room, no candles, no oaths delivered on the blade of some fallen hero's sabre. And Traugutt himself, a small, bespectacled, sober-looking individual, made no display of emotion or passion. He merely accepted a post that few wanted, and set about making the best of an impossible predicament. He united the Whites and the Reds, sacked incompetent commanders and worked hard to supply the effective ones with a modicum of arms. He insisted that people face up to the fact that there would be no help from abroad, and that they must count only on their own forces, and did everything he could to increase these by drawing the masses into the struggle. He was moderately successful, but it was too late in the day, and although it guttered on until the spring of 1864, nothing short of a miracle could have saved the rising from collapse.

The whole reckless enterprise had been a costly catastrophe, yet it was seen as a triumph of faith and hope. There had been over a thousand military engagements, in which some 25,000 insurgents had lost their lives. Although only a fraction of the population had taken part, all segments had been drawn in at some point, and the very last engagement had been fought by a detachment composed entirely of peasants, so the myth of the nation in arms was safe. The Russians executed 669 people, sent 38,000 to forced labour in Siberia, and another 7,000 to serve in the ranks of Russian regiments. On 5 August 1864 the five members of the insurrectionary government, including Traugutt, were led out on to a bastion of the Warsaw Citadel, where five gibbets had been erected. A crowd of 30,000 knelt and chanted patriotic hymns as the five were hanged, in what was more of a sacrament than an execution.

21

Last Rites

The hero of Turgenev's novel *On the Eve*, published in 1860, is a Bulgarian freedom-fighter who maintains that a man cannot say he loves his country before he has died for it. Two years later, Turgenev published *Fathers and Sons*, whose main protagonist, Bazarov, utterly rejects such 'romantic rubbish' along with anything that cannot be proved by hard fact. This 'nihilist', who scorns the principles and beliefs of an earlier generation, marked the emergence of a new kind of political activist. While Turgenev's latest novel was being acridly debated by writers and critics, one of them, Nikolay Chernyshevsky, was prevented from taking part as he was locked up in the Peter and Paul Fortress. But he was employing his time in captivity to write his own novel, which appeared in 1863 under the title *What is to be Done?*; in it he paints a portrait of the revolutionary of the future, cold, disciplined and single-mindedly bent on one specific political purpose.

When Herzen went to Geneva in 1865 he was chilled to meet many such 'new men', who laughed contemptuously at his faith in liberalism and constitutional democracy, men whose only goal was the delivery of violent revolution which was to be implemented as though it were a form of political surgery. A year later, in 1866, one of them, Dimitry Karakozov, tried to assassinate the Tsar in St Petersburg. In the same year the Irish Republican Brotherhood, known as the Fenians, recently founded in New York, launched its first assault on British rule, in Canada. Modern terrorism had arrived. Dostoyevsky savaged its values in his novel *The Possessed*, and a horrified Herzen contemplated a future of politics through violence.

But he accepted an element of responsibility, referring to it as 'this syphilis of our revolutionary lusts'.[1]

The old lovers of the cause mostly ignored such frightening developments. On Caprera, Garibaldi tilled his rocky soil and ruminated on the various possibilities of striking another blow for Italy, carefully watched from the decks of a couple of Italian ironclads which patrolled the waters around the island. In 1864 Bakunin turned up, bent on founding an International Secret Society for the Emancipation of Humanity. A few months later came General Hauke-Bosak, fresh from London, where he and Mazzini had dreamed up a grandiose project for a Carpathian League which would bring the Poles, the Hungarians and the Romanians together in a grand military alliance. The methodical Gustav Struve wrote, inviting Garibaldi to preside over a great conference of revolutionaries of all nations, for which he had the perfect venue. This great bonding session could take place at a sanatorium in Switzerland owned by his brother, which would provide fresh air, fine views and exhilarating walks to accompany their deliberations – 'Would it not be charming!' he enthused.[2] Garibaldi may not have agreed, but by now he was so restless that he actually considered going off to Mexico to help the populist leader Benito Juárez in his struggle against the Emperor Maximilian.

The year 1866 opened up all sorts of new prospects and aroused fresh hope in emigrés of every hue. The crisis that led to war between Austria and Prussia necessarily concerned the Hungarians and the Italians, whose respective loyalty and neutrality were essential to Austria. Klapka recruited a Hungarian Legion under the wing of the Prussian army, while a Polish Legion began forming in Paris and another in Turin under Hauke-Bosak with the intention of going to the aid of an expected Hungarian rising. Garibaldi quickly mustered a force which took the field in north-eastern Italy.

Austria had attempted to bribe Italy to remain neutral by offering her Venice, but Victor Emmanuel refused. So far, every square inch of Italian soil acquired by his monarchy had been courtesy of Mazzini, Garibaldi or Napoleon III, and he was determined to capture something himself for once. With Austria being hammered by the Prussians, he could expect to be successful. But he was wrong. His army was given a drubbing at Custozza (again), his navy was defeated at Lissa, and he was only saved from actually losing territory by Prussia's crushing defeat of the Austrians at Sadowa. The single Italian victory of the whole campaign was won by

Garibaldi. But Garibaldi was not happy. He was depressed by the lack of enthusiasm for the national cause he encountered everywhere, and shocked by the peace settlement. Austria was obliged to give up Venice, but instead of ceding it to Italy, haughtily handed it to France, which passed it on like a tip. The wider picture was no more comforting.

When Klapka marched into Hungary at the head of his legion he met with indifference. The spirit of 1848 was dead, and the church was beginning to splinter. Some 2,000 *garibaldini* went off to Crete to foment a rising against the Turks. Langiewicz was in Istanbul fostering a Young Turkey movement. Klapka and others accepted the Austrian compromise of the dual monarchy, and went back to their homelands. The smaller Slav nations took refuge under the wing of the Tsars, at the first Pan-Slav congress, held in Moscow in 1867. In Poland, a new realist tendency condemned the insurrectionary tradition and preached organic self-improvement. In Germany, the exclusive nationalism that had raised its head in 1848 had become institutionalized. It was philosophically elaborated by Moritz Arndt's pupil Heinrich von Treitschke, who taught his countrymen to pursue the interests of the German state by any means and to increase its power through war, which he held up as a natural and wholesome condition.

None of this could deter the wild old man of Caprera. One night early in 1867, he slipped off his island in a skiff and landed on the mainland, where he began to rally volunteers for a march to liberate Rome, but he was promptly arrested by Italian troops and sent back home. At the beginning of October the volunteers he had raised marched into the Papal States without him. They were at first ignored, and then rounded on by those they had come to deliver, and had to take refuge in flight. Hearing of this, Garibaldi decided that he was needed. He went to Florence, the new capital of the kingdom of Italy, and began calling his men to arms. Several of his friends advised him against a new march on Rome, but he was confident that his presence would galvanize the populace and undermine the enemy's morale. On 22 October he led his volunteers into the Papal States, issuing stirring proclamations, and on 3 November, at Mentana, he came up against Papal units supported by a detachment of French troops. His men were no match for the French regulars, armed with their deadly new '*chassepot*' rifles, and Garibaldi was forced to withdraw after suffering heavy casualties. For the first time, the magic had failed to work. Roughly arrested and manhandled back to

Caprera once again by the Italian authorities, he settled down to writing bad novels on the theme of Italian regeneration.

'And you, Mazzini, Garibaldi, last of the saints, last of the Mohicans, fold your hands and take your rest,' wrote Herzen from Genoa on the last day of 1867. 'You are not needed now. You have done your part. Make room now for madness, for the frenzy of blood in which either Europe will slay herself or the Reaction will. What will you do with your hundred republicans and your volunteers with two or three cases of contraband guns? Now there are a million from here and a million from there with needle-guns and other artifices. Now there will be lakes of blood, seas of blood, mountains of corpses . . .'[3]

That same year of 1867 had seen the Great Exhibition in Paris, an eloquent measure of how much the world had changed. It was not only an extraordinary display of the dominance of the material over the spiritual, but also a remarkable demonstration of a new cosmopolitanism in action. It was held on the Champ de Mars, where so many revolutionary festivals had taken place. But the dozens of pavilions featuring the arts and crafts of nations as varied as Japan and Mexico, Finland and Morocco, expunged any lingering ghosts of 1789. All the trappings of an aggressive modernity were on show, including new discoveries and inventions: aluminium (which so impressed Napoleon III that he ordered a dinner service in it), petroleum, and Krupp's new steel cannon. The idea that this last object would be used in Europe seemed absurd as the wealthy middle classes of every nation on the Continent happily jostled at the exhibition. The king of Prussia and the tsar of Russia were among the visitors, drawn as much by the lure of Paris as by the exhibition itself. The city was one of the wonders of the world. It had been tidied and beautified under the direction of Baron Haussmann, with grand boulevards, public buildings and monuments. It was a city of light and cleanliness, with magnificent new foot-pavements, sewers and public conveniences. Visitors admired the *Halles*, a triumph of science and hygiene, as much as the fabled department stores in which almost anything could be purchased, and the splendid modern hotels. But it was also the Paris of Offenbach, a city of 20,000 cafés and a reputed 100,000 whores, the first tourist trap, the eldorado of the hedonist. Those who had flocked to Paris in the closing decades of the eighteenth century had come to partake of intellectual and aesthetic excellence, to drink in the *Zeitgeist* at its source. Those who trundled into the French capital in their thousands on the railways of the 1860s came to gape at the wonders of material progress, to buy consumer goods, to stuff their bellies and to get laid. They came not in quest of regeneration, but in search of gratification.

France was still culturally a beacon for the rest of Europe, but its most respected and authoritative writers no longer dominated the Parisian scene, and Victor Hugo thundered against it from self-imposed exile on Jersey. With the cult of progress in the ascendant, the cult of salvation went underground. The *Marseillaise* was sung only in prisons and on penal colonies, by convicts gathering for their evening assembly, for which reason it became known as the *Prière du Soir*. Even the old liberty tree in the Luxembourg Gardens, which had somehow survived the Restoration, was chopped down and replaced with a sensual sculpture by Carpeaux.

While idealists bemoaned the materialism and vulgarity of this brave new world, many did at least take comfort from the thought that it made old-style wars increasingly unlikely. The very idea of the pleasure-loving inhabitants of Paris marching off to fight the equally comfort-loving English or Germans seemed as ridiculous as any notion that those tourists who came to spend their money in Parisian restaurants and brothels wanted to destroy the place. These people had far more reason to fear the poorest workers in their own countries than each other. Tensions there were aplenty, with the occasional diplomatic hiccup as some foreign initiative designed to caress public opinion at home in one country collided with a similar ploy in another. Many Frenchmen were, it is true, deeply uneasy about the gradual unification of the German lands under the Prussian sceptre. The military in particular raged about the implied German threat. But there were no real bones of contention. And the sort of footling excuses, often involving pointless dynastic claims and counter-claims, that had launched wars under the *ancien régime*, could surely not provide a credible *casus belli* after all that had happened since 1789. Or so it seemed.

At the beginning of July 1870 the Prussian chancellor Otto von Bismarck suggested a minor Hohenzollern prince as a candidate for the empty throne of Spain. In France, this was immediately seen as an attempt at 'encirclement', something that used to bother Louis XIV a great deal in the seventeenth century, but was a meaningless concept in the nineteenth. The reaction of the French was nevertheless so violent that the candidacy was immediately withdrawn. But that did nothing to appease the fears and passions aroused. The French had taken pleasure in Napoleon

III's imperial foreign policy and approved of involvement in the Crimean War and in Italy. They had even enjoyed the extraordinary imperial escapade in Mexico, and they felt keenly the shame of its failure. The presumption inherent in Prussia's suggestion was seen as an affront to France's position, and, given the recent rise of Prussian power and influence, as a challenge. The whole country suddenly seized on the idea of war as a general panacea for all that was wrong with the international situation and the state of the nation itself. The ailing emperor was swept on a tide of public opinion into demanding from the Prussian king a humble retraction of the Spanish proposal. When this was refused, Napoleon III declared war, on 15 July 1870.

A few days earlier, Michelet had published an impassioned manifesto. 'Let us plant the flag of peace,' he concluded. 'War alone to those who could wish war in this world.' He signed an appeal composed by Karl Marx, Louis Blanc and all the eminent French and German emigrés in London calling on their respective peoples to foil the plans of the tyrants by refusing to fight each other. Their plea ended with the words of the *Marseillaise*: 'The people are for us brethren, and the tyrants enemies'.[4] They were labouring under the misapprehension that the war was the tyrant Napoleon's doing. It was not.

The *Marseillaise* was being sung everywhere in a quite different mood, the tricolor was waved and venerated as it had not been for decades. Theatres staged plays on the theme of 1792, tableaux with the Goddess of Liberty holding the tricolor and real soldiers on stage, while audiences knelt and joined in the choruses. The desire for war was strong and deep. 'At last we are going to know the delights of massacre,' wrote one columnist. 'Let the blood of Prussians flow in torrents, in waterfalls, with the divine fury of the flood! Let the wretch who merely dares to utter the word "peace" be immediately shot like a dog and flung into the sewer!'[5] In such circumstances it would have been a brave man who raised the possibility of defeat. Yet the French army was in poor shape, its officer corps was stuck in a set of rigid attitudes, and its infrastructure was incapable of dealing with the transport and supply problems of modern warfare. The Prussians quickly gained the upper hand, as a result of good organization as much as anything else. On 31 August, after a desultory campaign, Napoleon III was obliged to surrender with the main body of his army at Sedan. That should have been the end of that, particularly in view of what now took place in Paris.

When, on 3 September, news of the disaster of Sedan was announced in the capital, crowds spilled out on to the streets. The following day they overran the Palais Bourbon, and, in a repeat of the events of 1848, then marched to the Hôtel de Ville, where a provisional government was formed and the Second Republic proclaimed. A carnival atmosphere spread through the city. Somewhat disingenuously considering the strident jingoism of the preceding weeks, the people of France now adopted the line that the war had been launched by the wicked emperor, and that since he was no more the French could reach out to the Germans with an olive branch. Naively, they imagined that this would be accepted with no hard feelings, and that everything would return to normal.

The Germans could not see it like that. As Bismarck had foreseen and counted on, the war stirred ancient animosities which a couple of victories did little to appease. The mood of 1813 was abroad in Germany, intensified by the aggressive posturing of the French, and strengthened in its righteousness by the early success of German arms. The victories of 1813 had failed to assuage the wounded pride or to resolve the cultural complexes of the Germans. But those of 1870 were of a different order, and the date of Sedan was proposed as the German national day. This is revealing; in their choice of national holiday, nations usually chose not an anniversary of conquest, but one of liberation. The Germans of 1870 did see in the humiliation of the French at Sedan a liberation from their cultural ascendancy. Richard Wagner, who worked himself into a paroxysm of excitement over the German victories, felt confident enough to write a comedy (sic) in which he mocked the French.

The war had been launched with no territorial aims, but the victories naturally awakened German greed, and demands for the annexation of Alsace and Lorraine were voiced. At a practical level, no German government could consider settling for anything less than a new frontier that would guarantee safety from French belligerence in the future. At the popular level, Germany required the total humiliation of France as a nation.

The unthinkable had happened. What had started as a war between two monarchs had turned into war to the death between two peoples. As in 1813, the German cause was draped in the cloak of spiritual mission, with the German press baying for the destruction of the 'modern Babylon' that was Paris, of which no stone should remain standing. But this only thinly veiled their real joy at humiliating a nation that had for so long made them feel culturally inferior. An equally dubious figleaf covered what was in effect no more or less than France's struggle for survival as a power. On 5 September, the day after the declaration of the republic, Victor Hugo steamed into the Gare du Nord from exile, greeted by a vast crowd. His arrival was a statement. It proclaimed that France had reassumed her role as the torch-bearer of liberty and the guardian of the values of 1789, and that her cause was once again the cause of humanity. 'When France fights for the Republic, she fights for the liberty of the world', in the words of one journalist. All the rhetoric and the imagery of 1792 were trotted out, and there was much talk of a *guerre à outrance*, a war to the end based on the Spanish model of 1808.

As the German armies closed in on Paris, to which they laid siege on 23 September, part of the provisional government and the army command retired to Tours where, under the leadership of the Minister of the Interior, Léon Gambetta, it struggled to marshal the forces of France. The situation was by no means desperate, since only a fraction of the country's potential had been mobilized to date, and there were still plenty of troops holding out in fortresses such as Belfort and Metz in the German rear.

Volunteers of every kind crawled out of the towns and the villages, representing the whole spectrum of French politics, from white-flag-waving legitimists in the Vendée to black anarchists. Suspicious of the French army, which was disdainful of them, they formed up companies of *francs-tireurs*, which allowed them to operate according to their own political convictions and express their aesthetic preferences through unusual uniforms and bizarre names. But the overwhelming majority of the population remained apathetic, and even most of the officer corps had lost faith in the possibility of victory.

But if this was not Spain in 1808, there was enough irregular skirmishing to give the Germans the impression that the French were not playing fair. They had started off very correctly, paying for supplies and refraining from rapine, but as they started to suffer losses from the activities of *francs-tireurs* and even civilians, they began to exact reprisals. They were encouraged in this by the American Civil War General William Tecumseh Sherman, who was observing the proceedings as a guest of the German staff. 'The proper strategy', Sherman declared after Sedan, 'consists in inflicting as telling blows as possible on the enemy's army, and then in causing the inhabitants so much suffering that they must long for peace, and force the government to demand it. The people must be left nothing but their eyes to weep with over the war.'[6] Bismarck saw the logic of this and recommended stern measures, though he stopped short of military terrorism and rebuked his wife when she wrote that all the French should be 'shot and stabbed to death, down to the little babies'.[7] All captured *francs-tireurs* were nevertheless denied combatant status and shot out of hand, and treatment of civilians grew progressively harsher.

At the start of the war, Kossuth telegraphed Bismarck offering a Hungarian Legion to fight on the German side.[8] Garibaldi had welcomed the thought of 'the noble Germanic nation at last rewarding Napoleon for all his villainies'. He had never liked the French. But once the republic had been declared he saw in France only the cradle of 1789 and a sister nation in peril, and on 6 September he wrote offering his sword in her service.[9] He was whisked off Caprera in a private yacht by French disciples, and came ashore at Marseille on 7 October, cheered by crowds lining the dockside. He went straight to Tours to see Gambetta.

Garibaldi was not the only one to rally to the cause of France. Her dramatic defeat rekindled affection in many hearts. In his poem *Quia Multum Amavit*, Swinburne encapsulates the feelings of many, representing France as a daughter of heaven who has fallen and become a harlot, but, like a repentant Magdalen, is forgiven because she has loved deeply. From distant Mexico, Benito Juárez offered helpful suggestions on how to organize a *guerilla*.[10] On 14 September Bakunin, horrified at the idea of German soldiers trampling the holy ground that had nourished the seed of 1789, arrived in Lyon, where he established a 'Committee for Saving France'. He made rousing speeches which were cheered to the rafters, and on 26 September issued a manifesto declaring the state to have been abolished. 'The French people resumes full control of its destinies,' he announced.[11] Astonishingly, it took a full two weeks before the whole enterprise disintegrated into farce and Bakunin was forced to slip away. He then went to Marseille, where a sister non-state had been founded by some of his acolytes.

Equally astonishing is that Gambetta managed to survive the enthusiastic attentions of all those coming to offer their services. They included the regular cast of Italians, Poles, Spaniards, Irishmen and Americans, led by Mierosławski and Wysocki with rival schemes. Gambetta was severely tested by the arrival of Garibaldi; his very name was an offence to French Catholics and conservatives, and he was regarded as an enemy bandit by the army establishment. Gambetta offered him the command of a few hundred Italian volunteers who had gathered at Chambéry. Realizing that he was being sidelined, Garibaldi threatened to return to Caprera. Much as he would have liked to be rid of the old hero, Gambetta knew that this would reflect poorly on France – Garibaldi was still a worldwide legend. So he gave him command of all the *francs-tireurs* operating in eastern France, whom he was to form up into a single corps, to be known as the Armée des Vosges.

By 14 October Garibaldi was at his headquarters in Dôle, and set about organizing the various volunteer units he found there. He was assisted by Jean Philippe Bordone, who had served under him in the Cacciatori delle Alpi and in Sicily in 1860, and who now became chief of staff of the Armée des Vosges. Two days later, Hauke-Bosak arrived on the scene. Garibaldi gave him command of the first of his four brigades, the strongest, with some 4,250 men. The second was entrusted to Cristiano Lobbia, the third and fourth to Garibaldi's sons Menotti and Ricciotti respectively.

The assemblage of men under Garibaldi's command did not promise much. Numbers varied considerably, but never rose higher than about 16,000. They were armed with a dozen different makes of rifle, uniformed in as many different styles, and commanded in all the languages of Europe. There was a core of Gardes Mobiles, conscripts of little military value; some French volunteer units whose names, such as Les Franc-Tireurs de la Mort and Les Enfants Perdus, suggest their outlook, and about 1,000 redshirts, made up of the usual assortment of young Italian poets, students and adventurers, as well as veteran *garibaldini*. There were a couple of hundred Poles, and Bosak's brigade included an English company and a Spanish one. Hanging about Garibaldi's headquarters was Fra' Pantaleo from Sicily, and there to nurse the wounded, faithful as ever, was Jesse White Mario. But, as one French officer put it, 'in the Armée des Vosges, there was faith'.[12]

Garibaldi's never wavered. In his letter to the French government Garibaldi had offered 'what remains of myself', and that was indeed not very much.[13] His ox-like constitution undermined by a life of hardship and privation, one leg rendered virtually unusable by two bad wounds that had never been allowed to heal properly, and his whole body gripped by arthritis, he needed to be carried about on a stretcher much of the time. But he never lost heart. In letter after letter, he expressed his firm conviction that the people of France, aided by the faithful from other lands, would triumph. The scale of the struggle only promised a more glorious conclusion – perhaps the shock of defeat would bring down the tyrants of Germany, and, after them, those of Austria and Russia. At the end of October, when his army had more or less taken shape, he issued a proclamation which spelt out their doctrine. 'Drawn up under the banners of human brotherhood, all national differences must disappear, and we must march together to conquer a liberty which alone can bring to life the great humanitarian principle.'[14]

The Armée des Vosges went into action at the beginning of November 1870. Garibaldi moved up to Autun, from where he began to launch probing attacks on the Germans occupying Dijon. On 14 November Ricciotti's brigade made a lightning raid into the German rear at Châtillon, defeating a column of General von Werder's corps, and on 26 November Garibaldi attacked Dijon itself. He was initially successful and entered the town. But the German armies of 1870 were not Neapolitan or Papal levies. They had been thrown at first by the unexpected manoeuvres and the sheer dash of the *garibaldini*, but once they had recovered from their surprise, they moved against them in force. And, out in the open, Garibaldi's volunteers were no match for the regulars. After a bloody two-day battle they were forced to abandon Dijon and fall back.

The French had meanwhile assembled a large army under General Bourbaki which was to move eastwards out of central France, relieve the fortress of Belfort and then sweep up into the rear of the German forces besieging Paris. The Armée des Vosges was assigned the task of covering its rear. Accordingly, Garibaldi advanced in a northerly direction, and on 29 December took up positions around Dijon, which had been vacated by the Germans. His brief was to prevent General Manteuffel from sweeping up from the west and threatening the rear of Bourbaki, who had just marched through in a north-easterly direction towards Belfort.

'Never, dear ones, have I desired as I desire now to be twenty years younger,' he wrote to friends in Genoa on the last day of 1870. 'I consider this war as the most important one of my life. I am thankful to see the cause of the Republic take a favourable turn. I have never doubted of the final triumph, and now doubt less than ever. The spirit of these populations has revived. Men of all ages rally to the standard. You see from my writing that my hand is infirm, but for the rest I am in excellent health, and can mount horse without difficulty.'[15] But the next day he fell ill, and over the next two weeks the Armée des Vosges adopted a largely defensive role. This was partly due to supply problems (they were all freezing without greatcoats in one of the worst winters on record) and partly because the French regular forces on his wings consistently refused to cooperate with him.

On 21 January Garibaldi's forces were vigorously attacked by a strong German army under General Kettler. Garibaldi was so ill that he was obliged to exercise command from a carriage. His men fought magnificently, twice repulsing the Germans, and pursuing them as far as Pouilly, where they captured a regimental colour. But these heroics were of little avail. While Kettler was being given a hard time by Garibaldi, Manteuffel marched past behind him and fell on Bourbaki's rear. Worse, they had taken a terrible toll in Garibaldi's ranks, picking off the bravest and the best. On 21 January, at Hauteville outside Dijon, Józef Hauke-Bosak was killed by a bullet in the chest while leading his men to the attack. When they recovered his body they observed that he had died with a beatific smile on his face. But if he had found peace at last, his death was a terrible blow to the cause.

An equally painful, and more poignant, loss was that of the young poet Giorgio Imbriani. Born in Naples during the revolution of 1848, he was named after Washington. The defeat of the revolution forced his family to flee, and he was brought up in Piedmont. He attended the military academy in Turin, but rejected an army career in favour of literature. In 1866 the eighteen-year-old enlisted under Garibaldi, and was as disgusted by the diplomatic outcome of the war as his commander. In a letter to a friend he said he wished he had died in battle rather than having to witness the shame. The following year he marched into the Papal States with Garibaldi and experienced the humiliation of Mentana. But his faith remained unshaken, and he had preceded Garibaldi to France, where he donned the red shirt. 'We are face to face with the enemy,' he wrote to his father from Dôle on 31 October, 'never before have there been soldiers more convinced and more dedicated to a more noble cause.' His letters home reproduce feelings little short of ecstasy. 'I am here at my post of honour,' he wrote on 12 November, 'at the post assigned to me by my convictions and my faith, at the post of glory and danger.' He died at his post outside Dijon on the same day as Hauke-Bosak, aged twenty-two. 'He had the faith of a martyr, the love and the passion of an apostle,' in the words of one of his friends.[16]

As they mourned their heroes, the redshirts heard the news that on 29 January Paris had capitulated and an armistice had been signed. With the fighting stopped, the provisional government held elections to a new National Assembly, to meet at Bordeaux for practical reasons. Garibaldi was among those elected (he had been put forward in Paris), as were other prominent figures of the revolutionary tradition such as Victor Hugo. But the overwhelming majority of the vote had gone to candidates from the Right, including monarchists. When Garibaldi walked into the Chamber on 13 February, he was met with a hurricane of invective from the other Deputies, who questioned his right as a foreigner to represent Frenchmen. After vainly trying to make himself heard through the shouting, he resigned his seat and left for Caprera. Victor Hugo spoke up for him, pointing out that he had been the only general on the French side to capture an enemy standard, but this provoked uproar and accusations of insulting the French nation. He too eventually went off in disgust.

There was more to Hugo's and Garibaldi's gestures than personal pique. Both were violently opposed to the armistice, which ceded Alsace and Lorraine to Germany (the king of Prussia had been acclaimed emperor of a unified Germany at Versailles during the siege of Paris), and imposed humiliating restrictions and reparations on France. They saw it as a betrayal of the nation, and the ratification of the armistice by the Assembly did nothing to change this view, which was shared by many patriots and by large sections of the population of Paris, which had been deeply affected by the four months of the siege.

The process had begun with the reconstitution of the National Guard, abolished by Napoleon III. A total of 300,000 men were called up from all classes of the population, which meant that the National Guard would no longer be a middle-class force for law and order. It grew more radical in spirit during the siege as several hundred foreigners joined its ranks, some of them members of the Workers' International who had homed in on Paris after the proclamation of the republic.

The moment the spirit of 1792 had been invoked, some began to contemplate going on to 1793. The first attempt at armed revolt had come just ten days after the start of the siege. It was whipped up and led by Gustave Flourens, a figure symptomatic of the inchoate political scene in the capital, a spoilt middle-class boy, intelligent but restless of spirit. In 1866 he had gone to Crete in support of the rebellion against Turkish rule. Back in Paris, he made such a nuisance of himself that he was forced to flee to England in 1869 to avoid prison, and he returned to a hero's welcome after the declaration of the Second Republic on 4 September

1870. Tall and slender, with blond hair and piercing blue eyes, he cut a dashing, if slightly androgynous figure. He joined the National Guard and got himself elected commander of one of the Belleville battalions. Scorning the regulation blue uniform, he had a 'Cretan' one made, and, having somehow procured the finest horses looted from the imperial stables, assumed a quite unwarranted prominence as he pranced about on them. On 2 October he led five battalions of the National Guard on the Hôtel de Ville, seat of the provisional government, but withdrew after a certain amount of bluster. He tried again on 31 October, when news of the fall of Metz reached the capital, with little more success. As the siege ground on, most Parisians were more interested in where their next meal was coming from than political upheaval, and they greeted the armistice with relief.

But there was no avoiding the humiliation, particularly as the Germans demanded the right to march triumphally into Paris as a symbol of their victory. And the workers of the poor *quartiers* saw in the armistice not so much the coming of peace as the probable destruction of their revolutionary work. They were a much stronger force than they had been in 1848, and while they were not very articulate in political terms, they were fired by a sense of patriotism and felt the shame of the capitulation as keenly as anyone. So did a number of junior army officers and intellectuals, and sundry others with nothing to lose or determined to lose everything, including their lives. Paris began to draw in free spirits of every kind, such as the nobleman Arthur de Fonvielle, who had previously gone all the way to the Caucasus to fight under Shamil for the freedom of the hill-tribes; François Rochebrune, erstwhile commander of the 'Zouaves of Death'; and the beautiful Elizabeth Dimitriev, who had left her husband and befriended Marx, who sent her to Paris to promote revolution. To such people, Paris had become, in the words of the journalist and minor novelist Jules Vallès, the 'Fatherland of honour, city of salvation, bivouac of the revolution'.[17]

The ignominious capitulation of 28 January and the humiliation of the German parade (after which Parisians went out and scrubbed the cobbles they had marched over with soap and bleach) combined with the February general election, which showed that the provinces were overwhelmingly right-wing, to generate a profound sense of alienation in the capital. And this was to be ignited into revolution by the actions of the government formed by the former Orleanist minister Adolphe Thiers, which had taken up temporary abode in Versailles. It began clamping down on left-wing activity, suspending publications and arresting key figures. It nominated an unpopular general to command the National Guard, and set about drawing its teeth.

On the morning of 18 March the army was ordered to remove from the custody of the National Guard a couple of hundred cannon left over from the siege and parked innocuously on the Butte Montmartre. The troops marched in, but while they were wondering how to drag the guns out of town, a crowd gathered. The soldiers began to fraternize with the civilians, and then with members of the National Guard who came to defend their cannon. Officers were shot, two generals were butchered, and the mood of the streets grew increasingly ugly. That evening the remainder of troops loyal to the government withdrew from the city, along with all its representatives. The red flag was hoisted on the Hôtel de Ville, and ten days later the Paris Commune formally installed itself, in a carnivalesque atmosphere of rejoicing which somehow obliterated the shame of the capitulation. Even the whores appeared on the streets dressed as *cantinières* of 1792. And it was in this festive spirit of blind optimism that Paris entered on the worst two months of its history.

On 2 April the Versailles government's troops took up offensive positions to the west and south-west of Paris, and on the following day the forces of the Commune marched out to confront them. There was an unreal quality to this sortie, with Flourens striking brave attitudes and waving his scimitar. They marched out in the belief that they only had to show themselves for the *versaillais* to turn and flee, a belief rooted in the mythology of Valmy. But a single salvo from the heavy guns in the fortress of Mont Valérien cut the column in half and sent the second half scuttling back in disarray, while the other extricated itself as best it could from the advancing *versaillais*. Flourens, who was among the latter group, achieved his moment of glory in death.

After this débâcle, the Commune nominated a new commander-in-chief, Gustave Cluseret, a regular French officer who had won the Légion d'Honneur for putting down the revolution in Paris in June 1848, he had served in the Crimea, where he was wounded, and then in Algeria, where he was cashiered for pilfering. He had then gone to seek his fortune in America, and in 1860 he brought a group of Americans to join Garibaldi in Sicily. The following year he volunteered for the Union Army, passing out with the rank of brigadier-general. He had then fallen in with the

Fenians and plotted insurrection in Canada in support of Ireland's liberty, subsequently taking the struggle closer to home, by playing a part in the 1867 attack on Chester gaol. While in London, he had teamed up with Bakunin, helping him to stage his coup in Lyon in September 1870. After being forced to leave that city, Cluseret proclaimed the Commune at Marseille and nominated himself 'Commander of the Armies of the South'. 'He appeared to have neither fixed principles, depth of knowledge nor serious experience,' according to his chief of staff. 'A distinguished youth, he had grown into a mediocre man.'[18] Cluseret whipped the National Guard into shape by tightening discipline, dismissing inefficient officers, banning some of the more outlandish uniforms, and generally introducing a sense of professionalism. He then put in place a command structure.

As his chief of staff he chose one of the most able French soldiers of his time, a man who in other circumstances would certainly have had a stunning career – Louis Nathaniel Rossel. Rossel had everything of the young Bonaparte about him. Dark and fine-featured, he was hard-working, taciturn and apparently uninterested in the pursuit of pleasure. Spiritually, he was a child of Michelet – devoted to a republican mother-France. By the age of twenty-five he was a captain of engineers, and a year later, in 1870, he found himself besieged with Marshal Bazaine's army in the fortress of Metz. He tried to stage a coup by junior officers to wrench command from the passive brass hats, and escaped when Bazaine surrendered the fortress. He made his way via Belgium to Tours, where he offered his services to Gambetta.

'The future is mine, as much and more than anyone else's,' Rossel wrote to his sister in December 1870, 'nobody understands war and few desire it; I desire it and I understand it.'[19] He was all the more sickened by the armistice signed a month later, and when he heard of the events of 18 March in Paris, he resigned his commission and offered his services to the Commune. He was not driven by any political sympathy for it. 'My departure [for Paris] was a sacrifice more than anything else,' he explained. 'In the midst of the disaster and given the collapse of morale throughout the country, the Parisian revolutionary faction was the only possible cause left.'[20]

To command the 1st Army, defending the western approaches of Paris against the main thrust of the *versaillais* attack, Cluseret chose Jarosław Dąbrowski, the man intended to lead the rising in Poland eight years before. He had been arrested by the Russians before its outbreak, but as they could pin nothing on him, he was only sentenced to fifteen years' hard labour. Like Rossel, he was a young man in a hurry, and he managed to escape from the prison convoy as it passed through Moscow. Evading the Tsarist police, he made his way to Stockholm and then Paris. In 1866 he had started raising a Polish Legion there to take advantage of the Austro-Prussian War and assist a planned insurrection in Hungary, and in 1870 he joined the Paris National Guard. Dąbrowski was small, with an agile physique tempered in battle with the hill tribes of the Caucasus as a Tsarist officer in the late 1850s. He looked much younger than his thirty-five years but exuded an almost dictatorial authority, and his subordinates jumped to his commands. 'There was good, quiet, firm, undemonstrative stuff here, whatever there might be elsewhere,' noted a British journalist on visiting his Neuilly headquarters.[21]

On 29 April the *versaillais* managed to storm the fort of Issy, dominating the south-western sector of the city's defences, and although Cluseret personally led the attack that recaptured it, he was nevertheless arrested by the Committee of Public Safety which had taken over the running of the Commune. His post was assumed by Rossel, who left Dąbrowski in command of all the right-bank defences, including the main front at Neuilly. The south-western sector he gave to General Napoleon La Cecilia, the son of a Neapolitan officer and veteran of the 1820 rising. A mathematics teacher by profession, La Cecilia had sailed with Garibaldi as one of the Thousand at the age of twenty-five. He had commanded the artillery at the Battle of Palermo and distinguished himself in various engagements, so much so that he had been offered rank in the Piedmontese army. He refused, and gave himself over to teaching Sanskrit in Naples and later mathematics at the university of Ulm. In 1870 he had volunteered to fight for France as a *franc-tireur.* One year older than Dąbrowski, he was his antithesis in every way. Thin and gangly, balding and hideously pock-marked, he bubbled with energy and enthusiasm.

The southern sector Rossel gave to another Pole, General Walery Wróblewski. A minor nobleman from Poland's eastern marches like Dąbrowski, he was born in the same year, and the two had become friends at university. He had commanded a cavalry unit in the January Insurrection and been badly wounded, but had escaped and made his way to France. Rossel's new chief of staff was General August Okołowicz, who had served in the Polish Legion in the Crimean War and in the Armée des Vosges.

This preponderance of Poles in the highest posts reflects the problems Rossel was having in finding Frenchmen prepared to serve the Commune. As the *versaillais* troops closed in, the leaders of the Commune grew more radical (even adopting the old revolutionary calendar and turning May 1871 into Floréal of the year 79), and the majority of the inhabitants drifted further away from it. Instead of defending the city, many went into hiding and prayed for the speedy success of the government troops. By 7 May Rossel was convinced of the pointlessness of defending the cause, and two days later, tipped off that he was about to be arrested, went into hiding himself.

His place in overall command was taken by Dąbrowski, and on the following day Wróblewski took over the sector of La Cecilia, who had fallen ill. So by 10 May the forces of the Commune were under the command of two 35-year-old Polish minor nobles whose every trait betrayed their descent from those who had left their small estates in Lithuania and Volhynia in 1768 to fight for the holy cause in the Confederation of Bar. Aside from some four hundred of their own countrymen, a clutch of other foreigners and a handful of middle-class or aristocratic idealists, such as the Comte de Beaufort, who commanded a unit of communards, they were leading people with whom they had nothing in common. The forces of the Commune were now made up primarily of the National Guards from the poorer *quartiers*, the grimy and stunted denizens of Belleville, who had no option but to die in the defence of their revolution.

Over the next ten days, the forces of the Commune managed to repel all the attacks of the *versaillais*, and to retake all forts temporarily lost. This they did despite heavy shelling from the big guns trained on them from the heights outside Paris, and in defiance of the reality that spelled out the ultimate hopelessness of their cause.

On 21 May government troops managed to penetrate the perimeter defences. Once inside, they proved impossible to expel, and began a gradual advance into the heart of the city. Although there was an intricate system of concentric defences in place, based on barricades built across streets, it was now only a matter of days before the Commune was crushed. Dąbrowski's forces began to melt away as the men went off, individually or in groups, to look to the defence of their own *quartiers*. Requests for reinforcements were ignored by the Committee of Public Safety, which was adopting a Neronian attitude; while the *versaillais* troops advanced, blasting barricade after barricade with their cannon, the Commune embarked on a cultural purge of the capital under the direction of the painter Gustave Courbet, who saw himself as a latter-day David. The column in the Place Vendôme was ceremonially toppled and smashed to pieces, with guardsmen who should have been manning the barricades taking turns to spit on the prone statue of Napoleon; the Tuileries were burned down, and Notre Dame only escaped destruction for lack of time.

On 22 May, Dąbrowski contacted the Germans surrounding the northern and eastern perimeter of the city, requesting free passage for himself and other Polish officers.[22] There could have been no more eloquent admission that they no longer had a cause to fight for in Paris. When permission was refused, he courted death by leading a company of communard sailors to recapture a barricade on the rue Myrrha. Mortally wounded, he was taken to the Lariboisière Hospital, where he died. His body was covered with a red flag and borne ceremonially, with National Guards presenting arms, to the Hôtel de Ville, where it lay in state the whole of that night and the following day. On the evening of 24 May it was carried in procession to the cemetery of Père Lachaise. When it reached the Place de la Bastille, the cortège was halted and Dąbrowski's body was laid out at the foot of the great column. There it lay, illuminated by flaming torches, while hundreds of communard soldiers filed past to pay their last respects, many of them kneeling to kiss his brow.

The *versaillais* advanced inexorably from the west and swept round the northern *quartiers*, towards the eastern communard seedbeds of Belleville and the Faubourg St-Antoine. Only in the south were they being held at bay. Wróblewski had carried on an energetic defence, personally leading bayonet charges to recapture lost territory, but as the numbers of his troops dwindled, he was forced to fall back on the forts of Montrouge, Bicêtre and Ivry, and then on the small rise called the Butte aux Cailles, from which he held off the *versaillais* for four more days. On 25 May he reluctantly obeyed the command to evacuate the left bank, and withdrew across the Pont d'Austerlitz with his last 1,000 men and all his cannon. Wróblewski was offered overall command, but when he realized the extent of the rout, he declined. He took a rifle and went off to fight as a simple soldier to the end. This came on 28 May. The remaining forces of the Commune made a final stand on the barricade of the Château d'Eau, led by a huge *garibaldino* clutching the red flag. The last shots were fired by communards who knew they had no way out, among the graves of the great Romantics in the cemetery of Père Lachaise.

22
Afterlife

Karl Marx hailed the Paris Commune as the fulfilment of the promise of 1830 and 1848, a vital stage in the continuous process begun in 1789, and 'a new point of departure of world-historic importance'.[1] The extent to which his followers accepted this vision of it as a new dawn can be gauged from the fact that Lenin was wrapped in a communard flag at his obsequies, and the first Russian spacecraft carried on board a ribbon from a communard banner. But these gestures tell us more about the seedy, relic-obsessed culture of Soviet Russia than about the essence of the Commune which Flaubert, perhaps more appropriately, described as 'the last manifestation of the Middle Ages'.[2]

There was certainly something of the convulsive spasm about it, and it was, in part at least, the final manifestation of the religious cult of the nation, whose cause had expired back in 1848. Few had understood the lessons of that year with the same intense clarity and pain as Herzen. 'Everything sacred that we loved, for which we struggled, for which we made sacrifices, has been betrayed by life, betrayed by history, betrayed for her own ends – she needs madmen as a ferment, and cares not what becomes of them when they recover; they have served her turn – let them live out their crippled lives in hospital!' he almost ranted in his despair.[3]

Many of his peers had hung on to their faith grimly and refused to be confined in the hospitals, coming forward every time the bugle sounded the call to battle. But each time there were fewer of them. Some died, some lost their faith, some gave up, some faced up to their failure – like Harro Harring, who ended his life in 1870 in a shabby hotel room in

London by swallowing phosphorus matches. After 1871 there were no believers left – even Mazzini and Garibaldi had lost their faith.

'I had hoped to evoke the soul of Italy,' Mazzini wrote from exile in Switzerland, 'and instead find merely her inanimate corpse.'[4] Italy was united, but she had not been reborn in an act of self-sacrifice – unification had been achieved through a series of '*combinazioni*'. It had been an opportunistic, low-cost business: the total losses in all the risings and military operations since 1815 added up to less than those of one day in the Franco-Prussian War.[5] The process was hailed as the Risorgimento, the national resurgence, but it was nothing of the sort: a handful of patriots had been manipulated by a jackal monarchy and its pragmatic ministers. And the last act of 1870 had been the most opportunistic of all.

With Garibaldi safely out of the way in Dôle and all French troops called back to defend their motherland, Victor Emmanuel had marched into the Papal States. His agents fomented a small insurrection in the city by supporters of Mazzini and Garibaldi, so that he could pose as the champion of its people. At the same time he assured the Pope that he was only coming to protect him. To lend credibility to this argument, he had 30,000 of the insurgents and other assorted suspects put to death, while accepting 'the will of the people' that he should make Rome the capital of his kingdom.[6]

'It was a different Italy that I had dreamed of all my life,' Garibaldi admitted a couple of years before his death.[7] And when this came, in 1882, he was betrayed once more. He had left detailed instructions that his body should be burned on a pyre on Caprera, but the Italian government overruled his will and staged a pompous funeral for its own propaganda purposes. Mazzini received no such honours. He remained an exile, and people continued to be arrested for reading his books just as they had been in the days of the hated Austrians. When he died, Italian police confiscated wreaths placed outside his birthplace in Genoa and banned public manifestations of grief. In official accounts the authorities described him as a dangerous enemy of Italian unification.

In the circumstances, it is hardly surprising that some of the old crusaders went a little mad. 'I am learning to bark, as I am conversing aloud only with dogs,' wrote Kossuth, who was living alone outside Turin, 'I also whisper to flowers the way lovers do.'[8] Others had to be restrained in asylums. Bakunin went off at a tangent of Romantic anarchism that allowed Marx to secure his exclusion from the International. There was no room for such spiritual errantry in the new scientific politics.

The Quixotic tradition did not die out entirely. Some former *garibaldini* went out to fight for the republican cause in Spain in 1874, a few redshirts were to be found supporting the rising against the Turks in Bosnia-Herzegovina the following year, there were Poles fighting for Cuban independence and an international force of red-shirted volunteers in the Cretan rising of 1897, not to mention a couple of hundred Russian volunteers who went out to support the Boers in their struggle against British oppression. Lone acts of heroism or lunacy, often both, continued to be perpetrated by people clinging to the wreckage of the great ark of national redemption. The man who assassinated Archduke Charles at Sarajevo in 1914 was a member of a movement calling itself Young Bosnia. There have been haunting visitations even more recently.

On 8 October 1967 a battalion of Bolivian Army Rangers trapped a group of *guerrilleros* in a scrubby gully east of Sucre. Two were captured alive: a Bolivian fighter known as 'Willy' and Ernest 'Che' Guevara, hero of the Cuban revolution. 'What made you decide to operate in our country?' asked the Bolivian colonel interrogating him. ' Can't you see the state in which the peasants live?' retorted Che, 'they are almost like savages, living in a state of poverty that depresses the heart, having only one room in which to sleep and cook and no clothing to wear, abandoned like animals . . .' The colonel pointed out that conditions on Cuba were no better. 'No. That's not true,' Che fired back. 'I don't deny that in Cuba poverty exists, but [at least] the peasants there have an illusion of progress, whereas the Bolivian lives without hope . . .'[9] This determination to foist their own illusions and their own hopes on others, whether they like it or not, is a characteristic of believers.

In 1781 Lafayette's friend Ségur was very taken with the simple way of life of the Shakers of Newport, Rhode Island, and particularly with one of them, Polly Leiton. 'Her dress was as white as her complexion; the muslin of her ample kerchief, the jealous batiste which almost denied me the sight of her blond hair, and all the attributes of a pure and intelligent maiden seemed to combine vainly to hide from us the most seductive attractions,' he records. 'Her eyes seemed to reflect, like two mirrors, the gentleness of a pure and tender heart; she received us with a confident naivety which charmed me, and the familiarity prescribed by the sect to which she belonged gave our fresh acquaintance the appearance of an old friendship. I doubt whether any masterpiece of art could have eclipsed this masterpiece of nature.' Wishing to establish his credentials as a dashing paladin, Ségur explained that he had given up everything in order to come and defend her liberty against the English. 'The English have done you no wrong, and our liberty does not concern you,' she retorted. 'One should never involve oneself in the affairs of others, unless it should be to make peace and prevent the shedding of blood.'[10]

This reply should not have surprised a young man who had certainly read Voltaire's *Candide* – assuming he had understood its message. But it did, because Ségur and Lafayette could not accept the rationalism of Voltaire. They were Romantics. They rejected the head in favour of the heart; they recoiled, not just from reason but from unbelief. And they were aristocrats, not in the habit of asking the lower orders for an opinion. That was why they did not pause to consider whether the majority of the North American continent's inhabitants would benefit from their chivalrous intervention. Whether Polly Leiton liked it or not, they would deliver into the world a miraculous new nation.

Like true crusaders, they sailed off home with a light conscience, blissfully oblivious of the fact that they might have done more harm than good – it is idle to speculate, but worth remembering that the slave trade was abolished by Britain half a century before the land of the free got round to it. More to the point, these young men bent on bringing into being a prelapsarian utopia had helped to create a state which not only carried all the taints of the old world they were so desperate to save it from, but which also felt obliged to ape it by reproducing hierarchies and mythologies in which it revels to this day. Paul Revere spurs are as numerous in American museums today as the proverbial fragments of the True Cross in medieval Europe, and millions of pilgrims every year visit the house of Betsy Ross, who made the American flag, resolutely ignoring the reality that it was not her house and that she did not make the flag. Much the same kind of dubious mythological baggage has been harnessed in support of all supposedly modern and secular forms of government. And where new states have come into being, they have invariably swaddled themselves in sacred symbols and shibboleths forged in more dedicated struggles, beginning with an often random tricolor and a national anthem of no resonance.

The hundred years following the death of Lafayette have gone down in history as the age of nationalism, with the two world wars standing as monuments to the horrors it can lead to. But this is a very different kind of nationalism from that which fired the gallant marquis. It made itself felt first in Germany, in 1813. It was a distorted offshoot of the compulsion to seek salvation through national regeneration, and grew into its very negation by seeking it through the assertion of a single nation over others. A not dissimilar reflex caused a Russian society cut off from the mainstream and ashamed of its backwardness to take refuge in a paranoid redemptive vision of a holy essence within Russia that led inexorably to state-worship and a zealous contempt for the allegedly corrupt rest of the world.

Even France, *La Grande Nation* and cradle of the faith, drifted into a defensive nationalism after the trauma of 1870–1. In the 1880s Ernest Renan, a spiritual heir to Michelet, attempted to define a more up-to-date and secular version of the national faith, as 'a great solidarity, based on the awareness of the sacrifices which one has made and those which one is prepared to make'.[11] At first, the French concentrated on the memories. Paul Déroulède founded the Ligue des Patriotes, which went on pilgrimages to the battlefields of the Franco-Prussian War, pausing to pray on each one as though they had been stations of the cross. But this obituary cult grew exclusive and xenophobic, and when, in the next decade, the Dreyfus affair suggested that the army (which, since 1790, *was* the nation) was being infiltrated and corrupted by Jews, it exploded into aggressive racism. The new nationalism henceforth defined itself against the German and the Jewish threat, and lost whatever was left of the spirit of 1792 during the *débandade* of 1940.

Similar distortions took place elsewhere. In Poland, the Left continued to pursue the vision of a brotherhood of nations, but in the last decade of the nineteenth century a new form of exclusive nationalism, based on language and religion, emerged in definition against the perceived threat posed by Germans, Ruthenes and Jews. In Italy, where national sentiment remained the preserve of an educated minority, Mussolini would apply Rousseau in an effort to create the nation Mazzini had imagined. The attempt was ostensibly successful, but it rested on too many fictions and relied too heavily on the military element; when nemesis came the whole structure fell apart, and Italy went back to being something of a geographical expression. To walk through the sanctuary of banners in the bowels of the Victor Emmanuel monument in Rome today is to enter the temple of a dead civilization.

All the efforts of Lafayette, Kościuszko and Garibaldi, and all the faith of Mazzini, Mickiewicz and Michelet, were defeated by the fundamental truth that the people they sought to liberate and make happy were, like Polly Leiton, simply not interested. At the same time, the defenders of the *status quo* reacted with such vehemence to the ideological threat posed by these relatively innocuous idealists, that they drove them and particularly their heirs towards more extreme ideas and more ruthless methods of carrying them through.

Unable to establish the nation's sovereignty through some kind of ecstatic self-fulfilment, many sought to assert it through cultural or racial superiority. The National Guards and militias which incarnated the active citizen and should have stood in defence of civil liberty turned into populist pretorians assuming the role of saviour of the nation's honour and guardian of its spiritual purity from the supposed corruption of allegedly venal politicians, paving the way for militarist dictatorships of the Right and the Left, from Bonaparte to Hitler and from Bolívar to Pinochet.

In view of the impossibility of achieving spiritual nirvana for the people, a new generation of crusaders embraced socialism. They brought to it the internationalism preached by Mazzini and Mickiewicz, thereby endowing it with not only universal relevance but also a sacred duty to subvert the world. They imbued it with the sense of brotherhood that united the members of all the secret societies from the Carbonari to Young Europe, which was later turned into the dominance of the collective over the individual. They inspired it with their sense of self-immolatory mission, along with their hallucinatory vision of heaven on earth.

It was where the military tradition came together with this pseudo-religious socialism that the results were most devastating. In the Soviet Union they created a parody of Rousseau in which everything was sacralized, down to the economic system, and in which sacrifice in the service of the community led to self-extermination on a massive scale. It also helped the Red Army emulate the élan of 1792 in defence of the socialist motherland in the 1940s and the Soviet Union to act out its own version of the dream of *La Grande Nation*.

All of this was also in evidence in the Third Reich, which subverted much of the Romantic canon. Its elaborate rites and rituals fed on the earlier quest for alternative states of being and the desire for fulfilment, confusing its own aims with some great destiny. The Nazi rallies consciously drew on the tradition of Wartburg and Hambach, and the Nazi regime carried on the pedigree-hunting and myth-making of the previous century with grotesque thoroughness. In 1944 there were still units which could have been more usefully employed elsewhere attending to such arcane pursuits as scouring northern Italy in search of the earliest copy of Tacitus's *Germania* as bombs were falling about the ears of the Thousand-Year Reich.

What these regimes did was to carry to their logical extremity Rousseau's ideas on the need to replace God in the workings of human society with something else that would motivate people in the desired direction. But regimes which applied the ideas of Rousseau somehow always seemed to inherit along with them something of the obsessive self-pitying paranoia of the man himself, and usually ended up destroying themselves through their own instruments of control and repression. They signally failed to implant the absolute and unstinting faith that Rousseau wrote so passionately about, the faith that equated true happiness with serving the interests of the community. They did manage to instil zeal and the spirit of sacrifice in their populations, but only in conditions of crisis and war. When peace descended, they could count at best only on a degree of superstitious piety and on fear.

Lafayette and his peers, on the other hand, were natural believers. Most of them left the Christian Church at some stage, but they never eradicated God from their minds. They sought Him in nature, in art, in everything but religion. Some found Him in humanity, as represented by the nation. Robespierre described this faith as a 'tender, imperious, irresistible passion, the torment and delight of magnanimous souls', just as the great ecstatic saints had described their love of God. For him, 'this sacred love of the *Patrie*, this most sublime and holy love of humanity,' would one day find its spiritual consummation in the contemplation of 'the ravishing spectacle of universal happiness'.[12] For Michelet, faith in the nation meant 'the salvation of all by all'. He hated Catholicism because it saved people individually, thereby undermining the love of the nation. 'No more individual incarnation; God in all and all Messiahs!'[13] he preached. In other words, salvation could only be achieved by, with and through the nation. 'We shall bring about the freedom of nations all over the world,' wrote Słowacki in November of the terrible year 1848, 'our blood and our body is the property of the world and will be its nourishment, strengthening those who have grown weak under oppression.'[14]

These were no mere rebels; they aspired to emulate Christ by immolating themselves for the sake of humanity. And they offered hope, not political solutions. The wars and revolutions they started or embraced were acts of faith. They were for the most part born of vague longing not specific grievance, and that was why they lingered in the memory as glorious acts however dismal their outcome: grievances can fail to be righted, but hope can never be defeated.

Devotion to the cause became the only and all-embracing purpose of their lives, more important than the achievement of its end. They sublimated the mission itself. They accepted its purpose without question, because to question it would have made nonsense of their sacrifices and their whole lives. This made them fear and denounce everything that smacked of lukewarm belief or heresy. In order to fortify themselves in the faith, they leaned on ritual, invoked exemplars and martyrs, and venerated relics. They had, in fact, created a faith and a church of their own, with all the trappings of the Christian one they affected to despise. And, as with all faiths, the ultimate longing, because it provided escape into another, and necessarily better, world, was death in the service of the cause. They were certainly all a little mad, but theirs was a devoted and holy madness.

'Do not smile, future reader,' wrote Heinrich Heine. 'Each century believes its fight to be weightier than that of all others preceding it. This is a faith proper to the century, in which it lives and dies. And we also desire to live and die in this religion of liberty, which perhaps deserves the name of religion more than the hollow and exhausted soul-spectre which we still so name from habit. Our holy war seems to us the weightiest of all that have hitherto been waged upon this earth, notwithstanding that historical forecasts tell us that, at a future date, our grandchildren will view this struggle with the same feelings of indifference wherewith we review the struggles of primitive man, who had to fight against greedy monsters, dragons and giants.'[15]

In the 1990s, two centuries after the birth of the Romantic concept of the nation, the world has been visited by eruptions of nationalist violence of a kind that brings to mind Herzen's phrase about the syphilis of earlier lusts. Public opinion has been strident in its condemnation and sometimes paranoid in its assessments of the nature and scale of the phenomenon, leading to hysterical reaction. Yet if these pages have illustrated anything, it is that the national instinct is a natural one where religious belief-systems have failed, and that it inherits from these not only crude fanaticism, but also a spark of divinity, for it is, ultimately, a kind of mission. That is why it cannot be persuaded out of existence by the reasonable arguments of capitalist liberalism. However different the brutal gunmen of today may be from the noble Marquis de Lafayette, all those who rally to the cause of some real or invented nation carry within themselves an instinctual religious germ, and they too see themselves as valorous knights defending their world against greedy monsters, dragons and giants.

Notes

1: Our Lord Mankind

1 Albert Camus, *L'Homme Révolté*, Paris 1951, pp. 156–7.

2 ibid., p. 153; see also Susan Dunn, *The Deaths of Louis XVI. Regicide and the French Political Imagination*, Princeton 1994.

3 Baron D'Holbach, *Système de la Nature, ou des lois du monde physique et du monde moral*, Paris 1821, p. V; and Bonnot de Mably, *De la législation ou principes des lois*, Lausanne 1777, Vol. I, pp. 32, 45. For the background, see also: Carl L. Becker, *The Heavenly City of the Eighteenth-Century Philosophers*, Yale 1968; Jean Touchard, *Histoire des Idées Politiques*, Vol. II, Paris 1973; Arthur O. Lovejoy, *Essays in the History of Ideas*, Baltimore 1948; Peter Gay, *The Enlightenment, an Interpretation*, 2 vols, London 1967; David Hume, *The Natural History of Religion*, Oxford 1976.

4 Mary Wollstonecraft, *A Historical and Moral View of the French Revolution*, in *Works*, ed. Janet Todd and Marilyn Butler, Vol. VI, London 1989, p. 235. See also: David Denby, *Sentimental Narrative and the Social Order in France 1760–1820*, Cambridge 1994; Howard Mumford Jones, *Revolution and Romanticism*, Oxford 1974; Jean Starobinski, *The Invention of Liberty*, tr. Bernard C. Swift, Geneva 1964.

2: The American Parable

1 Quoted in Louis Gottschalk, *Lafayette Comes to America*, Chicago 1935, p. 135. On the background to Lafayette's expedition, see also: Chevalier de Pontgibaud, *A French Volunteer of the War of Independence*, tr. Robert B. Douglas, Paris 1898; and Gilles Perrault, *Le Secret du Roi*, Paris 1992.

2 Quoted in René Gonnard, *La Légende du Bon Sauvage*, Paris 1946, p. 74. On

European perceptions of America, the noble savage myth, etc., see also: Gilbert Chinard, *L'Amérique et le Rêve Éxotique dans la Littérature Française au XVIIe et au XVIIIe siècles*, Paris 1934; *Coup d'Oeuil sur la Grande Bretagne*, London 1776; Marquis F. J. de Chastellux, *De la Félicité Publique*, 2 vols, Amsterdam 1772.

3 Guillaume-Thomas Raynal, *Histoire Philosophique et Politique des Établissements et du Commerce Européens dans les Deux Indes*, Geneva 1780, Vol. IX, pp. 194, 193. For the wider context, see: R.R. Palmer, *The Age of Democratic Revolution. A Political History of Europe and America 1760–1800*, Vol. I; Princeton 1959, Robert Middlekauf, *The Glorious Cause*, Oxford 1982; Esmond Wright, *The Search for Liberty* (Vol. I of *A History of the United States of America*, Oxford 1995).

4 M.R. Hilliard d'Auberteuil, *Éssais Historiques et Politiques sur les Anglo-Américains*, Brussels 1782, Vol. II, pp. 119–20. On French attitudes to the colonists and their cause, see: Bernard Fay, *L'Esprit Révolutionnaire en France et aux États-Unis à la fin du XVIIIe siècle*, Paris 1925; Marquis de Castellane, *Gentilshommes Democrates*, Paris 1891; Henri Carré, *La Noblesse de France et l'Opinion Publique au XVIIIe Siècle*, Paris 1920; J.J. Jusserand, *En Amérique Jadis et Maintenant*, Paris 1919.

5 J. Hector St John Crevecoeur, *Letters from an American Farmer*, London 1908, p. 77. See also: William Penn, *Some Fruits of Solitude*, in *The Peace of Europe and Other Writings*, London 1993.

6 Quoted in Hans Kohn, *American Nationalism*, New York 1957, p. 11.

7 Comte de Ségur, *Mémoires ou Souvenirs et Anecdotes*, Paris 1824, Vol. I, pp. 86–7. On Franklin, see: Richard Deacon, *British Secret Service*, London 1991, pp. 88–90; also Cecil B. Currey, *Road to Revolution; Benjamin Franklin in England 1765–1775*, New York 1969, and *Code Number 72: Ben Franklin: Patriot or Spy?*, Englewood Cliffs, NJ, 1972; David T. Morgan, *The Devious Mr Franklin, Colonial Agent*, Macon, GA, 1996.

8 Quoted in Louis Gottschalk, *Lafayette Joins the American Army*, Chicago 1937, p. 7.

9 Quoted in Louis Gottschalk, ibid., p. 38.

10 Hans Kohn, *The Idea of Nationalism, A Study in its Origins and Background*, New York 1945, p. 271.

11 Hans Kohn, ibid., p. 283.

12 J.C.D. Clark, *The Language of Liberty 1660–1832*, Cambridge 1994, p. 261.

13 Quoted in R.R. Palmer, op. cit., Vol. I, pp. 144, 145.

14 Quoted in Hans Kohn, *The Idea of Nationalism*, p. 277.

15 John Dickinson, *Letters from a Farmer in Pennsylvania to the Inhabitants of the British Colonies*, Philadelphia 1768, p. 15. For the wider context of changing

attitudes, see also: Emory Elliott, *Revolutionary Writers: Literature and Authority in the New Republic 1725–1810*, Oxford 1986; G. Adolf Koch, *Republican Religion, The American Revolution and the Cult of Reason*, New York 1933; Jared Brown, *The Theatre in America during the Revolution*, Cambridge 1995; Robert Allen Rutland, *The Birth of the Bill of Rights 1776–1791*, Boston 1983.

16 Quoted in Middlekauf, op. cit., p. 261. For British attitudes to the issue, see: Linda Colley, *Britons. Forging the Nation 1707–1837*, Yale 1992.

17 Quoted in Arthur Johnston, *Myths and Facts of the American Revolution*, Toronto 1908, p. 96; see also J.H. Plumb, *In the Light of History*, Boston 1973, pp. 70–88; William H. Nelson, *The American Tory*, Oxford 1961.

18 See David Hackett Fischer, *Paul Revere's Ride*, Oxford 1994, p. 275.

19 See David Hackett Fischer, ibid., pp. 109, 110.

20 See David Hackett Fischer, ibid., p. 211; also James Hunter, *A Dance Called America. The Scottish Highlands, the United States and Canada*, Edinburgh 1994; and Esmond Wright, *The Search for Liberty*, pp. 465–6. On Washington, see: Paul K. Longmore, *The Invention of George Washington*, Berkeley 1988; Garry Wills, *Cincinnatus: George Washington and the Enlightenment*, Columbia 1984; Richard Brookhiser, *Founding Father, Rediscovering George Washington*, New York 1996.

21 See William H. Nelson, op. cit., pp. 89, 111–12, 92; J.C.D. Clark, op. cit.; also Harold Nicolson, *The Desire to Please, A Story of Hamilton Rowan and the United Irishmen*, London 1943, p. 43.

22 Thomas Paine, *Common Sense; Addressed to the Inhabitants of America*, London 1776, p. 15. See also: John Keane, *Tom Paine, a Political Life*, London 1995.

23 Quoted in Bernard Fay, op. cit., p. 133.

24 Quoted in Bernard Fay, op. cit., p. 57.

25 Quoted in Eugene Pivany, *Hungarian-American Historical Connections*, Budapest 1927, p. 18. See also: Guillaume-Thomas Raynal, *The Revolution of America*, London 1781; Vittorio Alfieri, *Opere*, Asti 1966, Vol. IV, pp. 77, 81, 99.

26 Alexis de Tocqueville, *L'Ancien Régime et la Révolution*, Paris 1856, p. 223.

27 See Louis Gottschalk, *Lafayette Joins the American Army*, Chicago 1937, pp. 75, 67–9.

28 Ségur, *Mémoires*, Vol. I, p. 189.

3: ARTICLES OF FAITH

1 J.J. Rousseau, *Oeuvres Complètes, Bibliothèque de la Pleiade, Paris 1964,* Vol. III, pp. 943, 919. On the subject of eighteenth-century French utopias, see Bronisław Baczko, *Utopian Lights, The Evolution of the Idea of Social Progress*, tr. by Judith Greenberg, New York 1989; Morelly, *Code de la Nature*, Paris 1841. On Corsica, and Rousseau's ideas on the subject, see: J.M. Biancamaria, *La*

Corse dans sa Gloire, ses Luttes, et ses Souffrances, Paris 1963; Alfred Cobban, *Rousseau and the Modern State*, London 1934.

2 James Boswell, *État de la Corse, suivi d'un journal d'un Voyage dans l'Isle, et des Mémoires de Pascal Paoli*, London 1769, p. 216.

3 See Yves Benot, *Diderot, de l'Athéisme à l'Anticolonialisme*, Paris 1970, pp. 153, 207.

4 See Jan Gintel, ed., *Cudzoziemcy o Polsce*, Vol. II, Kraków 1971, p. 289.

5 For the text of Pułaski's speech, see: Bibliothèque Polonaise, Paris, Ms BP 111, p. 51. See also Władysław Konopczyński, *Kazimierz Pułaski*, Kraków 1931; *Pułaski, Hero of the American Revolution*, American Revolution Bicentennial, 1776–1976, Chicago 1975.

6 Jean-Jacques Rousseau, *Oeuvres Complètes*, Vol. III, p. 499. See also Bronisław Baczko, op. cit., for Rousseau's extrapolations.

7 See Johann Heinrich Pestalozzi, *Leonard and Gertrude*, tr. by Eva Channing, London 1885, p. 181.

8 Quoted in Hans Kohn, *The Idea of Nationalism*, p. 385.

9 See Ignacy Krasicki, *Hymn do Miłości Ojczyzny*; see also Zdzisław Libera, *Poezja Polska XVIII wieku*, Warsaw 1983, p. 133.

10 Quoted in Louis Gottschalk, *Lafayette Joins the American Army*, p. 276.

11 Quoted in *Dla Dobra Rzeczypospolitej. Antologia Myśli Państwowej*, ed. Krzysztof Budziło and Jan Pruszyński, Warsaw 1996, p. 131. For the French volunteers, see: Gilles Perrault, *Le Secret du Roi*, Vol. III, *La Revanche Américaine*, Paris 1996; Claude Manceron, *Les Hommes de la Liberté*, Vol. I, *Les Vingt Ans du Roi*, Paris 1972.

12 See Gilles Perrault, *La Revanche Américaine*, Paris, 1996, pp. 459, 466; also Manceron, op cit., Vol. II, *Le Vent d'Amérique*, pp. 79, 170.

13 See Esmond Wright, op. cit., p. 464.

14 Henri de Rouvroy, Comte de Saint Simon, *Oeuvres*, Vol. I, Paris 1865, p. 12.

15 Richard Price, *Observations on the Importance of the American Revolution*, Boston 1818, p. 4.

16 Quoted in J.J. Jusserand, op. cit., p. 233.

17 Quoted in Claude Manceron, op. cit, Vol. III, *Le Bon Plaisir*, Paris 1976, p. 121.

18 Quoted by Marianne Elliott in Otto Dann and John Dinwiddy, eds, *Nationalism in the Age of the French Revolution*, London 1988, p. 77.

19 See Hans Kohn, *The Idea of Nationalism*, p. 472.

20 Quoted in Harold Nicolson, op. cit., p. 67.

21 Quoted in Simon Schama, *Patriots and Liberators, Revolution in the Netherlands 1780–1813*, London 1977, p. 60. See also: Bernard H.M. Vlekke, *Evolution of the Dutch Nation*, London 1951; Simon Schama, *The Enlightenment in the*

Netherlands; in Roy Porter and Mikulas Teich, eds, *The Enlightenment in National Context*, Cambridge 1981; Friedrich Edler, *The Dutch Republic and the American Revolution*, Baltimore 1911.

22 Simon Schama, *Patriots and Liberators*, p. 74.

23 ibid., p. 95. For French intervention plans, see: Jacques Étiennie Macdonald, *Souvenirs du Maréchal Macdonald*, Paris 1892, p. 6; Mathieu Dumas, *Souvenirs du Général Comte Mathieu Dumas de 1770 à 1836*, Paris 1839, Vol. I, pp. 411–18.

24 Quoted in G.P. Gooch, *Germany and the French Revolution*, London 1920, p. 423.

25 See L. Wolff, *The Vatican and Poland in the age of the Partitions*, Boulder 1988, p. 185.

4: FALSE GODS

1 See R.R. Palmer, op. cit., Vol. I, pp. 155–7. On the situation in America after 1783, see: Guillaume-Thomas Raynal, *The Revolution of America*, London 1781; Emory Elliott, op. cit.

2 J. Hector St John Crevecoeur, *Letters from an American Farmer*, London 1782, p. 287.

3 Quoted by J.C.D. Clark, *The Language of Liberty 1660–1832*, Cambridge 1994, p. 388.

4 See Paul K. Longmore, op. cit., pp. 197, 201, 204, 210; Howard Mumford Jones, *Revolution and Romanticism*, p. 213; Esmond Wright, op. cit., p. 464.

5 R.R. Palmer, op. cit., Vol. I, p. 254, quoted from J.B. Mailhe, *Discours qui a remporté le prix de l'Académie des Jeux Floreaux en 1784*, etc., Toulouse 1784.

6 Quoted by Bernard Fay, op. cit., p. 192.

7 R.R. Palmer, op. cit., Vol. I, p. 260, quoted from J.B. Brissot de Warville, *Éxamen critique* etc., London 1786.

8 See Ségur, op. cit., Vol. I, pp. 454, 518. See also: Mathieu Dumas, op. cit.

9 See Pierre Trahard, *La Sensibilité Révolutionnaire 1789–1794*, Paris 1936, pp. 139, 31–2.

10 See Henri Carré, op. cit., p. 312.

11 See James J. Sheehan, *German History 1770–1866*, Oxford, 1989, p. 72. See also: Joachim Whaley, *The Protestant Enlightenment in Germany*, and T.C.W. Blanning, *The Enlightenment in Catholic Germany*, both in Roy Porter and Mikulas Teich, op. cit.

12 See Arnold Hauser, *The Social History of Art*, Vol. II, London 1951, p. 609.

13 See Harro Segeberg in Otto Dann and John Dinwiddy, op. cit., p. 142.

14 Quoted by Richard Friedenthal, *Goethe. His Life and Times*, London 1993, p. 82.

15 Maurice Cranston, *The Romantic Movement*, Oxford 1994, p. 31.
16 See Richard Friedenthal, op. cit., pp. 106, 112.
17 *The Poems of Ossian, translated by James Macpherson, Esq.*, London 1805, Vol. I, p. 28.
18 See Harro Segeberg, op. cit., p. 143.
19 Norman Hampson, *The Enlightenment*, London 1990, pp. 201–2.
20 See Harro Segeberg, op. cit., p. 144.
21 See Richard Friedenthal, op. cit., p. 143.
22 See G.P. Gooch, op. cit., p. 36.
23 Quoted in R.R. Palmer, op. cit., p. 257.
24 Johann Wolfgang Goethe, *Italian Journey*, tr. W.H. Auden and Elizabeth Mayer, London 1962, pp. 39, 147, 377, 426; Richard Friedenthal, op. cit., p. 241. See also: Johann Joachim Winckelmann, *Writings on Art*, ed. David Irwin, London 1972.
25 Friedrich Schiller, *Essays Aesthetical and Philosophical*, London 1884, Letter VI, p. 38.
26 Quoted in E.M. Butler, *The Tyranny of Greece over Germany*, Cambridge 1935, p. 215.
27 See ibid., p. 210.
28 Alexis de Tocqueville, op. cit., p. 236.
29 Gérard de Nerval, *Jacques Cazotte*, in Jacques Cazotte, *Le Diable Amoureux*, Paris 1979, p. 151.
30 See Jean Touchard, op. cit., Vol. I, p. 386; also Reinhard Bendix, *Kings or People. Power and the Mandate to Rule*, Berkeley, 1978, p. 361.
31 See Auguste Viatte, *Les Sources Occultes du Romantisme*, Paris 1928, Vol. I, pp. 72–90. For more information on Freemasonry, the Illuminati and the occult during this period, see: J.M. Roberts, *The Mythology of the Secret Societies*, London 1972; Albert Mathiez, *Contributions à l'Histoire Religieuse de la Révolution Française*, Paris 1907; Isabel de Madariaga, *Freemasonry in Eighteenth-century Russian Society*, in *Politics and Culture in Eighteenth-century Russia*, London 1998; J.P.L. Luchet, *Éssai sur la secte des Illuminés*, Paris 1789; G.P. Gooch, op. cit. , pp. 30ff, 66; Jacques Droz, *L'Allemagne et la Révolution Française*, Paris 1949, pp. 400–4, and *Le Romantisme Allemand et l'État*, Paris 1966, pp. 21–33; also R.R. Palmer, op. cit., Vol. II, pp. 142, 144, 163, 454; Le Forestier, *Les Illuminés de Bavière et la franc-maçonnerie allemande*; Renato Soriga, *Le Società Segrete, l'emigrazione politica e i primi moti per l'inde Pendenza*, Modena 1942.
32 Quoted in Ralph Lerner, *Revolutions Revisited*, Chapel Hill 1994, p. 4.
33 Alexis de Tocqueville, op. cit., p. xii.

5: Civil Rites

1 Quoted in J.J. Jusserand, op. cit., p. 246. For the fall of the Bastille, see: Simon Schama, *Citizens, A Chronicle of the French Revolution*, London 1989; M. Dusaulx, *De l'insurréction parisienne, et de la prise de la Bastille*, in *Mémoires de Linguet sur la Bastille et de Dusaulx sur le 14 juillet*, Paris 1821.

2 Thomas Paine, *The Rights of Man*, ed. London 1993, p. 22; see also William Cowper, *The Task. The Winter Morning Walk.*

3 Mary Wollstonecraft, op. cit., in *Works*, ed. Janet Todd and Marilyn Butler, Vol. VI, London 1989, p. 146.

4 Ségur, op. cit., Vol. III, p. 508.

5 Albert Camus, op. cit., pp. 152–3.

6 On the subject of the liberty tree, see Simon Schama, *Landscape and Memory*, London 1995, pp. 245ff, and note, p. 595; see also Aileen Ribeiro, *Fashion in the French Revolution*, London 1988, p. 68; Emmet Kennedy, *A Cultural History of the French Revolution*, New Haven 1989; Harold T. Parker, *The Cult of Antiquity and the French Revolutionaries*, New York 1965; Jan Baszkiewicz, *Nowy Człowiek, nowy naród, nowy świat. Mitologia i rzeczywistość rewolucji francuskiej*, Warsaw 1993.

7 See A.E. Ghibelin, *De l'Origine et de la Forme du Bonnet de la Liberté*, Paris 1796.

8 See Julien Tiersot, *Les Fêtes et les Chants de la Révolution Française*, Paris 1908, p. 31; also Mona Ozouf, *La Fête Révolutionnaire*, Paris 1976, pp. 71ff. On revolutionary festivals and cults, see also: Michel Vovelle, *Les Métamorphoses de la Fête en Provence de 1750 à 1820*, Paris 1976; Albert Mathiez, *Les Origines des Cultes Révolutionnaires*, Paris 1904; Henri Grégoire, *Mémoires*, 2 vols, Paris 1837; *Principes de Mably sur la Nécessité de la Religion et d'un Culte Public*, Paris An III (1795); K. Twiss, *A Trip to Paris in July and August 1792*, Dublin 1793; Michel Delon, ed., *Le Chansonnier Révolutionnaire*, Paris 1989; Helen Maria Williams, *Sketches of the State of Manners and Opinions in the French Republic, etc*, London 1810.

9 See James H. Billington, *Fire in the Minds of Men. Origins of the Revolutionary Faith*, London 1980 p. 20.

10 For the French revolutionary calendar see: Bronisław Baczko, *Le Calendrier Républicain, Décréter l'Éternité*, in Pierre Nora, ed., *Les Lieux de Mémoire*, Vol. I, *La République*, Paris 1984; also Bronisław Baczko, *Utopian Lights*, pp. 159–171; Mona Ozouf, *Calendrier* in François Furet and Mona Ozouf, *Dictionnaire Critique de la Révolution Française, Institutions et Créations*, Paris 1992, pp. 91–106; Jan Baszkiewicz, op. cit., pp. 156 ff; Henri Grégoire, op. cit.

11 Quoted by Bronisław Baczko in Pierre Nora, op. cit., Vol. I, *La République*, p. 43.

12 Quoted in Hans Kohn, *The Idea of Nationalism*, p. 237.
13 Hans Kohn, ibid., p. 255.
14 Quoted in Hans Kohn, ibid., p. 252.
15 Jean-Jacques Rousseau, *Du Contrat Social*, Chapter VII, in *Oeuvres Complètes*, Vol. III, p. 465.
16 Quoted in Hans Kohn, *The Idea of Nationalism*, p. 242.
17 Alexis de Tocqueville, op. cit., p. 19.
18 See Gilbert Chinard, ed., *L'Apothéose de Benjamin Franklin, Collection de Textes*, Paris 1955, pp. 18, 35, 36, 41–2, 42–3, 47, 162.
19 See Emmet Kennedy, *A Cultural History of the French Revolution*, New Haven 1989, pp. 333–6.
20 Quoted in Carl L. Becker, op. cit., p. 150.
21 ibid., pp. 142–3.
22 Quoted in Charles Vellay, *Discours et Rapports de Robespierre*, Paris 1908, p. 351.
23 Quoted in Arnold Hauser, op. cit., Vol. II, p. 638.
24 See R.R. Palmer, op. cit., Vol. II, p. 127.
25 Marc-Antoine Jullien, *From Jacobin to Liberal, Marc-Antoine Jullien, 1775–1848*, ed. R.R. Palmer, Princeton 1993, pp. 45–6. See also: Jean François de La Harpe, *Du Fanatisme dans la Langue Révolutionnaire*, Paris 1797; Clive Emsley, *Nationalist Rhetoric and Nationalist Sentiment in Revolutionary France*, in Otto Dann and John Dinwiddy, op. cit.
26 Alexis de Tocqueville, op. cit., p. 19.

6: Holy War

1 Quoted in W. Cobbett, *The Parliamentary History of England from the Earliest Period to the Year 1803*, Vol. XXIX, London 1817, p. 826.
2 Frank MacDermot, *Theobald Wolfe Tone*, London 1939, p. 100; also Harold Nicolson, op. cit., p. 92.
3 Klemens von Metternich, *Mémoires, Documents et Écrits Divers Laissés par le Prince de Metternich*, Vol. I, Paris 1880, pp. 8–9.
4 Quoted in G.P. Gooch, op. cit., p. 317.
5 Quoted in Erik Lonroth, in Otto Dann and John Dinwiddy, op. cit., p. 110.
6 See Evelyne Lever, *Philippe Égalité*, Paris 1996, p. 452.
7 Quoted in Jacques Godechot, *La Grande Nation; L'Expansion Révolutionnaire de la France dans le Monde de 1789 à 1799*, Paris 1956, Vol. I, p. 71.
8 Quoted in Jennifer M. Welsh, *Edmund Burke and International Relations, The Commonwealth of Europe and the Crusade against the French Revolution*, London 1995, p. 73.
9 Quoted in Jacques Godechot, op. cit., Vol. I, p. 71.

10 Quoted in G.P. Gooch, op. cit., p. 476.
11 Quoted ibid., p. 323.
12 Quoted in Norman Hampson, *Prelude to Terror*, Oxford 1988, p. 128.
13 Quoted R.R. Palmer, op. cit., Vol. II, p. 60.
14 See *La Convention Nationale au Peuple Français*, October 1792, pp. 7–8.
15 On the legions, see Jacques Godechot, op. cit., Vol. II, pp. 611–15; also Alexis de Tocqueville, op. cit., p. 19.
16 See Richard Friedenthal, op. cit., p. 313; also R.R. Palmer, op. cit., Vol. II, p. 444.
17 Quoted in Richard Friedenthal, op. cit., p. 303.
18 See R.R. Palmer, op. cit., Vol. II, p. 444.
19 François-René de Chateaubriand, *Mémoires d'Outre-tombe*, Paris 1951, Vol. II, p. 747.
20 See William Augustus Miles, *Correspondence on the French Revolution*, London 1890, Vol. I. p. 345.
21 See R.R. Palmer, op. cit., Vol. II, pp. 251–3.
22 See Henryk Kocój, *Wielka Rewolucja Francuska a Polska*, Warsaw 1987, p. 66.
23 See Joseph de Maistre, *Considérations sur la France*, London 1797, p. 76. On the supposed activities of the Jacobins, Illuminati and other sects, see: James H. Billington, op. cit., p. 180; Bela K. Kiraly, *Hungary in the Late Eighteenth Century*, New York 1969, pp. 198, 211; J.M. Roberts, *The Mythology of the Secret Societies*, London 1972; R.R. Palmer, op. cit., Vol. II, pp. 51–2; Adam Zamoyski, *The Last King of Poland*, London 1992, pp. 437, 443–8; Raoul Girardet, *Mythes et Mythologies Politiques*, Paris 1986; Robert M. Ryan, *The Romantic Reformation*, Cambridge 1992, p. 27.
24 Quoted in Jennifer M. Welsh, op. cit., p. 106.
25 Gilbert du Motier, Marquis de Lafayette, *Lettres de Prison*, ed. J. Thomas, Paris 1907, pp. 192, 200, 182–6.
26 Marquis de Lafayette, op. cit., pp. 203–5.

7: Dying to be Free

1 See Thomas K. Gorman, *America and Belgium. A Study in the Influence of the United States upon the Belgian Revolution of 1789–90*, London 1925, p. 187.
2 Archiwum Główne Akt Dawnych, Warsaw; AKP 203, ff. 26–9. See also: B. Leśnodorski, *Polscy Jakobini*, Warsaw 1960.
3 Quoted in W. Smoleński, *Konfederacja Targowicka*, Kraków 1913, p. 377.
4 Quoted in Henryk Kocój, op. cit., p. 120; also Helena Rządkowska, *Stosunek Polskiej Opinii Publicznej do Rewolucji Francuskiej*, Warsaw 1948, p. 113.
5 Quoted by Z. Góralski, *Stanisław August w Insurekcji Kościuszkowskiej*, Wrocław

1979, p. 127. On the 1794 Insurrection, see also: A. Zamoyski, op. cit.; J. Kopczewski, ed., *Tadeusz Kościuszko w Historii i Tradycji*, Warsaw 1968; J. Zajączek, *Histoire de la Révolution de Pologne en 1794 par un Témoin Oculaire*, Paris 1797.

6 Tadeusz Kościuszko, *Listy, Odezwy, Wspomnienia*, ed. Henryk Mościcki, Warsaw 1917, p. 53.

7 Quoted in Andrzej Walicki, *The Enlightenment and the Birth of Modern Nationhood*, Notre Dame 1989, p. 27.

8 See Hortense de St Albin, *Jenerała Józefa Sułkowskiego Życie i Pamiętniki*, tr. Ludwik Miłkowski, Poznań 1864, p. 73.

9 ibid., p. 117.

10 Quoted in Hans Kohn, *The Idea of Nationalism*, p. 532. See also Andrew C. Janos, *The Politics of Backwardness in Hungary*, Princeton 1982.

11 Quoted in Henry Marczali, *Hungary in the Eighteenth Century*, Cambridge 1910, p. 235.

12 See Peter F. Sugar, *The Influence of the Enlightenment and the French Revolution in Eighteenth-century Hungary*, in *Journal of Central European Affairs*, Vol. XVII, No. 4, Boulder, January 1958, p. 334.

13 Domokos Kosary, *Culture and Society in Eighteenth-century Hungary*, Budapest 1987, p. 161.

14 Quoted in Bela K. Kiraly, op. cit., p. 157.

15 Quoted ibid., p. 9. On the Jacobin rising, see: Paul Bödy, *The Hungarian Jacobin Conspiracy of 1794–5* in *Journal of Central European Affairs*, Vol. XXII, Boulder 1962, No. 1.

16 See Alfred Cobban, ed., *The Debate on the French Revolution 1789–1800*, London 1950, p. 42.

17 Quoted in H.C. Fairchild, *The Romantic Quest*, New York, 1931, p. 24. For repercussions of the French Revolution in Britain, see also: Robert Birley, *The English Jacobins from 1789 to 1802*, Oxford 1924; Alfred Owen Aldridge, *Man of Reason, The Life of Thomas Paine*, Philadelphia 1959; Roger Wells, *Insurrection, the British Experience*, Gloucester 1983.

18 Quoted in H.C. Fairchild, op. cit., p. 50.

19 Quoted in H.C. Fairchild, op. cit., p. 54.

20 On Wales, see: Gwyn A. Williams, *The Search for Beulah Land, The Welsh and the Atlantic Revolution*, London 1980; *Romanticism in Wales*, in Roy Porter and Mikulas Teich, op. cit.; Prys Morgan, *From a Death to a View: the Hunt for the Welsh Past in the Romantic Period*, in Eric Hobsbawm and Terence Ranger, ed., *The Invention of Tradition*, Cambridge 1983.

21 See Harold Nicolson, op. cit., pp. 87, 84.

22 See R.F. Foster, *Modern Ireland 1600–1972*, London 1988, p. 265. Also: David Dickson, Daire Keogh and Kevin Whelan, eds., *The United Irishmen: Repub-*

licanism Radicalism and Rebellion, Dublin 1996; and Stella Tillyard, *Citizen Lord*, London 1997.

23 Theobald Wolfe Tone, *The Life of Theobald Wolfe Tone, written by himself*, London 1831, p. 63.

24 Quoted in Harold Nicolson, op. cit., pp. 151–2.

25 Quoted by Frank McDermot, *Theobald Wolfe Tone*, London 1939, pp. 171, 176.

26 Quoted by Marianne Elliott in Otto Dann and John Dinwiddy, op. cit., p. 79.

27 See R.F. Foster, op. cit., p. 273.

28 Quoted in Frank McDermot, op. cit., p. 199. On the 1798 rebellion, see also: Thomas Pakenham, *The Year of Liberty*, London 1969; Liam Kelly, *A Flame Now Quenched: Rebels and Frenchmen in Leitrim 1793–1798*, Dublin 1998; Daire Keogh and Nicholas Furlong, eds, *The Mighty Wave; the 1798 Rebellion in Wexford*, Blackrock 1996.

8: La Grande Nation

1 Quoted in Norman Hampson, *The French Revolution and the Nationalisation of Honour*, in *War and Society*, ed. M.R.D. Foot, London 1973, p. 210.

2 Quoted in George Rudé, *Revolutionary Europe 1783–1815*, London 1985, p. 215. See also: Dino Carpanetto and Giuseppe Ricuperati, *Italy in the Age of Reform*, London 1987; Marco Meriggi in Otto Dann and John Dinwiddy, op. cit.

3 Emiliana Pasha Noether, *Seeds of Italian Nationalism*, Columbia U.P. 1951, p. 93.

4 Emiliana Pasha Noether, ibid., pp. 52–60.

5 Vittorio Alfieri, *Memoirs*, Oxford 1961, p. 261.

6 Emiliana Pasha Noether, op. cit., pp. 149–50.

7 Quoted in R.R. Palmer, op. cit., Vol. II, p. 241.

8 See R.R. Palmer, op. cit., Vol. II, p. 339.

9 See Marc-Antoine Jullien, op. cit., pp. 83–5.

10 See Paul Hazard, *La Révolution Française et les Lettres Italiennes 1789–1815*, Paris 1910, pp. 77ff.

11 See R.R. Palmer, op. cit., Vol. II, p. 379.

12 Vincenzo Cuoco, *Saggio Storico sulla Rivoluzione Napoletana del 1799*, Bari 1913, p. 94.

13 See Richard Clogg, ed., *The Movement for Greek Independence 1770–1821, A Collection of Documents*, London 1976, p. 163.

14 See *Voyages de Dimo et Nicolo Stephanopoli en Grèce pendant les années 1797 et 1798*, London 1800, Vol. I, p. 113.

15 See Stanisław Wasylewski, *Życie Polskie w XIX wieku*, Kraków 1962, pp. 44–5.

On revolutionary and military activities in the Balkans, see also: Jacques Godechot, op. cit., Vol. I, p. 199; Jan Henryk Dąbrowski, *Pamiętnik Wojskowy Legionów Polskich we Włoszech*, Poznań 1864; Antoni Rolle, *Nowe Opowiadania Historyczne*, Lwów 1878, pp. 337–75; Aleksander Kraushar, *Albert Sarmata* in *Obrazy i Wizerunki Historyczne*, Warsaw 1906, pp. 4–27.

16 Quoted in Richard Clogg, op. cit., p. 61.

17 See Pamphile de Lacroix, *Mémoires pour servir à l'histoire de la Révolution de Saint-Domingue*, Paris 1819, Vol. I, p. 10. See also C.L.R. James, *The Black Jacobins*, London 1938.

18 Quoted in Wenda Parkinson, *This Gilded African, Toussaint L'Ouverture*, London 1978, p. 155.

19 See T. Lothrop Stoddard, *The French Revolution in San Domingo*, Boston 1914, pp. 304, 332. See also: Jan Pachoński and Reuel K. Wilson, *Poland's Caribbean Tragedy. A Study of the Polish Legions in the Haitian War of Independence 1802–1803*, Boulder 1986; Hubert Cole, *Christophe: King of Haiti*, London 1967.

9: Un Pueblo Americano

1 See John Rydjord, *Foreign Interest in the Independence of New Spain*, Durham, NC, 1935, pp. 61, 72, 66.

2 ibid., pp. 97, 99.

3 See Salvador de Madariaga, *Bolivar*, London 1952, pp. 38–40; also Victor Andrés Belaunde, *Bolivar and the Political Thought of the Spanish American Revolution*, Baltimore 1938, p. 79; also Salvador de Madariaga, *The Fall of the Spanish American Empire*, London 1947, pp. 339, 195.

4 See Salvador de Madariaga, *The Fall of the Spanish American Empire*, p. 347; also C. Parra-Perez, *Miranda et la Révolution Française*, Paris 1925; William Spence Robertson, *Francisco de Miranda and the Revolutionizing of Spanish America*, in *Annual Report of the American Historical Association*, Vol. I, Washington 1908, p. 234; Salvador de Madariaga, *Bolivar*, pp. 18–19; and Francisco de Miranda, *The Diary of Francisco de Miranda, Tour of the United States*, New York 1928.

5 Quoted in W.S. Robertson, op. cit., p. 250.

6 Quoted ibid.

7 See Salvador de Madariaga, *The Fall of the Spanish American Empire*, p. 353; also Irene Nicholson, *The Liberators*, London 1969, p. 61.

8 See W.S. Robertson, op. cit., p. 291.

9 Salvador de Madariaga, *Bolivar*, p. 152.

10 See C. Parra-Perez, op. cit., pp. 381–2; also Marius André, *La Fin de l'Empire Espagnol d'Amérique*, Paris 1922, p. 39.

11 See W.S. Robertson, op. cit., Vol. I, p. 235.

12 See Salvador de Madariaga, *Bolivar*, p. 108.
13 Quoted by Irene Nicholson, op. cit., p. 74.
14 See W.S. Robertson, op. cit., p. 151.
15 See John Rydjord, op. cit., p. 246.
16 Quoted in Salvador de Madariaga, *Bolivar*, p. 95.
17 See ibid., pp. 97, 98.
18 See ibid., p. 86.
19 See John Rydjord, op. cit., p. 268.
20 Quoted in Victor Andrés Belaunde, op. cit., p. 105.
21 See ibid., pp. 102, 105.
22 See Irene Nicholson, op. cit., p. 231.
23 ibid, p. 232.
24 See D.A. Brading, *Classical Republicanism and Creole Patriotism: Simon Bolivar and the Spanish American Revolution*, Cambridge 1983, pp. 5, 7; Lester D. Langley, *The Americas in the Age of Revolution 1750–1850*, Yale 1996, pp. 184–5.
25 Quoted by Lester D. Langley, op. cit., p. 171; see also Marius Andre, op. cit., pp. 43–4.
26 Quoted by Bernard Moses, *The Intellectual Background of the Revolution in South America 1810–1824*, New York 1926, pp. 102–4.
27 Quoted by Lester D. Langley, op. cit., p. 171. See also: Ricardo Salvatore, *The Breakdown of Social Discipline in the Banda Oriental and the Littoral 1790–1820*, in Mark D. Szuchman and Jonathan C. Brown, eds, *Revolution and Restoration: the Rearrangement of Power in Argentina 1776–1860*, Lincoln, Nebraska, 1995. As a curiosum, see: Miriam Williford, *Jeremy Bentham on Spanish America*, Baton Rouge 1980.
28 Quoted by Salvador de Madariaga, *Bolivar*, pp. 67, 68.
29 See ibid., p. 155.
30 See ibid., p. 181.
31 See ibid., pp. 182–4, 189–90.
32 Quoted ibid, pp. 199, 201.
33 Quoted ibid, p. 202.

10: The World Spirit

1 Alexandre Dumas, *Mes Mémoires*, Paris 1989, p. 44.
2 See Émile Haumant, *La Formation de la Yougoslavie*, Paris 1930, p. 258.
3 See Kveta Mejdrička, *Les Paysans Tchèques et la Révolution Française*, in *Annales Historiques de la Révolution Française*, no. 154, Nancy 1958, pp. 68–9.
4 See Heinrich Heine, *Italian Travel Sketches*, tr. Elizabeth A. Sharp, London 1892, p. 81.

5 Quoted in Hans Kohn, *The Idea of Nationalism*, p. 387.
6 See G.P. Gooch, op. cit., pp. 312, 313; also Jacques Droz, *L'Allemagne et la Révolution Française*, pp. 197, 208, 210; Franz Dumont, *The Rhineland*, in Otto Dann and John Dinwiddy, op. cit.; Frederick C. Beiser, *Enlightenment, Revolution and Romanticism. The Genesis of Modern German Political Thought 1790–1800*, Harvard 1992.
7 Quoted by R.R. Palmer, op. cit., Vol. II, p. 448; see also Jean Touchard, op. cit., Vol. II, p. 486.
8 Quoted by Norman Hampson, *The Enlightenment*, p. 277.
9 Quoted by R.R. Palmer, op. cit., Vol. II, p. 442.
10 See G.P. Gooch, op. cit., pp. 474, 483, 485.
11 Jean Touchard, op. cit., Vol. II, p. 496.
12 Hans Kohn, *The Age of Nationalism*, New York 1962, p. 9.
13 ibid., p. 60.
14 See Hugh Honour, *Romanticism*, London 1991, pp. 157, 160; also Richard Friedenthal, op. cit., pp. 453–4.
15 See Golo Mann, *The History of Germany since 1789*, tr. Marian Jackson, London 1996, p. 58.
16 Norman Hampson, *The Enlightenment*, p. 281.
17 Jacques Droz, *L'Allemagne et la Révolution Française*, pp. 108, 107.
18 Quoted in Jacques Droz, *Le Romantisme Allemand et l'État*, Paris 1966, p. 195.
19 Quoted by Geoffrey Best, *Honour Among Men and Nations, Transformations of an Idea*, Toronto 1982, p. 25.
20 Quoted in James Sheehan, op. cit., p. 314.
21 Golo Mann, op. cit., p. 38.
22 See James Sheehan, op. cit., pp. 384–5.
23 See Richard Friedenthal, op. cit., pp. 453–4.
24 Quoted by Hugh Honour, op. cit., p. 225.
25 See Germaine de Staël, *Ten Years' Exile*, London 1812, p. 179.
26 On Russia, see: Hans Rogger, *National Consciousness in Eighteenth-century Russia*, Harvard 1960; M.M. Shtrange, *Russkoye Obshestvo i Frantsuzkaya Revolyutsia 1789–1794*, Moscow 1956, and *Demokraticheskaya Intelligentsia Rossyi w XVIII vyekhe*, Moscow 1965; Paul Dukes, *Russia*, in Porter and Tiech, op. cit.; Evgenii Plimak and Vladimir Khoros, *La Révolution Française et la Tradition Révolutionnaire en Russie*, in *La Révolution Française et la Russie*, Moscow 1989.
27 See John Dinwiddy, in Otto Dann and John Dinwiddy, op. cit., p. 53.
28 See Hugh Trevor-Roper, *The Highland Tradition of Scotland*, in Eric Hobsbawm and Terence Ranger, eds, op. cit.; also Robert Clyde, *From Rebel to Hero, the Image of the Highlander 1745–1830*, East Linton 1995.

11: Golgotha

1 François-René de Chateaubriand, op. cit., Vol. I, p. 962.
2 Encyclopedia Britannica, 11th Ed., *Holy Alliance*, Vol. XIII, p. 621.
3 Jacques Droz, *Europe Between Revolutions*, p. 217; also George Rudé, *Revolutionary Europe*, p. 285.
4 Quoted in Frederick B. Artz, *Reaction and Revolution*, New York 1966, p. 195.
5 Denis Mack Smith, *Il Risorgimento Italiano*, Bari 1968, p. 20.
6 Quoted in H.A. Straus, *The Attitude of the Congress of Vienna toward Nationalism in Germany, Italy and Poland*, New York 1949, pp. 97, 106. On the secret societies in Italy, see: Derek Beales, *The Risorgimento and the Unification of Italy*, London 1971; Rene Albrecht-Carrie, *Italy from Napoleon to Mussolini*, New York 1950; John Rath, *The Carbonari*, in *The American Historical Review*, Vol. LXIX, No. 2, January 1964, Washington; also Renato Soriga, op. cit.; *Memoirs of the Secret Societies of the South of Italy, particularly the Carbonari*, London 1821; J.M. Roberts, op. cit., London 1972; Carlo Francovich, *L'Azione rivoluzionaria risorgimentale e i movimenti delle nazionalità in Europe prima del 1848*, in *Nuove Question i de Storia del Risorgimento e dell'Unita d'Italia*, Milano 1961, Vol. I. For the secret societies under the Restoration see: Georges Sencier, *Le Babouvisme après Babeuf*, pp. 36ff; Alexandre Dumas, op. cit., Vol. I pp. 444–6; John Plamenatz, *The Revolutionary Movement in France 1815–1871*, pp. 22–4; Herbert Vivian, *Secret Societies Old and New*, London 1927.
7 Heinrich Heine, *Italian Travel Sketches*, p. 76.
8 Alfonse de Lamartine, *Jeanne d'Arc*, Brussels 1852, p. 15.
9 Jacques Étienne Macdonald, op. cit., p. 313.
10 Mathieu Dumas, op. cit., p. 583.
11 Quoted in Jean Touchard, op. cit., Vol. II, p. 433. On the changing role of the soldier see also: Jonathan Swift, *Gulliver's Travels*, Oxford 1928, p. 281; M.H. Beyle (Stendhal), *Vie de Napoléon*, Paris 1929, p. 224; *Catéchisme des Décadis*, Paris 1795, p. 70.
12 Alfred de Vigny, *Servitude et Grandeurs Militaires*, Paris 1872, p. 25.
13 Alexandre Dumas, op. cit., Vol. I, pp. 216, 274.
14 Alfred de Musset, *La Confession d'un Enfant du Siècle*, Paris 1891, p. 4.
15 Alfred de Vigny, op. cit., pp. 6, 14–15.
16 ibid, p. 346.
17 François-René de Chateaubriand, op. cit., II, p. 3; Vol. I, pp. 894, 490.
18 F.S. Dmochowski, *Wspomnienia od 1806 do 1830 roku*, Warsaw 1858, p. 41.
19 For the cult of Napoleon, see: Robert Gildea, *The Past in French History*, Yale 1994, pp. 92–4; Jean Touchard, op. cit., Vol. II, pp. 522; also Sergio Luzzato, *European Visions of the French Revolution*, in Isser Woloch (ed.), *Revolution and the Meanings of Freedom in the Nineteenth Century*, Stanford 1996, pp. 34–5.

20 See Henry Lachouque, *The Anatomy of Glory*, London 1961, p. 502.

21 See Andrew Motion, *Keats*, London 1998, p. 68; also Simon Bainbridge, *Napoleon and English Romanticism*, Cambridge 1995.

22 Walter Scott, *France and Belgium*, Edinburgh 1855, p. 149.

23 Quoted in H.A. Straus, op. cit., p. 70.

24 François-René de Chateaubriand, op. cit., Vol. I, p. 845.

25 M.H. Beyle (Stendhal), *Rome, Naples et Florence*, Paris 1919, Vol. II, p. 223.

26 See Félix Ponteil, *L'Éveil des Nationalités et le Mouvement Libéral (1815–1848)*, Paris 1960, p. 111.

27 Quoted in James Sheehan, op. cit., p. 575.

28 See Paul C. Weber, *America in Imaginative German Literature in the First Half of the Nineteenth Century*, New York 1926, pp. 59, 71.

29 Quoted in Hans Kohn, *American Nationalism*, p. 13.

30 Quoted in Alfred Owen Aldridge, op. cit., p. 275. On America see: Lloyd S. Kramer, *The French Revolution and the Creation of American Political Culture*, in Joseph Klaits and Michael Haltzel, eds., *The Global Ramifications of the French Revolution*, Cambridge 1994; J.J. Jusserand, op. cit., pp. 165–78; François-René de Chateaubriand, op. cit., Vol. I, p. 277; Steven C. Bullock, *Revolutionary Brotherhood. Freemasonry and the Transformation of the American Social Order 1730–1840*, Chapel Hill, 1996, pp. 51, 109, 129.

31 See John Rydjord, op. cit., p. 114.

32 Quoted by Golo Mann, op. cit., p. 60.

33 Johann Joseph von Görres, *Germany and the Revolution*, tr. John Black, London 1820, p. 4.

34 See James Sheehan, op. cit., p. 445.

35 Germaine de Staël, op. cit., p. 267.

36 See Maria Janion and Maria Żmigrodzka, *Romantyzm i Historia*, Warsaw 1978, p. 215.

37 Aleksander Fredro, *Trzy po Trzy*, Krakow 1949, p. 41.

38 See Maria Janion and Maria Żmigrodzka, op. cit., p. 213.

39 Natalia Kicka, *Pamiętniki*, Warsaw 1972, p. 198.

40 Natalia Kicka, ibid, p. 375.

12: PHANTOM CAUSES

1 Quoted in Salvador de Madariaga, *Bolivar*, p. 379. On the subject of leadership in Spanish America, see: John Lynch, *Caudillos in Spanish America 1800–1850*, Oxford 1992; Edouard Clavéry, *Trois Précurseurs de l'Indépendance des Démocraties Sud-Américaines*, Paris 1932; J.C.J. Metford, *San Martin the Liberator*, Oxford 1950; Wilfred Hardy Callcott, *Santa Anna. The Story of an Enigma who once was Mexico*, Norman, Oklahoma, 1936.

2 Salvador de Madariaga, ibid., p. 273.
3 Quoted ibid., p. 280.
4 See François Dalencour, *Alexandre Pétion Devant l'Humanité*, Port-au-Prince 1928, p. 17.
5 See Salvador de Madariaga, *Bolivar*, p. 319; also Victor Andrés Belaunde, op. cit., p. 184. See also: Bernard Moses, *The Intellectual Background of the Revolution in South America 1810–1824*, New York 1926.
6 See Maurice Persat, *Mémoires du Commandant Persat*, Paris 1910, p. 41.
7 ibid., p. 52.
8 See George Laval Chesterton, *Peace, War, and Adventure*, London 1853, Vol. II, p. 23.
9 See Alfred Hasbrouck, *Foreign Legionaries in the Liberation of Spanish South America*, New York, 1928; also Michael G. Mulhall, *The English in South America*, Buenos Aires and London 1978.
10 Gustavus Hippisley, *A Narrative of the Expedition to the Rivers Orinoco and Apure in South America*, London 1819, p. 13.
11 Gustavus Hippisley, op. cit., p. 3.
12 Quoted by Alfred Hasbrouck, op. cit., p. 146.
13 See Alfred Hasbrouck, op. cit., pp. 164–7; also Salvador de Madariaga, *Bolivar*, pp. 355–6.
14 See Alfred Hasbrouck, op. cit., pp. 288–9. See also: *Recollections of a Service of Three Years during the War of Extermination in the Republics of Venezuela and Colombia, by an Officer of the Colombian Navy*, London 1828.
15 See Alfred Hasbrouck, op. cit., p. 203.
16 See Giuseppe Pecchio, *Semi-Serious Observations of an Italian Exile during his Residence in England*, London 1833, p. 171; also Denis Mack Smith, *Il Risorgimento Italiano*, p. 23. On Italy during this period, see also: George T. Romani, *The Neapolitan Revolution of 1820–1821*, Evanston 1950; M.H. Beyle, *Rome, Naples et Florence*; Lord Byron, *Letters and Journals*, London 1978, Vol. VIII, pp. 39, 40.
17 See Giuseppe Pecchio, *Six Mois en Espagne*, Paris 1822, p. 6.
18 ibid., p. 95. See also Louis Jullian, *Précis Historique des Principaux Évènements Politiques et Militaires qui ont Amené la Révolution d'Espagne*, Paris 1821.
19 Quoted by Raymond Carr, *Spain 1808–1939*, Oxford 1966, p. 129.
20 Quoted in Geoffroy de Grandmaison, *L'Éxpédition Française d'Espagne en 1823*, Paris 1928, pp. 63–4.
21 See Geoffroy de Grandmaison, op. cit., p. 92; also Persat, op. cit., pp. 130–3.
22 Quoted by Raymond Carr, op. cit., p. 141.
23 Giuseppe Pecchio, *Lettres Historiques et Politiques sur le Portugal*, Paris, n.d., p. 120, and *Journal of Military and Political Events in Spain*, London 1824, p. 133.

24 Giuseppe Pecchio, *Semi-Serious Observations*, pp. 150–1.
25 See William Spence Robertson, *Iturbide of Mexico*, Durham, North Carolina, 1952, pp. 93, 95, 98, 99. See also: Augustin de Iturbide, *Mémoires Autographes*, tr. J. T. Parisot, Paris 1824; Charles de Beneski, *A Narrative of the Last Moments of the Life of Don Augustine de Iturbide*, New York 1825.
26 Quoted William Spence Robertson, op. cit., p. 102.
27 See ibid., 129, 130, 133.
28 See William St Clair, *That Greece Might Still be Free*, London 1972, pp. 304–5.
29 See Brian Vale, *Independence or Death! British Sailors and Brazilian Independence 1822–1825*, London 1996, pp. 8, 18.
30 Quoted in Salvador de Madariaga, *Bolivar*, p. 516; see also p. 551.

13: Glorious Exertions

1 See C.M. Woodhouse, *The Philhellenes*, London 1969, p. 46. For the background, see notes to earlier chapters, and: Jean-Jacques Barthélémy, *Voyage du Jeune Anacharsis en Grèce*, Paris 1788; A. Boppe, *L'Albanie et Napoléon 1797–1814*, Paris 1914; C.W. Crawley, *The Question of Greek Independence*, Cambridge 1930; Richard Clogg, ed., *The Struggle for Greek Independence*, London 1973; George Finlay, *History of the Greek Revolution*, 2 vols, London 1861.
2 Quoted in Olga Augustinos, *French Odysseys, Greece in French Travel Literature from the Renaissance to the Romantic Era*, Baltimore 1994, p. 178.
3 Richard Clogg, *The Movement for Greek Independence*, p. xi; Douglas Dakin, *British and American Philhellenes during the War of Greek Independence 1821–1833*, Thessaloniki 1955, p. 8; Korais quoted in Richard Clogg, *The Struggle for Greek Independence*, p. 80.
4 Quoted in William St Clair, op. cit., p. 23.
5 Quoted ibid., p. 13.
6 Quoted ibid., p. 54.
7 Quoted in Stephen A. Larrabee, *Hellas Observed, The American experience in Greece, 1775–1865*, New York 1957, p. 55.
8 Quoted in William St Clair, op. cit., p. 24.
9 See William St Clair, op. cit., pp. 67, 72; also Walter Grab, *Odysseus der Freiheit – Harro Harring – ein nordfriesischer Revolutionsdichter*, in *Mitteilungen der Harro – Harring – Gesselschaft*, 1, Husum 1982.
10 See Stephen A. Larrabee, op. cit., pp. 66, 67.
11 See François Dalencour, op. cit., p. 23.
12 See Giuseppe Pecchio, *Semi-Serious Observations*, pp. 174, 284.
13 Alerino Palma di Cesnola, *Greece Vindicated in Two Letters*, London 1826, p. 9.

14 See Douglas Dakin, op. cit., pp. 28–9; also, William St Clair, op. cit., p. 45.
15 See *A Picture of Greece in 1825; as exhibited in the Narratives of James Emerson, Esq., Count Pecchio, and W.H. Humphries*, London 1826, Vol. II, p. 7.
16 See Maurice Persat, op. cit., pp. 77, 79–80, 90, 123.
17 See William St Clair, op. cit., p. 37, for fighting tactics of Greeks.
18 Quoted in F. Rosen, *Bentham, Byron and Greece. Constitutionalism, Nationalism and Early Liberal Political Thought*, Oxford 1992, p. 137.
19 See William St Clair, op. cit. pp. 218–19.
20 See Frederick B. Artz, op. cit., p. 149.
21 See Douglas Dakin, op. cit., p. 86.
22 See Lord Byron, *Letters*, ed. R.G. Howarth, London 1971, p. 358.
23 See Alexandre Dumas, op. cit., Vol. I, p. 709.
24 Quoted in Charles Christopher Lloyd, *Lord Cochrane, Seaman-Radical-Liberator*, London 1947, pp. 188–9.
25 See Marc Raeff, *The Decembrist Movement*, Englewood Cliffs, N.J., 1966, p. 43. For the historical background of the Decembrist revolt, see: Yu. G. Oksman and S.N. Chernov, *Vospominania i Raskazy Deyateliey Taynykh Obshestv 1820 – tykh godov*, 2 vols, Moscow 1931. M.V. Nyechkina, *Vosstanye 14 Dekabrya 1825*, Moscow 1951, and *Dvizhenie Dekabristov*, 2 vols, Moscow 1955.
26 See Marc Raeff, op. cit., p. 60. For the cast of mind of the young men involved, see also: Yu. M. Lotman, *The Decembrist in Daily Life*, in *The Semiotics of Russian Cultural History*, ed. Alexander D. Nakhimovsky and Alice Stone Nakhimovsky, Ithaca 1985.
27 Quoted in Anatole G. Mazour, *The First Russian Revolution*, Berkeley 1937, p. 132.
28 Quoted in A. Mazour, op. cit., p. 151.
29 See A. Mazour, op. cit., p. 164.
30 See Marc Raef, op. cit., p. 177.
31 See Alexander Herzen, *My Past and Thoughts*, tr. Constance Garnett, London 1924, Vol. I, pp. 87 and 91.

14: Glory Days

1 Quoted in Maurice Cranston, *The Romantic Movement*, Oxford 1994, p. 95.
2 Ralph Waldo Emerson, *Essays and Poems*, London 1992, pp. 182, 183, 184, 195.
3 See James H. Billington, op. cit., p. 154.
4 Quoted in Paul Johnson, *The Birth of the Modern*, London 1991, p. 117.
5 See Arnold Hauser, op. cit., Vol. II, p. 684.
6 Heinrich Heine, *Italian Travel Sketches*, p. 90.

7 See Anthony Arblaster, *Viva la Liberta! Politics in Opera*, London 1992, p. 30.
8 See Jane F. Fulcher, *The Nation's Image, French Grand Opera as Politics and Politicized Art*, Cambridge 1987, p. 31.
9 Alexandre Dumas, op. cit., Vol. II, p. 75.
10 Hector Berlioz, *Memoirs*, tr. David Cairns, London 1970, pp. 156–8.
11 Alexandre Dumas, op. cit., Vol. II, p. 56.
12 Maurice Persat, op. cit., p. 219.
13 See Alexandre Dumas, op. cit., Vol. II, p. 91.
14 See Pierre Nora, op. cit., Vol. I, *La République*, p. 19.
15 See John Stuart Mill, *Autobiography*, London 1873, p. 172.
16 Quoted in Frederick B. Artz, op. cit., p. 277.
17 See Adolphe Bartels, *Les Flandres et la Révolution Belge*, Brussels 1834, p. 339.
18 See James H. Billington, op. cit., p. 156.
19 See Adolphe Bartels, op. cit., p. 2.
20 See ibid. , p. 1.
21 Quoted in R. Demoulin, *Les Journées de Septembre à Bruxelles et en Province*, Liège 1934, p. 71.
22 Quoted by Jacques-Robert Leconte, *La Formation Historique de l'Armée Belge 1830–1853*, Paris 1949, p. 15; see also Don Juan Van Halen, *Memoirs*, 2 vols, London 1830.
23 See R. Demoulin, *La Révolution de 1830*, Brussels 1950, p. 68.
24 Quoted ibid., p. 139. On the candidates to the Belgian throne, see Adolphe Bartels, op. cit., pp. 531–2; W. Toporowski, *25-lecie Panowania króla Belgii Baldwina I*, in *Dziennik Polski*, London, Nr. 270, 1976; Władysław Rostocki, *Z Badań nad kontaktami Polsko-Belgijskimi w drugiej ćwierci XIX wieku*, in *Roczniki Humanistyczne*, Vol. 22, Zeszyt 2, Warsaw 1974, pp. 169–70.
25 See Tadeusz Łepkowski, *Piotr Wysocki*, Warsaw 1981, pp. 38–9.
26 See Ernest Łuniński, *Wspominki. Z dni historycznych kart kilka*, Warsaw 1910.
27 See Józef Dutkiewicz, *Francja a Polska w 1831 r.*, Łódź 1950, pp. 28–30; also Mark Liam Brown, *The Polish Question and Public Opinion in France 1830–1846*, in *Antemurale*, Vol. XXIV, Rome 1980, p. 114.
28 See Stanisław Szenic, *Ani Triumf ani Zgon*, Warsaw 1974, p. 48.
29 See Kazimierz Lewandowski, *Pamiętnik Wychodźca Polskiego*, Warsaw 1977, p. 55.
30 Quoted in Maria Janion, *Płacz Generała. Esejo o Wojnie*, Warsaw 1998, p. 11.
31 See Zbigniew Sudolski, *Słowacki, Opowieść Biograficzna*, Warsaw 1996, p. 67.
32 See Andrzej Walicki, *Philosophy and Romantic Nationalism*, Oxford 1982, p. 78.
33 Quoted in Jerzy Robert Nowak, *Myśli o Polsce i Polakach*, Katowice 1994, pp. 98, 99.

34 Quoted in A.J.P. Taylor, *The Trouble Makers. Dissent over Foreign Policy 1792–1939*, London 1957, p. 44.
35 Quoted in Jerzy Robert Nowak, op. cit., p. 124.
36 See Richard Wagner, *My Life*, Vol. I, London 1911, p. 72; see also Henry Weisser, *British Working-Class Movements and Europe 1815–1848*, Manchester 1975, p. 32.
37 See A. Lewak, *Generał M.R. La Fayette o Polsce*, Warsaw 1934, pp. 31, 45, 49, 70.
38 See Józef Dutkiewicz, op. cit., pp. 135–8.

15: Apostles and Martyrs

1 Heinrich Heine quoted in Jan Gintel, op. cit., Vol. II, p. 323; Thomas Campbell, *Complete Poetical Works*, London 1907, pp. 218, 223; for Lamennais, see Christian Seneschal, *La Pologne de 1830 à 1846 dans la Poésie Romantique Française*, Paris 1937, p. 34.
2 See Jacques-Robert Leconte, op. cit., p. 41. See also: Ryszard Bender, *Polacy w Armii Belgijskiej w latach 1830–1853*, in Henryk Zins, ed., *Polska w Europie*, Lublin 1968.
3 See Christian Seneschal, op. cit., pp. 19–20.
4 Quoted in Krzysztof Budziło and Jan Pruszyński, op. cit., p. 156.
5 See Kazimierz Lewandowski, op. cit. , p. 30; Maria Janion, *Płacz Generała*, p. 12; Zbigniew Sudolski, *Słowacki*, p. 94.
6 See Karol Borkowski, *Pamiętnik Historyczny o Wyprawie Partyzanckiej do Polski w Roku 1833*, Leipzig 1863, p. 4.
7 Denis Mack Smith, *Mazzini*, Yale 1994, p. 26. See also Roland Sarti, *Mazzini. A Life for the Religion of Politics*, Westport 1997.
8 Heinrich Heine, *Italian Travel Sketches*, p. 77.
9 See Felice Orsini, *The Austrian Dungeons in Italy*, London 1856, p. 53.
10 See Derek Beales, op. cit., p. 45.
11 Quoted in Denis Mack Smith, *Mazzini*, p. 121.
12 See Duke Litta-Visconti-Arese, ed., *The Birth of Modern Italy. The posthumous papers of Jesse White Mario*, London 1909, p. 8.
13 Giuseppe Mazzini, *Essays*, tr. Thomas Okey, London 1894, pp. 7, 19.
14 Quoted in Jean Touchard, op. cit., Vol. II, p. 535.
15 Giuseppe Mazzini, *Essays*, p. 85.
16 Quoted in Denis Mack Smith, *Mazzini*, p. 33.
17 See E. Helleniusz, *Wspomnienia Narodowe*, Paris 1861, pp. 330, 340–1, 351.
18 Karol Borkowski, op. cit., p. 107. See also: *Roman Sanguszko, Zesłaniec na Sybir z r. 1831, w świetle pamiętnika matki*, Warsaw 1927.
19 Alexander Herzen, *My Past and Thoughts*, Vol. I, p. 214; Vol. II, p. 99.

20 See George Macaulay Trevelyan, *Garibaldi and the Thousand*, London 1928, p. 153.

21 See Andrzej Walicki, *Philosophy and Romantic Nationalism*, pp. 49, 58. On communes, see: Lidia and Adam Ciołkosz, *Zarys Dziejów Socjalizmu Polskiego*, London 1966, Vol. I, p. 124; Maria Janion and Maria Żmigrodzka, op. cit., pp. 114–5.

22 See Felice Orsini, op. cit., p. 53.

23 Quoted in Emmanuel Halicz, *Polish National Liberation Struggles and the Genesis of the Modern Nation. Collected Papers*, trs. Roger Clark, Odense 1982, p. 86.

24 Quoted in Hans Kohn, *The Making of the Modern French Mind*, New York 1955, p. 40; see also Rainer S. Elkar, *Young Germans and Young Germany*, in *Generations in Conflict*, ed. Mark Roseman, Cambridge 1995.

25 See R. Hinton Thomas, *Liberalism, Nationalism and the German Intellectuals (1822–1847), an Analysis of the Academic and Scientific Conferences of the Period*, Cambridge 1951, p. 40.

26 See R. Hinton Thomas, op. cit., p. 6.

27 See Paul Harro Harring, *Epistel an Lord Goderich*, n.p. 1833.

28 Quoted by Golo Mann, op. cit., p. 65; see also Félix Ponteil, op. cit., p. 330; James Sheehan, op. cit., p. 610.

29 Paul Harro Harring, *Mémoires sur la Jeune Italie et sur les derniers évènements de Savoie*, Milan 1918, p. 112.

30 Paul Harro Harring, ibid, p. 266.

31 See E.E.Y. Hales, *Mazzini and the Secret Societies. The Making of a Myth*, London 1956, p. 144.

32 Quoted in W.J. Linton, *European Republicans*, London 1893, p. 42.

33 Giuseppe Mazzini, *Essays*, pp. 67, 72.

34 See Leo Morabito, ed., *Daniel O'Connell, Atti del Convegno di Studi nel 1400 Anniversaria della morte*, Genoa 1990, p. 91. Also, H. Keller, *Das Junge Europa 1834–1836*, Zurich 1938.

35 Giuseppe Mazzini, *Essays*, p. 75.

36 ibid., *Essays*, p. 85.

37 See W.J. Linton, *European Republicans*, p. 12.

38 Felice Orsini, op. cit., p. 53.

39 Quoted by J.M. Roberts, op. cit., p. 301; see also A.J.P. Taylor in François Fejtö, *The Opening of an Era: 1848*, London 1948, p. 10.

40 Quoted in Denis Mack Smith, *Mazzini*, p. 41.

41 See W.J. Linton, *European Republicans*, pp. 184–5.

42 See Maria Janion and Maria Żmigrodzka, op. cit., p. 366.

43 ibid., p. 404.

44 ibid., p. 417.

16: Resurrection of the Spirit

1 See Marie d'Agoult (Daniel Stern) *Histoire de la Révolution de 1848*, Paris 1862, Vol. I, p. 54.

2 Quoted by Jacques Droz, *Europe Between Revolutions, 1815–1848*, p. 70.

3 Quoted by J.L. Talmon, *Political Messianism. The Romantic Phase*, London 1960 p. 138. See also: Maxime Leroy, *La Vie Véritable du Comte Henri de Saint-Simon*, Paris 1925; Paul Bénichou, *Le Temps des Prophètes. Doctrines de l'Age Romantique*, Paris 1977.

4 Alexandre Dumas, op. cit., Vol. II, pp. 412–25.

5 See Jules Garson, *Béranger et La Légende Napoléonienne*, Brussels 1897, p. 43.

6 Louis-Napoléon Bonaparte, *L'Idée Napoléonienne*, in *Oeuvres*, Vol. I, Paris 1859, pp. 31, 7.

7 For the relationship between Lamennais and Mickiewicz, see Manfred Kridl, *Mickiewicz i Lamennais*, Warsaw 1909.

8 See Hans Kohn, *Prophets and Peoples, Studies in Nineteenth-century Nationalism*, New York 1946, p. 55; also W.J. Linton, *European Republicans*, p. 211. See also Paul Viallaneix, *Michelet, les Travaux et les Jours*, Paris 1998.

9 Quoted in Jean Touchard, op. cit., p. 549.

10 Félicité de Lamennais, *La Pologne*, in *Paroles d'un Croyant*, Paris n.d., p. 203.

11 Quoted in Andrzej Walicki, *Philosophy and Romantic Nationalism*, p. 245.

12 Félicité de Lamennais, *Le Livre du Peuple*, Paris 1838, p. 145.

13 Quoted in Susan Dunn, op. cit., p. 52.

14 Quoted in Jean Touchard, op. cit., p. 536.

15 A. de Lamartine, *Jeanne d'Arc*, Brussels 1852, pp. 132–3.

16 Quoted in Noel Parker, *Portrayals of Revolution. Images, Debates and Patterns of Thought on the French Revolution*, London 1990, p. 140.

17 Jules Michelet, *Le Peuple*, Brussels 1846, pp. 305, 306, 308, 328, 335.

18 Quoted in Robert Gildea, op. cit., p. 138.

19 Victor Hugo, *La Légende des Siècles*, Paris 1912, Vol. I, p. 14; Vol. II, p. 131.

20 Quoted in Lloyd S. Kramer, *Threshold of a New World, Intellectuals and the Exile Experience in Paris 1830–1848*, Ithaca 1988, p. 74.

21 Hans Kohn, *Prophets and Peoples*, p. 83.

22 Quoted in Eric Hobsbawm, *The Age of Revolution*, p. 164.

23 See John Chancellor, *Wagner*, p. 77. See also: James J. Sheehan, *The German States and the European Revolution*, in Isser Woloch, op. cit.

24 Heinrich Heine, *Deutschland. A Winter's Tale*, tr. T.J. Read, London 1986, p. 92.

25 See Golo Mann, op. cit., p. 74.

26 See Golo Mann, op. cit., p. 82.
27 Quoted in Lloyd S. Kramer, op. cit., p. 32.
28 See Robert Joseph Kerner, *Bohemia in the Eighteenth Century*, New York 1932; H. Jelinek, *Histoire de la Littérature Tchèque*, Vol. I, *Des Origines à 1850*, Paris 1930; Mikulas Teich, *Bohemia: From Darkness into Light*, in Roy Porter and Mikulas Teich, op. cit.; Louis Léger, *La Renaissance Tchèque au Dix-neuvième Siècle*, Paris 1911; Hans Kohn, *The Idea of Nationalism*, and *Pan-Slavism, Its History and Ideology*, Notre Dame, Indiana, 1953; Derek Sayer, *The Coasts of Bohemia, a Czech History*, Princeton 1998.
29 Quoted in Hans Schenk, *The Mind of the European Romantics*, London 1966, p. 16.
30 See H. Jelinek, op. cit., pp. 289, 295.
31 See Hans Kohn, *Pan-Slavism*, p. 15.
32 See Vladimir Macula, *Problems and Paradoxes of the National Revival*, in Mikulas Teich, ed., *Bohemia in History*, Cambridge 1998, pp. 182, 193–4.
33 See H. Jelinek, op. cit., p. 272.
34 See Hans Kohn, *Pan-Slavism*, p. 16.
35 ibid., p. 19.
36 See Frederick B. Artz, op. cit., p. 244.
37 Stefan Kozak, *Ukrainscy Spiskowcy i Mesjanisci Bractwa Cyryla i Metodego*, Warsaw 1990, pp. 189–90.
38 ibid., p. 165.
39 ibid., p. 162.
40 Quoted in Hans Kohn, *Pan-Slavism*, p. 19.
41 Quoted in Andrzej Walicki, *Philosophy and Romantic Nationalism*, p. 81.
42 Quoted in Hans Kohn, *Pan-Slavism*, p. 111.
43 See Alexander Herzen, *My Past and Thoughts*, Vol. II, p. 273.
44 Stefan Kozak, op. cit., p. 135.
45 Quoted in Hans Kohn, *Pan-Slavism*, p. 112.
46 Quoted ibid., p. 125.
47 ibid., p. 127.
48 Quoted in Otto Zarek, *Kossuth*, London 1937, pp. 68–9.
49 See Istvan Deak, *The Lawful Revolution, Louis Kossuth and the Hungarians, 1848–1849*, New York 1979, pp. 45, 119; also Lorant Czigany, *The Oxford Book of Hungarian Literature*, Oxford 1984, p. 122.
50 Quoted in Zbigniew Sudolski, *Mickiewicz. Opowieść Biograficzna*, Warsaw 1995, p. 562.
51 Adam Mickiewicz, *Les Slaves, Cours Professé au Collège de France (1842–1844)*, Paris 1914, pp. 347–9.

17: ON THE THRESHOLD OF PARADISE

1 Quoted in Guy Antonetti, *Louis-Philippe*, Paris 1994, p. 906.
2 Quoted in J.L. Talmon, op. cit., p. 394.
3 See Guy Antonetti, op. cit., Paris 1994, p. 887.
4 Quoted in J.L. Talmon, op. cit., p. 479.
5 Quoted in Hans Kohn, *Prophets and Peoples*, p. 56.
6 See Maria Janion and Maria Żmigrodzka, op. cit., p. 490.
7 See Ferdynand Gregorovius, *Idea Polskości. Dwie księgi martyrologii polskiej*, Olsztyn 1991, pp. 96–7.
8 See Michel Vovelle, *La Marseillaise, La Guerre ou la Paix*, in Pierre Nora, op. cit., Vol. I, *République*, p. 114; also Alexander Herzen, *From the Other Shore*, trs. Moura Budberg, Oxford 1979, p. 43.
9 Quoted in James H. Billington, op. cit., p. 238.
10 Quoted in Lewis Namier, *The Revolution of the Intellectuals*, Oxford 1946, p. 9.
11 See W.J. Linton, *Memories*, London 1895, p. 105.
12 Quoted in Marie d'Agoult, op. cit., Vol. II, pp. 148–50.
13 Quoted in Reinhard Bendix, op. cit., p. 270.
14 Quoted in Lorant Czigany, op. cit., p. 190.
15 Sandor Petöfi, *The Apostle*, translated by Victor Clement, Budapest 1961, p. 8.
16 Quoted in James Eastwood and Paul Tabori, *'48. The Year of Revolutions*, London 1948, p. 130.
17 Sandor Petöfi, op. cit., p. 97.
18 See Ferdynand Gregorovius, op. cit., p. 108.
19 Quoted in Lewis Namier, op. cit., p. 57.
20 Quoted by Benjamin Goriely in François Fejtö, op. cit., p. 368.
21 See Zbigniew Sudolski, *Słowacki*, p. 304.
22 See Derek Beales, op. cit., p. 149.
23 See Janusz Ruszkowski, *Adam Mickiewicz i Ostatnia Krucjata. Studium romantycznego millenaryzmu*, Wrocław 1996, p. 212.
24 See Zbigniew Sudolski, *Mickiewicz*, p. 688.
25 Władysław Zamoyski, *Pamiętniki*, Vol. V, Poznań 1922, p. 96.
26 See Dorota Zamojska, *Bursz-Cygan-Legionista, Józef Bogdan Dziekoński 1816–1855*, Warsaw 1995, p. 77.
27 Quoted in Derek Beales, op. cit., p. 147.
28 See Istvan Deak, *Lawful Revolutions and the Many Meanings of Freedom in the Habsburg Monarchy*, in Isser Woloch, op. cit., p. 291.
29 See Lewis Namier, op. cit., p. 119.
30 Istvan Deak, *Lawful Revolutions*, p. 291.

31 For quotation from Marx, see ibid.; for Grillparzer quote see Golo Mann, op. cit., p. 117.
32 Quoted in C. Edmund Maurice, *The Revolutionary Movement of 1848*, London 1887, p. 322.
33 Quoted in Hans Kohn, *Pan-Slavism*, p. 72.
34 Ibid., p. 73.
35 See François Fejtö, op. cit., p. 421.
36 Jules Michelet, *Principautés Danubiennes*, in *Légendes Démocratiques du Nord*, Paris 1854, p. 304.
37 See: D.A. Stourdza, *Actes et Documents relatifs à la régénération de la Roumanie*, Bucharest 1910; *L'Année 1848 dans les principautés roumaines, actes et documents*, Bucharest 1902; Keith Hitchins, *The Rumanian National Movement in Transylvania 1780–1849*, Harvard 1969; Michael Roller, *The Rumanians in 1848*, in François Fejtö, op. cit.; Józef Feldman, *Sprawa Polska w 1848 roku*, Kraków 1933, pp. 283–4.
38 See Marie d'Agoult, op. cit., Vol. II, p. 256 (note).
39 Quoted in Guy Antonetti, op. cit., p. 919.
40 Hector Berlioz, op. cit., p. 51.
41 Alexander Herzen, *My Past and Thoughts*, Vol. III, pp. 91–2.
42 See Priscilla Robertson, *Revolutions of 1848: A Social History*, Princeton 1952, p. 142.
43 Quoted in Lewis Namier, op. cit., p. 88.
44 ibid., p. 86.
45 Quoted in Golo Mann, op. cit., pp. 116–17.
46 Quoted in James J. Sheehan, *German History*, p. 565.
47 See James Eastwood and Paul Tabori, op. cit., p. 56.

18: SUSTAINING LEGENDS

1 See Priscilla Robertson, op. cit., p. 390.
2 Giuseppe Garibaldi, *Autobiography*, tr. A. Werner, London 1889, Vol. I, p. 54.
3 Giuseppe Garibaldi, op. cit., Vol. I, p. 258.
4 Quoted in K. Morawski, *Polacy i Sprawa Polska w Dziejach Italii w Latach 1830–1866*, Warsaw 1937, p. 133.
5 See Albert Boime, *The Art of the Macchia and the Risorgimento*, Chicago 1993, p. 29.
6 See Christopher Hibbert, *Garibaldi and his Enemies*, London 1987, p. 44.
7 Adam Mickiewicz, *La Tribune Des Peuples*, Paris 1907, p. 151.
8 See Stefan Kieniewicz, *Legion Mickiewicza 1848–1849*, Warsaw 1955, p. 145.

See also Henryk Batowski, *Legion Mickiewicza w Kampanii Włosko-Austriackiej 1848 roku*, Warsaw 1956.

9 Quoted by Christopher Hibbert, op. cit., p. 51.

10 ibid., p. 85.

11 See István Deák, *The Lawful Revolution*, p. 57.

12 See James Sheehan, *German History*, p. 698.

13 Quoted in István Deák, op. cit., p. 218.

14 ibid., p. 274.

15 ibid., p. 293.

16 ibid., pp. 296–7.

17 Władysław Zamoyski, op. cit., Vol. V, p. 236. See also Gyorgy Klapka, *Memoirs of the War of Independence in Hungary*, London 1850.

18 Quoted by Otto Zarek, op. cit., p. 238.

19 Quoted by István Deák, op. cit., p. 328.

20 See Franciszek Bagieński, *Wspomnienia Starego Wołyniaka*, Warsaw 1987. For Kossuth's trip to the United States, see Francis and Theresa Pulszky, *White Red Black, Sketches of Society in the United States*, 3 vols., London 1853, and Eugene Pivany, *Hungarian American Historical Connections*, Budapest 1927.

19: BEARING WITNESS

1 Hector Berlioz, op. cit., p. 51.

2 Alexander Herzen, *My Past and Thoughts*, Vol. IV, pp. 196, 206.

3 Giuseppe Garibaldi, *Autobiography*, Vol. II, p. 59; see also G.M. Trevelyan, op. cit., p. 27.

4 Alexander Herzen, *My Past and Thoughts*, Vol. IV, p. 149; Vol. III, p. 72.

5 Quoted in Judith E. Zimmerman, *Midpassage, Alexander Herzen and European Revolution 1847–1852*, Pittsburgh 1989, p. 191.

6 See Władysław Zamoyski, op. cit., Vol. VI, p. 13.

7 Alexander Herzen, *My Past and Thoughts*, Vol. IV, p. 187.

8 W.J. Linton, *European Republicans*, p. 337; Alexander Herzen, *My Past and Thoughts*, Vol. IV, p. 162.

9 Carlo Pisacane, *Guerra Combattuta in Italia negli Anni 1848–1849*, Rome 1906, p. 308; also Denis Mack Smith, *Il Risorgimento Italiano*, p. 416.

10 See Denis Mack Smith, *Garibaldi*, London 1957, p. 85; G.M. Trevelyan, op. cit., p. 28; Giuseppe Garibaldi, *Autobiography*, Vol. III, Supplement by Jessie White Mario, p. 140.

11 See Denis Mack Smith, *Mazzini*, p. 131.

12 Quoted in Mary Jane Phillips-Matz, *Verdi. A Biography*, Oxford 1993, p. 392.

13 See Christopher Hibbert, op. cit., pp. 272–3.

14 Giuseppe Garibaldi, *Autobiography*, Vol. II, p. 90.

15 Quoted in G.M. Trevelyan, op. cit., p. 105.
16 Quoted ibid., p. 112.
17 See Denis Mack Smith, *Garibaldi*, p. 94; also G.M. Trevelyan, op. cit., pp. 203, 215–6.
18 Quoted by G.M. Trevelyan, op. cit., p. 209.
19 Quoted by Denis Mack Smith, *Garibaldi*, p. 93.
20 See Christopher Hibbert, op. cit., p. 213.
21 See A.R. Schoyen, *The Chartist Challenge. A Portrait of Julian Harney*, London 1958, p. 257.
22 See Alexandre Dumas, *Les Garibaldiens*, Paris 1861, p. 37. See also Maxime Du Camp, *Expédition des Deux Siciles*, Paris 1861.

20: Keeping the Faith

1 Alexander Herzen, *My Past and Thoughts*, Vol. V, p. 131.
2 E.H. Carr, *The Romantic Exiles. A Nineteenth-century Portrait Gallery*, London 1949, p. 252.
3 See Andrea Viotti, *Garibaldi, the Revolutionary and his Men*, Poole 1979, p. 135. See also Eugene Pivany, *Hungarians in the American Civil War*, Cleveland 1913.
4 Giuseppe Garibaldi, *Autobiography*, Vol. II, p. 147.
5 See Mary Jane Phillips-Matz, op. cit., p. 409.
6 *Dottrina di Giuseppe Garibaldi*, Torino, Muzeo del Risorgimento, S.I.G. 123.
7 For Garibaldi's visit to England, see: Denis Mack Smith, *Garibaldi*, pp. 140–5; Christopher Hibbert, op. cit., pp. 339–50; Alexander Herzen, *My Past and Thoughts*, Vol. V, pp. 36–65. For Marx quote, see Denis Mack Smith, *Garibaldi*, p. 141.
8 Alexander Herzen, *My Past and Thoughts*, Vol. V, p. 36.
9 See Andrea Viotti, op. cit., p. 11.
10 Quoted in Maria Janion and Maria Żmigrodzka, op. cit., p. 490.
11 ibid., p. 541.
12 See Stefan Kieniewicz, *Powstanie Styczniowe*, Warsaw 1972, p. 138.
13 See Maria Janion and Maria Żmigrodzka, op. cit., p. 548.
14 Comte de Montalembert, *Une Nation en Deuil, La Pologne en 1861*, Paris 1861, pp. 13, 15.
15 Algernon Charles Swinburne, *Collected Poetical Works*, London 1924, Vol. I, p. 677.
16 See Stefan Kieniewicz, op. cit., p. 180.
17 ibid., p. 334.
18 See Maryan Langiewicz, *Relacye o kampanii własnej w r. 1863*, in Kwartalnik History czng, Vol. XIX, Warsaw, 1905, p. 255.

19 ibid., p. 252.

20 Quoted in Maria Janion and Maria Żmigrodzka, op. cit., p. 554.

21 See E.H. Carr, op. cit., p. 272.

22 See Stefan Kieniewicz, op. cit.; also Zbigniew Gnat-Wieteska, *Generałowie Powstania Styczniowego*, Pruszków 1994, pp. 63–4; also E.H. Carr, op. cit., 273; also Alexander Herzen, *My Past and Thoughts*, Vol. V, p. 169.

23 See Denis Mack Smith, *Mazzini*, p. 158.

21: LAST RITES

1 See E.H. Carr, op. cit., p. 306.

2 See Marie E. von Schwarz, *Garibaldi, Recollections of his Public and Private Life*, London 1887, pp. 344–5.

3 Alexander Herzen, *My Past and Thoughts*, Vol. V, p. 274.

4 See Hans Kohn, *Prophets and Peoples*, p. 73.

5 Quoted in Rupert Christiansen, *Tales of the New Babylon, Paris 1869–1875*, London 1994, p. 138.

6 See Michael Howard, *The Franco–Prussian War*, London 1981, p. 380.

7 Quoted ibid., p. 381.

8 See Otto Zarek, op. cit., p. 284.

9 See Christopher Hibbert, op. cit., p. 360; also Giuseppe Garibaldi, op. cit., Vol. II, p. 317.

10 See Stewart Edwards, *The Paris Commune*, London 1971, p. 97.

11 See E.H. Carr, op. cit., p. 375.

12 P.A. Dormoy, *Souvenirs d'Avant-Garde*, Vol. II, *Chatillon*, Paris 1887, pp. 8–11; also J. Bordone, *Garibaldi, Sa Vie, Ses Aventures, ses Combats*, Paris 1878.

13 Giuseppe Garibaldi, op. cit., Vol. II, p. 399.

14 ibid., Vol. III, *Supplement by Jesse White Mario*, p. 404; and J. Bordone, *Garibaldi et l'Armée des Vosges*, Paris 1877, p. 46.

15 Quoted in Giuseppe Garibaldi, op. cit., Vol. III, *Supplement by Jesse White Mario*, p. 406.

16 Quoted by Nunzio Coppola, op. cit., pp. 70, 71, 7.

17 Quoted by Eugen Weber, in review of Roger Bellet, *Jules Vallès*, in *Times Literary Supplement*, 21 April 1995, p. 4.

18 See Louis Nathaniel Rossel, *Mémoires, Procès et Correspondance*, ed. Roger Stéphane, Paris 1960, p. 289.

19 ibid., p. 104.

20 ibid., p. 107.

21 See Archibald Forbes, *What I saw of the Paris Commune*, in *The Century Magazine*, October 1892, p. 808.

22 See Krystyna Wyczańska, *Polacy w Komunie Paryskiej 1871r*, Warsaw 1957, pp. 92, 106.

22: AFTERLIFE

1 Quoted by Alastair Horne, *The Fall of Paris*, London 1965, p. 429.
2 Quoted by Rupert Christiansen, op. cit., p. 330.
3 Alexander Herzen, *My Past and Thoughts*, Vol. IV, p. 16.
4 Denis Mack Smith, *Mazzini*, p. 212.
5 See Denis Mack Smith, *Il Risorgimento Italiano*, p. xx; also Frank J. Coppa, *The Origin of the Italian Wars of Independence*, London 1992, p. 150.
6 Denis Mack Smith, *Mazzini*, p. 211.
7 Quoted ibid., p. 212.
8 Quoted in István Déak, *The Lawful Revolution*, p. 349.
9 See Alberto Manguel, *Hero of Our Time*, in *Times Literary Supplement*, 2 May 1997, p. 4.
10 Ségur, op. cit., Vol. I, pp. 424–5.
11 Ernest Renan, *Qu'est-ce qu'une nation?*, Paris 1882, pp. 29, 26–7.
12 Quoted in J.L. Talmon, *The Origins of Totalitarian Democracy*, London 1952, p. 68.
13 Jules Michelet, *Légendes Démocratiques du Nord*, p. 134.
14 Juliusz Słowacki, *Notatki z Dziennika z lat 1847–9* in *Dzieła Wszystkie*, Vol. 15, Wrocław 1955, p. 488.
15 Heinrich Heine, *Italian Travel Sketches*, p. 84.

Index